KRISHNA:

This exhaustless doctrine of Yoga I formerly taught unto Vivaswat; Vivaswat communicated it to Manu and Manu made it known unto Ikshwaku; and being thus transmitted from one unto another it was studied by the Rajarshees, until at length in the course of time the mighty art was lost, O harasser of thy foes! It is even the same exhaustless, secret, eternal doctrine I have this day communicated unto thee because thou art my devotee and my friend."

ARJUNA:

Seeing that thy birth is posterior to the life of Ikshwaku, how am I to understand that thou wert in the beginning the teacher of this doctrine?"

KRISHNA:

"Both I and thou have passed through many births, O harasser of thy foes! Mine are known unto me, but thou knowest not of thine.

"Even though myself unborn, of changeless essence, and the lord of all existence, yet in presiding over nature - which is mine - I am born but through my own *maya*, the mystic power of self-ideation, the eternal thought in the eternal mind. I produce myself among creatures, O son of Bharata, whenever there is a decline of virtue and an insurrection of vice and injustice in the world; and thus I incarnate from age to age for the preservation of the just, the destruction of the wicked, and the establishment of righteousness. Whoever, O Arjuna, knoweth my divine birth and actions to be even so doth not upon quitting his mortal frame enter into another, for he entereth into me. Many who were free from craving, fear, and anger, filled with my spirit, and who depended upon me, having been purified by the ascetic fire of knowledge, have entered into my being. In whatever way men approach me, in that way do I assist them; but whatever the path taken by mankind, that path is mine, O son of Pritha. Those who wish for success to their works in this life sacrifice to the gods; and in this world success from their actions soon cometh to pass.

Baghavad-Gita, IV

Other Theosophy Trust Books

by H.P. Blavatsky
The Key to Theosophy
The Voice of the Silence
The Secret Doctrine, Vols. I & II

by Raghavan Iyer
Wisdom in Action
The Dawning of Wisdom
Meditation and Self-Study
The Yoga Sutras of Patanjali
Mahatma Gandhi and Buddha's Path to Enlightenment
Self-Actualization and Spiritual Self-Regeneration

by William Q. Judge
The Ocean of Theosophy
The Bhagavad-Gita with Notes on the Bhagavad-Gita
and Gita Yoga

by Elton Hall
Teachers of the Eternal Doctrine

by Helen Valborg
Symbols of the Eternal Doctrine

by the Editorial Board of Theosophy Trust
Evolution and Intelligent Design
in *The Secret Doctrine*
The Origins of Self-Consciousness
in *The Secret Doctrine*
Theosophy ~ The Wisdom Religion

ISIS UNVEILED

A MASTER-KEY

TO THE

MYSTERIES OF ANCIENT AND MODERN

SCIENCE AND THEOLOGY

BY
H. P. BLAVATSKY,

CORRESPONDING SECRETARY OF THE THEOSOPHICAL SOCIETY

"Cecy est un livre de bonne Foy." — MONTAIGNE

————

VOL. I – SCIENCE

————

Isis Unveiled

Volume 1

Theosophy Trust books may be ordered through Amazon.com, CreateSpace.com, and other retail outlets, or by visiting:

https://www.Theosophytrust.org/online_books.php

ISBN-13: 978-0-9992382-1-9

ISBN-10: 0-9992382-1-3

Library of Congress Control Number: 2017957743

Printed in the United States of America

THE AUTHOR

DEDICATES THESE VOLUMES

TO THE

THEOSOPHICAL SOCIETY,

WHICH WAS FOUNDED AT NEW YORK, A.D. 1875,

TO STUDY THE SUBJECTS ON WHICH THEY TREAT.

PUBLISHER'S PREFACE

One could ask the same question that we asked in the Theosophy Trust editions of *The Secret Doctrine*, "Why publish yet another version of *Isis Unveiled*, when there are several very accessible editions (not to mention the facsimile version of the Original Edition) already available in print? What does this Theosophy Trust Books edition offer that the others do not?"

The answer is simply a higher degree of readability. Our editorial group agreed that, though the Original Edition was a spectacular work, given that the enormous complexity of the content – with a range of drawings, and a complex mixture of Sanskrit, Hebrew and Greek words – along with a very complex arrangement of the subject matter, presents uniquely difficult challenges. More recent editions have tried to remedy some of the problems found in the O.E., but some introduced other difficulties as well, such as editorial "explanations" and comments, as well as sectarian subject matter. The aim of this edition is to preserve all of the original content and modes of presentation – including even the archaic use of punctuation in the headings – while improving upon the accessibility and usefulness to the reader.

To this end, we have included several features that may prove to be useful improvements. First, we have inserted a new set of minor section headers that indicate what that particular section discusses. These minor section headings do not replace the original section headers that also appear as line items in the Table of Contents; they simply provide some convenient reference points for the reader, and do not disturb the listings in the original Table of Contents.

Second, the headers more consistently reflect the chapters where they are located. Third, we have selected a larger format book to allow us to set the entire book in 10 point Palatino Linotype, an elegant and highly readable typeface, replacing the original edition's 8 pt. font. Fourth, as the footnotes contain some of the most interesting and provocative statements in the book, we have numbered all of the footnotes (all 907 of them) with consecutive numbers, so that the reader will more easily be able to retrace their path to these remarkable statements. In addition, we were able to employ a specialized Theosophical font containing all of the figures that H.P. Blavatsky used in the Original Edition, as a result of a valuable gift from our friends and colleagues, the Philalethian Society of the U.K. Theosophy Trust is greatly indebted to the Philalethian Society for this very useful font.

Although employing these purely schematic and somewhat mechanical aids, we have sought in this work to remain entirely faithful to all of the content in the 1877 Original Edition of *Isis Unveiled*, without introducing any new errors. The content of this volume has been laboriously proofed and all known errors corrected by comparison to the O.E., but there are sure to be some that diligent attention paid to fidelity has missed; therefore, we beg the reader who finds any such to communicate their findings to us via our website or email at Editor@theosophytrust.org. Subsequent releases will contain all corrections noted to date.

We would be remiss not to mention that one of our objectives in publishing this work is to add to our overall portfolio of Theosophical works that we put into the hands of inmates in state prisons in Texas, Florida, North and South Carolina, and Missouri. Our Books for Prisoners initiative sends - by request - dozens of free books weekly to prisoners there, and publishing our own edition will lower the cost and make it more feasible to send copies of *Isis* to prisoners who request it. *Isis Unveiled* continues to be in high demand among this indigent group of our nation's population.

Finally, like *The Secret Doctrine*, this is a marvelously profound work, the diligent study of which will reward the student with the riches of the Eternal Doctrine – *Sanatana Dharma* – and a growing awareness that the understanding of these truths is an ageless. Each life brings the opportunity – and none is greater than the present cycle, in which these teachings have been made public for the first time in recorded history - for every immortal soul to enjoy greater access to the ontological plenty of the realm of higher *Manas*. Such is the generosity and sacrifice of those Masters of Wisdom who stood behind and beside HP Blavatsky to roll back before the world again the veil of Isis.

Editor, Theosophy Trust Books

NOTE: Free downloads of MOBI (Kindle), ePub and PDF versions of this work, along with the other classics of the Theosophical Movement, may be found at our website: http://www.theosophytrust.org/

PREFACE

THE work now submitted to public judgment is the fruit of a somewhat intimate acquaintance with Eastern adepts and study of their science. It is offered to such as are willing to accept truth wherever it may be found, and to defend it, even looking popular prejudice straight in the face. It is an attempt to aid the student to detect the vital principles which underlie the philosophical systems of old.

The book is written in all sincerity. It is meant to do even justice, and to speak the truth alike without malice or prejudice. But it shows neither mercy for enthroned error, nor reverence for usurped authority. It demands for a spoliated past, that credit for its achievements which has been too long withheld. It calls for a restitution of borrowed robes, and the vindication of calumniated but glorious reputations. Toward no form of worship, no religious faith, no scientific hypothesis has its criticism been directed in any other spirit. Men and parties, sects and schools are but the mere ephemera of the world's day. TRUTH, high-seated upon its rock of adamant, is alone eternal and supreme.

We believe in no Magic which transcends the scope and capacity of the human mind, nor in "miracle," whether divine or diabolical, if such imply a transgression of the laws of nature instituted from all eternity. Nevertheless, we accept the saying of the gifted author of *Festus*, that the human heart has not yet fully uttered itself, and that we have never attained or even understood the extent of its powers. Is it too much to believe that man should be developing new sensibilities and a closer relation with nature? The logic of evolution must teach as much, if carried to its legitimate conclusions. If, somewhere, in the line of ascent from vegetable or ascidian to the noblest man a soul was evolved, gifted with intellectual qualities, it cannot be unreasonable to infer and believe that a faculty of perception is also growing in man, enabling him to descry facts and truths even beyond our ordinary ken. Yet we do not hesitate to accept the assertion of Biffé, that "the essential is forever the same. Whether we cut away the marble inward that hides the statue in the block, or pile stone upon stone outward till the temple is completed, our NEW result is only an *old idea*. The latest of all the eternities will find its destined other half-soul in the earliest." When, years ago, we first travelled over the East, exploring the penetralia of its deserted sanctuaries, two saddening and ever-recurring questions oppressed our thoughts: *Where*, WHO, WHAT *is* GOD? *Who ever saw the* IMMORTAL SPIRIT *of man, so as to be able to assure himself of man's immortality?*

It was while most anxious to solve these perplexing problems that we came into contact with certain men, endowed with such mysterious powers and such profound knowledge that we may truly designate them as the sages of the Orient. To their instructions we lent a ready ear. They showed us that by combining science with religion, the existence of God and immortality of man's spirit may be demonstrated like a problem of Euclid. For the first time we received the assurance that the Oriental philosophy has room for no other faith than an absolute and immovable faith in the omnipotence of man's own immortal self. We were taught that this omnipotence comes from the kinship of man's spirit with the

Universal Soul — God! The latter, they said, can never be demonstrated but by the former. Man-spirit proves God-spirit, as the one drop of water proves a source from which it must have come. Tell one who had never seen water, that there is an ocean of water, and he must accept it on faith or reject it altogether. But let one drop fall upon his hand, and he then has the fact from which all the rest may be inferred. After that he could by degrees understand that a boundless and fathomless ocean of water existed. Blind faith would no longer be necessary; he would have supplanted it with KNOWLEDGE. When one sees mortal man displaying tremendous capabilities, controlling the forces of nature and opening up to view the world of spirit, the reflective mind is overwhelmed with the conviction that if one man's spiritual *Ego* can do this much, the capabilities of the FATHER SPIRIT must be relatively as much vaster as the whole ocean surpasses the single drop in volume and potency. *Ex nihilo nihil fit;* prove the soul of man by its wondrous powers — you have proved God! In our studies, mysteries were shown to be no mysteries. Names and places that to the Western mind have only a significance derived from Eastern fable, were shown to be realities. Reverently we stepped in spirit within the temple of Isis; to lift aside the veil of "the one that is and was and shall be" at Saïs; to look through the rent curtain of the Sanctum Sanctorum at Jerusalem; and even to interrogate within the crypts which once existed beneath the sacred edifice, the mysterious Bath-Kol. The *Filia Vocis* — the daughter of the divine voice — responded from the mercy-seat within the veil,[1] and science, theology, every human hypothesis and conception born of imperfect knowledge, lost forever their authoritative character in our sight. The one-living God had spoken through his oracle—man, and we were satisfied. Such knowledge is priceless; and it has been hidden only from those who overlooked it, derided it, or denied its existence.

From such as these we apprehend criticism, censure, and perhaps hostility, although the obstacles in our way neither spring from the validity of proof, the authenticated facts of history, nor the lack of common sense among the public whom we address. The drift of modern thought is palpably in the direction of liberalism in religion as well as science. Each day brings the reactionists nearer to the point where they must surrender the despotic authority over the public conscience, which they have so long enjoyed and exercised. When the Pope can go to the extreme of fulminating anathemas against all who maintain the liberty of the Press and of speech, or who insist that in the conflict of laws, civil and ecclesiastical, the civil law should prevail, or that any method of instruction solely secular, may be approved;[2] and Mr. Tyndall, as the mouth-piece of nineteenth century science, says, ". . . the impregnable position of science may be stated in a few words: we claim, and we shall wrest from theology, the entire domain of cosmological theory"[3]—the end is not difficult to foresee.

Centuries of subjection have not quite congealed the life-blood of men into crystals around the nucleus of blind faith; and the nineteenth is witnessing the struggles of the giant

---

1 Lightfoot assures us that this voice, which had been used in times past for a testimony from heaven, "was indeed performed by magic art" (vol. ii., p. 128). This latter term is used as a supercilious expression, just because it was and is still misunderstood. It is the object of this work to correct the erroneous opinions concerning "magic art."

2 Encyclical of 1864.

3 *"Fragments of Science."*

as he shakes off the Liliputian cordage and rises to his feet. Even the Protestant communion of England and America, now engaged in the revision of the text of its *Oracles*, will be compelled to show the origin and merits of the text itself. The day of domineering over men with dogmas has reached its gloaming.

Our work, then, is a plea for the recognition of the Hermetic philosophy, the anciently universal Wisdom-Religion, as the only possible key to the Absolute in science and theology. To show that we do not at all conceal from ourselves the gravity of our undertaking, we may say in advance that it would not be strange if the following classes should array themselves against us:

The Christians, who will see that we question the evidences of the genuineness of their faith. The Scientists, who will find their pretensions placed in the same bundle with those of the Roman Catholic Church for infallibility, and, in certain particulars, the sages and philosophers of the ancient world classed higher than they. Pseudo-Scientists will, of course, denounce us furiously. Broad Churchmen and Freethinkers will find that we do not accept what they do, but demand the recognition of the whole truth. Men of letters and various *authorities*, who hide their real belief in deference to popular prejudices. The mercenaries and parasites of the Press, who prostitute its more than royal power, and dishonor a noble profession, will find it easy to mock at things too wonderful for them to understand; for to them the price of a paragraph is more than the value of sincerity. From many will come honest criticism; from many — cant. But we look to the future. The contest now going on between the party of public conscience and the party of reaction, has already developed a healthier tone of thought. It will hardly fail to result ultimately in the overthrow of error and the triumph of Truth. We repeat again — we are laboring for the brighter morrow. And yet, when we consider the bitter opposition that we are called upon to face, who is better entitled than we upon entering the arena to write upon our shield the hail of the Roman gladiator to Cæsar: MORITURUS TE SALUTÂT!

New York, September, 1877

TABLE OF CONTENTS

———————

BEFORE THE VEIL

———————

VOLUME FIRST

THE "INFALLIBILITY" OF MODERN SCIENCE

———————

CHAPTER I

OLD THINGS WITH NEW NAMES

CHAPTER II

PHENOMENA AND FORCES

CHAPTER III

BLIND LEADERS OF THE BLIND

CHAPTER IV

THEORIES RESPECTING PSYCHIC PHENOMENA

CHAPTER V

THE ETHER, OR "ASTRAL LIGHT"

CHAPTER VI

PSYCHO-PHYSICAL PHENOMENA

CHAPTER VII

THE ELEMENTS, ELEMENTALS, AND ELEMENTARIES

CHAPTER VIII

SOME MYSTERIES OF NATURE

CHAPTER IX

CYCLIC PHENOMENA

CHAPTER X

THE INNER AND OUTER MAN

CHAPTER XI

PSYCHOLOGICAL AND PHYSICAL MARVELS

CHAPTER XII

THE "IMPASSABLE CHASM"

CHAPTER XIII

REALITIES AND ILLUSION

CHAPTER XIV

EGYPTIAN WISDOM

CHAPTER XV

INDIA THE CRADLE OF THE RACE

BEFORE THE VEIL

Joan. — Advance our waving colors on the walls!

King Henry VI. Act IV

"My life has been devoted to the study of man, his destiny and his happiness."

J. R. BUCHANAN, M.D.
Outlines of Lectures on Anthropology

IT is nineteen centuries since, as we are told, the night of Heathenism and Paganism was first dispelled by the divine light of Christianity; and two-and-a-half centuries since the bright lamp of Modern Science began to shine on the darkness of the ignorance of the ages. Within these respective epochs, we are required to believe, the true moral and intellectual progress of the race has occurred. The ancient philosophers were well enough for their respective generations, but they were illiterate as compared with modern men of science.

DOGMATIC ASSUMPTIONS OF MODERN SCIENCE AND THEOLOGY

The ethics of Paganism perhaps met the wants of the uncultivated people of antiquity, but not until the advent of the luminous "Star of Bethlehem," was the true road to moral perfection and the way to salvation made plain. Of old, brutishness was the rule, virtue and spirituality the exception. Now, the dullest may read the will of God in His revealed word; men have every incentive to be good, and are constantly becoming better.

This is the assumption; what are the facts? On the one hand an unspiritual, dogmatic, too often debauched clergy; a host of sects, and three warring great religions; discord instead of union, dogmas without proofs, sensation-loving preachers, and wealth and pleasure-seeking parishioners' hypocrisy and bigotry, begotten by the tyrannical exigencies of respectability, the rule of the day, sincerity and real piety exceptional. On the other hand, scientific hypotheses built on sand; no accord upon a single question; rancorous quarrels and jealousy; a general drift into materialism. A death-grapple of Science with Theology for infallibility — "a conflict of ages."

At Rome, the self-styled seat of Christianity, the putative successor to the chair of Peter is undermining social order with his invisible but omnipresent net-work of bigoted agents, and incites them to revolutionize Europe for his temporal as well as spiritual supremacy. We see him who calls himself the "Vicar of Christ," fraternizing with the anti-Christian Moslem against another Christian nation, publicly invoking the blessing of God upon the arms of those who have for centuries withstood, with fire and sword, the pretensions of his Christ to Godhood! At Berlin — one of the great seats of learning — professors of modern *exact* sciences, turning their backs on the boasted results of enlightenment of the post-Galileonian period, are quietly snuffing out the candle of the great Florentine; seeking, in short, to prove the heliocentric system, and even the earth's rotation, but the dreams of deluded scientists, Newton a visionary, and all past and present astronomers but clever calculators of unverifiable problems.[4]

---

4 See the last chapter of this volume, p. 622.

Between these two conflicting Titans — Science and Theology — is a bewildered public, fast losing all belief in man's personal immortality, in a deity of any kind, and rapidly descending to the level of a mere animal existence. Such is the picture of the hour, illumined by the bright noonday sun of this Christian and scientific era!

Would it be strict justice to condemn to critical lapidation the most humble and modest of authors for *entirely rejecting the authority of both these combatants?* Are we not bound rather to take as the true aphorism of this century, the declaration of Horace Greeley: "I accept *unreservedly* the views of no man, living or dead"? [5] Such, at all events, will be our motto, and we mean that principle to be our constant guide throughout this work.

Among the many phenomenal outgrowths of our century, the strange creed of the so-called Spiritualists has arisen amid the tottering ruins of self-styled revealed religions and materialistic philosophies; and yet it alone offers a possible last refuge of compromise between the two. That this unexpected ghost of pre-Christian days finds poor welcome from our sober and positive century, is not surprising. Times have strangely changed; and it is but recently that a well-known Brooklyn preacher pointedly remarked in a sermon, that could Jesus come back and behave in the streets of New York, as he did in those of Jerusalem, he would find himself confined in the prison of the Tombs.[6] What sort of welcome, then, could Spiritualism ever expect? True enough, the weird stranger seems neither attractive nor promising at first sight. Shapeless and uncouth, like an infant attended by seven nurses, it is coming out of its teens lame and mutilated. The name of its enemies is legion; its friends and protectors are a handful. But what of that? When was ever truth accepted *a priori*? Because the champions of Spiritualism have in their fanaticism magnified its qualities, and remained blind to its imperfections, that gives no excuse to doubt its reality. A forgery is impossible when we have no model to forge after. The fanaticism of Spiritualists is itself a proof of the genuineness and possibility of their phenomena. They give us facts that we may investigate, not assertions that we must believe without proof. Millions of reasonable men and women do not so easily succumb to collective hallucination. And so, while the clergy, following their own interpretations of the *Bible,* and science its self-made *Codex* of possibilities in nature, refuse it a fair hearing, *real* science and *true* religion are silent, and gravely wait further developments.

THE PLATONIC PHILOSOPHY AFFORDS THE ONLY MIDDLE GROUND

The whole question of phenomena rests on the correct comprehension of old philosophies. Whither, then, should we turn, in our perplexity, but to the ancient sages, since, on the pretext of superstition, we are refused an explanation by the modern? Let us ask them what they know of genuine science and religion; not in the matter of mere details, but in all the broad conception of these twin truths — so strong in their unity, so weak when divided. Besides, we may find our profit in comparing this boasted modern science with ancient ignorance; this improved modern theology with the "Secret doctrines" of the ancient universal religion. Perhaps we may thus discover a neutral ground whence we can reach and profit by both.

---

5 *"Recollections of a Busy Life,"* p. 147.
6 Henry Ward Beecher.

It is the Platonic philosophy, the most elaborate compend of the abstruse systems of old India, that can alone afford us this middle ground. Although twenty-two and a quarter centuries have elapsed since the death of Plato, the great minds of the world are still occupied with his writings. He was, in the fullest sense of the word, the world's interpreter. And the greatest philosopher of the pre-Christian era mirrored faithfully in his works the spiritualism of the Vedic philosophers who lived thousands of years before himself, and its metaphysical expression. Vyasa, Djeminy, Kapila, Vrihaspati, Sumati, and so many others, will be found to have transmitted their indelible imprint through the intervening centuries upon Plato and his school. Thus is warranted the inference that to Plato and the ancient Hindu sages was alike revealed the same wisdom. So surviving the shock of time, what can this wisdom be but divine and eternal?

Plato taught justice as subsisting in the soul of its possessor and his greatest good. "Men, in proportion to their intellect, have admitted his transcendent claims." Yet his commentators, almost with one consent, shrink from every passage which implies that his metaphysics are based on a solid foundation, and not on ideal conceptions.

But Plato could not accept a philosophy destitute of spiritual aspirations; the two were at one with him. For the old Grecian sage there was a single object of attainment: REAL KNOWLEDGE. He considered those only to be genuine philosophers, or students of truth, who possess the knowledge of the really-existing, in opposition to the mere seeing; of the *always-existing*, in opposition to the transitory; and of that which exists *permanently*, in opposition to that which waxes, wanes, and is developed and destroyed alternately. "Beyond all finite existences and secondary causes, all laws, ideas, and principles, there is an INTELLIGENCE or MIND [νοῦς, *nous* , the spirit], the first principle of all principles, the Supreme Idea on which all other ideas are grounded; the Monarch and Lawgiver of the universe; the ultimate substance from which all things derive their being and essence, the first and efficient Cause of all the order, and harmony, and beauty, and excellency, and goodness, which pervades the universe — who is called, by way of preëminence and excellence, the Supreme Good, the God (ὁ θεὸς) 'the God over all' (ὁ επι πασι θεὸς)."[7] He is not the truth nor the intelligence, but "the father of it." Though this eternal essence of things may not be perceptible by our physical senses, it may be apprehended by the mind of those who are not wilfully obtuse. "To you," said Jesus to his elect disciples, "it is given to know the mysteries of the Kingdom of God, but to them [the πολλοὶ] it is not given; . . . therefore speak I to them in parables [or allegories]; because they seeing, see not, and hearing, they hear not, neither do they understand."[8]

The philosophy of Plato, we are assured by Porphyry, of the Neoplatonic School was taught and illustrated in the MYSTERIES. Many have questioned and even denied this; and Lobeck, in his *Aglaophomus*, has gone to the extreme of representing the sacred orgies as little more than an empty show to captivate the imagination. As though Athens and Greece would for twenty centuries and more have repaired every fifth year to Eleusis to witness a solemn religious farce! Augustine, the papa-bishop of Hippo, has resolved such assertions. He declares that the doctrines of the Alexandrian Platonists were the original esoteric doctrines of the first followers of Plato, and describes Plotinus as a Plato resuscitated. He

---

7 Cocker, "*Christianity and Greek Philosophy*," xi., p. 377.
8 *Gospel According to Matthew*, xiii. 11, 13.

also explains the motives of the great philosopher for veiling the interior sense of what he taught.[9]

As to the *myths,* Plato declares in the *Gorgias* and the *Phædon* that they were the vehicles of great truths well worth the seeking. But commentators are so little *en rapport* with the great philosopher as to be compelled to acknowledge that they are ignorant where "the doctrinal ends, and the mythical begins." Plato put to flight the popular superstition concerning magic and dæmons, and developed the exaggerated notions of the time into rational theories and metaphysical conceptions. Perhaps these would not quite stand the inductive method of reasoning established by Aristotle; nevertheless they are satisfactory in the highest degree to those who apprehend the existence of that higher faculty of insight or intuition, as affording a criterion for ascertaining truth.

Basing all his doctrines upon the presence of the Supreme Mind, Plato taught that the *nous,* spirit, or rational soul of man, being "generated by the Divine Father," possessed a nature kindred, or even homogeneous, with the Divinity, and was capable of beholding the eternal realities. This faculty of contemplating reality in a direct and immediate manner belongs to God alone; the aspiration for this knowledge constitutes what is really meant by *philosophy* — the love of wisdom. The love of truth is inherently the love of good; and so predominating over every desire of the soul, purifying it and assimilating it to the divine, thus governing every act of the individual, it raises man to a participation and communion with Divinity, and restores him to the likeness of God. "This flight," says Plato in the *Theætetus,* "consists in becoming like God, and this assimilation is the becoming just and holy with wisdom."

The basis of this assimilation is always asserted to be the preëxistence of the spirit or *nous.* In the allegory of the chariot and winged steeds, given in the *Phædrus,* he represents the psychical nature as composite and two-fold; the *thumos,* or *epithumetic* part, formed from the substances of the world of phenomena; and the θυμοιδές, *thumoeides,* the essence of which is linked to the eternal world. The present earth-life is a fall and punishment. The soul dwells in "the grave which we call *the body,*" and in its incorporate state, and previous to the discipline of education, the noetic or spiritual element is "asleep." Life is thus a dream, rather than a reality. Like the captives in the subterranean cave, described in *The Republic,* the back is turned to the light, we perceive only the shadows of objects, and think them the

---

9 "The accusations of atheism, the introducing of foreign deities, and corrupting of the Athenian youth, which were made against Socrates, afforded ample justification for Plato to conceal the arcane preaching of his doctrines. Doubtless the peculiar diction or 'jargon' of the alchemists was employed for a like purpose. The dungeon, the rack, and the fagot were employed without scruple by Christians of every shade, the Roman Catholics especially, against all who taught even natural science contrary to the theories entertained by the Church. Pope Gregory the Great even inhibited the grammatical use of Latin as heathenish. The offense of Socrates consisted in unfolding to his disciples the arcane doctrine concerning the gods, which was taught in the Mysteries and was a capital crime. He also was charged by Aristophanes with introducing the new god Dinos into the republic as the demiurgos or artificer, and the lord of the solar universe. The Heliocentric system was also a doctrine of the Mysteries; and hence, when Aristarchus the Pythagorean taught it openly, Cleanthes declared that the Greeks ought to have called him to account and condemned him for blasphemy against the gods," — ("Plutarch"). But Socrates had never been initiated, and hence divulged nothing which had ever been imparted to him.

actual realities. Is not this the idea of *Maya*, or the illusion of the senses in physical life, which is so marked a feature in Buddhistical philosophy? But these shadows, if we have not given ourselves up absolutely to the sensuous nature, arouse in us the reminiscence of that higher world that we once inhabited. "The interior spirit has some dim and shadowy recollection of its antenatal state of bliss, and some instinctive and proleptic yearnings for its return." It is the province of the discipline of philosophy to disinthrall it from the bondage of sense, and raise it into the empyrean of pure thought, to the vision of eternal truth, goodness, and beauty. "The soul," says Plato, in the *Theætetus*, "cannot come into the form of a man if it has never seen the truth. This is a recollection of those things which our soul formerly saw when journeying with Deity, despising the things which we now say *are*, and looking up to that which REALLY IS. Wherefore the *nous*, or spirit, of the philosopher (or student of the higher truth) alone is furnished with wings; because he, to the best of his ability, keeps these things in mind, of which the contemplation renders even Deity itself divine. By making the right use of these things remembered from the former life, by constantly perfecting himself in the perfect mysteries, a man becomes truly perfect — an initiate into the diviner wisdom."

Hence we may understand why the sublimer scenes in the Mysteries were always in the night. The life of the interior spirit is the death of the external nature; and the night of the physical world denotes the day of the spiritual. Dionysus, the night-sun, is, therefore, worshipped rather than Helios, orb of day. In the Mysteries were symbolized the preëxistent condition of the spirit and soul, and the lapse of the latter into earth-life and Hades, the miseries of that life, the purification of the soul, and its restoration to divine bliss, or reunion with spirit. Theon, of Smyrna, aptly compares the philosophical discipline to the mystic rites: "Philosophy," says he, "may be called the initiation into the true arcana, and the instruction in the genuine Mysteries. There are five parts of this initiation: I., the previous purification; II., the admission to participation in the arcane rites; III., the epoptic revelation; IV., the investiture or enthroning; V. — the fifth, which is produced from all these, is friendship and interior communion with God, and the enjoyment of that felicity which arises from intimate converse with divine beings. . . . Plato denominates the *epopteia*, or personal view, the perfect contemplation of things which are apprehended intuitively, absolute truths and ideas. He also considers the binding of the head and crowning as analogous to the authority which any one receives from his instructors, of leading others into the same contemplation. The fifth gradation is the most perfect felicity arising from hence, and, according to Plato, an assimilation to divinity as far as is possible to human beings."[10]

REVIEW OF THE ANCIENT PHILOSOPHICAL SYSTEMS

Such is Platonism. "Out of Plato," says Ralph Waldo Emerson, "come all things that are still written and debated among men of thought." He absorbed the learning of his times — of Greece from Philolaus to Socrates; then of Pythagoras in Italy; then what he could procure from Egypt and the East. He was so broad that all philosophy, European and Asiatic, was in his doctrines; and to culture and contemplation he added the nature and qualities of the poet.

---

10 See Thomas Taylor, *"Eleusinian and Bacchic Mysteries,"* p. 47. New York: J. W. Bouton, 1875.

The followers of Plato generally adhered strictly to his psychological theories. Several, however, like Xenocrates, ventured into bolder speculations. Speusippus, the nephew and successor of the great philosopher, was the author of the *Numerical Analysis,* a treatise on the Pythagorean numbers. Some of his speculations are not found in the written *Dialogues;* but as he was a listener to the unwritten lectures of Plato, the judgment of Enfield is doubtless correct, that he did not differ from his master. He was evidently, though not named, the antagonist whom Aristotle criticised, when professing to cite the argument of Plato against the doctrine of Pythagoras, that all things were in themselves numbers, or rather, inseparable from the idea of numbers. He especially endeavored to show that the Platonic doctrine of ideas differed essentially from the Pythagorean, in that it presupposed numbers and magnitudes to exist apart from things. He also asserted that Plato taught that there could be no *real* knowledge, if the object of that knowledge was not carried beyond or above the sensible.

But Aristotle was no trustworthy witness. He misrepresented Plato, and he almost caricatured the doctrines of Pythagoras. There is a canon of interpretation, which should guide us in our examinations of every philosophical opinion: "The human mind has, under the necessary operation of its own laws, been compelled to entertain the same fundamental ideas, and the human heart to cherish the same feelings in all ages." It is certain that Pythagoras awakened the deepest intellectual sympathy of his age, and that his doctrines exerted a powerful influence upon the mind of Plato. His cardinal idea was that there existed a permanent principle of unity beneath the forms, changes, and other phenomena of the universe. Aristotle asserted that he taught that "numbers are the first principles of all entities." Ritter has expressed the opinion that the formula of Pythagoras should be taken symbolically, which is doubtless correct. Aristotle goes on to associate these *numbers* with the "forms" and "ideas" of Plato. He even declares that Plato said: "forms are numbers," and that "ideas are substantial existences — real beings." Yet Plato did not so teach. He declared that the final cause was the Supreme Goodness — τo $\dot{\alpha}\gamma\alpha\theta\acute{o}\nu$. "Ideas are objects of pure conception for the human reason, and they are attributes of the Divine Reason."[11] Nor did he ever say that "forms are numbers." What he did say may be found in the *Timæus:* "God formed things as they first arose according to forms and numbers."

It is recognized by modern science that all the higher laws of nature assume the form of quantitative statement. This is perhaps a fuller elaboration or more explicit affirmation of the Pythagorean doctrine. Numbers were regarded as the best representations of the laws of harmony which pervade the cosmos. We know too that in chemistry the doctrine of atoms and the laws of combination are actually and, as it were, arbitrarily defined by numbers. As Mr. W. Archer Butler has expressed it: "The world is, then, through all its departments, a living arithmetic in its development, a realized geometry in its repose."

The key to the Pythagorean dogmas is the general formula of unity in multiplicity, the one evolving the many and pervading the many. This is the ancient doctrine of emanation in few words. Even the apostle Paul accepted it as true. "$E\xi$ $\alpha\nu\tauo\hat{\nu}$, $\kappa\alpha\iota$ $\delta\iota'$ $\alpha\nu\tauo\hat{\nu}$, $\kappa\alpha\iota$ $\epsilon\iota\varsigma$ $\alpha\nu\tau\grave{o}\nu$ $\tau\alpha$ $\pi\grave{\alpha}\nu\tau\alpha$" — Out of him and through him and in him all things are. This, as we can see by the following quotation, is purely Hindu and Brahmanical:

---

11 Cousin, *"History of Philosophy,"* I., ix.

"When the dissolution — Pralaya — had arrived at its term, the great Being — Para-Atma or Para-Purusha — the Lord existing through himself, out of whom and through whom all things were, and are and will be . . . resolved to emanate from his own substance the various creatures" (*Manava-Dharma-Sastra*, book i., slokas 6 and 7).

The mystic Decad 1 + 2 + 3 + 4 = 10 is a way of expressing this idea. The One is God, the Two, matter; the Three, combining Monad and Duad, and partaking of the nature of both, is the phenomenal world; the Tetrad, or form of perfection, expresses the emptiness of all; and the Decad, or sum of all, involves the entire cosmos. The universe is the combination of a thousand elements, and yet the expression of a single spirit — a chaos to the sense, a cosmos to the reason.

The whole of this combination of the progression of numbers in the idea of creation is Hindu. The Being existing through himself, Swayambhu or Swayambhuva, as he is called by some, is one. He emanates from himself the creative faculty, Brahma or Purusha (the divine male), and the one becomes Two; out of this Duad, union of the purely intellectual principle with the principle of matter, evolves a third, which is Viradj, the phenomenal world. It is out of this invisible and incomprehensible trinity, the Brahmanic Trimurty, that evolves the second triad which represents the three faculties — the creative, the conservative, and the transforming. These are typified by Brahma, Vishnu, and Siva, but are again and ever blended into one. Unity, Brahma, or as the Vedas called him, Tridandi, is the god triply manifested, which gave rise to the symbolical *Aum* or the abbreviated Trimurty. It is but under this trinity, ever active and tangible to all our senses, that the invisible and unknown Monas can manifest itself to the world of mortals. When he becomes *Sarira*, or he who puts on a visible form, he typifies all the principles of matter, all the germs of life, he is Purusha, the god of the three visages, or triple power, the essence of the Vedic triad. "Let the Brahmas know the sacred Syllable (Aum), the three words of the Savitri, and read the *Vedas* daily" (*Manu*, book iv., sloka 125).

> "After having produced the universe, He whose power is incomprehensible vanished again, absorbed in the Supreme Soul. . . . . Having retired into the primitive darkness, the great Soul remains within the unknown, and is void of all form. . . . .
>
> "When having again reunited the subtile elementary principles, it introduces itself into either a vegetable or animal seed, it assumes at each a new form."
>
> "It is thus that, by an alternative waking and rest, the Immutable Being causes to revive and die eternally all the existing creatures, active and inert"
>
> (*Manu*, book i., sloka 50, and others).

He who has studied Pythagoras and his speculations on the Monad, which, after having emanated the Duad retires into silence and darkness, and thus creates the Triad can realize whence came the philosophy of the great Samian Sage, and after him that of Socrates and Plato.

Speusippus seems to have taught that the psychical or thumetic soul was immortal as well as the spirit or rational soul, and further on we will show his reasons. He also — like Philolaus and Aristotle, in his disquisitions upon the soul — makes of æther an element; so that there were five principal elements to correspond with the five regular figures in

Geometry. This became also a doctrine of the Alexandrian school.[12] Indeed, there was much in the doctrines of the *Philaletheans* which did not appear in the works of the older Platonists, but was doubtless taught in substance by the philosopher himself, but with his usual reticence was not committed to writing as being too arcane for promiscuous publication. Speusippus and Xenocrates after him, held, like their great master, that the *anima mundi,* or world-soul, was not the Deity, but a manifestation. Those philosophers never conceived of the One as an *animate nature.*[13] The original One did not *exist,* as we understand the term. Not till he had united with the many — emanated existence (the monad and duad) was a being produced. The τίμιον, honored — the something manifested, dwells in the centre as in the circumference, but it is only the reflection of the Deity — the World-Soul.[14] In this doctrine we find the spirit of esoteric Buddhism.

A man's idea of God, is that image of blinding light that he sees reflected in the concave mirror of his own soul, and yet this is not, in very truth, God, but only His reflection. His glory is there, but, it is the light of his own Spirit that the man sees, and it is all he can bear to look upon. *The clearer the mirror, the brighter will be the divine image.* But the external world cannot be witnessed in it at the same moment. In the ecstatic Yogin, in the illuminated Seer, the spirit will shine like the noonday sun; in the debased victim of earthly attraction, the radiance has disappeared, for the mirror is obscured with the stains of matter. Such men deny their God, and would willingly deprive humanity of soul at one blow.

No GOD, No SOUL? Dreadful, annihilating thought! The maddening nightmare of a lunatic — Atheist; presenting before his fevered vision, a hideous, ceaseless procession of sparks of cosmic matter created by *no one;* self-appearing, self-existent, and self-developing; this Self *no Self,* for it is *nothing* and *nobody;* floating onward from *nowhence,* it is propelled by no Cause, for there is none, and it rushes *nowhither.* And this in a circle of Eternity blind, inert, and — CAUSELESS. What is even the erroneous conception of the Buddhistic Nirvana in comparison! The Nirvana is preceded by numberless spiritual transformations and metempsychoses, during which the entity loses not for a second the sense of its own individuality, and which may last for millions of ages before the Final *No*-Thing is reached.

Though some have considered Speusippus as inferior to Aristotle, the world is nevertheless indebted to him for defining and expounding many things that Plato had left obscure in his doctrine of the Sensible and Ideal. His maxim was "The Immaterial is known by means of scientific thought, the Material by scientific perception."[15]

Xenocrates expounded many of the unwritten theories and teachings of his master. He too held the Pythagorean doctrine, and his system of numerals and mathematics in the highest estimation. Recognizing but three degrees of knowledge—*Thought, Perception,* and *Envisagement* (or knowledge by *Intuition*), he made the former busy itself with all that which is *beyond* the heavens; Perception with things in the heavens; Intuition with the heavens themselves.

---

12 "*Theol. Arithme.,*" p. 62, "On Pythag. Numbers."
13 Plato, "*Parmenid.,*" 141 E.
14 See Stobœus' "*Ecl.,*" i., 862.
15 Sextus, "*Math.,*" vii.

We find again these theories, and nearly in the same language in the *Manava-Dharma-Sastra,* when speaking of the creation of man: "He (the Supreme) drew from his own essence the immortal breath which *perisheth not in the being,* and to this soul of the being he gave the Ahancara (conscience of the *ego*) sovereign guide." Then he gave to that soul of the being (man) the intellect formed of *the three qualities,* and the five organs of the outward perception."

These three qualities are Intelligence, Conscience, and Will; answering to the Thought, Perception, and Envisagement of Xenocrates. The relation of numbers to Ideas was developed by him further than by Speusippus, and he surpassed Plato in his definition of the doctrine of Indivisible Magnitudes. Reducing them to their ideal primary elements, he demonstrated that every figure and form originated out of the smallest indivisible line. That Xenocrates held the same theories as Plato in relation to the human soul (supposed to be a number) is evident, though Aristotle contradicts this, like every other teaching of this philosopher.[16] This is conclusive evidence that many of Plato's doctrines were delivered orally, even were it shown that Xenocrates and not Plato was the first to originate the theory of indivisible magnitudes. He derives the Soul from the first Duad, and calls it a self-moved number.[17] Theophrastus remarks that he entered and eliminated this Soul-theory more than any other Platonist. He built upon it the cosmological doctrine, and proved the necessary existence in every part of the universal space of a successive and progressive series of animated and thinking though spiritual beings.[18] The Human Soul with him is a compound of the most spiritual properties of the Monad and the Duad, possessing the highest principles of both. If, like Plato and Prodicus, he refers to the Elements as to Divine Powers, and calls them gods, neither himself nor others connected any anthropomorphic idea with the appellation. Krische remarks that he called them gods only that these elementary powers should not be confounded with the dæmons of the nether world[19] (the Elementary Spirits). As the Soul of the World permeates the whole Cosmos, even beasts must have in them something divine.[20] This, also, is the doctrine of Buddhists and the Hermetists, and Manu endows with a living soul even the plants and the tiniest blade of grass. —

The dæmons, according to this theory, are intermediate beings between the divine perfection and human sinfulness,[21] and he divides them into classes, each subdivided in many others. But he states expressly that the individual or personal soul is the leading guardian dæmon of every man, and that no dæmon has more power over us than our own. Thus the *Daimonion* of Socrates is the god or Divine Entity which inspired him all his life. It depends on man either to open or close his perceptions to the Divine voice. Like Speusippus he ascribed immortality to the $\psi v \chi \eta$, psychical body, or irrational soul. But some Hermetic philosophers have taught that the soul has a separate continued existence only so long as in its passage through the spheres any material or earthly particles remain incorporated in it;

---

16 "*Metaph.,*" 407, a. 3.
17 Appendix to "*Timæus.*"
18 Stob., "*Ecl.,*" i., 62.
19 Krische, "*Forsch.,*" p. 322, etc.
20 Clem., "*Alex. Stro.,*" v., 590.
21 Plutarch, "*De Isid,*" chap. 25, p. 360.

and that when absolutely purified, the latter are *annihilated*, and the quintessence of the soul alone becomes blended with its *divine* spirit (the *Rational*), and the two are thenceforth one.

Zeller states that Xenocrates forbade the eating of animal food, not because he saw in beasts something akin to man, as he ascribed to them a dim consciousness of God, but, "for the opposite reason, lest the irrationality of animal souls might thereby obtain a certain influence over us."[22] But we believe that it was rather because, like Pythagoras, he had had the Hindu sages for his masters and models. Cicero depicted Xenocrates utterly despising everything except the highest virtue;[23] and describes the stainlessness and severe austerity of his character.[24] "To free ourselves from the subjection of sensuous existence, to conquer the Titanic elements in our terrestrial nature through the Divine one, is our problem." Zeller makes him say:[25] "Purity, even in the secret longings of our heart, is the greatest duty, and only philosophy and the initiation into the Mysteries help toward the attainment of this object."

Crantor, another philosopher associated with the earliest days of Plato's Academy, conceived the human soul as formed out of the primary substance of all things, the Monad or *One*, and the Duad or the *Two*. Plutarch speaks at length of this philosopher, who like his master believed in souls being distributed in earthly bodies as an exile and punishment.

Herakleides, though some critics do not believe him to have strictly adhered to Plato's primal philosophy,[26] taught the same ethics. Zeller presents him to us imparting, like Hiçetas and Eçphantus, the Pythagorean doctrine of the diurnal rotation of the earth and the immobility of the fixed stars, but adds that he was ignorant of the annual revolution of the earth around the sun, and of the heliocentric system.[27] But we have good evidence that the latter system was taught in the Mysteries, and that Socrates died for *atheism, i.e.,* for divulging this sacred knowledge. Herakleides adopted fully the Pythagorean and Platonic views of the human soul, its faculties and its capabilities. He describes it as a luminous, highly ethereal essence. He affirms that souls inhabit the milky way before descending "into generation" or sublunary existence. His dæmons or spirits are airy and vaporous bodies.

In the *Epinomis* is fully stated the doctrine of the Pythagorean numbers in relation to created things. As a true Platonist, its author maintains that wisdom can only be attained by a thorough inquiry into the occult nature of the creation; it alone assures us an existence of bliss after death. The immortality of the soul is greatly speculated upon in this treatise; but its author adds that we can attain to this knowledge only through a complete comprehension of the numbers; for the man, unable to distinguish the straight line from a curved one will never have wisdom enough to secure a mathematical demonstration of the *invisible, i.e.,* we must assure ourselves of the objective existence of our soul (astral body) before we learn that we are in possession of a divine and immortal spirit. Iamblichus says the same thing; adding, moreover, that it is a secret belonging to the highest initiation. The Divine Power, he says, always felt indignant with those "who rendered manifest the

---

22 "*Plato und die Alt. Akademie.*"
23 "*Tusc.,*" v., 18, 51.
24 Ibid. Cf. p. 559.
25 "*Plato und die Alt. Akademie.*"
26 Ed. Zeller, "*Philos. der Griech.*"
27 "*Plato und die Alt. Akademie.*"

composition of the *icostagonus*," viz., who delivered the method of inscribing in a sphere the dodecahedron.[28]

The idea that "numbers" possessing the greatest virtue, produce always what is good and never what is evil, refers to justice, equanimity of temper, and everything that is harmonious. When the author speaks of every star as an individual soul, he only means what the Hindu initiates and the Hermetists taught before and after him, viz.: that every star is an independent planet, which, like our earth, has a soul of its own, every atom of matter being impregnated with the divine influx of the soul of the world. It breathes and lives; it feels and suffers as well as enjoys life in its way. What naturalist is prepared to dispute it on good evidence? Therefore, we must consider the celestial bodies as the images of gods; as partaking of the divine powers in their substance; and though they are not immortal in their soul-entity, their agency in the economy of the universe is entitled to divine honors, such as we pay to minor gods. The idea is plain, and one must be malevolent indeed to misrepresent it. If the author of *Epinomis* places these fiery gods higher than the animals, plants, and even mankind, all of which, as earthly creatures, are assigned by him a lower place, who can prove him wholly wrong? One must needs go deep indeed into the profundity of the abstract metaphysics of the old philosophies, who would understand that their various embodiments of their conceptions are, after all, based upon an identical apprehension of the nature of the First Cause, its attributes and method.

Again when the author of *Epinomis* locates between these highest and lowest gods (embodied souls) three classes of dæmons, and peoples the universe with invisible beings, he is more rational than our modern scientists, who make between the two extremes one vast hiatus of being, the playground of blind forces. Of these three classes the first two are invisible; their bodies are pure ether and fire (*planetary spirits*); the dæmons of the third class are clothed with vapory bodies; they are usually invisible, but sometimes making themselves concrete become visible for a few seconds. These are the earthly spirits, or our astral souls.

It is these doctrines, which, studied analogically, and on the principle of correspondence, led the ancient, and may now lead the modern Philaletheian step by step toward the solution of the greatest mysteries. On the brink of the dark chasm separating the spiritual from the physical world stands modern science, with eyes closed and head averted, pronouncing the gulf impassable and bottomless, though she holds in her hand a torch which she need only lower into the depths to show her her mistake. But across this chasm, the patient student of Hermetic philosophy has constructed a bridge.

In his *Fragments of Science* Tyndall makes the following sad confession: "If you ask me whether science has solved, or is likely in our day to solve the problem of this universe, I must shake my head in doubt." If moved by an afterthought, he corrects himself later, and assures his audience that experimental evidence has helped him to discover, in the opprobrium-covered matter, the "promise and potency of every quality of life," he only jokes. It would be as difficult for Professor Tyndall to offer any ultimate and irrefutable proofs of what he asserts, as it was for Job to insert a hook into the nose of the leviathan.

---

28 One of the five solid figures in Geometry.

To avoid confusion that might easily arise by the frequent employment of certain terms in a sense different from that familiar to the reader, a few explanations will be timely. We desire to leave no pretext either for misunderstanding or misrepresentation. Magic may have one signification to one class of readers and another to another class. We shall give it the meaning which it has in the minds of its Oriental students and practitioners. And so with the words *Hermetic Science, Occultism, Hierophant, Adept, Sorcerer*, etc.; there has been little agreement of late as to their meaning. Though the distinctions between the terms are very often insignificant — merely ethnic — still, it may be useful to the general reader to know just what that is. We give a few alphabetically.

ÆTHROBACY, is the Greek name for walking or being lifted in the air; *levitation*, so called, among modern spiritualists. It may be either conscious or unconscious; in the one case, it is magic; in the other, either disease or a power which requires a few words of elucidation.

A Syriac Manuscript on Simon Magus

A symbolical explanation of æthrobacy is given in an old Syriac manuscript which was translated in the fifteenth century by one Malchus, an alchemist. In connection with the case of Simon Magus, one passage reads thus:

"Simon, laying his face upon the ground, whispered in her ear, 'O mother Earth, give me, I pray thee, some of thy breath; and I will give thee mine; *let me loose*, O mother, that I may carry thy words to the stars, and I will return faithfully to thee after a while.' And the Earth strengthening her status, none to her detriment, sent her genius to breathe of her *breath* on Simon, *while he breathed on her*; and the stars rejoiced to be visited by the mighty One."

The starting-point here is the recognized electro-chemical principle that bodies similarly electrified repel each other, while those differently electrified mutually attract. "The most elementary knowledge of chemistry," says Professor Cooke, "shows that, while radicals of opposite natures combine most eagerly together, two metals, or two closely-allied metalloids, show but little affinity for each other."

Glossary of Terms Used in This Book

The earth is a magnetic body; in fact, as some scientists have found, it is one vast magnet, as Paracelsus affirmed some 300 years ago. It is charged with one form of electricity — let us call it positive — which it evolves continuously by spontaneous action, in its interior or centre of motion. Human bodies, in common with all other forms of matter, are charged with the opposite form of electricity — negative. That is to say, organic or inorganic bodies, if left to themselves will constantly and involuntarily charge themselves with, and evolve the form of electricity opposed to that of the earth itself. Now, what is weight? Simply the attraction of the earth. "Without the attractions of the earth you would have no weight," says Professor Stewart;[29] "and if you had an earth twice as heavy as this, you would have double the attraction." How then, can we get rid of this attraction? According to the electrical law above stated, there is an attraction between our planet and the organisms

---

29 *"The Sun and the Earth."*

upon it, which holds them upon the surface of the ground. But the law of gravitation has been counteracted in many instances, by levitations of persons and inanimate objects; how account for this? The condition of our physical systems, say theurgic philosophers, is largely dependent upon the action of our will. If well-regulated, it can produce "miracles"; among others a change of this electrical polarity from negative to positive; the man's relations with the earth-magnet would then become repellent, and "gravity" for him would have ceased to exist. It would then be as natural for him to rush into the air until the repellent force had exhausted itself, as, before, it had been for him to remain upon the ground. The altitude of his levitation would be measured by his ability, greater or less, to charge his body with positive electricity. This control over the physical forces once obtained, alteration of his levity or gravity would be as easy as breathing.

The study of nervous diseases has established that even in ordinary somnambulism, as well as in mesmerized somnambulists, the weight of the body seems to be diminished. Professor Perty mentions a somnambulist, Koehler, who when in the water could not sink, but floated. The seeress of Prevorst rose to the surface of the bath and could not be kept seated in it. He speaks of Anna Fleisher, who being subject to epileptic fits, was often seen by the Superintendent to rise in the air; and was once, in the presence of two trustworthy witnesses (two deans) and others, raised two and a half yards from her bed in a horizontal position. The similar case of Margaret Rule is cited by Upham in his *History of Salem Witchcraft*. "In ecstatic subjects," adds Professor Perty, "the rising in the air occurs much more frequently than with somnambulists. We are so accustomed to consider gravitation as being a something absolute and unalterable, that the idea of a complete or partial rising in opposition to it seems inadmissible; nevertheless, there are phenomena in which, by means of material forces, gravitation is overcome. In several diseases — as, for instance, nervous fever — the weight of the human body seems to be increased, but in all ecstatic conditions to be diminished. And there may, likewise, be other forces than material ones which can counteract this power."

A Madrid journal, *El Criterio Espiritista*, of a recent date, reports the case of a young peasant girl near Santiago, which possesses a peculiar interest in this connection. "Two bars of magnetized iron held over her horizontally, half a metre distant, was sufficient to suspend her body in the air."

Were our physicians to experiment on such levitated subjects, it would be found that they are strongly charged with a similar form of electricity to that of the spot, which, according to the law of gravitation, ought to *attract* them, or rather prevent their levitation. And, if some physical nervous disorder, as well as spiritual ecstasy produce unconsciously to the subject the same effects, it proves that if this force in nature were properly studied, it could be regulated at will.

ALCHEMISTS — From *Al* and *Chemi*, fire, or the god and patriarch, *Kham*, also, the name of Egypt. The Rosicrucians of the middle ages, such as Robertus de Fluctibus (Robert Fludd), Paracelsus, Thomas Vaughan (Eugenius Philalethes), Van Helmont, and others, were all alchemists, who sought for the *hidden spirit* in every inorganic matter. Some people — nay, the great majority — have accused alchemists of charlatanry and false pretending. Surely such men as Roger Bacon, Agrippa, Henry Kunrath, and the Arabian Geber (the first to introduce into Europe some of the secrets of chemistry), can hardly be treated as impostors — least of all as fools. Scientists who are reforming the science of physics upon the basis of the atomic theory of Demokritus, as restated by John Dalton, conveniently forget that Demokritus, of Abdera, was an alchemist, and that the mind that was capable of penetrating so far into the secret operations of nature in one direction must have had good reasons to study and become a Hermetic philosopher. Olaus Borrichias says, that the cradle of alchemy is to be sought in the most distant times.

ASTRAL LIGHT — The same as the *sidereal light* of Paracelsus and other Hermetic philosophers. Physically, it is the ether of modern science. Metaphysically, and in its spiritual, or occult sense, ether is a great deal more than is often imagined. In occult physics, and alchemy, it is well demonstrated to enclose within its shoreless waves not only Mr. Tyndall's "*promise* and potency of every quality of life," but also the *realization* of the potency of every quality of spirit. Alchemists and Hermetists believe that their astral, or sidereal ether, besides the above properties of sulphur, and white and red magnesia, or *magnes,* is the *anima mundi,* the workshop of Nature and of all the cosmos, spiritually, as well as physically. The "grand magisterium" asserts itself in the phenomenon of mesmerism, in the "levitation" of human and inert objects; and may be called the ether from its spiritual aspect.

The designation *astral* is ancient, and was used by some of the Neoplatonists. Porphyry describes the celestial body which is always joined with the soul as "immortal, luminous, and star-like." The root of this word may be found, perhaps, in the Scythic *aistaer* — which means star, or the Assyrian *Istar,* which, according to Burnouf has the same sense. As the Rosicrucians regarded the real, as the direct opposite of the apparent, and taught that what seems light to *matter,* is darkness to *spirit,* they searched for the latter in the astral ocean of invisible fire which encompasses the world; and claim to have traced the equally invisible divine spirit, which overshadows every man and is erroneously called *soul,* to the very throne of the Invisible and Unknown God. As the great cause must always remain invisible and imponderable, they could prove their assertions merely by demonstration of its effects in this world of matter, by calling them forth from the unknowable down into the knowable universe of effects. That this astral light permeates the whole cosmos, lurking in its latent state even in the minutest particle of rock, they demonstrate by the phenomenon of the spark from flint and from every other stone, whose spirit when forcibly disturbed springs to sight spark-like, and immediately disappears in the realms of the unknowable.

Paracelsus named it the *sidereal light,* taking the term from the Latin. He regarded the starry host (our earth included) as the *condensed* portions of the astral light which "fell down into generation and matter," but whose magnetic or spiritual emanations kept constantly a never-ceasing intercommunication between themselves and the parent-fount of all — the astral light. "The stars attract from us to themselves, and we again from them to us," he says. The body is wood and the life is fire, which comes like the light from the stars and from heaven. "Magic is the philosophy of alchemy," he says again.[30] Everything pertaining to the spiritual world must come to us through the stars, and if we are in friendship with them, we may attain the greatest *magical* effects.

"As fire passes through an iron stove, so do the stars pass through man with all their properties and go into him as the rain into the earth, which gives fruit out of that same rain. Now observe that the stars *surround* the whole earth, *as a shell does the egg;* through the shell comes the air, and penetrates to the centre of the world." The human body is subjected as

---

30 "*De Ente Spirituali,*" lib. iv.; "*de Ente Astrorum,*" book i.; and *opera omnia,* vol. i., pp. 634 and 699.

well as the earth, and planets, and stars, to a double law; it attracts and repels, for it is saturated through with double magnetism, the influx of the astral light. Everything is double in nature; magnetism is positive and negative, active and passive, male and female. Night rests humanity from the day's activity, and restores the equilibrium of human as well as of cosmic nature. When the mesmerizer will have learned the grand secret of polarizing the action and endowing his fluid with a bisexual force he will have become the greatest magician living. Thus the astral light is androgyne, for equilibrium is the resultant of two opposing forces eternally reacting upon each other. The result of this is LIFE. *When the two forces are expanded and remain so long inactive, as to equal one another and so come to a complete rest, the condition is* DEATH. A human being can blow either a hot or a cold breath; and can absorb either cold or hot air. Every child knows how to regulate the temperature of his breath; but how to protect one's self from either hot or cold air, no physiologist has yet learned with certainty. The astral light alone, as the chief agent in magic, can discover to us all secrets of nature. The astral light is identical with the Hindu *akâsa*, a word which we will now explain.

AKÂSA — Literally the word means in Sanscrit *sky*, but in its mystic sense it signifies the *invisible* sky; or, as the Brahmans term it in the Soma-sacrifice (the *Gyotishtoma Agnishtoma*), the god Akâsa, or god Sky. The language of the *Vedas* shows that the Hindus of fifty centuries ago ascribed to it the same properties as do the Thibetan lamas of the present day; that they regarded it as the source of life, the reservoir of all energy, and the propeller of every change of matter. In its latent state it tallies exactly with our idea of the universal ether; in its active state it became the Akâsa, the all-directing and omnipotent god. In the Brahmanical sacrificial mysteries it plays the part of Sadasya, or superintendent over the magical effects of the religious performance, and it had its own appointed Hotar (or priest), who took its name. In India, as in other countries in ancient times, the priests are the representatives on earth of different gods; each taking the name of the deity in whose name he acts.

The Akâsa is the indispensable agent of every Kritya (magical performance) either religious or profane. The Brahmanical expression "to stir up the Brahma" — *Brahma jinvati* — means to stir up the power which lies latent at the bottom of every such magical operation, for the Vedic sacrifices are but ceremonial magic. This power is the Akâsa or the *occult* electricity; the alkahest of the alchemists in one sense, or the universal solvent, the same *anima mundi* as the astral light. At the moment of the sacrifice, the latter becomes imbued with the spirit of Brahma, and so for the time being is Brahma himself. This is the evident origin of the Christian dogma of transubstantiation. As to the most general effects of the Akâsa, the author of one of the most modern works on the occult philosophy, *Art-Magic*, gives for the first time to the world a most intelligible and interesting explanation of the Akâsa in connection with the phenomena attributed to its influence by the fakirs and lamas.

ANTHROPOLOGY — The science of man; embracing among other things:

Physiology, or that branch of natural science which discloses the mysteries of the organs and their functions in men, animals, and plants; and also, and especially,

Psychology, or the great, and in our days, so neglected science of the soul, both as an entity distinct from the spirit and in its relations with the spirit and body. In modern science, psychology relates only or principally to conditions of the nervous system, and almost absolutely ignores the psychical essence and nature. Physicians denominate the science of insanity *psychology*, and name the lunatic chair in medical colleges by that designation.

CHALDEANS, or Kasdim — At first a tribe, then a caste of learned kabalists. They were the savants, the magians of Babylonia, astrologers and diviners. The famous Hillel, the precursor of Jesus in philosophy and in ethics, was a Chaldean. Franck in his *Kabbala* points to the close resemblance of the "secret doctrine" found in the *Avesta* and the religious metaphysics of the Chaldees.

DACTYLS (*daktulos*, a finger). — A name given to the priests attached to the worship of *Kybelé* (Cybelè). Some archæologists derive the name from δάκτυλος, finger, because they were ten, the same in number as the fingers of the hand. But we do not believe the latter hypothesis is the correct one.

DÆMONS — A name given by the ancient people, and especially the philosophers of the Alexandrian school, to all kinds of spirits, whether good or bad, human or otherwise. The appellation is often synonymous with that of gods or angels. But some philosophers tried, with good reason, to make a just distinction between the many classes.

DEMIURGOS, or Demiurge — Artificer; the Supernal Power which built the universe. Freemasons derive from this word their phrase of "Supreme Architect." The chief magistrates of certain Greek cities bore the title.

DERVISHES, or the "whirling charmers," as they are called. Apart from the austerities of life, prayer and contemplation, the Mahometan devotee presents but little similarity with the Hindu fakir. The latter may become a sannyasi, or saint and holy mendicant; the former will never reach beyond his second class of occult manifestations. The dervish may also be a strong mesmerizer, but he will never voluntarily submit to the abominable and almost incredible self-punishment which the fakir invents for himself with an ever-increasing avidity, until nature succumbs and he dies in slow and excruciating tortures. The most dreadful operations, such as flaying the limbs alive; cutting off the toes, feet, and legs; tearing out the eyes; and causing one's self to be buried alive up to the chin in the earth, and passing whole months in this posture, seem child's play to them. One of the most common tortures is that of Tshiddy-Parvady.[31] It consists in suspending the fakir to one of the mobile arms of a kind of gallows to be seen in the vicinity of many of the temples. At the end of each of these arms is fixed a pulley over which passes a rope terminated by an iron hook. This hook is inserted into the bare back of the fakir, who inundating the soil with blood is hoisted up in the air and then whirled round the gallows. From the first moment of this cruel operation until he is either unhooked or the flesh of his back tears out under the weight of the body and the fakir is hurled down on the heads of the crowd, not a muscle of his face will move. He remains calm and serious and as composed as if taking a refreshing bath. The fakir will laugh to scorn every imaginable torture, persuaded that the more his outer body is mortified, the brighter and holier becomes his *inner*, spiritual body. But the Dervish, neither in India, nor in other Mahometan lands, will ever submit to such operations.

DRUIDS — A sacerdotal caste which flourished in Britain and Gaul.

---

31 Or more commonly chārkh pūjā.

ELEMENTAL SPIRITS — The creatures evolved in the four kingdoms of earth, air, fire, and water, and called by the kabalists gnomes, sylphs, salamanders, and undines. They may be termed the forces of nature, and will either operate effects as the servile agents of general law, or may be employed by the disembodied spirits — whether pure or impure — and by living adepts of magic and sorcery, to produce desired phenomenal results. Such beings never become men.[32]

Under the general designation of fairies, and fays, these spirits of the elements appear in the myth, fable, tradition, or poetry of all nations, ancient and modern. Their names are legion — peris, devs, djins, sylvans, satyrs, fauns, elves, dwarfs, trolls, norns, nisses, kobolds, brownies, necks, stromkarls, undines, nixies, salamanders, goblins, ponkes, banshees, kelpies, pixies, moss people, good people, good neighbors, wild women, men of peace, white ladies — and many more. They have been seen, feared, blessed, banned, and invoked in every quarter of the globe and in every age. Shall we then concede that all who have met them were hallucinated?

These elementals are the principal agents of disembodied but *never visible* spirits at seances, and the producers of all the phenomena except the subjective.

ELEMENTARY SPIRITS — Properly, the disembodied *souls* of the depraved; these souls having at some time prior to death separated from themselves their divine spirits, and so lost their chance for immortality. Eliphas Levi and some other kabalists make little distinction between elementary spirits who have been men, and those beings which people the elements, and are the blind forces of nature. Once divorced from their bodies, these souls (also called "astral bodies") of purely materialistic persons, are irresistibly attracted to the earth, where they live a temporary and finite life amid elements congenial to their gross natures. From having never, during their natural lives, cultivated their spirituality, but subordinated it to the material and gross, they are now unfitted for the lofty career of the pure, disembodied being, for whom the atmosphere of earth is stifling and mephitic, and whose attractions are all away from it. After a more or less prolonged period of time these material souls will begin to disintegrate, and finally, like a column of mist, be dissolved, atom by atom, in the surrounding elements.

ESSENES — from *Asa*, a healer. A sect of Jews said by Pliny to have lived near the Dead Sea *"per millia sæculorum"* — for thousands of ages. Some have supposed them to be extreme Pharisees; and others — which may be the true theory — the descendants of the *Benim-nabim* of the *Bible*, and think they were "Kenites" and "*Nazarites*." They had many Buddhistic ideas and practices; and it is noteworthy that the priests of the *Great Mother* at Ephesus, Diana-Bhavani with many breasts, were also so denominated. Eusebius, and after him De Quincey, declared them to be the same as the early Christians, which is more than probable.

---

32 Persons who believe in the clairvoyant power, but are disposed to discredit the existence of any other spirits in nature than disembodied human spirits, will be interested in an account of certain clairvoyant observations which appeared in the *London Spiritualist* of June 29, 1877. A thunder-storm approaching, the seeress saw "a bright spirit emerge from a dark cloud and pass with lightning speed across the sky, and, a few minutes after, a diagonal line of dark spirits in the clouds." These are the *Maruts* of the "Vedas" (See Max Müller's *"Rig-Veda Sanhita"*).

The well-known and respected lecturer, author, and clairvoyant, Mrs. Emma Hardinge Britten, has published accounts of her frequent experiences with these elemental spirits.

The title "brother," used in the early Church, was Essenean: they were a fraternity, or a *koinobion* or community like the early converts. It is noticeable that only the Sadducees, or Zadokites, the priest-caste and their partisans, persecuted the Christians; the Pharisees were generally scholastic and mild, and often sided with the latter. James the Just was a Pharisee till his death; but Paul or *Aher* was esteemed a schismatic.

EVOLUTION — The development of higher orders of animals from the lower. Modern, or so-called *exact* science, holds but to a one-sided physical evolution, prudently avoiding and ignoring the higher or spiritual evolution, which would force our contemporaries to confess the superiority of the ancient philosophers and psychologists over themselves. The ancient sages, ascending to the UNKNOWABLE, made their starting-point from the first manifestation of the unseen, the unavoidable, and from a strict logical reasoning, the absolutely necessary creative Being, the Demiurgos of the universe. Evolution began with them from pure spirit, which descending lower and lower down, assumed at last a visible and comprehensible form, and became matter. Arrived at this point, they speculated in the Darwinian method, but on a far more large and comprehensive basis.

In the *Rig-Veda-Sanhita*, the oldest book of the World[33] (to which even our most prudent Indiologists and Sanscrit scholars assign an antiquity of between two and three thousand years B.C.), in the first book, "Hymns to the Maruts," it is said:

"*Not-being* and *Being* are in the highest heaven, in the birthplace of Daksha, in the lap of Aditi" (*Mandala*, i, Sukta 166).

"In the first age of the gods, Being (the comprehensible Deity) was born from Not-being (whom no intellect can comprehend); after it were born the Regions (the invisible), from them Uttânapada."

"From Uttânapad the Earth was born, the Regions (those that are visible) were born from the Earth. Daksha was born of Aditi, and Aditi from Daksha" (Ibid.).

Aditi is the Infinite, and Daksha is *dakska-pitarah*, literally meaning *the father of gods*, but understood by Max Müller and Roth to mean *the fathers of strength*, "preserving, possessing, granting faculties." Therefore, it is easy to see that "Daksha, born of Aditi and Aditi from Daksha," means what the moderns understand by "correlation of forces"; the more so as we find in this passage (translated by Prof. Müller):

"I place Agni, the source of all beings, the father of strength" (iii., 27, 2), a clear and identical idea which prevailed so much in the doctrines of the Zoroastrians, the Magians, and the mediæval fire-philosophers. Agni is god of fire, of the Spiritual Ether, the very substance of the divine essence of the Invisible God present in every atom of His creation and called by the Rosicrucians the "Celestial Fire." If we only carefully compare the verses from this Mandala, one of which runs thus: "The Sky is your father, the Earth your mother, Soma your brother, Aditi your sister" (i., 191, 6),[34] with the inscription on the *Smaragdine Tablet* of Hermes, we will find the same substratum of metaphysical philosophy, the identical doctrines!

---

33 Translated by Max Müller, Professor of Comparative Philology at the Oxford University, England.
34 "Dyarih vah pitâ, prithivi mâtâ sômah bhrâtâ âditih svasâ."

"As all things were produced by the mediation of one being, so all things were produced from this one thing by adaptation: 'Its father is the sun; its mother is the moon'. . . . etc. Separate the earth from the fire, the *subtile from the gross*. . . . What I had to say about the operation of the *sun* is completed" (*Smaragdine Tablet*).[35]

Professor Max Müller sees in this *Mandala* "at last, something like a theogony, though full of contradictions."[36] The alchemists, kabalists, and students of mystic philosophy will find therein a perfectly defined system of Evolution in the Cosmogony of a people who lived a score of thousands of years before our era. They will find in it, moreover, a perfect identity of thought and even doctrine with the Hermetic philosophy, and also that of Pythagoras and Plato.

In Evolution, as it is now beginning to be understood, there is supposed to be in all matter an impulse to take on a higher form — a supposition clearly expressed by Manu and other Hindu philosophers of the highest antiquity. The philosopher's tree illustrates it in the case of the zinc solution. The controversy between the followers of this school and the Emanationists may be briefly stated thus: The Evolutionist stops all inquiry at the borders of "the Unknowable"; the Emanationist believes that nothing can be evolved — or, as the word means, unwombed or born — except it has first been involved, thus indicating that life is from a spiritual potency above the whole.

FAKIRS — Religious devotees in East India. They are generally attached to Brahmanical pagodas and follow the laws of Manu. A strictly religious fakir will go absolutely naked, with the exception of a small piece of linen called *dhoti*, around his loins. They wear their hair long, and it serves them as a pocket, as they stick in it various objects — such as a pipe, a small flute called *vagudah*, the sounds of which throw the serpents into a cataleptic torpor, and sometimes their bamboo-stick (about one foot long) with *the seven mystical knots* on it. This magical stick, or rather *rod*, the fakir receives from his guru on the day of his initiation, together with the three *mantrams*, which are communicated to him "mouth to ear." No fakir will be seen without this powerful adjunct of his calling. It is, as they all claim, the divining rod, the cause of every occult phenomenon produced by them.[37] The Brahmanical fakir is entirely distinct from the Mussulman mendicant of India, also called fakirs in some parts of the British territory.

HERMETIST— From Hermes, the god of Wisdom, known in Egypt, Syria, and Phœnicia as Thoth, Tat, Adad, Seth, and Sat-an (the latter *not to be taken* in the sense applied to it by Moslems and Christians), and in Greece as Kadmus. The kabalists identify him with Adam *Kadmon*, the first manifestation of the Divine Power, and with Enoch. There were two Hermes: the elder was the Trismegistus, and the second an emanation, or "permutation" of

---

35 As the perfect identity of the philosophical and religious doctrines of antiquity will be fully treated upon in subsequent chapters, we limit our explanations for the present.

36 "*Rig-Veda-Anhita*," p. 234.

37 Philostratus assures us that the Brahmins were able, in his time, to perform the most wonderful cures by merely pronouncing certain magical words. "The Indian Brahmans carry a staff and a ring, by means of which they are able to do almost anything." Origenes states the same ("*Contra Celsum*"). But if a strong mesmeric fluid — say projected from the eye, and without any other contact — is not added, no magical words would be efficacious.

himself; the friend and instructor of Isis and Osiris. Hermes is the god of the priestly wisdom, like Mazeus.

HIEROPHANT — Discloser of sacred learning. The Old Man, the Chief of the Adepts at the initiations, who explained the arcane knowledge to the neophytes, bore this title. In Hebrew and Chaldaic the term was *Peter,* or opener, discloser; hence, the Pope, as the successor of the hierophant of the ancient Mysteries, sits in the Pagan chair of "St. Peter." The vindictiveness of the Catholic Church toward the alchemists, and to arcane and astronomical science, is explained by the fact that such knowledge was the ancient prerogative of the hierophant, or representative of Peter, who kept the mysteries of life and death. Men like Bruno, Galileo, and Kepler, therefore, and even Cagliostro, trespassed on the preserves of the Church, and were accordingly murdered.

Every nation had its Mysteries and hierophants. Even the Jews had their Peter — Tanaïm or Rabbin, like Hillel, Akiba,[38] and other famous kabalists, who alone could impart the awful knowledge contained in the *Merkaba.* In India, there was in ancient times one, and now there are several hierophants scattered about the country, attached to the principal pagodas, who are known as the Brahma-âtmas. In Thibet the chief hierophant is the Dalay, or Taley-Lama of Lha-ssa.[39] Among Christian nations, the Catholics alone have preserved this "heathen" custom, in the person of their Pope, albeit they have sadly disfigured its majesty and the dignity of the sacred office.

INITIATES — In times of antiquity, those who had been initiated into the arcane knowledge taught by the hierophants of the Mysteries; and in our modern days those who have been initiated by the adepts of mystic lore into the mysterious knowledge, which, notwithstanding the lapse of ages, has yet a few real votaries on earth.

KABALIST, from קבלה, KABALA; an unwritten or oral tradition. The kabalist is a student of "secret science," one who interprets the hidden meaning of the Scriptures with the help of the symbolical *Kabala,* and explains the real one by these means. The Tanaim were the first kabalists among the Jews; they appeared at Jerusalem about the beginning of the third century before the Christian era. The Books of *Ezekiel, Daniel, Henoch,* and the *Revelation* of St. John, are purely kabalistical. This secret doctrine is identical with that of the Chaldeans, and includes at the same time much of the Persian wisdom, or "magic."

LAMAS — Buddhist monks belonging to the Lamaic religion of Thibet, as, for instance, friars are the monks belonging to the Popish or Roman Catholic religion. Every lama is subject to the grand Taley-Lama, the Buddhist pope of Thibet, who holds his residence at Lha-ssa, and is a reincarnation of Buddha.

MAGE, or *Magian;* from *Mag* or *Maha.* The word is the root of the word magician. The Maha-âtma (the great Soul or Spirit) in India had its priests in the pre-Vedic times. The Magians were priests of the fire-god; we find them among the Assyrians and Babylonians, as well as among the Persian fire-worshippers. The three magi, also denominated kings, that are said to have made gifts of gold, incense, and myrrh to the infant Jesus, were fire-

---

38 Akiba was a friend of Aher, said to have been the Apostle Paul of Christian story. Both are depicted as having visited Paradise. Aher took branches from the Tree of Knowledge, and so fell from the true (Jewish) religion. Akiba came away in peace. See *2d Epistle to the Corinthians,* chapter xii.
39 Taley means ocean or sea.

worshippers like the rest, and astrologers; for they saw his star. The high priest of the Parsis, at Surat, is called *Mobed,* others derived the word from Megh; Meh-ab signifying something grand and noble. Zoroaster's disciples were called *Meghestom,* according to Kleuker.

MAGICIAN — This term, once a title of renown and distinction, has come to be wholly perverted from its true meaning. Once the synonym of all that was honorable and reverent, of a possessor of learning and wisdom, it has become degraded into an epithet to designate one who is a pretender and a juggler; a charlatan, in short, or one who has "sold his soul to the Evil One"; who misuses his knowledge, and employs it for low and dangerous uses, according to the teachings of the clergy, and a mass of superstitious fools who believe the magician a sorcerer and an enchanter. But Christians forget, apparently, that Moses was also a magician, and Daniel, "*Master* of the magicians, astrologers, Chaldeans, and soothsayers" (*Daniel,* v. II).

The word magician then, scientifically speaking, is derived from *Magh, Mah,* Hindu or *Sanscrit* Maha — great; a man well versed in the secret or esoteric knowledge; properly a Sacerdote.

MANTICISM, or mantic frenzy. During this state was developed the gift of prophecy. The two words are nearly synonymous. One was as honored as the other. Pythagoras and Plato held it in high esteem, and Socrates advised his disciples to study Manticism. The Church Fathers, who condemned so severely the *mantic frenzy* in Pagan priests and Pythiæ, were not above applying it to their own uses. The Montanists, who took their name from Montanus, a bishop of Phrygia, who was considered divinely inspired, rivalled with the *manteis* or prophets. "Tertullian, Augustine, and the martyrs of Carthage, were of the number," says the author of *Prophecy, Ancient and Modern.* "The Montanists seem to have resembled the *Bacchantes* in the wild enthusiasm that characterized their orgies," he adds. There is a diversity of opinion as to the origin of the word *Manticism.* There was the famous Mantis the Seer, in the days of Melampus and Prœtus, King of Argos; and there was Manto, the daughter of the prophet of Thebes, herself a prophetess. Cicero describes prophecy and mantic frenzy by saying that "in the inner recesses of the mind is divine prophecy hidden and confined, a divine impulse, which when it burns more vividly is called furor" (frenzy, madness).

But there is still another etymology possible for the word *mantis,* and to which we doubt if the attention of the philologists was ever drawn. The mantic frenzy may, perchance, have a still earlier origin. The two sacrificial cups of the Soma-mystery used during the religious rites, and generally known as grahas, are respectively called *Sukra* and *Manti.*[40]

It is in the latter manti or manthi cup that Brahma is said to be "stirred up." While the initiate drinks (albeit sparingly) of this sacred soma-juice, the Brahma, or rather his "spirit," personified by the god Soma, enters into the man and takes *possession* of him. Hence, ecstatic vision, clairvoyance, and the gift of prophecy. Both kinds of divination — the natural and the artificial — are aroused by the Soma. The *Sukra*-cup awakens that which is given to every man by nature. It unites both spirit and soul, and these, from their own nature and essence, which are divine, have a foreknowledge of future things, as dreams, unexpected visions, and presentiments, well prove. The contents of the other cup, the manti, which

---

40 See "*Aytareya Brahmanan,*" 3, I.

"stirs the Brahma," put thereby the soul in communication not only with the minor gods — the well-informed but not omniscient spirits — but actually with the highest divine essence itself. The soul receives a direct illumination from the presence of its "god"; but as it is not allowed to remember certain things, well known only in heaven, the initiated person is generally seized with a kind of sacred frenzy, and upon recovering from it, only remembers that which is allowed to him. As to the other kind of seers and diviners — those who make a profession of and a living by it — they are usually held to be possessed by a *gandharva*, a deity which is nowhere so little honored as in India.

MANTRA — A *Sanskrit* word conveying the same idea as the "Ineffable Name." Some mantras, when pronounced according to magical formula taught in the *Atharva-Veda*, produce an instantaneous and wonderful effect. In its general sense, though, a mantra is either simply a prayer to the gods and powers of heaven, as taught by the Brahmanical books, and especially Manu, or else a magical charm. In its esoteric sense, the "word" of the mantra, or mystic speech, is called by the Brahmans *Vâch*. It resides in the mantra, which literally means those parts of the sacred books which are considered as the *Sruti*, or direct divine revelation.

MARABUT — A Mahometan pilgrim who has been to Mekka; a saint, after whose death his body is placed in an open sepulchre built on the surface, like other buildings, but in the middle of the streets and public places of populated cities. Placed inside the small and only room of the tomb (and several such public sarcophagi of brick and mortar may be seen to this day in the streets and squares of Cairo), the devotion of the wayfarers keeps a lamp ever burning at his head. The tombs of some of these marabuts have a great fame for the miracles they are alleged to perform.

MATERIALIZATION — A word employed by spiritualists to indicate the phenomenon of "a spirit clothing himself with a material form." The far less objectionable term, "form-manifestation," has been recently suggested by Mr. Stainton-Moses, of London. When the real nature of these apparitions is better comprehended, a still more appropriate name will doubtless be adopted. To call them materialized spirits is inadmissible, for they are not spirits but animated portrait-statues.

MAZDEANS, from (Ahura) Mazda. (See Spiegel's *Yasna*, xl.) They were the ancient Persian nobles who worshipped Ormazd, and, rejecting images, inspired the Jews with the same horror for every concrete representation of the Deity. "They seem in Herodotus's time to have been superseded by the Magian religionists. The Parsis and Ghebers *geberim*, mighty men, of *Genesis* vi. and x. 8) appear to be Magian religionists. . . . By a curious muddling of ideas, Zoro-Aster (*Zero*, a circle, a son or priest, Aster, Ishtar, or Astarte — in Aryan dialect, a star), the title of the head of the Magians and fire-worshippers, or Surya-ishtara, the sun-worshipper, is often confounded in modern times with Zara-tustra, the reputed Mazdean apostle" (Zoroaster).

METEMPSYCHOSIS — The progress of the soul from one stage of existence to another. Symbolized and vulgarly believed to be rebirths in animal bodies. A term generally misunderstood by every class of European and American society, including many scientists. The kabalistic axiom, "A stone becomes a plant, a plant an animal, an animal a man, a man a spirit, and a spirit a god," receives an explanation in Manu's *Manava-Dharma-Sastra*, and other Brahmanical books.

MYSTERIES — Greek *teletai*, or finishings, as analogous to *teleuteia* or death. They were observances, generally kept secret from the profane and uninitiated, in which were taught by dramatic representation and other methods, the origin of things, the nature of the human spirit, its relations to the body, and the method of its purification and restoration to higher life. Physical science, medicine, the laws of music, divination, were all taught in the same manner. The Hippocratic oath was but a mystic obligation. Hippocrates was a priest of Asklepios, some of whose writings chanced to become public. But the Asklepiades were initiates of the Æsculapian serpent-worship, as the Bacchantes were of the Dionysia; and both rites were eventually incorporated with the Eleusinia. We will treat of the Mysteries fully in the subsequent chapters.

MYSTICS — Those initiated. But in the mediæval and later periods the term was applied to men like Bœhmén the Theosophist, Molinos the Quietist, Nicholas of Basle, and others who believed in a direct interior communion with God, analogous to the inspiration of the prophets.

NABIA — Seership, soothsaying. This oldest and most respected of mystic phenomena, is the name given to prophecy in the *Bible,* and is correctly included among the spiritual powers, such as divination, clairvoyant visions, trance-conditions, and oracles. But while enchanters, diviners, and even astrologers are strictly condemned in the Mosaic books, prophecy, seership, and nabia appear as the special gifts of heaven. In early ages they were all termed *Epoptai*, the Greek word for seers, clairvoyants; after which they were designated as *Nebim*, "the plural of Nebo, the Babylonian god of wisdom." The kabalist distinguishes between the *seer* and the *magician*; one is passive, the other active; *Nebirah*, is one who looks into futurity and a clairvoyant; *Nebi-poel*, he who possesses *magic powers.* We notice that Elijah and Apollonius resorted to the same means to isolate themselves from the disturbing influences of the outer world, viz.: wrapping their heads entirely in a woolen mantle; from its being an electric non-conductor we must suppose.

OCCULTIST — One who studies the various branches of occult science. The term is used by the French kabalists (See Eliphas Levi's works). Occultism embraces the whole range of psychological, physiological, cosmical, physical, and spiritual phenomena. From the word *occult*, hidden or secret; applying therefore to the study of the *Kabala*, astrology, alchemy, and all arcane sciences.

PAGAN GODS — This term gods is erroneously understood by most of the reading public, to mean idols. The idea attached to them is *not* that of something objective or anthropomorphical. With the exception of occasions when "gods" mean either divine planetary entities (angels), or disembodied spirits of pure men, the term simply conveys to the mind of the mystic — whether Hindu Hotar, Mazdean Mage, Egyptian hierophant, or disciple of the Greek philosophers — the idea of a visible or cognized manifestation of an invisible potency of nature. And such occult potencies are invoked under the appellation of various gods, who, for the time being, are personating these powers. Thus every one of the numberless deities of the Hindu, Greek, and Egyptian Pantheons, are simply Powers of the "Unseen Universe." When the officiating Brahman invokes Aditya — who, in her cosmic character, is the goddess-sun — he simply *commands* that potency (personified in some god), which, as he asserts, "resides in the Mantra, as the sacred *Vâch*." These god-powers are allegorically regarded as the divine *Hotars* of the Supreme One; while the priest (Brahman) is the human Hotar who officiates on earth, and representing that particular Power becomes, ambassador-like, invested with the very potency which he personates.

PITRIS — It is generally believed that the Hindu term *Pitris* means the spirits of our direct ancestors; of disembodied people. Hence the argument of some spiritualists that fakirs, and other Eastern wonder-workers, are *mediums;* that they themselves confess to being unable to produce anything without the help of the *Pitris,* of whom they are the obedient instruments. This is in more than one sense erroneous. The *Pitris* are not the ancestors of the present living men, but those of the human kind or Adamic race; the spirits of *human* races which, on the great scale of descending evolution, preceded our races of men, and were physically, as well as spiritually, far superior to our modern pigmies. In *Manava-Dharma-Sastra* they are called the *Lunar* ancestors.

PYTHIA, or Pythoness. — Webster dismisses the word very briefly by saying that it was the name of one who delivered the oracles at the Temple of Delphi, and "any female supposed to have the spirit of divination in her — *a witch,*" which is neither complimentary, exact, nor just. A Pythia, upon the authority of Plutarch, Iamblichus, Lamprias, and others, was a nervous sensitive; she was chosen from among the poorest class, young and pure. Attached to the temple, within whose precincts she had a room, secluded from every other, and to which no one but the priest, or seer, had admittance, she had no communications with the outside world, and her life was more strict and ascetic than that of a Catholic nun. Sitting on a tripod of brass placed over a fissure in the ground, through which arose intoxicating vapors, these subterranean exhalations penetrating her whole system produced the prophetic mania. In this abnormal state she delivered oracles. She was sometimes called *ventriloqua vates,*[41] the ventriloquist-prophetess.

The ancients placed the astral soul of man, $\psi\upsilon\chi\eta$, or his self-consciousness, in the pit of the stomach. The Brahmans shared this belief with Plato and other philosophers. Thus we find in the fourth verse of the second *Nabhânedishtha Hymn* it is said: "Hear, O sons of the gods (spirits) one who speaks through his navel (nâbhâ) for he hails you in your dwellings!"

Many of the Sanscrit scholars agree that this belief is one of the most ancient among the Hindus. The modern fakirs, as well as the ancient gymnosophists, unite themselves with their Âtman and the Deity by remaining motionless in contemplation and concentrating their whole thought on their navel. As in modern somnambulic phenomena, the navel was regarded as "the circle of the sun," the seat of internal divine light.[42] Is the fact of a number of modern somnambulists being enabled to read letters, hear, smell, and see, through that part of their body to be regarded again as a simple "coincidence," or shall we admit at last that the old sages knew something more of physiological and psychological mysteries than our modern Academicians? In modern Persia, when a "magician" (often simply a mesmerizer) is consulted upon occasions of theft and other puzzling occurrences, he makes his manipulations over the pit of his stomach, and so brings himself into a state of clairvoyance. Among the modern Parsis, remarks a translator of the *Rig-vedas,* there exists a

---

41 See Pantheon, "*Myths,*" p. 31; also Aristophanes in "*Vœstas,*" i., reg. 28.

42 The oracle of Apollo was at Delphos, the city of the "delfu," womb or abdomen; the place of the temple was denominated the *omphalos* or navel. The symbols are female and lunary; reminding us that the Arcadians were called Proseleni, pre-Hellenic or more ancient than the period when Ionian and Olympian lunar worship was introduced.

belief up to the present day that their adepts have a flame in their navel, which enlightens to them all darkness and discloses the spiritual world, as well as all things unseen, or at a distance. They call it the lamp of *the Deshtur*, or high priest; the light of the Dikshita (the initiate), and otherwise designate it by many other names.

SAMOTHRACES — A designation of the Fane-gods worshipped at Samothracia in the Mysteries. They are considered as identical with the Kabeiri, Dioskuri, and Korybantes. Their names were mystical — denoting Pluto, Ceres or Proserpina, Bacchus, and Æsculapius or Hermes.

SHAMANS, or Samaneans. — An order of Buddhists among the Tartars, especially those of Siberia. They are possibly akin to the philosophers anciently known as *Brachmanes*, mistaken sometimes for Brahmans.[43] They are all *magicians*, or rather sensitives or mediums artificially developed. At present those who act as priests among the Tartars are generally very ignorant, and far below the fakirs in knowledge and education. Both men and women may be Shamans.

SOMA— This Hindu sacred beverage answers to the Greek ambrosia or nectar, drunk by the gods of Olympus. A cup of kykeon was also quaffed by the mysta at the Eleusinian initiation. He who drinks it easily reaches *Bradhna,* or place of splendor (Heaven). The soma-drink known to Europeans is not the *genuine* beverage, but its substitute; for the initiated priests alone can taste of the real soma; and even kings and rajas, when sacrificing, receive the substitute. Haug shows by his own confession, in his *Aytareya Brahmanan,* that it was not the Soma that he tasted and found nasty, but the juice from the roots of the Nyagradha, a plant or bush which grows on the hills of Poona. We were positively informed that the majority of the sacrificial priests of the Dekkan have lost the secret of the true soma. It can be found neither in the ritual books nor through oral information. The true followers of the primitive Vedic religion are very few; these are the alleged descendants from the *Rishis,* the real Agnihôtris, the initiates of the great Mysteries. The soma-drink is also commemorated in the Hindu Pantheon, for it is called the King-Soma. He who drinks of it is made to participate in the heavenly king, because he becomes filled with it, as the Christian apostles and their converts became filled with the Holy Ghost, and purified of their sins. The soma makes a new man of the initiate; he is reborn and transformed, and his spiritual nature overcomes the physical; it gives the divine power of inspiration, and develops the clairvoyant faculty to the utmost. According to the exoteric explanation the soma is a plant, but, at the same time it is an angel. It forcibly connects the *inner,* highest "spirit" of man, which spirit is an angel like the mystical soma, with his "irrational soul," or astral body, and thus united by the power of the magic drink, they soar together above physical nature, and participate during life in the beatitude and ineffable glories of Heaven.

Thus the Hindu soma is mystically, and in all respects the same that the Eucharistic supper is to the Christian. The idea is similar. By means of the sacrificial prayers — the mantras — this liquor is supposed to be transformed on the spot into real soma— — or the

---

43 From the accounts of Strabo and Megasthenes, who visited Palibothras, it would seem that the persons termed by him Samanean, or Brachmane priests, were simply Buddhists. "The singularly subtle replies of the Samanean or Brahman philosophers, in their interview with the conqueror, will be found to contain the spirit of the Buddhist doctrine," remarks Upham. (See the "*History and Doctrine of Buddhism*"; and Hale's "*Chronology,*" vol. iii, p. 238.)

angel, and even into Brahma himself. Some missionaries have expressed themselves very indignantly about this ceremony, the more so, that, generally speaking, the Brahmans use a *kind of spirituous liquor* as a substitute. But do the Christians believe less fervently in the transubstantiation of the communion-wine into the blood of Christ, because this wine happens to be more or less spirituous? Is not the idea of the symbol attached to it the same? But the missionaries say that this hour of soma-drinking is the golden hour of Satan, who lurks at the bottom of the Hindu sacrificial cup.[44]

SPIRIT — The lack of any mutual agreement between writers in the use of this word has resulted in dire confusion. It is commonly made synonymous with *soul;* and the lexicographers countenance the usage. This is the natural result of our ignorance of the other word, and repudiation of the classification adopted by the ancients. Elsewhere we attempt to make clear the distinction between the terms "spirit" and "soul." There are no more important passages in this work. Meanwhile, we will only add that "spirit" is the voῦς of Plato, the immortal, immaterial, and purely *divine* principle in man — the crown of the human *Triad*; whereas,

SOUL is the ψυχη, or the *nephesh* of the *Bible;* the vital principle, or the breath of life, which every animal, down to the infusoria, shares with man. In the translated *Bible* it stands indifferently for *life*, blood, and soul. "Let us *not kill* his nephesh," says the original text: "let us not kill *him*," translate the Christians (*Genesis* xxxvii. 21), and so on.

THEOSOPHISTS— In the mediæval ages it was the name by which were known the disciples of Paracelsus of the sixteenth century, the so-called fire-philosophers or *Philosophi per ignem*. As well as the Platonists they regarded the soul, (ψυχη), and the divine spirit, *nous* (voῦς), as a particle of the great Archos — a fire taken from the eternal ocean of light.

The Theosophical Society, to which these volumes are dedicated by the author as a mark of affectionate regard, was organized at New York in 1875. The object of its founders was to experiment practically in the occult powers of Nature, and to collect and disseminate among Christians information about the Oriental religious philosophies. Later, it has determined to spread among the "poor benighted heathen" such evidences as to the practical results of Christianity as will at least give both sides of the story to the communities among which missionaries are at work. With this view it has established relations with associations and individuals throughout the East, to whom it furnishes authenticated reports of the ecclesiastical crimes and misdemeanors, schisms and heresies, controversies and litigations, doctrinal differences and biblical criticisms and revisions, with which the press of Christian Europe and America constantly teems. Christendom has been long and minutely informed of the degradation and brutishness into which Buddhism, Brahmanism, and Confucianism have plunged their deluded votaries, and many millions have been lavished upon foreign missions under such false representations. The Theosophical Society, seeing daily exemplifications of this very state of things as the sequence of Christian teaching and example — the latter especially — thought it simple justice to make the facts known in

---

44 In their turn, the heathen may well ask the missionaries what sort of a spirit lurks at the bottom of the sacrificial beer-bottle. That evangelical New York journal, the "Independent," says: "A late English traveller found a simple-minded Baptist mission church, in far-off Burmah, using for the communion service, and we doubt not with God's blessing, Bass's pale ale instead of wine." Circumstances alter cases, it seems!

Palestine, India, Ceylon, Cashmere, Tartary, Thibet, China, and Japan, in all which countries it has influential correspondents. It may also in time have much to say about the conduct of the missionaries to those who contribute to their support.

THEURGIST — From $\theta\varepsilon o\varsigma$, god, and $\varepsilon\rho\gamma o\nu$, work. The first school of practical theurgy in the Christian period was founded by Iamblichus among the Alexandrian Platonists; but the priests attached to the temples of Egypt, Assyria, and Babylonia, and who took an active part in the evocations of the gods during the Sacred Mysteries, were known by this name from the earliest archaic period. The purpose of it was to make spirits visible to the eyes of mortals. A theurgist was one expert in the esoteric learning of the Sanctuaries of all the great countries. The Neoplatonists of the school of Iamblichus were called theurgists, for they performed the so-called "ceremonial magic," and evoked the "spirits" of the departed heroes, "gods," and Daimonia ($\delta\alpha\iota\mu o\nu\iota\alpha$, divine, spiritual entities). In the rare cases when the presence of a *tangible* and *visible* spirit was required, the theurgist had to furnish the weird apparition with a portion of his own flesh and blood — he had to perform the *theopœa*, or the "creation of gods," by a mysterious process well known to the modern fakirs and initiated Brahmans of India. This is what is said in the *Book of Evocations* of the pagodas. It shows the perfect identity of rites and ceremonial between the oldest Brahmanic theurgy and that of the Alexandrian Platonists:

"The Brahman Grihasta (the evocator) must be in a state of complete purity before he ventures to call forth the Pitris."

After having prepared a lamp, some sandal, incense, etc., and having traced the magic circles taught to him by the superior guru, in order to keep away *bad* spirits, he "ceases to breathe, and calls *the fire* to his help to disperse his body." He pronounces a certain number of times the sacred word, and "his soul escapes from his body, and his body disappears, and the soul of the evoked spirit descends into the *double* body and animates it." Then "His (Grihasta's) soul reënters into his body, whose subtile particles have again been aggregating, after having formed of their emanations an aërial body to the spirit he evoked."

And now, that he has formed for the Pitri a body with the particles the most essential and pure of his own, the grihasta is allowed, after the ceremonial sacrifice is over, to "converse with the souls of the ancestors and the Pitris, and offer them questions on the mysteries of the *Being* and the transformations of the *imperishable*."

"Then after having blown out his lamp he must light it again, and set at liberty the bad spirits shut out from the place by the magical circles, and leave the sanctuary of the Pitris."[45]

The school of Iamblichus was distinct from that of Plotinus and Porphyry, who were strongly against ceremonial magic and practical theurgy as dangerous, though these two eminent men firmly believed in both. "The *theurgic* or *benevolent* magic, the Goëtic, or dark and evil necromancy, were alike in preëminent repute *during the first century* of the Christian era."[46] But never have any of the highly moral and pious philosophers, whose fame has descended to us spotless of any evil deed, practiced any other kind of magic than the theurgic, or *benevolent,* as Bulwer-Lytton terms it. "Whoever is acquainted with the nature *of divinely luminous appearances* ($\varphi\alpha\sigma\mu\alpha\tau\alpha$) knows also on what account it is requisite to abstain

---

45 *"Book of Brahmanical Evocations,"* part iii.
46 Bulwer-Lytton, *"Last Days of Pompeii,"* p. 147.

from all birds (animal food), and especially for him who hastens to be liberated from terrestrial concerns and to be established with the celestial gods," says Porphyry.[47]

Though he refused to practice theurgy himself, Porphyry, in his *Life of Plotinus*, mentions a priest of Egypt, who, "at the request of a certain friend of Plotinus (which friend was perhaps Porphyry himself, remarks T. Taylor), exhibited to Plotinus, in the temple of Isis at Rome, the familiar daimon, or, in modern language, the *guardian angel* of that philosopher."[48]

The popular, prevailing idea was that the theurgists, as well as the magicians, worked wonders, such as evoking the souls or shadows of the heroes and gods, and doing other thaumaturgic works by supernatural powers.

YAJNA — "The Yajna," say the Brahmans, exists from eternity, for it proceeded forth from the Supreme One, the *Brahma-Prajapâti*, in whom it lay dormant from "*no* beginning." It is the key to the TRAIVIDYA, the thrice sacred science contained in the Rig verses, which teaches the Yagus or sacrificial mysteries. "The Yajna" exists as an invisible thing at all times; it is like the latent power of electricity in an electrifying machine, requiring only the operation of a suitable apparatus in order to be elicited. It is supposed to extend from the *Ahavaniya* or sacrificial fire to the heavens, forming a bridge or ladder by means of which the sacrificer can communicate with the world of gods and spirits, and even ascend when alive to their abodes.[49]

This *Yajna* is again one of the forms of the Akâsa, and the mystic word calling it into existence and pronounced mentally by the initiated Priest is the *Lost Word* receiving impulse through WILL-POWER.

To complete the list, we will now add that in the course of the following chapters, whenever we use the term *Archaic*, we mean before the time of Pythagoras; when *Ancient*, before the time of Mahomet; and when *Mediæval*, the period between Mahomet and Martin Luther. It will only be necessary to infringe the rule when from time to time we may have to speak of nations of a pre-Pythagorean antiquity, and will adopt the common custom of calling them "ancient."

Before closing this initial chapter, we venture to say a few words in explanation of the plan of this work. Its object is not to force upon the public the personal views or theories of its author; nor has it the pretensions of a scientific work, which aims at creating a revolution in some department of thought. It is rather a brief summary of the religions, philosophies, and universal traditions of human kind, and the exegesis of the same, in the spirit of those secret doctrines, of which none — thanks to prejudice and bigotry — have reached Christendom in so unmutilated a form, as to secure it a fair judgment. Since the days of the unlucky mediæval philosophers, the last to write upon these secret doctrines of which they were the depositaries, few men have dared to brave persecution and prejudice by placing their knowledge upon record. And these few have never, as a rule, written for the public, but only for those of their own and succeeding times who possessed the key to their jargon.

----

47 *"Select Works,"* p. 159.
48 Ibid., p. 92.
49 *"Aitareya Brahmanam,"* Introduction.

The multitude, not understanding them or their doctrines, have been accustomed to regard them *en masse* as either charlatans or dreamers. Hence the unmerited contempt into which the study of the noblest of sciences — that of the spiritual man — has gradually fallen.

In undertaking to inquire into the assumed infallibility of Modern Science and Theology, the author has been forced, even at the risk of being thought discursive, to make constant comparison of the ideas, achievements, and pretensions of their representatives, with those of the ancient philosophers and religious teachers. Things the most widely separated as to time, have thus been brought into immediate juxtaposition, for only thus could the priority and parentage of discoveries and dogmas be determined. In discussing the merits of our scientific contemporaries, their own confessions of failure in experimental research, of baffling mysteries, of missing links in their chains of theory, of inability to comprehend natural phenomena, of ignorance of the laws of the causal world, have furnished the basis for the present study. Especially (since Psychology has been so much neglected, and the East is so far away that few of our investigators will ever get there to study that science where alone it is understood), we will review the speculations and policy of noted authorities in connection with those modern psychological phenomena which began at Rochester and have now overspread the world. *We wish to show how inevitable were their innumerable failures, and how they must continue until these pretended authorities of the West go to the Brahmans and Lamaists of the far Orient, and respectfully ask them to impart the alphabet of true science.* We have laid no charge against scientists that is not supported by their own published admissions, and if our citations from the records of antiquity rob some of what they have hitherto viewed as well-earned laurels, the fault is not ours but Truth's. No man worthy of the name of philosopher would care to wear honors that rightfully belong to another.

Deeply sensible of the Titanic struggle that is now in progress between materialism and the spiritual aspirations of mankind, our constant endeavor has been to gather into our several chapters, like weapons into armories, every fact and argument that can be used to aid the latter in defeating the former. Sickly and deformed child as it now is, the materialism of To-Day is born of the brutal Yesterday. Unless its growth is arrested, it may become our master. It is the bastard progeny of the French Revolution and its reaction against ages of religious bigotry and repression. To prevent the crushing of these spiritual aspirations, the blighting of these hopes, and the deadening of that intuition which teaches us of a God and a hereafter, we must show our false theologies in their naked deformity, and distinguish between divine religion and human dogmas. Our voice is raised for spiritual freedom, and our plea made for enfranchisement from all tyranny, whether of SCIENCE or THEOLOGY.

THE VEIL OF ISIS

PART ONE — SCIENCE

CHAPTER I

"Ego sum qui sum."

An axiom of Hermetic Philosophy

"We commenced research where modern conjecture closes its faithless wings. And with us, those were the common elements of science which the sages of to-day disdain as wild chimeras, or despair of as unfathomable mysteries." —

BULWER'S "ZANONI"

THE ORIENTAL KABALA

THERE exists somewhere in this wide world an old Book — so very old that our modern antiquarians might ponder over its pages an indefinite time, and still not quite agree as to the nature of the fabric upon which it is written. It is the only original copy now in existence. The most ancient Hebrew document on occult learning — the *Siphra Dzeniouta* — was compiled from it, and that at a time when the former was already considered in the light of a literary relic. One of its illustrations represents the Divine Essence emanating from ADAM[50] like a luminous arc proceeding to form a circle; and then, having attained the highest point of its circumference, the ineffable Glory bends back again, and returns to earth, bringing a higher type of humanity in its vortex. As it approaches nearer and nearer to our planet, the Emanation becomes more and more shadowy, until upon touching the ground it is as black as night. A conviction, founded upon *seventy* thousand years of experience,[51] as they allege, has been entertained by hermetic philosophers of all periods that matter has in time become, through sin, more gross and dense than it was at man's first formation; that, at the beginning, the human body was of a half-ethereal nature; and that, before the fall, mankind communed freely with the now unseen universes. But since that time matter has become the formidable barrier between us and the world of spirits. The oldest esoteric traditions also teach that, before the mystic Adam, many races of human beings lived and died out, each giving place in its turn to another. Were these precedent types more perfect? Did any of them belong to the *winged* race of men mentioned by Plato in *Phædrus?* It is the special province of science to solve the problem. The caves of France and the relics of the stone age afford a point at which to begin.

---

50 The name is used in the sense of the Greek word ανθρωπος.
51 The traditions of the Oriental Kabalists claim their science to be older than that. Modern scientists may doubt and reject the assertion. They *cannot* prove it false.

As the cycle proceeded, man's eyes were more and more opened, until he came to know "good and evil" as well as the Elohim themselves. Having reached its summit, the cycle began to go downward. When the arc attained a certain point which brought it parallel with the fixed line of our terrestrial plane, the man was furnished by nature with "coats of *skin*," and the Lord God "clothed them."

This same belief in the pre-existence of a far more spiritual race than the one to which we now belong can be traced back to the earliest traditions of nearly every people. In the ancient Quiche manuscript, published by Brasseur de Bourbourg — the *Popol Vuh* — the first men are mentioned as a race that could reason and speak, whose sight was unlimited, and who knew all things at once. According to Philo Judæus, the air is filled with an invisible host of spirits, some of whom are free from evil and immortal, and others are pernicious and mortal. "From the sons of EL we are descended, and sons of EL must we become again." And the unequivocal statement of the anonymous Gnostic who wrote *The Gospel according to John*, that "as many as received Him," *i.e.*, who followed practically the esoteric doctrine of Jesus, would "become the sons of God," points to the same belief. (i., 12.) "Know ye not, ye are *gods?*" exclaimed the Master. Plato describes admirably in *Phædrus* the state in which man once was, and what he will become again: before, and after the "loss of his wings"; when "he lived among the gods, a god himself in the airy world." From the remotest periods religious philosophies taught that the whole universe was filled with divine and spiritual beings of divers races. From one of these evolved, in the course of time, ADAM, the primitive man.

The Kalmucks and some tribes of Siberia also describe in their legends earlier creations than our present race. These beings, they say, were possessed of almost boundless knowledge, and in their audacity even threatened rebellion against the Great Chief Spirit. To punish their presumption and humble them, he imprisoned them *in bodies*, and so shut in their senses. From these they can escape but through long repentance, self-purification, and development. Their *Shamans*, they think, occasionally enjoy the divine powers originally possessed by all human beings.

ANCIENT TRADITIONS SUPPORTED BY MODERN RESEARCH

The Astor Library of New York has recently been enriched by a facsimile of an Egyptian Medical Treatise, written in the sixteenth century B.C. (or, more precisely, 1552 B.C.), which, according to the commonly received chronology, is the time when Moses was just twenty-one years of age. The original is written upon the inner bark of *Cyperus papyrus*, and has been pronounced by Professor Schenk, of Leipsig, not only genuine, but also the most perfect ever seen. It consists of a single sheet of yellow-brown papyrus of finest quality, three-tenths of a metre wide, more than twenty metres long, and forming one roll divided into one hundred and ten pages, all carefully numbered. It was purchased in Egypt, in 1872-3, by the archæologist Ebers, of "a well-to-do Arab from Luxor." The New York *Tribune*, commenting upon the circumstance, says: The papyrus "bears internal evidence of being one of the six *Hermetic Books on Medicine*, named by Clement of Alexandria."

The editor further says: "At the time of Iamblichus, A.D. 363, the priests of Egypt showed forty-two books which they attributed to Hermes (Thuti). Of these, according to that author, thirty-six contained the history of all human knowledge; the last six treated of anatomy, of pathology, of affections of the eye, instruments of surgery, and of medicines.[52] The *Papyrus Ebers* is indisputably one of these ancient Hermetic works."

If so clear a ray of light has been thrown upon ancient Egyptian science, by the accidental (?) encounter of the German archæologist with one "well-to-do Arab" from Luxor, how can we know what sunshine may be let in upon the dark crypts of history by an equally accidental meeting between some other prosperous Egyptian and another enterprising student of antiquity!

The discoveries of modern science do not disagree with the oldest traditions which claim an incredible antiquity for our race. Within the last few years geology, which previously had only conceded that man could be traced as far back as the tertiary period, has found unanswerable proofs that human existence antedates the last glaciation of Europe — over 250,000 years! A hard nut, this, for Patristic Theology to crack; but an accepted fact with the ancient philosophers.

Moreover, fossil implements have been exhumed together with human remains, which show that man hunted in those remote times, and knew how to build a fire. But the forward step has not yet been taken in this search for the origin of the race; science comes to a dead stop, and waits for future proofs. Unfortunately, anthropology and psychology possess no Cuvier; neither geologists nor archæologists are able to construct, from the fragmentary bits hitherto discovered, the perfect skeleton of the triple man — physical, intellectual, and spiritual. Because the fossil implements of man are found to become more rough and uncouth as geology penetrates deeper into the bowels of the earth, it seems a proof to science that the closer we come to the origin of man, the more savage and brute-like he must be. Strange logic! Does the finding of the remains in the cave of Devon prove that there were no contemporary races then who were highly civilized? When the present population of the earth have disappeared, and some archæologist belonging to the "coming race" of the distant future shall excavate the domestic implements of one of our Indian or Andaman Island tribes, will he be justified in concluding that mankind in the nineteenth century was "just emerging from the Stone Age"?

It has lately been the fashion to speak of "the untenable conceptions of an uncultivated past." *As though it were possible to hide behind an epigram the intellectual quarries out of which the reputations of so many modern philosophers have been carved!* Just as Tyndall is ever ready to disparage ancient philosophers — for a dressing-up of whose ideas more than one distinguished scientist has derived honor and credit — so the geologists seem more and more inclined to take for granted that all of the archaic races were contemporaneously in a state of dense barbarism. But not all of our best authorities agree in this opinion. Some of the most eminent maintain exactly the reverse. Max Müller, for instance, says: "Many things are still unintelligible to us, and the hieroglyphic language of antiquity records but half of the mind's unconscious intentions. Yet more and more the image of man, in whatever clime we meet him, rises before us, noble and pure from the very beginning; even his errors we learn to understand, even his dreams we begin to interpret. As far as we can trace back the footsteps of man, even on the lowest strata of history, we see the divine gift of a sound and

---

52 Clement of Alexandria asserted that in his day the Egyptian priests possessed forty-two Canonical Books.

sober intellect belonging to him from the very first, and the idea of a humanity emerging slowly from the depths of an animal brutality can never be maintained again."[53]

THE PROGRESS OF MANKIND MARKED BY CYCLES

As it is claimed to be unphilosophical to inquire into first causes, scientists now occupy themselves with considering their physical effects. The field of scientific investigation is therefore bounded by physical nature. When once its limits are reached, enquiry must stop, and their work be recommenced. With all due respect to our learned men, they are like the squirrel upon its revolving wheel, for they are doomed to turn their "matter" over and over again. Science is a mighty potency, and it is not for us pigmies to question her. But the "*scientists*" are not themselves science embodied any more than the men of our planet are the planet itself. We have neither the right to demand, nor power to compel our "modern-day philosopher" to accept without challenge a geographical description of the dark side of the moon. But, if in some lunar cataclysm one of her inhabitants should be hurled thence into the attraction of our atmosphere, and land, safe and sound, at Dr. Carpenter's door, he would be indictable as recreant to professional duty if he should fail to set the physical problem at rest.

For a man of science to refuse an opportunity to investigate any new phenomenon, whether it comes to him in the shape of a man from the moon, or a ghost from the Eddy homestead, is alike reprehensible.

Whether arrived at by the method of Aristotle, or that of Plato, we need not stop to inquire; but it is a fact that both the inner and outer natures of man are claimed to have been thoroughly understood by the ancient andrologists. Notwithstanding the superficial hypotheses of geologists, we are beginning to have almost daily proofs in corroboration of the assertions of those philosophers.

They divided the interminable periods of human existence on this planet into cycles, during each of which mankind gradually reached the culminating point of highest civilization and gradually relapsed into abject barbarism. To what eminence the race in its progress had several times arrived may be feebly surmised by the wonderful monuments of old, still visible, and the descriptions given by Herodotus of other marvels of which no traces now remain. Even in his days the gigantic structures of many pyramids and world-famous temples were but masses of ruins. Scattered by the unrelenting hand of time, they are described by the Father of History as "these venerable witnesses of the long bygone glory of departed ancestors." He "shrinks from speaking of divine things," and gives to posterity but an imperfect description from hearsay of some marvellous subterranean chambers of the Labyrinth, where lay — and now lie — concealed, the sacred remains of the King-Initiates.

We can judge, moreover, of the lofty civilization reached in some periods of antiquity by the historical descriptions of the ages of the Ptolemies, yet in that epoch the arts and sciences were considered to be degenerating, and the secret of a number of the former had been already lost. In the recent excavations of Mariette-Bey, at the foot of the Pyramids, statues of wood and other relics have been exhumed, which show that long before the period of the first dynasties the Egyptians had attained to a refinement and perfection

53 "*Chips from a German Work-shop,*" vol. ii., p. 7. "*Comparative Mythology.*"

which is calculated to excite the wonder of even the most ardent admirers of Grecian art. Bayard Taylor describes these statues in one of his lectures, and tells us that the beauty of the heads, ornamented with eyes of precious stones and copper eyelids, is unsurpassed. Far below the stratum of sand in which lay the remains gathered into the collections of Lepsius, Abbott, and the British Museum, were found buried the tangible proofs of the hermetic doctrine of cycles which has been already explained.

Dr. Schliemann, the enthusiastic Hellenist, has recently found, in his excavations in the Troad, abundant evidences of the same gradual change from barbarism to civilization, and from civilization to barbarism again. Why then should we feel so reluctant to admit the possibility that, if the antediluvians were so much better versed than ourselves in certain sciences as to have been perfectly acquainted with important arts, which we now term *lost,* they might have equally excelled in psychological knowledge? Such a hypothesis must be considered as reasonable as any other until some countervailing evidence shall be discovered to destroy it.

Every true *savant* admits that in many respects human knowledge is yet in its infancy. Can it be that our cycle began in ages comparatively recent? *These cycles,* according to the Chaldean philosophy, *do not embrace all mankind at one and the same time.* Professor Draper partially corroborates this view by saying that the periods into which geology has "found it convenient to divide the progress of man in civilization are not abrupt epochs which hold good simultaneously for the whole human race"; giving as an instance the "wandering Indians of America," who "are only at the present moment emerging from the stone age." Thus more than once scientific men have unwittingly confirmed the testimony of the ancients.

ANCIENT CRYPTIC SCIENCE

Any Kabalist well acquainted with the Pythagorean system of numerals and geometry can demonstrate that the metaphysical views of Plato were based upon the strictest mathematical principles. "True mathematics," says the *Magicon,* "is something with which all higher sciences are connected; common mathematics is but a deceitful phantasmagoria, whose much-praised infallibility only arises from this — that materials, conditions, and references are made its foundation." Scientists who believe they have adopted the Aristotelian method only because they creep when they do not run from demonstrated particulars to universals, glorify this method of inductive philosophy, and reject that of Plato, which they treat as unsubstantial. Professor Draper laments that such speculative mystics as Ammonius Saccas and Plotinus should have taken the place "of the severe geometers of the old museum."[54] He forgets that geometry, of all sciences the only one which proceeds from universals to particulars, was precisely the method employed by Plato in his philosophy. As long as exact science confines its observations to physical conditions and proceeds Aristotle-like, it certainly cannot fail. But notwithstanding that the world of matter is boundless for us, it still is finite; and thus materialism will turn forever in this vitiated circle, unable to soar higher than the circumference will permit. The cosmological theory of numerals which Pythagoras learned from the Egyptian hierophants, is alone able

---

54 *"Conflict between Religion and Science,"* ch. i.

to reconcile the two units, matter and spirit, and cause each to demonstrate the other mathematically.

The sacred numbers of the universe in their esoteric combination solve the great problem and explain the theory of radiation and the cycle of the emanations. The lower orders before they develop into higher ones must emanate from the higher spiritual ones, and when arrived at the turning-point, be reabsorbed again into the infinite.

Physiology, like everything else in this world of constant evolution, is subject to the cyclic revolution. As it now seems to be hardly emerging from the shadows of the lower arc, so it may be one day proved to have been at the highest point of the circumference of the circle far earlier than the days of Pythagoras.

Mochus, the Sidonian, the physiologist and teacher of the science of anatomy, flourished long before the Sage of Samos; and the latter received the sacred instructions from his disciples and descendants. Pythagoras, the pure philosopher, the deeply-versed in the profounder phenomena of nature, the noble inheritor of the ancient lore, whose great aim was to free the soul from the fetters of sense and force it to realize its powers, must live eternally in human memory.

The impenetrable veil of arcane secrecy was thrown over the sciences taught in the sanctuary. This is the cause of the modern depreciating of the ancient philosophies. Even Plato and Philo Judæus have been accused by many a commentator of absurd inconsistencies, whereas the design which underlies the maze of metaphysical contradictions so perplexing to the reader of the *Timæus,* is but too evident. But has Plato ever been read understandingly by one of the expounders of the classics? This is a question warranted by the criticisms to be found in such authors as Stalbaum, Schleirmacher, Ficinus (Latin translation), Heindorf, Sydenham, Buttmann, Taylor and Burges, to say nothing of lesser authorities. The covert allusions of the Greek philosopher to esoteric things have manifestly baffled these commentators to the last degree. They not only with unblushing coolness suggest as to certain difficult passages that another phraseology was evidently intended, but they audaciously make the changes! The Orphic line:

"Of the song, the order of the *sixth race* close" —

which can only be interpreted as a reference to the *sixth* race evolved in the consecutive evolution of the spheres,[55] Burges says: ". . . was evidently taken from a cosmogony *where man was feigned to be created the last.*" [56]— Ought not one who undertakes to edit another's works at least understand what his author means? Indeed, the ancient philosophers seem to be generally held, even by the least prejudiced of our modern critics, to have lacked that profundity and thorough knowledge in the exact sciences of which our century is so boastful. It is even questioned whether they understood that basic scientific principle: *ex nihilo nihil fit.* If they suspected the indestructibility of matter at all, — say these commentators — it was not in consequence of a firmly-established formula but only through an intuitional reasoning and by analogy. We hold to the contrary opinion. The speculations of these philosophers upon matter were open to public criticism: but their

---

55 In another place, we explain with some minuteness the Hermetic philosophy of the evolution of the spheres and their several races.

56 J. Burges, *"The Works of Plato,"* p. 207, note.

teachings in regard to spiritual things were profoundly esoteric. Being thus sworn to secrecy and religious silence upon abstruse subjects involving the relations of spirit and matter, they rivalled each other in their ingenious methods for concealing their real opinions. The doctrine of *Metempsychosis* has been abundantly ridiculed by men of science and rejected by theologians, yet if it had been properly understood in its application to the indestructibility of matter and the immortality of spirit, it would have been perceived that it is a sublime conception. Should we not first regard the subject from the stand-point of the ancients before venturing to disparage its teachers? The solution of the great problem of *eternity* belongs neither to religious superstition nor to gross materialism. The harmony and mathematical equiformity of the double evolution — spiritual and physical — are elucidated only in the universal numerals of Pythagoras, who built his system entirely upon the so-called "metrical speech" of the Hindu *Vedas*. It is but lately that one of the most zealous Sanskrit scholars, Martin Haug, undertook the translation of the *Aitareya Brahmana* of the *Rig-Veda*. It had been till that time entirely unknown; these explanations indicate beyond dispute the identity of the Pythagorean and Brahmanical systems. In both, the esoteric significance is derived from the number: in the former, from the mystic relation of every number to everything intelligible to the human mind; in the latter, from the number of syllables of which each verse in the *Mantras* consists. Plato, the ardent disciple of Pythagoras, realized it so fully as to maintain that the Dodecahedron was the geometrical figure employed by the *Demiurgus* in constructing the universe. Some of these figures had a peculiarly solemn significance. For instance *four*, of which the Dodecahedron is the trine, was held sacred by the Pythagoreans. It is the perfect square, and neither of the bounding lines exceeds the other in length, by a single point. It is the emblem of moral justice and divine equity geometrically expressed. All the powers and great symphonies of physical and spiritual nature lie inscribed within the perfect square; and the ineffable name of Him, which name otherwise, would remain unutterable, was replaced by this sacred number **4** the most binding and solemn oath with the ancient mystics — the *Tetractys*.

If the Pythagorean metempsychosis should be thoroughly explained and compared with the modern theory of evolution, it would be found to supply every "missing link" in the chain of the latter. But who of our scientists would consent to lose his precious time over the vagaries of the ancients. Notwithstanding proofs to the contrary, they not only deny that the nations of the archaic periods, but even the ancient philosophers had any positive knowledge of the Heliocentric system. The "Venerable Bedes," the Augustines and Lactantii appear to have smothered, with their dogmatic ignorance, all faith in the more ancient theologists of the pre-Christian centuries. But now philology and a closer acquaintance with Sanskrit literature have partially enabled us to vindicate them from these unmerited imputations. In the *Vedas*, for instance, we find positive proof that so long ago as 2000 B.C., the Hindu sages and scholars must have been acquainted with the rotundity of our globe and the Heliocentric system. Hence, Pythagoras and Plato knew well this astronomical truth; for Pythagoras obtained his knowledge in India, or from men who had been there, and Plato faithfully echoed his teachings. We will quote two passages from the *Aitareya Brahmana:*

In the "*Serpent-Mantra*,"[57] the *Brahmana* declares as follows: that this *Mantra* is that one which was seen by the Queen of the Serpents, *Sarpa-râjni*; because the earth (*iyam*) is the Queen of the Serpents, as she is the mother and queen of all that moves (*sarpat*). In the beginning she (the earth) was but one head (round), without hair (*bald*), *i.e.*, without vegetation. She then perceived this *Mantra* which confers upon him who knows it, the power of assuming any form which he might desire. She "pronounced the *Mantra*," *i.e.*, sacrificed to the gods; and, in consequence, immediately obtained a motley appearance; she became variegated, and able to produce any form she might like, *changing one form into another*. This *Mantra* begins with the words: "*Ayam gaûh pris'nir akramit*" (x., 189).

The description of the earth in the shape of a *round* and *bald* head, which was *soft* at first, and became hard only from being breathed upon by the god Vayu, the lord of the air, forcibly suggests the idea that the authors of the sacred Vedic books knew the earth to be *round* or spherical; moreover, that it had been a *gelatinous* mass at first, which gradually cooled off under the influence of the air and time. So much for their knowledge about our globe's sphericity; and now we will present the testimony upon which we base our assertion, that the Hindus were perfectly acquainted with the Heliocentric system, at least 2000 years B.C.

In the same treatise the *Hotar*, (priest), is taught how the *Shastras* should be repeated, and how the phenomena of sunrise and sunset are to be explained. It says: "The Agnishtoma is that one (that god) who burns. The sun *never sets nor rises*. When people think the sun is setting, it is *not so*; they are mistaken. For after having arrived at the end of the day, it produces two opposite effects, making night to what is below, and day to what is on the other side. When they (the people) believe it rises in the morning, the sun only does thus: having reached the end of the night, it makes itself produce two opposite effects, making day to what is below, and night to what is on the other side. In fact the sun never sets; nor does it set for him who has such a knowledge. . ."[58] This sentence is so conclusive, that even the translator of the *Rig-Veda*, Dr. Haug, was forced to remark it. He says this passage contains "the *denial* of the existence of sunrise and sunset," and that the author supposes the sun "to remain always in its high position."[59]

In one of the earliest *Nivids*, Rishi Kutsa, a Hindu sage of the remotest antiquity, explains the allegory of the first laws given to the celestial bodies. For doing "what she ought not to do," Anahit (Anaitis or Nana, the Persian Venus), representing the earth in the legend, is sentenced to turn round the sun. The *Sattras*, or sacrificial sessions[60] prove undoubtedly that so early as in the eighteenth or twentieth century B.C., the Hindus had made considerable progress in astronomical science. The *Sattras* lasted one year, and were "nothing but an imitation of the sun's yearly course. They were divided, says Haug, into two distinct parts, each consisting of six months of thirty days each; in the midst of both was the *Vishuvan* (equator or central day), cutting the whole *Sattras* into two halves, etc."[61] This scholar,

---

57 From the Sanskrit text of the Aitareya Brahmanam. Rig-Veda, v., ch. ii., verse 23.
58 *Aitareya Brahmanam*, book iii., c. v., 44.
59 *Ait. Brahm.*, vol. ii., p. 242.
60 *Ait. Brahm.*, book iv.
61 Septenary Institutions, "*Stone him to Death*," p. 20.

although he ascribes the composition of the bulk of the *Brahmanas* to the period 1400-1200 B.C., is of opinion that the oldest of the hymns may be placed at the very commencement of Vedic literature, between the years 2400-2000, B.C. He finds no reason for considering the *Vedas* less ancient than the sacred books of the Chinese. As the *Shu-King* or *Book of History*, and the sacrificial songs of the *Shi-King*, or *Book of Odes*, have been proved to have an antiquity as early as 2200, B.C., our philologists may yet be compelled before long to acknowledge, that in astronomical knowledge, the antediluvian Hindus were their masters.

At all events, there are facts which prove that certain astronomical calculations were as correct with the Chaldeans in the days of Julius Cæsar as they are now. When the calendar was reformed by the Conqueror, the civil year was found to correspond so little with the seasons, that summer had merged into the autumn months, and the autumn months into full winter. It was Sosigenes, the Chaldean astronomer, who restored order into the confusion, by putting back the 25th of March ninety days, thus making it correspond with the vernal equinox; and it was Sosigenes, again, who fixed the lengths of the months *as they now remain.*

In America, it was found by the Montezuman army, that the calendar of the Aztecs gave an equal number of days and weeks to each month. The extreme accuracy of their astronomical calculations was so great, that *no error* has been discovered in their reckoning by subsequent verifications; while the Europeans, who landed in Mexico in 1519, were, by the Julian calendar, nearly eleven days in advance of the exact time.

It is to the priceless and accurate translations of the Vedic Books, and to the personal researches of Dr. Haug, that we are indebted for the corroboration of the claims of the hermetic philosophers. That the period of Zarathustra Spitama (Zoroaster) was of untold antiquity, can be easily proved. The *Brahmanas*, to which Haug ascribes four thousand years, describe the religious contest between the ancient Hindus, who lived in the pre-Vedic period, and the Iranians. The battles between the *Devas* and the *Asuras* — the former representing the *Hindus* and the latter the Iranians — are described at length in the sacred books. As the Iranian prophet was the first to raise himself against what he called the "idolatry" of the Brahmans, and to designate them as the *Devas* (devils), how far back must then have been this religious crisis?

PRICELESS VALUE OF THE VEDAS

"This contest," answers Dr. Haug, "must have appeared to the authors of the *Brahmanas* as old as the feats of King Arthur appear to English writers of the nineteenth century."

There was not a philosopher of any notoriety who did not hold to this doctrine of metempsychosis, as taught by the Brahmans, Buddhists, and later by the Pythagoreans, in its esoteric sense, whether he expressed it more or less intelligibly. Origen and Clemens Alexandrinus, Synesius and Chalcidius, all believed in it; and the Gnostics, who are unhesitatingly proclaimed by history as a body of the most refined, learned, and enlightened men,[62] were all believers in metempsychosis. Socrates entertained opinions identical with those of Pythagoras; and both, as the penalty of their divine philosophy, were put to a violent death. The rabble has been the same in all ages. Materialism has been, and

---

62 See Gibbon's "*Decline and Fall of the Roman Empire.*"

will ever be blind to spiritual truths. These philosophers held, with the Hindus, that God had infused into matter a portion of his own Divine Spirit, which animates and moves every particle. They taught that men have *two souls,* of separate and quite different natures: the one perishable — the Astral Soul, or the inner, fluidic body — the other incorruptible and immortal — the *Augoeides,* or portion of the Divine Spirit; that the mortal or Astral Soul perishes at each gradual change at the threshold of every new sphere, becoming with every transmigration more purified. The astral man, intangible and invisible as he might be to our mortal, earthly senses, is still constituted of matter, though sublimated. Aristotle, notwithstanding that for political reasons of his own he maintained a prudent silence as to certain esoteric matters, expressed very clearly his opinion on the subject. It was his belief that human souls are emanations of God, that are finally re-absorbed into Divinity. Zeno, the founder of the Stoics, taught that there are "two eternal qualities throughout nature: the one active, or male; the other passive, or female: that the former is pure, subtile ether, or Divine Spirit; the other entirely inert in itself till united with the active principle. That the Divine Spirit acting upon matter produced fire, water, earth, and air; and that it is the sole efficient principle by which all nature is moved. The Stoics, like the Hindu sages, believed in the final absorption. St. Justin believed in the emanation of these souls from Divinity, and Tatian, the Assyrian, his disciple, declared that "man was as immortal as God himself."[63]

MUTILATIONS OF THE JEWISH SACRED BOOKS IN TRANSLATION

That profoundly significant verse of the *Genesis,* "And to every beast of the earth, and to every fowl of the air, and to everything that creepeth upon the earth, I gave *a living soul,* . . . ." should arrest the attention of every Hebrew scholar capable of reading the Scripture in its original, instead of following the erroneous translation, in which the phrase reads, "wherein *there is life.*"[64]

From the first to the last chapters, the translators of the Jewish Sacred Books misconstrued this meaning. They have even changed the spelling of the name of God, as Sir W. Drummond proves. Thus *El,* if written correctly, would read *Al,* for it stands in the original la— Al, and, according to Higgins, this word means the god Mithra, the *Sun,* the preserver and savior. Sir W. Drummond shows that *Beth-El* means the House of the *Sun* in its literal translation, and not of God. "*El,* in the composition of these Canaanite names, does not signify *Deus,* but *Sol.*"[65] Thus Theology has disfigured ancient Theosophy, and Science ancient Philosophy.[66]

---

63 See Turner; also G. Higgins's "*Anacalypsis.*"

64 *Genesis,* i, 30.

65 Sir William Drummond, "*Œdipus Judicus,*" p. 250.

66 The absolute necessity for the perpetration of such pious frauds by the early fathers and later theologians becomes apparent, if we consider that if they had allowed the word *Al* to remain as in the original, it would have become but too evident — except for the initiated — that the *Jehovah* of Moses and the sun were identical. The multitudes, which ignore that the ancient hierophant considered our *visible* sun but as an emblem of the central, invisible, and spiritual Sun, would have accused Moses — as many of our modern commentators have already done — of worshipping the planetary bodies; in short, of actual Zabaism.

For lack of comprehension of this great philosophical principle, the methods of modern science, however exact, must end in nullity. In no one branch can it demonstrate the origin and ultimate of things. Instead of tracing the effect from its primal source, its progress is the reverse. Its higher types, as it teaches, are all evolved from antecedent lower ones. It starts from the bottom of the cycle, led on step by step in the great labyrinth of nature by a thread of matter. As soon as this breaks and the clue is lost, it recoils in affright from the Incomprehensible, and confesses itself *powerless*. Not so did Plato and his disciples. With him *the lower types were but the concrete images of the higher abstract ones*. The soul, which is immortal, has an arithmetical, as the body has a geometrical, beginning. This beginning, as the reflection of the great universal ARCHÆUS, is self-moving, and from the centre diffuses itself over the whole body of the microcosm.

It was the sad perception of this truth that made Tyndall confess how powerless is science, even over the world of matter. "The first marshalling of the atoms, on which all subsequent action depends, baffles a keener power than that of the microscope." "Through pure excess of complexity, and long before observation can have any voice in the matter, the most highly trained intellect, the most refined and disciplined imagination, *retires in bewilderment from the contemplation of the problem*. We are struck dumb by an astonishment which no microscope can relieve, doubting not only the power of our instrument, but even whether we ourselves possess the intellectual elements which will ever enable us to grapple with the ultimate structural energies of nature."

The fundamental geometrical figure of the Kabala — that figure which tradition and the esoteric doctrines tell us was given by the Deity itself to Moses on Mount Sinai[67] — contains in its grandiose, because simple combination, the key to the universal problem. This figure contains in itself all the others. For those who are able to master it, there is no need to exercise imagination. No earthly microscope can be compared with the keenness of the spiritual perception. And even for those who are unacquainted with the GREAT SCIENCE, the description given by a well-trained child-psychometer of the genesis of a grain, a fragment of crystal, or any other object — is worth all the telescopes and microscopes of "exact science."

There may be more truth in the adventurous pangenesis of Darwin — whom Tyndall calls a "soaring speculator" — than in the cautious, line-bound hypothesis of the latter; who, in common with other thinkers of his class, surrounds his imagination "by the firm frontiers of reason." The theory of a microscopic germ which contains in itself "a world of minor germs," soars in one sense at least into the infinite. It oversteps the world of matter, and begins unconsciously busying itself in the world of spirit. If we accept Darwin's theory of the development of species, we find that his starting-point is placed in front of an open door. We are at liberty with him, to either remain within, or cross the threshold, beyond which lies the limitless and the incomprehensible, or rather the *Unutterable*. If our mortal language is inadequate to express what our spirit dimly foresees in the great "*Beyond*" — while on this earth — it *must* realize it at some point in the timeless Eternity.

Not so with Professor Huxley's theory of the "Physical Basis of Life." Regardless of the formidable majority of "nays" from his German brother-scientists, he creates a universal

---

67 *Exodus*, xxv., 40.

protoplasm and appoints its cells to become henceforth the sacred founts of the principle of all *life*. By making the latter identical in living man, "dead mutton," a nettle-sting, and a lobster; by shutting in, in the molecular cell of the protoplasm, the life-principle, and by shutting out from it the divine influx which comes with subsequent evolution, he closes every door against any possible escape. Like an able tactician he converts his "*laws* and *facts*" into sentries whom he causes to mount guard over every issue. The standard under which he rallies them is inscribed with the word "necessity"; but hardly is it unfurled when he mocks the legend and calls it "an empty shadow of my own imagination."[68]

The fundamental doctrines of spiritualism, he says, "lie outside the limits of philosophical inquiry." We will be bold enough to contradict this assertion, and say that they lie a great deal more within such inquiry than Mr. Huxley's protoplasm. Insomuch that they present evident and palpable facts of the existence of *spirit*, and the protoplasmic cells, *once dead*, present none whatever of being the originators or the bases of life, as this one of the few "foremost thinkers of the day" wants us to believe.[69]

The ancient Kabalist rested upon no hypothesis till he could lay its basis upon the firm rock of recorded experiment.

But the too great dependence upon physical facts led to a growth of materialism and a decadence of spirituality and faith. At the time of Aristotle, this was the prevailing tendency of thought. And though the Delphic commandment was not as yet completely eliminated from Grecian thought; and some philosophers still held that "in order to know what man *is*, we ought to know what man *was*" — still materialism had already begun to gnaw at the root of faith. The Mysteries themselves had degenerated in a very great degree into mere priestly speculations and religious fraud. Few were the true adepts and initiates, the heirs and descendants of those who had been dispersed by the conquering swords of various invaders of Old Egypt.

The time predicted by the great Hermes in his dialogue with Æsculapius had indeed come; the time when impious foreigners would accuse Egypt of adoring monsters, and naught but the letters engraved in stone upon her monuments would survive — enigmas incredible to posterity. Their sacred scribes and hierophants were wanderers upon the face of the earth. Obliged from fear of a profanation of the sacred mysteries to seek refuge among the Hermetic fraternities — known later as the *Essenes* — their esoteric knowledge was buried deeper than ever. The triumphant brand of Aristotle's pupil swept away from his path of conquest every vestige of a once pure religion, and Aristotle himself, the type and child of his epoch, though instructed in the secret science of the Egyptians, knew but little of this crowning result of millenniums of esoteric studies.

As well as those who lived in the days of the Psammetics, our present-day philosophers "lift the Veil of Isis" — for Isis is but the symbol of nature. But, they see only her physical forms. The soul within escapes their view; and the Divine Mother has no answer for them. There are anatomists, who, uncovering to sight no indwelling spirit under the layers of muscles, the network of nerves, or the cineritious matter, which they lift with the point of the scalpel, assert that man has no soul. Such are as purblind in sophistry as the student,

---

68 "*The Physical Basis of Life*," a Lecture by T. H. Huxley.
69 Huxley, "*Physical Basis of Life*."

who, confining his research to the cold letter of the Kabala, dares say it has no vivifying spirit. To see the true man who once inhabited the subject which lies before him, on the dissecting table, the surgeon must use other eyes than those of his body. So, the glorious truth covered up in the hieratic writings of the ancient papyri can be revealed only to him who possesses the faculty of intuition — which, if we call reason the eye of the mind, may be defined as the eye of the soul.

Our modern science acknowledges a Supreme Power, an Invisible Principle, but denies a Supreme Being, or Personal God.[70] Logically, the difference between the two might be questioned; for in this case *the Power and the Being are identical.* Human reason can hardly imagine to itself an Intelligent Supreme Power without associating it with the idea of an Intelligent Being. The masses can never be expected to have a clear conception of the omnipotence and omnipresence of a supreme God, without investing with those attributes a gigantic projection of their own personality. But the kabalists have never looked upon the invisible EN-SOPH otherwise than as a *Power.*

So far our modern positivists have been anticipated by thousands of ages, in their cautious philosophy. What the hermetic adept claims to demonstrate is, that simple common sense precludes the possibility that the universe is the result of mere chance. Such an idea appears to him more absurd than to think that the problems of Euclid were unconsciously formed by a monkey playing with geometrical figures.

Very few Christians understand, if indeed they know anything at all, of the Jewish Theology. The *Talmud* is the darkest of enigmas even for most Jews, while those Hebrew scholars who do comprehend it do not boast of their knowledge. Their kabalistic books are still less understood by them; for in our days more Christian than Jewish students are engrossed in the elimination of their great truths. How much less is definitely known of the Oriental, or the universal Kabala! Its adepts are few; but these heirs elect of the sages who first discovered "the starry truths which shone on the great Shemaia of the Chaldean lore"[71] have solved the "absolute" and are now resting from their grand labor. They cannot go beyond that which is given to mortals of this earth to know; and no one, not even these elect, can trespass beyond the line drawn by the finger of the Divinity itself. Travellers have met these adepts on the shores of the sacred Ganges, brushed against them in the silent ruins of Thebes, and in the mysterious deserted chambers of Luxor. Within the halls upon whose blue and golden vaults the weird signs attract attention, but whose secret meaning is never penetrated by the idle gazers, they have been seen but seldom recognized. Historical memoirs have recorded their presence in the brilliantly illuminated *salons* of European aristocracy. They have been encountered again on the arid and desolate plains of the Great Sahara, as in the caves of Elephanta. They may be found everywhere, but make themselves known only to those who have devoted their lives to unselfish study, and are not likely to turn back.

Maimonides, the great Jewish theologian and historian, who at one time was almost deified by his countrymen and afterward treated as a heretic, remarks, that the more absurd and void of sense the *Talmud* seems the more sublime is the secret meaning. This learned

---

70 Prof. J. W. Draper, *"Conflict Between Religion and Science."*
71 Bulwer's *"Zanoni."*

man has successfully demonstrated that the Chaldean Magic, the science of Moses and other learned thaumaturgists was wholly based on an extensive knowledge of the various and now forgotten branches of natural science. Thoroughly acquainted with all the resources of the vegetable, animal, and mineral kingdoms, experts in occult chemistry and physics, psychologists as well as physiologists, why wonder that the graduates or adepts instructed in the mysterious sanctuaries of the temples, could perform wonders, which even in our days of enlightenment would appear supernatural? It is an insult to human nature to brand magic and the occult science with the name of imposture. To believe that for so many thousands of years, one-half of mankind practiced deception and fraud on the other half, is equivalent to saying that the human race was composed only of knaves and incurable idiots. Where is the country in which magic was not practised? At what age was it wholly forgotten?

In the oldest documents now in our possession — the *Vedas* and the older laws of Manu — we find many magical rites practiced and permitted by the Brahmans.[72] Thibet, Japan and China teach in the present age that which was taught by the oldest Chaldeans. The clergy of these respective countries, prove moreover what they teach, namely: that the practice of moral and physical purity, and of certain austerities, developes the vital soulpower of self-illumination. Affording to man the control over his own immortal spirit, it gives him truly magical powers over the elementary spirits inferior to himself. In the West we find magic of as high an antiquity as in the East. The Druids of Great Britain practised it in the silent crypts of their deep caves; and Pliny devotes many a chapter to the "wisdom"[73] of the leaders of the Celts. The Semothees, — the Druids of the Gauls, expounded the physical as well as the spiritual sciences. They taught the secrets of the universe, the harmonious progress of the heavenly bodies, the formation of the earth, and above all — the immortality of the soul.[74] Into their sacred groves — natural academies built by the hand of the Invisible Architect — the initiates assembled at the still hour of midnight to learn about what man once was and what he will be.[75] They needed no artificial illumination, nor life-drawing gas, to light up their temples, for the chaste goddess of night beamed her most silvery rays on their oak-crowned heads; and their white-robed sacred bards knew how to converse with the solitary queen of the starry vault.[76]

On the dead soil of the long by-gone past stand their sacred oaks, now dried up and stripped of their spiritual meaning by the venomous breath of materialism. But for the student of occult learning, their vegetation is still as verdant and luxuriant, and as full of deep and sacred truths, as at that hour when the arch-druid performed his magical cures, and waving the branch of mistletoe, severed with his golden sickle the green bough from its mother oak-tree. *Magic is as old as man.* It is as impossible to name the time when it sprang into existence as to indicate on what day the first man himself was born. Whenever a writer has started with the idea of connecting its first foundation in a country with some historical character, further research has proved his views groundless. Odin, the Scandinavian priest

---

72 See the Code published by Sir William Jones, chap. ix., p. 11.

73 Pliny, "*Hist. Nat.*," xxx. I: Ib., xvi., 14; xxv., 9, etc.

74 Pomponius ascribes to them the knowledge of the highest sciences.

75 Cæsar, iii., 14.

76 Pliny, xxx.

and monarch, was thought by many to have originated the practice of magic some seventy years B.C. But it was easily demonstrated that the mysterious rites of the priestesses called *Voïlers, Valas,* were greatly anterior to his age.[77] Some modern authors were bent on proving that Zoroaster was the founder of magic, because he was the founder of the Magian religion. Ammianus Marcellinus, Arnobius, Pliny, and other ancient historians demonstrated conclusively that he was but a reformer of Magic as practiced by the Chaldeans and Egyptians.[78]

The greatest teachers of divinity agree that nearly all ancient books were written symbolically and in a language intelligible only to the initiated. The biographical sketch of Apollonius of Tyana affords an example. As every Kabalist knows, it embraces the whole of the Hermetic philosophy, being a counterpart in many respects of the traditions left us of King Solomon. It reads like a fairy story, but, as in the case of the latter, sometimes facts and historical events are presented to the world under the colors of a fiction. The journey to India represents allegorically the trials of a neophyte. His long discourses with the Brahmans, their sage advice, and the dialogues with the Corinthian Menippus would, if interpreted, give the esoteric catechism. His visit to the empire of the wise men, and interview with their king Hiarchas, the oracle of Amphiaraus, explain symbolically many of the secret dogmas of Hermes. They would disclose, if understood, some of the most important secrets of nature. Eliphas Levi points out the great resemblance which exists between King Hiarchas and the fabulous Hiram, of whom Solomon procured the cedars of Lebanon and the gold of Ophir. We would like to know whether modern Masons, even "Grand Lecturers" and the most intelligent craftsmen belonging to important lodges, understand who the *Hiram* is whose death they combine together to avenge?

Putting aside the purely metaphysical teachings of the *Kabala,* if one would devote himself but to physical occultism, to the so-called branch of therapeutics, the results might benefit some of our modern sciences; such as chemistry and medicine. Says Professor Draper: "Sometimes, not without surprise, we meet with ideas *which we flatter ourselves originated in our own times.*" This remark, uttered in relation to the scientific writings of the Saracens, would apply still better to the more secret *Treatises* of the ancients. Modern medicine, while it has gained largely in anatomy, physiology, and pathology, and even in therapeutics, has lost immensely by its narrowness of spirit, its rigid materialism, its sectarian dogmatism. One school in its purblindness sternly ignores whatever is developed by other schools; and all unite in ignoring every grand conception of man or nature, developed by Mesmerism, or by American experiments on the brain — every principle which does not conform to a stolid materialism. It would require a convocation of the hostile physicians of the several different schools to bring together what is now known of medical science, and it too often happens that after the best practitioners have vainly exhausted their art upon a patient, a mesmerist or a "healing medium" will effect a cure! The explorers of old medical literature, from the time of Hippocrates to that of Paracelsus and Van Helmont, will find a vast number of well-attested physiological and psychological facts and of measures or medicines for healing the sick which modern physicians superciliously

---

77 Munter, on the most ancient religion of the North before the time of Odin. *Memoires de la Société des Antiquaires de France.* Tome ii., p. 230.
78 Ammianus Marcellinus, xxvi., 6.

refuse to employ.[79] Even with respect to surgery, modern practitioners have humbly and publicly confessed the total impossibility of their approximating to anything like the marvellous skill displayed in the art of bandaging by ancient Egyptians. The many hundred yards of ligature enveloping a mummy from its ears down to every separate toe, were studied by the chief surgical operators in Paris, and, notwithstanding that the models were before their eyes, they were unable to accomplish anything like it.

In the Abbott Egyptological collection, in New York City, may be seen numerous evidences of the skill of the ancients in various handicrafts; among others the art of lace-making; and, as it could hardly be expected but that the signs of woman's vanity should go side by side with those of man's strength, there are also specimens of artificial hair, and gold ornaments of different kinds. The New York *Tribune*, reviewing the contents of the *Ebers Papyrus*, says: — "Verily, there is no new thing under the sun. . . . Chapters 65, 66, 79, and 89 show that hair invigorators, hair dyes, pain-killers, and flea-powders were desiderata 3,400 years ago."

How few of our recent alleged discoveries are in reality new, and how many belong to the ancients, is again most fairly and eloquently though but in part stated by our eminent philosophical writer, Professor John W. Draper. His *Conflict between Religion and Science* — a great book with a very bad title — swarms with such facts. At page 13, he cites a few of the achievements of ancient philosophers, which excited the admiration of Greece. In Babylon was a series of Chaldean astronomical observations, ranging back through nineteen hundred and three years, which Callisthenes sent to Aristotle. Ptolemy, the Egyptian king-astronomer possessed a Babylonian record of eclipses going back seven hundred and forty-seven years before our era. As Prof. Draper truly remarks: "Long-continued and close observations were necessary before some of these astronomical results that have reached our times could have been ascertained. Thus, the Babylonians had fixed the length of a tropical year within twenty-five seconds of the truth; their estimate of the sidereal year was barely two minutes in excess. They had detected the precession of the equinoxes. They knew the causes of eclipses, and, by the aid of their cycle, called *saros*, could predict them. Their estimate of the value of that cycle, which is more than 6,585 days, was within nineteen and a half minutes of the truth."

"Such facts furnish incontrovertible proof of the patience and skill with which astronomy had been cultivated in Mesopotamia, and that, with very inadequate instrumental means, it had reached no inconsiderable perfection. These old observers had made a catalogue of the stars, had divided the zodiac into twelve signs; they had parted the day into twelve hours, the night into twelve. They had, as Aristotle says, for a long time devoted themselves to

---

79 In some respects our modern philosophers, who think they make new discoveries can be compared to "the very clever, learned, and civil gentleman" whom Hippocrates having met at Samos one day, describes very good-naturedly. "He informed me," the Father of Medicine proceeds to say, "that he had lately discovered an herb never before known in Europe or Asia, and that no disease, however malignant or chronic, could resist its marvellous properties. Wishing to be civil in turn, I permitted myself to be persuaded to accompany him to the conservatory in which he had transplanted the wonderful specific. What I found was one of the commonest plants in Greece, namely, garlic — the plant which above all others has least pretensions to healing virtues." Hippocrates, "De optima prædicandi ratione item judicii operum magni." I.

observations of star-occultations by the moon. They had correct views of the structure of the solar system, and knew the order of emplacement of the planets. They constructed sundials, clepsydras, astrolabes, gnomons."

Speaking of the world of eternal truths that lies "within the world of transient delusions and unrealities," Professor Draper says: "That world is not to be discovered through the vain traditions that have brought down to us the opinion of men who lived in the morning of civilization, nor in the *dreams of mystics* who thought that they were inspired. It is to be discovered by the investigations *of geometry, and by the practical interrogations of nature.*"

Precisely. The issue could not be better stated. This eloquent writer tells us a profound truth. He does not, however, tell us *the whole* truth, because he does not know it. He has not described the nature or extent of the knowledge imparted in the Mysteries. No subsequent people has been so proficient in geometry as the builders of the Pyramids and other Titanic monuments, antediluvian and postdiluvian. On the other hand, none has ever equalled them in the practical interrogation of nature.

An undeniable proof of this is the significance of their countless symbols. *Every one of these symbols is an embodied idea, — combining the conception of the Divine Invisible with the earthly and visible.* The former is derived from the latter strictly through analogy according to the hermetic formula — "as below, so it is above." Their symbols show great knowledge of natural sciences and a practical study of cosmical power.

As to practical results to be obtained by "the investigations of geometry," very fortunately for students who are coming upon the stage of action, we are no longer forced to content ourselves with mere conjectures. In our own times, an American, Mr. George H. Felt, of New York, who, if he continues as he has begun, may one day be recognized as the greatest geometer of the age, has been enabled, by the sole help of the premises established by the ancient Egyptians, to arrive at results which we will give in his own language. "Firstly," says Mr. Felt, "the fundamental diagram to which all science of elementary geometry, both plane and solid, is referable; to produce arithmetical systems of proportion in a geometrical manner; to identify this figure with all the remains of architecture and sculpture, in all which it had been followed in a marvellously exact manner; to determine that the Egyptians had used it as the basis of all their astronomical calculations, on which their religious symbolism was almost entirely founded; to find its traces among all the remnants of art and architecture of the Greeks; to discover its traces so strongly among the Jewish sacred records, as to prove conclusively that it was founded thereon; to find that the whole system had been discovered by the Egyptians after researches of tens of thousands of years into the laws of nature, and that it might truly be called the science of the Universe." Further it enabled him "to determine with precision problems in physiology heretofore only surmised; to first develop such a Masonic philosophy as showed it to be conclusively the first science and religion, as it will be the last"; and we may add, lastly, to prove by ocular demonstrations that the Egyptian sculptors and architects obtained the models for the quaint figures which adorn the facades and vestibules of their temples, not in the disordered fantasies of their own brains, but from the "viewless races of the air," and other kingdoms of nature, whom he, like them, *claims* to make visible by resort to their own chemical and kabalistical processes.

Schweigger proves that the symbols of all the mythologies have a scientific foundation and substance.[80] It is only through recent discoveries of the physical electro-magnetical powers of nature that such experts in Mesmerism as Ennemoser, Schweigger and Bart, in Germany, Baron Du Potet and Regazzoni, in France and Italy, were enabled to trace with almost faultless accuracy the true relation which each *Theomythos* bore to some one of these powers. The Idæic finger, which had such importance in the magic art of healing, means an iron finger, which is attracted and repulsed in turn by magnetic, natural forces. It produced, in Samothrace, wonders of healing by restoring affected organs to their normal condition.

Bart goes deeper than Schweigger into the significations of the old myths, and studies the subject from both its spiritual and physical aspects. He treats at length of the Phrygian Dactyls, those "magicians and exorcists of sickness," and of the Cabeirian Theurgists. He says: "While we treat of the close union of the Dactyls and magnetic forces, we are not necessarily confined to the magnetic stone, and our views of nature but take a glance at magnetism in its whole meaning. Then it is clear how the initiated, who called themselves *Dactyls*, created astonishment in the people through their magic arts, working as they did, miracles of a healing nature. To this united themselves many other things which the priesthood of antiquity was wont to practice; the cultivation of the land and of morals, the advancement of art and science, mysteries, and secret consecrations. All this was done by the priestly Cabeirians, and *wherefore not guided and supported by the mysterious spirits of nature?*"[81] Schweigger is of the same opinion, and demonstrates that the phenomena of ancient Theurgy were produced by magnetic powers "under the guidance of spirits."

Despite their apparent Polytheism, the ancients — those of the educated class at all events — were entirely monotheistical; and this, too, ages upon ages before the days of Moses. In the *Ebers Papyrus* this fact is shown conclusively in the following words, translated from the first four lines of Plate I.: "I came from Heliopolis with the great ones from Het-aat, the Lords of Protection, the masters of eternity and salvation. I came from Sais with the Mother-goddesses, who extended to me protection. *The Lord of the Universe* told me how to free the gods from all murderous diseases." *Eminent men were called gods by the ancients.* The deification of mortal men and supposititious gods is no more a proof against their monotheism than the monument-building of modern Christians, who erect statues to their heroes, is proof of their polytheism. Americans of the present century would consider it absurd in their posterity 3,000 years hence to classify them as idolaters for having built statues to their god Washington. So shrouded in mystery was the Hermetic Philosophy that Volney asserted that the ancient peoples worshipped their gross material symbols as divine in themselves; whereas these were only considered as representing esoteric principles. Dupuis, also, after devoting many years of study to the problem, mistook the symbolic circle, and attributed their religion solely to astronomy. Eberhart (*Berliner Monatschrift*) and many other German writers of the last and present centuries, dispose of magic most unceremoniously, and think it due to the Platonic mythos of the *Timæus*. But how, without possessing a knowledge of the mysteries, was it possible for these men or any others not endowed with the finer intuition of a Champollion, to discover the esoteric half of that which was concealed, behind the veil of Isis, from all except the adepts?

---

80 Schweigger, "*Introduction to Mythology through Natural History.*"
81 Ennemoser, "*History of Magic,*" i, 3.

The merit of Champollion as an Egyptologist none will question. He declares that everything demonstrates the ancient Egyptians to have been profoundly monotheistical. The accuracy of the writings of the mysterious Hermes Trismegistus, whose antiquity runs back into the night of time, is corroborated by him to their minutest details. Ennemoser also says: "Into Egypt and the East went Herodotus, Thales, Parmenides, Empedocles, Orpheus, and Pythagoras, to instruct themselves in Natural Philosophy and Theology." There, too, Moses acquired his wisdom, and Jesus passed the earlier years of his life.

Thither gathered the students of all countries before Alexandria was founded. "How comes it," Ennemoser goes on to say, "that so little has become known of these mysteries? through so many ages and amongst so many different times and people? The answer is that it is owing to the universally strict silence of the initiated. Another cause may be found in the destruction and total loss of all the written memorials of the secret knowledge of the remotest antiquity." Numa's books, described by Livy, consisting of treatises upon natural philosophy, were found in his tomb; but they were not allowed to be made known, lest they should reveal the most secret mysteries of the state religion. The senate and the tribune of the people determined that the books themselves should be burned, which was done in public.[82]

MAGIC ALWAYS REGARDED AS A DIVINE SCIENCE

Magic was considered a divine science which led to a participation in the attributes of Divinity itself. "It unveils the operations of nature," says Philo Judæus, "and leads to the contemplation of celestial powers."[83] In later periods its abuse and degeneration into sorcery made it an object of general abhorrence. We must therefore deal with it only as it was in the remote past, during those ages when every true religion was based on a knowledge of the occult powers of nature. It was not the sacerdotal class in ancient Persia that established magic, as it is commonly thought, but the Magi, who derive their name from it. The Mobeds, priests of the Parsis — the ancient Ghebers — are named, even at the present day, Magoï, in the dialect of the Pehlvi.[84] *Magic appeared in the world with the earlier races of men.* Cassien mentions a treatise, well-known in the fourth and fifth centuries, which was accredited to Ham, the son of Noah, who in his turn was reputed to have received it from Jared, the fourth generation from Seth, the son of Adam.[85]

ACHIEVEMENTS OF ITS ADEPTS AND HYPOTHESES OF THEIR MODERN DETRACTORS

Moses was indebted for his knowledge to the mother of the Egyptian princess, Thermuthis, who saved him from the waters of the Nile. The wife of Pharaoh,[86] Batria, was an initiate herself, and the Jews owe to her the possession of their prophet, "learned in all

---

82 "*Hist. of Magic*," vol. i, p. 3.
83 Philo Jud., "*De Specialibus Legibus.*"
84 Zend-Avesta, vol. ii., p. 506.
85 Cassian, "*Conference,*" i., 21.
86 "*De Vita et Morte Mosis,*" p. 199.

the wisdom of the Egyptians, and mighty in words and deeds."[87] Justin Martyr, giving as his authority Trogus Pompeius, shows Joseph as having acquired a great knowledge in magical arts with the high priests of Egypt.[88]

The ancients knew more concerning certain sciences than our modern savants have yet discovered. Reluctant as many are to confess as much, it has been acknowledged by more than one scientist. "The degree of scientific knowledge existing in an early period of society was much greater than the moderns are willing to admit"; says Dr. A. Todd Thomson, the editor of *Occult Sciences,* by Salverte; "but," he adds, "it was confined to the temples, carefully veiled from the eyes of the people and opposed only to the priesthood." Speaking of the *Kabala,* the learned Franz von Baader remarks that "not only our salvation and wisdom, but our science itself came to us from the Jews." But why not complete the sentence and tell the reader from whom the Jews got their wisdom? Origen, who had belonged to the Alexandrian school of Platonists, declares that Moses, besides the teachings of the covenant, communicated some very important secrets "from the hidden depths of the law" to the seventy elders. These he enjoined them to impart only to persons whom they found worthy.

St. Jerome names the Jews of Tiberias and Lydda as the only teachers of the mystical manner of interpretation. Finally, Ennemoser expresses a strong opinion that "the writings of Dionysius Areopagita have palpably been grounded on the Jewish *Kabala.*" When we take in consideration that the Gnostics, or early Christians, were but the followers of the old Essenes under a new name, this fact is nothing to be wondered at. Professor Molitor gives the *Kabala* its just due. He says:

"The age of inconsequence and shallowness, in theology as well as in sciences, is past, and since that revolutionary rationalism has left nothing behind but its own emptiness, after having destroyed everything positive, it seems now to be the time to direct our attention anew to that mysterious revelation which is the living spring whence our salvation must come. . . the Mysteries of ancient Israel, which contain all secrets of modern Israel, would be particularly calculated to . . . found the fabric of theology upon its deepest theosophical principles, and to gain *a firm basis* to all ideal sciences. It would open a new path . . . to the obscure labyrinth of the myths, mysteries and constitutions of primitive nations. . .In these traditions alone are contained the system of the schools of the prophets, which the prophet Samuel did not found, *but only restored,* whose end was no other than to lead the scholars to wisdom and the highest knowledge, and when they had been found worthy, to induct them *into deeper mysteries.* Classed with these mysteries was *magic,* which was of a double nature — divine magic, and evil magic, or the black art. Each of these is again divisible into two kinds, the active and seeing; in the first, man endeavors to place himself *en rapport* with the world to learn hidden things; in the latter he endeavors to gain power over spirits; in the former, to perform *good and beneficial* acts; in the latter to do all kinds of diabolical and unnatural deeds."[89]

The clergy of the three most prominent Christian bodies, the Greek, Roman Catholic, and Protestant, discountenance every spiritual phenomenon manifesting itself through the

---

87 *Acts of the Apostles,* vii., 22.
88 Justin, xxxvi., 2.
89 Molitor, "*Philosophy of History and Traditions,*" Howitt's Translation, p. 285

so-called "mediums." A very brief period, indeed, has elapsed since both the two latter ecclesiastical corporations burned, hanged, and otherwise murdered every helpless victim through whose organism spirits — and sometimes blind and as yet unexplained forces of nature — manifested themselves. At the head of these three churches, pre-eminent stands the Church of Rome. Her hands are scarlet with the innocent blood of countless victims shed in the name of the Moloch-like divinity at the head of her creed. She is ready and eager to begin again. But she is bound hand and foot by that nineteenth century spirit of progress and religious freedom which she reviles and blasphemes daily. The Græco-Russian Church is the most amiable and Christ-like in her primitive, simple, though blind faith. Despite the fact that there has been no practical union between the Greek and Latin Churches, and that the two parted company long centuries ago, the Roman Pontiffs seem to invariably ignore the fact. They have in the most impudent manner possible arrogated to themselves jurisdiction not only over the countries within the Greek communion but also over all Protestants as well. "The Church insists," says Professor Draper, "that the state has no rights over anything which it declares to be within its domain, and that Protestantism being a mere rebellion, has no rights at all; that even in Protestant communities the Catholic bishop *is the only lawful* spiritual pastor."[90] Decrees unheeded, encyclical letters unread, invitations to ecumenical councils unnoticed, excommunications laughed at — all these have seemed to make no difference. Their persistence has only been matched by their effrontery. In 1864, the culmination of absurdity was attained when Pius IX. excommunicated and fulminated publicly his anathemas against the Russian Emperor, as a "*schismatic* cast out from the bosom of the Holy Mother Church."[91] Neither he nor his ancestors, nor Russia since it was Christianized, a thousand years ago, have ever consented to join the Roman Catholics. Why not claim ecclesiastical jurisdiction over the Buddhists of Thibet, or the shadows of the ancient Hyk-Sos?

The mediumistic phenomena have manifested themselves at all times in Russia as well as in other countries. This force ignores religious differences; it laughs at nationalities; and invades unasked any individuality, whether of a crowned head or a poor beggar.

Not even the present Vice-God, Pius IX., himself, could avoid the unwelcome guest. For the last fifty years his Holiness has been known to be subject to very extraordinary fits. Inside the Vatican they are termed *Divine visions;* outside, physicians call them epileptic fits; and popular rumor attributes them to an obsession by the ghosts of Peruggia, Castelfidardo, and Mentana!

> "The lights burn blue: it is now dead midnight,
> Cold fearful drops stand on my trembling flesh,
> Methought the souls of all that I caused to be murdered Came. . . . "[92]

The Prince of Hohenlohe, so famous during the first quarter of our century for his healing powers, was himself a great medium. Indeed, these phenomena and powers belong to no particular age or country. They form a portion of the psychological attributes of man — the Microcosmos.

---

90 "*Conflict between Religion and Science,*" p. 329.
91 See "*Gazette du Midi,*" and "*Le Monde,*" of 3 May, 1864.
92 Shakespere, "*Richard III.*"

For centuries have the *Klikouchy*,[93] *the Yourodevoÿ*,[94] and other miserable creatures been afflicted with strange disorders, which the Russian clergy and the populace attribute to possession by the devil. They throng the entrances of the cathedrals, without daring to trust themselves inside, lest their self-willed controlling demons might fling them on the ground. Voroneg, Kiew, Kazan, and all cities which possess the thaumaturgical relics of canonized saints, abound with such unconscious mediums. One can always find numbers of them, congregating in hideous groups, and hanging about the gates and porches. At certain stages of the celebration of the mass by the officiating clergy, such as the appearance of the sacraments, or the beginning of the prayer and chorus, "*Ejey Cheroúvim*," these half-maniacs, half-mediums, begin crowing like cocks, barking, bellowing and braying, and, finally, fall down in fearful convulsions. "The *unclean one* cannot bear the holy prayer," is the pious explanation. Moved by pity, some charitable souls administer restoratives to the "afflicted ones," and distribute alms among them. Occasionally, a priest is invited to exorcise, in which event he either performs the ceremony for the sake of love and charity, or the alluring prospect of a twenty-copeck silver bit, according to his Christian impulses. But these miserable creatures — who are mediums, for they prophesy and see visions sometimes, when the fit is genuine § — are never molested because of their misfortune. Why should the clergy persecute them, or people hate and denounce them as damnable witches or wizards? Common sense and justice surely suggest that if any are to be punished it is certainly not the victims who cannot help themselves, but the demon who is alleged to control their actions. The worst that happens to the patient is, that the priest inundates him or her with holy water, and causes the poor creature to catch cold. This failing in efficacy, the *Klikoucha* is left to the will of God, and taken care of in love and pity. Superstitious and blind as it is, a faith conducted on such principles certainly deserves some respect, and can never be offensive, either to man or the *true* God. Not so with that of the Roman Catholics; and hence, it is they, and secondarily, the Protestant clergy — with the exception of some foremost thinkers among them — that we purpose questioning in this work. We want to know upon what grounds they base their right to treat Hindus and Chinese spiritualists and kabalists in the way they do; denouncing them, in company with the infidels — creatures of their own making — as so many convicts sentenced to the inextinguishable fires of hell.

Far from us be the thought of the slightest irreverence — let alone blasphemy — toward the Divine Power which called into being all things, visible and invisible. Of its majesty and boundless perfection we dare not even think. It is enough for us to know that *It* exists and that *It* is all wise. Enough that in common with our fellow creatures we possess a spark of *Its* essence. The supreme power whom we revere is the boundless and endless one — the grand "CENTRAL SPIRITUAL SUN" by whose attributes and the visible effects of whose inaudible WILL we are surrounded — the God of the ancient and the God of modern seers. His nature can be studied only in the worlds called forth by his mighty FIAT. His revelation is traced with his own finger in imperishable figures of universal harmony upon the face of the Cosmos. It is the only INFALLIBLE gospel we recognize.

---

93 Literally, the *screaming* or the howling ones.
94 The half-demented, the *idiots*. But such is not always the case, for some among these beggars make a regular and profitable trade of it.

Speaking of ancient geographers, Plutarch remarks in *Theseus*, that they "crowd into the edges of their maps parts of the world which they do not know about, adding notes in the margin to the effect that beyond this lies nothing but sandy deserts *full of wild beasts* and *unapproachable bogs.*" Do not our theologians and scientists do the same? While the former people the invisible world with either angels or devils, our philosophers try to persuade their disciples that where there is no *matter* there is *nothing.*

How many of our inveterate skeptics belong, notwithstanding their materialism, to Masonic Lodges? The brothers of the Rosie-Cross, mysterious practitioners of the mediæval ages, still live — but in name only. They may "shed tears at the grave of their respectable Master, Hiram Abiff "; but vainly will they search for the true locality, "where the sprig of myrtle was placed." The dead letter remains alone, the spirit has fled. They are like the English or German chorus of the Italian opera, who descend in the fourth act of *Ernani* into the crypt of Charlemagne, singing their conspiracy in a tongue utterly unknown to them. So, our modern knights of the Sacred Arch may descend every night if they choose "through the nine arches into the bowels of the earth," — they "will never discover the sacred Delta of Enoch." The "Sir Knights in the South Valley" and those in "the North Valley" may try to assure themselves that "enlightenment dawns upon their minds," and that as they progress in Masonry "the veil of superstition, despotism, tyranny" and so on, no longer obscures the visions of their minds. But these are all empty words so long as they neglect their mother Magic, and turn their backs upon its twin sister, Spiritualism. Verily, "Sir Knights of the Orient," you may "leave your stations and sit upon the floor in attitudes of grief, with your heads resting upon your hands," for you have cause to bewail and mourn your fate. Since Philippe le Bel destroyed the Knights-Templars, not one has appeared to clear up your doubts notwithstanding all claims to the contrary. Truly, you are "wanderers from Jerusalem, seeking the lost treasure of the holy place." Have you found it? Alas, no! for the holy place is profaned; the pillars of wisdom, strength and beauty are destroyed. Henceforth, "you must wander in darkness," and "travel in humility," among the woods and mountains in search of the "lost word." "Pass on!" — you will never find it so long as you limit your journeys to *seven* or even seven times seven; because you are "travelling in darkness," and this darkness can only be dispelled by the light of the blazing torch of truth which alone the right descendants of Ormasd carry. They alone can teach you the true pronunciation of the name revealed to Enoch, Jacob and Moses. "Pass on! Till your R. S. W. shall learn to multiply 333, and *strike* instead 666 — the number of the Apocalyptic Beast, you may just as well observe prudence and act "*sub rosa.*"

In order to demonstrate that the notions which the ancients entertained about dividing human history into cycles were not utterly devoid of a philosophical basis, we will close this chapter by introducing to the reader one of the oldest traditions of antiquity as to the evolution of our planet.

At the close of each "great year," called by Aristotle — according to Censorinus — the *greatest*, and which consists of six *sars*[95] our planet is subjected to a thorough physical

---

95 Webster declares very erroneously that the Chaldeans called *saros*, the cycle of eclipses, a period of about 6,586 years, "the time of revolution of the moon's node." Berosus, himself a Chaldean astrologer,

revolution. The polar and equatorial climates gradually exchange places; the former moving slowly toward the Line, and the tropical zone, with its exuberant vegetation and swarming animal life, replacing the forbidding wastes of the icy poles. This change of climate is necessarily attended by cataclysms, earthquakes, and other cosmical throes.[96] As the beds of the ocean are displaced, at the end of every decimillennium and about one neros, a semi-universal deluge like the legendary Noachian flood is brought about. This year was called the *Heliacal* by the Greeks; but no one outside the sanctuary knew anything certain either as to its duration or particulars. The winter of this year was called the Cataclysm or the Deluge, — the Summer, the Ecpyrosis. The popular traditions taught that at these alternate seasons the world was in turn burned and deluged. This is what we learn at least from the *Astronomical Fragments* of Censorinus and Seneca. So uncertain were the commentators about the length of this year, that none except Herodotus and Linus, who assigned to it, the former 10,800, and the latter 13,984, came near the truth.[97] According to the claims of the Babylonian priests, corroborated by Eupolemus,[98] "the city of Babylon, owes its foundation to those who were saved from the catastrophe of the deluge; *they were the giants* and they built the tower which is noticed in history."[99] These giants who were great astrologers and had received moreover from their fathers, "the sons of God," every instruction pertaining to secret matters, instructed the priests in their turn, and left in the temples all the records of the periodical cataclysm that they had witnessed themselves. This is how the high priests came by the knowledge of the *great* years. When we remember, moreover, that Plato in the *Timæus* cites the old Egyptian priest rebuking Solon for his ignorance of the fact that there were several such deluges as the great one of Ogyges, we can easily ascertain that this belief in the *Heliakos* was a doctrine held by the initiated priests the world over.

The Neroses, the Vrihaspati, or the periods called yugas or kalpas, are life-problems to solve. The Satya-yug and Buddhistic cycles of chronology would make a mathematician stand aghast at the array of ciphers. The Maha-kalpa embraces an untold number of periods far back in the antediluvian ages. Their system comprises a kalpa or grand period of 4,320,000,000 years, which they divide into four lesser yugas, running as follows:

---

at the Temple of Belus, at Babylon, gives the duration of the sar, or sarus, 3,600 years; a neros 600; and a sossus 60. (See, Berosus from Abydenus, "*Of the Chaldaean Kings and the Deluge.*" See also Eusebius, and Cory's *MS*. Ex. Cod. reg. gall. gr. No. 2360, fol. 154.)

96 Before scientists reject such a theory — traditional as it is — it would be in order for them to demonstrate why, at the end of the tertiary period, the Northern Hemisphere had undergone such a reduction of temperature as to utterly change the torrid zone to a Siberian climate? Let us bear in mind that the *heliocentric system came to us from upper India;* and that the germs of all great astronomical truths were brought thence by Pythagoras. So long as we lack a mathematically correct demonstration, one hypothesis is as good as another.

97 Censorinus, "*De Natal Die.*" Seneca, "*Nat. Quæst.,*" iii., 29.

98 Euseb., "*Præp. Evan.*" Of the Tower of Babel and Abraham.

99 This is in flat contradiction of the Bible narrative, which tells us that the deluge was sent for the special destruction of these *giants*. The Babylon priests had *no* object to invent lies.

1st — Satya yug . . . . 1,728,000 years

2d — Tretya yug. . . . 1,296,000   "

3d — Dvapa yug 864,000   "

4th —Kali yug . . . . <u>432,000</u> "

      Total. 4,320,000

which make one divine age or Maha-yug; seventy-one Maha-yugs make 306,720,000 years, to which is added a sandhi (or the time when day and night border on each other, morning and evening twilight), equal to a Satya-yug, 1,728,000, make a manwantara of 308,448,000 years;[100] fourteen manwantaras make 4,318,272,000 years; to which must be added a sandhi to begin the kalpa, 1,728,000 years, making the kalpa or grand period of 4,320,000,000 of years. As we are now only in the Kali-yug of the twenty-eighth age of the seventh manwantara of 308,448,000 years, we have yet sufficient time before us to wait before we reach even half of the time allotted to the world.

These ciphers are not fanciful, but founded upon actual astronomical calculations, as has been demonstrated by S. Davis.[101] Many a scientist, Higgins among others, notwithstanding their researches, has been utterly perplexed as to which of these was the *secret* cycle. Bunsen has demonstrated that the Egyptian priests, who made the cyclic notations, kept them always in the profoundest mystery.[102] Perhaps their difficulty arose from the fact that the calculations of the ancients applied equally to the spiritual progress of humanity as to the physical. It will not be difficult to understand the close correspondence drawn by the ancients between the cycles of nature and of mankind, if we keep in mind their belief in the constant and all-potent influences of the planets upon the fortunes of humanity. Higgins justly believed that the cycle of the Indian system, of 432,000, is the true key of the secret cycle. But his failure in trying to decipher it was made apparent; for as it pertained to the mystery of the creation, this cycle was the most inviolable of all. It was repeated in symbolic figures only in the Chaldean *Book of Numbers*, the original of which, if now extant, is certainly not to be found in libraries, as it formed one of the most ancient Books of Hermes,[103] the number of which is at present undetermined.

---

100 Coleman, who makes this calculation, allowed a serious error to escape the proofreader; the length of the manwantara is given at 368,448,000, which is just sixty million years too much.

101 S. Davis, "*Essay in the Asiatic Researches*"; and Higgins's "*Anacalypsis*"; also see Coleman's "*Mythology of the Hindus,*" Preface, p. xiii.

102 Bunsen, "*Egypte,*" vol. i.

103 The forty-two Sacred Books of the Egyptians mentioned by Clement of Alexandria as having existed in his time, were but a portion of the Books of Hermes. Iamblichus, on the authority of the Egyptian priest Abammon, attributes 1200 of such books to Hermes, and Manetho 36,000. But the testimony of Iamblichus as a neo-Platonist and theurgist is of course rejected by modern critics. Manetho, who is held by Bunsen in the highest consideration as a "purely historical personage" . . . with whom "none of the later native historians can be compared . . . ." (See "Egypte," i, p. 97), suddenly becomes a Pseudo-Manetho, as soon as the ideas propounded by him clash with the scientific prejudices against magic and the occult knowledge claimed by the ancient priests. However, none of the archeologists doubt for a moment the almost incredible antiquity of the Hermetic books. Champollion shows the greatest regard for their authenticity and great truthfulness, corroborated as it is by many of the oldest monuments. And Bunsen brings irrefutable proofs of their age. From his

Calculating by the secret period of the Great Neros and the Hindu Kalpas, some kabalists, mathematicians and archeologists who knew naught of the secret computations made the above number of 21,000 years to be 24,000 years, for the length of the great year, as it was to the renewal only of our globe that they thought the last period of 6,000 years applied. Higgins gives as a reason for it, that it was anciently thought that the equinoxes preceded only after the rate of 2,000, not 2,160, years in a sign; for thus it would allow for the length of the great year four times 6,000 or 24,000 years. "Hence," he says, "might arise their immensely-lengthened cycles; because, it would be the same with this great year as with the common year, till it travelled round an immensely-lengthened circle, when it would come to the old point again." He therefore accounts for the 24,000 in the following manner: "If the angle which the plane of the ecliptic makes with the plane of the equator had decreased gradually and regularly, as it was till very lately supposed to do, the two planes would have coincided in about ten ages, 6,000 years; in ten ages, 6,000 years more, the sun would have been situated relatively to the Southern Hemisphere as he is now to the Northern; in ten ages, 6,000 years more, the two planes would coincide again; and, in ten ages, 6,000 years more, he would be situated as he is now, after a lapse of about twenty-four or twenty-five thousand years in all. When the sun arrived at the equator, the ten ages or six thousand years would end, and the world would be destroyed *by fire;* when he arrived at the southern point, it would be destroyed by water. And thus, it would be destroyed at the end of every 6,000 years, or ten neroses."[104] This method of calculating by the *neroses,* without allowing any consideration for the secrecy in which the ancient philosophers, who were exclusively of the sacerdotal order, held their knowledge, gave rise to the greatest errors. It led the Jews, as well as some of the Christian Platonists, to maintain that the world would be destroyed at the end of six thousand years. Gale shows how firmly this belief was rooted in the Jews. It has also led modern scientists to discredit entirely the hypothesis of the ancients. It has given rise to the formation of different religious sects, which, like the Adventists of our century, are always living in the expectation of the approaching destruction of the world.

As our planet revolves once every year around the sun and at the same time turns once in every twenty-four hours upon its own axis, thus traversing minor circles within a larger one, so is the work of the smaller cyclic periods accomplished and recommenced, within the Great Saros.

---

researches, for instance, we learn that there was a line of sixty-one kings before the days of Moses, who preceded the Mosaic period by a clearly-traceable civilization of several thousand years. Thus we are warranted in believing that the works of Hermes Trismegistus were extant many ages before the birth of the Jewish law-giver. "Styli and inkstands were found on monuments of the fourth Dynasty, the oldest in the world," says Bunsen. If the eminent Egyptologist rejects the period of 48,863 years before Alexander, to which Diogenes Laertius carries back the records of the priests, he is evidently more embarrassed with the ten thousand of astronomical observations, and remarks that "if they were actual observations, they *must have* extended over 10,000 years" (p. 14). "We learn, however," he adds, "from one of their own old chronological works . . . that the genuine Egyptian traditions concerning the mythological period, treated of *myriads* of years." ("*Egypte,*" i, p. 15).
104 Higgins, "*Anacalypsis.*"

The revolution of the physical world, according to the ancient doctrine, is attended by a like revolution in the world of intellect — the spiritual evolution of the world proceeding in cycles, like the physical one.

Thus we see in history a regular alternation of ebb and flow in the tide of human progress. The great kingdoms and empires of the world, after reaching the culmination of their greatness, descend again, in accordance with the same law by which they ascended; till, having reached the lowest point, humanity reasserts itself and mounts up once more, the height of its attainment being, by this law of ascending progression by cycles, somewhat higher than the point from which it had before descended.

The division of the history of mankind into Golden, Silver, Copper and Iron Ages, is not a fiction. We see the same thing in the literature of peoples. An age of great inspiration and unconscious productiveness is invariably followed by an age of criticism and consciousness. The one affords material for the analyzing and critical intellect of the other. Thus, all those great characters who tower like giants in the history of mankind, like Buddha-Siddartha, and Jesus, in the realm of spiritual, and Alexander the Macedonian and Napoleon the Great, in the realm of physical conquests, were but reflexed images of human types which had existed ten thousand years before, in the preceding decimillennium, reproduced by the mysterious powers controlling the destinies of our world. There is no prominent character in all the annals of sacred or profane history whose prototype we cannot find in the half-fictitious and half-real traditions of bygone religions and mythologies. As the star, glimmering at an immeasurable distance above our heads, in the boundless immensity of the sky, reflects itself in the smooth waters of a lake, so does the imagery of men of the antediluvian ages reflect itself in the periods we can embrace in an historical retrospect.

"As above, so it is below. That which has been, will return again. As in heaven, so on earth."

The world is always ungrateful to its great men. Florence has built a statue to Galileo, but hardly even mentions Pythagoras. The former had a ready guide in the treatises of Copernicus, who had been obliged to contend against the universally established Ptolemaic system. But neither Galileo nor modern astronomy discovered the emplacement of the planetary bodies. Thousands of ages before, it was taught by the sages of Middle Asia, and brought thence by Pythagoras, not as a speculation, but as a demonstrated science. "The numerals of Pythagoras," says Porphyry, "were hieroglyphical symbols, by means whereof he explained all ideas concerning the nature of *all* things."[105]

Verily, then, to antiquity alone have we to look for the origin of all things. How well Hargrave Jennings expresses himself when speaking of Pyramids, and how true are his words when he asks: "Is it at all reasonable to conclude, at a period when knowledge was at the highest, and when the human powers were, in comparison with ours at the present time, prodigious, that all these indomitable, *scarcely believable* physical effects — that such achievements as those of the Egyptians — were devoted to a mistake? that the myriads of the Nile were fools laboring in the dark, and that all the magic of their great men was forgery, and that we, in despising that which we call their superstition and wasted power, are alone the wise? No! there is much more in these old religions than probably — in the audacity of modern denial, in the confidence of these superficial-science times, and in the

---

105 *"De Vite Pythag."*

derision of these days without faith — is in the least degree supposed. We do not understand the old time. . . . Thus we see how classic practice and heathen teaching may be made to reconcile — how even the Gentile and the Hebrew, the mythological and the Christian doctrine harmonize in the general faith founded on Magic. That Magic is indeed possible is the moral of this book."[106]

It is possible. Thirty years ago, when the first rappings of Rochester awakened slumbering attention to the reality of an invisible world; when the gentle shower of raps gradually became a torrent which overflowed the whole globe, spiritualists had to contend but against two potencies — theology and science. But the theosophists have, in addition to these, to meet the world at large and the spiritualists first of all.

"There is a *personal* God, and there is a *personal* Devil!" thunders the Christian preacher. "Let him be anathema who dares say nay!" "There is no personal God, except the gray matter in our brain," contemptuously replies the materialist. "And there is no Devil. Let him be considered thrice an idiot who says aye." Meanwhile the occultists and *true* philosophers heed neither of the two combatants, but keep perseveringly at their work. None of them believe in the absurd, passionate, and fickle God of superstition, but all of them believe in good and evil. Our human reason, the emanation of our finite mind, is certainly incapable of comprehending a divine intelligence, an endless and infinite entity; and, according to strict logic, that which transcends our understanding and would remain thoroughly incomprehensible to our senses cannot exist for us; hence, it does *not* exist. So far finite reason agrees with science, and says: "There is no God." But, on the other hand, our *Ego,* that which lives and thinks and feels independently of us in our mortal casket, does more than believe. It *knows* that there exists a God in nature, for the sole and invincible Artificer of all lives in us as we live in Him. No dogmatic faith or exact science is able to uproot that intuitional feeling inherent in man, when he has once fully realized it in himself.

Human nature is like universal nature in its abhorrence of a vacuum. It feels an intuitional yearning for a Supreme Power. Without a God, the cosmos would seem to it but like a soulless corpse. Being forbidden to search for Him where alone His traces would be found, man filled the aching void with the personal God whom his spiritual teachers built up for him from the crumbling ruins of heathen myths and hoary philosophies of old. How otherwise explain the mushroom growth of new sects, some of them absurd beyond degree? Mankind have one innate, irrepressible craving, that *must* be satisfied in any religion that would supplant the dogmatic, undemonstrated and undemonstrable theology of our Christian ages. This is the yearning after the proofs of immortality. As Sir Thomas Browne has expressed it: . . . . "it is the heaviest stone that melancholy can throw at a man, to tell him that he is at the end of his nature, or that there is no future state to come, unto which this seems progressive, and otherwise made in vain." Let any religion offer itself that can supply these proofs in the shape of scientific facts, and the established system will be driven to the alternative of fortifying its dogmas with such facts, or of passing out of the reverence and affection of Christendom. Many a Christian divine has been forced to acknowledge that there is *no authentic* source whence the assurance of a future state could have been derived by man. How could then such a belief have stood for countless ages, were it not that among

---

106 "*The Rosicrucians,*" etc., by Hargrave Jennings.

all nations, whether civilized or savage, man *has been* allowed the demonstrative proof? Is not the very existence of such a belief an evidence that thinking philosopher and unreasoning savage have both been compelled to acknowledge the testimony of their senses? That if, in isolated instances, spectral illusion may have resulted from physical causes, on the other hand, in thousands of instances, apparitions of persons have held converse with several individuals at once, who saw and heard them collectively, and could not all have been diseased in mind?

MAN'S YEARNING FOR IMMORTALITY

The greatest thinkers of Greece and Rome regarded such matters as demonstrated facts. They distinguished the apparitions by the names of *manes, anima* and *umbra*: the *manes* descending after the decease of the individual into the Underworld; the *anima*, or pure spirit, ascending to heaven; and the restless *umbra* (earth-bound spirit), hovering about its tomb, because the attraction of matter and love of its earthly body prevailed in it and prevented its ascension to higher regions.

> "Terra legit *carnem* tumulum circumvolet *umbra*,
> Orcus habet *manes, spiritus* astra petit,"

says Ovid, speaking of the threefold constituents of souls.

But all such definitions must be subjected to the careful analysis of philosophy. Too many of our thinkers do not consider that the numerous changes in language, the allegorical phraseology and evident secretiveness of old Mystic writers, who were generally under an obligation never to divulge the solemn secrets of the sanctuary, might have sadly misled translators and commentators. The phrases of the mediæval alchemist they read literally; and even the veiled symbololy of Plato is commonly misunderstood by the modern scholar. One day they may learn to know better, and so become aware that the method of extreme necessarianism was practiced in ancient as well as in modern philosophy; that from the first ages of man, the fundamental truths of all that we are permitted to know on earth was in the safe keeping of the adepts of the sanctuary; that the difference in creeds and religious practice was only external; and that those guardians of the primitive divine revelation, who had solved every problem that is within the grasp of human intellect, were bound together by a universal freemasonry of science and philosophy, which formed one unbroken chain around the globe. It is for philology and psychology to find the end of the thread. That done, it will then be ascertained that, by relaxing one single loop of the old religious systems, the chain of mystery may be disentangled.

The neglect and withholding of these proofs have driven such eminent minds as Hare and Wallace, and other men of power, into the fold of modern spiritualism. At the same time it has forced others, congenitally devoid of spiritual intuitions, into a gross materialism that figures under various names.

But we see no utility in prosecuting the subject further. For, though in the opinion of most of our contemporaries, there has been but one day of learning, in whose twilight stood the older philosophers, and whose noontide brightness is all our own; and though the testimony of scores of ancient and mediæval thinkers has proved valueless to modern experimenters, as though the world dated from A.D. I , and all knowledge were of recent growth, we will not lose hope or courage. The moment is more opportune than ever for the review of old philosophies. Archæologists, philologists, astronomers, chemists and physicists are getting nearer and nearer to the point where they will be forced to consider them. Physical science has already reached its limits of exploration; dogmatic theology sees the springs of its inspiration dry. Unless we mistake the signs, the day is approaching when the world will receive the proofs that only ancient religions were in harmony with nature, and ancient science embraced all that can be known. Secrets long kept may be revealed; books long forgotten and arts long time lost may be brought out to light again; papyri and parchments of inestimable importance will turn up in the hands of men who pretend to have unrolled them from mummies, or stumbled upon them in buried crypts; tablets and pillars, whose sculptured revelations will stagger theologians and confound scientists, may yet be excavated and interpreted. Who knows the possibilities of the future? An era of disenchantment and rebuilding will soon begin — nay, has already begun. The cycle has almost run its course; a new one is about to begin, and the future pages of history may contain full evidence, and convey full proof that

> "If ancestry can be in aught believed,
> Descending spirits have conversed with man,
> And told him secrets of the world unknown."

———

CHAPTER II

"Pride, where wit fails, steps in to our defence
And fills up all the mighty void of sense. . . . "

PORE

"But why should the operations of nature be changed? There may be a deeper philosophy than we dream of — a philosophy that discovers the secrets of nature, *but does not alter, by penetrating them, its course.*"

BULWER

THE SERVILITY OF SOCIETY

IS it enough for man to know that he exists? Is it enough to be formed a human being to enable him to deserve the appellation of MAN? It is our decided impression and conviction, that to become a genuine spiritual entity, which that designation implies, man must first *create* himself anew, so to speak — *i.e.,* thoroughly eliminate from his mind and spirit, not only the dominating influence of selfishness and other impurity, but also the infection of superstition and prejudice. The latter is far different from what we commonly term *antipathy* or *sympathy.* We are at first irresistibly or unwittingly drawn within its dark circle by that peculiar influence, that powerful current of magnetism which emanates from ideas as well as from physical bodies. By this we are surrounded, and finally prevented through moral cowardice — fear of public opinion — from stepping out of it. It is rare that men regard a thing in either its true or false light, accepting the conclusion by the free action of their own judgment. Quite the reverse. The conclusion is more commonly reached by blindly adopting the opinion current at the hour among those with whom they associate. A church member will not pay an absurdly high price for his pew any more than a materialist will go twice to listen to Mr. Huxley's talk on evolution, because they think that it is right to do so; but merely because Mr. and Mrs. So-and-so have done it, and these personages are THE S — AND S—'s.

The same holds good with everything else. If psychology had had its Darwin, the descent of man as regards moral qualities might have been found inseparably linked with that of his physical form. Society in its servile condition suggests to the intelligent observer of its mimicry a kinship between the Simia and human beings even more striking than is exhibited in the external marks pointed out by the great anthropologist.

PREJUDICE AND BIGOTRY OF MEN OF SCIENCE

The many varieties of the ape — "mocking presentments of ourselves" — appear to have been evolved on purpose to supply a certain class of expensively-dressed persons with the material for genealogical trees.

Science is daily and rapidly moving toward the great discoveries in chemistry and physics, organology, and anthropology. Learned men ought to be free from preconceptions and prejudices of every kind; yet, although thought and opinion are now free, scientists are still the same men as of old. An Utopian dreamer is he who thinks that man ever changes with the evolution and development of new ideas. The soil may be well fertilized and made to yield with every year a greater and better variety of fruit; but, dig a little deeper than the stratum required for the crop, and the same earth will be found in the subsoil as was there before the first furrow was turned.

Not many years ago, the person who questioned the infallibility of some theological dogma was branded at once an iconoclast and an infidel. *Væ victis!* . . . Science has conquered. But in its turn the victor claims the same infallibility, though it equally fails to prove its right. "*Tempora mutantur et nos mutamur in illis,*" the saying of the good old Lotharius, applies to the case. Nevertheless, we feel as if we had some right to question the high-priests of science.

For many years we have watched the development and growth of that apple of discord — MODERN SPIRITUALISM. Familiar with its literature both in Europe and America, we have closely and eagerly witnessed its interminable controversies and compared its contradictory hypotheses. Many educated men and women — heterodox spiritualists, of course — have tried to fathom the Protean phenomena. The only result was that they came to the following conclusion: whatever may be the reason of these constant failures — whether such are to be laid at the door of the investigators themselves, or of the secret Force at work — it is at least proved that, in proportion as the psychological manifestations increase in frequency and variety, the darkness surrounding their origin becomes more impenetrable.

That phenomena are actually witnessed, mysterious in their nature — generally and perhaps wrongly termed spiritual — it is now idle to deny. Allowing a large discount for clever fraud, what remains is quite serious enough to demand the careful scrutiny of science. "*E pur se muove,*" the sentence spoken ages since, has passed into the category of household words. The courage of Galileo is not now required to fling it into the face of the Academy. Psychological phenomena are already on the offensive.

THEY ARE CHASED BY PSYCHICAL PHENOMENA

The position assumed by modern scientists is that even though the occurrence of certain mysterious phenomena in the presence of the mediums be a fact, there is no proof that they are not due to some abnormal nervous condition of those individuals. The possibility that they may be produced by returning human spirits need not be considered until the other question is decided. Little exception can be taken to this position. Unquestionably, the burden of proof rests upon those who assert the agency of spirits. If the scientists would grapple with the subject in good faith, showing an earnest desire to solve the perplexing mystery, instead of treating it with undignified and unprofessional contempt, they would be open to no censure. True, the great majority of "spiritual" communications are calculated to disgust investigators of even moderate intelligence. Even when genuine they are trivial, commonplace, and often vulgar. During the past twenty years we have received through various mediums messages purporting to be from Shakespeare, Byron, Franklin, Peter the Great, Napoleon and Josephine, and even from Voltaire. The general impression made upon us was that the French conqueror and his consort seemed to have forgotten how to spell words correctly; Shakespeare and Byron had become chronic inebriates; and Voltaire had turned an imbecile. Who can blame men trained to habits of exactitude, or even simply well-educated persons, for hastily concluding that when so much palpable fraud lies upon the surface, there could hardly be truth if they should go to the bottom? The huckstering about of pompous names attached to idiotic communications has given the scientific stomach such an indigestion that it cannot assimilate even the great truth which lies on the telegraphic plateaux of this ocean of psychological phenomena. They judge by its surface, covered with froth and scum. But they might with equal propriety deny that there is any clear water in the depths of the sea when an oily scum was floating upon the surface. Therefore, if on one hand we cannot very well blame them for stepping back at the first sight of what seems really repulsive, we do, and have a right to censure them for their unwillingness to explore deeper. Neither pearls nor cut diamonds are to be found lying loose on the ground; and these persons act as unwisely as would a professional diver, who should reject an oyster on account of its filthy and slimy appearance, when by opening it he might find a precious pearl inside the shell.

Even the just and severe rebukes of some of their leading men are of no avail and the fear on the part of men of science to investigate such an unpopular subject, seems to have now become a general panic. "*The phenomena chase the scientists, and the scientists run away from the phenomena,*" very pointedly remarks M.A.N. Aksakof in an able article on Mediumism and the St. Petersburg Scientific Committee. The attitude of this body of professors toward the subject which they had pledged themselves to investigate was throughout simply disgraceful. Their premature and *prearranged* report was so evidently partial and inconclusive as to call out a scornful protest even from unbelievers.

The inconsistency of the logic of our learned gentlemen against the philosophy of spiritualism proper is admirably pointed out by Professor John Fisk — one of their own body. In a recent philosophical work, *The Unseen World,* while showing that from the very definition of the terms , *matter* and *spirit,* the existence of spirit cannot be demonstrated to the senses, and that thus no theory is amenable to *scientific test*s, he deals a severe blow at his colleagues in the following lines:

"The testimony in such a case," he says, "must, under the conditions of the present life, be forever inaccessible. It lies wholly outside the range of experience. However abundant it may be, we cannot expect to meet it. And, accordingly, our failure to produce it does not raise even the slightest presumption against our theory. When conceived in this way, the belief in the future life is without scientific support, but at the same time it is placed beyond the need of scientific support and the range of scientific criticism. It is a belief which no imaginable future advance of physical discovery can in any way impugn. It is a belief which is in no sense irrational, and which may be logically entertained without in the least affecting our scientific habit of mind, or influencing our scientific conclusions." "If now," he adds, "men of science will accept the position that spirit is not matter, nor governed by the laws of matter, and refrain from speculations concerning it restricted by their knowledge of material things, they will withdraw what is to men of religion, at present, their principal cause of irritation."

But, they will do no such thing. They feel incensed at the brave, loyal, and highly commendable surrender of such superior men as Wallace, and refuse to accept even the prudent and restrictive policy of Mr. Crookes.

No other claim is advanced for a hearing of the opinions contained in the present work than that they are based upon many years' study of both ancient magic and its modern form, Spiritualism. The former, even now, when phenomena of the same nature have become so familiar to all, is commonly set down as clever jugglery. The latter, when overwhelming evidence precludes the possibility of truthfully declaring it charlatanry, is denominated an universal hallucination.

Many years of wandering among "heathen" and "Christian" magicians, occultists, mesmerisers; and the *tutti quanti* of white and black art, ought to be sufficient, we think, to give us a certain right to feel competent to take a practical view of this doubted and very complicated question. We have associated with the fakirs, the holy men of India, and seen them when in intercourse with the *Pitris.* We have watched the proceedings and *modus operandi* of the howling and dancing dervishes; held friendly communications with the marabouts of European and Asiatic Turkey; and the serpent-charmers of Damascus and Benares have but few secrets that we have not had the fortune to study. Therefore, when scientists who have never had an opportunity of living among these oriental jugglers and can judge at the best but superficially, tell us that there is naught in their performances but mere tricks of prestidigitation, we cannot help feeling a profound regret for such hasty conclusions. That such pretentious claims should be made to a thorough analysis of the powers of nature, and at the same time such unpardonable neglect displayed of questions of purely physiological and psychological character, and astounding phenomena rejected without either examination or appeal, is an exhibition of inconsistency, strongly savoring of timidity, if not of moral obliquity.

If, therefore, we should ever receive from some contemporaneous Faraday the same fling that that gentleman made years since, when, with more sincerity than good breeding, he said that "many *dogs* have the power of coming to much more logical conclusions than some spiritualists,"[107] we fear we must still persist. Abuse is not argument, least of all, proof. Because such men as Huxley and Tyndall denominate spiritualism "a degrading belief" and oriental magic "jugglery," they cannot thereby take from truth its verity. Skepticism, whether it proceeds from a scientific or an ignorant brain, is unable to overturn the immortality of our souls — if such immortality is a fact — and plunge them into *post-mortem* annihilation. "Reason is subject to error," says Aristotle; so is opinion; and the personal views of the most learned philosopher are often more liable to be proved erroneous, than the plain common sense of his own illiterate cook. In the *Tales of the Impious Khalif,* Barrachias-Hassan-Oglu, the Arabian sage holds a wise discourse: "Beware, O my son, of self-incense," he says. "It is the most dangerous, on account of its agreeable intoxication. Profit by thy own wisdom, but learn to respect the wisdom of thy fathers likewise. And remember, O my beloved, that the light of Allah's truth will often penetrate much easier an empty head, than one that is so crammed with learning that many a silver ray is crowded out for want of space; . . . such is the case with our over-wise Kadi."

These representatives of modern science in both hemispheres seem never to have exhibited more scorn, or to have felt more bitterly toward the unsolvable mystery, than since Mr. Crookes began the investigation of the phenomena, in London. This courageous gentleman was the first to introduce to the public one of those alleged "materialized" sentries that guard the forbidden gates. Following after him, several other learned members

---

107 W. Crookes, F.R.S., "*Researches in the Phenomena of Spiritualism.*"

of the scientific body had the rare integrity, combined with a degree of courage, which, in view of the unpopularity of the subject, may be deemed heroic, to take the phenomena in hand.

But, alas! although the spirit, indeed, was willing, the mortal flesh proved weak. Ridicule was more than the majority of them could bear; and so, the heaviest burden was thrown upon the shoulders of Mr. Crookes. An account of the benefit this gentleman reaped from his disinterested investigations, and the thanks he received from his own brother scientists, can be found in his three pamphlets, entitled, *Researches in the Phenomena of Spiritualism.*

After a while, the members appointed on the Committee of the Dialectical Society and Mr. Crookes, who had applied to his mediums the most crucial tests, were forced by an impatient public to report in so many plain words what they had seen. But what could they say, except the truth? Thus, they were compelled to acknowledge: 1st. That the phenomena which *they,* at least, had witnessed, were genuine, and impossible to simulate; thus showing that manifestations produced by some unknown force, could and did happen. 2d. That, whether the phenomena were produced by disembodied spirits or other analogous entities, they could not tell; but that manifestations, thoroughly upsetting many preconceived theories as to natural laws, did happen and were undeniable. Several of these occurred in their own families. 3d. That, notwithstanding all their combined efforts to the contrary, beyond the indisputable fact of the reality of the phenomena, "glimpses of natural action not yet reduced to law,"[108] they, to borrow the expression of the Count de Gabalis, "could make neither head nor tail on't."

Now this was precisely what a skeptical public had not bargained for. The discomfiture of the believers in spiritualism had been impatiently anticipated before the conclusions of Messrs. Crookes, Varley, and the Dialectical Society were announced. Such a confession on the part of their brother-scientists was too humiliating for the pride of even those who had timorously abstained from investigation. It was regarded as really too much, that such vulgar and repulsive manifestations of phenomena which had always, by common consent of educated people, been regarded as nursery tales, fit only to amuse hysterical servant-girls and afford revenue to professional somnambulists — that manifestations which had been consigned by the Academy and Institute of Paris to oblivion, should so impertinently elude detection at the hands of experts in physical sciences.

A tornado of indignation followed the confession. Mr. Crookes depicts it in his pamphlet on *Psychic Force.* He heads it very pointedly with the quotation from Galvani: "I am attacked by two very opposite sects — the scientists and the *know-nothings,* yet I know that I have discovered one of the greatest forces in nature. . . . " He then proceeds:

"It was taken for granted that the results of my experiments would be in accordance with their preconceptions. What they really desired was not *the truth,* but an additional witness in favor of their own foregone conclusions. When they found the facts which that investigation established could not be made to fit those opinions, why,. . . so much the worse for the facts. They try to creep out of their own confident recommendations of the inquiry, by declaring 'that Mr. Home is a clever conjurer who has duped us all.' 'Mr. Crookes might, with equal propriety, examine the performances of an Indian juggler.' 'Mr.

---

108 W. Crookes, *"Experiments on Psychic Force,"* page 25.

Crookes must get better witnesses before he can be believed.' 'The thing is too absurd to be treated seriously.' 'It is impossible, and therefore can't be.'. . . (I never said it was impossible, I only said it was true.) 'The observers have all been biologized, and fancy they saw things occur which really *never* took place,' etc., etc., etc."[109]

After expending their energy on such puerile theories as "unconscious cerebration," "involuntary muscular contraction," and the sublimely ridiculous one of the "cracking knee-joints" (*le muscle craqueur*); after meeting ignominious failures by the obstinate survival of the new force, and finally, after every desperate effort to compass its obliteration, these *filii diffidentiæ* — as St. Paul calls their class — thought best to give up the whole thing in disgust. Sacrificing their courageously persevering brethren as a holocaust on the altar of public opinion, they withdrew in dignified silence. Leaving the arena of investigation to more fearless champions, these unlucky experimenters are not likely to ever enter it again.[110] It is easier by far to deny the reality of such manifestations from a secure distance, than find for them a proper place among the classes of natural phenomena accepted by exact science. And how can they, since all such phenomena pertain to psychology, and the latter, with its occult and mysterious powers, is a *terra incognita* for modern science. Thus, powerless to explain that which proceeds directly from the nature of the human soul itself — the existence of which most of them deny — unwilling at the same time to confess their ignorance, scientists retaliate very unjustly on those who believe in the evidence of their senses without any pretence to science.

"A kick from thee, O Jupiter! is sweet," says the poet Tretiakowsky, in an old Russian tragedy. Rude as those Jupiters of science may be occasionally toward us credulous mortals, their vast learning — in less abstruse questions, we mean — if not their manners, entitles them to public respect. But unfortunately it is not the gods who shout the loudest.

The eloquent Tertullian, speaking of Satan and his imps, whom he accuses of ever mimicking the Creator's works, denominates them the "monkeys of God." It is fortunate for the philosophicules that we have no modern Tertullian to consign them to an immortality of contempt as the "monkeys of science."

But to return to genuine scientists. "Phenomena of a merely objective character," says A. N. Aksakof, "force themselves upon the representatives of exact sciences for investigation and explanation; but the high-priests of science, in the face of apparently such a simple question . . . are totally disconcerted! This subject seems to have the privilege of forcing them to betray, not only the highest code of morality — truth, but also the supreme law of science — *experiment!* . . . They feel that there is something too serious underlying it. The cases of Hare, Crookes, de Morgan, Varley, Wallace, and Butleroff create a panic! They fear that as soon as they concede one step, they will have to yield the whole ground. Time-honored principles, the contemplative speculations of a whole life, of a long line of generations, are all staked on a single card!"[111]

In the face of such experience as that of Crookes and the Dialectical Society, of Wallace and the late Professor Hare, what can we expect from our luminaries of erudition? Their

---

109 W. Crookes, *"Spiritualism Viewed by the Light of Modern Science."* See *"Quarterly Journal of Science."*
110 A. Aksakof, *"Phenomena of Mediumism."*
111 A. N. Aksakof, *"Phenomena of Mediumism."*

attitude toward the undeniable phenomena is in itself another phenomenon. It is simply incomprehensible, unless we admit the possibility of another psychological disease, as mysterious and contagious as hydrophobia. Although we claim no honor for this new discovery, we nevertheless propose to recognize it under the name of *scientific psychophobia*.

They ought to have learned by this time, in the school of bitter experience, that they can rely on the self-sufficiency of the positive sciences only to a certain point; and that, so long as there remains one single unexplained mystery in nature, the word "*impossible*" is a dangerous word for them to pronounce.

In the *Researches on the Phenomena of Spiritualism*, Mr. Crookes submits to the option of the reader eight theories "to account for the phenomena observed."

These theories run as follows: "*First Theory.* — The phenomena are all the result of tricks, clever mechanical arrangements, or legerdemain; the mediums are impostors, and the rest of the company fools. "*Second Theory.* — The persons at a seance are the victims of a sort of mania, or delusion, and imagine phenomena to occur which have no real objective existence. "*Third Theory.* — The whole is the result of conscious or unconscious cerebral action. "*Fourth Theory.* — The result of the spirit of the medium, perhaps in association with the spirits of some or all of the people present. "*Fifth Theory.* — The actions of evil spirits, or devils, personifying whom or what they please, in order to undermine Christianity, and ruin men's souls. (Theory of our theologians.) "*Sixth Theory.* — The actions of a separate order of beings living on this earth, but invisible and immaterial to us. Able, however, occasionally to manifest their presence, known in almost all countries and ages as demons (not necessarily bad), gnomes, fairies, kobolds, elves, goblins, Puck, etc. (One of the claims of the kabalists.) "*Seventh Theory.* — The actions of departed human beings. (The spiritual theory *par excellence*.) "*Eighth Theory.* — (The psychic force) . . . an adjunct to the fourth, fifth, sixth, and seventh theories."

The first of these theories having been proved valid only in exceptional, though unfortunately still too frequent cases, must be ruled out as having no material bearing upon the phenomena themselves. Theories the *second* and the *third* are the last crumbling entrenchments of the guerilla of skeptics and materialists, and remain, as lawyers say, "*Adhuc sub judice lis est.*" Thus, we can deal in this work but with the four remaining ones, the last, eighth, theory being according to Mr. Crookes's opinion, but "a necessary adjunct" of the others.

How subject even a scientific opinion is to error, we may see, if we only compare the several articles on spiritual phenomena from the able pen of that gentleman, which appeared from 1870 to 1875. In one of the first we read: . . . "the increased employment of scientific methods will promote exact observations and greater love of truths among inquirers, and will produce a race of observers *who will drive the worthless residuum of spiritualism hence into the unknown limbo of magic and necromancy.*" And in 1875, we read, over his own signature, minute and most interesting descriptions of the materialized spirit — Katie King![112]

---

112 "*The Last of Katie King,*" pamphlet iii., p. 119.

It is hardly possible to suppose that Mr. Crookes could be under electro-biological influence or hallucination for two or three consecutive years. The "spirit" appeared in his own house, in his library, under the most crucial tests, and was seen, felt, and heard by hundreds of persons.

But Mr. Crookes denies that he ever took Katie King for a disembodied spirit. What was it then? If it was not Miss Florence Cook, and his word is our sufficient guarantee for it — then it was either the spirit of one who had lived on earth, or one of those that come directly under the sixth theory of the eight the eminent scientist offers to the public choice. It must have been one of the classes named: Fairies, Kobolds, Gnomes, Elves, Goblins, or a Puck.[113]

Yes; Katie King must have been a fairy — a Titania. For to a fairy only could be applied with propriety the following poetic effusion which Mr. Crookes quotes in describing this wonderful spirit:

> "Round her she made an atmosphere of life;
>
> The very air seemed lighter from her eyes;
>
> They were so soft and beautiful and rife
>
> With all we can imagine of the skies;
>
> Her overpowering presence makes you feel
>
> It would *not be idolatry to kneel!*"[114]

And thus, after having written, in 1870, his severe sentence against spiritualism and magic; after saying that even at that moment he believed "the whole affair a superstition, or, at least, an unexplained trick — a delusion of the senses;"[115] Mr. Crookes, in 1875, closes his letter with the following memorable words: — "To imagine, I say, the Katie King of the last three years to be the result of imposture does more violence to one's reason and common sense than to believe her to be what she herself affirms."[116] This last remark, moreover, conclusively proves that : 1. Notwithstanding Mr. Crookes's full convictions that the somebody calling herself Katie King was neither the medium nor some confederate, but on the contrary an unknown force in nature, which — like love — "laughs at locksmiths"; 2. That that hitherto unrecognized form of Force, albeit it had become with him "not a matter of opinion, but of absolute knowledge," — the eminent investigator still did not abandon to the last his skeptical attitude toward the question. In short, he firmly believes in the phenomenon, but cannot accept the idea of its being the human spirit of a departed *somebody*.

LOST ARTS

It seems to us, that, as far as *public prejudice goes,* Mr. Crookes solves one mystery by creating a still deeper one: the *obscurum per obscurius.* In other words, rejecting "*the worthless residuum of spiritualism,*" the courageous scientist fearlessly plunges into his own "*unknown limbo of magic* and *necromancy!*"

---

113 Ibid., pam. i., p. 7.
114 *"The Last of Katie King,"* pamp. iii., p. 112.
115 Ibid., p. 112.
116 *"Researches in the Phenomena of Spiritualism,"* p. 45.

The recognized laws of physical science account for but a few of the more objective of the so-called spiritual phenomena. While proving the reality of certain visible effects of an unknown force, they have not thus far enabled scientists to control at will even this portion of the phenomena. The truth is that the professors have not yet discovered the necessary conditions of their occurrence. They must go as deeply into the study of the triple nature of man — physiological, psychological, and *divine* — as did their predecessors, the magicians, theurgists, and thaumaturgists of old. Until the present moment, even those who have investigated the phenomena as thoroughly and impartially as Mr. Crookes, have set aside the cause as something not to be discovered now, if ever. They have troubled themselves no more about that than about the first cause of the cosmic phenomena of the correlation of forces, whose endless effects they are at such pains to observe and classify. Their course has been as unwise as that of a man who should attempt to discover the sources of a river by exploring toward its mouth. It has so narrowed their views of the possibilities of natural law that very simple forms of occult phenomena have necessitated their denial that they can occur unless miracles were possible; and this being a scientific absurdity the result has been that physical science has latterly been losing prestige. If scientists had studied the so-called "miracles" instead of denying them, many secret laws of nature comprehended by the ancients would have been again discovered. "Conviction," says Bacon, "comes not through arguments but through experiments."

The ancients were always distinguished — especially the Chaldean astrologers and Magians — for their ardent love and pursuit of knowledge in every branch of science. They tried to penetrate the secrets of nature in the same way as our modern naturalists, and by the only method by which this object can be obtained, namely: by experimental researches and reason. If our modern philosophers cannot apprehend the fact that they penetrated deeper than themselves into the mysteries of the universe, this does not constitute a valid reason why the credit of possessing this knowledge should be denied them or the imputation of superstition laid at their door. Nothing warrants the charge; and every new archæological discovery militates against the assumption. As chemists they were unequalled, and in his famous lecture on *The Lost Arts*, Wendell Phillips says: "The chemistry of the most ancient period had reached a point which *we have never even approached.*" The secret of the malleable glass, which, "if supported by one end by its own weight, in twenty hours dwindles down to a fine line that you can curve around your wrist," would be as difficult to rediscover in our civilized countries as to fly to the moon.

The fabrication of a cup of glass which was brought by an exile to Rome in the reign of Tiberius, — a cup "which he dashed upon the marble pavement, and it was not crushed nor broken by the fall," and which, as it got "dented some" was easily brought into shape again with a hammer, is a historic fact. If it is doubted now it is merely because the moderns cannot do the same. And yet, in Samarkand and some monasteries of Thibet such cups and glass-ware may be found to this day; nay, there are persons who claim that they can make the same by virtue of their knowledge of the much-ridiculed and ever-doubted *alkahest* — the universal solvent. This agent that Paracelsus and Van Helmont maintain to be a certain fluid in nature, "capable of reducing all sublunary bodies, as well homogeneous as mixed, into their *ens primum*, or the original matter of which they are composed; or into an uniform, equable, and potable liquor, that will unite with water, and the juices of all bodies, and yet retain its own radical virtues; and, if again mixed with itself will thereby be converted into pure elementary water": what impossibilities prevent our crediting the statement? Why should it not exist and why the idea be considered Utopian? Is it again because our modern chemists are unable to produce it? But surely it may be conceived without any great effort of imagination that all bodies must have originally come from some first matter, and that this matter, according to the lessons of astronomy, geology and physics, must have been a fluid. Why should not gold — of whose genesis our scientists know so little — have been originally a primitive or *basic matter of gold*, a ponderous fluid which, as says Van Helmont, "from its own nature, or a strong cohesion between its particles, acquired afterward a solid form?"

There seems to be very little absurdity to believe in a "universal *ens* that resolves all bodies into their *ens genitale*." Van Helmont calls it "the highest and most successful of all salts; which having obtained the supreme degree of simplicity, purity, subtilty, enjoys alone the faculty of remaining unchanged and unimpaired by the subjects it works upon, and of dissolving the most stubborn and untractable bodies; as stones, gems, glass, earth, sulphur, metals, etc., into red salt, equal in weight to the matter dissolved; and this with as much ease as hot water melts down snow."

It is into this fluid that the makers of malleable glass claimed, and now claim, that they immersed common glass for several hours, to acquire the property of malleability.

We have a ready and palpable proof of such possibilities. A foreign correspondent of the Theosophical Society, a well-known medical practitioner, and one who has studied the occult sciences for upward of thirty years, has succeeded in obtaining what he terms the "true oil of gold," *i.e.*, the primal element. Chemists and physicists have seen and examined it, and were driven to confess that they neither knew *how* it was obtained nor could they do the same. That he desires his name to remain unknown is not to be wondered at; ridicule and public prejudice are more dangerous sometimes than the inquisition of old. This "Adamic earth" is next-door neighbor to the alkahest, and one of the most important secrets of the alchemists. No Kabalist will reveal it to the world, for, as he expresses it in the well-known jargon: "it would explain *the eagles* of the alchemists, and how the eagles' wings are clipped," a secret that it took Thomas Vaughan (Eugenius Philalethes) twenty years to learn.

As the dawn of physical science broke into a glaring day-light, the spiritual sciences merged deeper and deeper into night, and in their turn they were denied. So, now, these greatest masters in psychology are looked upon as "ignorant and superstitious ancestors"; as mountebanks and jugglers, because, forsooth, the sun of modern learning shines to-day so bright, it has become an axiom that the philosophers and men of science of the olden time knew nothing, and lived in a night of superstition. But their traducers forget that the sun of to-day will seem dark by comparison with the luminary of to-morrow, whether justly or not; and as the men of our century think their ancestors ignorant, so will perhaps their descendants count them for *know-nothings*. The world moves in cycles. The coming races will be but the reproductions of races long bygone; as we, perhaps, are the images of those who lived a hundred centuries ago. The time will come when those who now in public slander the hermetists, but ponder in secret their dust-covered volumes; who plagiarize their ideas, assimilate and give them out as their own — will receive their dues. "Who," honestly exclaims Pfaff — "what man has ever taken more comprehensive views of nature than Paracelsus? He was the bold creator of chemical medicines; the founder of courageous parties; victorious in controversy, belonging to those spirits who have created amongst us a new mode of thinking on the natural existence of things. What he scattered through his writings on the philosopher's stone, on pigmies and spirits of the mines; on signs, on homunculi, and the elixir of life, and which are employed by many to lower his estimation, cannot extinguish our grateful remembrance of his general works, nor our admiration of his free, bold exertions, and his noble, intellectual life."[117]

More than one pathologist, chemist, homoeopathist, and magnetist has quenched his thirst for knowledge in the books of Paracelsus. Frederick Hufeland got his theoretical doctrines on infection from this mediæval "quack," as Sprengel delights in calling one who was immeasurably higher than himself. Hemman, who endeavors to vindicate this great philosopher, and nobly tries to redress his slandered memory, speaks of him as the "*greatest* chemist of his time."[118] So do Professor Molitor,[119] and Dr. Ennemoser, the eminent German psychologist.[120] According to their criticisms on the labors of this Hermetist, Paracelsus is the most "wondrous intellect of his age," a "noble genius." But our modern lights assume to know better, and the ideas of the Rosicrucians about the elementary spirits, the goblins and the elves, have sunk into the "limbo of magic" and fairy tales for early childhoods.[121]

We are quite ready to concede to skeptics that one-half, and even more, of seeming phenomena, are but more or less clever fraud. Recent exposures, especially of "materializing" mediums, but too well prove the fact. Unquestionably numerous others are still in store, and this will continue until tests have become so perfect and spiritualists so reasonable as no longer to furnish opportunity to mediums or weapons to adversaries.

What should sensible spiritualists think of the character of *angel* guides, who after monopolizing, perhaps for years, a poor medium's time, health and means, suddenly abandon him when he most needs their help? None but creatures *without soul or conscience* would be guilty of such injustice. Conditions? — Mere sophistry. What sort of spirits must they be who would not summon if necessary an army of spirit-friends (if such there be) to snatch the innocent medium from the pit dug for his feet? Such things happened in the olden time, such may happen now. *There were apparitions before modern spiritualism, and phenomena like ours in every previous age.* If modern manifestations are a reality and palpable facts, so must have been the so-called "miracles" and thaumaturgic exploits of old; or if the latter are but fictions of superstition so must be the former, for they rest on no better testimony.

---

117 Pfaff's "*Astrology*," Berl.

118 "*Medico-Surgical Essays*."

119 "*The Philosophy of Hist.*"

120 *On Theoph. Paracelsus — Magic.*

121 Kemshead says in his "*Inorganic Chemistry*" that "the element *hydrogen* was first mentioned in the sixteenth century by Paracelsus, but very little was known of it in any way." (P. 66.) And why not be fair and confess at once that Paracelsus was the *re*-discoverer of hydrogen as he was the *re*-discoverer of the hidden properties of the magnet and animal magnetism? It is easy to show that according to the strict vows of secrecy taken and faithfully observed by every Rosicrucian (and especially by the alchemist) he kept his knowledge secret. Perhaps it would not prove a very difficult task for any chemist well versed in the works of Paracelsus to demonstrate that *oxygen*, the discovery of which is credited to Priestley, was known to the Rosicrucian alchemists as well as hydrogen.

But, in this daily-increasing torrent of occult phenomena that rushes from one end of the globe to the other, though two-thirds of the manifestations are proved spurious, what of those which are proved genuine beyond doubt or cavil? Among these may be found communications coming through non-professional as well as professional mediums, which are sublime and divinely grand. Often, through young children, and simple-minded ignorant persons, we receive philosophical teachings and precepts, poetry and inspirational orations, music and paintings that are fully worthy of the reputations of their alleged authors. Their prophecies are often verified and their moral disquisitions beneficent, though the latter is of rarer occurrence. Who are those spirits, what those powers or intelligences which are evidently *outside* of the medium proper and entities *per se?* These *intelligences* deserve the appellation; and they differ as widely from the generality of spooks and goblins that hover around the cabinets for physical manifestations, as day from night.

We must confess that the situation appears to be very grave. The control of mediums by such unprincipled and lying "spirits" is constantly becoming more and more general; and the pernicious effects of *seeming* diabolism constantly multiply. Some of the best mediums are abandoning the public rostrum and retiring from this influence; and the movement is drifting churchward. We venture the prediction that unless spiritualists set about the study of ancient philosophy, so as to learn to discriminate between spirits and to guard themselves against the baser sort, twenty-five years more will not elapse before they will have to fly to the Romish communion to escape these "guides" and "controls" that they have fondled so long. The signs of this catastrophe already exhibit themselves. At a recent convention at Philadelphia, it was seriously proposed to organize a sect of *Christian* Spiritualists! This is because, having withdrawn from the church and learned nothing of the philosophy of the phenomena, or the nature of their spirits, they are drifting about on a sea of uncertainty like a ship without compass or rudder. They cannot escape the dilemma; they must choose between Porphyry and Pio Nono.

While men of genuine science, such as Wallace, Crookes, Wagner, Butlerof, Varley, Buchanan, Hare, Reichenbach, Thury, Perty, de Morgan, Hoffmann, Goldschmidt, W. Gregory, Flammarion, Sergeant Cox and many others, firmly believe in the current phenomena, many of the above named reject the theory of departed spirits. Therefore, it seems but logical to think that if the London "Katie King," the only materialized *something* which the public is obliged more or less to credit out of respect to science, — is not the spirit of an ex-mortal, then it must be the astral solidified shadow of either one of the Rosicrucian spooks — "fantasies of superstition" — or of some as yet unexplained force in nature. Be it however a "spirit of health or goblin damn'd" it is of little consequence; for if it be once proved that its organism is not solid matter, then it must be and is a "spirit," an apparition, a *breath.* It is an intelligence which acts outside our organisms and therefore must belong to some existing even though unseen race of beings. But what is it? What is this something which thinks and even speaks but yet is not human; that is impalpable and yet not a disembodied spirit; that simulates affection, passion, remorse, fear, joy, but yet feels neither? What is this canting creature which rejoices in cheating the truthful inquirer and mocking at sacred human feeling? For, if not Mr. Crookes's Katie King, other similar creatures have done all these. Who can fathom the mystery? The true psychologist alone. And where should he go for his text-books but to the neglected alcoves of libraries where the works of despised hermetists and theurgists have been gathering dust these many years.

Says Henry More, the revered English Platonist, in his answer to an attack on the believers of spiritual and magic phenomena by a skeptic of that age, named Webster:[122] "As for that other opinion, that the greater part of the reformed divines hold, that it was the Devil that appeared in Samuel's shape, it is beneath contempt; for though I do not doubt but that in many of these necromantic apparitions, they are *ludicrous spirits, not the souls of the deceased that appear*, yet I am clear for the appearing of the soul of Samuel, and as clear that in other necromancies, it may be such kinds of spirits, as Porphyrius above describes, 'that change themselves into omnifarious forms and shapes, and one while act the parts of dæmons, another while of angels or gods, and another while *of the souls of the departed*.' And I confess such a spirit as this might *personate* Samuel here, for anything Webster alleged to the contrary, for his arguments indeed are wonderfully weak and wooden."

When such a metaphysician and philosopher as Henry More gives such testimony as this, we may well assume our point to have been well taken. Learned investigators, all very skeptical as to spirits in general and "departed human spirits" in particular, during the last twenty years have taxed their brains to invent new names for an old thing. Thus, with Mr. Crookes and Sergeant Cox, it is the "psychic force." Professor Thury of Geneva calls it the "psychode" or *ectenic* force; Professor Balfour Stewart, the "electro-biological power"; Faraday, the "great master of experimental philosophy in physics," but apparently a novice in psychology, superciliously termed it an "unconscious muscular action," an "unconscious cerebration," and what not? Sir William Hamilton, a "latent thought"; Dr. Carpenter, "the ideo-motor principle," etc., etc. So many scientists — so many names.

Years ago the old German philosopher, Schopenhauer, disposed of this force and matter at the same time; and since the conversion of Mr. Wallace, the great anthropologist has evidently adopted his ideas. Schopenhauer's doctrine is that the universe is but the manifestation of the will. Every force in nature is also an effect of will, representing a higher or lower degree of its objectiveness. It is the teaching of Plato, who stated distinctly that everything visible was created or evolved out of the invisible and eternal WILL, and after its fashion. Our Heaven — he says — was produced according to the eternal pattern of the "Ideal World," contained, as everything else, in the dodecahedron, the geometrical model used by the Deity.[123] With Plato, the Primal Being is an emanation of the Demiurgic Mind (*Nous*), which contains from the eternity the "*idea*" of the "to be created world" within itself, and which idea he produces out of himself.[124] The laws of nature are the established relations of this *idea* to the forms of its manifestations; "these forms," says Schopenhauer, "are time, space, and causality. Through time and space the idea varies in its numberless manifestations." These ideas are far from being new, and even with Plato they were not original. This is what we read in the *Chaldean Oracles*:[125] "The works of nature co-exist with

---

122 "Letter to J. Glanvil, chaplain to the king and a fellow of the Royal Society." Glanvil was the author of the celebrated work on Apparitions and Demonology entitled "*Sadducismus Triumphatus, or a full and plain evidence concerning witches and apparitions*," in two parts, "proving partly by Scripture, and partly by a choice collection of modern relations, the real existence of apparitions, spirits and witches." — 1700.
123 Plato, "*Timæus Soerius*," 97.
124 See Movers' "*Explanations*," 268.
125 Cory, "*Chaldean Oracles*," 243.

the intellectual [νοἑρῷ], spiritual Light of the Father. For it is the soul [ψυχη] which adorned the great heaven, and which adorns it after the Father." "The incorporeal world then was already completed, having its seat in the Divine Reason," says Philo[126] who is erroneously accused of deriving his philosophy from Plato's. In the *Theogony* of Mochus, we find Æther first, and then the air; the two principles from which Ulom, the *intelligible* [νοῆτος] God (the visible universe of matter) is born.[127] In the Orphic hymns, the Eros-Phanes evolves from the Spiritual Egg, which the Æthereal winds impregnate, Wind[128] being "the spirit of God," who is said to move in Æther, "brooding over the Chaos" — the Divine "Idea." In the Hindu *Katakopanisad,* Purusha, the Divine Spirit, already stands before the original matter, from whose union springs the great Soul of the World, "Maha = Atma, Brahm, the Spirit of Life";[129] these latter appellations are identical with the Universal Soul, or *Anima Mundi,* and the Astral Light of the theurgists and kabalists. Pythagoras brought his doctrines from the eastern sanctuaries, and Plato compiled them into a form more intelligible than the mysterious numerals of the sage — whose doctrines he had fully embraced — to the uninitiated mind. Thus, the *Cosmos* is "the Son" with Plato, having for his father and mother the Divine Thought and Matter.[130] "The Egyptians," says Dunlap,[131] "distinguish between an older and younger Horus, the former the *brother* of Osiris, the latter the *son* of Osiris and Isis." The first is the *Idea* of the world remaining in the Demiurgic Mind, "born in darkness before the creation of the world." The second Horus is this "Idea" going forth from the *Logos,* becoming clothed with matter, and assuming an actual existence.[132] "The mundane God, eternal, boundless, young and old, of winding form,"[133] say the *Chaldean Oracles.*

This "winding form" is a figure to express the vibratory motion of the Astral Light, with which the ancient priests were perfectly well acquainted, though they may have differed in views of ether, with modern scientists; for in the Æther they placed the Eternal Idea pervading the Universe, or the *Will* which becomes *Force,* and creates or organizes *matter.*

THE HUMAN WILL THE MASTER-FORCE OF FORCES

"The will," says Van Helmont, "is the first of all powers. For through the will of the Creator all things were made and put in motion. . . . The will is the property of all spiritual beings, and displays itself in them the more actively the more they are freed from matter." And Paracelsus, "the divine," as he was called, adds in the same strain: "*Faith* must confirm the imagination, for faith establishes the *will.* . . . Determined will is a beginning of all magical operations. . . . Because men do not perfectly imagine and believe the result, is that the arts are uncertain, while they might be perfectly certain."

---

126 Philo Judæus, *"On the Creation,"* x.

127 Movers, *"Phoinizer,"* 282.

128 K. O. Müller, 236.

129 Weber, *"Akad. Vorles,"* 213, 214, etc.

130 Plutarch, *"Isis and Osiris,"* i., vi.

131 *"Spirit History of Man,"* p. 88.

132 Movers, *"Phoinizer,"* 268.

133 Cory, *"Fragments,"* 240.

The opposing power alone of unbelief and skepticism, if projected in a current of equal force, can check the other, and sometimes completely neutralize it. Why should spiritualists wonder that the presence of some strong skeptics, or of those who, feeling bitterly opposed to the phenomenon, unconsciously exercise their will-power in opposition, hinders and often stops altogether the manifestations? If there is no *conscious* power on earth but sometimes finds another to interfere with or even counterbalance it, why wonder when the *unconscious*, passive power of a medium is suddenly paralyzed in its effects by another opposing one, though it also be as unconsciously exercised? Professors Faraday and Tyndall boasted that their presence at a circle would stop at once every manifestation. This fact alone ought to have proved to the eminent scientists that there was some force in these phenomena worthy to arrest their attention. As a scientist, Prof. Tyndall was perhaps pre-eminent in the circle of those who were present at the seance; as a shrewd observer, one not easily deceived by a tricking medium, he was perhaps no better, if as clever, as others in the room, and if the manifestations were but a fraud so ingenious as to deceive the others, they would not have stopped, even on *his* account. What medium can ever boast of such phenomena as were produced by Jesus, and the apostle Paul after him? Yet even Jesus met with cases where the unconscious force of resistance overpowered even his so well directed current of will. "And he did not many mighty works there, because of their unbelief."

There is a reflection of every one of these views in Schopenhauer's philosophy. Our "investigating" scientists might consult his works with profit. They will find therein many a strange hypothesis founded on old ideas, speculations on the "new" phenomena, which may prove as reasonable as any, and be saved the useless trouble of inventing new theories. The psychic and ectenic forces, the "ideo-motor" and "electro-biological powers"; "latent thought" and even "unconscious cerebration" theories, can be condensed in two words: the kabalistic Astral Light.

The bold theories and opinions expressed in Schopenhauer's works differ widely with those of the majority of our orthodox scientists. "In reality," remarks this daring speculator, "there is neither *matter* nor *spirit*. The tendency to gravitation in a stone is as unexplainable as thought in human brain. . . . If matter can — no one knows why — fall to the ground, then it can also — no one knows why — think. . . . As soon, even in mechanics, as we trespass beyond the purely mathematical, as soon as we reach the inscrutable, adhesion, gravitation, and so on, we are faced by phenomena which are to our senses as mysterious as the Will and Thought in man — we find ourselves facing the incomprehensible, for such is every force in nature. Where is then that *matter* which you all pretend to know so well; and from which — being so familiar with it — you draw all your conclusions and explanations, and attribute to it all things? That, which can be fully realized by our reason and senses, is but the superficial: they can never reach the true inner substance of things. Such was the opinion of Kant. If you consider that there is in a human head some sort of a *spirit*, then you are obliged to concede the same to a stone. If your dead and utterly passive matter can manifest a tendency toward gravitation, or, like electricity, attract and repel, and send out sparks — then, as well as the brain, it can also think. In short, every particle of the so-called spirit, we can replace with an equivalent of matter, and every particle of matter replace with spirit. . . . Thus, it is not the Cartesian division of all things into matter and spirit that can ever be found philosophically exact; but only if we divide them into *will* and *manifestation*, which form of division has naught to do with the former, for it spiritualizes everything: all that, which is in the first instance real and objective — body and matter — it transforms into a representation, and every manifestation into will."[134]

These views corroborate what we have expressed about the various names given to the same thing. The disputants are battling about mere words. Call the phenomena force, energy, electricity or magnetism, will, or spirit-power, it will ever be the partial manifestation of the *soul*, whether disembodied or imprisoned for a while in its body — of a portion of that intelligent, omnipotent, and individual WILL, pervading all nature, and known, through the insufficiency of human language to express correctly psychological images, as — **GOD**.

The ideas of some of our schoolmen about matter are, from the kabalistic standing-point, in many a way erroneous. Hartmann calls their views "an *instinctual* prejudice." Furthermore, he demonstrates that no experimenter can have anything to do with matter properly termed, but only with the forces into which he divides it. The visible effects of matter are but the effects of force. He concludes thereby, that that which is now called matter is nothing but the aggregation of atomic forces, to express which the word *matter* is used: outside of that, for science matter is but a word void of sense. Notwithstanding many an honest confession on the part of our specialists — physicists, physiologists and chemists — that they know nothing whatever of matter,[135] *they deify it.* Every new phenomenon which they find themselves unable to explain, is triturated, compounded into incense, and burned on the altar of the goddess who patronizes modern scientists.

No one can better treat his subject than does Schopenhauer in his Parerga. In this work he discusses at length animal magnetism, clairvoyance, sympathetic cures, seership, magic, omens, ghost-seeing, and other spiritual matters. "All these manifestations," he says, "are branches of one and the same tree, and furnish us with irrefutable proofs of the existence of a chain of beings which is based on quite a different order of things than that nature which has at its foundation laws of space, time and adaptability. This other order of things is far deeper, for it is the original and the direct one; in its presence the common laws of nature, which are simply formal, are unavailing; therefore, under its immediate action neither time nor space can separate any longer the individuals, and the separation impendent on these forms presents no more insurmountable barriers for the intercourse of thoughts and the immediate action of the will. In this manner changes may be wrought by quite a different course than the course of physical causality, *i.e.*, through an action of the manifestation of the will exhibited in a peculiar way and outside the individual himself. Therefore the peculiar character of all the aforesaid manifestations is the *visio in distante et actio in distante* (vision and action at a distance) in its relation to time as well as in its relation to space. Such an action at a distance is just what constitutes the fundamental character of what is called *magical;* for such is the immediate action of our will, an action liberated from the causal conditions of physical action, viz., contact."

"Besides that," continues Schopenhauer, "these manifestations present to us a substantial and perfectly logical contradiction to materialism, and even to naturalism, because in the light of such manifestations, that order of things in nature which both these philosophies

---

134 "*Parerga,*" ii., pp. 111, 112.
135 See Huxley, "*Physical Basis of Life.*"

seek to present as absolute and the only genuine, appears before us on the contrary purely phenomenal and superficial, and containing at the bottom of it a substance of things *à parte* and perfectly independent of its own laws. That is why these manifestations — at least from a purely philosophical point of view — among all the facts which are presented to us in the domain of experiment, are beyond any comparison the most important. Therefore, it is the duty of every scientist to acquaint himself with them."[136]

SUPERFICIAL GENERALIZATIONS OF THE FRENCH SAVANTS

To pass from the philosophical speculations of a man like Schopenhauer to the superficial generalizations of some of the French Academicians, would be profitless but for the fact that it enables us to estimate the intellectual grasp of the two schools of learning. What the German makes of profound psychological questions, we have seen. Compare with it the best that the astronomer Babinet and the chemist Boussingault can offer by way of explaining an important spiritualistic phenomenon. In 1854-5 these distinguished specialists presented to the Academy a *memoire*, or monograph, whose evident object was to corroborate and at the same time make clearer Dr. Chevreuil's too complicated theory in explanation of the turning-tables, of the commission for the investigation of which he was a member. Here it is *verbatim:* "As to the movements and oscillations *alleged* to happen with certain tables, they can have no cause other than the *invisible* and involuntary vibrations of the experimenter's muscular system; the extended contraction of the muscles manifesting itself at such time by a series of vibrations, and becoming thus a *visible tremor* which communicates to the object a circumrotary motion. This rotation is thus enabled to manifest itself with a considerable energy, by a gradually quickening motion, or by a strong resistance, whenever it is required to stop. Hence the physical explanation of the phenomenon becomes clear and does not offer the slightest difficulty."[137]

None whatever. This scientific hypothesis — or demonstration shall we say? — is as clear as one of M. Babinet's nebulæ examined on a foggy night.

And still, clear as it may be, it lacks an important feature, *i.e.*, common sense. We are at a loss to decide whether or not Babinet accepts *en desespoir de cause* Hartmann's proposition that "the visible *effects of matter* are nothing but the *effects of a force*," and, that in order to form a clear conception of matter, one must first form one of force. The philosophy to the school of which belongs Hartmann, and which is partly accepted by several of the greatest German scientists, teaches that the problem of matter can only be solved by that invisible Force, acquaintance with which Schopenhauer terms the "magical knowledge," and "magical effect or action of Will." Thus, we must first ascertain whether the "involuntary vibrations of the experimenter's muscular system," which are but "actions of matter," are influenced by a will *within* the experimenter or *without.* In the former case Babinet makes of him an unconscious epileptic; the latter, as we will further see, he rejects altogether, and attributes all intelligent answers of the tipping or rapping tables to "unconscious ventriloquism."

---

136 Schopenhauer, "*Parerga.*" Art. on "*Will in Nature.*"
137 "*Revue des Deux Mondes,*" Jan. 15, 1855, p. 108.

We know that every exertion of will results in *force,* and that, according to the above-named German school, the manifestations of atomic forces are individual actions of will, resulting in the unconscious rushing of atoms into the concrete image already subjectively created by the will. Democritus taught, after his instructor Leucippus, that the first principles of all things contained in the universe were atoms and a *vacuum.* In its kabalistic sense, the *vacuum* means in this instance the *latent* Deity, or latent force, which at its first manifestation became WILL, and thus communicated the first impulse to these atoms — whose agglomeration, is matter. This vacuum was but another name for chaos, and an unsatisfactory one, for, according to the Peripatetics "nature abhors a vacuum."

That before Democritus the ancients were familiar with the idea of the indestructibility of matter is proved by their allegories and numerous other facts. Movers gives a definition of the Phœnician idea of the ideal sun-light as a spiritual influence issuing from the highest God, IAO, "the light conceivable only by intellect — the physical and spiritual Principle of all things; out of which the soul emanates." It was the male Essence, or Wisdom, while the primitive matter or *Chaos* was the female. Thus the two first principles — co-eternal and infinite, were already with the primitive Phœnicians, spirit and matter. Therefore the theory is as old as the world; for Democritus was not the first philosopher who taught it; and intuition existed in man before the ultimate development of his reason. But it is in the denial of the boundless and endless Entity, possessor of that invisible Will which we for lack of a better term call GOD, that lies the powerlessness of every materialistic science to explain the occult phenomena. It is in the rejection *a priori* of everything which might force them to cross the boundary of exact science and step into the domain of psychological, or, if we prefer, metaphysical physiology, that we find the secret cause of their discomfiture by the manifestations, and their absurd theories to account for them. The ancient philosophy affirmed that it is in consequence of the manifestation of that Will — termed by Plato *the Divine Idea* — that everything visible and invisible sprung into existence. As that Intelligent Idea, which, by directing its sole will-power toward a centre of localized forces called objective forms into being, so can man, the microcosm of the great Macrocosm, do the same in proportion with the development of his will-power. The imaginary atoms — a figure of speech employed by Democritus, and gratefully seized upon by the materialists — are like automatic workmen moved inwardly by the influx of that Universal Will directed upon them, and which, manifesting itself as force, sets them into activity. The plan of the structure to be erected is in the brain of the Architect, and reflects his will; abstract as yet, from the instant of the conception it becomes concrete through these atoms which follow faithfully every line, point and figure traced in the imagination of the Divine Geometer.

As God creates, so man can create. Given a certain intensity of will, and the shapes created by the mind become subjective. Hallucinations, they are called, although to their creator they are real as any visible object is to any one else. Given a more intense and intelligent concentration of this will, and the form becomes concrete, visible, objective; the man has learned the secret of secrets; he is a MAGICIAN.

The materialist should not object to this logic, for he regards thought as matter. Conceding it to be so, the cunning mechanism contrived by the inventor; the fairy scenes born in the poet's brain; the gorgeous painting limned by the artist's fancy; the peerless statue chiselled in ether by the sculptor; the palaces and castles built in air by the architect — all these, though invisible and subjective, must exist, for they are matter, shaped and moulded. Who shall say, then, that there are not some men of such imperial will as to be able to drag these air-drawn fancies into view, enveloped in the hard casing of gross substance to make them tangible?

If the French scientists reaped no laurels in the new field of investigation, what more was done in England, until the day when Mr. Crookes offered himself in atonement for the sins of the learned body? Why, Mr. Faraday, some twenty years ago, actually condescended to be spoken to once or twice upon the subject. Faraday, whose name is pronounced by the anti-spiritualists in every discussion upon the phenomena, as a sort of scientific charm against the evil-eye of Spiritualism, Faraday, who "blushed" for having published his researches upon such a degrading belief, is now proved on good authority to have never sat at a tipping table himself at all! We have but to open a few stray numbers of the *Journal des Debats*, published while a noted Scotch medium was in England, to recall the past events in all their primitive freshness. In one of these numbers, Dr. Foucault, of Paris, comes out as a champion for the eminent English experimenter. "Pray, do not imagine," says he, "that the grand physicist had ever himself condescended so far as to sit prosaically at a jumping table." Whence, then, came the "blushes" which suffused the cheeks of the "Father of Experimental Philosophy"? Remembering this fact, we will now examine the nature of Faraday's beautiful "Indicator," the extraordinary "Medium-Catcher," invented by him for the detection of mediumistic fraud. That complicated machine, the memory of which haunts like a nightmare the dreams of dishonest mediums, is carefully described in Comte de Mirville's *Question des Esprits.*

The better to prove to the experimenters the reality of their own impulsion, Professor Faraday placed several card-board disks, united to each other and stuck to the table by a half-soft glue, which, making the whole adhere for a time together, would, nevertheless, yield to a continuous pressure. Now, the table having turned — yes, actually *having dared to turn before Mr. Faraday*, which fact is of some value, at least — the disks were examined; and, as they were found to have gradually displaced themselves by slipping in the same direction as the table, it thus became an unquestionable proof that the experimenters had *pushed* the tables themselves.

Another of the so-called scientific tests, so useful in a phenomenon alleged to be either spiritual or psychical, consisted of a small instrument which immediately warned the witnesses of the slightest personal impulsion on their part, or rather, according to Mr. Faraday's own expression, "it warned them when they changed from the passive to the active state." This needle which betrayed the active motion proved but one thing, viz.: the action of a force which either emanated from the sitters or controlled them. And who has ever said that there is no such force? Every one admits so much, whether this force passes through the operator, as it is generally shown, or acts independently of him, as is so often the case. "The whole mystery consisted in the disproportion of the force employed by the operators, who pushed because they were forced to push, with certain effects of rotation, or rather, of a really marvellous race. In the presence of such prodigious effects, how could any one imagine that the Lilliputian experiments of that kind could have any value in this newly discovered Land of Giants?"[138]

---

138 Comte de Mirville, "*Question des Esprits.*"

Professor Agassiz, who occupied in America nearly the same eminent position as a scientist which Mr. Faraday did in England, acted with a still greater unfairness. Professor J. R. Buchanan, the distinguished anthropologist, who has treated Spiritualism in some respects more scientifically than any one else in America, speaks of Agassiz, in a recent article, with a very just indignation. For, of all other men, Professor Agassiz ought to believe in a phenomenon to which he had been a subject himself. But now that both Faraday and Agassiz are themselves *disembodied,* we can do better by questioning the living than the dead.

Thus a force whose secret powers were thoroughly familiar to the ancient theurgists, is denied by modern skeptics. The antediluvian children — who perhaps played with it, using it as the boys in Bulwer-Lytton's *Coming Race,* use the tremendous *"vril"* — called it the "Water of Phtha"; their descendants named it the *Anima Mundi,* the soul of the universe; and still later the mediæval hermetists termed it "sidereal light," or the "Milk of the Celestial Virgin," the "Magnes," and many other names. But our modern learned men will neither accept nor recognize it under such appellations; for it pertains to *magic,* and magic is, in their conception, a disgraceful superstition.

Apollonius and Iamblichus held that it was not "in the knowledge of things *without,* but in the perfection of the soul *within,* that lies the empire of man, aspiring to be more than men."[139] Thus they had arrived at a perfect cognizance of their godlike souls, the powers of which they used with all the wisdom, outgrowth of esoteric study of the hermetic lore, inherited by them from their forefathers. But our philosophers, tightly shutting themselves up in their shells of flesh, cannot or dare not carry their timid gaze beyond the *comprehensible.* For them there is no future life; there are no godlike dreams, they scorn them as unscientific; for them the men of old are but "ignorant ancestors," as they express it; and whenever they meet during their physiological researches with an author who believes that this mysterious yearning after spiritual knowledge is inherent in every human being, and cannot have been given us utterly in vain, they regard him with contemptuous pity.

Says a Persian proverb: "The darker the sky is, the brighter the stars will shine." Thus, on the dark firmament of the mediæval ages began appearing the mysterious Brothers of the Rosie Cross. They formed no associations, they built no colleges; for, hunted up and down like so many wild beasts, when caught by the Christian Church, they were unceremoniously roasted. "As religion forbids it," says Bayle, "to spill blood," therefore, "to elude the maxim, *Ecclesia non novit sanguinem,* they burned human beings, as burning a man does not *shed his blood!*"

Many of these mystics, by following what they were taught by some treatises, secretly preserved from one generation to another, achieved discoveries which would not be despised even in our modern days of exact sciences. Roger Bacon, the friar, was laughed at as a quack, and is now generally numbered among "pretenders" to magic art; but his discoveries were nevertheless accepted, and are now used by those who ridicule him the most. Roger Bacon belonged by right if not by fact to that Brotherhood which includes all those who study the occult sciences. Living in the thirteenth century, almost a contemporary, therefore, of Albertus Magnus and Thomas Aquinas, his discoveries — such

---

139 Bulwer-Lytton, "*Zanoni.*"

as gunpowder and optical glasses, and his mechanical achievements — were considered by every one as so many miracles. He was accused of having made a compact with the Evil One.

In the legendary history of Friar Bacon, as "well as in an old play written by Robert Green, a dramatist in the days of Queen Elizabeth, it is recounted, that, having been summoned before the king, the friar was induced to show" some of his skill before her majesty the queen. So he waved his hand (*his wand*, says the text), and "presently was heard such excellent music, that they all said they had never heard the like." Then there was heard a still louder music and four apparitions suddenly presented themselves and danced until they vanished and disappeared in the air. Then he waved his wand again, and suddenly there was such a smell "as if all the rich perfumes in the whole world had been there prepared in the best manner that art could set them out." Then Roger Bacon having promised a gentleman to show him his sweetheart, he pulled a hanging in the king's apartment aside and every one in the room saw "a kitchen-maid with a basting-ladle in her hand." The proud gentleman, although he recognized the maiden who disappeared as suddenly as she had appeared, was enraged at the humiliating spectacle, and threatened the friar with his revenge. What does the magician do? He simply answers: "Threaten not, lest I do you more shame; and do you take heed how you give *scholars* the lie again!"

As a commentary on this, the modern historian[140] remarks: "This may be taken as a sort of exemplification of the class of exhibitions which were probably the result of a *superior knowledge* of natural sciences." No one ever doubted that it was the result of precisely such a knowledge, and the hermetists, magicians, astrologers and alchemists never claimed anything else. It certainly was not their fault that the ignorant masses, under the influence of an unscrupulous and fanatical clergy, should have attributed all such works to the agency of the devil. In view of the atrocious tortures provided by the Inquisition for all suspected of either black or white magic, it is not strange that these philosophers neither boasted nor even acknowledged the fact of such an intercourse. On the contrary, their own writings prove that they held that magic is "no more than the application of natural active causes to passive things or subjects; by means thereof, many tremendously surprising but yet natural effects are produced."

The phenomena of the mystic odors and music, exhibited by Roger Bacon, have been often observed in our own time. To say nothing of our personal experience, we are informed by English correspondents of the Theosophical Society that they have heard strains of the most ravishing music, coming from no visible instrument, and inhaled a succession of delightful odors produced, as they believed, by spirit-agency. One correspondent tells us that so powerful was one of these familiar odors — that of sandal-wood — that the house would be impregnated with it for weeks after the seance. The medium in this case was a member of a private family, and the experiments were all made within the domestic circle. Another describes what he calls a "*musical* rap." The potencies that are now capable of producing these phenomena must have existed and been equally efficacious in the days of Roger Bacon. As to the apparitions, it suffices to say that they are evoked now in

---

140 T. Wright, "*Narratives of Sorcery and Magic.*"

spiritualistic circles, and guaranteed by scientists, and their evocation by Roger Bacon is thus made more probable than ever.

Baptista Porta, in his treatise on *Natural Magic*, enumerates a whole catalogue of secret formulæ for producing extraordinary effects by employing the occult powers of nature. Although the "magicians" believed as firmly as our spiritualists in a world of invisible spirits, none of them claimed to produce his effects under their control or through their sole help. They knew too well how difficult it is to keep away the elementary creatures when they have once found the door wide open. Even the magic of the ancient Chaldeans was but a profound knowledge of the powers of simples and minerals. It was only when the theurgist desired *divine* help in spiritual and earthly matters that he sought direct communication through religious rites, with pure spiritual beings. With them, even, those spirits who remain invisible and communicate with mortals through their awakened inner senses, as in clairvoyance, clairaudience and trance, could only be evoked *subjectively* and as a result of purity of life and prayer. But all physical phenomena were produced simply by applying a knowledge of natural forces, although certainly not by the method of legerdemain, practiced in our days by conjurers.

Men possessed of such knowledge and exercising such powers patiently toiled for something better than the vain glory of a passing fame. Seeking it not, they became immortal, as do all who labor for the good of the race, forgetful of mean self. Illuminated with the light of eternal truth, these rich-poor alchemists fixed their attention upon the things that lie beyond the common ken, recognizing nothing inscrutable but the First Cause, and finding no question unsolvable. To dare, to know, to will, and REMAIN SILENT, was their constant rule; to be beneficent, unselfish, and unpretending, were, with them, spontaneous impulses. Disdaining the rewards of petty traffic, spurning wealth, luxury, pomp, and worldly power, they aspired to knowledge as the most satisfying of all acquisitions. They esteemed poverty, hunger, toil, and the evil report of men, as none too great a price to pay for its achievement. They, who might have lain on downy, velvet-covered beds, suffered themselves to die in hospitals and by the wayside, rather than debase their souls and allow the profane cupidity of those who tempted them to triumph over their sacred vows. The lives of Paracelsus, Cornelius Agrippa, and Philalethes are too well known to repeat the old, sad story.

MEDIUMISTIC PHENOMENA, TO WHAT ATTRIBUTABLE

If spiritualists are anxious to keep strictly dogmatic in their notions of the "spirit-world," they must not set *scientists* to investigate their phenomena in the true experimental spirit. The attempt would most surely result in a partial re-discovery of the magic of old — that of Moses and Paracelsus. Under the deceptive beauty of some of their apparitions, they might find some day the sylphs and fair Undines of the Rosicrucians playing in the currents of *psychic* and *odic* force.

Already Mr. Crookes, who fully credits the *being*, feels that under the fair skin of Katie, covering a simulacrum of heart borrowed partially from the medium and the circle, there is *no soul!* And the learned authors of *The Unseen Universe*, abandoning their "electro-biological" theory, begin to perceive in the universal ether the *possibility* that it is a photographic album of EN-SOPH — the Boundless.

We are far from believing that all the spirits that communicate at circles are of the classes called "Elemental," and "Elementary." Many — especially among those who control the medium subjectively to speak, write, and otherwise act in various ways — are human, disembodied spirits. Whether the majority of such spirits are good or *bad*, largely depends on the private morality of the medium, much on the circle present, and a great deal on the intensity and object of their purpose. If this object is merely to gratify curiosity and to pass the time, it is useless to expect anything serious. But, in any case, human spirits can *never* materialize themselves in *propriâ personâ*. These can never appear to the investigator clothed with warm, solid flesh, sweating hands and faces, and grossly-material bodies. The most they can do is to project their æthereal reflection on the atmospheric waves, and if the touch of their hands and clothing can become upon rare occasions objective to the senses of a living mortal, it will be felt as a passing breeze gently sweeping over the touched spot, not as a human hand or material body. It is useless to plead that the "materialized spirits" that have exhibited themselves with beating hearts and loud voices (with or without a trumpet) are *human* spirits. The voices — if such sound can be termed a voice at all — of a spiritual apparition once heard can hardly be forgotten. That of a pure spirit is like the tremulous murmur of an Æolian harp echoed from a distance; the voice of a suffering, hence impure, if not utterly bad spirit, may be assimilated to a human voice issuing from an empty barrel.

This is not *our* philosophy, but that of the numberless generations of theurgists and magicians, and based upon their practical experience. The testimony of antiquity is positive on this subject: Δαιμονιῶν.φωναὶ ἄναρθροι εἰσί . . .[141] The voices of spirits are not articulated. The spirit-voice consists of a series of sounds which conveys the impression of a column of compressed air ascending from beneath upward, and spreading around the living interlocutor. The many eye-witnesses who testified in the case of Elizabeth Eslinger, namely:[142] the deputy-governor of the prison of Weinsberg, Mayer, Eckhart, Theurer, and Knorr (sworn evidence), Duttenhofer, and Kapff, the mathematician, testified that they saw the apparition *like a pillar of clouds.* For the space of eleven weeks, Doctor Kerner and his sons, several Lutheran ministers, the advocate Fraas, the engraver Duttenhofer, two physicians, Siefer and Sicherer, the judge Heyd, and the Baron von Hugel, with many others, followed this manifestation daily. During the time it lasted, the prisoner Elizabeth prayed with a loud voice uninterruptedly; therefore, as the "spirit" was talking at the same time, it could be no ventriloquism; and that voice, they say, "had nothing *human* in it; no one could imitate its sounds."

Further on we will give abundant proofs from ancient authors concerning this neglected truism. We will now only again assert that no spirit claimed by the spiritualists to be human was ever proved to be such on sufficient testimony. The influence of the *disembodied* ones can be felt, and communicated *subjectively* by them to sensitives. They can produce *objective* manifestations, but they cannot produce *themselves* otherwise than as described above. They can control the body of a medium, and express their desires and ideas in various modes well known to spiritualists; but not *materialize* what is matterless and purely spiritual — their *divine essence.* Thus every so-called "materialization" — when genuine — is either produced (*perhaps*) by the will of that spirit whom the "appearance" is claimed to be but can

---

141 See Des Mousseaux's "*Dodone*," and "*Dieu et les dieux*," p. 326.
142 "*Apparitions*," translated by C. Crowe, pp. 388, 391, 399.

only personate at best, or by the elementary goblins themselves, which are generally too stupid to deserve the honor of being called devils. Upon rare occasions the spirits are able to subdue and control these soulless beings, which are ever ready to assume pompous names if left to themselves, in such a way that the mischievous spirit "of the air," shaped in the real image of the *human* spirit, will be moved by the latter like a marionette, and unable to either act or utter other words than those imposed on him by the "immortal soul." But this requires many conditions generally unknown to the circles of even spiritualists most in the habit of regularly attending seances. Not every one can attract *human* spirits who likes. One of the most powerful attractions of our departed ones is their strong affection for those whom they have left on earth. It draws them irresistibly, by degrees, into the current of the Astral Light vibrating between the person sympathetic to them and the Universal Soul. Another very important condition is harmony, and the magnetic purity of the persons present.

If this philosophy is wrong, if all the "materialized" forms emerging *in darkened* rooms from still *darker* cabinets, are spirits of men who once lived upon this earth, why such a difference between them and the *ghosts* that appear unexpectedly — *ex abrupto* — without either cabinet or medium? Who ever heard of the apparitions, unrestful "souls," hovering about the spots where they were murdered, or coming back for some other mysterious reasons of their own, with "warm hands" feeling *like living flesh*, and but that they are known to be dead and buried, not distinguishable from living mortals? We have well-attested facts of such apparitions making themselves suddenly visible, but never, until the beginning of the era of the "materializations," did we see anything like them. In the *Medium and Day Break*, of September 8, 1876, we read a letter from "a lady travelling on the continent," narrating a circumstance that happened in a haunted house. She says: ". . . A strange sound proceeded from a darkened corner of the library . . . on looking up she perceived a *cloud or column of luminous vapor*; . . .the earth-bound spirit was hovering about the spot rendered accursed by his evil deed. . ." As this spirit was doubtless a *genuine* elementary apparition, which made itself visible of its own free will — in short, an *umbra* — it was, as every respectable shadow should be, visible but impalpable, or if palpable at all, communicating to the feeling of touch the sensation of a mass of water suddenly clasped in the hand, or of condensed but cold steam. It was *luminous* and *vapory*; for aught we can tell it might have been the real personal umbra of the "spirit," persecuted, and earth-bound, either by its own remorse and crimes or those of another person or spirit. The mysteries of after-death are many, and modern "materializations" only make them cheap and ridiculous in the eyes of the indifferent.

To these assertions may be opposed a fact well known among spiritualists: *The writer has publicly certified to having seen such materialized forms.* We have most assuredly done so, and are ready to repeat the testimony. We have recognized such figures as the visible representations of acquaintances, friends, and even relatives. We have, in company with many other spectators, heard them pronounce words in languages unfamiliar not only to the medium and to every one else in the room, except ourselves, but, in some cases, to almost if not quite every medium in America and Europe, for they were the tongues of Eastern tribes and peoples. At the time, these instances were justly regarded as conclusive proofs of the genuine mediumship of the uneducated Vermont farmer who sat in the "cabinet." But, nevertheless, these figures were *not* the forms of the persons they appeared to be. They were simply their portrait statues, constructed, animated and operated by the elementaries. If we have not previously elucidated this point, it was because the spiritualistic public was not then ready to even listen to the fundamental proposition that there are elemental and elementary spirits. Since that time this subject has been broached and more or less widely discussed. There is less hazard now in attempting to launch upon the restless sea of criticism the hoary philosophy of the ancient sages, for there has been some preparation of the public mind to consider it with impartiality and deliberation. Two years of agitation have effected a marked change for the better.

Pausanias writes that four hundred years after the battle of Marathon, there were still heard in the place where it was fought, the *neighing of horses* and the shouts of shadowy soldiers. Supposing that the spectres of the slaughtered soldiers were their genuine spirits, they looked like "shadows," not materialized men. Who, then, or what, produced the neighing of horses? *Equine* "spirits"? And if it be pronounced untrue that horses have spirits — which assuredly no one among zoologists, physiologists or psychologists, or even spiritualists, can either prove or disprove — then must we take it for granted that it was the "immortal souls" of men which produced the neighing at Marathon to make the historical battle scene more vivid and dramatic? The phantoms of dogs, cats, and various other animals have been repeatedly seen, and the world-wide testimony is as trustworthy upon this point as that with respect to human apparitions. Who or *what* personates, if we are allowed such an expression, the ghosts of departed animals? Is it, again, human spirits? As the matter now stands, there is no side issue; we have either to admit that animals have surviving spirits and souls as well as ourselves, or hold with Porphyry that there are in the *invisible* world a kind of tricky and malicious demons, intermediary beings between living men and "gods," spirits that delight in appearing under every imaginable shape, beginning with the human form, and ending with those of multifarious animals.[143]

THEIR RELATION TO CRIME

Before venturing to decide the question whether the spectral animal forms so frequently seen and attested are the returning spirits of dead beasts, we must carefully consider their reported behavior. Do these spectres act according to the habits and display the same instincts, as the animals during life? Do the spectral beasts of prey lie in wait for victims, and timid animals flee before the presence of man; or do the latter show a malevolence and disposition to annoy, quite foreign to their natures? Many victims of these obsessions — notably, the afflicted persons of Salem and other historical witchcrafts — testify to having seen dogs, cats, pigs, and other animals, entering their rooms, biting them, trampling upon their sleeping bodies, and *talking* to them; *often inciting them to suicide and other crimes.* In the well-attested case of Elizabeth Eslinger, mentioned by Dr. Kerner, the apparition of the ancient priest of Wimmenthal[144] was accompanied by a large black dog, which he called *his father,* and which dog in the presence of numerous witnesses jumped on all the beds of the prisoners. At another time the priest appeared with a lamb, and sometimes with two lambs. Most of those accused at Salem were charged by the seeresses with consulting and plotting

---

143 *"De Abstinentia,"* etc.
144 C. Crowe, *"On Apparitions,"* p. 398.

mischief with yellow birds, which would sit on their shoulder or on the beams overhead.[145] And unless we discredit the testimony of thousands of witnesses, in all parts of the world, and in all ages, and allow a monopoly of seership to modern mediums, spectre-animals do appear and manifest all the worst traits of depraved human nature, without themselves being human. What, then, can they be but elementals?

Descartes was one of the few who believed and dared say that to occult medicine we shall owe discoveries "destined to extend the domain of philosophy"; and Brierre de Boismont not only shared in these hopes but openly avowed his sympathy with "supernaturalism," which he considered the universal "grand creed." ". . . We think with Guizot," he says, "that the existence of society is bound up in it. It *is in vain* that modern reason, which, notwithstanding its *positivism,* cannot explain the intimate cause of any phenomena, *rejects the supernatural*; it is universal, and at the root of all hearts. The most elevated minds are frequently its most ardent disciples."[146]

Christopher Columbus discovered America, and Americus Vespucius reaped the glory and usurped his dues. Theophrastus Paracelsus rediscovered the occult properties of the magnet — "the bone of Horus" which, twelve centuries before his time, had played such an important part in the theurgic mysteries — and he very naturally became the founder of the school of magnetism and of mediæval magico-theurgy. But Mesmer, who lived nearly three hundred years after him, and as a disciple of his school brought the magnetic wonders before the public, reaped the glory that was due to the fire-philosopher, while the great master died in a hospital!

So goes the world: new discoveries, evolving from old sciences; new men — the same old nature!

---

145 Upham, "*Salem Witchcraft.*"
146 Brierre de Boismont, "*On Hallucinations,*" p. 60.

CHAPTER III

"The mirror of the soul cannot reflect both earth and heaven; and the one vanishes from its surface, as the other is glassed upon its deep."

ZANONI

"Qui, donc, t'a donne la mission d'annoncer au peuple que la Divinite n'existe pas — quel avantage trouves tu a persuader a l'homme qu'une force aveugle preside a ses destinees et frappe au hasard le crime et la vertu?"

ROBESPIERRE (Discours)

May 7, 1794

WE believe that few of those physical phenomena which are genuine are caused by disembodied human spirits. Still, even those that are produced by occult forces of nature, such as happen through a few genuine mediums, and are consciously employed by the so-called "jugglers" of India and Egypt, deserve a careful and serious investigation by science; especially now that a number of respected authorities have testified that in many cases the hypothesis of fraud does not hold. No doubt, there are professed "conjurors" who can perform cleverer tricks than all the American and English "John Kings" together. Robert Houdin unquestionably could, but this did not prevent his laughing outright in the face of the academicians, when they desired him to assert in the newspapers, that he could make a table move, or rap answers to questions, without contact of hands, unless the table was a prepared one.[147] The fact alone, that a now notorious London juggler refused to accept a challenge for £1,000 offered him by Mr. Algernon Joy,[148] to produce such manifestations as are usually obtained through mediums, unless he was left unbound and free from the hands of a committee, negatives his expose of the occult phenomena. Clever as he may be, we defy and challenge him to reproduce, under the same conditions, the "tricks" exhibited even by a common Indian juggler. For instance, the spot to be chosen by the investigators at the moment of the performance, and the juggler to know nothing of the choice; the experiment to be made in broad daylight, without the least preparations for it; without any confederate but a boy absolutely naked, and the juggler to be in a condition of semi-nudity. After that, we should select out of a variety three tricks, the most common among such public jugglers, and that were recently exhibited to some gentlemen belonging to the suite of the Prince of Wales: 1. To transform a rupee — firmly clasped in the hand of a skeptic — into a living cobra, the bite of which would prove fatal, as an examination of its fangs would show. 2. To cause a seed chosen at random by the spectators, and planted in the first semblance of a flower-pot, furnished by the same skeptics, to grow, mature, and bear fruit in less than a quarter of an hour. 3. To stretch himself on three swords, stuck perpendicularly in the ground at their hilts, the sharp points upward; after that, to have removed first one of the swords, then the other, and, after an interval of a few seconds, the last one, the juggler remaining, finally, lying on nothing — on the air, miraculously suspended at about one yard from the ground. When any prestidigitateur, to begin with Houdin and end with the

---

147 See de Mirville's "*Question des Esprits,*" and the works on the "*Phenomenes Spirites,*" by de Gasparin.
148 Honorary Secretary to the National Association of Spiritualists of London.

last trickster who has secured gratuitous advertisement by attacking spiritualism, does the same, then — but only then — we will train ourselves to believe that mankind has been evolved out of the hind-toe of Mr. Huxley's Eocene Orohippus.

HUXLEY'S DERIVATION FROM THE OROHIPPUS

We assert again, in full confidence, that there does not exist a professional wizard, either of the North, South or West, who can compete with anything approaching success, with these untutored, naked sons of the East. These require no Egyptian Hall for their performances, nor any preparations or rehearsals; but are ever ready, at a moment's notice, to evoke to their help the hidden powers of nature, which, for European prestidigitateurs as well as for scientists, are a closed book. Verily, as Elihu puts it, "great men are not always wise; neither do the aged understand judgment."[149] To repeat the remark of the English divine, Dr. Henry More, we may well say: ". . . indeed, if there were any modesty left in mankind, the histories of the Bible might abundantly assure men of the existence of angels and spirits." The same eminent man adds, "I look upon it as a special piece of Providence that . . . fresh examples of apparitions may awaken our benumbed and lethargic minds into an assurance that there are other intelligent beings besides those that are clothed in heavy earth or clay . . . for this evidence, showing that there are bad spirits, will necessarily open a door to the belief that there are good ones, and lastly, that there is a God." The instance above given carries a moral with it, not only to scientists, but theologians. Men who have made their mark in the pulpit and in professors' chairs, are continually showing the lay public that they really know so little of psychology, as to take up with any plausible schemer who comes their way, and so make themselves ridiculous in the eyes of the thoughtful student. Public opinion upon this subject has been manufactured by jugglers and self-styled savants, unworthy of respectful consideration.

COMTE, HIS SYSTEM AND DISCIPLES

The development of psychological science has been retarded far more by the ridicule of this class of pretenders, than by the inherent difficulties of its study. The empty laugh of the scientific nursling or of the fools of fashion, has done more to keep man ignorant of his imperial psychical powers, than the obscurities, the obstacles and the dangers that cluster about the subject. This is especially the case with spiritualistic phenomena. That their investigation has been so largely confined to incapables, is due to the fact that men of science, who might and would have studied them, have been frightened off by the boasted exposures, the paltry jokes, and the impertinent clamor of those who are not worthy to tie their shoes. There are moral cowards even in university chairs. The inherent vitality of modern spiritualism is proven in its survival of the neglect of the scientific body, and of the obstreperous boasting of its pretended exposers. If we begin with the contemptuous sneers of the patriarchs of science, such as Faraday and Brewster, and end with the professional (?) *exposes* of the successful mimicker of the phenomena, —, of London, we will not find them furnishing one single, well-established argument against the occurrence of spiritual manifestations. "My theory is," says this individual, in his recent *soi-disant* "*expose*," "that Mr.

---

149 Job.

Williams dressed up and personified John King and Peter. Nobody can prove that it wasn't so." Thus it appears that, notwithstanding the bold tone of assertion, it is but a theory after all, and spiritualists might well retort upon the exposer, and demand that he should prove that it is so.

But the most inveterate, uncompromising enemies of Spiritualism are a class very fortunately composed of but few members, who, nevertheless, declaim the louder and assert their views with a clamorousness worthy of a better cause. These are the *pretenders* to science of young America — a mongrel class of pseudo-philosophers, mentioned at the opening of this chapter, with sometimes no better right to be regarded as scholars than the possession of an electrical machine, or the delivery of a puerile lecture on insanity and mediomania. Such men are — if you believe them — profound thinkers and physiologists; there is none of your metaphysical nonsense about them; they are Positivists — the mental sucklings of Auguste Comte, whose bosoms swell at the thought of plucking deluded humanity from the dark abyss of superstition, and rebuilding the cosmos on improved principles. Irascible psychophobists, no more cutting insult can be offered them than to suggest that they may be endowed with immortal spirits. To hear them, one would fancy that there can be no other souls in men and women than "scientific" or "unscientific souls"; whatever that kind of soul may be.[150]

Some thirty or forty years ago, in France, Auguste Comte — a pupil of the *Ecole Polytechnique,* who had remained for years at that establishment as a *repetiteur* of Transcendant Analysis and Rationalistic Mechanics — awoke one fine morning with the very irrational idea of becoming a prophet. In America, prophets can be met with at every street-corner; in Europe, they are as rare as black swans. But France is the land of novelties. Auguste Comte became a prophet; and so infectious is fashion, sometimes, that even in sober England he was considered, for a certain time, the Newton of the nineteenth century.

The epidemic extended, and for the time being, it spread like wildfire over Germany, England, and America. It found adepts in France, but the excitement did not last long with these. The prophet needed money: the disciples were unwilling to furnish it. The fever of admiration for a religion without a God cooled off as quickly as it had come on; of all the enthusiastic apostles of the prophet, there remained but one worthy of any attention. It was the famous philologist Littre, a member of the French Institute, and a *would-be* member of the Imperial Academy of Sciences, but whom the archbishop of Orleans maliciously prevented from becoming one of the "Immortals."[151]

The philosopher-mathematician — the high-priest of the "religion of the future" — taught his doctrine as do all his brother-prophets of our modern days. He deified "woman," and furnished her with an altar; but the goddess had to pay for its use. The rationalists had laughed at the mental aberration of Fourier; they had laughed at the St. Simonists; and their scorn for Spiritualism knew no bounds. The same rationalists and materialists were caught, like so many empty-headed sparrows, by the bird-lime of the new prophet's rhetoric. A longing for some kind of divinity, a craving for the "unknown," is a feeling congenital in

---

150 See Dr. F. R. Marvin's *"Lectures on Mediomania and Insanity."*

151 Vapereau, *"Biographie Contemporaine,"* art. Littre; and Des Mousseaux, *"Les Hauts Phenomenes de la Magie,"* ch. 6.

man; hence the worst atheists seem not to be exempt from it. Deceived by the outward brilliancy of this *ignus fatuus,* the disciples followed it until they found themselves floundering in a bottomless morass.

Covering themselves with the mask of a pretended erudition, the Positivists of this country have organized themselves into clubs and committees with the design of uprooting Spiritualism, while pretending to impartially investigate it.

Too timid to openly challenge the churches and the Christian doctrine, they endeavor to sap that upon which all religion is based — man's faith in God and his own immortality. Their policy is to ridicule that which affords an unusual basis for such a faith — phenomenal Spiritualism.

Attacking it at its weakest side, they make the most of its lack of an inductive method, and of the exaggerations that are to be found in the transcendental doctrines of its propagandists. Taking advantage of its unpopularity, and displaying a courage as furious and out of place as that of the errant knight of La Mancha, they claim recognition as philanthropists and benefactors who would crush out a monstrous superstition.

Let us see in what degree Comte's boasted religion of the future is superior to Spiritualism, and how much less likely its advocates are to need the refuge of those lunatic asylums which they officiously recommend for the mediums whom they have been so solicitous about. Before beginning, let us call attention to the fact that three-fourths of the disgraceful features exhibited in modern Spiritualism are directly traceable to the materialistic adventurers pretending to be spiritualists. Comte has fulsomely depicted the "artificially-fecundated" woman of the future. She is but elder sister to the Cyprian ideal of the free-lovers. The immunity against the future offered by the teachings of his moonstruck disciples, has inoculated some pseudo-spiritualists to such an extent as to lead them to form communistic associations. None, however, have proved long-lived. Their leading feature being generally a materialistic animalism, gilded over with a thin leaf of Dutch-metal philosophy and tricked out with a combination of hard Greek names, the community could not prove anything else than a failure.

Plato, in the fifth book of the *Republic,* suggests a method for improving the human race by the elimination of the unhealthy or deformed individuals, and by coupling the better specimens of both sexes. It was not to be expected that the "genius of our century," even were he a prophet, would squeeze out of his brain anything entirely new.

Comte was a mathematician. Cleverly combining several old utopias, he colored the whole, and, improving on Plato's idea, materialized it, and presented the world with the greatest monstrosity that ever emanated from a human mind!

We beg the reader to keep in view, that we do not attack Comte as a philosopher, but as a professed reformer. In the irremediable darkness of his political, philosophical and religious views, we often meet with isolated observations and remarks in which profound logic and judiciousness of thought rival the brilliancy of their interpretation. But then, these dazzle you like flashes of lightning on a gloomy night, to leave you, the next moment, more in the dark than ever. If condensed and repunctuated, his several works might produce, on the whole, a volume of very original aphorisms, giving a very clear and really clever definition of most of our social evils; but it would be vain to seek, either through the tedious circumlocution of the six volumes of his *Cours de Philosophie Positive*, or in that parody on priesthood, in the form of a dialogue — *The Catechism of the Religion of Positivism* — any idea suggestive of even provisional remedies for such evils. His disciples suggest that the sublime doctrines of their prophet were not intended *for the vulgar*. Comparing the dogmas preached by Positivism with their practical exemplifications by its apostles, we must confess the possibility of some very achromatic doctrine being at the bottom of it. While the "high-priest" preaches that "woman must cease to be the *female* of the man";[152] while the theory of the positivist legislators on marriage and the family, chiefly consists in making the woman the "mere companion of man by ridding her of every maternal function";[153] and while they are preparing against the future a substitute for that function by applying "to the *chaste woman*" "a *latent force*,"[154] some of its lay priests openly preach polygamy, and others affirm that their doctrines are the quintessence of spiritual philosophy.

In the opinion of the Romish clergy, who labor under a chronic nightmare of the devil, Comte offers his "woman of the future" to the possession of the "incubi."[155] In the opinion of more prosaic persons, the *Divinity* of Positivism, must henceforth be regarded as a biped broodmare. Even Littre, made prudent restrictions while accepting the apostleship of this marvellous religion. This is what he wrote in 1859: "M. Comte not only thought that he found the principles, traced the outlines, and furnished the method, but that he had deduced the consequences and constructed the social and religious edifice of the future. It is in this *second* division that we make our reservations, declaring, at the same time, that we accept as an inheritance, the whole of the first."[156]

Further, he says: "M. Comte, in a grand work entitled the *System of the Positive Philosophy*, established the basis of a philosophy [?] which must finally supplant every theology and the whole of metaphysics. Such a work necessarily contains a direct application to the government of societies; as it *has nothing arbitrary in it* [?] and as we find therein a *real science* [?], my adhesion to the principles involves my adhesion to the essential consequences."

M. Littre has shown himself in the light of a true son of his prophet. Indeed the whole system of Comte appears to us to have been built on a play of words. When they say "*Positivism*," read *Nihilism*; when you hear the word *chastity*, know that it means *impudicity*; and so on. Being a religion based on a theory of negation, its adherents can hardly carry it out practically without saying white when meaning black!

"Positive Philosophy," continues Littre, "does not accept atheism, for the atheist is not a really-emancipated mind, but is, in his own way, a theologian still; he gives his explanation about the essence of things; *he knows* how they began! . . . Atheism is Pantheism; this system is quite theological yet, and thus belongs to the ancient party."[157]

It really would be losing time to quote any more of these paradoxical dissertations. Comte attained to the apotheosis of absurdity and inconsistency when, after inventing his

---

152 A. Comte, "*Systeme de Politique Positive*," vol. i., p. 203, etc.
153 Ibid.
154 Ibid.
155 See des Mousseaux, "*Hauts Phenomenes de la Magie*," chap. 6.
156 Littre, "*Paroles de Philosophie Positive*."
157 Littre, "*Paroles de Philosophie Positive*," vii., 57.

philosophy, he named it a "Religion." And, as is usually the case, the disciples have surpassed the reformer — in absurdity. Supposititious philosophers, who shine in the American academies of Comte, like a *lampyris noctiluca* beside a planet, leave us in no doubt as to their belief, and contrast "that system of thought and life" elaborated by the French apostle with the "idiocy" of Spiritualism; of course to the advantage of the former. "To destroy, you must replace"; exclaims the author of the *Catechism of the Religion of Positivism*, quoting Cassaudiere, by the way, without crediting him with the thought; and his disciples proceed to show by what sort of a loathsome system they are anxious to replace Christianity, Spiritualism, and even Science.

"Positivism," perorates one of them, "is an *integral* doctrine. It rejects completely all forms of theological and metaphysical belief; all forms of supernaturalism, and thus — Spiritualism. The true positive spirit consists in substituting the study of the invariable laws of phenomena for that of their so-called causes, whether proximate or primary. On this ground it equally rejects atheism; *for the atheist is at bottom a theologian*," he adds, plagiarizing sentences from Littre's works: "the atheist does not reject the problems of theology, only the solution of these, and so he is illogical. We *Positivists* reject the problem in our turn on the ground that it is utterly inaccessible to the intellect, and we would only waste our strength in a vain search for first and final causes. As you see, Positivism gives a complete explanation [?] of the world, of man, his duty and destiny . . . . "![158]

Very brilliant this; and now, by way of contrast, we will quote what a really great scientist, Professor Hare, thinks of this system. "Comte's positive philosophy," he says, "after all, is merely negative. It is admitted by Comte, that he knows nothing of *the sources* and *causes* of nature's laws; that their origination is so perfectly inscrutable as to make it idle to — take up time in any scrutiny for that purpose. . . . Of course his doctrine makes him avowedly a thorough ignoramus, as to the causes of laws, or the means by which they are established, and can have no basis but the *negative* argument above stated, in objecting to the facts ascertained in relation to the spiritual creation. Thus, while allowing the atheist his material dominion, Spiritualism will erect within and above the same space a dominion of an importance as much greater as eternity is to the average duration of human life, and as the boundless regions of the fixed stars are to the habitable area of this globe."[159]

In short, Positivism proposes to itself to destroy Theology, Metaphysics, Spiritualism, Atheism, Materialism, Pantheism, and Science, and it must finally end in destroying itself. De Mirville thinks that according to Positivism, "order will begin to reign in the human mind only on the day when psychology will become a sort of *cerebral physics*, and history a kind of social physics." The modern Mohammed first disburdens man and woman of God and their own soul, and then unwittingly disembowels his own doctrine with the too sharp sword of metaphysics, which all the time he thought he was avoiding, thus letting out every vestige of philosophy.

In 1864, M. Paul Janet, a member of the Institute, pronounced a discourse upon Positivism, in which occur the following remarkable words:

---

158 "*Spiritualism and Charlatanism.*"
159 Prof. Hare, "*On Positivism,*" p. 29.

"There are some minds which were brought up and fed on exact and positive sciences, but which feel nevertheless, a sort of instinctive impulse for philosophy. They can satisfy this instinct but with elements that they have already on hand. Ignorant in psychological sciences, having studied only the rudiments of metaphysics, they nevertheless are determined to fight these same metaphysics as well as psychology, of which they know as little as of the other. After this is done, they will imagine themselves to have founded a Positive Science, while the truth is that they have only built up a new mutilated and incomplete metaphysical theory. They arrogate to themselves the authority and infallibility properly belonging alone to the true sciences, those which are based on experience and calculations; but they lack such an authority, for their ideas, defective as they may be, nevertheless belong to the same class as those which they attack. Hence the weakness of their situation, the final ruin of their ideas, which are soon scattered to the four winds."[160]

The Positivists of America have joined hands in their untiring efforts to overthrow Spiritualism. To show their impartiality, though, they propound such novel queries as follows: " . . . how much rationality is there in the dogmas of the Immaculate Conception, the Trinity and Transubstantiation, if submitted to the tests of physiology, mathematics, and chemistry?" and they "undertake to say, that the vagaries of Spiritualism do not surpass in absurdity these eminently respectable beliefs." Very well. But there is neither theological absurdity nor spiritualistic delusion that can match in depravity and imbecility that positivist notion of "artificial fecundation." Denying to themselves all thought on primal and final causes, they apply their insane theories to the construction of an impossible woman for the worship of future generations; the living, immortal companion of man they would replace with the Indian female fetich of the Obeah, the wooden idol that is stuffed every day with serpents' eggs, to be hatched by the heat of the sun!

And now, if we are permitted to ask in the name of common-sense, why should Christian mystics be taxed with credulity or the spiritualists be consigned to Bedlam, when a *religion* embodying such revolting absurdity finds disciples even among Academicians? — when such insane rhapsodies as the following can be uttered by the mouth of Comte and admired by his followers: "My eyes are dazzled; — they open each day more and more to the increasing coincidence between the social advent of the *feminine mystery*, and the mental decadence of the eucharistical sacrament. Already the Virgin has dethroned God in the minds of Southern Catholics! Positivism realizes the Utopia of the mediæval ages, by representing all the members of the great family as the issue of a *virgin mother without a husband*. . . ." And again, after giving the *modus operandi*: "The development of the *new process* would soon cause to spring up a caste without heredity, better adapted than vulgar procreation to the recruitment of spiritual chiefs, or even temporal ones, whose authority would then rest upon an origin truly superior, which would not *shrink from an investigation*."[161]

To this we might inquire with propriety, whether there has ever been found in the "vagaries of Spiritualism," or the mysteries of Christianity, anything more preposterous than this ideal "coming race." If the tendency of materialism is not grossly belied by the

---

160 "*Journal des Debats*," 1864. See also des Mousseaux's "*Hauts Phen. de la Magie*."
161 "*Philosophie Positive*," Vol. iv., p. 279.

behavior of some of its advocates, those who publicly preach polygamy, we fancy that whether or not there will ever be a sacerdotal stirp so begotten, we shall see no end of progeny, — the offspring of "mothers without husbands."

How natural that a philosophy which could engender such a caste of didactic incubi, should express through the pen of one of its most garrulous essayists, the following sentiments: "This is a sad, a very sad age,[162] full of dead and dying faiths; full of idle prayers sent out in vain search for the departing gods. But oh! it is a glorious age, full of the golden light which streams from the ascending sun of science! What shall we do for those who are shipwrecked in faith, *bankrupt in intellect,* but . . . who seek comfort in the *mirage of spiritualism,* the delusions of transcendentalism, or the *will o' the wisp* of mesmerism? . . ."

The *ignis fatuus,* now so favorite an image with many dwarf philosophers, had itself to struggle for recognition. It is not so long since the now familiar phenomenon was stoutly denied by a correspondent of the London *Times,* whose assertions carried weight, till the work of Dr. Phipson, supported by the testimony of Beccaria, Humboldt, and other naturalists, set the question at rest.[163] The Positivists should choose some happier expression, and follow the discoveries of science at the same time. As to mesmerism, it has been adopted in many parts of Germany, and is publicly used with undeniable success in more than one hospital; its occult properties have been proved and are believed in by physicians, whose eminence, learning, and merited fame, the self-complacent lecturer on mediums and insanity cannot well hope to equal.

We have to add but a few more words before we drop this unpleasant subject. We have found Positivists particularly happy in the delusion that the *greatest scientists* of Europe were Comtists. How far their claims may be just, as regards other *savants,* we do not know, but Huxley, whom all Europe considers one of her greatest scientists, most decidedly declines that honor, and Dr. Maudsley, of London, follows suit. In a lecture delivered by the former gentleman in 1868, in Edinburgh, on *The Physical Basis of Life,* he even appears to be very much shocked at the liberty taken by the Archbishop of York, in identifying him with Comte's philosophy. "So far as I am concerned," says Mr. Huxley, "the most reverend prelate might dialectically hew Mr. Comte in pieces, as a modern Agag, and I would not attempt to stay his hand. In so far as my study of what specially characterizes the positive philosophy has led me, I find, therein, little or nothing of any scientific value, and a great deal which is *as thoroughly antagonistic to the very essence of science as anything in ultramontane Catholicism.* In fact, Comte's philosophy in practice might be compendiously described as *Catholicism minus Christianity.*" Further, Huxley even becomes wrathful, and falls to accusing Scotchmen of ingratitude for having allowed the Bishop to mistake Comte for the founder of a philosophy which belonged by right to Hume. "It was enough," exclaims the professor, "to make David Hume turn in his grave, that here, almost within earshot of his house, an interested audience should have listened, without a murmur, whilst his most characteristic doctrines were attributed to a French writer of fifty years later date, in whose *dreary and verbose pages we miss alike the vigor of thought and the clearness of style.* . . ."[164]

---

162 Dr. F. R. Marvin, *"Lecture on Insanity."*
163 See Howitt, *"History of the Supernatural,"* vol. ii.
164 Prof. Huxley, *"Physical Basis of Life."*

Poor Comte! It appears that the highest representatives of his philosophy are now reduced, at least in this country, to "one physicist, one physician who has made a specialty of nervous diseases, and one lawyer." A very witty critic nicknamed this desperate trio, "*an anomalistic triad,* which, amid its arduous labors, finds no time to acquaint itself with the principles and laws of their language."[165]

To close the question, the Positivists neglect no means to overthrow Spiritualism in favor of their *religion.* Their high priests are made to blow their trumpets untiringly; and though the walls of no modern Jericho are ever likely to tumble down in dust before their blast, still they neglect no means to attain the desired object. Their paradoxes are unique, and their accusations against spiritualists irresistible in logic. In a recent lecture, for instance, it was remarked that: "The exclusive exercise of *religious* instinct is productive of sexual immorality. Priests, monks, nuns, saints, *media,* ecstatics, and devotees are famous for their impurities."[166]

We are happy to remark that, while Positivism loudly proclaims itself a religion, Spiritualism has never pretended to be anything more than a science, a growing philosophy, or rather a research in hidden and as yet unexplained forces in nature. The objectiveness of its various phenomena has been demonstrated by more than one genuine representative of science, and as ineffectually denied by her "monkeys." Finally, it may be remarked of our Positivists who deal so unceremoniously with every psychological phenomenon, that they are like Samuel Butler's rhetorician, who

". . . . could not ope
His mouth, but out there flew a *trope.*"

We would there were no occasion to extend the critic's glance beyond the circle of triflers and pedants who improperly wear the title of men of science. But it is also undeniable that the treatment of new subjects by those whose rank is high in the scientific world but too often passes unchallenged, when it is amenable to censure. The cautiousness bred of a fixed habit of experimental research, the tentative advance from opinion to opinion, the weight accorded to recognized authorities — all foster a conservatism of thought which naturally runs into dogmatism. The price of scientific progress is too commonly the martyrdom or ostracism of the innovator. The reformer of the laboratory must, so to speak, carry the citadel of custom and prejudice at the point of the bayonet. It is rare that even a postern-door is left ajar by a friendly hand. The noisy protests and impertinent criticisms of the little people of the antechamber of science, he can afford to let pass unnoticed; the hostility of the other class is a real peril that the innovator must face and overcome. Knowledge does increase apace, but the great body of scientists are not entitled to the credit. In every instance they have done their best to shipwreck the new discovery, together with the discoverer. The palm is to him who has won it by individual courage, intuitiveness, and persistency. Few are the forces in nature which, when first announced, were not laughed at,

---

165 Reference is made to a card which appeared some time since in a New York paper, signed by three persons styling themselves as above, and assuming to be a scientific committee appointed two years before to investigate spiritual phenomena. The criticism on the triad appeared in the "*New Era*" magazine.
166 Dr. Marvin, "*Lecture on Insanity,*" N. Y., 1875.

and then set aside as absurd and unscientific. Humbling the pride of those who had not discovered anything, the just claims of those who have been denied a hearing until negation was no longer prudent, and then — alas for poor, selfish humanity! these very discoverers too often became the opponents and oppressors, in their turn, of still more recent explorers in the domain of natural law! So, step by step, mankind move around their circumscribed circle of knowledge, science constantly correcting its mistakes, and readjusting on the following day the erroneous theories of the preceding one. This has been the case, not merely with questions pertaining to psychology, such as mesmerism, in its dual sense of a physical and spiritual phenomenon, but even with such discoveries as directly related to exact sciences, and have been easy to demonstrate.

What can we do? Shall we recall the disagreeable past? Shall we point to mediæval scholars conniving with the clergy to deny the Heliocentric theory, for fear of hurting an ecclesiastical dogma? Must we recall how learned conchologists once denied that the fossil shells, found scattered over the face of the earth, were ever inhabited by living animals at all? How the naturalists of the eighteenth century declared these but mere *fac-similes* of animals? And how these naturalists fought and quarrelled and battled and called each other names, over these venerable mummies of the ancient ages for nearly a century, until Buffon settled the question by proving to the negators that they were mistaken? Surely an oyster-shell is anything but transcendental, and ought to be quite a palpable subject for any exact study; and if the scientists could not agree on that, we can hardly expect them to believe at all that evanescent forms, — of hands, faces, and whole bodies sometimes — appear at the seances of spiritual mediums, when the latter are honest.

THE LONDON MATERIALISTS

There exists a certain work which might afford very profitable reading for the leisure hours of skeptical men of science. It is a book published by Flourens, the Perpetual Secretary of the French Academy, called *Histoire des Recherches de Buffon*. The author shows in it how the great naturalist combated and finally conquered the advocates of the *fac-simile* theory; and how they still went on denying everything under the sun, until at times the learned body fell into a fury, an epidemic of negation. It denied Franklin and his refined electricity; laughed at Fulton and his concentrated steam; voted the engineer Perdormet a strait-jacket for his offer to build railroads; stared Harvey out of countenance; and proclaimed Bernard de Palissy "as stupid as one of his own pots!"

In his oft-quoted work, *Conflict between Religion and Science*, Professor Draper shows a decided propensity to kick the beam of the scales of justice, and lay all such impediments to the progress of science at the door of the clergy alone. With all respect and admiration due to this eloquent writer and scientist, we must protest and give every one his just due. Many of the above-enumerated discoveries are mentioned by the author of the *Conflict*. In every case he denounces the bitter resistance on the part of the clergy, and keeps silent on the like opposition invariably experienced by every new discoverer at the hands of science. His claim on behalf of science that "knowledge is power" is undoubtedly just. But abuse of power, whether it proceeds from excess of wisdom or ignorance is alike obnoxious in its effects. Besides, the clergy are silenced now. Their protests would at this day be scarcely noticed in the world of science. But while theology is kept in the background, the scientists have seized the sceptre of despotism with both hands, and they use it, like the cherubim and flaming sword of Eden, to keep the people away from the tree of immortal life and within this world of perishable matter.

The editor of the London *Spiritualist*, in answer to Dr. Gully's criticism of Mr. Tyndall's fire-mist theory, remarks that if the entire body of spiritualists are not roasting alive at Smithfield in the present century, it is to science alone that we are indebted for this crowning mercy. Well, let us admit that the scientists are indirectly public benefactors in this case, to the extent that the burning of erudite scholars is no longer fashionable. But is it unfair to ask whether the disposition manifested toward the spiritualistic doctrine by Faraday, Tyndall, Huxley, Agassiz, and others, does not warrant the suspicion that if these learned gentlemen and their following had the unlimited power once held by the Inquisition, spiritualists would not have reason to feel as easy as they do now? Even supposing that they should not roast believers in the existence of a spirit-world — it being unlawful to cremate people alive — would they not send every spiritualist they could to Bedlam? Do they not call us "incurable monomaniacs," "hallucinated fools," "fetich-worshippers," and like characteristic names? Really, we cannot see what should have stimulated to such extent the gratitude of the editor of the London *Spiritualist*, for the benevolent tutelage of the men of science. We believe that the recent Lankester-Donkin-Slade prosecution in London ought at last to open the eyes of hopeful spiritualists, and show them that stubborn materialism is often more stupidly bigoted than religious fanaticism itself.

One of the cleverest productions of Professor Tyndall's pen is his caustic essay upon *Martineau and Materialism*. At the same time it is one which in future years the author will doubtless be only too ready to trim of certain unpardonable grossnesses of expression. For the moment, however, we will not deal with these, but consider what he has to say of the phenomenon of consciousness. He quotes this question from Mr. Martineau: "A man can say 'I feel, I think, I love'; but how does consciousness infuse itself into the problem?" And thus answers: "The passage from the physics of the brain to the corresponding facts of consciousness is unthinkable. Granted that a definite thought and a molecular action in the brain occur simultaneously; we do not possess the intellectual organ nor apparently any rudiments of the organ, which would enable us to pass by a process of reasoning from one to the other. They appear together, but *we do not know why*. Were our minds and senses so expanded, strengthened and illuminated, as to enable us to see and feel the very molecules of the brain; were we capable of following all their motions, all their groupings, all their electric discharges, if such there be; and were we intimately acquainted with the corresponding states of thought and feeling, we should be as far as ever from the solution of the problem, 'How are these physical processes connected with the facts of consciousness?' The chasm between the two classes of phenomena would still remain intellectually impassable."[167]

This chasm, as impassable to Professor Tyndall as the fire-mist where the scientist is confronted with his unknowable cause, is a barrier only to men without spiritual intuitions. Professor Buchanan's *Outlines of Lectures on the Neurological System of Anthropology*, a work

---

167 Tyndall, "*Fragments of Science.*"

written so far back as 1854, contains suggestions that, if the sciolists would only heed them, would show how a bridge can be thrown across this dreadful abyss. It is one of the bins in which the thought-seed of future harvests is stored up by a frugal present. But the edifice of materialism is based entirely upon that gross sub-structure — the reason. *When they have stretched its capabilities to their utmost limits, its teachers can at best only disclose to us an universe of molecules animated by an occult impulse.* What better diagnosis of the ailment of our scientists could be asked than can be derived from Professor Tyndall's analysis of the mental state of the Ultramontane clergy by a very slight change of names. For "spiritual guides" read "scientists," for "prescientific past" substitute "materialistic present," say "spirit" for "science," and in the following paragraph we have a life portrait of the modern man of science drawn by the hand of a master:

" . . . Their spiritual guides live so exclusively in the prescientific past, that even the really strong intellects among them are reduced to atrophy as regards scientific truth. Eyes they have and see not; ears they have and hear not; for both eyes and ears are taken possession of by the sights and sounds of another age. In relation to science, the Ultramontane brain, through lack of exercise, is virtually the undeveloped brain of the child. And thus it is that as children in scientific knowledge, but as potent wielders of spiritual power among the ignorant, they countenance and enforce practices sufficient to bring the blush of shame to the cheeks of the more intelligent among themselves."[168] The Occultist holds this mirror up to science that it may see how it looks itself.

Since history recorded the first laws established by man, there never was yet a people, whose code did not hang the issues of the life and death of its citizens upon the testimony of two or three credible witnesses. "At the mouth of two witnesses, or three witnesses, shall he that is worthy of death be put to death,"[169] says Moses, the first legislator we meet in ancient history. "The laws which put to death a man on the deposition of one witness are fatal to freedom" — says Montesquieu. "Reason claims there should be two witnesses."[170]

Thus the value of evidence has been tacitly agreed upon and accepted in every country. But the scientists will not accept the evidence of the million against one. In vain do hundreds of thousands of men testify to facts. *Oculos habent et non vident!* They are determined to remain blind and deaf. Thirty years of practical demonstrations and the testimony of some millions of believers in America and Europe are certainly entitled to some degree of respect and attention. Especially so, when the verdict of twelve spiritualists, influenced by the evidence testified to by any two others, is competent to send even a scientist to swing on the gallows for a crime, perhaps committed under the impulse supplied by a commotion among the cerebral molecules unrestrained by a consciousness of future moral RETRIBUTION.

Toward science as a whole, as a divine goal, the whole civilized world ought to look with respect and veneration; for science alone can enable man to understand the Deity by the true appreciation of his works. "Science *is the understanding of truth or facts*," says Webster; "it is an investigation of truth *for its own sake* and a pursuit of pure knowledge." If

---

168 Tyndall, Preface to *"Fragments of Science."*
169 *Deuteronomy*, chap. xvii., 6.
170 Montesquieu, *Esprit des Lois I.*, xii., chap. 3.

the definition be correct, then the majority of our modern scholars have proved false to their goddess. "Truth for its own sake!" And where should the keys to every truth in nature be searched for, unless in the hitherto unexplored mystery of psychology? Alas! that in questioning nature so many men of science should daintily sort over her facts and choose only such for study as best bolster their prejudices.

Psychology has no worse enemies than the medical school denominated *allopathists*. It is in vain to remind them that of the so-called exact sciences, medicine, confessedly, least deserves the name. Although of all branches of medical knowledge, psychology ought more than any other to be studied by physicians, since without its help their practice degenerates into mere guess-work and chance-intuitions, they almost wholly neglect it. The least dissent from their promulgated doctrines is resented as a heresy, and though an unpopular and unrecognized curative method should be shown to save thousands, they seem, as a body, disposed to cling to accepted hypotheses and prescriptions, and decry both innovator and innovation until they get the mint-stamp of *regularity*. Thousands of unlucky patients may die meanwhile, but so long as professional honor is vindicated, this is a matter of secondary importance.

Theoretically the most benignant, at the same time no other school of science exhibits so many instances of petty prejudice, materialism, atheism, and malicious stubbornness as medicine. The predilections and patronage of the leading physicians are scarcely ever measured by the usefulness of a discovery. Bleeding, by leeching, cupping, and the lancet, had its epidemic of popularity, but at last fell into merited disgrace; water, now freely given to fevered patients, was once denied them, warm baths were superseded by cold water, and for a while hydropathy was a mania. Peruvian bark — which a modern defender of biblical authority seriously endeavors to identify with the paradisiacal "Tree of Life,"[171] and which was brought to Spain in 1632 — was neglected for years. The Church, for once, showed more discrimination than science. At the request of Cardinal de Lugo, Innocent X. gave it the prestige of his powerful name.

Borrowed Robes

In an old book entitled *Demonologia,* the author cites many instances of important remedies which being neglected at first afterward rose into notice through mere accident. He also shows that most of the new discoveries in medicine have turned out to be no more than "the revival and readoption of very ancient practices." During the last century, the root of the male fern was sold and widely advertised as a secret nostrum by a Madame Nouffleur, a female quack, for the effective cure of the tapeworm. The secret was bought by Louis XV. for a large sum of money; after which the physicians discovered that it was recommended and administered in that disease by Galen. The famous powder of the Duke of Portland for the gout, was the *diacentaureon* of Cælius Aurelianus. Later it was ascertained that it had been used by the earliest medical writers, who had found it in the writings of the old Greek philosophers. So with the *eau medicinale* of Dr. Husson, whose name it bears. This famous remedy for the gout was recognized under its new mask to be the *Colchicum autumnale,* or meadow saffron, which is identical with a plant called

---

171 C. B. Warring.

Hermodactylus, whose merits as a certain antidote to gout were recognized and defended by Oribasius, a great physician of the fourth century, and Ætius Amidenus, another eminent physician of Alexandria (fifth century). Subsequently it was abandoned and fell into disfavor only because it was *too old* to be considered good by the members of the medical faculties that flourished toward the end of the last century!

Even the great Magendie, the wise physiologist, was not above discovering that which had already been discovered and found good by the oldest physicians. His proposed remedy against consumption, namely, the use of prussic acid, may be found in the works of Linnæus, *Amenitates Academicæ,* vol. iv., in which he shows distilled laurel water to have been used with great profit in pulmonary consumption. Pliny also assures us that the extract of almonds and cherry-pits had cured the most obstinate coughs. As the author of *Demonologia* well remarks, it may be asserted with perfect safety that "all the various secret preparations of opium which have been lauded as the discovery of modern times, may be recognized in the works of ancient authors," who see themselves so discredited in our days.

It is admitted on all hands that from time immemorial the distant East was the land of knowledge. Not even in Egypt were botany and mineralogy so extensively studied as by the savants of archaic Middle Asia. Sprengel, unjust and prejudiced as he shows himself in everything else, confesses this much in his *Histoire de la Medicine.* And yet, notwithstanding this, whenever the subject of magic is discussed, that of India has rarely suggested itself to any one, for of its general practice in that country less is known than among any other ancient people. With the Hindus it was and is more esoteric, if possible, than it was even among the Egyptian priests. So sacred was it deemed that its existence was only half admitted, and it was only practiced in public emergencies. *It was more than a religious matter, for it was considered divine.* The Egyptian hierophants, notwithstanding the practice of a stern and pure morality, could not be compared for one moment with the ascetical Gymnosophists, either in holiness of life or miraculous powers developed in them by the supernatural adjuration of everything earthly. By those who knew them well they were held in still greater reverence than the magians of Chaldea. Denying themselves the simplest comforts of life, they dwelt in woods, and led the life of the most secluded hermits,[172] while their Egyptian brothers at least congregated together. Notwithstanding the slur thrown by history on all who practiced magic and divination, it has proclaimed them as possessing the greatest secrets in medical knowledge and unsurpassed skill in its practice. Numerous are the volumes preserved in Hindu convents, in which are recorded the proofs of their learning. To attempt to say whether these Gymnosophists were the real founders of magic in India, or whether they only practiced what had passed to them as an inheritance from the earliest Rishis[173]— the seven primeval sages — would be regarded as a mere speculation by exact scholars. "The care which they took in educating youth, in familiarizing it with generous and virtuous sentiments, did them peculiar honor, and their maxims and discourses, as recorded by historians, prove that they were expert in matters of philosophy,

---

172 Ammianus Marcellinus, xxiii., 6.

173 The Rishis were seven in number, and lived in days anteceding the Vedic period. They were known as sages, and held in reverence like demigods. Haug shows that they occupy in the Brahmanical religion a position answering to that of the twelve sons of Jacob in the Jewish Bible. The Brahmans claim to descend directly from these Rishis.

metaphysics, astronomy, morality, and religion," says a modern writer. They preserved their dignity under the sway of the most powerful princes, whom they would *not* condescend to visit, or to trouble for the slightest favor. If the latter desired the advice or the prayers of the holy men, they were either obliged to go themselves, or to send messengers. To these men no secret power of either plant or mineral was unknown. They had fathomed nature to its depths, while psychology and physiology were to them open books, and the result was that science or machagiotia that is now termed, so superciliously, *magic*.

While the miracles recorded in the Bible have become accepted facts with the Christians, to disbelieve which is regarded as infidelity, the narratives of wonders and prodigies found in the *Atharva-Veda*,[174] either provoke their contempt or are viewed as evidences of diabolism. And yet, in more than one respect, and notwithstanding the unwillingness of certain Sanscrit scholars, we can show the identity between the two. Moreover, as the Vedas have now been proved by scholars to antedate the Jewish *Bible* by many ages, the inference is an easy one that if one of them has borrowed from the other, the Hindu sacred books are not to be charged with plagiarism.

First of all, their cosmogony shows how erroneous has been the opinion prevalent among the civilized nations that Brahma was ever considered by the Hindus their chief or Supreme God. Brahma is a secondary deity, and like Jehovah is "a *mover of the waters.*" He is the *creating* god, and has in his allegorical representations four heads, answering to the four cardinal points. He is the demiurgos, the *architect* of the world. "In the primordiate state of the creation," says Polier's *Mythologie des Indous*, "the rudimental universe, submerged in water, reposed in the bosom of the Eternal. Sprang from this chaos and darkness, Brahma, the architect of the world, poised on a lotus-leaf floated (moved?) upon the waters, unable to discern anything but water and darkness." This is as identical as possible with the Egyptian cosmogony, which shows in its opening sentences Athtor[175] or Mother Night (which represents illimitable darkness) as the primeval element which covered the infinite abyss, animated by water and the universal spirit of the Eternal, dwelling alone in Chaos. As in the Jewish Scriptures, the history of the creation opens with the spirit of God and his creative emanation — another Deity.[176] Perceiving such a dismal state of things, Brahma soliloquizes in consternation: "Who am I? Whence came I?" Then he hears a voice: "Direct your prayer to Bhagavant — the Eternal, known, also, as Parabrahma." Brahma, rising from his natatory position, seats himself upon the lotus in an attitude of contemplation, and reflects upon the Eternal, who, pleased with this evidence of piety, disperses the primeval darkness and opens his understanding. "After this Brahma issues from the universal egg — (infinite chaos) as *light*, for his understanding is now opened, and he sets himself to work; he *moves* on the eternal waters, with the spirit of God within himself; in his capacity of *mover* of the waters he is *Narayana*."

The lotus, the sacred flower of the Egyptians, as well as the Hindus, is the symbol of Horus as it is that of Brahma. No temples in Thibet or Nepaul are found without it; and the meaning of this symbol is extremely suggestive. The sprig of *lilies* placed in the hand of the

---

174 The fourth Veda.
175 Orthography of the "Archaic Dictionary."
176 We do not mean the current or accepted Bible, but the *real* Jewish one explained kabalistically.

archangel, who offers them to the Virgin Mary, in the pictures of the "Annunciation," have in their esoteric symbolism precisely the same meaning. We refer the reader to Sir William Jones.[177] With the Hindus, the lotus is the emblem of the productive power of nature, through the agency of fire and water (spirit and matter). "Eternal!" says a verse in the *Bhagavad Gita*, "I see Brahma the creator enthroned in *thee* above the lotus!" and Sir W. Jones shows that the seeds of the lotus contain — even before they germinate — perfectly-formed leaves, the miniature shapes of what one day, as perfected plants, they will become; or, as the author of *The Heathen Religion*, has it — "nature thus giving us a specimen of the *preformation* of its productions"; adding further that "the seed of all *phœnogamous* plants bearing *proper* flowers, contain *an embryo plantlet ready formed*."[178]

EMANATION OF THE OBJECTIVE UNIVERSE FROM THE SUBJECTIVE

With the Buddhists, it has the same signification. Maha-Maya, or Maha-Deva, the mother of Gautama Buddha, had the birth of her son announced to her by Bhodisat (the spirit of Buddha), who appeared beside her couch with a *lotus* in his hand. Thus, also, Osiris and Horus are represented by the Egyptians constantly in association with the lotus-flower.

These facts all go to show the identical parentage of this idea in the three religious systems, Hindu, Egyptian and Judaico-Christian. Wherever the mystic water-lily (lotus) is employed, it signifies the emanation of the objective from the concealed, or subjective — the eternal thought of the ever-invisible Deity passing from the abstract into the concrete or visible form. For as soon as darkness was dispersed and "there was light," Brahma's understanding was opened, and he saw in the ideal world (which had hitherto lain eternally concealed in the Divine thought) the archetypal forms of all the infinite future things that would be called into existence, and hence become visible. At this first stage of action, Brahma had not yet become the architect, the builder of the universe, for he had, like the architect, to first acquaint himself with the plan, and realize the ideal forms which were buried in the bosom of the Eternal One, as the future lotus-leaves are concealed within the seed of that plant. And it is in this idea that we must look for the origin and explanation of the verse in the Jewish cosmogony, which reads: "And God said, Let the earth bring forth . . . the fruit-tree yielding fruit after his kind, *whose seed is in itself*." In all the primitive religions, the "Son of the Father" is the creative God — *i.e.*, His thought made visible; and before the Christian era, from the Trimurti of the Hindus down to the three kabalistic heads of the Jewish-explained scriptures, the triune godhead of each nation was fully defined and substantiated in its allegories. In the Christian creed we see but the artificial engrafting of a new branch upon the old trunk; and the adoption by the Greek and Roman churches of the lily-symbol held by the archangel at the moment of the Annunciation, shows a thought of precisely the same metaphysical significance.

The lotus is the product of fire (heat) and water, hence the dual symbol of spirit and matter. The God Brahma is the second person of the Trinity, as are Jehovah (Adam-Kadmon) and Osiris, or rather Pimander, or the Power of the Thought Divine, of Hermes; for it is Pimander who represents the root of all the Egyptian Sun-gods. The Eternal is the

---

177 *"Dissertations Relating to Asia."*
178 Dr. Gross, p. 195.

Spirit of Fire, which stirs up and fructifies and develops into a concrete form everything that is born of water or the primordial earth, evolved out of Brahma; but the universe is itself Brahma, and he is the universe. This is the philosophy of Spinoza, which he derived from that of Pythagoras; and it is the same for which Bruno died a martyr. How much Christian theology has gone astray from its point of departure, is demonstrated in this historical fact. Bruno was slaughtered for the exegesis of a symbol that was adopted by the earliest Christians, and expounded by the apostles! The sprig of water-lilies of Bhodisat, and later of Gabriel, typifying fire and water, or the idea of creation and generation, is worked into the earliest dogma of the baptismal sacrament.

Bruno's and Spinoza's doctrines are nearly identical, though the words of the latter are more veiled, and far more cautiously chosen than those to be found in the theories of the author of the *Causa Principio et Uno*, or the *Infinito Universo e Mondi*. Both Bruno, who confesses that the source of his information was Pythagoras, and Spinoza, who, without acknowledging it as frankly, allows his philosophy to betray the secret, view the First Cause from the same stand-point. With them, God is an Entity totally *per se*, an Infinite Spirit, and the only Being utterly free and independent of either effects or other causes; who, through that same Will which produced all things and gave the first impulse to every cosmic law, perpetually keeps in existence and order everything in the universe. As well as the Hindu Swâbhâvikas, erroneously called Atheists, who assume that all things, men as well as gods and spirits, were born from Swabhâva, or their own nature,[179] both Spinoza and Bruno were led to the conclusion that *God is to be sought for within nature and not without*. For, creation being proportional to the power of the Creator, the universe as well as its Creator must be infinite and eternal, one form emanating from its own essence, and creating in its turn another. The modern commentators affirm that Bruno, "*unsustained by the hope of another and better world*, still surrendered his life rather than his convictions"; thereby allowing it to be inferred that Giordano Bruno had no belief in the continued existence of man after death. Professor Draper asserts most positively that Bruno did not believe in the immortality of the soul. Speaking of the countless victims of the religious intolerance of the Popish Church, he remarks: "The passage from this life to the next, though through a hard trial, was the passage from a transient trouble to eternal happiness. . . . On his way through the dark valley, the martyr believed that there was an invisible hand that would lead him. . . . For Bruno there was no such support. The philosophical opinions, for the sake of which he surrendered his life, could give him no consolation."[180]

But Professor Draper seems to have a very superficial knowledge of the true belief of the philosophers. We can leave Spinoza out of the question, and even allow him to remain in the eyes of his critics an utter atheist and materialist; for the cautious reserve which he placed upon himself in his writings makes it extremely difficult for one who does not read him between the lines, and is not thoroughly acquainted with the hidden meaning of the

---

179 Brahma does *not* create the earth, *Mirtlok*, any more than the rest of the universe. Having evolved himself from the soul of the world, once separated from the First Cause, he emanates in his turn all nature out of himself. He does not stand above it, but is mixed up with it; and Brahma and the universe form one Being, each particle of which is in its essence Brahma himself, who proceeded out of himself. [Burnouf, "Introduction," p. 118.]

180 "*Conflict between Religion and Science*," 180.

Pythagorean metaphysics, to ascertain what his real sentiments were. But as for Giordano Bruno, if he adhered to the doctrines of Pythagoras he must have believed in another life, hence, he could not have been an atheist whose philosophy offered him no such "consolation." His accusation and subsequent confession, as given by Professor Domenico Berti, in his *Life of Bruno,* and compiled from original documents recently published, proved beyond doubt what were his *real* philosophy, creed and doctrines. In common with the Alexandrian Platonists, and the later Kabalists, he held that Jesus was a magician in the sense given to this appellation by Porphyry and Cicero, who call it the *divina sapientia* (divine knowledge), and by Philo Judæs, who described the Magi as the most wonderful inquirers into the hidden mysteries of nature, not in the degrading sense given to the word magic in our century. In his noble conception, *the Magi were holy men, who, setting themselves apart from everything else on this earth, contemplated the divine virtues and understood the divine nature of the gods and spirits, the more clearly; and so, initiated others into the same mysteries, which consist in one holding an uninterrupted intercourse with these invisible beings during life.* But we will show Bruno's inmost philosophical convictions better by quoting fragments from the *accusation* and his *own confession.*

The charges in the denunciation of Mocenigo, his accuser, are expressed in the following terms:

"I, Zuane Mocenigo, son of the most illustrious Ser Marcantonio, denounce to your very reverend fathership, by constraint of my conscience and by order of my confessor, that I have heard say by Giordano Bruno, several times when he discoursed with me in my house, that it is great blasphemy in Catholics to say that the bread transubstantiates itself into flesh; that he is opposed to the Mass; that no religion pleases him; that Christ was a wretch (*un tristo*), and that if he did wicked works to seduce the people he might well predict that He ought to be impaled; that there is no distinction of persons in God, and that it would be imperfection in God; that the world is eternal, and that there are infinite worlds, and that God makes them continually, because, he says, He desires all He can; that Christ did apparent miracles and was a *magician,* and so were the apostles, and that he had a mind to do as much and more than they did; that Christ showed an unwillingness to die, and shunned death all He could; that there is no punishment of sin, and that souls created by the operation of nature pass from one animal to another, and that as the brute animals are born of corruption, so also are men when after dissolution they come to be born again."

Perfidious as they are, the above words plainly indicate the belief of Bruno in the Pythagorean metempsychosis, which, misunderstood as it is, still shows a belief in the *survival* of man in one shape or another. Further, the accuser says:

"He has shown indications of wishing to make himself the author of a new sect, under the name of 'New Philosophy.' He has said that the Virgin could not have brought forth, and that our Catholic faith is all full of blasphemies against the majesty of God; that the monks ought to be deprived of the right of disputation and their revenues, because they pollute the world; that they are all asses, and that our opinions are doctrines of asses; that we have no proof that our faith has merit with God, and that not to do to others what we would not have done to ourselves suffices for a good life, and that he laughs at all other sins, and wonders how God can endure so many heresies in Catholics. He says that he means to apply himself to the art of divination, and make all the world run after him; that St. Thomas and all the Doctors knew nothing to compare with him, and that he could ask questions of all the first theologians of the world that they could not answer."

To this, the accused philosopher answered by the following profession of faith, which is that of every disciple of the ancient masters:

"I hold, in brief, to an infinite universe, that is, an effect of infinite divine power, because I esteemed it a thing unworthy of divine goodness and power, that being able to produce besides this world another and infinite others, it should produce a finite world. Thus I have declared that there are infinite particular worlds similar to this of the earth, which, with Pythagoras, I understand to be a star similar in nature with the moon, the other planets, and the other stars, which are infinite; and that all those bodies are worlds, and without number, which thus constitute the infinite universality in an infinite space, and this is called the infinite universe, in which are innumerable worlds, so that there is a double kind of infinite greatness in the universe, and of a multitude of worlds. Indirectly, this may be understood to be repugnant to the truth according to the true faith.

"Moreover, I place in this universe a universal Providence, by virtue of which everything lives, vegetates and moves, and stands in its perfection, and I understand it in two ways; one, in the mode in which the whole soul is present in the whole and every part of the body, and this I call nature, the shadow and footprint of divinity; the other, the ineffable mode in which God, by essence, presence, and power, is in all and above all, not as part, not as soul, but in mode inexplicable.

"Moreover, I understand all the attributes in divinity to be one and the same thing. Together with the theologians and great philosophers, I apprehend three attributes, power, wisdom, and goodness, or, rather, mind, intellect, love, with which things have first, being, through the mind; next, ordered and distinct being, through the intellect; and third, concord and symmetry, through love. Thus I understand being in all and over all, as there is nothing without participation in being, and there is no being without essence, just as nothing is beautiful without beauty being present; thus nothing can be free from the divine presence, and thus by way of reason, and not by way of substantial truth, do I understand distinction in divinity.

"Assuming then the world caused and produced, I understand that, according to all its being, it is dependent upon the first cause, so that it did not reject the name of creation, which I understand that Aristotle also has expressed, saying, 'God is that upon whom the world and all nature depends,' so that according to the explanation of St. Thomas, whether it be eternal or in time, it is, according to all its being, dependent on the first cause, and nothing in it is independent.

"Next, in regard to what belongs to the true faith, not speaking philosophically, to come to individuality about the divine persons, the wisdom and the son of the mind, called by philosophers intellect, and by theologians the word, which ought to be believed to have taken on human flesh. But I, abiding in the phrases of philosophy, have not understood it, but have doubted and held it with inconstant faith, not that I remember to have shown marks of it in writing nor in speech, except indirectly from other things, something of it may be gathered as by way of ingenuity and profession in regard to what may be proved by reason and concluded from natural light. Thus, in regard to the Holy Spirit in a third person, I have not been able to comprehend, as ought to be believed, but, according to the

Pythagoric manner, in conformity to the manner shown by Solomon, I have understood it as the soul of the universe, or adjoined to the universe according to the saying of the wisdom of Solomon: 'The spirit of God filled all the earth, and that which contains all things,' all which conforms equally to the Pythagoric doctrine explained by Virgil in the text of the *Æneid*:

> Principio coelum ac terras camposque liquentes,
> Lucentemque globum Lunæ, Titaniaque astra
> Spiritus intus alit, totamque infusa per artus
> Mens agitat molem;

and the lines following.

"From this spirit, then, which is called the life of the universe, I understand, in my philosophy, proceeds life and soul to everything which has life and soul, which, moreover, I understand to be immortal, as also to bodies, which, as to their substance, are all immortal, there being no other death than division and congregation, which doctrine seems expressed in *Ecclesiastes*, where it is said that 'there is nothing new under the sun; that which is is that which was.' "

Furthermore, Bruno confesses his inability to comprehend the doctrine of three persons in the godhead, and his doubts of the incarnation of God in Jesus, but firmly pronounces his belief in the *miracles* of Christ. How could he, being a Pythagorean philosopher, discredit them? If, under the merciless constraint of the Inquisition, he, like Galileo, subsequently recanted, and threw himself upon the clemency of his ecclesiastical persecutors, we must remember that he spoke like a man standing between the rack and the fagot, and human nature cannot always be heroic when the corporeal frame is debilitated by torture and imprisonment.

But for the opportune appearance of Berti's authoritative work, we would have continued to revere Bruno as a martyr, whose bust was deservedly set high in the Pantheon of Exact Science, crowned with laurel by the hand of Draper. But now we see that their hero of an hour is neither atheist, materialist, nor positivist, but simply a Pythagorean who taught the philosophy of Upper Asia, and claimed to possess the powers of the magicians, so despised by Draper's own school! Nothing more amusing than this *contretemps* has happened since the supposed statue of St. Peter was discovered by irreverent archæologists to be nothing else than the Jupiter of the Capitol, and Buddha's identity with the Catholic St. Josaphat was satisfactorily proven.

Thus, search where we may through the archives of history, we find that there is no fragment of modern philosophy — whether Newtonian, Cartesian, Huxleyian or any other — but has been dug from the Oriental mines. Even Positivism and Nihilism find their prototype in the exoteric portion of Kapila's philosophy, as is well remarked by Max Müller. It was the inspiration of the Hindu sages that penetrated the mysteries of Pragnâ Pâramitâ (perfect wisdom); their hands that rocked the cradle of the first ancestor of that feeble but noisy child that we have christened MODERN SCIENCE.

CHAPTER IV

"I choose the nobler part of Emerson, when, after various disenchantments, he exclaimed, 'I covet Truth.' The gladness of true heroism visits the heart of him who is really competent to say this."

TYNDALL

"A testimony is sufficient when it rests on:
1st. A great number of very sensible witnesses who agree in having seen *well*.
2d. Who are sane, bodily and mentally.
3d. Who are impartial and disinterested.
4th. Who unanimously agree.
5th. Who solemnly certify to the fact."

VOLTAIRE

Dictiannaire Philosophique

THE Count Agenor de Gasparin is a devoted Protestant. His battle with des Mousseaux, de Mirville and other fanatics who laid the whole of the spiritual phenomena at the door of Satan, was long and fierce. Two volumes of over fifteen hundred pages are the result, proving the *effects,* denying the *cause,* and employing superhuman efforts to invent every other possible explanation that could be suggested rather than the true one.

The severe rebuke received by the *Journal des Debats* from M. de Gasparin, was read by all civilized Europe.[181] After that gentleman had minutely described numerous manifestations that he had witnessed himself, this journal very impertinently proposed to the authorities in France to send all those who, after having read the *fine* analysis of the "spiritual hallucinations" published by Faraday, should insist on crediting this delusion, to the lunatic asylum for *Incurables.* "Take care," wrote de Gasparin in answer, "the representatives of the exact sciences are on their way to become . . . the *Inquisitors* of our days. . . . Facts are stronger than Academies. Rejected, denied, mocked, they nevertheless are facts, and *do* exist."[182]

THEORY OF DE GASPARIN

The following affirmations of physical phenomena, as witnessed by himself and Professor Thury, may be found in de Gasparin's voluminous work.

THEORY OF THURY

"The experimenters have often seen the legs of the table glued, so to say, to the floor, and, notwithstanding the excitement of those present, refuse to be moved from their place.

---

181 *"Des Tables,"* vol. i, p. 213.
182 Ibid., 216.

On other occasions they have seen the tables levitated in quite an energetic way. They heard, with their own ears, loud as well as gentle raps, the former threatening to shatter the table to pieces on account of their violence, the latter so soft as to become hardly perceptible. . . . As to Levitations Without Contact, we found means to produce them easily, and with success. . . . And such levitations do not pertain to isolated results. We have reproduced them over Thirty times. [183] . . . One day the table will turn, and lift its legs successively, its weight being augmented by a man weighing eighty-seven kilogrammes seated on it; another time it will remain motionless and immovable, notwithstanding that the person placed on it weighs but sixty..[184] . . On one occasion we willed it to turn upside down, and it turned over, with its legs in the air, notwithstanding that our fingers never touched it once." [185]

THEORY OF DES MOUSSEAUX, DE MIRVILLE

"It is certain," remarks de Mirville, "that a man who had repeatedly witnessed such a phenomenon, could not accept the *fine* analysis of the English physicist."[186]

Since 1850, des Mousseaux and de Mirville, uncompromising Roman Catholics, have published many volumes whose titles are cleverly contrived to attract public attention. They betray on the part of the authors a very serious alarm, which, moreover, they take no pains to conceal. Were it possible to consider the phenomena spurious, the church of Rome would never have gone so much out of her way to repress them.

Both sides having agreed upon the facts, leaving skeptics out of the question, people could divide themselves into but two parties: the believers in the direct agency of the devil, and the believers in disembodied and other spirits. The fact alone, that theology dreaded a great deal more the revelations which might come through this mysterious agency than all the threatening "conflicts" with Science and the categorical denials of the latter, ought to have opened the eyes of the most skeptical. The church of Rome has never been either credulous or cowardly, as is abundantly proved by the Machiavellism which marks her policy. Moreover, she has never troubled herself much about the clever prestidigitateurs whom she *knew* to be simply adepts in juggling. Robert Houdin, Comte, Hamilton and Bosco, slept secure in their beds, while she persecuted such men as Paracelsus, Cagliostro, and Mesmer, the Hermetic philosophers and mystics — and effectually stopped every genuine manifestation of an occult nature by killing the mediums.

Those who are unable to believe in a personal devil and the dogmas of the church must nevertheless accord to the clergy enough of shrewdness to prevent the compromising of her reputation for infallibility by making so much of manifestations which, if fraudulent, must inevitably be some day exposed. But the best testimony to the reality of this force was given by Robert Houdin himself, the king of jugglers, who, upon being called as an expert by the Academy to witness the wonderful *clairvoyant* powers and occasional mistakes of a table, said: "We jugglers never make mistakes, and my second-sight never failed me yet."

---

183 *"Des Tables,"* vol. i., p. 48.
184 Ibid., p. 24.
185 Ibid., p. 35.
186 De Mirville, *"Des Esprits,"* p. 26.

THEORY OF BABINET

The learned astronomer Babinet was not more fortunate in his selection of Comte, the celebrated ventriloquist, as an expert to testify against the phenomena of direct voices and the rappings. Comte, if we may believe the witnesses, laughed in the face of Babinet at the bare suggestion that the raps were produced by "*unconscious ventriloquism!*" The latter theory, worthy twin-sister of "*unconscious cerebration,*" caused many of the most skeptical academicians to blush. Its absurdity was too apparent.

"The problem of the supernatural," says de Gasparin, "such as it was presented by the middle ages, and as it stands now, is not among the number of those which we are permitted to despise; its breadth and grandeur escape the notice of no one. . . . Everything is profoundly serious in it, both the evil and the remedy, the superstitious recrudescency, and the physical fact which is destined to conquer the latter." [187]

THEORY OF HOUDIN

Further, he pronounces the following decisive opinion, to which he came, conquered by the various manifestations, as he says himself — "The number of facts which claim their place in the broad daylight of truth, has so much increased of late, that of two consequences one is henceforth inevitable: either the domain of natural sciences must consent to expand itself, or the domain of the supernatural will become so enlarged as to have no bounds." [188]

Among the multitude of books against spiritualism emanating from Catholic and Protestant sources, none have produced a more appalling effect than the works of de Mirville and des Mousseaux: *La Magie au XIXme Siecle — Mœurs et Pratiques des Demons — Hauts Phénoménes de la Magie — Les Mediateurs de la Magie — Des Esprits et de leurs Manifestations*, etc. They comprise the most cyclopædic biography of the devil and his imps that has appeared for the private delectation of good Catholics since the middle ages.

THEORY OF MM. ROYER AND JOBART DE LAMBALLE

According to the authors, *he* who was "a liar and murderer from the beginning," was also the principal motor of spiritual phenomena. He had been for thousands of years at the head of pagan theurgy; and it was he, again, who, encouraged by the increase of heresies, infidelity, and atheism, had reappeared in our century. The French Academy lifted up its voice in a general outcry of indignation, and M. de Gasparin even took it for a personal insult. "This is a declaration of war, a 'levée of shields' " — wrote he in his voluminous book of refutations. "The work of M. de Mirville is a real *manifesto*. . . . I would be glad to see in it the expression of a strictly individual opinion, but, in truth, it is *impossible*. The success of the work, these solemn adhesions, the faithful reproduction of its theses by the journals and writers of the party, the solidarity established throughout between them and the whole body of catholicity . . . everything goes to show a work which *is essentially an act, and has the*

---

187 "*Avant propos,*" pp. 12 and 16.
188 Vol. i., p. 244.

value of a collective labor. As it is, I felt that I had a duty to perform. . . . I felt obliged to pick up the glove. . . . and lift high the Protestant flag against the Ultramontane banner."[189]

The medical faculties, as might have been expected, assuming the part of the Greek chorus, echoed the various expostulations against the demonological authors. The *Medico-Psychological Annals,* edited by Drs. Brierre de Boismont and Cerise, published the following: "Outside these controversies of antagonistical parties, never in our country did a writer dare to face, with a more aggressive serenity, . . . the sarcasms, the scorn of what we term common sense; and, as if to defy and challenge at the same time thundering peals of laughter and shrugging of shoulders, the author strikes an attitude, and placing himself with effrontery before the members of the Academy . . . addresses to them what he modestly terms his *Memoire on the Devil!*"[190]

That was a cutting insult to the Academicians, to be sure; but ever since 1850 they seem to have been doomed to suffer in their pride more than most of them can bear. The idea of asking the attention of the forty "Immortals" to the pranks of the Devil! They vowed revenge, and, leaguing themselves together, propounded a theory which exceeded in absurdity even de Mirville's demonolatry! Dr. Royer and Jobart de Lamballe — both celebrities in their way — formed an alliance and presented to the Institute a German whose cleverness afforded, according to his statement, the key to all the knockings and rappings of both hemispheres. "We blush" — remarks the Marquis de Mirville — "to say that the whole of the trick consisted simply in the reiterated displacement of one of the muscular tendons of the legs. Great demonstration of the system in full sitting of the Institute — and on the spot . . . expressions of Academical gratitude for this *interesting* communication, and, a few days later, a full assurance given to the public by a professor of the medical faculty, that, scientists having pronounced their opinion, the mystery was at last unravelled!"[191]

But such *scientific* explanations neither prevented the phenomenon from quietly following its course, nor the two writers on demonology from proceeding to expound their strictly orthodox theories. Denying that the Church had anything to do with his books, des Mousseaux gravely gave the Academy, in addition to his *Memoire,* the following interesting and profoundly philosophical thoughts on Satan: "*The Devil is the chief pillar of Faith.* He is one of the grand personages whose life is closely allied to that of the church; and without his speech which issued out so triumphantly from the mouth of the Serpent, *his medium,* the fall of man could not have taken place. Thus, if it was not for him, the Saviour, the Crucified, the Redeemer, would be but the most ridiculous of supernumeraries, and the Cross an insult to good sense!"[192]

This writer, be it remembered, is only the faithful echo of the church, which anathematizes equally the one who denies God and him who doubts the objective existence of Satan. But the Marquis de Mirville carries this idea of God's partnership with the Devil still further. According to him it is a regular commercial affair, in which the senior "silent partner" suffers the active business of the firm to be transacted as it may please his junior

---

189 Vol. ii., p. 524.

190 "*Medico-Psychological Annals,*" Jan. 1, 1854.

191 De Mirville, "*Des Esprits,*" "*Constitutionnel,*" June 16, 1854.

192 Chevalier des Mousseaux, "*Moeurs et Pratiques des Demons,*" p. x.

associate, by whose audacity and industry he profits. Who could be of any other opinion, upon reading the following?

"At the moment of this spiritual invasion of 1853, so slightingly regarded, we had dared to pronounce the word of a 'threatening catastrophe.' The world was nevertheless at peace, but history showing us the same symptoms at all disastrous epochs, we had a presentiment of the sad effects of a law which Goerres has formulated thus: [vol. v., p. 356.] 'These mysterious apparitions have invariably indicated the chastening hand of God on earth.' "[193]

These guerilla-skirmishes between the champions of the clergy and the materialistic Academy of Science, prove abundantly how little the latter has done toward uprooting blind fanaticism from the minds of even very educated persons. *Evidently science has neither completely conquered nor muzzled theology.* She will master her only on that day when she will condescend to see in the spiritual phenomenon something besides mere hallucination and charlatanry. But how can she do it without investigating it thoroughly? Let us suppose that before the time when electro-magnetism was publicly acknowledged, the Copenhagen Professor Oersted, its discoverer, had been suffering from an attack of what we call *psychophobia,* or *pneumatophobia.* He notices that the wire along which a voltaic current is passing shows a tendency to turn the magnetic needle from its natural position to one perpendicular to the direction of the current. Suppose, moreover, that the professor had heard much of certain superstitious people who used that kind of magnetized needles to converse with unseen intelligences. That they received signals and even held correct conversations with them by means of the tippings of such a needle, and that in consequence he suddenly felt a scientific horror and disgust for such an ignorant belief, and refused, point-blank, to have anything to do with such a needle. What would have been the result? Electro-magnetism might not have been discovered till now, and our experimentalists would have been the principal losers thereby.

Babinet, Royer, and Jobert de Lamballe, all three members of the Institute, particularly distinguished themselves in this struggle between skepticism and supernaturalism, and most assuredly have reaped no laurels. The famous astronomer had imprudently risked himself on the battlefield of the phenomenon. He had *explained* scientifically the manifestations. But, emboldened by the fond belief among scientists that the new epidemic could not stand close investigation nor outlive the year, he had the still greater imprudence to publish two articles on them. As M. de Mirville very wittily remarks, if both of the articles had but a poor success in the scientific press, they had, on the other hand, none at all in the daily one.

M. Babinet began by accepting *a priori,* the rotation and movements of the furniture, which fact he declared to be "*hors de doute.*" "This rotation," he said, "being able to manifest itself with a considerable energy, either by a very great speed, or by a strong resistance when it is desired that it should stop."[194]

Now comes the explanation of the eminent scientist. "Gently pushed by little concordant impulsions of the hands laid upon it, the table begins to oscillate from right to left. . . . At the moment when, after more or less delay, a nervous trepidation is established in the hands

193 De Mirville, "*Des Esprits,*" p. 4.
194 Ibid., "*Revue des Deux Mondes,*" January 15, 1854, p. 108.

and the little individual impulses of all the experimenters have become harmonized, the table is set in motion."[195]

He finds it very simple, for "all muscular movements are determined over bodies by levers of the third order, in which the fulcrum is very near to the point where the force acts. This, consequently, communicates a great speed to the mobile parts for the very little distance which the motor force has to run. . . . Some persons are astonished to see a table subjected to the action of several well-disposed individuals in a fair way to *conquer powerful obstacles*, even break its legs, when suddenly stopped; but that is *very simple* if we consider the power of the *little concordant actions*. . . . Once more, the physical explanation offers no difficulty."[196]

In this dissertation, two results are clearly shown: the reality of the phenomena proved, and the scientific explanation made ridiculous. But M. Babinet can well afford to be laughed at a little; he knows, as an astronomer, that dark spots are to be found even in the sun.

There is one thing, though, that Babinet has always stoutly denied, viz.: the levitation of furniture without contact. De Mirville catches him proclaiming that such levitation is impossible: "simply *impossible*," he says, "as impossible as perpetual motion."[197]

The Twins "Unconscious Cerebration" and "Unconscious Ventriloquism"

Who can take upon himself, after such a declaration, to maintain that the word *impossible* pronounced by science is infallible? But the tables, after having waltzed, oscillated and turned, began tipping and rapping. The raps were sometimes as powerful as pistol-detonations. What of this? Listen: "The witnesses and investigators are *ventriloquists!*"

De Mirville refers us to the *Revue des Deux Mondes*, in which is published a very interesting dialogue, invented by M. Babinet speaking of himself to himself, like the Chaldean En-Soph of the Kabalists: "What can we finally say of all these facts brought under our observation? Are there such raps produced? Yes. Do such raps answer questions? Yes. Who produces these sounds? The mediums. By what means? *By the ordinary acoustic method of the ventriloquists.* But we were given to suppose that these sounds might result from the *cracking of the toes and fingers?* No; for then they would always proceed from the same point, and such is not the fact."[198]

"Now," asks de Mirville, "what are we to believe of the Americans, and their *thousands of mediums* who produce the same raps before millions of witnesses?" "*Ventriloquism*, to be sure," answers Babinet. "But how can you explain such an impossibility?" The easiest thing in the world; listen only: "All that was necessary to produce the first manifestation in the *first house* in America was, a street-boy knocking at the door of a mystified citizen, perhaps with a leaden ball attached to a string, and if Mr. Weekman (the first believer in America)

---

195 This is a repetition and variation of Faraday's theory.
196 "*Revue des Deux Mondes*," p. 410.
197 "*Revue des Deux Mondes*," January, 1854, p. 414.
198 "*Revue des Deux Mondes*," May 1, 1854, p. 531.

(?)[199] when he watched for the third time, heard no shouts of laughter in the street, it is because of the essential difference which exists between a French street-Arab, and an English or Trans-Atlantic one, the latter being amply provided with what we call a *sad merriment, "gaité triste."*[200]

Truly says de Mirville in his famous reply to the attacks of de Gasparin, Babinet, and other scientists: "and thus according to our great physicist, *the tables turn* very quickly, very energetically, resist likewise, and, as M. de Gasparin has proved, they *levitate without contact.* Said a minister: 'With three words of a man's handwriting, I take upon myself to have him hung.' With the above three lines, we take upon ourselves, in our turn, to throw into the greatest confusion the physicists of all the globe, or rather to revolutionize the world — if at least, M. de Babinet had taken the precaution of suggesting, like M. de Gasparin, some yet unknown law or force. For this would cover the whole ground."[201]

But it is in the notes embracing the "facts and physical theories," that we find the acme of the consistency and logic of Babinet as an expert investigator on the field of Spiritualism.

It would appear, that M. de Mirville in his narrative of the wonders manifested at the *Presbytere de Cideville,* § was much struck by the marvellousness of some facts. Though authenticated before the inquest and magistrates, they were of so miraculous a nature as to force the demonological author himself to shrink from the responsibility of publishing them.

These facts were as follows: "At the precise moment *predicted* by a *sorcerer"* — case of revenge — "a violent clap of thunder was heard above one of the chimneys of the presbytery, after which the *fluid* descended with a formidable noise through that passage, threw down believers as well as skeptics (as to the power of the sorcerer) who were warming themselves by the fire; and, having filled the room with a multitude of *fantastic animals,* returned to the chimney, and having reascended it, disappeared, after producing the same terrible noise. "As," adds de Mirville, "we were already but too rich in facts, we recoiled before this new enormity added to so many others."[202]

But Babinet, who in common with his learned colleagues had made such fun of the two writers on demonology, and who was determined, moreover, to prove the absurdity of all like stories, felt himself obliged to discredit the above-mentioned fact of the Cideville phenomena, by presenting one still more incredible. We yield the floor to M. Babinet, himself.

The following circumstance which he gave to the Academy of Sciences, on July 5, 1852, can be found *without further commentary,* and merely as an instance of a *sphere-like lightning,* in the "*Œuvres de F. Arago,*" vol. i., p. 52. We offer it *verbatim.*

"After a strong clap of thunder," says M. Babinet, "but not immediately following it, a tailor apprentice, living in the Rue St. Jacques, was just finishing his dinner, when he saw the paper-screen which shut the fireplace fall down as if pushed out of its place by a

199 We translate *verbatim.* We doubt whether Mr. Weekman was the first investigator.
200 Babinet, "*Revue des Deux Mondes,*" May 1, 1854, p. 511.
201 De Mirville, "*Des Esprits,*" p. 33.
202 Notes, "*Des Esprits,*" p. 38.

moderate gust of wind. Immediately after that he perceived a globe of fire, as large as the head of a child, come out *quietly* and *softly* from within the grate and slowly move about the room, without touching the bricks of the floor. The aspect of this fire-globe was that of a *young cat,* of middle size . . . moving itself without the use of its paws. The fire-globe was rather brilliant and luminous than hot or inflamed, and the tailor had no sensation of warmth. This globe approached his feet like a young cat which wishes to play and rub itself against the legs, as is habitual to these animals; but the apprentice withdrew his feet from it, and moving with great caution, avoided contact with the *meteor.* The latter remained for a few seconds moving about his legs, the tailor examining it with great curiosity and bending over it. After having tried several excursions in opposite directions, but without leaving the centre of the room, the fire-globe elevated itself vertically to the level of the man's head, who to avoid its contact with his face, threw himself backward on his chair. Arrived at about a yard from the floor the fire-globe slightly lengthened, took an oblique direction toward a hole in the wall over the fireplace, at about the height of a *metre* above the mantelpiece." This hole had been made for the purpose of admitting the pipe of a stove in winter; but, according to the expression of the tailor, "*the thunder could not see it,* for it was papered over like the rest of the wall. The fire-globe went directly to that hole, *unglued the paper without damaging it,* and reasscended the chimney . . . when it arrived at the top, which it did very slowly . . . at least sixty feet above ground . . . it produced a most frightful explosion, which partly destroyed the chimney, . . ." etc.

"It seems," remarks de Mirville in his review, "that we could apply to M. Babinet the following remark made by a very witty woman to Raynal, 'If you are not a Christian, it is not for lack of faith.' "[203]

It was not alone believers who wondered at the credulity displayed by M. Babinet, in persisting to call the manifestation a *meteor;* for Dr. Boudin mentions it very seriously in a work on *lightning* he was just then publishing. "If these details are exact," says the doctor, "as they seem to be, since they are admitted by MM. Babinet and Arago, it appears very difficult for the phenomenon to retain its appellation of *sphere-shaped lightning.* However, we leave it to others to explain, if they can, the *essence of a fire-globe emitting no sensation of heat, having the aspect of a cat, slowly promenading in a room, which finds means to escape by reascending the chimney through an aperture in the wall covered over with a paper which it unglues without damaging!*"[204]

"We are of the same opinion," adds the marquis, "as the learned doctor, on the difficulty of an exact definition, and we do not see why we should not have in future lightning in the shape of a dog, of a monkey, etc., etc. One shudders at the bare idea of a whole meteorological *menagerie,* which, thanks to *thunder,* might come down to our rooms to promenade themselves at will."

Says de Gasparin, in his monster volume of refutations: "In questions of testimony, certitude must absolutely cease the moment we cross the borders of the supernatural."[205]

---

203 De Mirville, "*Faits et Théories Physiques,*" p. 46.
204 See Monograph, "*Of the Lightning considered from the point of view of the history of Legal Medicine and Public Hygiene,*" by M. Boudin, Chief Surgeon of the Military Hospital of Boule.
205 De Gasparin, vol. i., page 288.

The line of demarcation not being sufficiently fixed and determined, which of the opponents is best fitted to take upon himself the difficult task? Which of the two is better entitled to become the public arbiter? Is it the party of superstition, which is supported in its testimony by the evidence of many thousands of people? For nearly two years they crowded the country where were daily manifested the unprecedented miracles of Cideville, now nearly forgotten among other countless spiritual phenomena; shall we believe them, or shall we bow to science, represented by Babinet, who, on the testimony of *one* man (the tailor), accepts the manifestation of the fire-globe, or the *meteor-cat*, and henceforth claims for it a place among the established facts of *natural* phenomena?

Mr. Crookes, in his first article in the *Quarterly Journal of Science*, October 1, 1871, mentions de Gasparin and his work *Science* v. *Spiritualism*. He remarks that "the author finally arrived at the conclusion that all these phenomena are to be accounted for by the action of natural causes, and do not require the supposition of miracles, nor the intervention of spirits and diabolical influences! Gasparin considers it as a fact fully established by his experiments, that *the will, in certain states of organism, can act at a distance on inert matter,* and most of his work is devoted to ascertaining the laws and conditions under which this action manifests itself."[206]

Precisely; but as the work of de Gasparin called forth numberless *Answers, Defenses,* and *Memoirs,* it was then demonstrated by his own work that as he was a Protestant, in point of religious fanaticism, he was as little to be relied upon as des Mousseaux and de Mirville. The former is a profoundly pious Calvinist, while the two latter are fanatical Roman Catholics. Moreover, the very words of de Gasparin betray the spirit of partisanship: — "I feel I have a duty to perform. . . . I lift high the Protestant flag against the Ultramontane banner!" etc.[207] In such matters as the nature of the so-called spiritual phenomena, no evidence can be relied upon, except the disinterested testimony of cold *unprejudiced* witnesses and science. Truth is one, and Legion is the name for religious sects; every one of which claims to have found the unadulterated truth; as "the Devil is the chief pillar of the (Catholic) Church," so all supernaturalism and miracles ceased, in de Gasparin's opinion, "with apostleship."

But Mr. Crookes mentioned another eminent scholar, Thury, of Geneva, professor of natural history, who was a brother-investigator with Gasparin in the phenomena of Valleyres. This professor contradicts point-blank the assertions of his colleague. "The first and most necessary condition," says Gasparin, "is the *will* of the experimenter; without the will, one would obtain nothing; you can form the chain (the circle) for twenty-four hours consecutively, without obtaining the least movement."[208]

The above proves only that de Gasparin makes no difference between phenomena purely magnetic, produced by the persevering will of the sitters among whom there may be not even a single medium, developed or undeveloped, and the so-called spiritual ones. While the first can be produced *consciously* by nearly every person, who has a firm and determined will, the latter overpowers the sensitive very often against his own consent, and

---

206 Crookes, "*Physical Force,*" page 26.
207 De Gasparin, "*Science* versus *Spirit,*" vol. i., p. 313.
208 Ibid., vol. i., p. 313.

always acts independently of him. *The mesmerizer wills a thing, and if he is powerful enough, that thing is done. The medium,* even if he had an honest purpose to succeed, *may get no manifestations at all; the less he exercises his will, the better the phenomena: the more he feels anxious, the less he is likely to get anything;* to mesmerize requires a positive nature, to be a medium a perfectly passive one. This is the Alphabet of Spiritualism, and no medium is ignorant of it.

The opinion of Thury, as we have said, disagrees entirely with Gasparin's theories of will-power. He states it in so many plain words, in a letter, in answer to the invitation of the count to modify the last article of his *mémoire.* As the book of Thury is not at hand, we translate the letter as it is found in the *résumé* of de Mirville's *Defense.* Thury's article which so shocked his religious friend, related to the possibility of the existence and intervention in those manifestations "of *wills* other than those of men and animals."

"I feel, sir, the justness of your observations in relation to the last pages of this *mémoire:* they may provoke a very bad feeling for me on the part of scientists in general. I regret it the more as my determination seems *to affect you so much;* nevertheless, I persist in my resolution, because I think it a duty, to shirk which would be a kind of treason.

"If, *against all expectations,* there were some truth in Spiritualism, by abstaining from saying on the part of science, as I conceive it to be, *that the absurdity of the belief in the intervention of spirits is not as yet demonstrated scientifically* (for such is the *résumé,* and the thesis of the past pages of my *mémoire*), by abstaining from saying it to those who, after having read my work, will feel inclined to experiment with the phenomena, I might risk to entice such persons on a path many issues of which are very *equivocal.*

"*Without leaving the domain of science,* as I esteem it, I will pursue my duty to the end, without any reticence to the profit of my own glory, and, to use your own words, 'as the great scandal lies there,' I do not wish to assume the shame of it. I, moreover, insist that 'this is as scientific as anything else.' If I wanted to sustain now the theory of the intervention of disembodied spirits, I would have no power for it, for the facts which are made known are not sufficient for the demonstration of such a hypothesis. As it is, and in the position I have assumed, I feel I am strong against every one. Willingly or not, all the scientists must learn, through experience and their own errors, to suspend their judgment as to things which they have not sufficiently examined. The lesson you gave them in this direction cannot be lost. "GENEVA, 21 *December,* 1854."

Let us analyze the above letter, and try to discover what the writer thinks, or rather what he does not think of this new force. One thing is certain, at least: Professor Thury, a distinguished physicist and naturalist, admits, and even scientifically proves that various manifestations take place. Like Mr. Crookes, he does not believe that they are produced by the interference of spirits or disembodied men who have lived and died on earth; for he says in his letter that nothing has demonstrated this theory. He certainly believes no more in the Catholic devils or demons, for de Mirville, who quotes this letter as a triumphant proof against de Gasparin's naturalistic theory, once arrived at the above sentence, hastens to emphasize it by a foot-note, which runs thus: "At Valleyres — *perhaps,* but everywhere else!"[209] showing himself anxious to convey the idea that the professor only meant the manifestations of Valleyres, when denying their being produced by demons.

The contradictions, and we are sorry to say, the absurdities in which de Gasparin allows himself to be caught, are numerous. While bitterly criticizing the pretensions of the learned Faradaysiacs, he attributes things which he declares *magical,* to causes perfectly natural. "If," he says, "we had to deal but with such phenomena (as witnessed and explained (?) by the great physicist), we might as well hold our tongues; but we have passed *beyond,* and what good can they do now, I would ask, these apparatus which demonstrate that an *unconscious pressure* explains the whole? It explains *all,* and the table resists pressure and guidance! It explains *all,* and a piece of furniture which *nobody touches* follows the fingers pointed at it; it *levitates* (without contact), and it turns itself *upside down*!"[210]

But for all that, he takes upon himself to *explain* the phenomena. "People will be advocating miracles, you say — magic! Every new law appears to them as a prodigy. Calm yourselves; I take upon myself the task to quiet those who are alarmed. In the face of such phenomena, we do not cross at all the boundaries of natural law."[211]

Most assuredly, we do not. But can the scientists assert that they have in their possession the keys to such law? M. de Gasparin thinks he has. Let us see. "I do not risk myself to explain anything; *it is no business of mine.* (?) To authenticate simple facts, and maintain a truth which science desires to smother, is all I pretend to do. Nevertheless, I cannot resist the temptation to point out to those who would treat us as so many *illuminati* or sorcerers, that the manifestation in question affords an interpretation which agrees with *the ordinary laws of science.*

"Suppose a fluid, emanating from the experimenters, and chiefly from *some of them;* suppose that the will determined the direction taken by the fluid, and you will readily understand the rotation and levitation of that one of the legs of the table toward which is ejected with every action of the will an excess of fluid. Suppose that the glass causes the fluid to escape, and you will understand how a tumbler placed on the table can interrupt its rotation, and that the tumbler, placed on one of its sides, causes the accumulation of the fluid in the opposite side, which, in consequence of that, *is lifted*!"

THEORY OF CROOKES

If every one of the experimenters were clever mesmerizers, the explanation, *minus* certain important details, might be acceptable. So much for the power of *human will* on inanimate matter, according to the learned minister of Louis Philippe. But how about the intelligence exhibited by the table? What explanation does he give as to answers obtained through the agency of this table to questions? answers which could not possibly have been the "reflections of the brain" of those present (one of the favorite theories of de Gasparin), for their own ideas were quite the reverse of the very *liberal* philosophy given by this wonderful table? On this he is silent. Anything but *spirits,* whether human, satanic, or elemental.

---

209 De Mirville pleads here the devil-theory, of course.
210 "*Des Tables,*" vol. i., p. 213.
211 Vol. i., p. 217.

Thus, the "simultaneous concentration of thought," and the "accumulation of fluid," will be found no better than "the unconscious cerebration" and "psychic force" of other scientists. We must try again; and we may predict beforehand that the thousand and one theories of science will prove of no avail until they will confess that this force, far from being a projection of the accumulated wills of the circle, is, on the contrary, a force which is abnormal, foreign to themselves, and *supra-intelligent*.

Professor Thury, who denies the theory of departed human spirits, rejects the Christian devil-doctrine, and shows himself unwilling to pronounce in favor of Crookes's theory (the 6th), that of the hermetists and ancient theurgists, adopts the one, which, he says in his letter, is "*the most prudent*, and makes him feel strong against every one." Moreover, he accepts as little of de Gasparin's hypothesis of "unconscious will-power." This is what he says in his work:

"As to the announced phenomena, such as the *levitation without contact*, and the displacement of furniture by invisible hands — unable to demonstrate their impossibility, *a priori*, no one has the right to treat as absurd the serious evidences which affirm their occurrence" (p. 9).

As to the theory proposed by M. de Gasparin, Thury judges it very severely. "While admitting that in the experiments of Valleyres," says de Mirville, "the seat of the *force* might have been in the *individual* — and we say that it was intrinsic and extrinsic at the same time — and that the will might be generally necessary (p. 20), he repeats but what he had said in his preface, to wit: 'M. de Gasparin presents us with crude facts, and the explanations following he offers for what they are worth. *Breathe on them*, and not many will be found standing after this. No, very little, if anything, will remain of his explanations. As to facts, they are *henceforth demonstrated*' " (p. 10).

As Mr. Crookes tells us, Professor Thury refutes "all these explanations, and considers the effects due to a peculiar substance, fluid, or agent, pervading in a manner similar to the luminiferous ether of the scientists, all matter, nervous, organic or inorganic, which he terms *psychode*. He enters into full discussion as to the properties of this state, or form, or matter, and proposes the term *ectenic* force . . . for the power exerted when the mind acts at a distance through the influence of the psychode."[212]

Mr. Crookes remarks further, that "Professor Thury's *ectenic* force, and his own 'psychic force' are evidently equivalent terms."

We certainly could very easily demonstrate that the two forces are identical, moreover, the astral or *sidereal* light as explained by the alchemists and Eliphas Levi, in his *Dogme et Rituel de la Haute Magie*; and that, under the name of AKASA, or life-principle, this all-pervading force was known to the gymnosophists, Hindu magicians, and adepts of all countries, thousands of years ago; and, that it is still known to them, and used at present by the Thibetan lamas, fakirs, thaumaturgists of all nationalities, and even by many of the Hindu "jugglers."

In many cases of trance, artificially induced by mesmerization, it is also quite possible, even quite probable, that it is the "spirit" of the subject which acts under the guidance of the

---

212 Crookes, "*Psychic Force*," part i., pp. 26-27.

operator's will. But, if the medium remains conscious, and psycho-physical phenomena occur which indicate a directing intelligence, then, unless it be conceded that he is a "magician," and can project his double, physical exhaustion can signify nothing more than nervous prostration. The proof that he is the passive instrument of unseen entities controlling occult potencies, seems conclusive. Even if Thury's *ectenic* and Crookes's *psychic* force are substantially of the same derivation, the respective discoverers seem to differ widely as to the properties and potencies of this force; while Professor Thury candidly admits that the phenomena are often produced by "wills *not* human," and so, of course, gives a qualified endorsement to Mr. Crookes's theory No. 6, the latter, admitting the genuineness of the phenomena, has as yet pronounced no definite opinion as to their cause. Thus, we find that neither M. Thury, who investigated these manifestations with de Gasparin in 1854, nor Mr. Crookes, who conceded their undeniable genuineness in 1874, have reached anything definite. Both are chemists, physicists, and very learned men. Both have given all their attention to the puzzling question; and besides these two scientists there were many others who, while coming to the same conclusion, have hitherto been as unable to furnish the world with a final solution. It follows then, that in twenty years none of the scientists have made a single step toward the unravelling of the mystery, which remains as immovable and impregnable as the walls of an enchanted castle in a fairy tale.

Would it be too impertinent to surmise that perhaps our modern scientists have got in what the French term *un cercle vicieux?* That, hampered by the weight of their materialism, and the insufficiency of what they name "the exact sciences" to demonstrate to them tangibly the existence of a spiritual universe, peopled and inhabited much more than our visible one, they are doomed forever to creep around *inside* that circle, unwilling rather than unable to penetrate beyond its enchanted ring, and explore it in its length and breadth? It is but prejudice which keeps them from making a compromise with well-established facts and seek alliance with such expert magnetists and mesmerizers as were Du Potet and Regazzoni.

"What, then, is produced from death?" inquired Socrates of Cebes. "*Life*," was the reply.[213] . . . "Can the soul, since it is immortal, be anything else than imperishable?"[214] The "seed cannot develop unless it is in part consumed," says Prof. Lecomte; "it is not quickened unless it die," says St. Paul.

A flower blossoms; then withers and dies. It leaves a fragrance behind, which, long after its delicate petals are but a little dust, still lingers in the air. Our material sense may not be cognizant of it, but it nevertheless exists. Let a note be struck on an instrument, and the faintest sound produces an eternal echo. A disturbance is created on the invisible waves of the shoreless ocean of space, and the vibration is never wholly lost. Its energy being once carried from the world of matter into the immaterial world will live for ever. And man, we are asked to believe, man, the living, thinking, reasoning entity, the indwelling deity of our nature's crowning masterpiece, will evacuate his casket and be no more! Would the principle of continuity which exists even for the so-called *inorganic* matter, for a floating atom, be denied to the spirit, whose attributes are consciousness, memory, mind, LOVE!

---

213 Plato, "*Phædo*," § 44
214 Ibid. § 128.

Really, the very idea is preposterous. The more we think and the more we learn, the more difficult it becomes for us to account for the atheism of the scientist. We may readily understand that a man ignorant of the laws of nature, unlearned in either chemistry or physics, may be fatally drawn into materialism through his very ignorance; his incapacity of understanding the philosophy of the exact sciences, or drawing any inference by analogy from the *visible* to the *invisible*. A natural-born metaphysician, an ignorant dreamer, may awake abruptly and say to himself: "I dreamed it; I have no tangible proof of that which I imagined; it is all illusion," etc. But for a man of science, acquainted with the characteristics of the universal energy, to maintain that *life* is merely a phenomenon of matter, a species of energy, amounts simply to a confession of his own incapability of analyzing and properly understanding the alpha and the omega even of that — matter.

Sincere skepticism as to the immortality of man's soul is a malady; a malformation of the physical brain, and has existed in every age. As there are infants born with a caul upon their heads, so there are men who are incapable to their last hour of ridding themselves of that kind of caul evidently enveloping their organs of spirituality. But it is quite another feeling which makes them reject the possibility of spiritual and magical phenomena. The true name for that feeling is — *vanity*. "We can neither produce nor explain it — hence, it *does not* exist, and moreover, could *never* have existed." Such is the irrefutable argument of our present-day philosophers. Some thirty years ago, E. Salverte startled the world of the "credulous" by his work, *The Philosophy of Magic*. The book claimed to unveil the whole of the miracles of the Bible as well as those of the Pagan sanctuaries. Its *resumé* ran thus: Long ages of observation; a great knowledge (for those days of ignorance) of natural sciences and philosophy; imposture; legerdemain; optics; phantasmagoria; exaggeration. Final and logical conclusion: Thaumaturgists, prophets, magicians, rascals, and knaves; the rest of the world, fools.

Among many other conclusive proofs, the reader can find him offering the following: "The enthusiastic disciples of Iamblichus affirmed that when he prayed, he was raised to the height of ten cubits from the ground; and *dupes* to the same metaphor, although Christians, have had the simplicity to attribute a similar miracle to St. Clare, and St. Francis of Assisi."[215]

Hundreds of travellers claimed to have seen fakirs produce the same phenomena, and they were all thought either liars or hallucinated. But it was but yesterday that the same phenomenon was witnessed and endorsed by a well-known scientist; it was produced under test conditions; declared by Mr. Crookes to be genuine, and to be *beyond* the possibility of an illusion or a trick. And so was it manifested many a time before and attested by numerous witnesses, though the latter are now invariably disbelieved.

THEORY OF FARADAY

Peace to thy scientific ashes, O credulous Eusebe Salverte! Who knows but before the close of the present century popular wisdom will have invented a new proverb: "As incredibly credulous as a scientist." Why should it appear so impossible that when the spirit is once separated from its body, it may have the power to animate some evanescent form, created out of that magical "psychic" or "ectenic" or "ethereal" force, with the help of the

---

215 "*Philosophy of Magic,*" English translation, p. 47.

elementaries who furnish it with the sublimated matter of their own bodies? The only difficulty is, to realize the fact that surrounding space is not an empty void, but a reservoir filled to repletion with the models of all things that ever were, that are, and that will be; and with beings of countless races, unlike our own. Seemingly supernatural facts — supernatural in that they openly contradict the demonstrated natural laws of gravitation, as in the above-mentioned instance of levitation — are recognized by many scientists. Every one who has dared to investigate with thoroughness has found himself compelled to admit their existence; only in their unsuccessful efforts to account for the phenomena on theories based on the laws of such forces as were already known, some of the highest representatives of science have involved themselves in inextricable difficulties!

In his *Resumé* de Mirville describes the argumentation of these adversaries of spiritualism as consisting of five paradoxes, which he terms *distractions*.

First distraction: that of Faraday, who explains the table phenomenon, by the table which *pushes* you "in consequence of the resistance which *pushes it back*."

Second distraction : that of Babinet, explaining all the communications (by raps) which are produced, as he says, "in good faith and with perfect conscientiousness, correct in every way and sense — by *ventriloquism*," the use of which faculty implies of necessity — *bad faith*.

THEORY OF CHEVREUIL

Third distraction: that of Dr. Chevreuil, explaining the faculty of moving furniture *without* contact, by the preliminary acquisition of that faculty.

Fourth distraction: that of the French Institute and its members, who consent to accept the miracles, on condition that the latter will not contradict in any way those natural laws with which they are acquainted.

Fifth distraction: that of M. de Gasparin, introducing as a very *simple* and perfectly *elementary* phenomenon that which every one rejects, precisely because no one ever saw the like of it.[216] While the great, world-known scientists indulge in such fantastic theories, some less known neurologists find an explanation for occult phenomena of every kind in an abnormal effluvium resulting from epilepsy.[217] Another would treat mediums — and poets, too, we may infer — with assafoetida and ammonia,[218] and declare every one of the believers in spiritual manifestations lunatics and hallucinated mystics.

THE MENDELEYEFF COMMISSION OF 1876

To the latter lecturer and professed pathologist is commended that sensible bit of advice to be found in the New Testament: "Physician, heal thyself." Truly, no sane man would so sweepingly charge insanity upon four hundred and forty-six millions of people in various parts of the world, who believe in the intercourse of spirits with ourselves!

---

216 De Mirville, "*Des Esprits*," p. 159.
217 See F. Gerry Fairfield's "*Ten Years with Spiritual Mediums*," New York, 1875.
218 Marvin, "*Lecture on Mediomania*."

Considering all this, it remains to us but to wonder at the preposterous presumption of these men, who claim to be regarded by right of learning as the high priests of science, to classify a phenomenon they know nothing about. Surely, several millions of their countrymen and women, if deluded, deserve at least as much attention as potato-bugs or grasshoppers! But, instead of that, what do we find? The Congress of the United States, at the demand of the American Association for the Advancement of Science, enacts statutes for organization of National Insect Commissions; chemists are busying themselves in boiling frogs and bugs; geologists amuse their leisure by osteological surveys of armor-plated *ganoids*, and discuss the odontology of the various species of *dinichtys*; and entomologists suffer their enthusiasm to carry them to the length of supping on grasshoppers boiled, fried, and in soup.[219] Meanwhile, millions of Americans are either losing themselves in the maze of "crazy delusions," according to the opinion of some of these very learned encyclopædists, or perishing physically from "nervous disorders," brought on or brought out by mediumistic diathesis.

At one time, there was reason to hope that Russian scientists would have undertaken the task of giving the phenomena a careful and impartial study. A commission was appointed by the Imperial University of St. Petersburg, with Professor Mendeleyeff, the great physicist, at its head. The advertised programme provided for a series of forty seances to test mediums, and invitations were extended to all of this class who chose to come to the Russian capital and submit their powers to examination. As a rule they refused — doubtless from a prevision of the trap that had been laid for them. After *eight* sittings, upon a shallow pretext, and just when the manifestations were becoming interesting, the commission prejudged the case, and published a decision adverse to the claims of mediumism. Instead of pursuing dignified, scientific methods, they set spies to peep through the key-holes. Professor Mendeleyeff declared in a public lecture that spiritualism, or any such belief in our souls' immortality, was a mixture of *superstition, delusion,* and *fraud;* adding that every "manifestation" of such nature — including mind-reading, trance, and other psychological phenomena, we must suppose — could be, and *was* produced by means of clever apparatus and machinery concealed under the clothing of mediums!

After such a public exhibition of ignorance and prejudice, Mr. Butlerof, Professor of Chemistry at the St. Petersburg University, and Mr. Aksakof, Counsellor of State in the same city, who had been invited to assist on the committee for mediums, became so disgusted that they withdrew. Having published their protests in the Russian papers, they were supported by the majority of the press, who did not spare either Mendeleyeff or his officious committee with their sarcasms. The public acted fairly in that case. One hundred and thirty names, of the most influential persons of the best society of St. Petersburg, many of them no spiritualists at all, but simply investigators, added their signatures to the well-deserved protest.

The inevitable result of such a procedure followed; universal attention was drawn to the question of spiritualism; private circles were organized throughout the empire; some of the most liberal journals began to discuss the subject; and, as we write, a new commission is being organized to finish the interrupted task.

---

219 *"Scientific American,"* N. Y., 1875.

But now — as a matter of course — they will do their duty less than ever. They have a better pretext than they ever had in the pretended *exposé* of the medium Slade, by Professor Lankester, of London. True, to the evidence of one scientist and his friend, — Messrs. Lankester and Donkin — the accused opposed the testimony of Wallace, Crookes, and a host of others, which totally nullifies an accusation based merely on circumstantial evidence and prejudice. As the *London Spectator* very pertinently observes:

"It is really a pure superstition and nothing else to assume that we are so fully acquainted with the laws of nature, that even carefully examined facts, attested by an experienced observer, ought to be cast aside as utterly unworthy of credit, only because they do not, at first sight, seem to be in keeping with what is most clearly known already. To assume, as Professor Lankester appears to do, that because there are fraud and credulity in plenty to be found in connection with these facts — as there is, no doubt, in connection with all nervous diseases — fraud and credulity will account for all the carefully attested statements of accurate and conscientious observers, is to saw away at the very branch of the tree of knowledge on which inductive science necessarily rests, and to bring the whole structure toppling to the ground."

But what matters all this to scientists? The torrent of superstition, which, according to them, sweeps away millions of bright intellects in its impetuous course, cannot reach them. The modern deluge called spiritualism is unable to affect their strong minds; and the muddy waves of the flood must expend their raging fury without wetting even the soles of their boots. Surely it must be but traditional stubbornness on the part of the Creator that prevents him from confessing what a poor chance his miracles have in our day in blinding professed scientists. By this time even He ought to know and take notice that long ago they decided to write on the porticoes of their universities and colleges:

Science commands that God shall not
Do miracles upon this spot![220]

Both the infidel spiritualists and the orthodox Roman Catholics seem to have leagued themselves this year against the iconoclastic pretensions of materialism. Increase of skepticism has developed of late a like increase of credulity. The champions of the Bible "divine" miracles rival the panegyrist's mediumistic phenomena, and the middle ages revive in the nineteenth century. Once more we see the Virgin Mary resume her epistolary correspondence with the faithful children of her church; and while the "angel friends" scribble messages to spiritualists through their mediums, the "mother of God" drops letters direct from heaven to earth. The shrine of Notre Dame de Lourdes has turned into a spiritualistic cabinet for "materializations," while the cabinets of popular American mediums are transformed into sacred shrines, into which Mohammed, Bishop Polk, Joan of Arc and other aristocratic spirits from over the "dark river," having descended, "materialize" in full light. And if the Virgin Mary is seen taking her daily walk in the woods about Lourdes in full human form, why not the Apostle of Islam, and the late Bishop of Louisiana? Either both "miracles" are possible, or both kinds of these manifestations, the

---

220 "De par le Roi, defense a Dieu, De faire miracle, en ces lieux." A satire that was found written upon the walls of the cemetery at the time of the Jansenist miracles and their prohibition by the police of France.

"divine" as well as the "spiritual," are arrant impostures. Time alone will prove which; but meanwhile, as science refuses the loan of her magic lamp to illuminate these mysteries, common people must go stumbling on whether they be mired or not.

The recent "miracles" at Lourdes having been unfavorably discussed in the London papers, Monsignor Capel communicates to the *Times* the views of the Roman Church in the following terms:

"As to the miraculous cures which are effected, I would refer your readers to the calm, judicious work, *La Grotte de Lourdes,* written by Dr. Dozous, an eminent resident practitioner, inspector of epidemic diseases for the district, and medical assistant of the Court of Justice. He prefaces a number of detailed cases of miraculous cures, which he says he has studied with great care and perseverance, with these words: 'I declare that these cures effected at the Sanctuary of Lourdes by means of the water of the fountain, have established their supernatural character in the eyes of men of good faith. I ought to confess that without these cures, my mind, little prone to listen to miraculous explanations of any kind, would have had great difficulty in accepting even this fact (the apparition), remarkable as it is from so many points of view. But the cures, of which I have been so often an ocular witness, have given to my mind a light which does not permit me to ignore the importance of the visits of Bernadette to the Grotto, and the reality of the apparitions with which she was favored.' The testimony of a distinguished medical man, who has carefully watched from the beginning Bernadette, and the miraculous cures at the Grotto, is at least worthy of respectful consideration. I may add, that the vast number of those who come to the Grotto do so to repent of their sins, to increase their piety, to pray for the regeneration of their country, to profess publicly their belief in the Son of God and his Immaculate Mother. Many come to be cured of bodily ailments; and on the testimony of eye-witnesses several return home freed from their sickness. To upbraid with non-belief, as does your article, those who use also the waters of the Pyrenees, is as reasonable as to charge with unbelief the magistrates who inflict punishment on the peculiar people for neglecting to have medical aid. Health obliged me to pass the winters of 1860 to 1867 at Pau. This gave me the opportunity of making the most minute inquiry into the apparition at Lourdes. After frequent and lengthened examinations of Bernadette and of some of the miracles effected, I am convinced that, *if facts are to be received on human testimony, then has the apparition at Lourdes every claim to be received as an undeniable fact.* It is, however, no part of the Catholic faith, and may be accepted or rejected by any Catholic without the least praise or condemnation."

Let the reader observe the sentence we have italicized. This makes it clear that the Catholic Church, despite her infallibility and her liberal postage convention with the Kingdom of Heaven, is content to accept even the validity of *divine* miracles upon human testimony. Now when we turn to the report of Mr. Huxley's recent New York lectures on evolution, we find him saying that it is upon "human historical evidence that we depend for the greater part of our knowledge for the doings of the past." In a lecture on Biology, he has said " . . . every man who has the interest of truth at heart must earnestly desire that every well-founded and just criticism that can be made should be made; but it is essential . . . that the critic should know what he is talking about." An aphorism that its author should recall when he undertakes to pronounce upon psychological subjects. Add this to his views, as expressed above, and who could ask a better platform upon which to meet him?

SOUL BLINDNESS

Here we have a representative materialist, and a representative Catholic prelate, enunciating an identical view of the sufficiency of *human testimony* to prove facts that it suits the prejudices of each to believe. After this, what need for either the student of occultism, or even the spiritualist, to hunt about for endorsements of the argument they have so long and so persistently advanced, that the psychological phenomena of ancient and modern thaumaturgists being superabundantly proven upon human testimony must be accepted as facts? Church and College having appealed to the tribunal of human evidence, they cannot deny the rest of mankind an equal privilege. One of the fruits of the recent agitation in London of the subject of mediumistic phenomena, is the expression of some remarkably liberal views on the part of the secular press. "In any case, we are for admitting spiritualism to a place among tolerated beliefs, and letting it alone accordingly," says the London *Daily News,* in 1876. "It has many votaries who are as intelligent as most of us, and to whom any obvious and palpable defect in the evidence meant to convince must have been obvious and palpable long ago. Some of *the wisest men in the world believed in ghosts,* and would have continued to do so even though half-a-dozen persons in succession had been convicted of frightening people with sham goblins."

It is not for the first time in the history of the world, that the invisible world has to contend against the materialistic skepticism of soul-blind Sadducees. Plato deplores such an unbelief, and refers to this pernicious tendency more than once in his works.

From Kapila, the Hindu philosopher, who many centuries before Christ demurred to the claim of the mystic Yogins, that in ecstasy a man has the power of seeing Deity face to face and conversing with the "highest" beings, down to the Voltaireans of the eighteenth century, who laughed at everything that was held sacred by other people, each age had its unbelieving Thomases. Did they ever succeed in checking the progress of truth? No more than the ignorant bigots who sat in judgment over Galileo checked the progress of the earth's rotation. No exposures whatever are able to vitally affect the stability or instability of a belief which humanity inherited from the first races of men, those, who — if we can believe in the evolution of spiritual man as in that of the physical one — had the great truth from the lips of their ancestors, the *gods of their fathers,* "that were on the other side of the flood." The identity of the Bible with the legends of the Hindu sacred books and the cosmogonies of other nations, must be demonstrated at some future day. *The fables of the mythopoeic ages will be found to have but allegorized the greatest truths of geology and anthropology.* It is in these ridiculously expressed fables that science will have to look for her "missing links."

Otherwise, whence such strange "coincidences" in the respective histories of nations and peoples so widely thrown apart? Whence that identity of primitive conceptions which, fables and legends though they are termed now, contain in them nevertheless the kernel of historical facts, of a truth thickly overgrown with the husks of popular embellishment, but still a truth? Compare only this verse of *Genesis* vi.: "And it came to pass, when *men began to multiply* on the face of the earth, and daughters were born unto them, that the sons of God saw the daughters of men that they were fair; and they took them wives of all which they chose. . . . There were *giants in the earth in those days,*" etc., with this part of the Hindu cosmogony, in the *Vedas,* which speaks of the descent of the Brahmans. The first Brahman complains of being *alone* among all his brethren without a wife. Notwithstanding that the Eternal advises him to devote his days solely to the study of the Sacred Knowledge (*Veda*), the *first-born* of mankind insists. Provoked at such ingratitude, the eternal gave Brahman a wife of the race of the *Daints,* or *giants,* from whom all the Brahmans maternally descend. Thus the entire Hindu priesthood is descended, on the one hand, from the *superior* spirits (the sons of God), and from *Daintany,* a daughter of the earthly giants, the primitive men.[221] "And they bare children to them; the same became mighty men which were of old; men of renown."[222]

The same is found in the Scandinavian cosmogonical fragment. In the *Edda* is given the description to Gangler by Har, one of the three informants (Har, Jafuhar, and Tredi) of the first man, called Bur, "the father of Bor, who took for wife Besla, a daughter of the giant Bolthara, of the race of the *primitive giants*." The full and interesting narrative may be found in the *Prose Edda,* sects. 4-8, in Mallett's *Northern Antiquities.*[223]

The same groundwork underlies the Grecian fables about the Titans; and may be found in the legend of the Mexicans — the four successive races of *Popol-Vuh*. It constitutes one of the many ends to be found in the entangled and seemingly inextricable skein of mankind, viewed as a psychological phenomenon. Belief in supernaturalism would be otherwise inexplicable. To say that it sprang up, and grew and developed throughout the countless ages, without either cause or the least firm basis to rest upon, but merely as an empty fancy, would be to utter as great an absurdity as the theological doctrine that the universe sprang into creation out of nothing.

It is too late now to kick against an evidence which manifests itself as in the full glare of noon. Liberal, as well as Christian papers, and the organs of the most advanced scientific authorities, begin to protest unanimously against the dogmatism and narrow prejudices of sciolism. The *Christian World,* a religious paper, adds its voice to that of the unbelieving London press. Following is a good specimen of its common sense:

"If a medium," it says,[224] "can be shown ever so conclusively to be an impostor, we shall still object to the disposition manifested by persons of some authority in scientific matters, to pooh-pooh and knock on the head all careful inquiry into those subjects of which Mr. Barrett took note in his paper before the British Association. Because spiritualists have committed themselves to many absurdities, that is no reason why the phenomena to which they appeal should be scouted as unworthy of examination. They may be mesmeric, or clairvoyant, or something else. But let our wise men tell us what they are, and not snub us, as ignorant people too often snub inquiring youth, by the easy but unsatisfactory apothegm, 'Little children should not ask questions.' "

---

221 Polier, "*Mythologie des Indous.*"

222 *Genesis* vi., 4.

223 Mallett, "*Northern Antiquities,*" Bohn's edition, pp. 401-405.

224 In the "*Quarterly Review*" of 1859, Graham gives a strange account of many now deserted Oriental cities, in which the stone doors are of enormous dimensions, often seemingly out of proportion with the buildings themselves, and remarks that dwellings and doors bear all of them the impress of an ancient race of giants.

Thus the time has come when the scientists have lost all right to be addressed with the Miltonian verse, "O thou who, for the testimony of truth, hast borne universal reproach!" Sad degeneration, and one that recalls the exclamation of that "doctor of physic" mentioned one hundred and eighty years ago by Dr. Henry More, and who, upon hearing the story told of the drummer of Tedworth and of Ann Walker, "*cryed* out presently, *If this be true, I have been in a wrong box all this time, and must begin my account anew.*"[225]

But in our century, notwithstanding Huxley's endorsement of the value of "human testimony," even Dr. Henry More has become "an enthusiast and a visionary, both of which, united in the same person, constitute a *canting madman*."[226]

What psychology has long lacked to make its mysterious laws better understood and applied to the ordinary as well as extraordinary affairs of life, is not facts. These it has had in abundance. The need has been for their recording and classification — for trained observers and competent analysts. From the scientific body these ought to have been supplied. If error has prevailed and superstition run riot these many centuries throughout Christendom, it is the misfortune of the common people, the reproach of science. The generations have come and gone, each furnishing its quota of martyrs to conscience and moral courage, and psychology is little better understood in our day than it was when the heavy hand of the Vatican sent those brave unfortunates to their untimely doom, and branded their memories with the stigma of heresy and sorcery.

---

225 Dr. More, *"Letter to Glanvil, author of 'Saducismus Triumphatus.'"*
226 J. S. Y., *"Demonologia, or Natural Knowledge Revealed,"* 1827, p. 219.

CHAPTER V

"Ich bin der Geist der stets verneint."
(I am the spirit which still denies.)

(Mephisto in FAUST)

"The Spirit of truth, whom the world cannot receive
because it seeth Him not; neither knoweth Him."

Gospel According to John, xiv, 17

"Millions of spiritual creatures walk the earth
Unseen, both when we wake and when we sleep."

MILTON

"Mere intellectual enlightenment cannot recognize the spiritual. As
the sun puts out a fire, so spirit puts out the eyes of mere intellect.

W. HOWITT

THERE has been an infinite confusion of names to express one and the same thing.

The chaos of the ancients; the Zoroastrian sacred fire, or the *Antusbyrum* of the Parsees; the Hermes-fire; the Elmes-fire of the ancient Germans; the lightning of Cybelè; the burning torch of Apollo; the flame on the altar of Pan; the inextinguishable fire in the temple on the Acropolis, and in that of Vesta; the fire-flame of Pluto's helm; the brilliant sparks on the hats of the Dioscuri, on the Gorgon head, the helm of Pallas, and the staff of Mercury; the πῦρ ἄσβεστος" ; the Egyptian Phtha, or Ra; the Grecian *Zeus Cataibates* (the descending);[227] the pentecostal fire-tongues; the burning bush of Moses; the pillar of fire of the *Exodus,* and the "burning lamp" of Abram; the eternal fire of the "bottomless pit"; the Delphic oracular vapors; the Sidereal light of the Rosicrucians; the AKASA of the Hindu adepts; the Astral light of Eliphas Levi; the nerve-aura and the fluid of the magnetists; the *od* of Reichenbach; the fire-globe, or meteor-*cat* of Babinet; the *Psychod* and ectenic force of Thury; the psychic force of Sergeant Cox and Mr. Crookes; the atmospheric magnetism of some naturalists; galvanism; and finally, electricity, are but various names for many different manifestations, or effects of the same mysterious, all-pervading cause — the Greek *Archeus,* or Ἀρχᾶιος" .

Sir E. Bulwer-Lytton, in his *Coming Race,* describes it as the VRIL,[228] used by the subterranean populations, and allowed his readers to take it for a fiction. "These people," he says, "consider that in the vril they had arrived at the unity in natural energic agencies"; and proceeds to show that Faraday intimated them "under the more cautious term of correlation," thus:

---

227 Pausanias, "*Eliæ,*" lib. i., cap. xiv.
228 We apprehend that the noble author coined his curious names by contracting words in classical languages. *Gy* would come from *gune; vril* from *virile.*

ONE PRIMAL FORCE, BUT MANY CORRELATIONS

"I have long held an opinion, almost amounting to a conviction, in common, I believe, with many other lovers of natural knowledge, that the various forms under which the forces of matter are made manifest, HAVE ONE COMMON ORIGIN; or, in other words, are so directly related and naturally dependent, that they are convertible, as it were, into one another, and possess equivalents of power in their action."

Absurd and unscientific as may appear our comparison of a fictitious *vril* invented by the great novelist, and the primal force of the equally great experimentalist, with the kabalistic astral light, it is nevertheless the true definition of this force. Discoveries are constantly being made to corroborate the statement thus boldly put forth. Since we began to write this part of our book, an announcement has been made in a number of papers of the supposed discovery of a new force by Mr. Edison, the electrician, of Newark, New Jersey, which force seems to have little in common with electricity, or galvanism, except the principle of conductivity. If demonstrated, it may remain for a long time under some pseudonymous scientific name; but, nevertheless, it will be but one of the numerous family of children brought forth from the commencement of time by our kabalistic mother, the *Astral Virgin*. In fact, the discoverer says that, "it is as distinct, and has as regular laws as heat, magnetism, or electricity." The journal which contains the first account of the discovery adds that, "Mr. Edison thinks that it exists in connection with heat, and that it can also be generated by independent and *as yet undiscovered means.*"

Another of the most startling of recent discoveries, is the possibility of annihilating distance between human voices — by means of the *telephone* (distance-sounder), an instrument invented by Professor A. Graham Bell. This possibility, first suggested by the little "lovers' telegraph," consisting of small tin cups with vellum and drug-twine apparatus, by which a conversation can be carried on at a distance of two hundred feet, has developed into the telephone, which will become the wonder of this age. A long conversation has taken place between Boston and Cambridgeport by telegraph; "every word being distinctly heard and perfectly understood, and the modulations of voices being quite distinguishable," according to the official report. *The voice is seized upon, so to say, and held in form by a magnet, and the sound-wave transmitted by electricity acting in unison and co-operating with the magnet.* The whole success depends upon a perfect control of the electric currents and the power of the magnets used, with which the former must co-operate. "The invention," reports the paper, "may be rudely described as a sort of trumpet, over the bell-mouth of which is drawn a delicate membrane, which, when the voice is thrown into the tube, swells outward in proportion to the force of the sound-wave. To the outer side of the membrane is attached a piece of metal, which, as the membrane swells outward, connects with a magnet, and this, with the electric circuit, is controlled by the operator. By some principle, not yet fully understood, the electric current transmits the sound-wave just as delivered by the voice in the trumpet, and the listener at the other end of the line, with a twin or facsimile trumpet at his ear, hears every word distinctly, and readily detects the modulations of the speaker's voice."

TYNDALL NARROWLY ESCAPES A GREAT DISCOVERY

Thus, in the presence of such wonderful discoveries of our age, and the further magical possibilities lying latent and yet undiscovered in the boundless realm of nature, and further, in view of the great probability that Edison's Force and Professor Graham Bell's Telephone may unsettle, if not utterly upset all our ideas of the imponderable fluids, would it not be well for such persons as may be tempted to traverse our statements, to wait and see whether they will be corroborated or refuted by further discoveries.

Only in connection with these *discoveries*, we may, perhaps, well remind our readers of the many hints to be found in the ancient histories as to a certain secret in the possession of the Egyptian priesthood, who could instantly communicate, during the celebration of the Mysteries, from one temple to another, even though the former were at Thebes and the latter at the other end of the country; the legends attributing it, as a matter of course, to the "invisible tribes" of the air, which carry messages for mortals. The author of *Pre-Adamite Man* quotes an instance, which being given merely on his own authority, and he seeming uncertain whether the story comes from Macrinus or some other writer, may be taken for what it is worth. He found good evidence, he says, during his stay in Egypt, that "one of the Cleopatras (?) sent news by a wire to all the cities, from Heliopolis to Elephantine, on the Upper Nile."[229]

It is not so long since Professor Tyndall ushered us into a new world, peopled with airy shapes of the most ravishing beauty.

"The discovery consists," he says, "in subjecting the vapors of volatile liquids to the action of concentrated sun-light, or to the concentrated beam of the electric light." The vapors of certain nitrites, iodides, and acids are subjected to the action of the light in an *experimental tube*, lying horizontally, and so arranged that the axis of the tube and that of the parallel beams issuing from the lamp are coincident. The vapors form clouds of gorgeous tints, and arrange themselves into the shapes of vases, of bottles and cones, in nests of six or more; of shells, of tulips, roses, sunflowers, leaves, and of involved scrolls. "In one case," he tells us, "the cloud-bud grew rapidly into a serpent's head; a mouth was formed, and from the cloud, a cord of cloud resembling a tongue was discharged." Finally, to cap the climax of marvels, "once it positively assumed the form of a fish, with eyes, gills, and feelers. The twoness of the animal form was displayed throughout, and no *disk, coil, or speck existed on one side that did not exist on the other*."

THE IMPOSSIBILITY OF MIRACLE

These phenomena may possibly be explained in part by the mechanical action of a beam of light, which Mr. Crookes has recently demonstrated. For instance, it is a supposable case, that the beams of light may have constituted a horizontal axis, about which the disturbed molecules of the vapors gathered into the forms of globes and spindles. But how account for the fish, the serpent's head, the vases, the flowers of different varieties, the shells? This seems to offer a dilemma to science as baffling as the meteor-cat of Babinet. We do not learn

---

229 P. B. Randolph, *"Pre-Adamite Man,"* p. 48.

that Tyndall ventured as absurd an explanation of his extraordinary phenomena as that of the Frenchman about his.

Those who have not given attention to the subject may be surprised to find how much was known in former days of that all-pervading, subtile principle which has recently been baptized THE UNIVERSAL ETHER.

Before proceeding, we desire once more to enunciate in two categorical propositions, what was hinted at before. These propositions were demonstrated laws with the ancient theurgists.

I. The so-called miracles, to begin with Moses and end with Cagliostro, when genuine, were as de Gasparin very justly insinuates in his work on the phenomena, "perfectly in accordance with natural law"; hence — no miracles. Electricity and magnetism were unquestionably used in the production of some of the prodigies; but now, the same as then, they are put in requisition by every sensitive, who is made to use *unconsciously* these powers by the peculiar nature of his or her organization, which serves as a conductor for some of these imponderable fluids, as yet so imperfectly known to science. This force is the prolific parent of numberless attributes and properties, many, or rather, most of which, are as yet unknown to modern physics.

II. The phenomena of natural magic to be witnessed in Siam, India, Egypt, and other Oriental countries, bear no relationship whatever to sleight of hand; the one being an absolute physical effect, due to the action of occult natural forces, the other, a mere deceptive result obtained by dexterous manipulations supplemented with confederacy.[230]

The thaumaturgists of all periods, schools, and countries, produced their wonders, because they were perfectly familiar with the imponderable — in their effects — but otherwise perfectly tangible waves of the astral light. They controlled the currents by guiding them with their will-power. The wonders were both of physical and psychological character; the former embracing effects produced upon material objects, the latter the mental phenomena of Mesmer and his successors. This class has been represented in our time by two illustrious men, Du Potet and Regazzoni, whose wonderful powers were well attested in France and other countries. Mesmerism is the most important branch of magic; and its phenomena are the effects of the universal agent which underlies all magic and has produced at all ages the so-called miracles.

The ancients called it *Chaos*; Plato and the Pythagoreans named it *the Soul of the World*. According to the Hindus, the Deity in the shape of Æther pervades all things. It is the invisible, but, as we have said before, too tangible Fluid. Among other names this universal Proteus — or "the nebulous Almighty," as de Mirville calls it in derision — was termed by

---

230 On this point at least we are on firm ground. Mr. Crookes's testimony corroborates our assertions. On page 84 of his pamphlet on "*Phenomenal Spiritualism*" he says: "The many hundreds of facts I am prepared to attest — facts which to imitate by known mechanics or physical means would baffle the skill of a Houdin, a Bosco, or an Anderson, backed with all the resources of elaborate machinery and the practice of years — have all taken place in my own house; at times appointed by myself and under circumstances which absolutely precluded the employment of the very simplest instrumental aids."

the theurgists "the living fire,"[231] the "Spirit of Light," and *Magnes*. This last appellation indicates its magnetic properties and shows its magical nature. For, as truly expressed by one of its enemies — μάγος and μάγνης are two branches growing from the same trunk, and shooting forth the same resultants.

Magnetism is a word for the derivation of which we have to look to an incredibly early epoch. The stone called *magnet* is believed by many to owe its name to Magnesia, a city or district in Thessaly, where these stones were found in quantity. We believe, however, the opinion of the Hermetists to be the correct one. The word *Magh, magus,* is derived from the Sanskrit *Mahaji,* the *great* or *wise* (the anointed by the divine wisdom). "Eumolpus is the *mythic* founder of the Eumolpidæ (priests); the priests traced their own wisdom to the Divine Intelligence."[232] The various cosmogonies show that the Archæal Universal Soul was held by every nation as the "mind" of the Demiurgic Creator, the *Sophia* of the Gnostics, or *the Holy Ghost as a female principle.* As the Magi derived their name from it, so the Magnesian stone or Magnet was called in their honor, for they were the first to discover its wonderful properties. Their temples dotted the country in all directions, and among these were some temples of Hercules,[233] — hence the stone, when it once became known that the priests used it for their curative and magical purposes, received the name of the Magnesian or Heraclean stone. Socrates, speaking of it, remarks: "Euripides calls it the Magnesian stone, but the common people, the Heraclean."[234] It was the country and stone which were called after the Magi, not the Magi after one or the other. Pliny informs us that the wedding-ring among the Romans was magnetized by the priests before the ceremony. The old Pagan historians are careful to keep silent on certain Mysteries of the "wise" (Magi) and Pausanias was warned in a dream, he says, not to unveil the holy rites of the temple of Demeter and Persephoneia at Athens.[235]

Modern science, after having ineffectually denied *animal magnetism,* has found herself forced to accept it as a fact. It is now a recognized property of human and animal organization; as to its psychological, occult influence, the Academies battle with it, in our century, more ferociously than ever. It is the more to be regretted and even wondered at, as the representatives of "exact science" are unable to either explain or even offer us anything like a reasonable hypothesis for the undeniable mysterious potency contained in a simple magnet. We begin to have daily proofs that these potencies underlie the theurgic mysteries, and therefore might perhaps explain the occult faculties possessed by ancient and modern

---

231 In this appellation, we may discover the meaning of the puzzling sentence to be found in the Zend-Avesta that "fire gives knowledge of the future, science, and amiable speech," as it develops an extraordinary eloquence in some sensitives.

232 Dunlap, "*Musah, His Mysteries,*" p. iii.

233 "Hercules was known as the king of the Musians," says Schwab, ii., 44; and Musien was the feast of "Spirit and Matter," Adonis and Venus, Bacchus and Ceres. (See Dunlap, "*Mystery of Adonis,*" p. 95.) Dunlap shows, on the authority of Julian and Anthon (67), Æsculapius, "the Savior of all," identical with Phtha (the creative Intellect, the Divine Wisdom), and with Apollo, Baal, Adonis, and Hercules (ibid., p. 93), and Phtha is the "Anima mundi," the Universal Soul, of Plato, the Holy Ghost of the Egyptians, and the Astral Light of the Kabalists. M. Michelet, however, regards the Grecian Herakles as a different character, the adversary of the Bacchic revellings and their attendant human sacrifices.

234 Plato, "*Ion*" (Burgess), vol. iv., p. 294.

235 "*Attica,*" i., xiv.

thaumaturgists as well as a good many of their most astounding achievements. Such were the gifts transmitted by Jesus to some of his disciples. At the moment of his miraculous cures, the Nazarene felt a *power* issuing from him. Socrates, in his dialogue with Theages,[236] telling him of his familiar god (demon), and his power of either imparting his (Socrates') wisdom to his disciples or preventing it from benefiting those he associates with, brings the following instance in corroboration of his words: "I will tell you, Socrates," says Aristides, "a thing incredible, indeed, by the gods, but true. I made a proficiency when I associated with you, even if I was only in the same house, though not in the same room; but more so, when I *was in the same room* . . . and much more when I *looked at you*. . . But I made by far the greatest proficiency when I sat near you and *touched you*."

This is the modern magnetism and mesmerism of Du Potet and other masters, who, when they have subjected a person to their *fluidic* influence, can impart to them all their thoughts even at a distance, and with an irresistible power force their subject to obey their *mental* orders. But how far better was this psychic force known to the ancient philosophers! We can glean some information on that subject from the earliest sources. Pythagoras taught his disciples that God is the universal *mind* diffused through all things, and that this mind by the sole virtue of its universal sameness could be communicated from one object to another and be made to create all things by the sole will-power of man. With the ancient Greeks, *Kurios* was the god-Mind (*Nous*). "Now Koros (Kurios) signifies the pure and unmixed nature of intellect — wisdom," says Plato.[237] Kurios is Mercury, the Divine Wisdom, and "Mercury is the Sol" (Sun),[238] from whom Thaut — Hermes — received this divine wisdom, which, in his turn, he imparted to the world in his books. Hercules is also the Sun — the celestial storehouse of the universal magnetism; § or rather Hercules is the magnetic light which, when having made its way through the "opened eye of heaven," enters into the regions of our planet and thus becomes the Creator. Hercules passes through the twelve labors, the valiant Titan! He is called "Father of All" and "self-born" "(*autophues*)."[239] Hercules, the Sun, is killed by the Devil, Typhon,[240] and so is Osiris, who is the father and brother of Horus, and at the same time is identical with him; and we must not forget that the magnet was called the "bone of Horus," and iron the "bone of Typhon." He is called "Hercules *Invictus*," only when he descends to Hades (the subterranean garden),

---

236 Plato, "*Theages*." Cicero renders this word daimonion, quiddam divinum, a divine something, not anything personal.
237 "*Cratylus*," p. 79.
238 "*Arnobius*," vi., xii. As we will show in subsequent chapters, the sun was not considered by the ancients as the direct cause of the light and heat, but only as an agent of the former, through which the light passes on its way to our sphere. Thus it was always called by the Egyptians "the eye of Osiris," who was himself the *Logos*, the First-begotten, or light made manifest to the world, "which is the mind and divine intellect of the Concealed." It is only that light of which we are cognizant that is the Demiurge, the *creator* of our planet and everything pertaining to it; with the invisible and unknown universes disseminated through space, none of the sun-gods had anything to do. The idea is expressed very clearly in the "*Books of Hermes*."
239 "*Orphic Hymn*," xii.; Hermann, Dunlap, "*Musah, His Mysteries*," p. 91.
240 Movers, 525. Dunlap, "*Mysteries of Adonis*," 94.

and plucking the "golden apples" from the "tree of life," slays the dragon.[241] The rough Titanic power, the "lining" of every sun-god, opposes its force of blind matter to the divine magnetic spirit, which tries to harmonize everything in nature.

All the sun-gods, with their symbol, the visible sun, are the creators of *physical* nature only. The *spiritual* is the work of the Highest God — the Concealed, the Central, Spiritual SUN, and of his Demiurge — the Divine Mind of Plato, and the Divine Wisdom of Hermes Trismegistus[242]— the wisdom effused from Oulom or Kronos.

"After the distribution of pure Fire, in the Samothracian Mysteries, a new life began."[243] This was the "new birth," that is alluded to by Jesus, in his nocturnal conversation with Nicodemus. "Initiated into the most blessed of all Mysteries, being ourselves pure . . . we become just and holy with wisdom."[244] "He *breathed* on them and saith unto them, 'Take the Holy Pneuma.' "[245] And this simple act of will-power was sufficient to impart vaticination in its nobler and most perfect form if both the initiator and the initiated were worthy of it. To deride this gift, even in its present aspect, "as the corrupt offspring and lingering remains of an ignorant age of superstition, and hastily to condemn it as unworthy of sober investigation, would be as unphilosophical as it is wrong," remarks the Rev. J. B. Gross. "To remove the veil which hides our vision from the future, has been attempted — in all ages of the world; and therefore the propensity to pry into the lap of time, contemplated as one of the faculties of human mind, comes recommended to us under the sanction of God. . . . Zuinglius, the Swiss reformer, attested the comprehensiveness of his faith in the providence of the Supreme Being, in the cosmopolitan doctrine that the Holy Ghost was not excluded from the more worthy portion of the heathen world. Admitting its truth, we cannot easily conceive a valid reason why a heathen, thus favored, should not be capable of true prophecy."[246]

NATURE OF THE PRIMORDIAL SUBSTANCE

Now, what is this mystic, primordial substance? In the book of Genesis, at the beginning of the first chapter, it is termed the "face of the waters," said to have been incubated by the "Spirit of God." Job mentions, in chap. xxvi., 5, that "dead things are formed from under the waters, and inhabitants thereof." In the original text, instead of "dead things," it is written dead Rephaim (giants, or mighty primitive men), from whom "Evolution" may one day trace our present race. In the Egyptian mythology, Kneph the Eternal unrevealed God is represented by a snake-emblem of eternity encircling a water-urn, with his head hovering over the waters, which it incubates with his breath. In this case the serpent is the

---

241 Preller, ii., 153. This is evidently the origin of the Christian dogma of Christ descending into hell and overcoming Satan.
242 This important fact accounts admirably for the gross polytheism of the masses, and the refined, highly-philosophical conception of *one* God, which was taught only in sanctuaries of the "pagan" temples.
243 Anthon,, "*Cabeiria.*"
244 Plato, "*Phædrus,*" Cary's translation.
245 *John* xx., 22.
246 "*Heathen Religion,*" 104.

Agathodaimon, the good spirit; in its opposite aspect it is the Kakodaimon — the bad one. In the Scandinavian Eddas, the honey-dew — the food of the gods and of the creative, busy Yggdrasill — bees — falls during the hours of night, when the atmosphere is impregnated with humidity; and in the Northern mythologies, as the passive principle of creation, it typifies the creation of the universe out of water; this dew is the astral light in one of its combinations and possesses creative as well as destructive properties. In the Chaldean legend of Berosus, Oannes or Dagon, the man-fish, instructing the people, shows the infant world created out of water and all beings originating from this prima materia. Moses teaches that only earth and water can bring a living soul; and we read in the Scriptures that herbs could not grow until the Eternal caused it to rain upon earth. In the Mexican Popol-Vuh man is created out of mud or clay (terre glaise), taken from under the water. Brahma creates Lomus, the great Muni (or first man), seated on his lotus, only after having called into being, spirits, who thus enjoyed among mortals a priority of existence, and he creates him out of water, air, and earth. Alchemists claim that primordial or pre-Adamic earth when reduced to its first substance is in its second stage of transformation like clear-water, the first being the alkahest[247] proper. This primordial substance is said to contain within itself the essence of all that goes to make up man; it has not only all the elements of his physical being, but even the "breath of life" itself in a latent state, ready to be awakened. This it derives from the "incubation" of the Spirit of God upon the face of the waters — chaos; in fact, this substance is chaos itself. From this it was that Paracelsus claimed to be able to make his "homunculi"; and this is why Thales, the great natural philosopher, maintained that *water* was the principle of all things in nature.

INTERPRETATION OF CERTAIN ANCIENT MYTHS

What is the primordial Chaos but Æther? The modern Ether; not such as is recognized by our scientists, but such as it was known to the ancient philosophers, long before the time of Moses; Ether, with all its mysterious and occult properties, containing in itself the germs of universal creation; Ether, the celestial virgin, the spiritual mother of every existing form and being, from whose bosom as soon as "incubated" by the Divine Spirit, are called into existence Matter and Life, Force and Action. Electricity, magnetism, heat, light, and chemical action are so little understood even now that fresh facts are constantly widening the range of our knowledge. Who knows where ends the power of this protean giant — Ether; or whence its mysterious origin? — Who, we mean, that denies the spirit that works in it and evolves out of it all visible forms?

It is an easy task to show that the cosmogonical legends all over the world are based on a knowledge by the ancients of those sciences which have allied themselves in our days to support the doctrine of evolution; and that further research may demonstrate that they were far better acquainted with the fact of evolution itself, embracing both its physical and spiritual aspects, than we are now. With the old philosophers, evolution was a universal theorem, a doctrine embracing the *whole,* and an established principle; while our modern evolutionists are enabled to present us merely with speculative theoretics; with *particular,* if not wholly *negative* theorems. It is idle for the representatives of our modern wisdom to

---

247 Alkahest, a word first used by Paracelsus, to denote the menstruum or universal solvent, that is capable of reducing all things.

close the debate and pretend that the question is settled, merely because the obscure phraseology of the Mosaic account clashes with the definite exegesis of "exact science."

One fact at least is proved: there is not a cosmogonical fragment, to whatever nation it may belong, but proves by this universal allegory of water and the spirit brooding over it, that no more than our modern physicists did any of them hold the universe to have sprung into existence out of nothing; for all their legends begin with that period when nascent vapors and Cimmerian darkness lay brooding over a fluid mass ready to start on its journey of activity at the first flutter of the breath of Him, who is the Unrevealed One. Him they felt, if they saw Him not. Their spiritual intuitions were not so darkened by the subtle sophistry of the forecoming ages as ours are now. If they talked less of the Silurian age slowly developing into the Mammalian, and if the Cenozoic time was only recorded by various allegories of the primitive man — the Adam of *our* race — it is but a negative proof after all that their "wise men" and leaders did not know of these successive periods as well as we do now.

In the days of Democritus and Aristotle, the cycle had already begun to enter on its downward path of progress. And if these two philosophers could discuss so well the atomic theory and trace the atom to its material or physical *point,* their ancestors may have gone further still and followed its genesis far beyond that limit where Mr. Tyndall and others seem rooted to the spot, not daring to cross the line of the "Incomprehensible." The *lost arts* are a sufficient proof that if even their achievements in physiography are now doubted, because of the unsatisfactory writings of their physicists and naturalists, — on the other hand their practical knowledge in phytochemistry and mineralogy far exceeded our own. Furthermore, they might have been perfectly acquainted with the physical history of our globe without publishing their knowledge to the ignorant masses in those ages of religious Mysteries.

Therefore, it is not only from the Mosaic books that we mean to adduce proof for our further arguments. The ancient Jews got all their knowledge — religious as well as profane — from the nations with which we see them mixed up from the earliest periods. Even the oldest of all sciences, their kabalistic "secret doctrine," may be traced in each detail to its primeval source, Upper India, or Turkestan, far before the time of a distinct separation between the Aryan and Semitic nations.

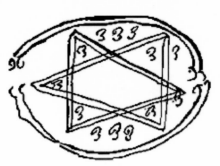

The King Solomon so celebrated by posterity, as Josephus the historian says,[248] for his magical skill, got his secret learning from India through Hiram, the king of Ophir, and perhaps Sheba. His ring, commonly known as "Solomon's seal," so celebrated for the potency of its sway over the various kinds of genii and demons, in all the popular legends, is equally of Hindu origin. Writing on the pretentious and abominable skill of the "devil-worshippers" of Travancore, the Rev. Samuel Mateer, of the London Missionary Society, claims at the same time to be in possession of a very old manuscript volume of

---

248 Josephus, "*Antiquities*," vol. viii., c. 2, 5.

magical incantations and spells in the Malayalim language, giving directions for effecting a great variety of purposes. Of course he adds, that "many of these are fearful in their malignity and obscenity," and gives in his work the fac-simile of some amulets bearing the magical figures and designs on them. We find among them one with the following legend: "To remove trembling arising from demoniacal possession — write this figure on a plant that has milky juice, and drive a nail through it; the trembling will cease."[249] The figure is the identical Solomon's seal, or double triangle of the Kabalists. Did the Hindu get it from the Jewish kabalist, or the latter from India, by inheritance from their great king-kabalist, the wise Solomon?[250] But we will leave this trifling dispute to continue the more interesting question of the astral light, and its unknown properties.

Admitting, then, that this mythical agent is Ether, we will proceed to see what and how much of it is known to science.

With respect to the various effects of the different solar rays, Robert Hunt, F. R. S., remarks, in his *Researches on Light in its Chemical Relations*, that:

"Those rays which give the *most* light — the yellow and the orange rays — will not produce change of color in the chloride of silver"; while "those rays which have the *least* illuminating power — the blue and violet — produce the greatest change, and in exceedingly short time. . . . The yellow glasses obstruct scarcely any light; the blue glasses may be so dark as to admit of the permeation of a very small quantity."

And still we see that under the *blue* ray both vegetable and animal life manifest an inordinate development, while under the yellow ray it is proportionately arrested. How is it

---

249 "*The Land of Charity*," p. 210.

250 The claims of certain "adepts," which do not agree with those of the students of the purely Jewish *Kabala,* and show that the "secret doctrine" has originated in India, from whence it was brought to Chaldea, passing subsequently into the hands of the Hebrew "Tanaim," are singularly corroborated by the researches of the Christian missionaries. These pious and learned travellers have inadvertently come to our help. Dr. Caldwell, in his "Comparative Grammar of the Dravidian Languages," p. 66, and Dr. Mateer, in the "Land of Charity," p. 83, fully support our assertions that the "wise" King Solomon got all his kabalistic lore from India, as the above-given magical figure well shows. The former missionary is desirous to prove that very old and huge specimens of the baobab-tree, which is not, as it appears, indigenous to India, but belongs to the African soil, and "found only at several ancient sites of foreign commerce (at Travancore), may, for aught we know," he adds, "have been introduced into India, and planted by the servants of King Solomon." The other proof is still more conclusive. Says Dr. Mateer, in his chapter on the Natural History of Travancore: "There is a curious fact connected with the name of this bird (the peacock) which throws some light upon Scripture history. King Solomon sent his navy to Tarshish (*I Kings*, x. 22), which returned once in three years, bringing 'gold and silver, ivory and apes, and peacocks.' Now the word used in the Hebrew Bible for peacock is '*tukki*,' and as the Jews had, of course, no word for these fine birds till they were first imported into Judea by King Solomon, there is no doubt that '*tukki*' is simply the old Tamil word '*toki*,' the name of the peacock. The ape or monkey also is, in Hebrew, called '*koph*,' the Indian word for which is '*kaphi*.' Ivory, we have seen, is abundant in South India, and gold is widely distributed in the rivers of the western coast. Hence the 'Tarshish' referred to was doubtless the western coast of India, and Solomon's ships were ancient 'East Indiamen.' " And hence also we may add, besides "the gold and silver, and apes and peacocks," King Solomon and his friend Hiram, of masonic renown, got their "magic" and "wisdom" from India.

possible to account for this satisfactorily upon any other hypothesis than that both animal and vegetable life are differently modified electrico-magnetic phenomena, as yet unknown in their fundamental principles?

Mr. Hunt finds that the undulatory theory does not account for the results of his experiments. Sir David Brewster, in his *Treatise on Optics*, showing that "the colors of vegetable life arise . . . from a specific attraction which the particles of these bodies exercise over the differently-colored rays of light," and that "it is by the light of the sun that the colored juices of plants are elaborated, that the colors of bodies are changed, etc. . . ." remarks that it is not easy to allow "that such effects can be produced by the mere vibration of an ethereal medium." And he is *forced*, he says, "by this class of facts, to reason as if light was *material* (?)." Professor Josiah P. Cooke, of Harvard University, says that he "cannot agree . . . with those who regard the wave-theory of light as an established principle of science."[251] Herschel's doctrine, that the intensity of light, in effect of each undulation, "is inversely as the square of the distance from the luminous body," if correct, damages a good deal if it does not kill the undulatory theory. That he is right, was proved repeatedly by experiments with photometers; and, though it begins to be much doubted, the undulatory theory is still alive.

As General Pleasonton, of Philadelphia, has undertaken to combat this anti-Pythagorean hypothesis, and has devoted to it a whole volume, we cannot do any better than refer the reader to his recent work on the *Blue Ray*, etc. We leave the theory of Thomas Young, who, according to Tyndall, "placed on an immovable basis the undulatory theory of light," to hold its own if it can, with the Philadelphia experimenter.

Eliphas Levi, the modern magician, describes the astral light in the following sentence: "We have said that to acquire magical power, two things are necessary: to disengage the will from all servitude, and to exercise it in control."

"The sovereign will is represented in our symbols by the woman who crushes the serpent's head, and by the resplendent angel who represses the dragon, and holds him under his foot and spear; the great magical agent, the dual current of light, the living and astral *fire* of the earth, has been represented in the ancient theogonies by the serpent with the head of a bull, a ram, or a dog. It is the double serpent of the *caduceus*, it is the Old Serpent of the *Genesis*, but it is also the *brazen serpent of Moses* entwined around the *tau*, that is to say, the generative *lingha*. It is also the goat of the witch-sabbath, and the Baphomet of the Templars; it is the *Hylé* of the Gnostics; it is the double-tail of serpent which forms the legs of the solar cock of the Abraxas; finally, it is the Devil of M. Eudes de Mirville. But in very fact it is the blind force which souls have to conquer to liberate themselves from the bonds of the earth; for if their will does not free "them from this *fatal attraction*, they will be absorbed in the current by the force which has produced them, and *will return to the central and eternal fire*."

This last kabalistic figure of speech, notwithstanding its strange phraseology, is precisely the one used by Jesus; and in his mind it could have had no other significance than the one attributed to it by the Gnostics and the Kabalists. Later the Christian theologians interpreted

---

251 Cooke, "*New Chemistry*," p. 22.

it differently, and with them it became the doctrine of Hell. Literally, though, it simply means what it says — the astral light, or the generator and destroyer of all forms.

"All the magical operations," continues Levi, "consist in freeing one's self from the coils of the Ancient Serpent; then to place the foot on its head, and lead it according to the operator's will. 'I will give unto thee,' says the Serpent, in the Gospel myth, 'all the kingdoms of the earth, if thou wilt fall down and worship me.' The initiate should reply to him, 'I will not fall down, but thou shalt crouch at my feet; thou wilt give me nothing, but I will make use of thee and take whatever I wish. For *I am thy Lord and Master*!' This is the real meaning of the ambiguous response made by Jesus to the tempter. . . . Thus, the Devil is not an Entity. It is an errant force, as the name signifies. An *odic or magnetic current* formed by a chain (a circle) of pernicious wills must create this evil spirit which the Gospel calls *legion*, and which forces into the sea a herd of swine — another evangelical allegory showing how base natures can be driven headlong by the blind forces set in motion by error and sin."[252]

EXPERIMENTS OF THE FAKIRS

In his extensive work on the mystical manifestations of human nature, the German naturalist and philosopher, Maximilian Perty, has devoted a whole chapter to the *Modern Forms of Magic*. "The manifestations of magical life," he says in his Preface, "partially repose on quite another order of things than the nature in which we are acquainted with time, space, and causality; these manifestations can be experimented with but little; they cannot be called out at our bidding, but may be observed and carefully followed whenever they occur in our presence; we can only group them by analogy under certain divisions, and deduce from them general principles and laws." Thus, for Professor Perty, who evidently belongs to the school of Schopenhauer, the possibility and *naturalness* of the phenomena which took place in the presence of Kavindasami, the fakir, and are described by Louis Jacolliot, the Orientalist, are fully demonstrated on that principle. The fakir was a man who, through the entire subjugation of the matter of his corporeal system has attained to that state of purification at which the spirit becomes nearly freed from its prison,[253] and can produce wonders. His *will*, nay, a simple desire of his has become creative force, and he can command the elements and powers of nature. His body is no more an impediment to him; hence he can converse "spirit to spirit, breath to breath." Under his extended palms, a seed, unknown to him (for Jacolliot has chosen it at random among a variety of seeds, from a bag, and planted it himself, after *marking* it, in a flower pot), will germinate instantly, and push its way through the soil. Developing in less than two hours' time to a size and height which, perhaps, under ordinary circumstances, would require several days or weeks, it grows miraculously under the very eyes of the perplexed experimenter, and mockingly upsets every accepted formula in Botany. Is this a miracle? By no means; it may be one, perhaps, if we take Webster's definition, that a miracle is "every event contrary to the *established*

---

252 Eliphas Levi, "*Dogme et Rituel de la Haute Magie*."

253 Plato hints at a ceremony used in the Mysteries during the performance of which the neophyte was taught that men are *in this life* in a kind of prison, and taught *how to escape from it temporarily*. As usual, the too-learned translators disfigured this passage, partially because they *could not* understand it, and partially because they *would not*. See *Phædo* § 16, and commentaries on it by Henry More, the well-known Mystic philosopher and Platonist.

constitution and course of things — a deviation from the *known* laws of nature." But are our naturalists prepared to support the claim that what they have once *established* on observation is infallible? Or that *every* law of nature is known to them? In this instance, the "miracle" is but a little *more* prominent than the now well-known experiments of General Pleasonton, of Philadelphia. While the vegetation and fruitage of his vines were stimulated to an incredible activity by the artificial violet light, the magnetic fluid emanating from the hands of the fakir effected still more intense and rapid changes in the vital function of the Indian plants. It attracted and concentrated the *akasa*, or life-principle, on the germ.[254] His magnetism, obeying his will, drew up the *akasa* in a concentrated current through the plant towards his hands, and by keeping up an unintermitted flow for the requisite space of time, the life-principle of the plant built up cell after cell, layer after layer, with preternatural activity, until the work was done. The life-principle is but a blind force obeying a controlling influence. In the ordinary course of nature the plant-protoplasm would have concentrated and directed it at a certain established rate. This rate would have been controlled by the prevalent atmospheric conditions; its growth being rapid or slow, and, in stalk or head, in proportion to the amount of light, heat, and moisture of the season. But the fakir, coming to the help of nature with his powerful will and spirit purified from the contact with matter,[255] condenses, so to speak, the essence of plant-life into its germ, and forces it to maturity ahead of its time. This blind force being totally submissive to his will, obeys it with servility. If he chose to *imagine* the plant as a monster, it would as surely become such, as ordinarily it would grow in its natural shape; for the concrete image — slave to the subjective model outlined in the imagination of the fakir — is forced to follow the original in its least detail, as the hand and brush of the painter follow the image which they copy from his mind. The will of the fakir-conjurer forms an invisible but yet, to it,

---

254 The *akasa* is a Sanscrit word which means sky, but it also designates the imponderable and intangible life-principle — the astral and celestial lights combined together, and which two form the *anima mundi,* and constitute the soul and spirit of man; the celestial light forming his nou;", pneuma , or divine spirit, and the other his fuch , soul or *astral* spirit. The grosser particles of the latter enter into the fabrication of his outward form — the body. *Akasa* is the mysterious fluid termed by scholastic science, "the all-pervading ether"; it enters into all the magical operations of nature, and produces mesmeric, magnetic, and spiritual phenomena. *As,* in Syria, Palestine, and India, meant the sky, *life,* and the *sun* at the same time; the sun being considered by the ancient sages as the great magnetic well of our universe. The softened pronunciation of this word was *Ah* — says Dunlap, for "the *s* continually softens to *h* from Greece to Calcutta." *Ah* is Iah, Ao, and Iao. God tells Moses that his name is "I am" (*Ahiah*), a reduplication of Ah or Iah. The word "As" Ah, or Iah means *life, existence,* and is evidently the root of the word *akasa,* which in Hindustan is pronounced a*h*asa, the life-principle, or Divine life-giving fluid or medium. It is the Hebrew *ruah,* and means the "wind," the breath, *the air in motion,* or "moving spirit," according to Parkhurst's *Lexicon;* and is identical with the spirit of God *moving* on the face of the waters.

255 Bear in mind that Kavindasami made Jacolliot swear that he would neither approach nor *touch* him during the time he was entranced. The least contact with *matter* would have paralyzed the action of the freed spirit, which, if we are permitted to use such an unpoetical comparison, would re-enter its dwelling like a frightened snail, drawing in its horns at the approach of any foreign substance. In some cases such a *brusque* interruption and oozing back of the spirit (sometimes it may suddenly and altogether break the delicate thread connecting it with the body) kills the entranced *subject.* See the several works of Baron du Potet and Puysegur on this question.

perfectly objective matrix, in which the vegetable matter is caused to deposit itself and assume the fixed shape. The will creates; for the will in motion is *force*, and force produces *matter*.

If some persons object to the explanation on the ground that the fakir could by no means create the model in his imagination, since he was kept ignorant by Jacolliot of the kind of seed he had selected for the experiment; to these we will answer that the spirit of man is like that of his Creator — omniscient in its essence. While in his natural state the fakir did *not*, and *could not* know whether it was a melon-seed, or seed of any other plant; once entranced, *i.e.*, bodily dead to all outward appearance — the spirit, for which there exist neither distance, material obstacle, nor space of time, experienced no difficulty in perceiving the melon-seed, whether as it lay deeply buried in the mud of the flower-pot, or reflected in the faithful picture-gallery of Jacolliot's brain. Our visions, portents, and other psychological phenomena, all of which exist in nature, are corroborative of the above fact.

And now, perhaps, we might as well meet at once another impending objection. Indian *jugglers,* they will tell us, do the same, and as well as the fakir, if we can believe newspapers and travellers' narratives. Undoubtedly so; and moreover these strolling jugglers are neither pure in their modes of living nor considered holy by any one; neither by foreigners nor their own people. *They are generally* FEARED *and despised by the natives,* for they are *sorcerers*; men practising the *black art*. While such a holy man as Kavindasami requires but the help of his own divine soul, closely united with the astral spirit, and the help of a few familiar *pitris* — pure, ethereal beings, who rally around their elect brother in flesh — the sorcerer can summon to his help but that class of spirits which we know as the elementals. Like attracts like; and greed for money, impure purposes, and selfish views, cannot attract any other spirits than those that the Hebrew kabalists know as the *klippoth*, dwellers of *Asiah*, the fourth world, and the Eastern magicians as the *afrits,* or elementary spirits of error, or the *devs.*

This is how an English paper describes the astounding *trick* of plant-growth, as performed by Indian *jugglers:*

"An empty flower-pot was now placed upon the floor by the juggler, who requested that his comrades might be allowed to bring up some garden mould from the little plot of ground below. Permission being accorded, the man went, and in two minutes returned with a small quantity of fresh earth tied up in a corner of his chudder, which was deposited in the flower-pot and lightly pressed down. Taking from his basket a dry mango-stone, and handing it round to the company that they might examine it, and satisfy themselves that it was really what it seemed to be, the juggler scooped out a little earth from the centre of the flower-pot and placed the stone in the cavity. He then turned the earth lightly over it, and, having poured a little water over the surface, shut the flower-pot out of view by means of a sheet thrown over a small triangle. And now, amid a full chorus of voices and rat-tat-tat accompaniment of the tabor, the stone germinated; presently a section of the cloth was drawn aside, and gave to view the tender shoot, characterized by two long leaves of a blackish-brown color. The cloth was readjusted, and the incantation resumed. Not long was it, however, before the cloth was a second time drawn aside, and it was then seen that the two first leaves had given place to several green ones, and that the plant now stood nine or ten inches high. A third time, and the foliage was much thicker, the sapling being about thirteen to fourteen inches in height. A fourth time, and the little miniature tree, now about eighteen inches in height, had ten or twelve mangoes about the size of walnuts hanging about its branches. Finally, after the lapse of three or four minutes, the cloth was altogether removed, and the fruit, having the perfection of size, though not of maturity, was plucked and handed to the spectators, and, on being tasted, was found to be approaching ripeness, being sweetly acid."

We may add to this, that we have witnessed the same experiment in India and Thibet, and that more than once we provided the flower-pot ourselves, by emptying an old tin box of some Liebig extracts. We filled it with earth with our own hands, and planted in it a small root handed to us by the conjurer, and until the experiment was ended never once removed our eyes from the pot, which was placed *in our own room.* The result was invariably the same as above described. Does the reader imagine that any prestidigitator could produce the same manifestation under the same conditions?

The learned Orioli, Corresponding Member of the Institute of France, gives a number of instances which show the marvellous effects produced by the will-power acting upon the invisible Proteus of the mesmerists. "I have seen," says he, "certain persons, who simply by pronouncing certain words, arrest wild bulls and horses at headlong speed, and suspend in its flight the arrow which cleaves the air." Thomas Bartholini affirms the same.

Says Du Potet: "When I trace upon the floor with chalk or charcoal this figure . . . a *fire*, a *light* fixes itself on it. Soon it attracts to itself the person who approaches it: it detains and fascinates him . . . and it is useless for him to try to cross the line. A *magic* power compels him to stand still. At the end of a few moments he yields, uttering sobs. . . . *The cause is not in me,* it is in this entirely kabalistic sign; in vain would you employ violence."[256]

In a series of remarkable experiments made by Regazzoni in the presence of certain well-known French physicians, at Paris, on the 18th of May, 1856, they assembled on one night together, and Regazzoni, with his finger, traced an imaginary kabalistic line upon the floor, over which he made a few rapid passes. It was agreed that the mesmeric subjects, selected by the investigators and the committee for the experiments, and all strangers to him, should be brought blindfold into the room, and caused to walk toward the line, without a word being spoken to indicate what was expected of them. The subjects moved along unsuspiciously till they came to the invisible barrier, when, as it is described, "their feet, *as if they had been suddenly seized and riveted,* adhere to the ground, while their bodies, carried forward by the rapid impulse of the motion, fall and strike the floor. The sudden rigidity of their limbs was like that of a frozen corpse, and their heels were rooted with mathematical precision upon the fatal line!"[257]

In another experiment it was agreed that upon one of the physicians giving a certain signal by a glance of the eye, the blindfolded girl should be made to fall on the ground, as if struck by lightning, by the magnetic fluid emitted by Regazzoni's will. She was placed at a distance from the magnetizer; the signal was given, and instantly the subject was felled to the earth, without a word being spoken or a gesture made. Involuntarily one of the spectators stretched out his hand as if to catch her; but Regazzoni, in a voice of thunder,

256 "*La Magie Devoilée,*" p. 147.
257 "*Magie au XIXme Siècle,*" p. 268.

exclaimed, "Do not touch her! Let her fall; a magnetized subject is never hurt by falling." Des Mousseaux, who tells the story, says that "marble is not more rigid than was her body; her head did not touch the ground; one of her arms remained stretched in the air; one of her legs was raised and the other horizontal. She remained in this unnatural posture an indefinite time. Less rigid is a statue of bronze."[258]

All the effects witnessed in the experiments of public lecturers upon mesmerism, were produced by Regazzoni in perfection, and without one spoken word to indicate what the subject was to do. He even by his silent will produced the most surprising effects upon the physical systems of persons totally unknown to him. Directions whispered by the committee in Regazzoni's ear were immediately obeyed by the subjects, whose ears were stuffed with cotton, and whose eyes were bandaged. Nay, in some cases it was not even necessary for them to express to the magnetizer what they desired, for their own mental requests were complied with with perfect fidelity.

Experiments of a similar character were made by Regazzoni in England, at a distance of three hundred paces from the subject brought to him. The *jettatura*, or evil eye, is nothing but the direction of this invisible fluid, charged with malicious will and hatred, from one person to another, and sent out with the intention of harming him. It may equally be employed for a good or evil purpose. *In the former case it is magic; in the latter, sorcery.*

What is the WILL? Can "exact science" tell? What is the nature of that intelligent, intangible, and powerful something which reigns supreme over all inert matter? The great Universal Idea willed, and the cosmos sprang into existence. I *will*, and my limbs obey. I *will*, and, my thought traversing space, which does not exist for it, envelops the body of another individual who is not a part of myself, penetrates through his pores, and, superseding his own faculties, if they are weaker, forces him to a predetermined action. It acts like the fluid of a galvanic battery on the limbs of a corpse. The mysterious effects of attraction and repulsion are the *unconscious* agents of that will; fascination, such as we see exercised by some animals, by serpents over birds, for instance, is a *conscious* action of it, and the result of thought. Sealing-wax, glass, and amber, when rubbed, *i.e.*, when the latent heat which exists in every substance is awakened, attract light bodies; they exercise unconsciously, *will*; for inorganic as well as organic matter possesses a particle of the *divine* essence in itself, however infinitesimally small it may be. And how could it be otherwise? Notwithstanding that in the progress of its evolution it may from beginning to end have passed through millions of various forms, it must ever retain its germ-point of that *preëxistent matter*, which is the first manifestation and emanation of the Deity itself. What is then this inexplicable power of attraction but an atomical portion of that essence that scientists and kabalists equally recognize as the "principle of life" — the *akasa*? Granted that the attraction exercised by such bodies may be blind; but as we ascend higher the scale of the organic beings in nature, we find this principle of life developing attributes and faculties which become more determined and marked with every rung of the endless ladder. Man, the most perfect of organized beings on earth, in whom matter and spirit — *i.e., will* — are the most developed and powerful, is alone allowed to give a conscious impulse to that principle which emanates from him; and only he can impart to the magnetic fluid opposite

---

258 Ibid.

and various impulses without limit as to the direction. "He wills," says Du Potet, "and *organized* matter obeys. It has *no poles.*"

Dr. Brierre de Boismont, in his volume on *Hallucinations,* reviews a wonderful variety of visions, apparitions, and ecstasies, generally termed hallucinations. "We cannot deny," he says, "that in certain diseases we see developed a great surexcitation of sensibility, which lends to the senses a prodigious acuteness of perception. Thus, some individuals will perceive at considerable distances, others will announce the approach of persons who are really on their way, although those present can neither hear nor see them coming."[259]

A lucid patient, lying in his bed, announces the arrival of persons to see whom he must possess *transmural vision,* and this faculty is termed by Brierre de Boismont — *hallucination.* In our ignorance, we have hitherto innocently supposed that in order to be rightly termed a *hallucination,* a vision must be subjective. It must have an existence only in the delirious brain of the patient. But if the latter announces the visit of a person, miles away, and this person arrives at the very moment predicted by the *seer,* then his vision was no more subjective, but on the contrary perfectly *objective,* for he saw that person in the act of coming. And how could the patient see, through solid bodies and space, an object shut out from the reach of our mortal sight, if he had not exercised his *spiritual* eyes on that occasion? Coincidence?

Cabanis speaks of certain nervous disorders in which the patients easily distinguished with the naked eye infusoria and other microscopical beings which others could only perceive through powerful lenses. "I have met subjects," he says, "who saw in Cimmerian darkness as well as in a lighted room; . . ." others "who followed persons, tracing them out like dogs, and recognizing by the smell objects belonging to such persons or even such as had been only touched by them, with a sagacity which was hitherto observed only in animals."[260] Exactly; because reason, which, as Cabanis says, develops only at the expense and loss of natural instinct, is a Chinese wall slowly rising on the soil of sophistry, and which finally shuts out man's spiritual perceptions of which the instinct is one of the most important examples. Arrived at certain stages of physical prostration, when mind and the reasoning faculties seem paralyzed through weakness and bodily exhaustion, instinct — the spiritual *unity* of the five senses — sees, hears, feels, tastes, and smells, unimpaired by either time or space. What do we know of the exact limits of mental action? How can a physician take upon himself to distinguish the imaginary from the real senses in a man who may be living a spiritual life, in a body so exhausted of its usual vitality that it actually is unable to prevent the soul from *oozing* out from its prison?

The divine light through which, unimpeded by matter, the soul perceives things past, present, and to come, as though their rays were focused in a mirror; the death-dealing bolt projected in an instant of fierce anger or at the climax of long-festering hate; the blessing wafted from a grateful or benevolent heart; and the curse hurled at an object — offender or

---

259 Brierre de Boismont, "*Des Hallucinations, ou Histoire raisonnee des apparitions, des songes, des visions, de l'extase du Magnetisme,*" 1845, p. 301 (French edition). See also Fairfield, "*Ten Years Among the Mediums.*"

260 Cabanis, seventh memoir, "*De l'Influence des Maladies sur la Formation des Idées,*" etc. A respected N. Y. legislator has this faculty.

victim — all have to pass through that universal agent, which under one impulse is the breath of God, and under another — the venom of the devil. It was *discovered* (?) by Baron Reichenbach and called OD, whether intentionally or otherwise we cannot say, but it is singular that a name should have been chosen which is mentioned in the most ancient books of the Kabala.

Our readers will certainly inquire what then is this invisible *all*? How is it that our scientific methods, however perfected, have never discovered any of the magical properties contained in it? To this we can answer, that it is no reason because modern scientists are ignorant of them that it should not possess all the properties with which the ancient philosophers endowed it. Science rejects many a thing to-day which she may find herself forced to accept to-morrow. A little less than a century ago the Academy denied Franklin's electricity, and, at the present day, we can hardly find a house without a conductor on its roof. Shooting at the barn-door, the Academy missed the barn itself. Modern scientists, by their wilful skepticism and learned ignorance, do this very frequently.

Emepht, the supreme, first principle, produced an egg; by brooding over which, and permeating the substance of it with its own vivifying essence, the germ contained within was developed; and *Phtha*, the active creative principle proceeded from it, and began his work. From the boundless expanse of cosmic matter, which had formed itself under his breath, or *will*, this cosmic matter — astral light, æther, fire-mist, principle of life — it matters not how we may call it, this creative principle, or, as our modern philosophy terms it, law of evolution, by setting in motion the potencies latent in it, formed suns and stars, and satellites; controlled their emplacement by the immutable law of harmony, and peopled them "with every form and quality of life." In the ancient Eastern mythologies, the cosmogonic myth states that there was but water (the father) and the prolific slime (the mother, *Ilus* or *Hyle*), from which crept forth the mundane snake-*matter*. It was the god *Phanes*, the revealed one, the Word, or *logos*. How willingly this myth was accepted, even by the Christians who compiled the New Testament, may be easily inferred from the following fact: Phanes, the revealed god, is represented in this snake-symbol as a *protogonos*, a being furnished with the heads of a *man*, a hawk or an eagle, a bull — *taurus*, and a lion, with wings on both sides. The heads relate to the zodiac, and typify the four seasons of the year, for the *mundane* serpent is the *mundane* year, while the serpent itself is the symbol of Kneph, the hidden, or *unrevealed* deity — God the Father. Time is winged, therefore the serpent is represented with wings. If we remember that each of the four evangelists is represented as having near him one of the described animals — grouped together in Solomon's triangle in the pentacle of Ezekiel, and to be found in the four cherubs or sphinxes of the sacred arch — we will perhaps understand the secret meaning, as well as the reason why the early Christians adopted this symbol; and how it is that the present Roman Catholics and the Greeks of the Oriental Church still represent these animals in the pictures of their evangelists which sometimes accompany the four *Gospels*. We will also understand why Irenæus, Bishop of Lyons, had so insisted upon the necessity of the *fourth* gospel; giving as a reason that there could not be less than four of them, as there were *four* zones in the world, and four principal winds coming from the four cardinal points, etc.[261]

---

261 Irenæus, Book iii., chap. ii., sec. 8.

According to one of the Egyptian myths, the phantom-form of the isle of Chemmis (*Chemi*, ancient Egypt), which floats on the ethereal waves of the empyrean sphere, was called into being by Horus-Apollo, the sun-god, who caused it to evolve out of the mundane egg.

In the cosmogonical poem of *Völuspa* (the song of the prophetess), which contains the Scandinavian legends of the very dawn of ages, the phantom-germ of the universe is represented as lying in the *Ginnungagap* — or the cup of illusion, a boundless and void abyss. In this world's matrix, formerly a region of night and desolation, *Nebelheim* (the Mist-place) dropped a ray of cold light (æther), which overflowed this cup and froze in it. Then the Invisible blew a scorching wind which dissolved the frozen waters and cleared the mist. These waters, called the streams of *Elivâgar*, distilled in vivifying drops which, falling down, created the earth and the giant *Ymir*, who only had "the semblance of man" (male principle). With him was created the cow, *Audhumla*[262] (female principle), from whose udder flowed *four* streams of milk,[263] which diffused themselves throughout space (the astral light in its purest emanation). The cow Audhumla produces a *superior* being, called Bur, handsome and powerful, by licking the stones that were covered with *mineral salt*.

Now, if we take into consideration that this mineral was universally regarded by ancient philosophers as one of the chief formative principles in organic creation; by the alchemists as the universal menstruum, which, they said, was to be wrought from water; and by every one else, even as it is regarded now by science as well as in the popular ideas, to be an indispensable ingredient for man and beast; we may readily comprehend the hidden wisdom of this allegory of the creation of man. Paracelsus calls salt "the centre of water, wherein metals ought to die," etc., and Van Helmont terms the *Alkahest*, "*summum et felicissimum omnium salium*," the most successful of all salts.

In the *Gospel according to Matthew,* Jesus says: "Ye are the *salt of the earth:* but if the salt have lost his savor, wherewith shall it be salted?" and following the parable he adds: "Ye are *the light* of the world" (v. 14). This is more than an allegory; these words point to a direct and unequivocal meaning in relation to the spiritual and physical organisms of man in his dual nature, and show, moreover, a knowledge of the "secret doctrine," the direct traces of which we find equally in the oldest ancient and current popular traditions, in both the Old and New Testaments, and in the writings of the ancient and mediæval mystics and philosophers.

But to return to our *Edda*-legend. Ymir, the giant, falls asleep, and sweats profusely. This perspiration causes the pit of his left arm to generate out of that place a man and a woman, while his foot produces a son for them. Thus, while the mythic "cow" gives being to a race of superior spiritual men, the giant Ymir begets a race of evil and depraved men, the Hrimthursen, or frost-giants. Comparing notes with the Hindu *Vedas*, we find it then, with slight modifications, the same cosmogonic legend in substance and details. Brahma, as soon

---

262 The cow is the symbol of prolific generation and of intellectual nature. She was sacred to Isis in Egypt; to Christna, in India, and to an infinity of other gods and goddesses personifying the various productive powers of nature. The cow was held, in short, as the impersonation of the Great Mother of all beings, both of the mortals and of the gods, of physical and spiritual generation of things.

263 In *Genesis* the river of Eden was parted, "and became into *four* heads" (*Gen.* ii., 5).

as Bhagaveda, the Supreme God, endows him with creative powers, produces animated beings, wholly spiritual at first. The Dejotas, inhabitants of the Surg's (the celestial) region, are unfit to live on earth, therefore Brahma creates the Daints (giants, who become the dwellers of the Patals, the lower regions of space), who are also unfit to inhabit Mirtlok (the earth). To palliate the evil, the creative power evolves *from his mouth* the first Brahman, who thus becomes the progenitor of our race; from his right arm Brahma creates Raettris, the warrior, and from his left Shaterany, the wife of Raettris. Then their son Bais springs from the right foot of the creator, and his wife Basany from the left. While in the Scandinavian legend Bur (the son of the cow Audhumla), a *superior* being, marries Besla, a daughter of the depraved race of giants, in the Hindu tradition the first Brahman marries Daintary, also a daughter of the race of the giants; and in *Genesis* we see the sons of God taking for wives the daughters of men, and likewise producing mighty men of old; the whole establishing an unquestionable identity of origin between the Christian inspired Book, and the heathen "fables" of Scandinavia and Hindustan. The traditions of nearly every other nation, if examined, will yield a like result.

What modern cosmogonist could compress within so simple a symbol as the Egyptian serpent in a circle such a world of meaning? Here we have, in this creature, the whole philosophy of the universe: matter vivified by spirit, and the two conjointly evolving out of chaos (Force) everything that was to be. To signify that the elements are fast bound in this cosmic matter, which the serpent symbolizes, the Egyptians tied its tail *into a knot.*

There is one more important emblem connected with the sloughing of the serpent's skin, which, so far as we are aware, has never been heretofore noticed by our symbolists. As the reptile upon casting his coat becomes freed from a casing of gross matter, which cramped a body grown too large for it, and resumes its existence with renewed activity, so *man, by casting off the gross material body, enters upon the next stage of his existence with enlarged powers and quickened vitality.* Inversely, the Chaldean Kabalists tell us that primeval man, who, contrary to the Darwinian theory was purer, wiser, and far more spiritual, as shown by the myths of the Scandinavian Bur, the Hindu Dejotas, and the Mosaic "sons of God," — in short, of a far higher nature than the man of the present Adamic race, became *despiritualized* or tainted with matter, and then, for the first time, was given the *fleshly body*, which is typified in *Genesis* in that profoundly-significant verse: "Unto Adam also and to his wife did the Lord God *make coats of skin,* and clothed them."[264] Unless the commentators would make of the First Cause a *celestial tailor,* what else can the apparently absurd words mean, but that the spiritual man had reached, through the progress of involution, to that point where matter, predominating over and conquering spirit, had transformed him into the physical man, or the second Adam, of the second chapter of *Genesis*?

This kabalistical doctrine is much more elaborated in the *Book of Jasher.*[265] In chapter vii., these garments of skin are taken by Noah into the ark, he having obtained them by

---

264 *Genesis* iii. 21.

265 This is claimed to be one of the missing books of the sacred Canon of the Jews, and is referred to in Joshua and II. Samuel. It was discovered by Sidras, an officer of Titus, during the sack of Jerusalem, and published in Venice in the seventeenth century, as alleged in its preface by the Consistory of Rabbins, but the American edition, as well as the English, is reputed by the modern Rabbis, to be a forgery of the twelfth century.

inheritance from Methuselah and Enoch, who had them from Adam and his wife. Ham steals them from his father Noah; gives them "in secret" to Cush, who conceals them from his sons and brothers, and passes them to Nimrod.

While some Kabalists, and even archæologists say that "Adam, Enoch, and Noah might, in outward appearance, be different men, but they were really the selfsame divine person."[266] Others explain that between Adam and Noah there intervened several cycles. That is to say, that every one of the antediluvian patriarchs stood as the representative of a race which had its place in a succession of cycles; and each of which races was less spiritual than its predecessor. Thus Noah, though a good man, could not have borne comparison with his ancestor, Enoch, who "walked with God and did not die." Hence the allegorical interpretation which makes Noah have this coat of skin by inheritance from the second Adam and Enoch, but not wear it himself, for if otherwise, Ham could not have stolen it. But Noah and his children bridged the flood; and while the former belonged to the old and still spiritual antediluvian generation, insomuch as he was selected from all mankind for his purity, his children were *post*-diluvian. The coat of skin worn by Cush "in secret," — *i.e.*, when his spiritual nature began to be tainted by the material — is placed on Nimrod, the most powerful and strongest of physical men on this side of the flood — the last remnant of the antediluvian giants.[267] In the Scandinavian legend, Ymir, the giant, is slain by the sons of Bur, and the streams of blood flowing from his wounds were so copious that the flood drowned the whole race of ice and frost giants, and Bergelmir alone of that race was saved, with his wife, by taking refuge in a bark; which fact permitted him to transmit a new branch of giants from the old stock. But all the sons of Bur remained untouched by the flood.[268]

When the symbolism of this diluvian legend is unravelled, one perceives at once the real meaning of the allegory. The giant Ymir typifies the primitive rude organic *matter*, the blind cosmical forces, in their chaotic state, before they received the intelligent impulse of the Divine Spirit which set them into a regular motion dependent on immovable laws. The progeny of Bur are the "sons of God," or the minor gods mentioned by Plato in the *Timæus*, and who were intrusted, as he expresses it, with the creation of men; for we see them taking the mangled remains of Ymir to the Ginnunga-gap, the chaotic abyss, and employing them for the creation of our world. His blood goes to form oceans and rivers; his bones, the mountains; his teeth, the rocks and cliffs; his hair, the trees, etc.; while his skull forms the heavenly vault, supported by four pillars representing the four cardinal points. From the eye-brows of Ymir was created the future abode of man — Midgard. This abode (the earth), says the *Edda*, in order to be correctly described in all its minute particulars, must be conceived as *round as a ring*, or as a disk, floating in the midst of the Celestial Ocean (Ether). It is encircled by Yormungand, the gigantic Midgard or Earth Serpent, holding its tail in its mouth. This is the mundane snake, matter and spirit, combined product and emanation of Ymir, the gross rudimental matter, and of the spirit of the "sons of God," who fashioned and created all forms. This emanation is the astral light of the Kabalists, and the as yet problematical, and hardly known, æther, or the "hypothetical agent of great elasticity" of our physicists.

---

266 See Godfrey Higgins, "*Anacalypsis*," quoting Faber.
267 See Cory's "*Ancient Fragments*." BEROSUS.
268 We refer the reader for further particulars to the "Prose Edda" in Mallett's "*Northern Antiquities*."

How sure the ancients were of this doctrine of man's trinitarian nature may be inferred from the same Scandinavian legend of the creation of mankind. According to the *Voluspa*, Odin, Honir, and Lodur, who are the progenitors of our race, found in one of their walks on the ocean-beach, two sticks floating on the waves, "powerless and without destiny." Odin breathed in them the breath of life; Honir endowed them with soul and motion; and Lodur with beauty, speech, sight, and hearing. The man they called *Askr* — the ash,[269] and the woman *Embla* — the alder. These first men are placed in Midgard (mid-garden, or Eden) and thus inherit, from their creators, matter or inorganic life; mind, or soul; and pure spirit; the first corresponding to that part of their organism which sprung from the remains of Ymir, the giant-matter, the second from the *Æsir*, or gods, the descendants of Bur, and the third from the *Vanr*, or the representative of pure spirit.

Another version of the *Edda* makes our visible universe spring from beneath the luxuriant branches of the mundane tree — the Yggdrasill, the tree with the *three* roots. Under the first root runs the fountain of life, Urdar; under the second is the famous well of Mimer, in which lie deeply buried Wit and Wisdom. Odin, the Alfadir, asks for a draught of this water; he gets it, but finds himself obliged to pledge one of his eyes for it; the eye being in this case the symbol of the Deity revealing itself in the wisdom of its own creation; for Odin leaves it at the bottom of the deep well. The care of the mundane tree is intrusted to three maidens (the Norns or Parcæ, Urdhr, Verdandi, and Skuld — or the Present, the Past, and the Future. Every morning, while fixing the term of human life, they draw water from the Urdar-fountain, and sprinkle with it the roots of the mundane tree, that it may live. The exhalations of the ash, Yggdrasill, condense, and falling down upon our earth call into existence and change of form every portion of the inanimate matter. This tree is the symbol of the *universal* Life, organic as well as inorganic; its emanations represent the spirit which vivifies every form of creation; and of its three roots, one extends to heaven, the second to the dwelling of the magicians — giants, inhabitants of the *lofty mountains* — and at the third, under which is the spring Hvergelmir, gnaws the monster Nidhogg, who constantly leads mankind into evil. The Thibetans have also their mundane tree, and the legend is of an untold antiquity. With them it is called *Zampun*. The first of its three roots also extends to heaven, to the top of the highest mountains; the second passes down to the lower region; the third remains midway, and reaches the east. The mundane tree of the Hindus is the *Aswatha*.[270] Its branches are the components of the visible world; and its leaves the *Mantras* of the Vedas, symbols of the universe in its intellectual or moral character.

Who can study carefully the ancient religious and cosmogonic myths without perceiving that this striking similitude of conceptions, in their exoteric form and esoteric spirit, is the result of no mere coincidence, but manifests a concurrent design? It shows that already in those ages which are shut out from our sight by the impenetrable mist of tradition, human religious thought developed in uniform sympathy in every portion of the globe. Christians call this adoration of nature in her most concealed verities — Pantheism. But if the latter, which worships and reveals to us God in space in His only possible objective form — that of visible nature — perpetually reminds humanity of Him who created it, and a religion of

---

269 It is worthy of attention that in the Mexican "Popol-Vuh" the human race is created out of a reed, and in Hesiod out of the ash-tree, as in the Scandinavian narrative.
270 See Kanne's "*Pantheum der Ältesten Philosophie.*"

theological dogmatism only serves to conceal Him the more from our sight, which is the better adapted to the needs of mankind?

EVOLUTION IN HINDU ALLEGORY

Modern science insists upon the doctrine of evolution; so do human reason and the "secret doctrine," and the idea is corroborated by the ancient legends and myths, and even by the Bible itself when it is read between the lines. We see a flower slowly developing from a bud, and the bud from its seed. But whence the latter, with all its predetermined programme of physical transformation, and its invisible, therefore spiritual forces which gradually develop its form, color, and odor? The word evolution speaks for itself. The germ of the present human race must have preexisted in the parent of this race, as the seed, in which lies hidden the flower of next summer, was developed in the capsule of its parent-flower; the parent may be but slightly different, but it still differs from its future progeny. The antediluvian ancestors of the present elephant and lizard were, perhaps, the mammoth and the plesiosaurus; why should not the progenitors of our human race have been the "giants" of the Vedas, the Völuspa, and the Book of Genesis? While it is positively absurd to believe the "transformation of species" to have taken place according to some of the more materialistic views of the evolutionists, it is but natural to think that each genus, beginning with the mollusks and ending with monkey-man, has modified from its own primordial and distinctive form. Supposing that we concede that "animals have descended from at most only four or five progenitors";[271] and that even *a la rigueur* "all the organic beings which have ever lived on *this earth* have descended from some one primordial form";[272] still no one but a stone-blind materialist, one utterly devoid of intuitiveness, can seriously expect to see "in the distant future . . . psychology based on a new foundation, that of the necessary acquirement of each mental power and capacity by gradation."[273]

Physical man, as a product of evolution, may be left in the hands of the man of exact science. None but he can throw light upon the *physical* origin of the race. But, we must positively deny the materialist the same privilege as to the question of man's psychical and spiritual evolution, for he and his highest faculties *cannot* be proved on any conclusive evidence to be "as much products of evolution as the humblest plant or the lowest worm."[274]

Having said so much, we will now proceed to show the evolution-hypothesis of the old Brahmans, as embodied by them in the allegory of the mundane tree. The Hindus represent their mythical tree, which they call *Aswatha,* in a way which differs from that of the Scandinavians. It is described by them as growing in a reversed position, the branches extending downward and the roots upward; the former typifying the external world of sense, *i.e.,* the visible cosmical universe, and the latter the invisible world of spirit, because the roots have their *genesis* in the heavenly regions where, from the world's creation, humanity has placed its invisible deity. The creative energy having originated in the

---

271 *"Origin of Species,"* p. 484.
272 Ibid. Which latter word we cannot accept unless that "primordial form" is conceded to be the primal concrete form that spirit assumed as the *revealed* Deity.
273 Ibid., p. 488.
274 Lecture by T. H. Huxley, F.R.S., *"Darwin and Hæckel."*

primordial point, the religious symbols of every people are so many illustrations of this metaphysical hypothesis expounded by Pythagoras, Plato, and other philosophers. "These Chaldeans," says Philo,[275] "were of opinion that the Kosmos, among the things that exist, is a single point, either being itself God (Theos) or that in it is God, comprehending the soul of all the things."

The Egyptian Pyramid also symbolically represents this idea of the mundane tree. Its apex is the mystic link between heaven and earth, and stands for the root, while the base represents the spreading branches, extending to the four cardinal points of the universe of matter. It conveys the idea that all things had their origin in spirit — evolution having originally begun from above and proceeded downward, instead of the reverse, as taught in the Darwinian theory. In other words, there has been a gradual materialization of forms until a fixed ultimate of debasement is reached. This point is that at which the doctrine of modern evolution enters into the arena of speculative hypothesis. Arrived at this period we will find it easier to understand Hæckel's *Anthropogeny*, which traces the pedigree of man "from its protoplasmic root, sodden in the mud of seas which existed before the oldest of the fossiliferous rocks were deposited," according to Professor Huxley's exposition. We may believe man evolved "by gradual modification of a mammal of ape-like organization" still easier when we remember that (though in a more condensed and less elegant, but still as comprehensible, phraseology) the same theory was said by Berosus to have been taught many thousands of years before his time by the man-fish Oannes or Dagon, the semi-demon of Babylonia.[276] We may add, as a fact of interest, that this ancient theory of evolution is not only embalmed in allegory and legend, but also depicted upon the walls of certain temples in India, and, in a fragmentary form, has been found in those of Egypt and on the slabs of Nimroud and Nineveh, excavated by Layard.

But what lies back of the Darwinian line of descent? So far as he is concerned nothing but "unverifiable hypotheses." For, as he puts it, he views all beings "as the lineal descendants of some few beings which lived long before the first bed of the Silurian system was deposited."[277] He does not attempt to show us who these "few beings" were. But it answers our purpose quite as well, for in the admission of their existence at all, resort to the ancients for corroboration and elaboration of the idea receives the stamp of scientific approbation. With all the changes that our globe has passed through as regards temperature, climate, soil, and — if we may be pardoned, in view of recent developments — its electromagnetic condition, he would be bold indeed who dare say that anything in present science contradicts the ancient hypothesis of ante-Silurian man. The flint-axes first found by Boucher de Perthes, in the valley of the Somme, prove that men must have existed at a period so remote as to be beyond calculation. If we believe Buchner, man must have lived even during and before the glacial epoch, a subdivision of the quaternary or diluvial period probably extending very far back in it. But who can tell what the next discovery has in store for us?

---

275 *"Migration of Abraham,"* § 32.
276 Cory, *"Ancient Fragments."*
277 *"Origin of Species,"* pp. 448, 489, first edition.

Now, if we have indisputable proof that man has existed so long as this, there must have been wonderful modifications of his physical system, corresponding with the changes of climate and atmosphere. Does not this seem to show by analogy that, tracing backward, there may have been other modifications, which fitted the most remote progenitors of the "frost-giants" to live even contemporaneously with the Devonian fishes or the Silurian mollusks? True, they left no flint-hatchets behind them, nor any bones or cave-deposits; but, if the ancients are correct, the races at that time were composed not only of giants, or "mighty men of renown," but also of "sons of God." If those who believe in the evolution of *spirit* as firmly as the materialists believe in that of *matter* are charged with teaching "unverifiable hypotheses," how readily can they retort upon their accusers by saying that, by *their* own confession, their physical evolution is still "an unverified, if not actually an unverifiable hypothesis."[278] The former have at least the inferential proof of legendary myth, the vast antiquity of which is admitted by both philologists and archæologists; while their antagonists have nothing of a similar nature, *unless they help themselves to a portion of the ancient picture-writings, and suppress the rest.*

It is more than fortunate that, while the works of some men of science — who have justly won their great reputations — will flatly contradict our hypotheses, the researches and labors of others not less eminent seem to fully confirm our views. In the recent work of Mr. Alfred R. Wallace, *The Geographical Distribution of Animals*, we find the author seriously favoring the idea of "some slow process of development" of the present species from others which have preceded them, his idea extending back over an innumerable series of cycles. And if animals, why not animal man, preceded still farther back by a thoroughly "spiritual" one — a "son of God"?

And now, we may once more return to the symbolology of the olden times, and their physico-religious myths. Before we close this work, we hope to demonstrate more or less successfully how closely the conceptions of the latter were allied with many of the achievements of modern science in physics and natural philosophy. Under the emblematical devices and peculiar phraseology of the priesthood of old lie latent hints of sciences as yet undiscovered during the present cycle. Well acquainted as may be a scholar with the hieratic writing and hieroglyphical system of the Egyptians, he must first of all learn to sift their records. He has to assure himself, compasses and rule in hand, that the picture-writing he is examining fits, to a line, certain fixed geometrical figures which are the hidden keys to such records, before he ventures on an interpretation.

But there are myths which speak for themselves. In this class we may include the double-sexed first creators, of every cosmogony. The Greek Zeus-Zen (æther), and Chthonia (the chaotic earth) and Metis (the water), his wives; Osiris and Isis-Latona — the former god representing also ether — the first emanation of the Supreme Deity, Amun, the primeval source of light; the goddess earth and water again; Mithras,[279] the rock-born god, the symbol of the male mundane-fire, or the personified primordial light, and Mithra, the fire-goddess, at once his mother and his wife; the pure element of fire (the active, or male principle) regarded as light and heat, in conjunction with earth and water, or matter (female or passive

---

278 Huxley, *"Darwin and Hæckel."*
279 Mithras was regarded among the Persians as the *Theos ek petros* — god of the rock.

elements of cosmical generation). Mithras is the son of Bordj, the Persian mundane mountain[280] from which he flashes out as a radiant ray of light. Brahma, the fire-god, and his prolific consort; and the Hindu *Unghi,* the refulgent deity, from whose body issue a thousand streams of glory and *seven* tongues of flame, and in whose honor the Sagniku Brahmans preserve to this day a *perpetual* fire; Siva, personated by the mundane mountain of the Hindus — the *Meru* (Himalaya). This terrific fire-god, who is said in the legend to have descended from heaven, like the Jewish Jehovah, *in a pillar of fire,* and a dozen of other archaic, double-sexed deities, all loudly proclaim their hidden meaning. And what can these dual myths mean but the physico-chemical principle of primordial creation? The first revelation of the Supreme Cause in its triple manifestation of spirit, force, and matter; the divine *correlation,* at its starting-point of evolution, allegorized as the marriage of *fire* and water, products of electrifying spirit, union of the male active principle with the female passive element, which become the parents of their tellurian child, cosmic matter, the *prima materia,* whose spirit is ether, the ASTRAL LIGHT!

Thus all the world-mountains and mundane eggs, the mundane trees, and the mundane snakes and pillars, may be shown to embody scientifically demonstrated truths of natural philosophy. All of these mountains contain, with very trifling variations, the allegorically-expressed description of primal cosmogony; the mundane trees, that of subsequent evolution of spirit and matter; the mundane snakes and pillars, symbolical memorials of the various attributes of this double evolution in its endless correlation of cosmic forces. Within the mysterious recesses of the mountain — the matrix of the universe — the gods (powers) prepare the atomic germs of organic life, and at the same time the life-drink, which, when tasted, awakens in man-matter the man-*spirit.* The soma, the sacrificial drink of the Hindus, is that sacred beverage. For, at the creation of the *prima materia,* while the grossest portions of it were used for the physical embryo-world, the more divine essence of it pervaded the universe, invisibly permeating and enclosing within its ethereal waves the newly-born infant, developing and stimulating it to activity as it slowly evolved out of the eternal chaos.

From the poetry of abstract conception, these mundane myths gradually passed into the concrete images of cosmic symbols, as archæology now finds them. The snake, which plays such a prominent part in the imagery of the ancients, was degraded by the absurd interpretation of the serpent of the Book of *Genesis* into a synonym of Satan, the Prince of Darkness, whereas it is the most ingenious of all the myths in its various symbolisms. For one, as *agathodaimon,* it is the emblem of the healing art and of the immortality of man. It encircles the images of most of the sanitary or hygienic gods. *The cup of health,* in the Egyptian Mysteries, was entwined by serpents. As evil can only arise from an extreme in good, the serpent, under some other aspects, became typical of matter; which, the more it recedes from its primal spiritual source, the more it becomes subject of evil. In the oldest Egyptian imagery, as in the cosmogonic allegories of Kneph, the mundane snake, when typifying matter, is usually represented as contained within a circle; he lies straight across its equator, thus indicating that the universe of astral light, out of which the physical world evolved, while bounding the latter, is itself bound by Emepht, or the Supreme First Cause. *Phtha* producing *Ra,* and the myriad forms to which he gives life, are shown as creeping out

---

280 Bordj is called a fire-mountain — a volcano; therefore it contains fire, rock, earth, and water — the male and active, and the female or passive elements. The myth is suggestive.

of the mundane egg, because it is the most familiar form of that in which is deposited and developed the germ of every living being. When the serpent represents eternity and immortality, it encircles the world, biting its tail, and thus offering no solution of continuity. It then becomes the astral light. The disciples of the school of Pherecydes taught that ether (Zeus or Zen) is the highest empyrean heaven, which encloses the supernal world, and its light (the astral) is the concentrated primordial element.

Such is the origin of the serpent, metamorphosed in Christian ages into Satan. It is the *Od*, the *Ob*, and the *Aour* of Moses and the Kabalists. When in its passive state, when it acts on those who are unwittingly drawn within its current, the astral light is the *Ob*, or Python. Moses was determined to exterminate all those who, sensitive to its influence, allowed themselves to fall under the easy control of the vicious beings which move in the astral waves like fish in the water; beings who surround us, and whom Bulwer-Lytton calls in *Zanoni* "the dwellers of the threshold." It becomes the *Od*, as soon as it is vivified by the *conscious efflux* of an immortal soul; for then the astral currents are acting under the guidance of either an adept, a pure spirit, or an able mesmerizer, who is pure himself and knows how to direct the blind forces. In such cases even a high Planetary Spirit, one of the class of beings that have never been embodied (though there are many among these hierarchies who have lived on our earth), descends occasionally to our sphere, and purifying the surrounding atmosphere enables the *subject* to see, and opens in him the springs of true divine prophecy. As to the term *Aour*, the word is used to designate certain occult properties of the universal agent. It pertains more directly to the domain of the alchemist, and is of no interest to the general public.

The author of the *Homoiomerian* system of philosophy, Anaxagoras of Clazomene, firmly believed that the spiritual prototypes of all things, as well as their elements, were to be found in the boundless ether, where they were generated, whence they evolved, and whither they returned from earth. In common with the Hindus who had personified their Akas'a (sky or ether) and made of it a deific entity, the Greeks and Latins had deified Æther. Virgil calls Zeus, *pater omnipotens æther*[281] *Magnus*, the great god, Ether.

These beings above alluded to are the elemental spirits of the Kabalists,[282] whom the Christian clergy denounce as "devils," the enemies of mankind.

---

281 Virgil, "*Georgica*," book ii.
282 Porphyry and other philosophers explain the nature of the *dwellers*. They are mischievous and deceitful, though some of them are perfectly gentle and harmless, but so weak as to have the greatest difficulty in communicating with mortals whose company they seek incessantly. The former are not wicked through intelligent malice. The law of spiritual evolution not having yet developed their instinct into intelligence, whose highest light belongs but to immortal spirits, their powers of reasoning are in a latent state and, therefore, they themselves, irresponsible. But the Latin Church contradicts the Kabalists. St. Augustine has even a discussion on that account with Porphyry, the Neo-platonist. "These spirits," he says, "are deceitful, *not by their nature*, as Porphyry, the theurgist, will have it, but through malice. They pass themselves off for *gods* and *for the souls of the defunct*" ("*Civit. Dei*," book x., ch. 2). So far Porphyry agrees with him; "but they do not claim to be *demons* [read devils], for they are such in reality!" adds the Bishop of Hippo. But then, under what class should we place the men *without heads*, whom Augustine wishes us to believe he saw himself? or the satyrs of St. Jerome, which he asserts were exhibited for a considerable length of time at Alexandria? They were,

"Already Tertullian," gravely remarks Des Mousseaux, in his chapter on the devils, "has *formally* discovered the secret of their cunning."

A priceless discovery, that. And now that we have learned so much of the mental labors of the holy fathers and their achievements in astral anthropology, need we be surprised at all, if, in the zeal of their spiritual explorations, they have so far neglected their own planet as at times to deny not only its right to motion but even its sphericity?

And this is what we find in Langhorne, the translator of *Plutarch:* Dionysius of Halicarnassus [L. ii.] is of opinion that Numa built the temple of Vesta in a *round* form, to represent the figure of the earth, for by Vesta they meant the earth." Moreover Philolaus, in common with all other Pythagoreans, held that the element of fire was placed in the centre of the universe; and Plutarch, speaking on the subject, remarks of the Pythagoreans that "the earth they suppose not to be without motion, *nor* situated in the centre of the world, but to make its revolution round the sphere of fire, being neither one of the most valuable, nor principal parts of the great machine." Plato, too, is reported to have been of the same opinion. It appears, therefore, that the Pythagoreans anticipated Galileo's *discovery.*

The existence of such an invisible universe being once admitted — as seems likely to be the fact if the speculations of the authors of the *Unseen Universe* are ever accepted by their colleagues — many of the phenomena, hitherto mysterious and inexplicable, become plain. It acts on the organism of the magnetized mediums, it penetrates and saturates them through and through, either directed by the powerful will of a mesmerizer, or by unseen beings who achieve the same result. Once that the silent operation is performed, the astral or sidereal phantom of the mesmerized subject quits its paralyzed, earthly casket, and, after having roamed in the boundless space, alights at the threshold of the mysterious "bourne." For it, the gates of the portal which marks the entrance to the "silent land," are now but partially ajar; they will fly wide open before the soul of the entranced somnambulist only on that day when, united with its higher immortal essence, it will have quitted forever its mortal frame. Until then, the seer or seeress can look but through a chink; it depends on the acuteness of the clairvoyant's spiritual sight to see more or less through it.

The trinity in unity is an idea which all the ancient nations held in common. The three Dejotas — the Hindu Trimurti; the *Three Heads* of the Jewish Kabala.[283] "Three heads are hewn in one another and over one another." The trinity of the Egyptians and that of the mythological Greeks were alike representations of the first triple emanation containing two male and one female principles. It is the union of the male *Logos,* or wisdom, the revealed Deity, with the female *Aura* or *Anima Mundi* — "the holy *Pneuma,*" which is the *Sephira* of the Kabalists and the *Sophia* of the refined Gnostics — that produced all things visible and invisible. While the true metaphysical interpretation of this universal dogma remained within the sanctuaries, the Greeks, with their poetical instincts, impersonated it in many charming myths. In the *Dionysiacs* of Nonnus, the god Bacchus, among other allegories, is represented as in love with the soft, genial breeze (the Holy Pneuma), under the name of

---

he tells us, "men with the legs and tails of goats"; and, if we may believe him, one of these Satyrs was actually *pickled* and sent in a cask to the Emperor Constantine!

283 "Tria capita exsculpta sunt, una intra alterum, et alterum supra alterum" — (Sohar; "*Idra Suta,*" sectio vii.)

Aura Placida.[284] And now we will leave Godfrey Higgins to speak: "When the *ignorant* Fathers were constructing their calendar, they made out of this gentle zephyr two Roman Catholic saints!! " SS. Aura and Placida; — nay, they even went so far as to transfer the jolly god into St. Bacchus, and actually *show his coffin and relics at Rome.* The festival of the two "blessed saints," Aura and Placida, occurs on the 5th of October, close to the festival of St. Bacchus.[285]

How far more poetical, and how much greater the religious spirit to be found in the "heathen" Norse legends of creation! In the boundless abyss of the mundane pit, the Ginnunga-gap, where rage in blind fury and conflict cosmic matter and the primordial forces, suddenly blows the thaw-wind. It is the "unrevealed God," who sends his beneficent breath from Muspellheim, the sphere of empyreal fire, within whose glowing rays dwells this great Being, far beyond the limits of the world of matter; and the *animus* of the Unseen, the Spirit brooding over the dark, abysmal waters, calls order out of chaos, and once having given the impulse to all creation the FIRST CAUSE retires, and remains for evermore in *statu abscondito!*[286]

There is both religion and science in these Scandinavian songs of heathendom. As an example of the latter, take the conception of Thor, the son of Odin. Whenever this Hercules of the North would grasp the handle of his terrible weapon, the thunderbolt or electric hammer, he is obliged to put on his *iron* gantlets. He also wears a magical belt known as the "*girdle of strength,*" which, whenever girded about his person, greatly augments his celestial power. He rides upon a car drawn by two rams with silver bridles, and his awful brow is encircled by a wreath of stars. His chariot has a pointed iron pole, and the spark-scattering wheels continually roll over rumbling thunder-clouds. He hurls his hammer with resistless force against the rebellious frost-giants, whom he dissolves and annihilates. When he repairs to the Urdar fountain, where the gods meet in conclave to decide the destinies of humanity, he alone goes on foot, the rest of the deities being mounted. He walks, for fear that in crossing Bifrost (the rainbow), the many-hued Æsirbridge, he might set it on fire with his thunder-car, at the same time causing the Urdar waters to boil.

Rendered into plain English, how can this myth be interpreted but as showing that the Norse legend-makers were thoroughly acquainted with electricity? Thor, the euhemerization of electricity, handles his peculiar element only when protected by gloves of *iron*, which is its natural conductor. His belt of strength is a closed circuit, around which the isolated current is compelled to run instead of diffusing itself through space. When he rushes with his car through the clouds, he is electricity in its *active* condition, as the sparks scattering from his wheels and the rumbling thunder of the clouds testify. The pointed iron pole of the chariot is suggestive of the lightning-rod; the two rams which serve as his coursers are the familiar ancient symbols of the male or generative power; their silver bridles typify the female principle, for silver is the metal of Luna, Astarte, Diana. Therefore in the ram and his bridle we see combined the active and passive principles of nature in opposition, one rushing forward, and the other restraining, while both are in subordination

---

284 Gentle gale (lit.)
285 Higgins, "*Anacalypsis*"; also "*Dupuis.*"
286 Mallett, "*Northern Antiquities,*" pp. 401-406, and "*The Songs of a Voluspa*" in the Edda.

to the world-permeating, electrical principle, which gives them their impulse. With the electricity supplying the impulse, and the male and female principle combining and recombining in endless correlation, the result is — evolution of visible nature, the crown-glory of which is the planetary system, which in the mythic Thor is allegorized by the circlet of glittering orbs which bedeck his brow. When in his active condition, his awful thunderbolts destroy everything, even the lesser other Titanic forces. But he goes afoot over the rainbow bridge, Bifrost, because to mingle with other less powerful gods than himself, he is obliged to be in a *latent* state, which he could not be in his car; otherwise he would set on fire and annihilate all. The meaning of the Urdar-fountain, that Thor is afraid to make boil, and the cause of his reluctance, will only be comprehended by our physicists when the reciprocal electro-magnetic relations of the innumerable members of the planetary system, now just suspected, shall be thoroughly determined. Glimpses of the truth are given in the recent scientific essays of Professors Mayer and Sterry Hunt. The ancient philosophers believed that not only volcanos, but boiling springs were caused by concentrations of underground electric currents, and that this same cause produced mineral deposits of various natures, which form curative springs. If it be objected that this fact is not distinctly stated by the ancient authors, who, in the opinion of our century were hardly acquainted with electricity, we may simply answer that not all the works embodying ancient wisdom are now extant among our scientists. The clear and cool waters of Urdar were required for the daily irrigation of the mystical mundane tree; and if they had been disturbed by Thor, or active electricity, they would have been converted into mineral springs unsuited for the purpose. Such examples as the above will support the ancient claim of the philosophers that *there is a logos in every mythos,* or a ground-work of truth in every fiction.

CHAPTER VI

"Hermes, who is of my ordinances ever the bearer . .
Then taking his staff, with which he the eyelids of mortals
Closes at will, and the sleeper, at will, reawakens."

— *Odyssey*, Book V

"I saw the Samothracian rings
Leap, and steel-filings boil in a brass dish
So soon as underneath it there was placed
The magnet-stone; and with wild terror seemed
The iron to flee from it in stern hate. . . ."
— *Lucretius*, Book VI

"But that which especially distinguishes the Brotherhood is
their marvellous knowledge of the resources of the medical art.
They work not by charms but by simples."

MS. Account of the Origin and Attributes of the True Rosicrucians

THE DEBT WE OWE TO PARACELSUS

ONE of the truest things ever said by a man of science is the remark made by Professor Cooke in his *New Chemistry.* "The history of Science shows that the age must be prepared before scientific truths can take root and grow. The barren premonitions of science have been barren because these seeds of truth fell upon unfruitful soil; and, as soon as the fulness of the time has come, the seed has taken root and the fruit has ripened . . . every student is surprised to find how very little is the share of new truth which even the greatest genius has added to the previous stock."

The revolution through which chemistry has recently passed, is well calculated to concentrate the attention of chemists upon this fact; and it would not be strange, if, in less time than it has required to effect it, the claims of the alchemists would be examined with impartiality, and studied from a rational point of view. To bridge over the narrow gulf which now separates the *new* chemistry from *old* alchemy, is little, if any harder than what they have done in going from dualism to the law of Avogadro.

As Ampère served to introduce Avogadro to our contemporary chemists, so Reichenbach will perhaps one day be found to have paved the way with his OD for the just appreciation of Paracelsus. It was more than fifty years before molecules were accepted as units of chemical calculations; it may require less than half that time to cause the superlative merits of the Swiss mystic to be acknowledged. The warning paragraph about healing mediums,[287] which will be found elsewhere, might have been written by one who had read his works. "You must understand," he says, "that the magnet is that spirit of life in man

---

287 From a London Spiritualist journal.

which the infected seeks, as both unite themselves with chaos from without. And thus the healthy are infected by the unhealthy through magnetic attraction."

The primal causes of the diseases afflicting mankind; the secret relations between physiology and psychology, vainly tortured by men of modern science for some clew to base their speculations upon; the specifics and remedies for every ailment of the human body — all are described and accounted for in his voluminous works. Electro-magnetism, the so-called *discovery* of Professor Oersted, had been used by Paracelsus three centuries before. This may be demonstrated by examining critically his mode of curing disease. Upon his achievements in chemistry there is no need to enlarge, for it is admitted by fair and unprejudiced writers that he was one of the greatest chemists of his time.[288] Brierre de Boismont terms him a "genius" and agrees with Deleuze that he created a new epoch in the history of medicine. The secret of his successful and, as they were called, magic cures lies in his sovereign contempt for the so-called learned "authorities" of his age. "Seeking for truth," says Paracelsus, "I considered with myself that if there were no teachers of medicine in this world, how would I set to learn the art? No otherwise than in the great open book of nature, written with the finger of God. . . . I am accused and denounced for not having entered in at the right door of art. But which is the right one? Galen, Avicenna, Mesue, Rhasis, or honest nature? I believe, the last! Through this door I entered, and the light of nature, and no apothecary's lamp directed me on my way."

This utter scorn for established laws and scientific formulas, this aspiration of mortal clay to commingle with the spirit of nature, and look to it alone for health, and help, and the light of truth, was the cause of the inveterate hatred shown by the contemporary pigmies to the fire-philosopher and alchemist. No wonder that he was accused of charlatanry and even drunkenness. Of the latter charge, Hemmann boldly and fearlessly exonerates him, and proves that the foul accusation proceeded from "Oporinus, who lived with him some time in order to learn his secrets, but his object was defeated; hence, the evil reports of his disciples and apothecaries." He was the founder of the School of Animal Magnetism and the discoverer of the occult properties of the magnet. He was branded by his age as a sorcerer, because the cures he made were marvellous. Three centuries later, Baron Du Potet was also accused of sorcery and demonolatry by the Church of Rome, and of charlatanry by the academicians of Europe. As the fire-philosophers say, it is not the chemist who will condescend to look upon the "living fire" otherwise than his colleagues do. "Thou hast forgotten what thy fathers taught thee about it — or rather, thou hast never known . . . it is *too loud* for thee!"[289]

MESMERISM — ITS PARENTAGE, RECEPTION, POTENTIALITY

A work upon magico-spiritual philosophy and occult science would be incomplete without a particular notice of the history of animal magnetism, as it stands since Paracelsus staggered with it the schoolmen of the latter half of the sixteenth century.

We will observe briefly its appearance in Paris when imported from Germany by Anton Mesmer. Let us peruse with care and caution the old papers now mouldering in the

---

288 Hemmann, "*Medico-Surgical Essays*," Berl., 1778.
289 Robert Fludd, "*Treatise III.*"

Academy of Sciences of that capital, for there we will find that, after having rejected in its turn every discovery that was ever made since Galileo, the *Immortals* capped the climax by turning their backs upon magnetism and mesmerism. They voluntarily shut the doors before themselves, the doors which led to those greatest mysteries of nature, which lie hid in the dark regions of the psychical as well as the physical world. The great universal solvent, the Alkahest, was within their reach — they passed it by; and now, after nearly a hundred years have elapsed, we read the following confession:

"Still it is true that, beyond the limits of direct observation, our science (chemistry) is not infallible, and our theories and systems, although they *may* all contain a kernel of truth, undergo frequent changes, and are often revolutionized."[290]

To assert so dogmatically that mesmerism and animal magnetism are but hallucinations, implies that it can be proved. But where are these proofs, which alone ought to have authority in science? Thousands of times the chance was given to the academicians to assure themselves of its truth; but, they have invariably declined. Vainly do mesmerists and healers invoke the testimony of the deaf, the lame, the diseased, the dying, who were cured or restored to life by simple manipulations and the apostolic "laying on of hands." "Coincidence" is the usual reply, when the fact is too evident to be absolutely denied; "will-o'-the-wisp," "exaggeration," "quackery," are favorite expressions, with our but too numerous Thomases. Newton, the well-known American healer, has performed more instantaneous cures than many a famous physician of New York City has had patients in all his life; Jacob, the Zouave, has had a like success in France. Must we then consider the accumulated testimony of the last forty years upon this subject to be all illusion, confederacy with clever charlatans, and lunacy? Even to breathe such a stupendous fallacy would be equivalent to a self-accusation of lunacy.

Notwithstanding the recent sentence of Leymarie, the scoffs of the skeptics and of a vast majority of physicians and scientists, the unpopularity of the subject, and, above all, the indefatigable persecutions of the Roman Catholic clergy, fighting in mesmerism woman's traditional enemy, so evident and unconquerable is the truth of its phenomena that even the French magistrature was forced tacitly, though very reluctantly, to admit the same. The famous *clairvoyante*, Madame Roger, was charged with obtaining money under false pretenses, in company with her mesmerist, Dr. Fortin. On May 18th, 1876, she was arraigned before the *Tribunal Correctionnel* of the Seine. Her witness was Baron Du Potet, the grand master of mesmerism in France for the last fifty years; her advocate, the no less famous Jules Favre. Truth for once triumphed — the accusation was abandoned. Was it the extraordinary eloquence of the orator, or bare facts incontrovertible and unimpeachable that won the day? But Leymarie, the editor of the *Revue Spirite*, had also facts in his favor; and, moreover, the evidence of over a hundred respectable witnesses, among whom were the first names of Europe. To this there is but one answer — the magistrates dared not question the facts of mesmerism. Spirit-photography, spirit-rapping, writing, moving, talking, and even spirit-materializations can be simulated; there is hardly a physical phenomenon now in Europe and America but could be imitated — with apparatus — by a clever juggler. The wonders of mesmerism and subjective phenomena alone defy tricksters, skepticism, stern

---

290 Prof. J. P. Cooke, "*New Chemistry.*"

science, and dishonest mediums; *the cataleptic state it is impossible to feign.* Spiritualists who are anxious to have their truths proclaimed and forced on science, cultivate the mesmeric phenomena. Place on the stage of Egyptian Hall a somnambulist plunged in a deep mesmeric sleep. Let her mesmerist send her freed spirit to all the places the public may suggest; test her clairvoyance and clairaudience; stick pins into any part of her body which the mesmerist may have made his passes over; thrust needles through the skin below her eyelids; burn her flesh and lacerate it with a sharp instrument. "Do not fear!" exclaim Regazzoni and Du Potet, Teste and Pierrard, Puysegur and Dolgorouky — "a mesmerized or entranced subject *is never hurt!*" And when all this is performed, invite any popular wizard of the day who thirsts for puffery, and is, or pretends to be, clever at mimicking every spiritual phenomenon, to submit *his* body to the same tests![291]

The speech of Jules Favre is reported to have lasted an hour and a half, and to have held the judges and the public spellbound by its eloquence. We who have heard Jules Favre believe it most readily; only the statement embodied in the last sentence of his argument was unfortunately premature and erroneous at the same time. "We are in the presence of a phenomenon which *science admits* without attempting to explain. *The public may smile at* it, but our most illustrious physicians regard it with gravity. Justice can no longer ignore what *science has acknowledged!*"

Were this sweeping declaration based upon fact and had mesmerism been impartially investigated by many instead of a few true men of science, more desirous of questioning nature than mere expediency, the public would *never* smile. The public is a docile and pious child, and readily goes whither the nurse leads it. It chooses its idols and fetishes, and worships them in proportion to the noise they make; and then turns round with a timid look of adulation to see whether the nurse, old Mrs. Public Opinion, is satisfied.

Lactantius, the old Christian father, is said to have remarked that no skeptic in his days would have dared to maintain before a magician that the soul did not survive the body, but died together with it; "for he would refute them on the spot by calling up the souls of the dead, rendering them visible to human eyes, and making them foretell future events."[292] So with the magistrates and bench in Madame Roger's case. Baron Du Potet was there, and they were *afraid* to see him mesmerize the somnambulist, and so force them not only to believe in the phenomenon, but to acknowledge it — which was far worse.

And now to the doctrine of Paracelsus. His incomprehensible, though lively style must be read like the biblio-rolls of Ezekiel, *"within and without."* The peril of propounding heterodox theories was great in those days; the Church was powerful, and sorcerers were burnt by the dozens. For this reason, we find Paracelsus, Agrippa, and Eugenius Philalethes as notable for their pious declarations as they were famous for their achievements in alchemy and magic. The full views of Paracelsus on the occult properties of the magnet are

---

291 In the *"Bulletin de l'Academie de Medecine,"* Paris, 1837, vol. i., p. 343 et seq., may be found the report of Dr. Oudet, who, to ascertain the state of insensibility of a lady in a magnetic sleep, pricked her with pins, introducing a long pin in the flesh up to its head, and held one of her fingers for some seconds in the flame of a candle. A cancer was extracted from the right breast of a Madame Plaintain. The operation lasted twelve minutes; during the whole time the patient talked very quietly with her mesmerizer, and never felt the slightest sensation (*"Bul. de l'Acad. de Med.,"* Tom. ii., p. 370).
292 *Prophecy, Ancient and Modern,* by A. Wilder, *"Phrenological Journal."*

explained partially in his famous book, *Archidaxarum,* in which he describes the wonderful tincture, a medicine extracted from the magnet and called *Magisterium Magnetis,* and partially in the *De Ente Dei,* and *De Ente Astrorum,* Lib. I. But the explanations are all given in a diction unintelligible to the profane. "Every peasant sees," said he, "that a magnet will attract iron, but a wise man must inquire for himself. . . . I have discovered that the magnet, besides this visible power, that of attracting iron, possesses another *and concealed* power."

He demonstrates further that in man lies hidden a *"sidereal force,"* which is that emanation from the stars and celestial bodies of which the spiritual form of man — the astral spirit — is composed. This identity of essence, which we may term the spirit of cometary matter, always stands in direct relation with the stars from which it was drawn, and thus there exists a mutual attraction between the two, both being magnets. The identical composition of the earth and all other planetary bodies and man's terrestrial body was a fundamental idea in his philosophy. "The body comes from the elements, the [astral] spirit from the stars. . . . Man eats and drinks of the elements, for the sustenance of his blood and flesh; from the stars are the intellect and thoughts sustained in his spirit." *The spectroscope has made good his theory as to the identical composition of man and stars; the physicists now lecture to their classes upon the magnetic attractions of the sun and planets.*[293]

Of the substances known to compose the body of man, there have been discovered in the stars already, hydrogen, sodium, calcium, magnesium and iron. In all the stars observed, numbering many hundreds, hydrogen was found, except in two. Now, if we recollect how they have deprecated Paracelsus and his theory of man and the stars being composed of like substances; how ridiculed he was by astronomers and physicists, for his ideas of chemical affinity and attraction between the two; and then realize that the spectroscope has vindicated one of his assertions at least, is it so absurd to prophesy that in time all the rest of his theories will be substantiated?

And now, a very natural question is suggested. How did Paracelsus come to learn anything of the composition of the stars, when, till a very recent period — till the discovery of the spectroscope in fact — the constituents of the heavenly bodies were utterly unknown to our learned academies? And even now, notwithstanding tele-spectroscope and other very important modern improvements, except a few elements and a hypothetical chromosphere, everything is yet a mystery for them in the stars. Could Paracelsus have been so sure of the nature of the starry host, unless he had means of which science knows nothing? Yet knowing nothing she will not even hear pronounced the very names of these means, which are — hermetic philosophy and alchemy.

We must bear in mind, moreover, that *Paracelsus was the discoverer of hydrogen, and knew well all its properties and composition* long before any of the orthodox academicians ever thought of it; that he had studied astrology and astronomy, as all the fire-philosophers did;

---

293 The theory that the sun is an incandescent globe is — as one of the magazines recently expressed it — "going out of fashion." It has been computed that if the sun — whose mass and diameter is known to us — "were a solid block of coal, and sufficient amount of oxygen could be supplied to burn at the rate necessary to produce the effects we see, it would be completely consumed in less than 5,000 years." And yet, till comparatively a few weeks ago, it was maintained — nay, is still maintained, that the sun is a reservoir of vaporized metals!

and that, if he did assert that man is in a direct affinity with the stars, he knew well what he asserted.

The next point for the physiologists to verify is his proposition that the nourishment of the body comes not merely through the stomach, "but also imperceptibly through the magnetic force, which resides in all nature and by which every individual member draws its specific nourishment to itself." Man, he further says, draws not only health from the elements when in equilibrium, but also disease when they are disturbed. Living bodies are subject to the laws of attraction and chemical affinity, as science admits; the most remarkable physical property of organic tissues, according to physiologists, is the property of *imbibition*. What more natural, then, than this theory of Paracelsus, that this absorbent, attractive, and chemical body of ours gathers into itself the astral or sidereal influences? "The sun and the stars attract from us to themselves, and we again from them to us." What objection can science offer to this? What it is that we give off, is shown in Baron Reichenbach's discovery of the odic emanations of man, which are identical with flames from magnets, crystals, and in fact from all vegetable organisms.

The unity of the universe was asserted by Paracelsus, who says that "the human body is possessed of primeval stuff" (or cosmic matter); the spectroscope has proved the assertion by showing that the same chemical elements which exist upon earth and in the sun, are also found in all the stars. The spectroscope does more: it shows that all the stars are *suns*, similar in constitution to our own;[294] and as we are told by Professor Mayer,[295] that the magnetic condition of the earth changes with every variation upon the sun's surface, and is said to be "in subjection to *emanations* from the sun," the stars being suns must also give off emanations which affect us in proportionate degrees.

"In our dreams," says Paracelsus, "we are like the plants, which have also the elementary and vital body, but possess not the spirit. In our sleep the astral body is free and can, by the elasticity of its nature, either hover round in proximity with its sleeping vehicle, or soar higher to hold converse with its starry parents, or even communicate with its brothers at great distances. Dreams of a prophetic character, prescience, and present wants, are the faculties of the astral spirit. To our elementary and grosser body, these gifts are not imparted, for at death it descends into the bosom of the earth and is reunited to the physical elements, while the several spirits return to the stars. The animals," he adds, "have also their presentiments, for they too have an astral body."

Van Helmont, who was a disciple of Paracelsus, says much the same, though his theories on magnetism are more largely developed, and still more carefully elaborated. The *Magnale Magnum*, the means by which the secret magnetic property "enables one person to affect another mutually, is attributed by him to that universal sympathy which exists between all things in nature. The cause produces the effect, the effect refers itself back to the cause, and both are reciprocated. "Magnetism," he says, "is an unknown property of a heavenly nature; very much resembling the stars, and not at all impeded by any boundaries of space or time.

---

294 See Youmans, "*Chemistry on the Basis of the New System — Spectrum Analysis.*"
295 Professor of Physics in the Stevens Institute of Technology. See his "*The Earth a Great Magnet,*" — a lecture delivered before the Yale Scientific Club, 1872. See, also, Prof. Balfour Stewart's lecture on "*The Sun and the Earth.*"

. . . Every created being possesses his own celestial power and is closely allied with heaven. This magic power of man, which thus can operate externally, lies, as it were, hidden in the inner man. This magical wisdom and strength thus sleeps, but, by a mere suggestion is roused into activity, and becomes more living, the more the outer man of flesh and the darkness is repressed . . . and this, I say, the kabalistic art effects; it brings back to the soul that magical yet natural strength which like a startled sleep had left it."[296]

Both Van Helmont and Paracelsus agree as to the great potency of the will in the state of ecstasy; they say that "the spirit is everywhere diffused; and the spirit is the medium of magnetism"; that pure primeval magic does not consist in superstitious practices and vain ceremonies but in the imperial will of man. "It is not the spirits of heaven and of hell which are the masters over physical nature, but the soul and spirit of man which are concealed in him as the fire is concealed in the flint."

The theory of the sidereal influence on man was enunciated by all the mediæval philosophers. "The stars consist equally of the elements of earthly bodies," says Cornelius Agrippa, "and therefore the ideas attract each other. . . . Influences only go forth through the help of the spirit; but this spirit is diffused through the whole universe and is in full accord with the human spirits. The magician who would acquire supernatural powers must possess *faith, love,* and *hope.* . . . In all things there is a secret power concealed, and thence come the miraculous powers of magic."

The modern theory of General Pleasonton[297] singularly coincides with the views of the fire-philosophers. His view of the positive and negative electricities of man and woman, and the mutual attraction and repulsion of everything in nature seems to be copied from that of Robert Fludd, the Grand Master of the Rosicrucians of England. "When two men approach each other," says the fire-philosopher, "their magnetism is either passive or active; that is, positive or negative. If the emanations which they send out are broken or thrown back, there arises antipathy. But when the emanations pass through each other from both sides, then there is positive magnetism, for the rays proceed from the centre to the circumference. In this case they not only affect sicknesses but also moral sentiments. This magnetism or sympathy is found not only among animals but also in plants and in minerals."[298]

And now we will notice how, when Mesmer had imported into France his "baquet" and system based entirely on the philosophy and doctrines of the Paracelsites — the great psychological and physiological discovery was treated by the physicians. It will demonstrate how much ignorance, superficiality, and prejudice can be displayed by a scientific body, when the subject clashes with their own cherished theories. It is the more important because, to the neglect of the committee of the French Academy of 1784 is probably due the present materialistic drift of the public mind; and certainly the gaps in the atomic philosophy which we have seen its most devoted teachers confessing to exist. The committee of 1784 comprised men of such eminence as Borie, Sallin, d'Arcet, and the famous Guillotin, to whom were subsequently added, Franklin, Leroi, Bailly, De Borg and

---

296 "*De Magnetica Vulner Curatione*," p. 722, 1. c.
297 See "*On the Influence of the Blue Ray.*"
298 Ennemoser, "*History of Magic.*"

Lavoisier. Borie died shortly afterward and Magault succeeded him. There can be no doubt of two things, viz.: that the committee began their work under strong prejudices and only because peremptorily ordered to do it by the king; and that their manner of observing the delicate facts of mesmerism was injudicious and illiberal. Their report, drawn by Bailly, was intended to be a death-blow to the new science. It was spread ostentatiously throughout all the schools and ranks of society, arousing the bitterest feelings among a large portion of the aristocracy and rich commercial class, who had patronized Mesmer and had been eye-witnesses of his cures. Ant. L. de Jussieu, an academician of the highest rank, who had thoroughly investigated the subject with the eminent court-physician, d'Eslon, published a counter-report drawn with minute exactness, in which he advocated the careful observation by the medical faculty of the therapeutic effects of the magnetic fluid and insisted upon the immediate publication of their discoveries and observations. His demand was met by the appearance of a great number of memoirs, polemical works, and dogmatical books developing new facts; and Thouret's works entitled *Recherches et Doutes sur le Magnetisme Animal*, displaying a vast erudition, stimulated research into the records of the past, and the magnetic phenomena of successive nations from the remotest antiquity were laid before the public.

The doctrine of Mesmer was simply a restatement of the doctrines of Paracelsus, Van Helmont, Santanelli, and Maxwell, the Scotchman; and he was even guilty of copying texts from the work of Bertrand, and enunciating them as his own principles.[299] In Professor Stewart's work,[300] the author regards our universe as composed of atoms with some sort of medium between them as the machine, and the laws of energy as the laws working this machine. Professor Youmans calls this "a modern doctrine," but we find among the twenty-seven propositions laid down by Mesmer, in 1775, just one century earlier, in his *Letter to a Foreign Physician*, the following: *1st. There exists a mutual influence between the heavenly bodies, the earth, and living bodies. 2d. A fluid, universally diffused and continued, so as to admit no vacuum, whose subtility is beyond all comparison, and which, from its nature, is capable of receiving, propagating, and communicating all the impressions of motion, is the medium of this influence.* It would appear from this, that the theory is not so modern after all. Professor Balfour Stewart says, "We may regard the universe in the light of a vast physical machine." And Mesmer: *3d. This reciprocal action is subject to mechanical laws, unknown up to the present time.*

Professor Mayer, reaffirming Gilbert's doctrine that the earth is a great magnet, remarks that the mysterious variations in the intensity of its force seem to be in subjection to emanations from the sun, "changing with the apparent daily and yearly revolutions of that orb, and pulsating in sympathy with the huge waves of fire which sweep over its surface." He speaks of "the constant fluctuation, the ebb and flow of the earth's directive influence." And Mesmer:

4th. "From this action result alternate effects which may be considered a flux and reflux."

6th. It is by this operation (the most universal of those presented to us by nature) that the relations of activity occur between the heavenly bodies, the earth, and its constituent parts.

There are two more which will be interesting reading to our modern scientists:

---

299 "*Du Magnetisme Animal, en France.*" Paris, 1826.
300 "*The Conservation of Energy.*" N. Y., 1875.

7th. The properties of matter, and of organized body, depend on this operation.

8th. The animal body experiences the alternate effects of this agent; and it is by insinuating itself into the substance of the nerves, that it immediately affects them.

Among other important works which appeared between 1798 and 1824, when the French Academy appointed its second commission to investigate mesmerism, the *Annales du Magnetisme Animal,* by the Baron d'Henin de Cuvillier, Lieutenant-General, Chevalier of St. Louis, member of the Academy of Sciences, and correspondent of many of the learned societies of Europe, may be consulted with great advantage. In 1820 the Prussian government instructed the Academy of Berlin to offer a prize of three hundred ducats in gold for the best thesis on mesmerism. The Royal Scientific Society of Paris, under the presidency of His Royal Highness the Duc d'Angouleme, offered a gold medal for the same purpose. The Marquis de la Place, peer of France, one of the *Forty* of the Academy of Sciences, and honorary member of the learned societies of all the principal European governments, issued a work entitled *Essai Philosophique sur les Probabilites,* in which this eminent scientist says: "Of all the instruments that we can employ to know the imperceptible agents of nature, the most sensitive are the nerves, especially when exceptional influences increase their sensibility. . . . The singular phenomena which result from this extreme nervous sensitiveness of certain individuals, have given birth to diverse opinions as to the existence of a new agent, which has been named animal magnetism. . . . We are so far from knowing all the agents of nature and their various modes of action that it would be hardly philosophical to deny the phenomena, simply because they are inexplicable, in the actual state of our information. It is simply our duty to examine them with an attention as much more scrupulous as it seems difficult to admit them." The experiments of Mesmer were vastly improved upon by the Marquis de Puysegur, who entirely dispensed with apparatus and produced remarkable cures among the tenants of his estate at Busancy. These being given to the public, many other educated men experimented with like success, and in 1825 M. Foissac proposed to the Academy of Medicine to institute a new inquiry. A special committee, consisting of Adelon, Parisey, Marc, Burdin, Sen., with Husson as reporter, united in a recommendation that the suggestion should be adopted. They make the manly avowal that "in science no decision whatever is absolute and irrevocable," and afford us the means to estimate the value which should be attached to the conclusions of the Franklin committee of 1784, by saying that "the experiments on which this judgment was founded appeared to have been conducted without the simultaneous and necessary assembling together of all the commissioners, and *also with moral predispositions,* which, according to the principles of the fact which they were appointed to examine, *must cause their complete failure.*"

What they say concerning magnetism as a secret remedy, has been said many times by the most respected writers upon modern Spiritualism, namely: "It is the duty of the Academy to study it, to subject it to trials; finally, to take away the use and practice of it from persons quite strangers to the art, who abuse this means, and make it an object of lucre and speculation."

This report provoked long debates, but in May, 1826, the Academy appointed a commission which comprised the following illustrious names: Leroux, Bourdois de la Motte, Double, Magendie, Guersant, Husson, Thillaye, Marc, Itard, Fouquier, and Guenau de Mussy. They began their labors immediately, and continued them five years, communicating, through Monsieur Husson, to the Academy the results of their observations. The report embraces accounts of phenomena classified under thirty-four different paragraphs, but as this work is not specially devoted to the science of magnetism, we must be content with a few brief extracts. They assert that neither contact of the hands, frictions, nor passes are invariably needed, since, on several occasions, the will, fixedness of stare, have sufficed to produce magnetic phenomena, even without the knowledge of the magnetized. "Well-attested and therapeutical phenomena" depend on magnetism alone, and are not reproduced without it. The state of somnambulism exists and "occasions the development of new faculties, which have received the denominations of *clairvoyance,* intuition, internal prevision." Sleep (the magnetic) has "been excited under circumstances where those magnetized could not see, and were entirely ignorant of the means employed to occasion it. The magnetizer, having once controlled his subject, may "put him completely into somnambulism, take him out of it without his knowledge, out of his sight, at a certain distance, and through closed doors." The external senses of the sleeper seem to be completely paralyzed, and a duplicate set to be brought into action. "Most of the time they are entirely strangers to the external and unexpected noise made in their ears, such as the sound of copper vessels, forcibly struck, the fall of any heavy substance, and so forth. . . . One may make them respire hydrochloric acid or ammonia without inconveniencing them by it, or without even a suspicion on their part." The committee could "tickle their feet, nostrils, and the angles of the eyes by the approach of a feather, pinch their skin so as to produce ecchymosis, prick it under the nails with pins plunged to a considerable depth, without the evincing of any pain, or by sign of being at all aware of it. In a word, we have seen one person who was insensible to one of the most painful operations of surgery, and whose countenance, pulse, or respiration did not manifest the slightest emotion."

So much for the external senses; now let us see what they have to say about the internal ones, which may fairly be considered as proving a marked difference between man and a mutton-protoplasm. "Whilst they are in this state of somnambulism," say the committee, "the magnetized persons we have observed, retain the exercise of the faculties which they have whilst awake. Their memory even appears to be more faithful and more extensive. . . . We have seen two somnambulists distinguish, width their eyes shut, the objects placed before them; they have told, without touching them, the color and value of the cards; they have read words traced with the hand, or some lines of books opened by mere chance. This phenomenon took place, even when the opening of the eyelids was accurately closed, by means of the fingers. We met, in two somnambulists, the power of foreseeing acts more or less complicated of the organism. One of them announced several days, nay, several months beforehand, the day, the hour, and the minute when epileptic fits would come on and return; the other declared the time of the cure. Their previsions were realized with remarkable exactness."

The commission say that "it has collected and communicated facts sufficiently important to induce it to think that the Academy should encourage the researches on magnetism as a very curious branch of psychology and natural history." The committee conclude by saying that the facts *are so extraordinary* that they scarcely imagine that the Academy will concede their reality, but protest that they have been throughout animated by motives of a lofty character, "the love of science and by the necessity of justifying the hopes which the Academy had entertained of our zeal and our devotion."

Their fears were fully justified by the conduct of at least one member of their own number, who had absented himself from the experiments, and, as M. Husson tells us, "did not deem it right to sign the report."

This was Magendie, the physiologist, who, despite the fact stated by the official report that he had not "been present at the experiments," did not hesitate to devote four pages of his famous work on *Human Physiology* to the subject of mesmerism, and after summarizing its alleged phenomena, without endorsing them as unreservedly as the erudition and scientific acquirements of his fellow committee-men would seem to have exacted, says: "Self-respect and the dignity of the profession demand circumspection on these points. He [the well-informed physician] will remember how readily mystery glides into charlatanry, and how apt the profession is to become degraded even by its semblance when countenanced by respectable practitioners." No word in the context lets his readers into the secret that he had been duly appointed by the Academy to serve on the commission of 1826; had absented himself from its sittings; had so failed to learn the truth about mesmeric phenomena, and was now pronouncing judgment ex parte. "Self-respect and the dignity of the profession" probably exacted silence!

Thirty-eight years later, an English scientist, whose specialty is the investigation of physics, and whose reputation is even greater than that of Magendie, stooped to as unfair a course of conduct. When the opportunity offered to investigate the spiritualistic phenomena, and aid in taking it out of the hands of ignorant or dishonest investigators, Professor John Tyndall avoided the subject; but in his *Fragments of Science*, he was guilty of the ungentlemanly expressions which we have quoted in another place.

But we are wrong; he made one attempt, and that sufficed. He tells us, in the *Fragments*, that he once got under a table, to see how the raps were made, and arose with a despair for humanity, such as he never felt before! Israel Putnam, crawling on hand and knee to kill the she-wolf in her den, partially affords a parallel by which to estimate the chemist's courage in groping in the dark after the ugly truth; but Putnam killed his wolf, and Tyndall was devoured by his! "*Sub mensa desperatio*" should be the motto on his shield.

Speaking of the report of the committee of 1824, Dr. Alphonse Teste, a distinguished contemporaneous scientist, says that it produced a great impression on the Academy, but few convictions: "No one could question the veracity of the commissioners, whose good faith as well as great knowledge were undeniable, but they were suspected of having been dupes. In fact, *there are certain unfortunate truths which compromise those who believe in them, and those especially who are so candid as to avow them publicly*." How true this is, let the records of history, from the earliest times to this very day, attest. When Professor Robert Hare announced the preliminary results of his spiritualistic investigations, he, albeit one of the most eminent chemists and physicists in the world, was, nevertheless, regarded as a dupe. When he proved that he was not, he was charged with having fallen into dotage; the Harvard professors denouncing "his insane adherence to the gigantic humbug."

When the professor began his investigations in 1853, he announced that he "felt called upon, as an act of duty to his fellow-creatures, to bring whatever influence he possessed to the attempt to stem the tide of popular madness, which, in defiance of reason and science, was fast setting in favor of the *gross delusion* called Spiritualism." Though, according to his declaration, he "entirely coincided with Faraday's theory of table-turning," he had the true greatness which characterizes the princes of science to make his investigation thorough, and then tell the truth. How he was rewarded by his life-long associates, let his own words tell. In an address delivered in New York, in September, 1854, he says that "he had been engaged in scientific pursuits for upwards of half a century, and his accuracy and precision had never been questioned, until he had become a spiritualist; while his integrity as a man had never in his life been assailed, until the Harvard professors fulminated their report against that which *he knew* to be true, and which they *did not know* to be false."

How much mournful pathos is expressed in these few words! An old man of seventy-six — a scientist of half a century, deserted for telling the truth! And now Mr. A. R. Wallace, who had previously been esteemed among the most illustrious of British scientists, having proclaimed his belief in spiritualism and mesmerism, is spoken of in terms of compassion. Professor Nicholas Wagner, of St. Petersburg, whose reputation as a zoologist is one of the most conspicuous, in his turn pays the penalty of his exceptional candor, in his outrageous treatment by the Russian scientists!

There are scientists and *scientists* and if the occult sciences suffer in the instance of modern spiritualism from the malice of one class, nevertheless, they have had their defenders at all times among men whose names have shed lustre upon science itself. In the first rank stands Isaac Newton, "the light of science," who was a thorough believer in magnetism, as taught by Paracelsus, Van Helmont, and by the fire-philosophers in general. No one will presume to deny that his doctrine of universal space and attraction is purely a theory of magnetism. If his own words mean anything at all, they mean that he based all his speculations upon the "soul of the world," the great universal, magnetic agent, which he called the *divine sensorium.*[301] "Here," he says, "the question is of a very subtile spirit which penetrates through all, even the hardest bodies, and which is concealed in their substance. Through the strength and activity of this spirit, bodies attract each other, and adhere together when brought into contact. Through it, electrical bodies operate at the remotest distance, as well as near at hand, attracting and repelling; through this spirit the light also flows, and is refracted and reflected, and warms bodies. All senses are excited by this spirit, and through it the animals move their limbs. But these things cannot be explained in few words, and we have not yet sufficient experience to determine fully the laws by which this universal spirit operates."

There are two kinds of magnetization; the first is purely *animal,* the other transcendent, and depending on the will and knowledge of the mesmerizer, as well as on the degree of spirituality of the subject, and his capacity to receive the impressions of the astral light. But now it is next to ascertain that clairvoyance depends a great deal more on the former than on the latter. To the power of an adept, like Du Potet, the most *positive* subject will have to submit. If his sight is ably directed by the mesmerizer, magician, or spirit, the light must yield up its most secret records to our scrutiny; for, if it is a book which is ever closed to those "who see and do not perceive," on the other hand it is ever opened for one who *wills* to see it opened. It keeps an unmutilated record of all that was, that is, or ever will be. The

---

301 *"Fundamental Principles of Natural Philosophy."*

minutest acts of our lives are imprinted on it, and even our thoughts rest photographed on its eternal tablets. It is the book which we see opened by the angel in the *Revelation*, "which is the Book of life, and out of which the dead are judged according to their works." It is, in short, the MEMORY of GOD!

"The oracles assert that the impression of thoughts, characters, men, and other divine visions, appear in the æther. . . . In this the things without figure are figured," says an ancient fragment of the *Chaldean Oracles* of Zoroaster.[302]

Thus, ancient as well as modern wisdom, vaticination and science, agree in corroborating the claims of the kabalists. It is on the indestructible tablets of the astral light that is stamped the impression of every thought we think, and every act we perform; and that future events — effects of long-forgotten causes — are already delineated as a vivid picture for the eye of the seer and prophet to follow. Memory — the despair of the materialist, the enigma of the psychologist, the sphinx of science — is to the student of old philosophies merely a name to express that power which man unconsciously exerts, and shares with many of the inferior animals — to look with inner sight into the astral light, and there behold the images of past sensations and incidents. Instead of searching the cerebral ganglia for "micrographs of the living and the dead, of scenes that we have visited, of incidents in which we have borne a part,"[303] they went to the vast repository where the records of every man's life as well as every pulsation of the visible cosmos are stored up for all Eternity!

That flash of memory which is traditionally supposed to show a drowning man every long-forgotten scene of his mortal life — as the landscape is revealed to the traveller by intermittent flashes of lightning — is simply the sudden glimpse which the struggling soul gets into the silent galleries where his history is depicted in imperishable colors.

The well-known fact — one corroborated by the personal experience of nine persons out of ten — that we often recognize as familiar to us, scenes, and landscapes, and conversations, which we see or hear for the first time, and sometimes in countries never visited before, is a result of the same causes. Believers in reïncarnation adduce this as an additional proof of our antecedent existence in other bodies. This recognition of men, countries, and things that we have never seen, is attributed by them to flashes of soul-memory of anterior experiences. But the men of old, in common with mediæval philosophers, firmly held to a contrary opinion.

They affirmed that though this psychological phenomenon was one of the greatest arguments in favor of immortality and the soul's preëxistence, yet the latter being endowed with an individual memory apart from that of our physical brain, it is no proof of reïncarnation. As Eliphas Levi beautifully expresses it, "nature shuts the door after everything that passes, and pushes life onward" in more perfected forms. The chrysalis becomes a butterfly; the latter can never become again a grub. In the stillness of the night-hours, when our bodily senses are fast locked in the fetters of sleep, and our elementary body rests, the astral form becomes free. It then *oozes* out of its earthly prison, and as Paracelsus has it — "confabulates with the outward world," and travels round the visible as

---

302 *"Simpl. in Phys.,"* 143; *"The Chaldean Oracles,"* Cory.
303 Draper, *"Conflict between Religion and Science."*

well as the invisible worlds. "In sleep," he says, "the astral body (soul) is in freer motion; then it soars to its parents, and holds converse with the stars." Dreams, forebodings, prescience, prognostications and presentiments are impressions left by our astral spirit on our brain, which receives them more or less distinctly, according to the proportion of blood with which it is supplied during the hours of sleep. The more the body is exhausted, the freer is the spiritual man, and the more vivid the impressions of our soul's memory. In heavy and robust sleep, dreamless and uninterrupted, upon awakening to outward consciousness, men may sometimes remember nothing. But the impressions of scenes and landscapes which the astral body saw in its peregrinations are still there, though lying latent under the pressure of matter. They may be awakened at any moment, and then, during such flashes of man's inner memory, there is an instantaneous interchange of energies between the visible and the invisible universes. Between the "micrographs" of the cerebral ganglia and the photo-scenographic galleries of the astral light, a current is established. And a man who knows that he has never visited in body, nor seen the landscape and person that he recognizes may well assert that still has he seen and knows them, for the acquaintance was formed while travelling in "spirit." To this the physiologists can have but one objection. They will answer that in natural sleep — perfect and deep, "half of our nature which is volitional is in the condition of inertia"; hence unable to travel; the more so as the existence of any such individual astral body or soul is considered by them little else than a poetical myth. Blumenbach assures us that in the state of sleep, all intercourse between mind and body is suspended; an assertion which is denied by Dr. Richardson, F. R. S., who honestly reminds the German scientist that "the precise limits and connections of mind and body being unknown" it is more than should be said. This confession, added to those of the French physiologist, Fournie, and the still more recent one of Dr. Allchin, an eminent London physician, who frankly avowed, in an address to students, that "of all scientific pursuits which practically concern the community, there is none perhaps which rests upon so uncertain and insecure a basis as medicine," gives us a certain right to offset the hypotheses of ancient scientists against those of the modern ones.

No man, however gross and material he may be, can avoid leading a double existence; one in the visible universe, the other in the invisible. The life-principle which animates his physical frame is chiefly in the astral body; and while the more animal portions of him rest, the more spiritual ones know neither limits nor obstacles. We are perfectly aware that many learned, as well as the unlearned, will object to such a novel theory of the distribution of the life-principle. They would prefer remaining in blissful ignorance and go on confessing that no one knows or can pretend to tell whence and whither this mysterious agent appears and disappears, than to give one moment's attention to what they consider old and exploded theories. Some might object on the ground taken by theology, that dumb brutes have no immortal souls, and hence, can have no astral spirits; for *theologians as well as laymen labor under the erroneous impression that soul and spirit are one and the same thing.*

But if we study Plato and other philosophers of old, we may readily perceive that while the "*irrational* soul," by which Plato meant our astral body, or the more ethereal representation of ourselves, can have at best only a more or less prolonged continuity of existence beyond the grave; the divine spirit — wrongly termed *soul,* by the Church — is immortal by its very essence. (Any Hebrew scholar will readily appreciate the distinction who comprehends the difference between the two words רוח *ruah* and נפש *nephesh.*) If the life-principle is something apart from the astral spirit and in no way connected with it, why is it that the intensity of the clairvoyant powers depends so much on the bodily prostration of the subject? The deeper the trance, the less signs of life the body shows, the clearer become the spiritual perceptions, and the more powerful are the soul's visions. The soul, disburdened of the bodily senses, shows activity of power in a far greater degree of intensity than it can in a strong, healthy body. Brierre de Boismont gives repeated instances of this fact. The organs of sight, smell, taste, touch, and hearing are proved to become far acuter in a mesmerized subject deprived of the possibility of exercising them bodily, than while he uses them in his normal state.

Such facts alone, once proved, ought to stand as invincible demonstrations of the continuity of individual life, at least for a certain period after the body has been left by us, either by reason of its being worn out or by accident. But though during its brief sojourn on earth our soul may be assimilated to a light hidden under a bushel, it still shines more or less bright and attracts to itself the influences of kindred spirits; and when a thought of good or evil import is begotten in our brain, it draws to it *impulses* of like nature as irresistibly as the magnet attracts iron filings. This attraction is also proportionate to the intensity with which the thought-impulse makes itself felt in the ether; and so it will be understood how one man may impress himself upon his own epoch so forcibly, that the influence may be carried — through the ever-interchanging currents of energy between the two worlds, the visible and the invisible — from one succeeding age to another, until it affects a large portion of mankind.

How much the authors of the famous work entitled the *Unseen Universe* may have allowed themselves to think in this direction, it would be difficult to say; but that they have not told *all* they might will be inferred from the following language:

"Regard it as you please, there can be no doubt that the properties of the ether are of a much higher order in the arcana of nature *than those of tangible matter*. And, as even the high priests of science still find the latter *far beyond* their comprehension, except in numerous but minute and often isolated particulars, it would not become us to speculate further. It is sufficient for our purpose to know from what the ether certainly does, that *it is capable of vastly more than any has yet ventured to say*."

One of the most interesting discoveries of modern times, is that of the faculty which enables a certain class of sensitive persons to receive from any object held in the hand or against the forehead impressions of the character or appearance of the individual, or any other object with which it has previously been in contact. Thus a manuscript, painting, article of clothing, or jewelry — no matter how ancient — conveys to the sensitive, a vivid picture of the writer, painter, or wearer; even though he lived in the days of Ptolemy or Enoch. Nay, more; a fragment of an ancient building will recall its history and even the scenes which transpired within or about it. A bit of ore will carry the soul-vision back to the time when it was in process of formation. This faculty is called by its discoverer — Professor J. R. Buchanan, of Louisville, Kentucky — *psychometry*. To him, the world is indebted for this most important addition to Psychological Sciences; and to him, perhaps, when skepticism is found felled to the ground by such accumulation of facts, posterity will have to elevate a statue. In announcing to the public his great discovery, Professor Buchanan, confining himself to the power of psychometry to delineate human character, says: "The mental and physiological influence imparted to writing appears to be imperishable, as the oldest specimens I have investigated gave their impressions with a distinctness and force, little impaired by time. Old manuscripts, requiring an antiquary to decipher their strange old penmanship, were easily interpreted by the psychometric power. . . . The property of retaining the impress of mind is not limited to writing. Drawings, paintings, everything upon which human contact, thought, and volition have been expended, may become linked with that thought and life, so as to recall them to the mind of another when in contact."

Without, perhaps, really knowing, at the early time of the grand discovery, the significance of his own prophetic words, the Professor adds: "This discovery, in its application to the arts and to history, will open a mine of interesting knowledge."[304]

The existence of this faculty was first experimentally demonstrated in 1841. It has since been verified by a thousand psychometers in different parts of the world. It proves that every occurrence in nature — no matter how minute or unimportant — leaves its indelible impress upon physical nature; and, as there has been no appreciable molecular disturbance, the only inference possible is, that these images have been produced by that invisible, universal force — Ether, or astral light.

"PSYCHOMETRY"

In his charming work, entitled *The Soul of Things*, Professor Denton, the geologist,[305] enters at great length into a discussion of this subject. He gives a multitude of examples of the psychometrical power, which Mrs. Denton possesses in a marked degree. A fragment of Cicero's house, at Tusculum, enabled her to describe, without the slightest intimation as to the nature of the object placed on her forehead, not only the great orator's surroundings, but also the previous owner of the building, Cornelius Sulla Felix, or, as he is usually called, Sulla the Dictator. A fragment of marble from the ancient Christian Church of Smyrna, brought before her its congregation and officiating priests. Specimens from Nineveh, China, Jerusalem, Greece, Ararat, and other places all over the world brought up scenes in the life of various personages, whose ashes had been scattered thousands of years ago. In many cases Professor Denton verified the statements by reference to historical records. More than this, a bit of the skeleton, or a fragment of the tooth of some antediluvian animal, caused the seeress to perceive the creature as it was when alive, and even live for a few brief moments its life, and experience its sensations. Before the eager quest of the psychometer, the most hidden recesses of the domain of nature yield up their secrets; and the events of the most remote epochs rival in vividness of impression the flitting circumstances of yesterday.

Says the author, in the same work: "Not a leaf waves, not an insect crawls, not a ripple moves, but each motion is recorded by a thousand faithful scribes in infallible and indelible scripture. This is just as true of all past time. From the dawn of light upon this infant globe, when round its cradle the steamy curtains hung, to this moment, nature has been busy photographing everything. What a picture-gallery is hers!"

---

304 J. R. Buchanan, M.D., "*Outlines of Lectures on the Neurological System of Anthropology.*"
305 W. and Elizabeth M. F. Denton, "*The Soul of Things; or Psychometric Researches and Discoveries,*" Boston, 1873.

It appears to us the height of impossibility to imagine that scenes in ancient Thebes, or in some temple of prehistoric times should be photographed only upon the substance of certain atoms. The images of the events are imbedded in that all-permeating, universal, and ever-retaining medium, which the philosophers call the "Soul of the World," and Mr. Denton "the Soul of Things." The psychometer, by applying the fragment of a substance to his forehead, brings his *inner-self* into relations with the inner soul of the object he handles. It is now admitted that the universal æther pervades all things in nature, even the most solid. It is beginning to be admitted, also, that this preserves the images of all things which transpire. When the psychometer examines his specimen, he is brought in contact with the current of the astral light, connected with that specimen, and which retains pictures of the events associated with its history. These, according to Denton, pass before his vision with the swiftness of light; scene after scene crowding upon each other so rapidly, that it is only by the supreme exercise of the will that he is able to hold any one in the field of vision long enough to describe it.

TIME, SPACE, ETERNITY

The psychometer is clairvoyant; that is, he sees with the inner eye. Unless his will-power is very strong, unless he has thoroughly trained himself to that particular phenomenon, and his knowledge of the capabilities of his sight are profound, his perceptions of places, persons, and events, must necessarily be very confused. But in the case of mesmerization, in which this same clairvoyant faculty is developed, the operator, whose will holds that of the subject under control, can force him to concentrate his attention upon a given picture long enough to observe all its minute details. Moreover, under the guidance of an experienced mesmerizer, the seer would excel the natural psychometer in having a prevision of future events, more distinct and clear than the latter. And to those who might object to the possibility of perceiving that which "yet is not," we may put the question: Why is it more impossible to see that which will be, than to bring back to sight that which is gone, and is no more? According to the kabalistic doctrine, the future exists in the astral light in embryo, as the present existed in embryo in the past. While man is free to act as he pleases, the manner in which he *will* act was foreknown from all time; not on the ground of fatalism or destiny, but simply on the principle of universal, unchangeable harmony; and, as it may be foreknown that, when a musical note is struck, its vibrations will not, and cannot change into those of another note. Besides, eternity can have neither past nor future, but only the present; as boundless space, in its strictly literal sense, can have neither distant nor proximate places. Our conceptions, limited to the narrow area of our experience, attempt to fit if not an end, at least a beginning of time and space; but neither of these exist in reality; for in such case time would not be eternal, nor space boundless. The past no more exists than the future, as we have said, only our memories survive; and our memories are but the glimpses that we catch of the reflections of this past in the currents of the astral light, as the psychometer catches them from the astral emanations of the object held by him.

Says Professor E. Hitchcock, when speaking of the influences of light upon bodies, and of the formation of pictures upon them by means of it: "It seems, then, that this photographic influence pervades all nature; nor can we say where it stops. We do not know but it may imprint upon the world around us our features, as they are modified by various passions, and thus fill nature with daguerreotype impressions of all our actions; . . . it may be, too, that there are tests by which nature, more skilful than any photographist, can bring out and fix these portraits, so that *acuter* senses than ours shall see them as on a great canvas, spread over the material universe. *Perhaps,* too, they may never fade from that canvas, but become specimens in the great picture-gallery of eternity."[306]

The "perhaps" of Professor Hitchcock is henceforth changed by the demonstration of psychometry into a triumphant certitude. Those who understand these psychological and clairvoyant faculties will take exception to Professor Hitchcock's idea, that acuter senses than ours are needed to see these pictures upon his supposed cosmic canvas, and maintain that he should have confined his limitations to the external senses of the body. *The human spirit, being of the Divine, immortal Spirit, appreciates neither past nor future, but sees all things as in the present.* These daguerreotypes referred to in the above quotation are imprinted upon the astral light, where, as we said before — and, according to the Hermetic teaching, the first portion of which is already accepted and demonstrated by science — is kept the record of all that was, is, or ever will be.

Of late, some of our learned men have given a particular attention to a subject hitherto branded with the mark of "superstition." They begin speculating on hypothetical and invisible worlds. The authors of the *Unseen Universe* were the first to boldly take the lead, and already they find a follower in Professor Fiske, whose speculations are given in the *Unseen World.* Evidently the scientists are probing the insecure ground of materialism, and, feeling it trembling under their feet, are preparing for a less dishonorable surrender of arms in case of defeat. Jevons confirms Babbage, and both firmly believe that every thought, displacing the particles of the brain and setting them in motion, scatters them throughout the universe, and think that "each particle of the existing matter must be a register of all that has happened."[307] On the other hand, Dr. Thomas Young, in his lectures on natural philosophy, most positively invites us to "speculate with freedom on the possibility of independent worlds; some existing in different parts, others *pervading each other, unseen and unknown,* in the same space, and others again to which space may not be a necessary mode of existence."

If scientists, proceeding from a strictly scientific point of view, such as the possibility of energy being transferred into the invisible universe — and on the principle of continuity, indulge in such speculations, why should occultists and spiritualists be refused the same privilege? Ganglionic impressions on the surface of polished metal, are registered and may be preserved for an indefinite space of time, according to science; and Professor Draper illustrates the fact most poetically. "A shadow," says he, "never falls upon a wall without leaving thereupon a permanent trace, a trace which might be made visible by resorting to proper processes. . . . The portraits of our friends, or landscape-views, may be hidden on the sensitive surface from the eye, but they are ready to make their appearance, as soon as proper developers are resorted to. A spectre is concealed on a silver or glassy surface, until, by our necromancy, we make it come forth into the visible world. Upon the walls of our most private apartments, where we think the eye of intrusion is altogether shut out, and our

---

306 *"Religion of Geology."*
307 *"Principles of Science,"* vol. ii., p. 455.

retirement can never be profaned, there exist the vestiges of all our acts, silhouettes of whatever we have done."[308]

TRANSFER OF ENERGY FROM THE VISIBLE TO THE INVISIBLE UNIVERSE

If an indelible impression may be thus obtained on inorganic matter, and if nothing is lost or passes completely out of existence in the universe, why such a scientific levee of arms against the authors of the *Unseen Universe?* And on what ground can they reject the hypothesis that *"Thought, conceived to affect the matter of another universe simultaneously with this, may explain a future state?"*[309]

In our opinion, if psychometry is one of the grandest proofs of the indestructibility of matter, retaining eternally the impressions of the outward world, the possession of that faculty by our inner sight is a still greater one in favor of the immortality of man's individual spirit. Capable of discerning events which took place hundreds of thousands of years ago, why would it not apply the same faculty to a future lost in the eternity, in which there can be neither past nor future, but only one boundless present?

Notwithstanding the confessions of stupendous ignorance in some things, made by the scientists themselves, they still deny the existence of that mysterious spiritual force, lying beyond the grasp of the ordinary physical laws. They still hope to be able to apply to living beings the same laws which they have found to answer in reference to dead matter. And, having discovered what the kabalists term "the gross purgations" of Ether — light, heat, electricity, and motion — they have rejoiced over their good fortune, counted its vibrations in producing the colors of the spectrum; and, proud of their achievements, refuse to see any further. Several men of science have pondered more or less over its protean essence, and unable to measure it with their photometers, called it "an *hypothetical* medium of great elasticity and extreme tenuity, *supposed* to pervade all space, the interior of solid bodies not excepted"; and, "to be the medium of transmission of light and heat" (Dictionary). Others, whom we will name "the will-o'-the-wisps" of science — her pseudo-sons — examined it also, and even went to the trouble of scrutinizing it "through powerful glasses," they tell us. But perceiving neither spirits nor ghosts in it, and failing equally to discover in its treacherous waves anything of a more scientific character, they turned round and called all believers in immortality in general, and spiritualists in particular, "insane fools" and "visionary lunatics" ;[310] the whole, in doleful accents, perfectly appropriate to the circumstance of such a sad failure.

Say the authors of the *Unseen Universe:*

> "We have driven the operation of that mystery called *Life* out of the objective universe. The mistake made, lies in imagining that by this process they completely get rid of a thing so driven before them, and that it disappears from the universe altogether. It does no such thing. It only disappears from that *small circle* of light which we may call the universe of *scientific perception.* Call it

---

308 J. W. Draper, "*Conflict between Religion and Science*," pp. 132, 133.
309 "*Unseen Universe*," p. 159.
310 F. R. Marvin, "*Lecture on Mediomania.*"

the trinity of mystery: mystery of matter, the mystery of life and — the mystery of God — and these three are One." [311]

Taking the ground that "the visible universe must *certainly, in transformable energy, and probably in matter,* come to an end," and "the principle of continuity . . . still demanding a continuance of the universe. . ." the authors of this remarkable work find themselves forced to believe "that there is something *beyond* that which is visible[312]. . . and that the visible system is not the whole universe but only, it may be, a very small part of it." Furthermore, looking back as well as forward to the origin of this visible universe, the authors urge that "if the visible universe is *all* that exists then the first abrupt manifestation of it is as truly a break of continuity as its final overthrow" (Art. 85). Therefore, as such a break is against the accepted law of continuity, the authors come to the following conclusion: "Now, is it not natural to imagine, that a universe of this nature, *which we have reason to think exists,* and is connected by bonds of energy with the visible universe, is also capable of receiving energy from it? . . . May we not regard Ether, or the medium, as not merely a bridge[313] between one order of things and another, forming as it were a species of cement, in virtue of which the various orders of the universe are welded together and made into one? In fine, what we generally called Ether, may be not a mere medium, but a medium *plus* the invisible order of things, so that when the motions of the visible universe are transferred into Ether, part of them are conveyed as by a *bridge* into the invisible universe, and are there made use of and stored up. Nay, is it even necessary to retain the conception of a bridge? May we not at once say that when energy is carried from matter into Ether, it is carried from the visible into the invisible; and that when it is carried from Ether to matter it is carried from the invisible into the visible?" — (Art. 198, *Unseen Universe.*)

Precisely; and were Science to take a few more steps in that direction and fathom more seriously the "hypothetical medium" who knows but Tyndall's impassable chasm between the physical processes of the brain and *consciousness,* might be — at least intellectually — passed with surprising ease and safety.

So far back as 1856, a man considered a savant in his days — Dr. Jobard of Paris, — had certainly the same ideas as the authors of the *Unseen Universe,* on ether, when he startled the press and the world of science by the following declaration: "I hold a discovery which frightens me. There are two kinds of electricity; one, brute and blind, is produced by the contact of metals and acids"; (the gross purgation) . . . "the other is intelligent and CLAIRVOYANT! . . . Electricity has bifurcated itself in the hands of Galvani, Nobili, and Matteuci. The brute force of the current has followed Jacobi, Bonelli, and Moncal, while the intellectual one was following Bois-Robert, Thilorier, and the Chevalier Duplanty. The electric ball or globular electricity contains a thought which disobeys Newton and Mariotte

---

311 "*Unseen Universe,*" p. 84, et seq.

312 Ibid., p. 89.

313 Behold! great scientists of the nineteenth century, corroborating the wisdom of the Scandinavian fable, cited in the preceding chapter. Several thousand years ago, the idea of a bridge between the visible and the invisible universes was allegorized by ignorant "heathen," in the "*Edda-Song of Voluspa,*" "*The Vision of Vala, the Seeress.*" For what is this bridge of Bifrost, the radiant rainbow, which leads the gods to their rendezvous, near the Urdar-fountain, but the same idea as that which is offered to the thoughtful student by the authors of the "*Unseen Universe*"?

to follow its own freaks. . . . We have, in the annals of the Academy, thousands of proofs *of the* INTELLIGENCE *of the electric bolt* . . . But I remark that I am permitting myself to become indiscreet. A little more and *I should have disclosed* to you the key which is about to discover to us the universal spirit."[314]

The foregoing, added to the wonderful confessions of science and what we have just quoted from the *Unseen Universe,* throw an additional lustre on the wisdom of the long departed ages. In one of the preceding chapters we have alluded to a quotation from Cory's translation of *Ancient Fragments,* in which it appears that one of the *Chaldean Oracles* expresses this self-same idea about ether, and in language singularly like that of the authors of the *Unseen Universe.* It states that from æther have come all things, and to it all will return; that the images of all things are indelibly impressed upon it; and that it is the store-house of the germs or of the remains of all visible forms, and even ideas. It appears as if this case strangely corroborates our assertion that whatever discoveries may be made in our days will be found to have been anticipated by many thousand years by our "simple-minded ancestors."

At the point at which we are now arrived, the attitude assumed by the materialists toward psychical phenomena being perfectly defined, we may assert with safety that were this key lying loose on the threshold of the "chasm" not one of our Tyndalls would stoop to pick it up.

How timid would appear to some kabalists these tentative efforts to solve the GREAT MYSTERY of the universal ether! although so far in advance of anything propounded by cotemporary philosophers, what the intelligent explorers of the *Unseen Universe* speculate upon, was to the masters of hermetic philosophy familiar science. To them ether was not merely a bridge connecting the seen and unseen sides of the universe, but across its span their daring feet followed the road that led through the mysterious gates which modern speculators either will not or *cannot* unlock.

The deeper the research of the modern explorer, the more often he comes face to face with the discoveries of the ancients. Does Elie de Beaumont, the great French geologist, venture a hint upon the terrestrial circulation, in relation to some elements in the earth's crust, he finds himself anticipated by the old philosophers. Do we demand of distinguished technologists, what are the most recent discoveries in regard to the origin of the metalliferous deposits? We hear one of them, Professor Sterry Hunt, in showing us how water is a *universal solvent,* enunciating the doctrine held and taught by the old Thales, more than two dozen centuries ago, that water was the principle of all things. We listen to the same professor, with de Beaumont as authority, expounding the terrestrial circulation, and the chemical and physical phenomena of the material world. While we read with pleasure that he is "not prepared to concede that we have in chemical and physical processes *the whole secret of organic life,*" we note with a still greater delight the following honest confession on his part: "Still we are, in many respects, approximating the phenomena of the organic world to those of the mineral kingdom; and we at the same time learn that these so far interest and depend upon each other that *we begin to see a certain truth* underlying the notion of those old philosophers, who extended to the mineral world the notion of a vital

---

314 "*L'Ami des Sciences,*" March 2, 1856, p. 67.

force, which led them to speak of the earth as a great *living* organism, and to look upon the various changes of its air, its waters, and its rocky depths, as processes belonging to the life of our planet."

Everything in this world must have a beginning. Things have latterly gone so far with scientists in the matter of prejudice, that it is quite a wonder that even so much as this should be conceded to ancient philosophy. The poor, honest primordial elements have long been exiled, and our ambitious men of science run races to determine who shall add one more to the fledgling brood of the sixty-three or more elementary substances. Meanwhile there rages a war in modern chemistry about terms. We are denied the right to call these substances "chemical elements," for they are not "primordial principles or self-existing essences out of which the universe was fashioned."[315] Such ideas associated with the word *element* were good enough for the "old Greek philosophy," but modern science rejects them; for, as Professor Cooke says, "they are unfortunate terms," and experimental science will have "nothing to do with any kind of essences except those which it can see, smell, or taste." It must have those that can be put in the eye, the nose, or the mouth! It leaves others to the metaphysicians.

Therefore, when Van Helmont tells us that, "though a homogeneal part of elementary earth may be artfully (artificially) converted into water," though he still denies "that the same can be done by nature alone; for no natural agent is able to transmute one element into another," offering as a reason that the elements always remain the same, we must believe him, if not quite an ignoramus, at least an unprogressed disciple of the mouldy "old Greek philosophy." Living and dying in blissful ignorance of the future sixty-three *substances,* what could either he or his old master, Paracelsus, achieve? Nothing, of course, but *metaphysical and crazy speculations,* clothed in a meaningless jargon common to all mediæval and ancient alchemists. Nevertheless, in comparing notes, we find in the latest of all works upon modern chemistry, the following: "The study of chemistry has revealed a remarkable class of substances, from no one of which a second substance has ever been produced by any chemical process which weighs less than the original substance . . . by no chemical process whatever can we obtain from iron a substance weighing less than the metal used in its production. In a word, we can *extract* from iron nothing but iron."[316] Moreover, it appears, according to Professor Cooke, that "*seventy-five years ago* men did not know there was any difference" between elementary and compound substances, for in old times alchemists *had never conceived* "that *weight is the measure of material,* and that, as thus measured, no material is ever lost; but, on the contrary, they imagined that in such experiments[317] as these the substances involved underwent a *mysterious transformation.* . . Centuries," in short "were wasted in vain attempts to transform the baser metals into gold."

Is Professor Cooke, so eminent in modern chemistry, equally proficient in the knowledge of what the alchemists did or did not know? Is he quite sure that he understands the meaning of the alchemical diction? We are not. But let us compare his views as above expressed with but sentences written in plain and good, albeit old English, from the

315 Cooke, "*New Chemistry,*" p. 113.
316 Ibid., pp. 110-111.
317 Ibid., p. 106.

translations of Van Helmont and Paracelsus. We learn from their own admissions that the alkahest induces the following changes:

"(1.) The alkahest never destroys the seminal virtues of the bodies thereby dissolved: for instance, gold, by its action, is reduced to a salt of gold, antimony to a salt of antimony, etc., of the same seminal virtues, or characters with the original concrete. (2.) The subject exposed to its operation is converted into its three principles, salt, sulphur, and mercury, and afterwards into salt alone, which then becomes volatile, and at length is wholly turned into clear water. (3.) Whatever it dissolves may be rendered volatile by a sand-heat; and if, after volatilizing the solvent, it be distilled therefrom, the body is left pure, insipid water, but always *equal in quantity to its original self.*" Further, we find Van Helmont, the elder, saying of this salt that it will dissolve the most untractable bodies into substances of the same seminal virtues, "*equal in weight to the matter dissolved*"; and he adds, "This salt, by being several times cohobated with Paracelsus' *sal circulatum*, loses all its fixedness, and at length becomes an insipid water, *equal in quantity* to the salt it was made from."[318]

The objection that might be made by Professor Cooke, in behalf of modern science, to the hermetic expressions, would equally apply to the Egyptian hieratic writings — they hide that which was meant to be concealed. If he would profit by the labors of the past, he must employ the cryptographer, and not the satirist. Paracelsus, like the rest, exhausted his ingenuity in transpositions of letters and abbreviations of words and sentences. For example, when he wrote *sutratur* he meant tartar, and *mutrin* meant nitrum, and so on. There was no end to the pretended explanations of the meaning of the alkahest. Some imagined that it was an alkaline of salt of tartar salatilized; others that it meant *algeist*, a German word which means all-spirit, or spirituous. Paracelsus usually termed salt "the centre of water wherein metals ought to die." This gave rise to the most absurd suppositions, and some persons — such as Glauber — thought that the alkahest was the spirit of salt. It requires no little hardihood to assert that Paracelsus and his colleagues were ignorant of the natures of elementary and compound substances; they may not be called by the same names as are now in fashion, but that they were known is proved by the results attained. What matters it by what name the gas given off when iron is dissolved in sulphuric acid was called by Paracelsus, since he is recognized, even by our standard authorities, as the discoverer of *hydrogen*?[319] His merit is the same; and though Van Helmont may have concealed, under the name "seminal virtues," his knowledge of the fact that elementary substances have their original properties, which the entering into compounds only temporarily modifies — never destroys — he was none the less the greatest chemist of his age, and the peer of modern scientists. He affirmed that the *aurum potabile* could be obtained with the alkahest, by converting the whole body of gold into salt, retaining its seminal virtues, and being soluble in water. When chemists learn what he meant by *aurum potabile*, alkahest, salt, and seminal virtues — what he really meant, not what he said he meant, nor what was thought he meant — then, and not before, can our chemists safely assume such airs toward the fire-philosophers and those ancient masters whose mystic

318 "*De Secretis Adeptorum,*" Werdenfelt; Philalethes; Van Helmont; Paracelsus.
319 Youmans, "*Chemistry,*" p. 169; and W. B. Kemshead, F. R. A. S., "*Inorganic Chemistry.*"

teachings they reverently studied. One thing is clear, at any rate. Taken merely in its exoteric form, this language of Van Helmont shows that he understood the solubility of metallic substances in water, which Sterry Hunt makes the basis of his theory of metalliferous deposits. We would like to see what sort of terms would be invented by our scientific contemporaries to conceal and yet half-reveal their audacious proposition that man's "only God is the cineritious matter of his brain," if in the basement of the new Court House or the cathedral on Fifth Avenue there were a torture-chamber, to which judge or cardinal could send them at will.

Professor Sterry Hunt says in one of his lectures:[320] "The alchemists sought in vain for a universal solvent; but we now know that water, aided in some cases by heat, pressure, and the presence of certain widely-distributed substances, such as carbonic acid and alkaline carbonates and sulphides, will dissolve the most insoluble bodies; so that it may, after all, be looked upon as the long-sought for alkahest or universal menstruum."

This reads almost like a paraphrase of Van Helmont, or Paracelsus himself! They knew the properties of water as a solvent as well as modern chemists, and what is more, made no concealment of the fact; which shows that this was not *their* universal solvent. Many commentaries and criticisms of their works are still extant, and one can hardly take up a book on the subject without finding at least one of their speculations of which they never thought of making a mystery. This is what we find in an old work on alchemists — a satire, moreover — of 1820, written at the beginning of our century when the new theories on the chemical potency of water were hardly in their embryonic state. "It may throw some light to observe, that Van Helmont, as well as Paracelsus, *took water for the universal instrument (agent?) of chymistry* and natural philosophy; and earth for the unchangeable basis of all things — that fire was assigned as the sufficient cause of all things — that Seminal impressions were lodged in the mechanism of the earth — that water, by dissolving and fermenting with this earth, as it does by means of fire, brings forth everything; whence originally proceeded animal, vegetable, and mineral kingdoms."[321] The alchemists understand well this universal potency of water. In the works of Paracelsus, Van Helmont, Philalethes, Pantatem, Tachenius, and even Boyle, "the great characteristic of the alkahest," "to dissolve and change all sublunary bodies — *water alone excepted,*" is explicitly stated. And is it possible to believe that Van Helmont, whose private character was unimpeachable, and whose great learning was universally recognized, should most solemnly declare himself possessed of the secret, were it but a vain boast![322] In a recent address at Nashville, Tennessee, Professor Huxley laid down a certain rule with respect to the validity of human testimony as a basis of history and science, which we are quite ready to apply to the present case. "It is impossible," he says, "that one's practical life should not be more or less influenced by the views which we may hold as to what has been the past history of things. One of them is *human testimony* in its various shapes — all testimony of eye-witnesses, traditional testimony from the lips of *those who have been eye-witnesses,* and the testimony of those who have put their impressions into writing and into print. . . . If you read Cæsar's *Commentaries,* wherever he gives an account of his battles with the Gauls, you place a certain

---

320 *"Origin of Metalliferous Deposits."*
321 John Bumpus, *"Alchemy and the Alkahest,"* 85, J. S. F., edition of 1820.
322 See Boyle's works.

amount of confidence in his statements. You take his testimony upon this. *You feel that Cæsar would not have made these statements unless he had believed them to be true.*" Now, we cannot in logic permit Mr. Huxley's philosophical rule to be applied in a one-sided manner to Cæsar. Either that personage was naturally truthful or a natural liar; and since Mr. Huxley has settled that point to his own satisfaction as regards the facts of military history in his favor, we insist that Cæsar is also a competent witness as to augurs, diviners, and psychological facts. So with Herodotus, and all other ancient authorities, unless they were by nature men of truth, they should not be believed even about civil or military affairs. *Falsus in uno, falsus in omnibus.* And equally, if they are credible as to physical things, they must be regarded as equally so as to spiritual things; for as Professor Huxley tells us, human nature was of old just as it is now. Men of intellect and conscience did not lie for the pleasure of bewildering or disgusting posterity.

The probabilities of falsification by such men having been defined so clearly by a man of science, we feel free from the necessity of discussing the question in connection with the names of Van Helmont and his illustrious but unfortunate master, the much-slandered Paracelsus. Deleuze, though finding in the works of the former many "mythic, illusory ideas" — perhaps only because he could not understand them — credits him nevertheless with a vast knowledge, "an acute judgment," and at the same time with having given to the world "great truths." "He was the first," he adds, "to give the name of *gas* to aerial fluids. Without him it is probable that steel would have given no new impulse to science."[323] By what application of the doctrine of chances could we discover the likelihood that experimentalists, capable of resolving and recombining chemical substances, as they are admitted to have done, were ignorant of the nature of elementary substances, their combining energies, and the solvent or solvents, that would disintegrate them when wanted? If they had the reputation only of theorists the case would stand differently and our argument would lose its force, but the chemical discoveries grudgingly accorded to them, by their worst enemies, form the basis for much stronger language than we have permitted ourselves, from a fear of being deemed over partial. And, as this work, moreover, is based on the idea that there is a higher nature of man, that his moral and intellectual faculties should be judged *psychologically,* we do not hesitate to reaffirm that since Van Helmont asserted, "most solemnly," that he was possessed of the secret of the alkahest, no modern critic has a right to set him down as either a liar or a visionary, until something more certain is known about the nature of this alleged *universal menstruum.*

"Facts are stubborn things," remarks Mr. A. R. Wallace, in his preface to *Miracles and Modern Spiritualism.* Therefore,[324] as facts must be our strongest allies, we will bring as many of these forward as the "miracles" of antiquity and those of our modern times will furnish us with. The authors of the *Unseen Universe* have *scientifically* demonstrated the possibility of certain alleged psychological phenomena through the medium of the universal ether. Mr. Wallace has as scientifically proved that the whole catalogue of assumptions to the contrary, including the sophisms of Hume, are untenable if brought face to face with strict logic. Mr. Crookes has given to the world of skepticism his own experiments, which lasted above

---

323 Deleuze, *"De l'Opinion de Van Helmont sur la Cause, la Nature et les Effets du Magnetisme,"* Anim. Vol. i., p. 45, and vol. ii., p. 198.
324 A. R. Wallace, *"An Answer to the Arguments of Hume, Lecky, etc., against Miracles."*

three years before he was conquered by the most undeniable of evidence — that of his own senses. A whole list could be made up of men of science who have recorded their testimony to that effect; and Camille Flammarion, the well-known French astronomer, and author of many works which, in the eyes of the skeptical, should send him to the ranks of the "deluded," in company with Wallace, Crookes, and Hare, corroborates our words in the following lines:

THE CROOKES EXPERIMENTS AND COX THEORY

"I do not hesitate to affirm my conviction, based on a personal examination of the subject, that any scientific man who declares the phenomena denominated 'magnetic,' 'somnambulic,' 'mediumic,' and others not yet explained by science, to be impossible, is one who speaks without knowing what he is talking about, and also any man accustomed, by his professional avocations, to scientific observations — provided that his mind be not biassed by pre-conceived opinions, nor his mental vision blinded by that opposite kind of illusion, unhappily too common in the learned world, which consists in imagining that the laws of Nature are already known to us, and that everything which appears to overstep the limit of our present formulas is impossible, may require a radical and absolute certainty of the reality of the facts alluded to."

In Mr. Crookes' *Notes of an Enquiry into the Phenomena called Spiritual*, on p. 101, this gentleman quotes Mr. Sergeant Cox, who having named this unknown force, *psychic*, explains it thus: "As the organism is itself moved and directed within the structure by a force — which either is, or is not controlled by — the soul, spirit, or mind . . . which constitutes the individual being we term 'the man,' it is an equally reasonable conclusion that the force which causes the motions beyond the limits of the body *is the same force that produces motion within the limits of the body*. And, as the external force is often directed by intelligence, it is an equally reasonable conclusion that the directing intelligence of the external force is the same intelligence that directs the force internally." In order to comprehend this theory the better, we may as well divide it in four propositions and show that Mr. Sergeant Cox believes:

1. That the force which produces physical phenomena proceeds *from* (consequently is generated *in*) the medium.

2. That the intelligence directing the force for the production of the phenomena (*a*) *may* sometimes be other than the intelligence of the medium; but of this the "proof" is "insufficient"; therefore, (*b*) the directing intelligence is probably that of the medium himself. This Mr. Cox calls "a reasonable conclusion."

3. He assumes that the force which moves the table is identical with the force which moves the medium's body itself.

4. He strongly disputes the spiritualistic theory, or rather assertion, that "spirits of the dead are the *sole* agents in the production of *all* the phenomena."

Before we fairly proceed on our analysis of such views we must remind the reader that we find ourselves placed between two extreme opposites represented by two parties — the believers and unbelievers in this agency of human spirits. Neither seem capable of deciding the point raised by Mr. Cox; for while the spiritualists are so omnivorous in their credulity as to believe every sound and movement in a *circle* to be produced by *disembodied* human beings, their antagonists dogmatically deny that anything can be produced by "spirits," for there are none. Hence, neither class is in a position to examine the subject without bias.

If they consider that force which "produces motion within the body" and the one "which causes the motion beyond the limits of the body" to be of *the same essence*, they may be right. But the identity of these two forces stops here. The life-principle which animates Mr. Cox's body is of the same nature as that of his medium; nevertheless he is not the medium, nor is the latter Mr. Cox.

This force, which, to please Mr. Cox and Mr. Crookes we may just as well call *psychic* as anything else, proceeds *through* not *from* the individual medium. In the latter case this force would be generated in the medium and we are ready to show that it cannot be so; neither in the instances of levitation of human bodies, the moving of furniture and other objects without contact, nor in such cases in which the force shows reason and intelligence. It is a well-known fact to both mediums and spiritualists, that the more the former is passive, the better the manifestations; and every one of the above-mentioned phenomena requires a *conscious* predetermined *will*. In cases of levitation, we should have to believe that this self-generated force would raise the inert mass off the ground, direct it through the air, and lower it down again, avoiding obstacles and thereby showing intelligence, and still act automatically, the medium remaining all the while *passive*. If such were the fact, the medium would be a conscious magician, and all pretense for being a passive instrument in the hands of invisible intelligences would become useless. As well plead that a quantity of steam sufficient to fill, without bursting, a boiler, will raise the boiler; or a Leyden jar, full of electricity, overcome the inertia of the jar, as such a mechanical absurdity. All analogy would seem to indicate that the force which operates in the presence of a medium upon external objects comes from a source back of the medium himself. We may rather compare it with the hydrogen which overcomes the inertia of the balloon. The gas, under the control of an intelligence, is accumulated in the receiver in sufficient volume to overcome the attraction of its combined mass. On the same principle this force moves articles of furniture, and performs other manifestations; and though identical in its essence with the astral spirit of the medium, it cannot be his spirit only, for the latter remains all the while in a kind of cataleptic torpor, when the mediumship is genuine. Mr. Cox's first point seems, therefore, not well taken; it is based upon an hypothesis mechanically untenable. Of course our argument proceeds upon the supposition that levitation is an observed fact. The theory of psychic force, to be perfect, must account for all "visible motions . . . in solid substances," and among these is levitation.

As to his second point, we deny that "the proof is insufficient" that the force which produces the phenomena is sometimes directed by other intelligences than the mind of the "psychic." On the contrary there is such an abundance of testimony to show that the mind of the medium, in a majority of cases, has nothing to do with the phenomena, that we cannot be content to let Mr. Cox's bold assertion go unchallenged.

Equally illogical do we conceive to be his third proposition; for if the medium's body be not the generator but simply the channel of the force which produces the phenomena — a question upon which Mr. Cox's researches throw no light whatever — then it does not follow that because the medium's "soul, spirit, or mind" directs the medium's organism, therefore this "soul, spirit, or mind," lifts a chair or raps at the call of the alphabet.

As to the fourth proposition, namely, that "spirits of the dead are the sole agents in the production of all the phenomena," we need not join issue at the present moment, inasmuch as the nature of the spirits producing mediumistic manifestations is treated at length in other chapters.

The philosophers, and especially those who were initiated into the Mysteries, held that the astral soul is the impalpable duplicate of the gross external form which we call body. It is the *perisprit* of the Kardecists and the *spirit-form* of the spiritualists. Above this internal duplicate, and illuminating it as the warm ray of the sun illuminates the earth, fructifying the germ and calling out to spiritual vivification the latent qualities dormant in it, hovers the divine spirit. The astral *perisprit* is contained and confined within the physical body as ether in a bottle, or magnetism in magnetized iron. It is a centre and engine of force, fed from the universal supply of force, and moved by the same general laws which pervade all nature and produce all cosmical phenomena. Its inherent activity causes the incessant physical operations of the animal organism and ultimately results in the destruction of the latter by overuse and its own escape. It is the prisoner, not the voluntary tenant, of the body. It has an attraction so powerful to the external universal force, that after wearing out its casing it finally escapes to it. The stronger, grosser, more material its encasing body, the longer is the term of its imprisonment. Some persons are born with organizations so exceptional, that the door which shuts other people in from communication with the world of the astral light, can be easily unbarred and opened, and their souls can look into, or even pass into that world, and return again. Those who do this consciously, and at will, are termed magicians, hierophants, seers, adepts; those who are made to do it, either through the fluid of the mesmerizer or of "spirits," are "mediums." The astral soul, when the barriers are once opened, is so powerfully attracted by the universal, astral magnet, that it sometimes lifts its encasement with it and keeps it suspended in mid-air, until the gravity of matter reasserts its supremacy, and the body redescends again to earth.

Every objective manifestation, whether it be the motion of a living limb, or the movement of some inorganic body, requires two conditions: will and force — plus *matter*, or that which makes the object so moved visible to our eye; and these three are all convertible forces, or the force-correlation of the scientists. In their turn they are directed or rather overshadowed by the Divine intelligence which these men so studiously leave out of the account, but without which not even the crawling of the smallest earth-worm could ever take place. The simplest as the most common of all natural phenomena, — the rustling of the leaves which tremble under the gentle contact of the breeze — requires a constant exercise of these faculties. Scientists may well call them cosmic laws, immutable and unchangeable. Behind these laws we must search for the intelligent cause, which once having created and set these laws in motion, has infused into them the essence of its own consciousness. Whether we call this the first cause, the universal will, or God, it must always bear intelligence.

And now we may ask, how can a will manifest itself intelligently and unconsciously at the same time? It is difficult, if not impossible, to conceive of intellection apart from consciousness. By consciousness we do not necessarily imply physical or corporeal consciousness. *Consciousness is a quality of the sentient principle, or, in other words, the soul; and the latter often displays activity even while the body is asleep or paralyzed.* When we lift our arm mechanically, we may imagine that we do it unconsciously because our superficial senses cannot appreciate the interval between the formulation of the purpose and its execution. Latent as it seemed to us, our vigilant will evolved force, and set our matter in motion. There is nothing in the nature of the most trivial of mediumistic phenomena to make Mr. Cox's theory plausible. If the intelligence manifested by this force is no proof that it belongs to a disembodied spirit, still less is it evidence that it is unconsciously given out by the medium; Mr. Crookes himself tells us of cases where the intelligence could not have emanated from any one in the room; as in the instance where the word "however," covered by his finger and unknown even to himself, was correctly written by planchette.[325] No explanation whatever can account for this case; the only hypothesis tenable — if we exclude the agency of a spirit-power — is that the clairvoyant faculties were brought into play. But scientists deny clairvoyance; and if, to escape the unwelcome alternative of accrediting the phenomena to a spiritual source, they concede to us the fact of clairvoyance, it then devolves upon them to either accept the kabalistic explanation of what this faculty is, or achieve the task hitherto impracticable of making a new theory to fit the facts.

Again, if for the sake of argument it should be admitted that Mr. Crookes' word "however" might have been clairvoyantly read, what shall we say of mediumistic communications having a prophetic character? Does any theory of mediumistic impulse account for the ability to foretell events beyond the possible knowledge of both speaker and listener? Mr. Cox will have to try again.

As we have said before, the modern psychic force, and the ancient oracular fluids, whether terrestrial or sidereal, are identical in essence — simply a blind force. So is air. And while in a dialogue the sound-waves produced by a conversation of the speakers affect the same body of air, that does not imply any doubt of the fact that there are two persons talking with each other. Is it any more reasonable to say that when a common agent is employed by medium and "spirit" to intercommunicate, there must necessarily be but one intelligence displaying itself? As the air is necessary for the mutual exchange of audible sounds, so are certain currents of astral light, or ether directed by an *Intelligence*, necessary for the production of the phenomena called spiritual. Place two interlocutors in the exhausted receiver of an air-pump, and, if they could live, their words would remain inarticulate thoughts, for there would be no air to vibrate, and hence no ripple of sound would reach their ears. Place the strongest medium in such isolating atmosphere as a powerful mesmerizer, familiar with the properties of the magical agent, can create around him, and no manifestations will take place until some opposing intelligence, more potential than the will-power of the mesmerizer, overcomes the latter and terminates the astral inertia.

The ancients were at no loss to discriminate between a blind force acting spontaneously and the same force when directed by an intelligence.

Plutarch, the priest of Apollo, when speaking of the oracular vapors which were but a subterranean gas, imbued with intoxicating magnetic properties, shows its nature to be

---

325 Crookes, *"Researches, etc.,"* p. 96.

dual, when he addresses it in these words: "And who art thou? without a God who creates and ripens thee; without a dæmon [spirit] who, acting under the orders of God, directs and governs thee; thou canst do nothing, thou art *nothing* but a vain breath."[326] Thus without the indwelling soul or intelligence, "Psychic Force" would be also but a "vain breath."

Aristotle maintains that this gas, or astral emanation, escaping from inside the earth, is the sole *sufficient cause*, acting from within outwardly for the vivification of every living being and plant upon the external crust. In answer to the skeptical negators of his century, Cicero, moved by a just wrath, exclaims: "And what can be more divine than the exhalations of the earth, which affect the human soul so as to enable her to predict the future? And could the hand of time evaporate such a virtue? Do you suppose you are talking of some kind of wine or salted meat?"[327] Do modern experimentalists claim to be wiser than Cicero, and say that this eternal force has evaporated, and that the springs of prophecy are dry?

All the prophets of old — inspired sensitives — were said to be uttering their prophecies under the same conditions, either by the direct outward efflux of the astral emanation, or a sort of damp fluxion, rising from the earth. It is this astral matter which serves as a temporary clothing of the souls who form themselves in this light. Cornelius Agrippa expresses the same views as to the nature of these phantoms by describing it as moist or humid: "*In spirito turbido* HUMIDOQUE."[328]

Prophecies are delivered in two ways — consciously, by magicians who are able to look into the astral light; and unconsciously, by those who act under what is called inspiration. To the latter class belonged and belong the Biblical prophets and the modern trance-speakers. So familiar with this fact was Plato, that of such prophets he says: "No man, when in his senses, attains prophetic truth and inspiration. . . but only when demented by some distemper or possession . . ." (by a daimonion or spirit).[329] "Some persons call them prophets; they do not know that they are only *repeaters* . . . and are not to be called prophets at all, but only *transmitters* of vision and prophecy," — he adds.

In continuation of his argument, Mr. Cox says: "The most ardent spiritualists practically admit the existence of psychic force, under the very inappropriate name of magnetism (to which it has no affinity whatever), for they assert that the spirits of the dead can only do the acts attributed to them by using the magnetism (that is, the psychic force) of the mediums."[330]

Here, again, a misunderstanding arises in consequence of different names being applied to what may prove to be one and the same imponderable compound. Because electricity did not become a science till the eighteenth century, no one will presume to say that this force has not existed since the creation; moreover, we are prepared to prove that even the ancient Hebrews were acquainted with it. But, merely because exact science did not happen before 1819 to stumble over the discovery which showed the intimate connection existing between magnetism and electricity, it does not at all prevent these two agents being identical. If a bar

---

326 Lucian, "*Pharsalia*," Book v.
327 "*De Divinatio*," Book i., chap. 3.
328 "*De Occulta Philosoph.*," p. 355.
329 Plato, "*Timæus*," vol. ii., p. 563.
330 Crookes, "*Researches, etc.*," p. 101.

of iron can be endowed with magnetic properties, by passing a current of voltaic electricity over some conductor placed in a certain way close to the bar, why not accept, as a provisional theory, that a medium may also be a *conductor,* and nothing more, at a seance? Is it unscientific to say that the intelligence of "psychic force," drawing currents of electricity from the waves of the ether, and employing the medium as a conductor, develops and calls into action the latent magnetism with which the atmosphere of the seance-room is saturated, so as to produce the desired effects? The word *magnetism* is as appropriate as any other, until science gives us something more than a merely hypothetical agent endowed with conjectural properties.

> "The difference between the advocates of psychic force and the spiritualists consists in this," says Sergeant Cox, "that we contend that there is as yet insufficient proof of any other directing agent than the intelligence of the medium, and *no proof whatever* of the agency of the 'spirits' of the dead."[331]

We fully agree with Mr. Cox as to the lack of proof that the agency is that of the spirits of the dead; as for the rest, it is a very extraordinary deduction from "a wealth of facts," according to the expression of Mr. Crookes, who remarks further, "On going over my notes, I find . . . such a superabundance of evidence, so overwhelming a mass of testimony . . .that I could fill several numbers of the *Quarterly.*"[332]

Now some of these facts of an "overwhelming evidence" are as follows: 1st. The movement of heavy bodies with contact, but without mechanical exertion. 2d. The phenomena of percussive and other sounds. 3d. The alteration of weight of bodies. 4th. Movements of heavy substances *when at a distance from the medium.* 5th. The rising of tables and chairs off the ground, *without contact with any person.* 6th. THE LEVITATION OF HUMAN BEINGS.[333] 7th. "Luminous apparitions." Says Mr. Crookes, "Under the strictest conditions, I have seen a solid self-luminous body, the size and nearly the shape of a turkey's egg, float noiselessly about the room, at one time higher than any one could reach on tiptoe, and then gently descend to the floor. It was visible for more than ten minutes, and before it faded away it struck the table three times with a sound like that of a hard, solid body."[334] (We must infer that the egg was of the same nature as M. Babinet's meteor-cat, which is classified with other natural phenomena in Arago's works.) 8th. The appearance of hands, either self-luminous or visible by ordinary light. 9th. "Direct writing" by these same luminous hands, detached, and evidently endowed with intelligence. (Psychic force?) 10th. "Phantom-forms and faces." In this instance, the psychic force comes "from a corner of the room" as a

---

331 Ibid., p. 101.

332 Crookes, "*Researches, etc.,*" p. 83.

333 In 1854, M. Foucault, an eminent physician and a member of the French Institute, one of the opponents of de Gasparin, rejecting the mere possibility of any such manifestations, wrote the following memorable words, "That day, when I should succeed in moving a straw under the action of my will only, I would feel terrified!" The word is ominous. About the same year, Babinet, the astronomer, repeated in his article in the "Revue des Deux Mondes," the following sentence to exhaustion: "The levitation of a body *without contact* is as *impossible* as the perpetual motion, because on the day it would be done, *the world would crumble down.*" Luckily, we see no sign as yet of such a cataclysm; yet bodies *are* levitated.

334 "*Researches, etc.,*" p. 91. § Ibid., pp. 86-97.

"phantom form," takes an accordeon in its hand, and then glides about the room, playing the instrument; Home, the medium, being in full view at the time. § The whole of the preceding Mr. Crookes witnessed and tested at his own house, and, having assured himself scientifically of the genuineness of the phenomenon, reported it to the Royal Society. Was he welcomed as the discoverer of natural phenomena of a new and important character? Let the reader consult his work for the answer.

In addition to these freaks played on human credulity by "psychic force," Mr. Crookes gives another class of phenomena, which he terms "special instances," which *seem* (?) to point to the agency of an *exterior* intelligence .[335]

"I have been," says Mr. Crookes, "with Miss Fox when she has been writing a message automatically to one person present, whilst a message to another person, on *another* subject, was being given alphabetically by means of 'raps,' and the whole time she was conversing freely with a third person, on a subject totally different from either. . . . During a seance with Mr. Home, a small lath moved across the table to me, *in the light,* and delivered a message to me by tapping my hand; I repeating the alphabet, and the lath tapping me at the right letters . . . being at a distance from Mr. Home's hands." The same lath, upon request of Mr. Crookes, gave him "a telegraphic message through the Morse alphabet, by taps on my hand" (the Morse code being quite unknown to any other person present, and but imperfectly to himself), "and," adds Mr. Crookes, "it convinced me that there was a good Morse operator at the other end of the line, WHEREVER THAT MIGHT BE."[336] Would it be undignified in the present case to suggest that Mr. Cox should search for the operator in his private principality — Psychic Land? But the same lath does more and better. In full light in Mr. Crookes' room *it* is asked to give a message, " . . . a pencil and some sheets of paper had been lying on the centre of the table; presently the *pencil rose on its point,* and after advancing by hesitating jerks to the paper, fell down. It then rose, and again fell. . . . After three unsuccessful attempts, a small wooden lath" (the Morse operator) "which was lying near upon the table, *slid towards the pencil,* and *rose* a few inches from the table; the pencil rose again, *and propping itself against the lath,* the two together made an effort to mark the paper. It fell, and then *a joint effort* was made again. After a third trial the lath gave it up, and *moved back to its place;* the pencil lay as it fell across the paper, and an alphabetic message told us: "We have tried to do as you asked, but *our power* is exhausted."[337] The word *our,* as the joint intelligent efforts of the friendly lath and pencil, would make us think that there were *two* psychic forces present.

In all this, is there any proof that the directing agent was "the intelligence of the medium"? Is there not, on the contrary, every indication that the movements of the lath and pencil were directed by spirits "of the dead," or at least of those of some other unseen intelligent entities?

Most certainly the word magnetism explains in this case as little as the term *psychic force;* howbeit, there is more reason to use the former than the latter, if it were but for the simple fact that the *transcendent* magnetism or mesmerism produces phenomena identical in effects

---

335 Ibid., p. 94.
336 Ibid., p. 95.
337 Ibid., p. 94.

with those of spiritualism. The phenomenon of the *enchanted* circle of Baron Du Potet and Regazzoni, is as contrary to the accepted laws of physiology as the rising of a table without contact is to the laws of natural philosophy. As strong men have often found it impossible to raise a small table weighing a few pounds, and broken it to pieces in the effort, so a dozen of experimenters, among them sometimes, academicians, were utterly unable to step across a chalk-line drawn on the floor by Du Potet. On one occasion a Russian general, well known for his skepticism, persisted until he fell on the ground in violent convulsions. In this case, the magnetic fluid which opposed such a resistance was Mr. Cox's psychic force, which endows the tables with an extraordinary and supernatural weight. If they produce the same psychological and physiological effects, there is good reason to believe them more or less identical. We do not think the deduction could be very reasonably objected to. Besides, were the fact even denied, this is no reason why it should not be so. Once upon a time, all the Academies in Christendom had agreed to deny that there were any mountains in the moon; and there was a certain time when, if any one had been so bold as to affirm that there was life in the superior regions of the atmosphere as well as in the fathomless depths of the ocean, he would have been set down as a fool or an ignoramus.

"The Devil affirms — it must be a lie!" the pious Abbé Almiguana used to say, in a discussion with a "spiritualized table." We will soon be warranted in paraphrasing the sentence and making it read — "Scientists deny — then it must be true."

CHAPTER VII

"Thou great First Cause, least understood."

POPE

"Whence this pleasing hope, this fond desire,
This longing after immortality?
Or whence this secret dread, and inward horror
Of falling into naught? Why shrinks the soul
Back on herself, and startles at destruction?
'Tis the divinity that stirs within us;
'Tis heaven itself that points out our hereafter
And intimates eternity to man.

ETERNITY! Thou pleasing, dreadful thought!"

ADDISON

"There is another and a better world."
KOTZEBUE, *The Stranger*

AFTER according so much space to the conflicting opinions of our men of science about certain occult phenomena of our modern period, it is but just that we give attention to the speculations of mediæval alchemists and certain other illustrious men. Almost without exception, ancient and mediæval scholars believed in the arcane doctrines of wisdom. These included Alchemy, the Chaldeo-Jewish Kabala, the esoteric systems of Pythagoras and the old Magi, and those of the later Platonic philosophers and theurgists.

We also propose in subsequent pages to treat of the Indian gymnosophists and the Chaldean astrologers. We must not neglect to show the grand truths underlying the misunderstood religions of the past. The four elements of our fathers, earth, air, water, and fire, contain for the student of alchemy and ancient psychology — or as it is now termed, *magic* — many things of which our philosophy has never dreamed. We must not forget that what is now called *Necromancy* by the Church, and *Spiritualism* by modern believers, and that includes the evoking of departed spirits, is a science which has, from remote antiquity, been almost universally diffused over the face of the globe.

ATTRACTION AND REPULSION UNIVERSAL IN ALL THE KINGDOMS OF NATURE

Although neither an alchemist, magician, nor astrologer, but simply a great philosopher, Henry More, of Cambridge University — a man universally esteemed, may be named as a shrewd logician, scientist, and metaphysician. His belief in witchcraft was firm throughout his life. His faith in immortality and able arguments in demonstration of the survival of man's spirit after death are all based on the Pythagorean system, adopted by Cardan, Van Helmont, and other mystics. The infinite and uncreated spirit that we usually call GOD, a substance of the highest virtue and excellency, produced everything else by *emanative causality*. God thus is the primary substance, the rest, the secondary; if the former created matter with a power of moving itself, he, the primary substance, is still the cause of that motion as well as of the matter, and yet we rightly say that it is matter which moves itself. "We may define this kind of spirit we speak of to be a substance indiscernible, that can move itself, that can penetrate, contract, and dilate itself, and can also penetrate, move, and alter matter,"[338] which is the third emanation. He firmly believed in apparitions, and stoutly defended the theory of the individuality of every soul in which "personality, memory, and conscience will surely continue in the future state." He divided the astral spirit of man after its exit from the body into two distinct entities: the "aërial" and the "æthereal vehicle." During the time that a disembodied man moves in its aërial clothing, he is subject to *Fate* — *i.e.*, evil and temptation, attached to its earthly interests, and therefore is not utterly pure; it is only when he casts off this garb of the first spheres and becomes ethereal that he becomes sure of his immortality. "For what shadow can that body cast that is a pure and transparent light, such as the ethereal vehicle is? And therefore that oracle is then fulfilled, when the soul has ascended into that condition we have already described, in which alone it is out of the reach of fate and mortality." He concludes his work by stating that this transcendent and divinely-pure condition was the only aim of the Pythagoreans.

As to the skeptics of his age, his language is contemptuous and severe. Speaking of Scot, Adie, and Webster, he terms them "our new inspired saints . . . sworn advocates of the witches, who thus madly and boldly, against all sense and reason, against all antiquity, all interpreters, and against the Scripture itself, will have even no Samuel in the scene, but a confederate knave! Whether the Scripture, or these inblown buffoons, puffed up with nothing but ignorance, vanity, and stupid infidelity, are to be believed, let any one judge," he adds.[339]

What kind of language would this eminent divine have used against our skeptics of the nineteenth century?

Descartes, although a worshipper of matter, was one of the most devoted teachers of the magnetic doctrine and, in a certain sense, even of Alchemy. His system of physics was very much like that of other great philosophers. Space, which is infinite, is composed, or rather filled up with a fluid and elementary matter, and is the sole fountain of all life, enclosing all the celestial globes and keeping them in perpetual motion. The magnet-streams of Mesmer are disguised by him into the Cartesian vortices, and both rest on the same principle. Ennemoser does not hesitate to say that both have more in common "than people suppose, who have not carefully examined the subject."[340]

The esteemed philosopher, Pierre Poiret Naude, was the warmest defender of the doctrines of occult magnetism and its first propounders,[341] in 1679. The magico-theosophical philosophy is fully vindicated in his works.

The well-known Dr. Hufeland has written a work on magic[342] in which he propounds the theory of the universal magnetic sympathy between men, animals, plants, and even minerals. The testimony of Campanella, Van Helmont, and Servius, is confirmed by him in

338 "*Antidote*," lib. i., cap. 4.
339 "Letter to Glanvil, the author of '*Sadducismus Triumphatus*,' May, 25, 1678."
340 "*History of Magic*," vol. ii., p. 272.
341 "Apologie pour tous les grands personnages faussement accuses de magie."
342 Berlin, 1817. § "*Nova Medicina Spirituum*," 1675.

relation to the sympathy existing between the different parts of the body as well as between the parts of all organic and even inorganic bodies.

Such also was the doctrine of Tenzel Wirdig. It may even be found expounded in his works, with far more clearness, logic, and vigor, than in those of other mystical authors who have treated of the same subject. In his famous treatise, *The New Spiritual Medicine*, he demonstrates, on the ground of the later-accepted fact of universal attraction and repulsion — now called "gravitation" — that the whole nature is *ensouled*. Wirdig calls this magnetic sympathy "the accordance of spirits." Everything is drawn to its like, and converges with natures congenial to itself. Out of this sympathy and antipathy arises a constant movement in the whole world, and in all its parts, and uninterrupted communion between heaven and earth, which produces universal harmony. Everything lives and perishes through magnetism; one thing affects another one, even at great distances, and its "congenitals" may be influenced to health and disease by the power of this sympathy, at any time, and notwithstanding the intervening space.§ "Hufeland," says Ennemoser, "gives the account of a nose which had been cut from the back of a porter, but which, when the porter died, died too and fell off from its artificial position. A piece of skin," adds Hufeland, "taken from a living head, had its hair turn gray at the same time as that on the head from which it was taken."[343]

Kepler, the forerunner of Newton in many great truths, even in that of the universal "gravitation" which he very justly attributed to magnetic attraction, notwithstanding that he terms astrology "the insane daughter of a most wise mother" — Astronomy, shares the kabalistic belief that the spirits of the stars are so many "intelligences." *He firmly believes that each planet is the seat of an intelligent principle, and that they are all inhabited by spiritual beings, who exercise influences over other beings inhabiting more gross and material spheres than their own and especially* our earth.[344] As Kepler's *spiritual* starry influences were superseded by the vortices of the more materialistic Descartes, whose atheistical tendencies did not prevent him from believing that he had found out a diet that would prolong his life five hundred years and more, so the vortices of the latter and his astronomical doctrines may some day give place to the *intelligent* magnetic streams which are directed by the *Anima Mundi.*

Baptista Porta, the learned Italian philosopher, notwithstanding his endeavors to show to the world the groundlessness of their accusations of magic being a superstition and sorcery, was treated by later critics with the same unfairness as his colleagues. This celebrated alchemist left a work on *Natural Magic,*[345] in which he bases all of the occult phenomena possible to man upon the world-soul which binds all with all. He shows that the astral light acts in harmony and sympathy with all nature; that it is the essence out of which our spirits are formed; and that by acting in unison with their parent-source, our sidereal bodies are rendered capable of producing magic wonders. The whole secret depends on our knowledge of kindred elements. He believed in the philosopher's stone, "of

---

343 *"History of Magic."*
344 It would be a useless and too long labor to enter here upon the defence of Kepler's theory of relation between the five regular solids of geometry and the magnitudes of the orbits of five principal planets, rather derided by Prof. Draper in his *"Conflict."* Many are the theories of the ancients that have been avenged by modern discovery. For the rest, we must bide our time.
345 *"Magia Naturalis,"* Lugduni, 1569.

which the world hath so great an opinion of, which hath been bragged of in so many ages and *happily attained unto by some.*" Finally, he throws out many valuable hints as to its "spiritual meaning." In 1643, there appeared among the mystics a monk, Father Kircher, who taught a complete philosophy of universal magnetism. His numerous works[346] embrace many of the subjects merely hinted at by Paracelsus. His definition of magnetism is very original, for he contradicted Gilbert's theory that the earth was a great magnet. He asserted that although every particle of matter, and even the intangible invisible "powers" were magnetic, they did not themselves constitute a magnet. *There is but one* MAGNET *in the universe, and from it proceeds the magnetization of everything existing.* This magnet is of course what the kabalists term the central Spiritual Sun, or God. The sun, moon, planets, and stars he affirmed are highly magnetic; but they have become so by induction from living in the universal magnetic fluid — the Spiritual light. He proves the mysterious sympathy existing between the bodies of the three principal kingdoms of nature, and strengthens his argument by a stupendous catalogue of instances. Many of these were verified by naturalists, but still more have remained unauthenticated; therefore, according to the traditional policy and very equivocal logic of our scientists, they are denied. For instance, he shows a difference between mineral magnetism and zoömagnetism, or animal magnetism. He demonstrates it in the fact that except in the case of the lodestone all the minerals are magnetized by the higher potency, the animal magnetism, while the latter enjoys it as the direct emanation from the first cause — the Creator. A needle can be magnetized by simply being held in the hand of a strong-willed man, and amber develops its powers more by the friction of the human hand than by any other object; therefore man can impart his own life, and, to a certain degree, *animate* inorganic objects. This, "in the eyes of the foolish, is sorcery." "The sun is the most magnetic of all bodies," he says; thus anticipating the theory of General Pleasonton by more than two centuries. "The ancient philosophers never denied the fact," he adds; "but have at all times perceived that the sun's emanations were binding all things to itself, and that it imparts this binding power to everything falling under its direct rays."

As a proof of it he brings the instance of a number of plants being especially attracted to the sun, and others to the moon, and showing their irresistible sympathy to the former by following its course in the heavens. The plant known as the *Githymal*,[347] faithfully follows its sovereign, even when it is invisible on account of the fog. The acacia uncloses its petals at its rising, and closes them at its setting. So does the Egyptian lotos and the common sunflower. The nightshade exhibits the same predilection for the moon.

As examples of antipathies or sympathies among plants, he instances the aversion which the vine feels for the cabbage, and its fondness toward the olive-tree; the love of the ranunculus for the water-lily, and of the rue for the fig. The antipathy which sometimes exists even among kindred substances is clearly demonstrated in the case of the Mexican pomegranate, whose shoots, when cut to pieces, repel each other with the "most extraordinary ferocity."

Kircher accounts for every feeling in human nature as results of changes in our magnetic condition. Anger, jealousy, friendship, love, and hatred, are all modifications of the

---

346 Athanasius Kircher, "*Magnes sive de arte magnetici, opus tripartitum*," Coloniae, 1654.
347 Lib. iii., p. 643.

magnetic atmosphere which is developed in us and constantly emanates from us. Love is one of the most variable, and therefore the aspects of it are numberless. Spiritual love, that of a mother for her child, of an artist for some particular art, love as pure friendship, are purely magnetic manifestations of sympathy in congenial natures. *The magnetism of pure love is the originator of every created thing.* In its ordinary sense love between the sexes is electricity, and he calls it *amor febris species,* the fever of species. There are two kinds of magnetic attraction: sympathy and fascination; the one holy and natural, the other evil and unnatural. To the latter, fascination, we must attribute the power of the poisonous toad, which upon merely opening its mouth, forces the passing reptile or insect to run into it to its destruction. The deer, as well as smaller animals, are attracted by the breath of the boa, and are made irresistibly to come within its reach. The electric fish, the torpedo, repels the arm with a shock that for a time benumbs it. To exercise such a power for beneficent purposes, man requires three conditions: 1, nobility of soul; 2, strong will and imaginative faculty; 3, a subject weaker than the magnetizer; otherwise he will resist. A man free from worldly incentives and sensuality, may cure in such a way the most "incurable" diseases, and his vision may become clear and prophetic.

A curious instance of the above-mentioned universal attraction between all the bodies of the planetary system and everything organic as well as inorganic pertaining to them, is found in a quaint old volume of the seventeenth century. It contains notes of travel and an official report to the King of France, by his Ambassador, de la Loubere, upon what he has seen in the kingdom of Siam. "At Siam," he says, "there are two species of fresh-water fish, which they respectively call *pal-out* and *pla-cadi* fish. Once salted and placed uncut (whole) in the pot, they are found to exactly follow the flux and reflux of the sea, growing higher and lower in the pot as the sea ebbs or flows."[348] De la Loubere experimented with this fish for a long time, together with a government engineer, named Vincent, and, therefore, vouches for the truth of this assertion, which at first had been dismissed as an idle fable. So powerful is this mysterious attraction that it affected the fishes even when their bodies became totally rotten and fell to pieces.

PSYCHICAL PHENOMENA DEPEND ON PHYSICAL SURROUNDINGS

It is especially in the countries unblessed with civilization that we should seek for an explanation of the nature, and observe the effects of that subtile power, which ancient philosophers called the "world's soul."

In the East only, and on the boundless tracts of unexplored Africa, will the student of psychology find abundant food for his truth-hungering soul. The reason is obvious. The atmosphere in populous neighborhoods is badly vitiated by the smoke and fumes of manufactories, steam-engines, railroads, and steamboats, and especially by the miasmatic exhalations of the living and the dead. Nature is as dependent as a human being upon conditions before she can work, and her mighty breathing, so to say, can be as easily interfered with, impeded, and arrested, and the correlation of her forces destroyed in a given spot, as though she were a man. Not only climate, but also occult influences daily felt

---

348 *"Notes from a New Historical Relation of the Kingdom of Siam,"* by de la Louere, French Ambassador to Siam in the years 1687-8. Edition of 1692.

not only modify the physio-psychological nature of man, but even alter the constitution of so-called inorganic matter in a degree not fairly realized by European science. Thus the London *Medical and Surgical Journal* advises surgeons not to carry lancets to Calcutta, because it has been found by personal experience "that English steel could not bear the atmosphere of India"; so a bunch of English or American keys will be completely covered with rust twenty-four hours after having been brought to Egypt; while objects made of native steel in those countries remain unoxidized. So, too, it has been found that a Siberian Shaman who has given stupendous proofs of his occult powers among his native Tschuktschen, is gradually and often completely deprived of such powers when coming into smoky and foggy London. Is the inner organism of man less sensitive to climatic influences than a bit of steel? If not, then why should we cast doubt upon the testimony of travellers who may have seen the Shaman, day after day, exhibit phenomena of the most astounding character in his native country, and deny the possibility of such powers and such phenomena, only because he cannot do as much in London or Paris? In his lecture on the *Lost Arts*, Wendell Phillips proves that besides the psychological nature of man being affected by a change of climate, Oriental people have physical senses far more acute than the Europeans. The French dyers of Lyons, whom no one can surpass in skill, he says, "have a theory that there is a certain delicate shade of blue that Europeans *cannot see.* . . . And in Cashmere, where the girls make shawls worth $30,000, they will show him (the dyer of Lyons) three hundred distinct colors, which he not only cannot make, but *cannot even distinguish.*" If there is such a vast difference between the acuteness of the external senses of two races, why should there not be the same in their psychological powers? Moreover, the eye of a Cashmere girl is able to see *objectively* a color which does exist, but which being inappreciable by the European, is therefore non-existent for him. Why then not concede, that some peculiarly-endowed organisms, which are thought to be possessed of that mysterious faculty called *second sight*, see their pictures as objectively as the girl sees the colors; and that therefore the former, instead of mere objective hallucinations called forth by imagination are, on the contrary, reflections of real things and persons impressed upon the astral ether, as explained by the old philosophy of the *Chaldean Oracles,* and surmised by those modern discoverers, Babbage, Jevons, and the authors of the *Unseen Universe?*

"Three spirits live and actuate man," teaches Paracelsus; "three worlds pour their beams upon him; but all three only as the image and echo of one and the same all-constructing and uniting principle of production. The first is the spirit of the elements (terrestrial body and vital force in its brute condition); the second, the spirit of the stars (sidereal or astral body — the soul); the third is the *Divine* spirit (*Augoeidés*)." Our human body, being possessed of "primeval earth-stuff," as Paracelsus calls it, we may readily accept the tendency of modern scientific research "to regard the processes of both animal and vegetable life as simply physical and chemical." This theory only the more corroborates the assertions of old philosophers and the *Mosaic Bible,* that from the dust of the ground our bodies were made, and to dust they will return. But we must remember that

" 'Dust thou art, to dust returnest,' Was not spoken of the soul."

Man is a little world — a microcosm inside the great universe. Like a fœtus, he is suspended, by all his *three* spirits, in the matrix of the macrocosmos; and while his terrestrial body is in constant sympathy with its parent earth, his astral soul lives in unison with the sidereal *anima mundi.* He is in it, as it is in him, for the world-pervading element fills all space, and *is* space itself, only shoreless and infinite. As to his third spirit, the divine, what is it but an infinitesimal ray, one of the countless radiations proceeding directly from the Highest Cause — the Spiritual Light of the World? This is the trinity of organic and inorganic nature — the spiritual and the physical, which are three in one, and of which Proclus says that "The first monad is the Eternal God; the second, eternity; the third, the paradigm, or pattern of the universe"; the three constituting the Intelligible Triad. Everything in this visible universe is the outflow of this Triad, and a microcosmic triad itself. And thus they move in majestic procession in the fields of eternity, around the spiritual sun, as in the heliocentric system the celestial bodies move round the visible suns. The Pythagorean *Monad*, which lives "in solitude and darkness," may remain on this earth forever invisible, impalpable, and undemonstrated by experimental science. Still the whole universe will be gravitating around it, as it did from the "beginning of time," and with every second, man and atom approach nearer to that solemn moment in the eternity, when the Invisible Presence will become clear to their spiritual sight. When every particle of matter, even the most sublimated, has been cast off from the last shape that forms the ultimate link of that chain of double evolution which, throughout millions of ages and successive transformations, has pushed the entity onward; and when it shall find itself reclothed in that primordial essence, identical with that of its Creator, then this once impalpable organic atom will have run its race, and the sons of God will once more "shout for joy" at the return of the pilgrim.

"Man," says Van Helmont, "is the mirror of the universe, and his triple nature stands in relationship to all things." The will of the Creator, through which all things were made and received their first impulse, is the property of every living being. Man, endowed with an additional spirituality, has the largest share of it on this planet. It depends on the proportion of matter in him whether he will exercise its magical faculty with more or less success. Sharing this divine potency in common with every inorganic atom, he exercises it through the course of his whole life, whether consciously or otherwise. In the former case, when in the full possession of his powers, he will be the master, and the *magnale magnum* (the universal soul) will be controlled and guided by him. In the cases of animals, plants, minerals, and even of the average of humanity, this ethereal fluid which pervades all things, finding no resistance, and being left to itself, moves them as its impulse directs. Every created being in this sublunary sphere, is formed out of the *magnale magnum*, and is related to it. Man possesses a double celestial power, and is allied to heaven. This power is "not only in the outer man, but to a degree also in the animals, and perhaps in all other things, as all things in the universe stand in a relation to each other; or, at least, God is in all things, as the ancients have observed it with a worthy correctness. It is necessary that the magic strength should be awakened in the outer as well as in the inner man. . . . And if we call this a magic power, the uninstructed only can be terrified by the expression. But, if you prefer it, you can call it a spiritual power — *spirituale robur vocitaveris*. There is, therefore, such magic power in the inner man. But, as there exists a certain relationship between the inner and the outer man, this strength must be diffused through the whole man."[349]

---

349 Baptist Van Helmont, "*Opera Omnia*," 1682, p. 720, and others.

OBSERVATIONS IN SIAM

In an extended description of the religious rites, monastic life, and "superstitions" of the Siamese, de la Loubere cites among other things the wonderful power possessed by the *Talapoin* (the monks, or the holy men of Buddha) over the wild beasts. "The Talapoin of Siam," he says, "will pass whole weeks in the dense woods under a small awning of branches and palm leaves, and never make a fire in the night to scare away the wild beasts, as all other people do who travel through the woods of this country." The people consider it a miracle that no Talapoin is ever devoured. The tigers, elephants, and rhinoceroses — with which the neighborhood abounds — respect him; and travellers placed in secure ambuscade have often seen these wild beasts lick the hands and feet of the sleeping Talapoin. "They all use magic," adds the French gentleman, "and think all nature animated (ensouled);[350] they believe in tutelar geniuses." But that which seems to shock the author most is the idea which prevails among the Siamese, "that all that man was in his bodily life, he will be after death." "When the Tartar, which now reigns at China," remarks de la Loubere, "would force the Chinese to shave their hair after the Tartarian fashion, several of them chose rather to suffer death than to go, they said, into the other world and appear before their ancestors without hair; imagining that they shaved the head of the soul also!"[351] "Now, what is altogether impertinent," adds the Ambassador, "in this absurd opinion is, that the Orientals attribute the human figure rather than any other to the soul." Without enlightening his reader as to the particular shape these benighted Orientals ought to select for their disembodied souls, de la Loubere proceeds to pour out his wrath on these "savages." Finally, he attacks the memory of the old king of Siam, the father of the one to whose court he was sent, by accusing him of having foolishly spent over two million livres in search of the philosopher's stone. "The Chinese," he says, "reputed so wise, have for three or four thousand years had the folly of believing in the existence, and of seeking out a universal remedy by which they hope to exempt themselves from the necessity of dying. They base themselves on some foolish traditions, concerning some *rare* persons that are reported to have made gold, and to have lived some ages; there are some very strongly established facts among the Chinese, the Siamese, and other Orientals, concerning those that know how to render themselves immortal, either absolutely, or in such a manner that they can die no otherwise than by violent death.[352] Wherefore, they name some persons who have withdrawn themselves from the sight of men to enjoy free and peaceable life. They relate wonders concerning the knowledge of these pretended immortals."

If Descartes, a Frenchman and a scientist, could, in the midst of civilization, firmly believe that such a universal remedy had been found, and that if possessed of it he could live at least five hundred years, why are not the Orientals entitled to the same belief? The master-problems of both life and death are still unsolved by occidental physiologists. Even sleep is a phenomenon about whose cause there is a great divergence of opinion among them. How, then, can they pretend to set limits to the possible, and define the impossible?

---

350 De la Loubere, "*Notes*," etc. (see *ante*), p. 115.
351 Ibid., p. 120.
352 Ibid., p. 63.

MUSIC IN NERVOUS DISORDERS

From the remotest ages the philosophers have maintained the singular power of music over certain diseases, especially of the nervous class. Kircher recommends it, having experienced its good effects in himself, and he gives an elaborate description of the instrument he employed. It was a harmonica composed of five tumblers of a very thin glass, placed in a row. In two of them were two different varieties of wine; in the third, brandy; in the fourth, oil; in the fifth, water. He extracted five melodious sounds from them in the usual way, by merely rubbing his finger on the edges of the tumblers. The sound has an attractive property; it draws out disease, which streams out to encounter the musical wave, and the two, blending together, disappear in space. Asclepiades employed music for the same purpose, some twenty centuries ago; he blew a trumpet to cure sciatica, and its prolonged sound making the fibres of the nerves to palpitate, the pain invariably subsided. Democritus in like manner affirmed that many diseases could be cured by the melodious sounds of a flute. Mesmer used this very harmonica described by Kircher for his magnetic cures. The celebrated Scotchman, Maxwell, offered to prove to various medical faculties that with certain magnetic means at his disposal, he would cure any of the diseases abandoned by them as incurable; such as epilepsy, impotence, insanity, lameness, dropsy, and the most obstinate fevers.[353]

The familiar story of the exorcism of the "evil spirit from God" that obsessed Saul, will recur to every one in this connection. It is thus related: "And it came to pass, when the evil spirit from God was upon Saul, that David took an harp, and played with his hand: *so Saul was refreshed, and was well,* and the evil spirit departed from him."[354]

Maxwell, in his *Medicina Magnetica,* expounds the following propositions, all which are the very doctrines of the alchemists and kabalists.

"That which men call the world-soul, is a life, as fire, spiritual, fleet, light, and ethereal as light itself. It is a life-spirit everywhere; and everywhere the same. . . All matter is destitute of action, except as it is ensouled by this spirit. This spirit maintains all things in their peculiar condition. It is found in nature free from all fetters; and he who understands how to unite it with a harmonizing body, possesses a treasure which exceeds all riches."

THE "WORLD-SOUL" AND ITS POTENTIALITIES

"This spirit is the common bond of all quarters of the earth, and lives through and in all — *adest in mundo quid commune omnibus mextis, in quo ipsa permanent.*" "He who knows this universal life-spirit and its application can prevent all injuries."[355] "If thou canst avail thyself of this spirit and fix it on some particular body thou wilt perform the mystery of magic." "He who knows how to operate on men by this universal spirit, can heal, and this at any distance that he

---

353 See his "*Conf.,*" xiii., 1. c. in præfatione.
354 *I Samuel,* xvi., 14-23.
355 "*Aphorisms,*" 22.

pleases."[356] "He who can invigorate the particular spirit through the universal one, *might continue his life to eternity.*"[357]

"There is a blending together of spirits, or of emanations, even when they are far separated from each other. And what is this blending together? It is an eternal and incessant outpouring of the rays of one body into another."

"In the meantime," says Maxwell, "it is not *without danger* to treat of this. Many abominable abuses of this may take place."

And now let us see what are these abuses of mesmeric and magnetic powers in some healing mediums.

Healing, to deserve the name, requires either faith in the patient, or robust health united with a strong will, in the operator. *With expectancy supplemented by faith, one can cure himself of almost any morbific condition.* The tomb of a saint; a holy relic; a talisman; a bit of paper or a garment that has been handled by the supposed healer; a nostrum; a penance, or a ceremonial; the laying on of hands, or a few words impressively pronounced — either will do. It is a question of temperament, imagination, self-cure. In thousands of instances, the doctor, the priest, or the relic has had credit for healings that were solely and simply due to the patient's unconscious will. The woman with the bloody issue who pressed through the throng to touch the robe of Jesus, was told that her "faith" had made her whole. The influence of mind over the body is so powerful that it has effected miracles at all ages. "How many unhoped-for, sudden, and prodigious cures have been effected by imagination," says Salverte. "Our medical books are filled with facts of this nature which would easily pass for miracles."[358]

HEALING BY TOUCH, AND HEALERS

But, if the patient has no faith, what then? If he is physically negative and receptive, and the healer strong, healthy, positive, determined, the disease may be extirpated by the imperative will of the operator, which, consciously or unconsciously, draws to and reinforces itself with the universal spirit of nature, and restores the disturbed equilibrium of the patient's aura. He may employ as an auxiliary, a crucifix — as Gassner did; or impose the hands and "will," like the French Zouave Jacob, like our celebrated American, Newton, the healer of many thousands of sufferers, and like many others; or like Jesus, and some apostles, he may cure by the word of command. The process in each case is the same.

In all these instances, the cure is radical and real, and without secondary ill-effects. But, when one who is himself physically diseased, attempts healing, he not only fails of that, but often imparts his illness to his patient, and robs him of what strength he may have. The decrepit King David reinforced his failing vigor with the healthy magnetism of the young Abishag;[359] and the medical works tell us of an aged lady of Bath, England, who broke down the constitutions of two maids in succession, in the same way. The old sages, and

---

356 Ibid., p. 69.
357 Ibid., p. 70.
358 *"Philosophie des Sciences Occultes."*
359 *I Kings*, i. 1-4, 15.

Paracelsus also, removed disease by applying a healthy organism to the afflicted part, and in the works of the above-said fire-philosopher, their theory is boldly and categorically set forth. If a diseased person — medium or not — attempts to heal, his force may be sufficiently robust to displace the disease, to disturb it in the present place, and cause it to shift to another, where shortly it will appear; the patient, meanwhile, thinking himself cured.

But, what if the healer be morally diseased? The consequences may be infinitely more mischievous; for it is easier to cure a bodily disease than cleanse a constitution infected with moral turpitude. The mystery of Morzine, Cevennes, and that of the Jansenists, is still as great a mystery for physiologists as for psychologists. If the gift of prophecy, as well as hysteria and convulsions, can be imparted by "infection," why not every vice? The healer, in such a case, conveys to his patient — who is now his victim — the moral poison that infects his own mind and heart. His magnetic touch is defilement; his glance, profanation. Against this insidious taint, there is no protection for the passively-receptive subject. The healer holds him under his power, spell-bound and powerless, as the serpent holds a poor, weak bird. The evil that one such "healing medium" can effect is incalculably great; and such healers there are by the hundred.

But, as we have said before, there are real and God-like healers, who, notwithstanding all the malice and skepticism of their bigoted opponents, have become famous in the world's history. Such are the Cure d'Ars, of Lyons, Jacob, and Newton. Such, also, were Gassner, the clergyman of Klorstele, and the well-known Valentine Greatrakes, the ignorant and poor Irishman, who was endorsed by the celebrated Robert Boyle, President of the Royal Society of London, in 1670. In 1870, he would have been sent to Bedlam, in company with other healers, if another president of the same society had had the disposal of the case, or Professor Lankester would have "summoned" him under the *Vagrant Act* for practicing upon Her Majesty's subjects "by *palmistry* or otherwise."

But, to close a list of witnesses which might be extended indefinitely, it will suffice to say that, from first to last, from Pythagoras down to Eliphas Levi, from highest to humblest, every one teaches *that the magical power is never possessed by those addicted to vicious indulgences.* Only the pure in heart "see God," or exercise divine gifts — only such can heal the ills of the body, and allow themselves, with relative security, to be guided by the "invisible powers." Such only can give peace to the disturbed spirits of their brothers and sisters, for the healing waters come from no poisonous source; grapes do not grow on thorns, and thistles bear no figs. But, for all this, "magic has nothing supernal in it"; it is a science, and even the power of "casting out devils" was a branch of it, of which the Initiates made a special study. "That skill which expels demons out of human bodies, is a science useful and sanative to men," says Josephus.[360]

The foregoing sketches are sufficient to show why we hold fast to the wisdom of the ages, in preference to any new theories that may have been hatched from the occurrences of our later days, respecting the laws of intermundane intercourse and the occult powers of man. While phenomena of a physical nature may have their value as a means of arousing the interest of materialists, and confirming, if not wholly, at least inferentially, our belief in

---

360 Josephus, "*Antiquities,*" viii., 2.

the survival of our souls and spirits, it is questionable whether, under their present aspect, the modern phenomena are not doing more harm than good. Many minds, hungering after proofs of immortality, are fast falling into fanaticism; and, as Stow remarks, "fanatics are governed rather by imagination than judgment."

"Diakka" and Porphyry's Bad Demons

Undoubtedly, believers in the modern phenomena can claim for themselves a diversity of endowments, but the "discerning of spirits" is evidently absent from this catalogue of "spiritual" gifts. Speaking of the "Diakka," whom he one fine morning had discovered in a shady corner of the "Summer Land," A. J. Davis, the great American seer, remarks: "A Diakka is one who takes insane delight in *playing parts*, in juggling *tricks*, in *personating* opposite characters; to whom prayer and profane utterances are of equi-value; surcharged with a passion for lyrical narrations; . . . morally deficient, he is without the active feelings of justice, philanthropy, or tender affection. He knows nothing of what men call the sentiment of gratitude; the ends of hate and love are the same to him; his motto is often fearful and terrible to others — SELF is the whole of private living, and exalted annihilation *the end of all private life.*[361]   Only yesterday, one said to a lady medium, signing himself *Swedenborg*, this: 'Whatsoever is, has been, will be, or may be, *that* I AM ; and private life is but the aggregative phantasms of thinking throblets, rushing in their rising onward to the central heart of eternal death!' "[362] Porphyry, whose works — to borrow the expression of an irritated phenomenalist — "are mouldering like every other antiquated trash in the closets of oblivion," speaks thus of these Diakka — if such be their name — rediscovered in the nineteenth century: "It is with the direct help of these bad demons, that every kind of sorcery is accomplished . . . it is the result of their operations, and men who injure their fellow-creatures by enchantments, usually pay great honors to these bad demons, and especially to their chief. These spirits pass their time in deceiving us, with a great display of cheap prodigies and *illusions;* their ambition is to be taken for gods, and their leader demands to be recognized as the supreme god."[363]

The spirit signing himself Swedenborg — just quoted from Davis's *Diakka,* and hinting that he is the I AM, singularly resembles this chief leader of Porphyry's bad demons. What more natural than this vilification of the ancient and experienced theurgists by certain mediums, when we find Iamblichus, the expositor of spiritualistic theurgy, strictly forbidding all endeavors to procure such phenomenal manifestations; unless, after a long preparation of moral and physical purification, and under the guidance of experienced theurgists. When, furthermore, he declares that, with very few exceptions, for *a person* "*to appear elongated or thicker, or be borne aloft in the air,*" is a sure mark of obsession by *bad* demons.[364]

---

361 "*The Diakka and their Victims; an Explanation of the False and Repulsive in Spiritualism.*"
362 See Chapter on the human spirits becoming the denizens of the *eighth* sphere, whose end is generally the *annihilation* of personal individuality.
363 Porphyry, "*On the Good and Bad Demons.*"
364 "*De Mysteriis Egyptorum,*" lib. iii., c. 5.

Everything in this world has its time, and truth, however based upon unimpeachable evidence, will not root or grow, unless, like a plant, it is thrown into soil in its proper season. "The age must be prepared," says Professor Cooke; and some thirty years ago this humble work would have been doomed to self-destruction by its own contents. But the modern phenomenon, notwithstanding the daily *exposes*, the ridicule with which it is crowned at the hand of every materialist, and its own numerous errors, grows and waxes strong in facts, if not in wisdom and spirit. What would have appeared twenty years ago simply preposterous, may well be listened to now that the phenomena are endorsed by great scientists. Unfortunately, if the manifestations increase in power daily, there is no corresponding improvement in philosophy. The discernment of spirits is still as wanting as ever.

Perhaps, among the whole body of spiritualist writers of our day, not one is held in higher esteem for character, education, sincerity, and ability, than Epes Sargent, of Boston, Massachusetts. His monograph entitled *The Proof Palpable of Immortality,* deservedly occupies a high rank among works upon the subject. With every disposition to be charitable and apologetic for mediums and their phenomena, Mr. Sargent is still compelled to use the following language: "The power of spirits to reproduce simulacra of persons who have passed from the earth-life, suggests the question — How far can we be assured of the identity of *any* spirit, let the tests be what they may? We have not yet arrived at that stage of enlightenment that would enable us to reply confidently to this inquiry. . . . There is much that is yet a puzzle in the language and action of this class of materialized spirits." As to the intellectual calibre of most of the spirits which lurk behind the physical phenomena, Mr. Sargent will unquestionably be accepted as a most competent judge, and he says, "the great majority, as in this world, are of the unintellectual sort." If it is a fair question, we would like to ask why they should be so lacking in intelligence, if they are human spirits? Either intelligent human spirits *cannot* materialize, or, the spirits that do materialize have not human intelligence, and, therefore, by Mr. Sargent's own showing, they may just as well be "elementary" spirits, who have ceased to be human altogether, or those demons, which, according to the Persian Magi and Plato, hold a middle rank between gods and disembodied men.

There is good evidence, that of Mr. Crookes for one, to show that many "materialized" spirits talk in an audible voice. Now, we have shown, on the testimony of ancients, that the voice of human spirits is not and *cannot* be articulated; being, as Emanuel Swedenborg declares, "a deep suspiration." Who of the two classes of witnesses may be trusted more safely? Is it the ancients who had the experience of so many ages in theurgical practices, or modern spiritualists, who have had none at all, and who have no facts upon which to base an opinion, except such as have been communicated by "spirits," whose identity they have no means of proving? There are mediums whose organisms have called out sometimes hundreds of these would-be "human" forms. And yet we do not recollect to have seen or heard of one expressing anything but the most commonplace ideas. This fact ought surely to arrest the attention of even the most uncritical spiritualist. If a spirit can speak at all, and if the way is opened to intelligent as well as to unintellectual beings, why should they not sometimes give us addresses in some remote degree approximating in quality to the communications we receive through the "direct writing"? Mr. Sargent puts forward a very suggestive and important idea in this sentence. "How far they are limited in their mental operations and in their recollections by the act of materialization, or how far by the intellectual horizon of the medium is still a question."[365] If the same kind of "spirits" materialize that produce the direct writing, and both manifest through mediums, and the one talk nonsense, while the other often give us sublime philosophical teachings, why should their mental operations be limited "by the intellectual horizon of the medium" in the one instance more than in the other? The materializing mediums — at least so far as our observation extends — are no more uneducated than many peasants and mechanics who at different times have, under supernal influences, given profound and sublime ideas to the world. The history of psychology teems with examples in illustration of this point, among which that of Boehme, the inspired but ignorant shoemaker, and our own Davis, are conspicuous. As to the matter of unintellectuality we presume that no more striking cases need be sought than those of the child-prophets of Cevennes, poets and seers, such as have been mentioned in previous chapters. When spirits have once furnished themselves with vocal organs to speak at all, it surely ought to be no more difficult for them to talk as persons of their assumed respective education, intelligence, and social rank would in life, instead of falling invariably into one monotonous tone of commonplace and, but too often, platitude. As to Mr. Sargent's hopeful remark, that "the science of Spiritualism being still in its infancy, we may hope for more light on this question," we fear we must reply, that *it is not through "dark cabinets" that this light will ever break.*[366]

It is simply ridiculous and absurd to require from every investigator who comes forward as a witness to the marvels of the day and psychological phenomena the diploma of a master of arts and sciences. The experience of the past forty years is an evidence that it is not always the minds which are the most "scientifically trained" that are the best in matters of simple common sense and honest truth. Nothing blinds like fanaticism, or a one-sided view of a question. We may take as an illustration Oriental magic or ancient spiritualism, as well as the modern phenomena. Hundreds, nay thousands of perfectly trustworthy witnesses, returning from residence and travels in the East, have testified to the fact that uneducated fakirs, sheiks, dervishes, and lamas have, in their presence, without confederates or mechanical appliances, produced wonders.

They have affirmed that the phenomena exhibited by them were in contravention of all the *known* laws of science, and thus tended to prove the existence of many yet unknown occult potencies in nature, seemingly directed by preterhuman intelligences. What has been the attitude assumed by our scientists toward this subject? How far did the testimony of the most "scientifically" trained minds make impression on their own? Did the investigations of Professors Hare and de Morgan, of Crookes and Wallace, de Gasparin and Thury, Wagner and Butlerof, etc., shake for one moment their skepticism? How were the personal experiences of Jacolliot with the fakirs of India received, or the psychological elucidations of Professor Perty, of Geneva, viewed? How far does the loud cry of mankind, craving for palpable and demonstrated signs of a God, an individual soul, and of eternity, affect them; and what is their response? They pull down and destroy every vestige of spiritual things, but they erect nothing. "We cannot get such signs with either retorts or crucibles," they say; "hence, it's all but a delusion!"

---

365 Epes Sargent, "*Proof Palpable of Immortality*," p. 45.
366 See *Matthew* xxiv. 26.

In this age of cold reason and prejudice, even the Church has to look to science for help. Creeds built on sand, and high-towering but rootless dogmas, crumble down under the cold breath of research, and pull down *true* religion in their fall. But the longing for some outward sign of a God and a life hereafter, remains as tenaciously as ever in the human heart. In vain is all sophistry of science; it can never stifle the voice of nature. Only her representatives have poisoned the pure waters of simple faith, and now humanity mirrors itself in waters made turbid with all the mud stirred up from the bottom of the once pure spring. The anthropomorphic God of our fathers is replaced by anthropomorphic monsters; and what is still worse, by the reflection of humanity itself in these waters, whose ripples send it back the distorted images of truth and facts as evoked by its misguided imagination.

"It is not a miracle that we want," writes the Reverend Brooke Herford, "but to find palpable evidence of the spiritual and the divine. It is not to the prophets that men cry for such a 'sign,' but rather to the scientists. Men feel as if all that groping about in the foremost verge or innermost recesses of creation should bring the investigator at length close to the deep, underlying facts of all things, to some unmistakable signs of God." The signs are there, and the scientists too; what can we expect more of them, now that they have done so well their duty? Have they not, these Titans of thought, dragged down God from His hiding-place, and given us instead a *protoplasm?*

At the Edinburgh meeting of the British Association, in 1871, Sir William Thomson said: "Science is bound by the everlasting law of honor to face fearlessly every problem which can fairly be presented to it." In his turn, Professor Huxley remarks: "With regard to the miracle-question, I can only say that the word 'impossible' is not, to my mind, applicable to matters of philosophy." The great Humboldt remarks that "a presumptuous skepticism that rejects facts without examination of their truth is, in some respects, more injurious than unquestioning credulity."

These men have proved untrue to their own teachings. The opportunity afforded them by the opening of the Orient, to investigate for themselves the phenomena alleged by every traveller to take place in those countries, has been rejected. Did our physiologists and pathologists ever so much as think of availing themselves of it to settle this most momentous subject of human thought? Oh, no; for they would never dare. It is not to be expected that the principal Academicians of Europe and America should undertake a joint journey to Thibet and India, and investigate the fakir marvel on the spot! And were one of them to go as a solitary pilgrim and witness all the miracles of creation, in that land of wonders, who, of his colleagues, could be expected to believe his testimony?

It would be as tedious as superfluous to begin a restatement of facts, so forcibly put by others, Mr. Wallace and W. Howitt,[367] have repeatedly and cleverly described the thousand and one absurd errors into which the learned societies of France and England have fallen, through their blind skepticism. If Cuvier could throw aside the fossil excavated in 1828 by Boue, the French geologist, only because the anatomist thought himself wiser than his colleague, and would not believe that human skeletons could be found eighty feet deep in the mud of the Rhine; and if the French Academy could discredit the assertions of Boucher de Perthes, in 1846, only to be criticised in its turn in 1860, when the truth of de Perthes'

---

367 See Wallace, *"Miracles and Modern Spiritualism,"* and W. Howitt, *"History of the Supernatural,"* vol. ii.

discoveries and observations was fully confirmed by the whole body of geologists finding flint weapons in the drift-gravels of northern France; and if McEnery's testimony, in 1825, to the fact that he had discovered worked flints, together with the remains of extinct animals, in Kent's Hole Cavern[368] was laughed at; and that of Godwin Austen to the same effect, in 1840, ridiculed still more, if that were possible; and all that excess of scientific skepticism and merriment could, in 1865, finally come to grief, and be shown to have been entirely uncalled for; when — says Mr. Wallace "all the previous reports for forty years were confirmed and shown to be even less wonderful than the reality;" — who can be so credulous as to believe in the infallibility of our science? And why wonder at the exhibition of such a lack of moral courage in individual members of this great and stubborn body known as modern science?

THE QUENCHLESS LAMP

Thus fact after fact has been discredited. From all sides we hear constant complaints. "Very little is known of psychology!" sighs one F. R. S. "We must confess that we know little, if anything, in physiology," says another. "Of all sciences, there is none which rests upon so uncertain a basis as medicine," reluctantly testifies a third. "What do we know about the presumed nervous fluids? . . . Nothing, as yet," puts in a fourth one; and so on in every branch of science. And, meanwhile, phenomena, surpassing in interest all others of nature, and to be solved only by physiology, psychology, and the "as yet unknown" fluids, are either rejected as delusions, or, if even true, "do not interest" scientists. Or, what is still worse, when a *subject*, whose organism exhibits in itself the most important features of such occult though natural potencies, offers his person for an investigation, instead of an honest experiment being attempted with him he finds himself entrapped by a scientist (?) and paid for his trouble with a sentence of three months' imprisonment! This is indeed promising.

It is easy to comprehend that a fact given in 1731, testifying to another fact which happened during the papacy of Paul III., for instance, is disbelieved in 1876. And when scientists are told that the Romans preserved lights in their sepulchres for countless years by the *oiliness of gold;* and that one of such ever-burning lamps was found brightly burning in the tomb of Tullia, the daughter of Cicero, notwithstanding that the tomb had been shut up fifteen hundred and fifty years,[369] — they have a certain right to doubt, and even disbelieve the statement, until they assure themselves, on the evidence of their own senses, that such a thing is possible. In such a case they can reject the testimony of all the ancient and mediæval philosophers. The burial of living fakirs and their subsequent resuscitation, after thirty days of inhumation, may have a suspicious look to them. So also with the self-infliction of mortal wounds, and the exhibition of their own bowels to the persons present by various lamas, who heal such wounds almost instantaneously.

For certain men who deny the evidence of their own senses as to phenomena produced in their own country, and before numerous witnesses, the narratives to be found in classical books, and in the notes of travellers, must of course seem absurd. But what we will never be able to understand is the collective stubbornness of the Academies, in the face of such bitter

---

368 See Wallace's paper read before the Dialectical Society, in 1871, "*Answer to Hume, etc.*"
369 "*Filologo*" (Bailey's), second edition.

lessons in the past, to these institutions which have so often "darkened counsel by words without knowledge." Like the Lord answering Job "out of the whirlwind," magic can say to modern science: "Where wast thou when I laid the foundations of the earth? declare, if thou hast understanding!" And, who art thou who dare say to nature, "Hitherto shalt thou come, but no further; and here shall thy proud waves be stayed"?

But what matters it if they do deny? Can they prevent phenomena taking place in the four corners of the world, if their skepticism were a thousand times more bitter? Fakirs will still be buried and resuscitated, gratifying the curiosity of European travellers; and lamas and Hindu ascetics will wound, mutilate, and even disembowel themselves, and find themselves all the better for it; and the denials of the whole world will not blow sufficiently to extinguish the perpetually-burning lamps in certain of the subterranean crypts of India, Thibet, and Japan. One of such lamps is mentioned by the Rev. S. Mateer, of the London Mission. In the temple of Trevandrum, in the kingdom of Travancore, South India, "there is a deep well inside the temple, into which immense riches are thrown year by year, and in another place, in a hollow covered by a stone, a great golden lamp, which was lit over 120 years ago, still continues burning," says this missionary in his description of the place. Catholic missionaries attribute these lamps, as a matter of course, to the obliging services of the devil. The more prudent Protestant divine mentions the fact, and makes no commentary. The Abbé Huc has seen and examined one of such lamps, and so have other people whose good luck it has been to win the confidence and friendship of Eastern lamas and divines. No more can be denied the wonders seen by Captain Lane in Egypt; the Benares experiences of Jacolliot and those of Sir Charles Napier; the levitations of human beings in broad daylight, and which can be accounted for only on the explanation given in the Introductory chapter of the present work.[370] Such levitations are testified to — besides Mr. Crookes — by Professor Perty, who shows them produced in open air, and lasting sometimes twenty minutes; all these phenomena and many more have happened, do, and will happen in every country of this globe, and that in spite of all the skeptics and scientists that ever were evolved out of the Silurian mud.

Among the ridiculed claims of alchemy is that of the *perpetual lamps.* If we tell the reader that we have seen such, we may be asked — in case that the sincerity of our personal belief is not questioned — how we can tell that the lamps we have observed are perpetual, as the period of our observation was but limited? Simply that, as we know the ingredients employed, and the manner of their construction, and the natural law applicable to the case, we are confident that our statement can be corroborated upon investigation in the proper quarter. What that quarter is, and from whom that knowledge can be learned, our critics must discover, by taking the pains we did. Meanwhile, however, we will quote a few of the 173 authorities who have written upon the subject. None of these, as we recollect, have asserted that these sepulchral lamps would burn perpetually, but only for an indefinite number of years, and instances are recorded of their continuing alight for many centuries. It will not be denied that, if there is a natural law by which a lamp can be made without replenishment to burn ten years, there is no reason why the same law could not cause the combustion to continue one hundred or one thousand years.

---

370 See Art. on "*Æthrobacy.*"

Among the many well-known personages who firmly believed and strenuously asserted that such sepulchral lamps burned for several hundreds of years, and would have continued to burn *may be* forever, had they not been extinguished, or the vessels broken by some accident, we may reckon the following names: Clemens Alexandrinus, Hermolaus Barbarus, Appian, Burattinus, Citesius, Cœlius, Foxius, Costæus, Casalius, Cedrenus, Delrius, Ericius, Gesnerus, Jacobonus, Leander, Libavius, Lazius, P. della Mirandola, Philalethes, Licetus, Maiolus, Maturantius, Baptista Porta, Pancirollus, Ruscellius, Scardeonius, Ludovicus Vives, Volateranus, Paracelsus, several Arabian alchemists, and finally, Pliny, Solinus, Kircher, and Albertus Magnus.

The discovery is claimed by the ancient Egyptians, those sons of the Land of Chemistry.[371] At least, they were a people who used these lamps far more than any other nation, on account of their religious doctrines. The astral soul of the mummy was believed to be lingering about the body for the whole space of the three thousand years of the circle of necessity. Attached to it by a magnetic thread, which could be broken but by its own exertion, the Egyptians hoped that the ever-burning lamp, symbol of their incorruptible and immortal spirit, would at last decide the more material soul to part with its earthly dwelling, and unite forever with its divine SELF. Therefore lamps were hung in the sepulchres of the rich. Such lamps are often found in the subterranean caves of the dead, and Licetus has written a large folio to prove that in his time, whenever a sepulchre was opened, a burning lamp was found within the tomb, but was instantaneously extinguished on account of the *desecration*. T. Livius, Burattinus, and Michael Schatta, in their letters to Kircher,[372] affirm that they found many lamps in the subterranean caves of old Memphis. Pausanias speaks of the golden lamp in the temple of Minerva at Athens, which he says was the workmanship of Callimachus, and burnt a whole year. Plutarch[373] affirms that he saw one in the temple of Jupiter Amun, and that the priests assured him that it had burnt continually for years, and though it stood in the open air, neither wind nor water could extinguish it. St. Augustine, the Catholic authority, also describes a lamp in the fane of Venus, of the same nature as the others, unextinguishable either by the strongest wind or by water. A lamp was found at Edessa, says Kedrenus, "which, being hidden at the top of a certain gate, burned 500 years." But of all such lamps, the one mentioned by Olybius Maximus of Padua is by far the more wonderful. It was found near Atteste, and Scardeonius[374] gives a glowing description of it: "In a large earthen urn was contained a lesser, and in that a burning lamp, which had continued so for 1500 years, by means of a most pure liquor contained in two bottles, one of gold and the other of silver. These are in the custody of Franciscus Maturantius, and are by him valued at an exceeding rate."

Taking no account of exaggerations, and putting aside as mere unsupported negation the affirmation by modern science of the impossibility of such lamps, we would ask whether, in case these inextinguishable fires are found to have really existed in the ages of "miracles," the lamps burning at Christian shrines and those of Jupiter, Minerva, and other Pagan deities, ought to be differently regarded. According to certain theologians, it would

---

371 *Psalm* cv. 23. "The Land of Ham," or *chem*, Greek chemi , whence the terms *alchemy* and *chemistry*.
372 "*Œdipi Ægyptiaci Theatrum Hieroglyphicum*," p. 544.
373 "*Lib. de Defectu Oraculorum*."
374 Lib. i., Class 3, *Cap. ult.*

appear that the former (for Christianity also claims such lamps) have burned by a *divine*, miraculous power, and that the light of the latter, made by "heathen" art, was supported by the wiles of the devil. Kircher and Licetus show that they were ordered in these two diverse ways. The lamp at Antioch, which burned 1500 years, in an open and public place, over the door of a church, was preserved by the "*power of God*," who "hath made so infinite a number of stars to burn with perpetual light." As to the Pagan lamps, St. Augustine assures us they were the work of the devil, "who deceives us in a thousand ways." What more easy for Satan to do than represent a flash of light, or a bright flame to them who first enter into such a subterranean cave? This was asserted by all good Christians during the Papacy of Paul III., when upon opening a tomb in the Appian Way, at Rome, there was found the entire body of a young girl swimming in a bright liquor which had so well preserved it, that the face was beautiful and like life itself. At her feet burned a lamp, whose flame vanished upon opening the sepulchre. From some engraved signs it was found to have been buried for over 1500 years, and supposed to have been the body of Tulliola, or Tullia, Cicero's daughter.[375]

Chemists and physicists deny that perpetual lamps are possible, alleging that whatever is resolved into vapor or smoke cannot be permanent, but must consume; and as the oily nutriment of a lighted lamp is exhaled into a vapor, hence the fire cannot be perpetual for want of food. Alchemists, on the other hand, deny that all the nourishment of kindled fire must of necessity be converted into vapor. They say that there are things in nature which will not only resist the force of fire and remain inconsumable, but will also prove inextinguishable by either wind or water. In an old chemical work of the year 1700, called NEKPOKHDEIA , the author gives a number of refutations of the claims of various alchemists. But though he denies that a fire can be made to burn *perpetually,* he is half-inclined to believe it possible that a lamp should burn several hundred years. Besides, we have a mass of testimony from alchemists who devoted years to these experiments and came to the conclusion that it was possible.

There are some peculiar preparations of gold, silver, and mercury; also of naphtha, petroleum, and other bituminous oils. Alchemists also name the oil of camphor and amber, the *Lapis asbestos seu Amianthus,* the *Lapis Carystius, Cyprius,* and *Linum vivum seu Creteum,* as employed for such lamps. They affirm that such matter can be prepared either of gold or silver, reduced to fluid, and indicate that gold is the fittest *pabulum* for their wondrous flame, as, of all metals, gold wastes the least when either heated or melted, and, moreover, can be made to reabsorb its oily humidity as soon as exhaled, so continuously feeding its own flame when it is once lighted. The Kabalists assert that the secret was known to Moses, who had learned it from the Egyptians; and that the lamp ordered by the "Lord" to burn on the tabernacle, was an inextinguishable lamp. "And thou shalt command the children of Israel, that they bring thee pure oil-olive beaten for the light, *to cause the lamp to burn always*" (Exod. xxvii. 20).

Licetus also denies that these lamps were prepared of metal, but on page 44 of his work mentions a preparation of quicksilver filtrated seven times through white sand by fire, of which, he says, lamps were made that would burn perpetually. Both Maturantius and Citesius firmly believe that such a work can be done by a purely chemical process. This

---

375 The details of this story may be found in the work of Erasmus Franciscus, who quotes from Pflaumerus, Pancirollus, and many others.

liquor of quicksilver was known among alchemists as *Aqua Mercurialis, Materia Metallorum, Perpetua Dispositio,* and *Materia prima Artis,* also *Oleum Vitri.* Tritenheim and Bartolomeo Korndorf both made preparations for the inextinguishable fire, and left their recipes for it.[376] Asbestos, which was known to the Greeks under the name of Ασβεστος, or *inextinguishable,* is a kind of stone, which once set on fire cannot be quenched, as Pliny and Solinus tell us. Albertus Magnus describes it as a stone of an iron color, found mostly in Arabia. It is generally found covered with a hardly-perceptible oleaginous moisture, which upon being approached with a lighted candle will immediately catch fire. Many were the experiments made by chemists to extract from it this indissoluble oil, but they are alleged to have all failed. But, are our chemists prepared to say that the above operation is utterly impracticable? If this oil could once be extracted there can be no question but it would afford a perpetual fuel. The ancients might well boast of having had the secret of it, for, we repeat, there are experimenters living at this day who have done so successfully. Chemists who have vainly tried it, have asserted that the fluid or liquor chemically extracted from

---

376 "*Sulphur. Alum* ust. a ℥ iv.; sublime them into flowers to ℥ ij., of which add of crystalline Venetian borax (powdered) ℥ j.; upon these affuse high rectified spirit of wine and digest it, then abstract it and pour on fresh; repeat this so often till the sulphur melts like wax without any smoke, upon a hot plate of brass: this is for the *pabulum,* but the wick is to be prepared after this manner: gather the threads or thrums of the *Lapis asbestos,* to the thickness of your middle and the length of your little finger, then put them into a Venetian glass, and covering them over with the aforesaid depurated sulphur or aliment, set the glass in sand for the space of twenty-four hours, so hot that the sulphur may bubble all the while. The wick being thus besmeared and anointed, is to be put into a glass like a scallop-shell, in such manner that some part of it may lie above the mass of prepared sulphur; then setting this glass upon hot sand, you must melt the sulphur, so that it may lay hold of the wick, and when it is lighted, it will burn with a perpetual flame and you may set this lamp in any place where you please."

The other is as follows: " ℞ . *Solis tosti,* lb. j.; affuse over it strong wine vinegar, and abstract it to the consistency of oil; then put on fresh vinegar and macerate and distill it as before. Repeat this four times successively, then put into this vinegar *vitr. antimonii subtilis loevigat,* lb. j.; set it on ashes in a close vessel for the space of six hours, to extract its tincture, decant the liquor, and put on fresh, and then extract it again; this repeat so often till you have got out all the redness. Coagulate your extractions to the consistency of oil, and then rectify them in Balneo Mariae (bain Marie). Then take the antimony, from which the tincture was extracted, and reduce it to a very fine meal, and so put it into a glass bolthead; pour upon it the rectified oil, which abstract and cohobate seven times, till such time as the powder has imbibed all the oil, and is quite dry. This extract again with spirit of wine, so often, till all the essence be got out of it, which put into a Venice matrass, well luted with paper five-fold, and then distill it so that the spirit being drawn off, there may remain at the bottom an inconsumable oil, to be used with a wick after the same manner with the sulphur we have described before."

"These are the eternal lights of Tritenheimus," says Libavius, his commentator, "which indeed, though they do not agree with the pertinacy of naphtha, yet these things can illustrate one another. Naphtha is not so durable as not to be burned, for it exhales and deflagrates, but if it be fixed by adding the juice of the *Lapis asbestinos* it can afford perpetual fuel," says this learned person.

We may add that we have ourselves seen a lamp so prepared, and we are told that since it was first lighted on May 2, 1871, it has not gone out. As we know the person who is making the experiment incapable to deceive any one, being himself an ardent experimenter in hermetic secrets, we have no reason to doubt his assertion.

that stone was more of a watery than oily nature, and so impure and feculent that it could not burn; others affirmed, on the contrary, that the oil, as soon as exposed to the air, became so thick and solid that it would hardly flow, and when lighted emitted no flame, but escaped in dark smoke; whereas the lamps of the ancients are alleged to have burned with the purest and brightest flame, without emitting the slightest smoke. Kircher, who shows the practicability of purifying it, thinks it so difficult as to be accessible only to the highest adepts of alchemy.

St. Augustine, who attributes the whole of these arts to the Christian scapegoat, the devil, is flatly contradicted by Ludovicus Vives,[377] who shows that all such would-be magical operations are the work of man's industry and deep study of the hidden secrets of nature, wonderful and miraculous as they may seem. Podocattarus, a Cypriote knight,[378] had both flax and linen made out of another asbestos, which *Porcacchius* says[379] he saw at the house of this knight. Pliny calls this flax *linum vinum*, and Indian flax, and says it is done out of *asbeston sive asbestinum*, a kind of flax of which they made cloth that was to be cleaned by throwing it in the fire. He adds that it was as precious as pearls and diamonds, for not only was it very rarely found but exceedingly difficult to be woven, on account of the shortness of the threads. Being beaten flat with a hammer, it is soaked in warm water, and when dried its filaments can be easily divided into threads like flax and woven into cloth. Pliny asserts he has seen some towels made of it, and assisted in an experiment of purifying them by fire. Baptista Porta also states that he found the same, at Venice, in the hands of a Cyprian lady; he calls this discovery of Alchemy a *secretum optimum.*

Dr. Grew, in his description of the curiosities in Gresham College (seventeenth century), believes the art, as well as the use of such linen, altogether lost, but it appears that it was not quite so, for we find the Museum Septalius boasting of the possession of thread, ropes, paper, and net-work done of this material as late as 1726; some of these articles made, moreover, by the own hand of Septalius, as we learn in Greenhill's *Art of Embalming,* p. 361. "Grew," says the author, "seems to make *Asbestinus Lapis* and *Amianthus* all one, and calls them in English the thrum-stone"; he says it grows in short threads or thrums, from about a quarter of an inch to an inch in length, parallel and glossy, as fine as those small, single threads the silk-worms spin, and very flexible like to flax or tow. That the secret is not altogether lost is proved by the fact that some Buddhist convents in China and Thibet are in possession of it. Whether made of the fibre of one or the other of such stones, we cannot say, but we have seen in a monastery of female Talapoins, a yellow gown, such as the Buddhist monks wear, thrown into a large pit, full of glowing coals, and taken out two hours afterward as clear as if it had been washed with soap and water.

Similar severe trials of asbestos having occurred in Europe and America in our own times, the substance is being applied to various industrial purposes, such as roofing-cloth, incombustible dresses and fireproof safes. A very valuable deposit on Staten Island, in New York harbor, yields the mineral in bundles, like dry wood, with fibres of several feet in

---

377 "*Commentary upon St. Augustine's 'Treatise de Civitate Dei.'* "
378 The author of "*De Rebus Cypriis,*" 1566 A. D.
379 "*Book of Ancient Funerals.*"

length. The finer variety of asbestos, called αμιαντος (undefiled) by the ancients, took its name from its white, satin-like lustre.

The ancients made the wick of their perpetual lamps from another stone also, which they called *Lapis Carystius.* The inhabitants of the city of Carystos seemed to have made no secret of it, as *Matthaeus Raderus* says in his work[380] that they "kemb'd, spun, and wove this downy stone into mantles, table-linen, and the like, which when foul they purified again with fire instead of water." Pausanias, in *Atticus,* and Plutarch[381] also assert that the wicks of lamps were made from this stone; but Plutarch adds that it was no more to be found in his time. Licetus is inclined to believe that the perpetual lamps used by the ancients in their sepulchres had no wicks at all, as very few have been found; but Ludovicus Vives is of a contrary opinion and affirms that he has seen quite a number of them.

Licetus, moreover, is firmly persuaded that a "pabulum for fire may be given with such an equal temperament as cannot be consumed but after a long series of ages, and so that neither the matter shall exhale but strongly resist the fire, nor the fire consume the matter, but be restrained by it, as it were with a chain, from flying upward." To this, Sir Thomas Browne,[382] speaking of lamps which have burned many hundred years, included in small bodies, observes that "this proceeds from the purity of the oil, which yields no fuliginous exhalations to suffocate the fire; for if air had nourished the flame, then it had not continued many minutes, for it would certainly in that case have been spent and wasted by the fire." But he adds, "the art of preparing this inconsumable oil is lost."

Not quite; and time will prove it, though all that we now write should be doomed to fail, like so many other truths.

We are told, in behalf of science, that she accepts no other mode of investigation than observation and experiment. Agreed; and have we not the records of say three thousand years of observation of facts going to prove the occult powers of man? As to experiment, what better opportunity could have been asked than the so-called modern phenomena have afforded? In 1869, various scientific Englishmen were invited by the London Dialectical Society to assist in an investigation of these phenomena. Let us see what our philosophers replied. Professor Huxley wrote: "I have no time for such an inquiry, which would involve much trouble and (unless it were unlike all inquiries of that kind I have known) much annoyance. . . . I take no interest in the subject . . . but supposing the phenomena to be genuine — they do not interest me."[383] Mr. George H. Lewes expresses a wise thing in the following sentence: "When any man says that phenomena are produced by no known physical laws, he declares he knows the laws by which they are produced."[384] Professor Tyndall expresses doubt as to the possibility of good results at any seance which he might attend. His presence, according to the opinion of Mr. Varley, throws everything in confusion.[385] Professor Carpenter writes, "I have satisfied myself by personal investigation,

---

380 "*Comment. on the 77th Epigram of the IXth Book of Martial.*"
381 "*De Defectu Oraculorum.*"
382 "*Vulgar Errors,*" p. 124.
383 "*London Dialectical Society's Report on Spiritualism,*" p. 229.
384 Ibid., p. 230.
385 Ibid., p. 265.

that, whilst a great number of what pass as such (*i.e.*, spiritual manifestations) are the results of intentional imposture, and many others of self-deception, there are certain phenomena which are quite genuine, and must be considered as fair subjects of scientific study . . . the source of these phenomena does not lie in any communication *ab-extra*, but depends upon the *subjective* condition of the individual which operates according to certain recognized physiological laws . . .the process to which I have given the name *'unconscious cerebration'*. . . performs a large part in the production of the phenomena known as spiritualistic."[386]

And it is thus that the world is apprised through the organ of exact science, that *unconscious cerebration* has acquired the faculty of making the guitars fly in the air and forcing furniture to perform various clownish tricks!

So much for the opinions of the English scientists. The Americans have not done much better. In 1857, a committee of Harvard University warned the public against investigating this subject, which "corrupts the morals and degrades the intellect." They called it, furthermore, "a contaminating influence, which surely tends to lessen the truth of man and the purity of woman." Later, when Professor Robert Hare, the great chemist, defying the opinions of his contemporaries, investigated spiritualism, and became a believer, he was immediately declared *non compos mentis;* and in 1874, when one of the New York daily papers addressed a circular letter to the principal scientists of this country, asking them to investigate, and offering to pay the expenses, they, like the guests bidden to the supper, "with one consent, began to make excuses."

Yet, despite the indifference of Huxley, the jocularity of Tyndall, and the "unconscious cerebration" of Carpenter, many a scientist as noted as either of them, has investigated the unwelcome subject, and, overwhelmed with the evidence, become converted. And another scientist, and a great author — although not a spiritualist — bears this honorable testimony: "That the spirits of the dead occasionally revisit the living, or haunt their former abodes, has been in all ages, in all European countries, a fixed belief, not confined to rustics, but participated in by the intelligent. . . . If human testimony on such subjects can be of any value, there is a body of evidence reaching from the remotest ages to the present time, as *extensive and unimpeachable as is to be found* in support of anything whatever."[387]

Unfortunately, human skepticism is a stronghold capable of defying any amount of testimony. And to begin with Mr. Huxley, our men of science accept of but so much as suits them, and no more.

"Oh shame to men! devil with devil damn'd Firm concord holds, — *men* only disagree Of creatures rational. . . ."[388]

How can we account for such divergence of views among men taught out of the same text-books and deriving their knowledge from the same source? Clearly, this is but one more corroboration of the truism that no two men see the same thing exactly alike. This idea is admirably formulated by Dr. J. J. Garth Wilkinson, in a letter to the Dialectical Society.

---

386 Ibid., p. 266.
387 Draper, *"Conflict between Religion and Science,"* p. 121.
388 Milton, *"Paradise Lost."*

"I have long," says he, "been convinced, by the experience of my life as a pioneer in several heterodoxies which are rapidly becoming orthodoxies, that nearly all truth is temperamental to us, or given in the affections and intuitions, and that discussion and inquiry do little more than feed temperament."

This profound observer might have added to his experience that of Bacon, who remarks that ". . . a *little* philosophy inclineth a man's mind to atheism, but *depth* in philosophy bringeth man's mind about to religion."

Professor Carpenter vaunts the advanced philosophy of the present day which "ignores no fact however strange that can be attested by valid evidence"; and yet he would be the first to reject the claims of the ancients to philosophical and scientific knowledge, although based upon evidence quite "as valid" as that which supports the pretensions of men of our times to philosophical or scientific distinction. In the department of science, let us take for example the subjects of electricity and electro-magnetism, which have exalted the names of Franklin and Morse to so high a place upon our roll of fame.

Six centuries before the Christian era, Thales is said to have discovered the electric properties of amber; and yet the later researches of Schweigger, as given in his extensive works on Symbolism, have thoroughly demonstrated that all the ancient mythologies were based on the science of natural philosophy, and show that the most occult properties of electricity and magnetism were known to the theurgists of the earliest Mysteries recorded in history, those of Samothrace. Diodorus, of Sicily, Herodotus, and Sanchoniathon, the Phœnician — the oldest of historians — tell us that these Mysteries originated in the night of time, centuries and probably thousands of years prior to the historical period. One of the best proofs of it we find in a most remarkable picture, in Raoul-Rochette's *Monuments d'Antiquité Figurés*, in which, like the "erect-haired Pan," all the figures have their hair streaming out in every direction — except the central figure of the Kabeirian Demeter, from whom the power issues, and one other, a kneeling man.[389] The picture, according to Schweigger, evidently represents a part of the ceremony of initiation. And yet it is not so long since the elementary works on natural philosophy began to be ornamented with cuts of *electrified* heads, with hair standing out in all directions, under the influence of the electric fluid. Schweigger shows that a *lost natural philosophy of antiquity* was connected with the most important religious ceremonies. He demonstrates in the amplest manner, that *magic* in the prehistoric periods had a part in the mysteries and that the greatest phenomena, the so-called miracles — whether Pagan, Jewish, or Christian — rested in fact on the arcane knowledge of the ancient priests of physics and all the branches of chemistry, or rather alchemy.

In Chapter XI., which is entirely devoted to the wonderful achievements of the ancients, we propose to demonstrate our assertions more fully. We will show, on the evidence of the most trustworthy classics, that at a period far anterior to the siege of Troy, the learned priests of the sanctuaries were thoroughly acquainted with electricity and even lightning-conductors. We will now add but a few more words before closing the subject.

---

389 See Ennemoser, *"History of Magic,"* vol. ii., and Schweigger, *"Introduction to Mythology through Natural History."*

The theurgists so well understood the minutest properties of magnetism, that, without possessing the lost key to their arcana, but depending wholly upon what was known in their modern days of electro-magnetism, Schweigger and Ennemoser have been able to trace the identity of the "twin brothers," the Dioskuri, with the polarity of electricity and magnetism. Symbolical myths, previously supposed to be meaningless fictions, are now found to be "the cleverest and at the same time most profound expressions of a strictly scientifically defined truth of nature," according to Ennemoser.[390]

Our physicists pride themselves on the achievements of our century and exchange antiphonal hymns of praise. The eloquent diction of their class-lectures, their flowery phraseology, require but a slight modification to change these lectures into melodious sonnets. Our modern Petrarchs, Dantes, and Torquato Tassos rival with the troubadours of old in poetical effusion. In their unbounded glorification of matter, they sing the amorous commingling of the wandering atoms, and the loving interchange of protoplasms, and lament the coquettish fickleness of "forces" which play so provokingly at hide-and-seek with our grave professors in the great drama of life, called by them "force-correlation." Proclaiming matter sole and autocratic sovereign of the Boundless Universe, they would forcibly divorce her from her consort, and place the widowed queen on the great throne of nature made vacant by the exiled spirit. And now, they try to make her appear as attractive as they can by incensing and worshipping at the shrine of their own building. Do they forget, or are they utterly unaware of the fact, that in the absence of its legitimate sovereign, this throne is but a whitened sepulchre, inside of which all is rottenness and corruption! That matter without the spirit which vivifies it, and of which it is but the "gross purgation," to use a hermetic expression, is nothing but a soulless corpse, whose limbs, in order to be moved in predetermined directions, require an intelligent operator at the great galvanic battery called LIFE!

In what particular is the knowledge of the present century so superior to that of the ancients? When we say knowledge we do not mean that brilliant and clear definition of our modern scholars of particulars to the most trifling detail in every branch of exact science; of that tuition which finds an appropriate term for every detail insignificant and microscopic as it may be; a name for every nerve and artery in human and animal organisms, an appellation for every cell, filament, and rib in a plant; but the philosophical and ultimate expression of every truth in nature.

The greatest ancient philosophers are accused of shallowness and a superficiality of knowledge of those details in exact sciences of which the moderns boast so much. Plato is declared by his various commentators to have been utterly ignorant of the anatomy and functions of the human body; to have known nothing of the uses of the nerves to convey sensations; and to have had nothing better to offer than vain speculations concerning physiological questions. He has simply generalized the divisions of the human body, they say, and given nothing reminding us of anatomical facts. As to his own views on the human frame, the microcosmos being in his ideas the image in miniature of the macrocosmos, they are much too transcendental to be given the least attention by our exact and materialistic skeptics. The idea of this frame being, as well as the universe, formed out of triangles, seems

---

390 *"History of Magic,"* vol. ii.

preposterously ridiculous to several of his translators. Alone of the latter, Professor Jowett, in his introduction to the *Timæus*, honestly remarks that the modern physical philosopher "hardly allows to his notions the merit of being 'the dead men's bones' out of which he has himself risen to a higher knowledge";[391] forgetting how much the metaphysics of olden times has helped the "physical" sciences of the present day. If, instead of quarrelling with the insufficiency and at times absence of terms and definitions strictly scientific in Plato's works, we analyze them carefully, the *Timæus*, alone, will be found to contain within its limited space the germs of every new discovery. The circulation of the blood and the law of gravitation are clearly mentioned, though the former fact, it may be, is not so clearly defined as to withstand the reiterated attacks of modern science; for according to Prof. Jowett, the specific discovery that the blood flows out at one side of the heart through the arteries, and returns through the veins at the other, was unknown to him, though Plato was perfectly aware "that blood is a fluid in constant motion."

MODERN IGNORANCE OF VITAL FORCE

Plato's method, like that of geometry, was to descend from universals to particulars. Modern science vainly seeks a first cause among the permutations of molecules; the former sought and found it amid the majestic sweep of worlds. For him it was enough to know the great scheme of creation and to be able to trace the mightiest movements of the universe through their changes to their ultimates. The petty details, whose observation and classification have so taxed and demonstrated the patience of modern scientists, occupied but little of the attention of the old philosophers. Hence, while a fifth-form boy of an English school can prate more learnedly about the little things of physical science than Plato himself, yet, on the other hand, the dullest of Plato's disciples could tell more about great cosmic laws and their mutual relations, and demonstrate a familiarity with and control over the occult forces which lie behind them, than the most learned professor in the most distinguished academy of our day.

This fact, so little appreciated and never dwelt upon by Plato's translators, accounts for the self-laudation in which we moderns indulge at the expense of that philosopher and his compeers. Their alleged mistakes in anatomy and physiology are magnified to an inordinate extent to gratify our self-love, until, in acquiring the idea of our own superior learning, we lose sight of the intellectual splendor which adorns the ages of the past; it is as if one should, in fancy, magnify the solar spots until he should believe the bright luminary to be totally eclipsed.

The unprofitableness of modern scientific research is evinced in the fact that while we have a name for the most trivial particle of mineral, plant, animal, and man, the wisest of our teachers are unable to tell us anything definite about the vital force which produces the changes in these several kingdoms. It is necessary to seek further for corroboration of this statement than the works of our highest scientific authorities themselves.

It requires no little moral courage in a man of eminent professional position to do justice to the acquirements of the ancients, in the face of a public sentiment which is content with nothing else than their abasement. When we meet with a case of the kind we gladly lay a

---

391 B. Jowett, M.A., "*The Dialogues of Plato,*" vol. ii., p. 508.

laurel at the feet of the bold and honest scholar. Such is Professor Jowett, Master of Balliol College, and Regius Professor of Greek in the University of Oxford, who, in his translation of Plato's works, speaking of "the physical philosophy of the ancients as a whole," gives them the following credit: 1. "That the nebular theory was the received belief of the early physicists." Therefore it could not have rested, as Draper asserts,[392] upon the telescopic discovery made by Herschel I. 2. "That the development of animals out of frogs who came to land, and of man out of the animals, was held by Anaximenes in the sixth century before Christ." The professor might have added that this theory antedated Anaximenes by some thousands of years, perhaps; that it was an accepted doctrine among Chaldeans, and that Darwin's evolution of species and monkey theory are of an antediluvian origin. 3. " . . . that, even by Philolaus and the early Pythagoreans, the earth was held to be a body like the other stars revolving in space."[393] Thus Galileo, studying some Pythagorean fragments, which are shown by Reuchlin to have yet existed in the days of the Florentine mathematician;[394] being, moreover, familiar with the doctrines of the old philosophers, but reasserted an astronomical doctrine which prevailed in India at the remotest antiquity. 4. The ancients " . . . thought that there was a sex in plants as well as in animals." Thus our modern naturalists had but to follow in the steps of their predecessors. 5. "That musical notes depended on the relative length or tension of the strings from which they were emitted, and were measured by ratios of number." 6. "That mathematical laws pervaded the world and even qualitative differences were supposed to have their origin in number"; and 7. "The annihilation of matter was denied by them, and held to be a *transformation* only."[395] "Although one of these discoveries might have been supposed to be a happy guess," adds Mr. Jowett, "we can hardly attribute them all to mere coincidences."[396]

In short, the Platonic philosophy was one of order, system, and proportion; it embraced the evolution of worlds and species, the correlation and conservation of energy, the transmutation of material form, the indestructibility of matter and of spirit. Their position in the latter respect being far in advance of modern science, and binding, the arch of their philosophical system with a keystone at once perfect and immovable. If science has made such colossal strides during these latter days — if we have such clearer ideas of natural law than the ancients — why are our inquiries as to the nature and source of life unanswered? If the modern laboratory is so much richer in the fruits of experimental research than those of the olden time, how comes it that we make no step except on paths that were trodden long before the Christian era? How does it happen that the most advanced standpoint that has

---

392 "*Conflict between Religion and Science*," p. 240.
393 "*Plutarch*," translated by Langhorne.
394 Some kabalistic scholars assert that the Greek original Pythagoric sentences of Sextus, which are now said to be lost, existed still, in a convent at Florence, at that time, and that Galileo was acquainted with these writings. They add, moreover, that a treatise on astronomy, a manuscript by Archytas, a direct disciple of Pythagoras, in which were noted all the most important doctrines of their school, was in the possession of Galileo. Had some *Ruffinas* got hold of it, he would no doubt have perverted it, as Presbyter Ruffinas has perverted the above-mentioned sentences of Sextus, replacing them with a fraudulent version, the authorship of which he sought to ascribe to a certain Bishop Sextus. See Taylor's Introduction to Iamblichus' "Life of Pythagoras," p. xvii.
395 Jowett, Introduction to the "*Timæus*," vol. ii., p. 508.
396 Ibid.

been reached in our times only enables us to see in the dim distance up the Alpine path of knowledge the monumental proofs that earlier explorers have left to mark the plateaux they had reached and occupied?

If modern masters are so much in advance of the old ones, why do they not restore to us the lost arts of our postdiluvian forefathers? Why do they not give us the unfading colors of Luxor — the Tyrian purple; the bright vermilion and dazzling blue which decorate the walls of this place, and are as bright as on the first day of their application? The indestructible cement of the pyramids and of ancient aqueducts; the Damascus blade, which can be turned like a corkscrew in its scabbard without breaking; the gorgeous, unparalleled tints of the stained glass that is found amid the dust of old ruins and beams in the windows of ancient cathedrals; and the secret of the true malleable glass? And if chemistry is so little able to rival even with the early mediæval ages in some arts, why boast of achievements which, according to strong probability, were perfectly known thousands of years ago? The more archæology and philology advance, the more humiliating to our pride are the discoveries which are daily made, the more glorious testimony do they bear in behalf of those who, perhaps on account of the distance of their remote antiquity, have been until now considered ignorant flounderers in the deepest mire of superstition.

Why should we forget that, ages before the prow of the adventurous Genoese clove the Western waters, the Phœnician vessels had circumnavigated the globe, and spread civilization in regions now silent and deserted? What archæologist will dare assert that the same hand which planned the Pyramids of Egypt, Karnak, and the thousand ruins now crumbling to oblivion on the sandy banks of the Nile, did *not* erect the monumental Nagkon-Wat of Cambodia? or trace the hieroglyphics on the obelisks and doors of the deserted Indian village, newly discovered in British Columbia by Lord Dufferin? or those on the ruins of Palenque and Uxmal, of Central America? Do not the relics we treasure in our museums — last mementos of the long "lost arts" — speak loudly in favor of ancient civilization? And do they not prove, over and over again, that nations and continents that have passed away have buried along with them arts and sciences, which neither the first crucible ever heated in a mediæval cloister, nor the last cracked by a modern chemist have revived, nor will — at least, in the present century.

"They were not without some knowledge of optics," Professor Draper magnanimously concedes to the ancients; others positively deny to them even that little. "The convex lens found at Nimroud shows that they were not unacquainted with magnifying instruments."[397] Indeed? If they were not, all the classical authors must have lied. For, when Cicero tells us that he had seen the entire *Iliad* written on skin of such a miniature size, that it could easily be rolled up inside a nut-shell, and Pliny asserts that Nero had a ring with a small glass in it, through which he watched the performance of the gladiators at a distance — could audacity go farther? Truly, when we are told that Mauritius could see from the promontory of Sicily over the entire sea to the coast of Africa, with an instrument called *nauscopite*, we must either think that all these witnesses lied, or that the ancients were more than slightly acquainted with optics and magnifying glasses. Wendell Phillips states that he has a friend who possesses an extraordinary ring "perhaps three-quarters of an inch in diameter, and on

---

397 "*Conflict between Religion and Science*," p. 14.

it is the naked figure of the god Hercules. By the aid of glasses, you can distinguish the interlacing muscles, and *count every separate hair on the eyebrows.*. . . Rawlinson brought home a stone about twenty inches long and ten wide, containing an entire treatise on mathematics. It would be perfectly illegible without glasses. . .In Dr. Abbott's Museum, there is a ring of Cheops, to which Bunsen assigns 500 B.C. The signet of the ring is about the size of a quarter of a dollar, and the engraving is *invisible* without the aid of glasses. . . At Parma, they will show you a gem once worn on the finger of Michael Angelo, of which the engraving is 2,000 years old, and on which there are the figures of *seven* women. You must have the aid of powerful glasses in order to distinguish the forms at all. . . So the microscope," adds the learned lecturer, "instead of dating from our time, finds its brothers in the Books of Moses — and these are infant brothers."

The foregoing facts do not seem to show that the ancients had merely "*some* knowledge of optics." Therefore, totally disagreeing in this particular with Professor Fiske and his criticism of Professor Draper's *Conflict* in his *Unseen World,* the only fault we find with the admirable book of Draper is that, as an historical critic, he sometimes uses his own optical instruments in the wrong place. While, in order to magnify the atheism of the Pythagorean Bruno, he looks through convex lenses; whenever talking of the knowledge of the ancients, he evidently sees things through *concave* ones.

ANTIQUITY OF THE THEORY OF FORCE-CORRELATION

It is simply worthy of admiration to follow in various modern works the cautious attempts of both pious Christians and skeptical, albeit very learned men, to draw a line of demarcation between what we are and what we are not to believe, in ancient authors. No credit is ever allowed them without being followed by a qualifying caution. If Strabo tells us that ancient Nineveh was forty-seven miles in circumference, and his testimony is accepted, why should it be otherwise the moment he testifies to the accomplishment of Sibylline prophecies? Where is the common sense in calling Herodotus the "Father of History," and then accusing him, in the same breath, of silly gibberish, whenever he recounts marvellous manifestations, of which he was an eye-witness? Perhaps, after all, such a caution is more than ever necessary, now that our epoch has been christened the Century of Discovery. The disenchantment may prove too cruel for Europe. Gunpowder, which has long been thought an invention of Bacon and Schwartz, is now shown in the school-books to have been used by the Chinese for levelling hills and blasting rocks, centuries before our era. "In the Museum of Alexandria," says Draper, "there was a machine invented by Hero, the mathematician, a little more than 100 years B.C. It revolved by the agency of steam, and was of the form that we should now call a reaction-engine. . . . Chance had nothing to do with the invention of the modern steam-engine."[398] Europe prides herself upon the discoveries of Copernicus and Galileo, and now we are told that the astronomical observations of the Chaldeans extend back to within a hundred years of the flood; and Bunsen fixes the flood at not less than 10,000 years before our era.[399] Moreover, a Chinese emperor, more than 2,000

---

398 *"Conflict between Religion and Science,"* p. 311.
399 *"Egypt's Place in Universal History,"* vol. v., p. 88.

years before the birth of Christ (*i.e.*, before Moses) put to death his two chief astronomers for not predicting an eclipse of the sun.

It may be noted, as an example of the inaccuracy of current notions as to the scientific claims of the present century, that the discoveries of the indestructibility of matter and force-correlation, especially the latter, are heralded as among our crowning triumphs. It is "the most important discovery of the present century," as Sir William Armstrong expressed it in his famous address as president of the British Association. But, this "important discovery" is no discovery after all. Its origin, apart from the undeniable traces of it to be found among the old philosophers, is lost in the dense shadows of prehistoric days. Its first vestiges are discovered in the dreamy speculations of Vedic theology, in the doctrine of emanation and absorption, the nirvana in short. John Erigena outlined it in his bold philosophy in the eighth century, and we invite any one to read his *De Divisione Naturæ*, who would convince himself of this truth. Science tells that when the theory of the indestructibility of matter (also a very, very old idea of Demokritus, by the way) was demonstrated, it became necessary to extend it to force. No material particle can ever be lost; no part of the force existing in nature can vanish; hence, force was likewise proved indestructible, and its various manifestations or forces, under divers aspects, were shown to be mutually convertible, and but different modes of motion of the material particles. And thus was rediscovered the force-correlation. Mr. Grove, so far back as 1842, gave to each of these forces, such as heat, electricity, magnetism, and light, the character of convertibility; making them capable of being at one moment a cause, and at the next an effect.[400] But whence come these forces, and whither do they go, when we lose sight of them? On this point science is silent.

The theory of "force-correlation," though it may be in the minds of our contemporaries "the greatest discovery of the age," can account for neither the beginning nor the end of one of such forces; neither can the theory point out the cause of it. Forces may be convertible, and one may produce the other, still, no exact science is able to explain the alpha and omega of the phenomenon. In what particular are we then in advance of Plato who, discussing in the *Timæus* the primary and secondary qualities of matter[401] and the feebleness of human intellect, makes Timæus say: "God knows the original qualities of things; man can only hope to attain to probability." We have but to open one of the several pamphlets of Huxley and Tyndall to find precisely the same confession; but they improve upon Plato by not allowing even God to know more than themselves; and perhaps it may be upon this that they base their claims of superiority? The ancient Hindus founded their doctrine of emanation and absorption on precisely that law. The Τὸ Ὂν, the primordial point in the boundless circle, "whose circumference is nowhere, and the centre everywhere," emanating from itself all things, and manifesting them in the visible universe under multifarious forms; the forms interchanging, commingling, and, after a gradual transformation from the pure spirit (or the Buddhistic "*nothing*"), into the grossest matter, beginning to recede and as gradually re-

---

400 W. R. Grove, "*Preface to the Correlation of Physical Forces.*"
401 "*Timæus,*" p. 22.

emerge into their primitive state, which is the absorption into Nirvana[402] — what else is this but correlation of forces?

Science tells us that heat may be shown to develop electricity, electricity produce heat; and magnetism to evolve electricity, and *vice versa*. Motion, they tell us, results from motion itself, and so on, *ad infinitum*. This is the A B C of occultism and of the earliest alchemists. The indestructibility of matter and force being discovered and proved, the great problem of eternity is solved. What need have we more of spirit? its uselessness is henceforth scientifically demonstrated!

Thus modern philosophers may be said not to have gone one step beyond what the priests of Samothrace, the Hindus, and even the Christian Gnostics well knew. The former have shown it in that wonderfully ingenious mythos of the Dioskuri, or "the sons of heaven"; the twin brothers, spoken of by Schweigger, "who constantly die and return to life together, while it is absolutely necessary *that one should die that the other may live.*" They knew as well as our physicists, that when a force has disappeared it has simply been converted into another force. Though archæology may not have discovered any ancient apparatus for such special conversions, it may nevertheless be affirmed with perfect reason and upon analogical deductions that nearly all the ancient religions were based on such indestructibility of matter and force — plus the emanation of the whole from an ethereal, spiritual fire — or the central sun, which is God or spirit, on the knowledge of whose potentiality is based ancient theurgic magic.

In the manuscript commentary of Proclus on magic he gives the following account: "In the same manner as lovers gradually advance from that beauty which is apparent in sensible forms, to that which is divine; so the ancient priests, when they considered that there is a certain alliance and sympathy in natural things to each other, and of things manifest to occult powers, and discovered that all things subsist in all, they fabricated a sacred science from this mutual sympathy and similarity. Thus they recognized things supreme in such as are subordinate, and the subordinate in the supreme; in the celestial regions, terrene properties subsisting in a causal and celestial manner; and in earth celestial properties, but according to a terrene condition."

Proclus then proceeds to point to certain mysterious peculiarities of plants, minerals, and animals, all of which are well known to our naturalists, but none of which are explained. Such are the rotatory motion of the sunflower, of the heliotrope, of the lotos — which, before the rising of the sun, folds its leaves, drawing the petals within itself, so to say, then expands them gradually, as the sun rises, and draws them in again as it descends to the west — of the sun and lunar stones and the helioselenus, of the cock and lion, and other animals. "Now the ancients," he says, "having contemplated this mutual sympathy of things

---

402 Beginning with Godfrey Higgins and ending with Max Müller, every archæologist and philologist who has fairly and seriously studied the old religions, has perceived that taken literally they could only lead them on a false track. Dr. Lardner disfigured and misrepresented the old doctrines — whether unwittingly or otherwise — in the grossest manner. The *pravritti*, or the existence of nature when alive, in activity, and the *nirvritti*, or the rest, the state of non-living, is the Buddhistic esoteric doctrine. The "pure nothing," or non-existence, if translated according to the esoteric sense, would mean the "pure spirit," the NAMELESS or something our intellect is unable to grasp, hence nothing. But we will speak of it further.

(celestial and terrestrial) applied them for occult purposes, both celestial and terrene natures, by means of which, through a certain similitude, they deduced divine virtues into this inferior abode. . . . All things are full of divine natures; terrestrial natures receiving the plenitude of such as are celestial, but celestial of *super*celestial essences, while every order of things proceeds gradually in a beautiful descent from *the highest to the lowest*.[403] For whatever particulars are collected into one above the order of things, are afterwards dilated in descending, *various souls being distributed under their various ruling divinities*."[404]

Evidently Proclus does not advocate here simply a superstition, but science; for notwithstanding that it is occult, and unknown to our scholars, who deny its possibilities, magic is still a science. It is firmly and solely based on the mysterious affinities existing between organic and inorganic bodies, the visible productions of the four kingdoms, and the invisible powers of the universe. That which science calls gravitation, the ancients and the mediæval hermetists called magnetism, attraction, affinity. It is the universal law, which is understood by Plato and explained in *Timæus* as the attraction of lesser bodies to larger ones, and of similar bodies to similar, the latter exhibiting a magnetic power rather than following the law of gravitation. The anti-Aristotelean formula that *gravity causes all bodies to descend with equal rapidity, without reference to their weight,* the difference being caused by some other *unknown* agency, would seem to point a great deal more forcibly to *magnetism* than to gravitation, the former attracting rather in virtue of the substance than of the weight. A thorough familiarity with the occult faculties of everything existing in nature, visible as well as invisible; their mutual relations, attractions, and repulsions; the cause of these, traced to the *spiritual* principle which pervades and animates all things; the ability to furnish the best conditions for this principle to manifest itself, in other words a profound and exhaustive knowledge of natural law — this *was* and *is* the basis of magic.

In his notes on *Ghosts and Goblins,* when reviewing some facts adduced by certain illustrious defenders of the spiritual phenomena, such as Professor de Morgan, Mr. Robert Dale Owen, and Mr. Wallace, among others — Mr. Richard A. Proctor says that he "cannot see any force in the following remarks by Professor Wallace: 'How is such evidence as this,' he (Wallace) says, speaking of one of Owen's stories, 'refuted or explained away? Scores, and even hundreds, of equally-attested facts are on record, but no attempt is made to explain them. They are simply ignored, and in many cases admitted to be inexplicable.' " To this Mr. Proctor jocularly replies that as "our philosophers declare that they have long ago decided these ghost stories to be all delusions; *therefore* they need only be ignored; and they feel much 'worritted' that fresh evidence should be adduced, and fresh converts made, some of whom are so unreasonable as to ask for a new trial on the ground that the former verdict was contrary to the evidence."

"All this," he goes on to say, "affords excellent reason why the 'converts' should not be ridiculed for their belief; but something more to the purpose must be urged before 'the philosophers' can be expected to devote much of their time to the inquiry suggested. It ought to be shown that *the well-being of the human race is to some important degree concerned in*

---

403 This is the exact opposite of the modern theory of evolution.
404 Ficinus, See *"Excerpta"* and *"Dissertation on Magic"*; Taylor, *"Plato,"* vol. i., p. 63.

the matter, whereas the trivial nature of all ghostly conduct hitherto recorded is admitted even by converts!"

Mrs. Emma Hardinge Britten has collected a great number of authenticated facts from secular and scientific journals, which show with what serious questions our scientists sometimes replace the vexed subject of "Ghosts and Goblins." She quotes from a Washington paper a report of one of these solemn conclaves, held on the evening of April 29th, 1854. Professor Hare, of Philadelphia, the venerable chemist, who was so universally respected for his individual character, as well as for his life-long labors for science, "was *bullied* into silence" by Professor Henry, as soon as he had touched the subject of spiritualism. "The impertinent action of one of the members of the 'American Scientific Association,' " says the authoress, "was sanctioned by the majority of that distinguished body and subsequently endorsed by all of them in their proceedings."[405] On the following morning, in the report of the session, the *Spiritual Telegraph* thus commented upon the events:

"It would seem that a subject like this" — (presented by Professor Hare) "was one which would lie peculiarly within the domain of 'science.' But the 'American Association for the Promotion of Science'[406] decided that it was either unworthy of their attention or dangerous for them to meddle with, and so they voted to put the invitation on the table. . . We cannot omit in this connection to mention that the 'American Association for *the Promotion of Science*' held a very learned, extended, grave, and profound discussion at the same session, *upon the cause why 'roosters crow between twelve and one o'clock at night!'* " A subject worthy of philosophers; and one, moreover, which must have been shown to effect "the well-being of the human race" in a *very* "*important* degree."

It is sufficient for one to express belief in the existence of a mysterious sympathy between the life of certain plants and that of human beings, to assure being made the subject of ridicule. Nevertheless, there are many well-authenticated cases going to show the reality of such an affinity. Persons have been known to fall sick simultaneously with the uprooting of a tree planted upon their natal day, and dying when the tree died. Reversing affairs, it has been known that a tree planted under the same circumstances withered and died simultaneously with the person whose twin brother, so to speak, it was. The former would be called by Mr. Proctor an "effect of the imagination"; the latter a "curious coincidence."

Max Müller gives a number of such cases in his essay *On Manners and Customs*. He shows this popular tradition existing in Central America, in India, and Germany. He traces it over nearly all Europe; finds it among the Maori Warriors, in British Guiana, and in Asia. Reviewing Tyler's *Researches into the Early History of Mankind*, a work in which are brought together quite a number of such traditions, the great philologist very justly remarks the following: "If it occurred in Indian and German tales only, we might consider it as ancient Aryan property; but when we find it again in Central America, nothing remains but either to admit a later communication between European settlers and native American story-

---

405 "*Modern American Spiritualism*," p. 119.
406 The full and correct name of this learned Society is — "The American Association for the *Advancement* of Science." It is, however, often called for brevity's sake, "The American Scientific Association."

tellers. . . or to inquire whether there is not some intelligible and truly human element in this supposed sympathy between the life of flowers and the life of man."

The present generation of men, who believe in nothing beyond the superficial evidence of their senses, will doubtless reject the very idea of such a sympathetic power existing in plants, animals, and even stones. The caul covering their inner sight allows them to see but that which they cannot well deny. The author of the *Asclepian Dialogue* furnishes us with a reason for it, that might perhaps fit the present period and account for this epidemic of unbelief. In our century, as then, "there is a lamentable departure of divinity from man, when nothing worthy of heaven or celestial concerns is heard or believed, and when every divine voice is by a *necessary* silence dumb."[407] Or, as the Emperor Julian has it, "the *little* soul" of the skeptic "is indeed acute, but sees nothing with a vision healthy and sound."

UNIVERSALITY OF BELIEF IN MAGIC

We are at the bottom of a cycle and evidently in a transitory state. Plato divides the intellectual progress of the universe during every cycle into fertile and barren periods. In the sublunary regions, the spheres of the various elements remain eternally in perfect harmony with the divine nature, he says; "but their parts," owing to a too close proximity to earth, and their commingling with the *earthly* (which is matter, and therefore the realm of evil), "are sometimes according, and sometimes contrary to (divine) nature." When those circulations — which Eliphas Levi calls "currents of the astral light" — in the universal ether which contains in itself every element, take place in harmony with the divine spirit, our earth and everything pertaining to it enjoys a fertile period. The occult powers of plants, animals, and minerals magically sympathize with the "superior natures," and the divine soul of man is in perfect intelligence with these "inferior" ones. But during the barren periods, the latter lose their magic sympathy, and the spiritual sight of the majority of mankind is so blinded as to lose every notion of the superior powers of its own divine spirit. We are in a barren period: the eighteenth century, during which the malignant fever of skepticism broke out so irrepressibly, has entailed unbelief as an hereditary disease upon the nineteenth. The divine intellect is veiled in man; his animal brain alone *philosophizes*.

Formerly, magic was a universal science, entirely in the hands of the sacerdotal savant. Though the focus was jealously guarded in the sanctuaries, its rays illuminated the whole of mankind. Otherwise, how are we to account for the extraordinary identity of "superstitions," customs, traditions, and even sentences, repeated in popular proverbs so widely scattered from one pole to the other that we find exactly the same ideas among the Tartars and Laplanders as among the southern nations of Europe, the inhabitants of the steppes of Russia, and the aborigines of North and South America? For instance, Tyler shows one of the ancient Pythagorean maxims, "Do not stir the fire with a sword," as popular among a number of nations which have not the slightest connection with each other. He quotes De Plano Carpini, who found this tradition prevailing among the Tartars so far back as in 1246. A Tartar will not consent for any amount of money to stick a knife into the fire, or touch it with any sharp or pointed instrument, for fear of cutting the "head of the fire."

---

407 See Taylor's translation of *"Select Works of Plotinus,"* p. 553, etc.

The Kamtchadal of North-eastern Asia consider it a great sin so to do. The Sioux Indians of North America dare not touch the fire with either needle, knife, or any sharp instrument. The Kalmucks entertain the same dread; and an Abyssinian would rather bury his bare arms to the elbows in blazing coals than use a knife or axe near them. All these facts Tyler also calls "simply curious coincidences." Max Müller, however, thinks that they lose much of their force by the fact "of the Pythagorean doctrine being at the bottom of it."

Every sentence of Pythagoras, like most of the ancient maxims, has a dual signification; and, while it had an occult physical meaning, expressed literally in its words, it embodied a moral precept, which is explained by Iamblichus in his *Life of Pythagoras*. This "Dig not fire with a sword," is the ninth symbol in the *Protreptics* of this Neo-platonist. "This symbol," he says, "exhorts to prudence." It shows "the propriety of not opposing sharp words to a man full of fire and wrath — not contending with him. For frequently by uncivil words you will agitate and disturb an ignorant man, and you will suffer yourself. . . Herakleitus also testifies to the truth of this symbol. For, he says, 'It is difficult to fight with anger, for whatever is necessary to be done redeems the soul.' And this he says truly. For many, by gratifying anger, have changed the condition of their soul, and have made death preferable to life. But by governing the tongue and being quiet, friendship is produced from strife, the fire of anger being extinguished, and you yourself will not appear to be destitute of intellect."[408]

We have had misgivings sometimes; we have questioned the impartiality of our own judgment, our ability to offer a respectful criticism upon the labors of such giants as some of our modern philosophers — Tyndall, Huxley, Spencer, Carpenter, and a few others. In our immoderate love for the "men of old" — the primitive sages — we were always afraid to trespass the boundaries of justice and refuse their dues to those who deserve them. Gradually this natural fear gave way before an unexpected reinforcement. We found out that we were but the feeble echo of public opinion, which, though suppressed, has sometimes found relief in able articles scattered throughout the periodicals of the country. One of such can be found in the *National Quarterly Review* of December, 1875, entitled "Our Sensational Present-Day Philosophers." It is a very able article, discussing fearlessly the claims of several of our scientists to new discoveries in regard to the nature of matter, the human soul, the mind, the universe; how the universe came into existence, etc. "The religious world has been much startled," the author proceeds to say, "and not a little excited by the utterances of men like Spencer, Tyndall, Huxley, Proctor, and a few others of the same school." Admitting very cheerfully how much science owes to each of those gentlemen, nevertheless the author "most emphatically" denies that they have made any discoveries at all. There is nothing new in the speculations, even of the most advanced of them; nothing which was not known and taught, in one form or another, thousands of years ago. He does not say that these scientists "put forward their theories as their own discoveries, but they leave the fact to be implied, and the newspapers do the rest. . . . The public, which has neither time nor the inclination to examine the facts, adopts the faith of the newspapers . . . and wonders what will come next! . . . The supposed originators of such startling theories are assailed in the newspapers. Sometimes the obnoxious scientists undertake to defend themselves, but we cannot recall a single instance in which they have

---

408 Iamblichus, "*De Vita Pythag.*," additional notes (Taylor).

candidly said, 'Gentlemen, be not angry with us; we are merely *revamping* stories which are nearly as old as the mountains.' " This would have been the simple truth; "but even scientists or philosophers," adds the author, "are not always proof against the weakness of encouraging any notion which they think may secure niches for them among the immortal Ones."[409]

Huxley, Tyndall, and even Spencer have become lately the great oracles, the "infallible popes" on the dogmas of protoplasm, molecules, primordial forms, and atoms. They have reaped more palms and laurels for their great discoveries than Lucretius, Cicero, Plutarch, and Seneca had hairs on their heads. Nevertheless, the works of the latter teem with ideas on the protoplasm, primordial forms, etc., let alone the atoms, which caused Demokritus to be called the *atomic* philosopher. In the same *Review* we find this very startling denunciation:

"Who, *among the innocent,* has not been astonished, even within the last year, at the wonderful results accomplished by oxygen? What an excitement Tyndall and Huxley have created by proclaiming, in their own ingenious, oracular way, just the very doctrines which we have just quoted from Liebig; yet, as early as 1840, Professor Lyon Playfair translated into English the most 'advanced' of Baron Liebig's works."[410]

"Another recent utterance," he says, "which startled a large number of innocent and pious persons, is, that every thought we express, or attempt to express, produces a certain wonderful change in the substance of the brain. But, for this and a good deal more of its kind, our philosophers had only to turn to the pages of Baron Liebig. Thus, for instance, that scientist proclaims: 'Physiology has sufficiently decisive grounds for the opinions, that *every thought, every sensation* is accompanied by a change in the composition of the *substance of the brain;* that every motion, every manifestation of force is the result of a transformation of the structure or of its substance.' "[411]

Thus, throughout the sensational lectures of Tyndall, we can trace, almost to a page, the whole of Liebig's speculations, interlined now and then with the still earlier views of Demokritus and other Pagan philosophers. A potpourri of old hypotheses elevated by the great authority of the day into quasi-demonstrated formulas, and delivered in that pathetic, picturesque, mellow, and thrillingly-eloquent phraseology so preeminently his own.

Further, the same reviewer shows us many of the identical ideas and all the material requisite to demonstrate the great discoveries of Tyndall and Huxley, in the works of Dr. Joseph Priestley, author of *Disquisitions on Matter and Spirit,* and even in Herder's *Philosophy of History.*

"Priestley," adds the author, "was not molested by government, simply because he had no ambition to obtain fame by proclaiming his atheistic views from the house-top. This philosopher . . . was the author of from seventy to eighty volumes, and the discoverer of oxygen." It is in these works that "he puts forward those identical ideas which have been declared so 'startling,' 'bold,' etc., as the utterances of our present-day philosophers."

---

409 *"The National Quarterly Review,"* Dec., 1875.
410 Ibid., p. 94.
411 *"Force and Matter,"* p. 151.

"Our readers," he proceeds to say, "remember what an excitement has been created by the utterances of some of our modern philosophers as to the origin and nature of ideas, but those utterances, like others that preceded and followed them, contain nothing new." "An idea," says Plutarch, "is a *being* incorporeal, which has no subsistence by itself, but gives figure and form unto shapeless matter, and *becomes the cause of its manifestation*" (*De Placitio Philosophorum*). Verily, no modern atheist, Mr. Huxley included, can outvie Epicurus in materialism; he can but mimic him. And what is his "protoplasm," but a *rechauffé* of the speculations of the Hindu Swâbhâvikas or Pantheists, who assert that all things, the gods as well as men and animals, are born from Swâbhâva or their own nature?[412] As to Epicurus, this is what Lucretius makes him say: "The soul, thus produced, must be *material*, because we trace it issuing from a material source; because it exists, and exists alone in a material system; is nourished by material food; grows with the growth of the body; becomes matured with its maturity; declines with its decay; and hence, whether belonging to man or brute, must die with its death." Nevertheless, we would remind the reader that Epicurus is here speaking of the *Astral Soul*, not of Divine Spirit. Still, if we rightly understand the above, Mr. Huxley's "mutton-protoplasm" is of a very ancient origin, and can claim for its birthplace, Athens, and for its cradle, the brain of old Epicurus.

Further, still, anxious not to be misunderstood or found guilty of depreciating the labor of any of our scientists, the author closes his essay by remarking, "We merely want to show that, at least, that portion of the public which considers itself intelligent and enlightened should cultivate its memory, or remember the 'advanced' thinkers of the past much better than it does. Especially should those do so who, whether from the desk, the rostrum, or the pulpit, undertake to instruct all willing to be instructed by them. There would then be much less groundless apprehension, much less charlatanism, and above all, much less plagiarism, than there is."[413]

Truly says Cudworth that the greatest ignorance of which our modern wiseacres accuse the ancients is their belief in the soul's immortality. Like the old skeptic of Greece, our scientists — to use an expression of the same Dr. Cudworth — are afraid that if they admit spirits and apparitions they must admit a God too; and there is nothing too absurd, he adds, for them to suppose, in order to keep out the existence of God. The great body of ancient materialists, skeptical as they now seem to us, thought otherwise, and Epicurus, who rejected the soul's immortality, believed still in a God, and Demokritus fully conceded the reality of apparitions. The preëxistence and God-like powers of the human spirit were believed in by most all the sages of ancient days. The magic of Babylon and Persia based upon it the doctrine of their *machagistia*. The *Chaldean Oracles*, on which Pletho and Psellus have so much commented, constantly expounded and amplified their testimony. Zoroaster, Pythagoras, Epicharmus, Empedocles, Kebes, Euripides, Plato, Euclid, Philo, Boehius, Virgil, Marcus Cicero, Plotinus, Iamblichus, Proclus, Psellus, Synesius, Origen, and, finally, *Aristotle* himself, far from denying our immortality, support it most emphatically. Like Cardon and Pompanatius, "who were no friends to the soul's immortality," as says Henry

---

412 Burnouf, "*Introduction*," p. 118.
413 "*The National Quarterly Review*," Dec., 1875, p. 96.

More, "Aristotle expressly concludes that the rational soul is both a distinct being from the soul of the world, though of the same essence," and that "it does preëxist before it comes into the body."[414]

Years have rolled away since the Count Joseph De Maistre wrote a sentence which, if appropriate to the Voltairean epoch in which he lived, applies with still more justice to our period of utter skepticism. "I have heard," writes this eminent man, "I have heard and read of myriads of good jokes on the ignorance of the ancients, who were always seeing spirits everywhere; methinks that we are a great deal more imbecile than our forefathers, in never perceiving any such now, anywhere."[415]

---

414 "*De Anima*," lib. i., cap. 3.
415 De Maistre, "*Soirées de St. Petersburg.*"

CHAPTER VIII

"Think not my magic wonders wrought by aid
Of Stygian angels summoned up from Hell;
Scorned and accursed by those who have essay'd
Her gloomy Divs and Afrites to compel.
But by perception of the secret powers
Of mineral springs, in nature's inmost cell,
Of herbs in curtain of her greenest bowers,
And of the moving stars o'er mountain tops and towers."

TASSO, Canto XIV, xliii

"Who dares think *one* thing and *another* tell
My heart detests him as the gates of Hell!"

POPE

"If man ceases to exist when he disappears in the grave, you must be compelled to affirm that he is the only creature in existence whom nature or providence has condescended to deceive and cheat by capacities for which there are no available objects."

BULWER-LYTTON, *Strange Story*

DO THE PLANETS AFFECT HUMAN DESTINY?

THE preface of Richard A. Proctor's latest work on astronomy, entitled *Our Place among Infinities,* contains the following extraordinary words: "It was their ignorance of the earth's place among infinities, which led the ancients to regard the heavenly bodies as ruling favorably or adversely the fates of men and nations, and to dedicate the days in sets of seven to the seven planets of their astrological system."

Mr. Proctor makes two distinct assertions in this sentence: 1. That the ancients were ignorant of the earth's place among infinities; and 2. That they regarded the heavenly bodies as ruling, favorably or adversely, the fates of men and nations.[416] We are very confident that there is at least good reason to suspect that the ancients were familiar with the movements, emplacement, and mutual relations of the heavenly bodies. The testimony of Plutarch, Professor Draper, and Jowett, are sufficiently explicit. But we would ask Mr. Proctor how it happens, if the ancient astronomers were so ignorant of the law of the birth and death of worlds that, in the fragmentary bits which the hand of time has spared us of ancient lore there should be — albeit couched in obscure language — so much information which the most recent discoveries of science have verified? Beginning with the tenth page of the work under notice, Mr. Proctor sketches for us the theory of the formation of our earth, and the successive changes through which it passed until it became habitable for man. In vivid

---

416 We need not go so far back as that to assure ourselves that many great men believed the same. Kepler, the eminent astronomer, fully credited the idea that the stars and all heavenly bodies, even our earth, are endowed with living and thinking souls.

colors he depicts the gradual accretion of cosmic matter into gaseous spheres surrounded with "a liquid non-permanent shell"; the condensation of both; the ultimate solidification of the external crust; the slow cooling of the mass; the chemical results following the action of intense heat upon the primitive earthy matter; the formation of soils and their distribution; the change in the constitution of the atmosphere; the appearance of vegetation and animal life; and, finally, the advent of man.

VERY CURIOUS PASSAGE FROM HERMES

Now, let us turn to the oldest written records left us by the Chaldeans, the Hermetic *Book of Numbers*,[417] and see what we shall find in the allegorical language of Hermes, Kadmus, or Thuti, the thrice great Trismegistus. "In the beginning of time the great invisible one had his holy hands full of celestial matter which he scattered throughout the infinity; and lo, behold! it became balls of fire and balls of clay; and they scattered like the moving metal[418] into many smaller balls, and began their ceaseless turning; and some of them which were balls of fire became balls of clay; and the balls of clay became balls of fire; and the balls of fire were waiting their time to become balls of clay; and the others envied them and bided their time to become balls of pure divine fire."

Could any one ask a clearer definition of the cosmic changes which Mr. Proctor so elegantly expounds?

Here we have the distribution of matter throughout space; then its concentration into the spherical form; the separation of smaller spheres from the greater ones; axial rotation; the gradual change of orbs from the incandescent to the earthy consistence; and, finally, the total loss of heat which marks their entrance into the stage of planetary death. The change of the balls of clay into balls of fire would be understood by materialists to indicate some such phenomenon as the sudden ignition of the star in Cassiopeia, A.D. 1572, and the one in Serpentarius, in 1604, which was noted by Kepler. But, do the Chaldeans evince in this expression a profounder philosophy than of our day? Does this change into balls of "pure divine fire" signify a continuous planetary existence, correspondent with the spirit-life of man, beyond the awful mystery of death? If worlds have, as the astronomers tell us, their periods of embryo, infancy, adolescence, maturity, decadence, and death, may they not, like man, have their continued existence in a sublimated, ethereal, or spiritual form? The magians so affirm. They tell us that the fecund mother Earth is subject to the same laws as every one of her children. At her appointed time she brings forth all created things; in the fulness of her days she is gathered to the tomb of worlds. Her gross, material body slowly parts with its atoms under the inexorable law which demands their new arrangement in other combinations. Her own perfected vivifying spirit obeys the eternal attraction which

---

417 We are not aware that a copy of this ancient work is embraced in the catalogue of any European library; but it is one of the "*Books of Hermes*," and it is referred to and quotations are made from it in the works of a number of ancient and mediæval philosophical authors. Among these authorities are Arnoldo di Villanova's "*Rosarium philosoph.*"; Francesco Arnolphim's "*Lucensis opus de Iapide.*" Hermes Trismegistus' "*Tractatus de transmutatione metallorum,*" "*Tabula smaragdina,*" and above all in the treatise of Raymond Lulli, "Ab angelis opus divinum de quinta essentia."
418 Quicksilver.

draws it toward that central spiritual sun from which it was originally evolved, and which we vaguely know under the name of GOD.

> "And the heaven was visible in seven circles, and the planets appeared with all their signs, in star-form, and the stars were divided and numbered with the rulers that were in them, and their *revolving* course was bounded with *the air,* and borne with a circular course, through the agency of the divine SPIRIT."[419]

We challenge any one to indicate a single passage in the works of Hermes which proves him guilty of that crowning absurdity of the Church of Rome which assumed, upon the geocentric theory of astronomy, that the heavenly bodies were made for our use and pleasure, and that it was worth while for the only son of God to descend upon this cosmic mote and die in expiation for our sins! Mr. Proctor tells us of a liquid non-permanent shell of uncongealed matter enclosing a "viscous plastic ocean," within which "there is another interior *solid globe* rotating." We, on our part, turn to the *Magia Adamica* of Eugenius Philalethes, published in 1650, and at page 12, we find him quoting from Trismegistus in the following terms: "Hermes affirmeth that in the *Beginning* the earth was a quackmire or quivering kind of jelly, it being nothing else but *water congealed* by the incubation and heat of the divine spirit; *cum adhuc* (sayeth he) *Terra tremula esset, Lucente sole compacta est.*"

In the same work Philalethes, speaking in his quaint, symbolical way, says, "The earth is invisible . . . on my soul it is so, and which is more, the *eye* of *man* never *saw* the *earth,* nor can it be *seen* without *art.* To make this *element invisible,* is the *greatest secret* in *magic* . . . as for this *fæculent,* gross *body* upon *which we walk,* it is a *compost,* and no earth *but it hath earth in it,* . . . in a word all the *elements* are *visible* but *one,* namely the *earth,* and when thou hast attained to so much *pefection* as to know why *God* hath placed the *earth in abscondito,*[420] thou hast an excellent figure whereby to know *God Himself,* and how He is *visible,* how *invisible.*"[421]

---

419 *"Hermes,"* iv. 6. Spirit here denotes the Deity — Pneuma, δθέος".
420 *"Magia Adamica,"* p. 11.
421 *The ignorance of the ancients of the earth's sphericity is assumed without warrant.* What proof have we of the fact? It was only the literati who exhibited such an ignorance. Even so early as the time of Pythagoras, the Pagans taught it, Plutarch testifies to it, and Socrates died for it. Besides, as we have stated repeatedly, all knowledge was concentrated in the sanctuaries of the temples from whence it very rarely spread itself among the uninitiated. If the sages and priests of the remotest antiquity were not aware of this astronomical truth, how is it that they represented Kneph, the spirit of the *first hour,* with an egg placed on his lips, the egg signifying our globe, to which he imparts life by his breath. Moreover, if, owing to the difficulty of consulting the Chaldean *"Book of Numbers,"* our critics should demand the citation of other authorities, we can refer them to Diogenes Laertius, who credits Manetho with having taught that the earth was in the shape of a ball. Besides, the same author, quoting most probably from the "Compendium of Natural Philosophy," gives the following statements of the Egyptian doctrine: "The beginning is matter Αρχὴν ρεὑ ἦἱναι ιλην, and from it the four elements separated. . . . The true form of God is unknown; but the world had a beginning and is therefore perishable. . . . The moon is eclipsed when it crosses the shadow of the earth" (Diogenes Laertius, *"Prœm,"* §§ 10, 11). Besides, Pythagoras is credited with having taught that the earth was round, that it rotated, and was but a planet like any other of these celestial bodies. (See Fenelon's *"Lives of the Philosophers."*) In the latest of Plato's translations (*"The Dialogues of Plato,"* by Professor Jowett), the author, in his introduction to "Timæus," notwithstanding "an unfortunate doubt" which arises in

Ages before our savants of the nineteenth century came into existence, a wise man of the Orient thus expressed himself, in addressing the invisible Deity: "For thy Almighty Hand, that made the world of *formless matter*."[422]

There is much more contained in this language than we are willing to explain, but we will say that the secret is worth the seeking; perhaps in this formless matter, the *pre-Adamite* earth, is contained a "potency" with which Messrs. Tyndall and Huxley would be glad to acquaint themselves.

THE RESTLESSNESS OF MATTER

But to descend from universals to particulars, from the ancient theory of planetary evolution to the evolution of plant and animal life, as opposed to the theory of special creation, what does Mr. Proctor call the following language of Hermes but an anticipation of the modern theory of evolution of species? "When God had filled his powerful hands with those things which are in nature, and in that which compasseth nature, then shutting them close again, he said: 'Receive from me, O holy earth! that art ordained to be the *mother of all*, lest thou shouldst want anything'; when presently opening such hands as it becomes a God to have, he poured down all that was necessary to the constitution of things." Here we have primeval matter imbued with "the promise and potency of every future form of life," and the earth declared to be the predestined mother of everything that should thenceforth spring from her bosom.

More definite is the language of Marcus Antoninus in his discourse to himself. "The nature of the universe delights not in anything so much as to alter all things, and present them under another form. This is her conceit to play one game and begin another. Matter is placed before her like a piece of wax and she shapes it to all forms and figures. Now she makes *a bird, then out of the bird a beast* — now a *flower*, then a frog, and she is pleased with her own magical performances as men are with their own fancies."[423]

Before any of our modern teachers thought of evolution, the ancients taught us, through Hermes, that nothing can be abrupt in nature; that she never proceeds by jumps and starts, that everything in her works is slow harmony, and that there is nothing sudden — not even violent death.

The slow development from preëxisting forms was a doctrine with the Rosicrucian Illuminati. The *Tres Matres* showed Hermes the mysterious progress of their work, before

---

consequence of the word ἵλλεσθαι, capable of being translated either "circling" or "compacted," feels inclined to credit Plato with having been familiar with the rotation of the earth. Plato's doctrine is expressed in the following words: "The earth which is our nurse (compacted or) *circling* around the pole which is extended through the universe." But if we are to believe Proclus and Simplicius, Aristotle understood this word in "Timæus" "to mean circling or revolving" (De Cœlo), and Mr. Jowett himself further admits that "Aristotle attributed to Plato the doctrine of the rotation of the earth." (See vol. ii. of "*Dial. of Plato.*" Introduction to "*Timæus*," pp. 501-2.) It would have been extraordinary, to say the least, that Plato, who was such an admirer of Pythagoras and who certainly must have had, as an initiate, access to the most secret doctrines of the great Samian, should be ignorant of such an elementary astronomical truth.

422 "*Wisdom of Solomon*," xi. 17.
423 Eugenius Philalethes, "*Magia Adamica.*"

they condescended to reveal themselves to mediæval alchemists. Now, in the Hermetic dialect, these three mothers are the symbol of light, heat, and electricity, or magnetism, the two latter being as convertible as the whole of the forces or agents which have a place assigned them in the modern "Force-correlation." Synesius mentions books of stone which he found in the temple of Memphis, on which was engraved the following sentence: "One *nature* delights in another, one nature overcomes another, one nature overrules another, and the whole of them are *one*."

The inherent restlessness of matter is embodied in the saying of Hermes: "Action is the life of Phta"; and Orpheus calls nature Πολυμμήχανος μᾱτηρ, "the mother that makes many things," or the ingenious, the contriving, the inventive mother.

Mr. Proctor says: "All that *that is upon and within the earth, all vegetable forms and* all animal forms, our bodies, our brains, are formed of materials which have been drawn in from those depths of space surrounding us on all sides." The Hermetists and the later Rosicrucians held that all things visible and invisible were produced by the contention of light with darkness, and that every particle of matter contains within itself a spark of the divine essence — or light, *spirit* — which, through its tendency to free itself from its entanglement and return to the central source, produced motion in the particles, and from motion forms were born. Says Hargrave Jennings, quoting Robertus di Fluctibus: "Thus all minerals in this spark of life have the rudimentary possibility of plants and growing organisms; thus all plants have rudimentary sensations which might (in the ages) enable them to perfect and transmute into locomotive new creatures, lesser or higher in their grade, or nobler or meaner in their functions; thus all plants, and all vegetation might pass off (by side roads) into more distinguished highways as it were, of independent, completer advance, allowing their original spark of light to expand and thrill with higher and more vivid force, and to urge forward with more abounding, informed purpose, all wrought by planetary influence directed by the unseen spirits (or workers) of the great original architect."[424]

Light — the first mentioned in *Genesis*, is termed by the kabalists, Sephira, or the Divine *Intelligence*, the mother of all the Sephiroth, while the *Concealed Wisdom* is the father. Light is the first begotten, and the first emanation of the Supreme, and Light is Life, says the evangelist. Both are electricity — the life-principle, the *anima mundi*, pervading the universe, the electric vivifier of all things. Light is the great Protean magician, and under the Divine Will of the architect, its multifarious, omnipotent waves gave birth to every form as well as to every living being. From its swelling, electric bosom, springs *matter* and *spirit*. Within its beams lie the beginnings of all physical and chemical action, and of all cosmic and spiritual phenomena; it vitalizes and disorganizes; it gives life and produces death, and from its primordial point gradually emerged into existence the myriads of worlds, visible and invisible celestial bodies. It was at the ray of this *First* mother, one in three, that God, according to Plato, "lighted a fire, which we now call the sun,"[425] and, which is *not* the cause of either light or heat, but merely the focus, or, as we might say, the lens, by which the rays of the primordial light become materialized, are concentrated upon our solar system, and produce all the correlations of forces.

---

424 Hargrave Jennings, "*The Rosicrucians.*"
425 "*Timæus.*"

So much for the first of Mr. Proctor's two propositions; now for the second.

The work which we have been noticing, comprises a series of twelve essays, of which the last is entitled *Thoughts on Astrology.* The author treats the subject with so much more consideration than is the custom of men of his class, that it is evident he has given it thoughtful attention. In fact, he goes so far as to say that, "If we consider the matter aright, we must concede . . . that of all the errors into which men have fallen in their desire to penetrate into futurity, astrology is the most respectable, we may even say the most reasonable."[426]

He admits that "The heavenly bodies *do* rule the fates of men and nations in the most unmistakable manner, seeing that without the controlling and beneficent influences of the chief among those orbs — the sun — every living creature on the earth must perish."[427] He admits, also, the influence of the moon, and sees nothing strange in the ancients reasoning by analogy, that if two among these heavenly bodies were thus potent in terrestrial influences, it was " . . . natural that the other moving bodies known to the ancients, should be thought to possess also their special powers."[428] Indeed, the professor sees nothing unreasonable in their supposition that the influences exerted by the slower moving planets "might be even more potent that those of the sun himself." Mr. Proctor thinks that the system of astrology "was formed gradually and perhaps tentatively." Some influences may have been inferred from observed events, the fate of this or that king or chief, guiding astrologers in assigning particular influences to such planetary aspects as were presented at the time of his nativity. Others may have been invented, and afterward have found general acceptance, because confirmed by some *curious coincidences.*

A witty joke may sound very prettily, even in a learned treatise, and the word "coincidence" may be applied to anything we are unwilling to accept. But a sophism is not a truism; still less is it a mathematical demonstration, which alone ought to serve as a beacon — to astronomers, at least. Astrology is a science *as infallible* as astronomy itself, with the condition, however, that its interpreters must be equally infallible; and it is this condition, *sine qua non,* so very difficult of realization, that has always proved a stumbling-block to both. Astrology is to exact astronomy what psychology is to exact physiology. In astrology and psychology one has to step beyond the visible world of matter, and enter into the domain of transcendent spirit. It is the old struggle between the Platonic and Aristotelean schools, and it is not in our century of Sadducean skepticism that the former will prevail over the latter. Mr. Proctor, in his professional capacity, is like the uncharitable person of the Sermon on the Mount, who is ever ready to attract public attention to the mote in his despised neighbor's eye, and overlook the beam in his own. Were we to record the failures and ridiculous blunders of astronomers, we are afraid they would outnumber by far those of the astrologers. Present events fully vindicate Nostradamus, who has been so much

---

426 *"Our Place among Infinities,"* p. 313.
427 Ibid.
428 Ibid., p. 314.

ridiculed by our skeptics. In an old book of prophecies, published in the fifteenth century (an edition of 1453), we read the following, among other astrological predictions:[429]

PROPHECY OF NOSTRADAMUS FULFILLED

"In twice two hundred years, the Bear
The Crescent will assail;
But if the Cock and Bull unite,
The Bear will not prevail.
In twice ten years again —
Let Islam know and fear —
The Cross shall stand, the Crescent wane,
Dissolve, and disappear."

In just twice two hundred years from the date of that prophecy, we had the Crimean war, during which the alliance of the Gallic Cock and English Bull interfered with the political designs of the Russian Bear. In 1856 the war was ended, and Turkey, or the Crescent, closely escaped destruction. In the present year (1876) the most unexpected events of a political character have just taken place, and *twice ten years* have elapsed since peace was proclaimed. Everything seems to bid fair for a fulfilment of the old prophecy; the future will tell whether the Moslem Crescent, which seems, indeed, to be *waning,* will irrevocably "wane, dissolve, and disappear," as the outcome of the present troubles.

In explaining away the heterodox facts which he appears to have encountered in his pursuit of knowledge, Mr. Proctor is obliged more than once in his work, to fall back upon these "curious coincidences." One of the most curious of these is stated by him in a foot-note (page 301) as follows: "I do not here dwell on the curious coincidence — if, indeed, Chaldean astrologers had not discovered the ring of Saturn — that they showed the god corresponding within a ring and *triple.* . . . Very moderate optical knowledge — such, indeed, as we may fairly infer from the presence of optical instruments among Assyrian remains — might have led to the discovery of Saturnal rings and Jupiter's moons. . . . Bel, the Assyrian Jupiter," he adds, "was represented sometimes with four star-tipped wings. *But it is possible that these are mere coincidences.*"

In short, Mr. Proctor's theory of coincidence becomes finally more suggestive of miracle than the facts themselves. For coincidences our friends the skeptics appear to have an unappeasable appetite. We have brought sufficient testimony in the preceding chapter to show that the ancients must have used as good optical instruments as we have now. Were the instruments in possession of Nebuchadnezzar of such moderate power, and the knowledge of his astronomers so very contemptible, when, according to Rawlinson's reading of the tiles, the Birs-Nimrud, or temple of Borsippa, had seven stages, symbolical of the concentric circles of the seven spheres, each built of tiles and metals to correspond with the color of the ruling planet of the sphere typified? Is it a coincidence again, that they

---

[429] The library of a relative of the writer contains a copy of a French edition of this unique work. The prophecies are given in the old French language, and are very difficult for the student of modern French to decipher. We give, therefore, an English version, which is said to be taken from a book in the possession of a gentleman in Somersetshire, England.

should have appropriated to each planet the color which our latest telescopic discoveries show to be the real one?[430] Or is it again a coincidence, that Plato should have indicated in the *Timæus* his knowledge of the indestructibility of matter, of conservation of energy, and correlation of forces? "The latest word of modern philosophy," says Jowett, "is continuity and development, but to Plato *this is the beginning and foundation of science.*"[431]

The radical element of the oldest religions was essentially *sabaistic*; and we maintain that their myths and allegories — if once correctly and thoroughly interpreted, will dovetail with the most exact astronomical notions of our day. We will say more; there is hardly a scientific law — whether pertaining to physical astronomy or physical geography — that could not be easily pointed out in the ingenious combinations of their fables. They allegorized the most important as well as the most trifling causes of the celestial motions; the nature of every phenomenon was personified; and in the mythical biographies of the Olympic gods and goddesses, one well acquainted with the latest principles of physics and chemistry can find their causes, inter-agencies, and mutual relations embodied in the deportment and course of action of the fickle deities. The atmospheric electricity in its neutral and latent states is embodied usually in demi-gods and goddesses, whose scene of action is more limited to earth and who, in their occasional flights to the higher deific regions, display their electric tempers always *in strict proportion with the increase of distance from the earth's surface:* the weapons of Hercules and Thor were never more mortal than when the gods soared into the clouds. We must bear in mind that before the time when the Olympian Jupiter was anthropomorphized by the genius of Pheidias into the Omnipotent God, the *Maximus,* the God of gods, and thus abandoned to the adoration of the multitudes, in the earliest and abstruse science of symbology he embodied in his person and attributes the whole of the cosmic forces. The Myth was less metaphysical and complicated, but more truly eloquent as an expression of natural philosophy. Zeus, the male element of the creation with Chthonia — Vesta (the earth), and Metis (the water) the first of the Oceanides (the feminine principles) — was viewed according to Porphyry and Proclus as the *zoon-ek-zoon,* the chief of living beings. In the Orphic theology, the oldest of all, metaphysically speaking, he represented both the *potentia* and *actus,* the unrevealed *cause* and the Demiurge, or the active creator as an emanation from the invisible potency. In the latter demiurgic capacity, in conjunction with his consorts, we find in him all the mightiest agents of cosmic evolution — chemical affinity, atmospheric electricity, attraction, and repulsion.

It is in following his representations in this physical qualification that we discover how well acquainted were the ancients with all the doctrines of physical science in their modern development. Later, in the Pythagorean speculations, Zeus became the metaphysical trinity; the monad evolving from its invisible SELF the *active* cause, effect, and intelligent will, the whole forming the *Tetractis*. Still later we find the earlier Neoplatonists leaving the primal monad aside, on the ground of its utter incomprehensibleness to human intellect, speculating merely on the *demiurgic triad* of this deity as visible and intelligible in its effects; and thus the metaphysical continuation by Plotinus, Porphyry, Proclus, and other philosophers of this view of Zeus the father, Zeus *Poseidon,* or *dunamis,* the son and power, and the spirit or *nous*. This triad was also accepted as a whole by the Irenæic school of the

---

430 See Rawlinson, vol. xvii., pp. 30-32, Revised edition.
431 Jowett, Introduction to *"Timæus," "Dial. of Plato,"* vol. i., p. 509.

second century; the more substantial difference between the doctrines of the Neo-platonists and the Christians being merely the forcible amalgamation by the latter of the incomprehensible monad with its actualized creative trinity.

In his astronomical aspect Zeus-Dionysus has his origin in the zodiac, the ancient solar year. In Libya he assumed the form of a ram, and is identical with the Egyptian Amun, who begat Osiris, the taurian god. Osiris is also a personified emanation of the Father-Sun, and himself the Sun in Taurus. The Parent-Sun being the Sun in Aries. As the latter, Jupiter, is in the guise of a ram, and as Jupiter-Dionysus or Jupiter-Osiris, he is the bull. This animal is, as it is well known, the symbol of the creative power; moreover the Kabala explains, through the medium of one of its chief expounders, Simon-Ben-Iochai,[432] the origin of this strange worship of the bulls and cows. It is neither Darwin nor Huxley — the founders of the doctrine of evolution and its necessary complement, the transformation of species — that can find anything against the rationality of this symbol, except, perhaps, a natural feeling of uneasiness upon finding that they were preceded by the ancients even in this particular modern discovery. Elsewhere, we will give the doctrine of the kabalists as taught by Simon-Ben-Iochai.

It may be easily proved that from time immemorial Saturn or Kronos, whose ring, most positively, *was* discovered by the Chaldean astrologers, and whose symbolism is no "coincidence," was considered the father of Zeus, before the latter became himself the father of all the gods, and was the highest deity. He was the Bel or Baal of the Chaldeans, and originally imported among them by the Akkadians. Rawlinson insists that the latter came from Armenia; but if so, how can we account for the fact that Bel is but a Babylonian personification of the Hindu Siva, or Bala, the fire-god, the omnipotent creative, and at the same time, destroying Deity, in many senses higher than Brahma himself?

"Zeus," says an Orphic hymn, "is the first and the last, the head, and the extremities; from him have proceeded all things. He is a man and an immortal nymph (male and female element); the soul of all things; and the principal motor in fire; he is the sun and the moon; the fountain of the ocean; the demiurgus of the universe; one power, one God; the mighty creator and governor of the cosmos. Everything, fire, water, earth, ether, night, the heavens, Metis, the primeval architecturess (the Sophia of the Gnostics, and the Sephira of the Kabalists), the beautiful Eros, Cupid, all is included within the vast dimensions of his glorious body!"[433]

This short hymn of laudation contains within itself the groundwork of every mythopoeic conception. The imagination of the ancients proved as boundless as the visible manifestations of the Deity itself which afforded them the themes for their allegories. Still the latter, exuberant as they seem, never departed from the two principal ideas which may be ever found running parallel in their sacred imagery; a strict adherence to the physical as well as moral or spiritual aspect of natural law. Their metaphysical researches never clashed with scientific truths, and their religions may be truly termed the psycho-physiological creeds of the priests and scientists, who built them on the traditions of the infant-world,

---

432 N. B. — He lived in the first century B. C.
433 Stobæus, "*Eclogues.*"

such as the unsophisticated minds of the primitive races received them, and on their own experimental knowledge, hoary with all the wisdom of the intervening ages.

SYMPATHIES BETWEEN PLANETS AND PLANTS

As the sun, what better image could be found for Jupiter emitting his golden rays than to personify this emanation in Diana, the all-illuminating virgin Artemis, whose oldest name was Diktynna, literally the emitted *ray*, from the word *dikein*. The moon is non-luminous, and it shines only by the reflected light of the sun; hence, the imagery of his daughter, the goddess of the moon, and herself, Luna, Astartè, or Diana. As the Cretan Diktynna, she wears a wreath made of the magic plant *diktamnon,* or *dictamnus*, the evergreen shrub whose contact is said, at the same time, to develop somnambulism and cure finally of it; and, as Eilithyia and Juno Pronuba, she is the goddess who presides over births; she is an Æsculapian deity, and the use of the dictamnus-wreath, in association with the moon, shows once more the profound observation of the ancients. This plant is known in botany as possessing strongly sedative properties; it grows on Mount Dicte, a Cretan mountain, in great abundance; on the other hand, the moon, according to the best authorities on animal magnetism, acts upon the juices and ganglionic system, or nerve-cells, the seat from whence proceed all the nerve-fibres which play such a prominent part in mesmerization. During childbirth the Cretan women were covered with this plant, and its roots were administered as best calculated to soothe acute pain, and allay the irritability so dangerous at this period. They were placed, moreover, within the precincts of the temple sacred to the goddess, and, if possible, under the direct rays of the resplendent daughter of Jupiter — the bright and warm Eastern moon.

The Hindu Brahmans and Buddhists have complicated theories on the influence of the sun and moon (the male and female elements), as containing the negative and positive principles, the opposites of the magnetic polarity. "The influence of the moon on women is well known," write all the old authors on magnetism; and Ennemoser, as well as Du Potet, confirm the theories of the Hindu seers in every particular.

HINDU KNOWLEDGE OF THE PROPERTIES OF COLORS

The marked respect paid by the Buddhists to the sapphire-stone — which was also sacred to Luna, in every other country — may be found based on something more scientifically exact than a mere groundless superstition. They ascribed to it a sacred magical power, which every student of psychological mesmerism will readily understand, for its polished and deep-blue surface produces extraordinary somnambulic phenomena. The varied influence of the prismatic colors on the growth of vegetation, and especially that of the "blue ray," has been recognized but recently. The Academicians quarrelled over the unequal heating power of the prismatic rays until a series of experimental demonstrations by General Pleasonton, proved that under the blue ray, the most electric of all, animal and vegetable growth was increased to a magical proportion. Thus Amoretti's investigations of the electric polarity of precious stones show that the diamond, the garnet, the amethyst, are

–E., while the sapphire is +E.[434] Thus, we are enabled to show that the latest experiments of science only corroborate that which was known to the Hindu sages before any of the modern academies were founded. An old Hindu legend says that Brahma-Prajapâti, having fallen in love with his own daughter, *Ushâs* (Heaven, sometimes the Dawn also), assumed the form of a buck (*ris'ya*) and Ushas that of a female deer (*rohit*) and thus committed the first sin.[435] Upon seeing such a desecration, the gods felt so terrified, that uniting their most fearful-looking bodies — each god possessing as many bodies as he desires — they produced Bhûtavan (the spirit of evil), who was created by them on purpose to destroy the *incarnation* of the first sin committed by the Brahma himself. Upon seeing this, Brahma-Hiranyagarbha[436] repented bitterly and began repeating the Mantras, or prayers of purification, and, in his grief, dropped on earth a tear, the *hottest* that ever fell from an eye; and from it was formed the first sapphire.

This half-sacred, half-popular legend shows that the Hindus knew which was the most electric of all the prismatic colors; moreover, the particular influence of the sapphire-stone was as well defined as that of all the other minerals. Orpheus teaches how it is possible to affect a whole audience by means of a lodestone; Pythagoras pays a particular attention to the color and nature of precious stones; while Apollonius of Tyana imparts to his disciples the secret virtues of each, and changes his jewelled rings daily, using a particular stone for every day of the month and according to the laws of judicial astrology. The Buddhists assert that the sapphire produces peace of mind, equanimity, and chases all evil thoughts by establishing a healthy circulation in man. So does an electric battery, with its well-directed fluid, say our electricians. "The sapphire," say the Buddhists, "will open barred doors and dwellings (for the spirit of man); it produces a desire for prayer, and brings with it more peace than any other gem; but he who would wear it must lead a pure and holy life."[437]

Diana-Luna is the daughter of Zeus by Proserpina, who represents the Earth in her active labor, and, according to Hesiod, as Diana Eilythia-Lucina she is Juno's daughter. But Juno, devoured by Kronos or Saturn, and restored back to life by the Oceanid Metis, is also known as the Earth. Saturn, as the evolution of Time, swallows the earth in one of the ante-historical cataclysms, and it is only when Metis (the waters) by retreating in her many beds, frees the continent, that Juno is said to be restored to her first shape. The idea is expressed in the 9th and 10th verses of the first chapter of *Genesis*. In the frequent matrimonial quarrels between Juno and Jupiter, Diana is always represented as turning her back on her mother and smiling upon her father, though she chides him for his numerous frolics. The Thessalian magicians are said to have been obliged, during such eclipses, to draw her attention to the earth by the power of their spells and incantations, and the Babylonian astrologers and magi never desisted in their spells until they brought about a reconciliation between the irritated couple, after which Juno "radiantly smiled on the bright goddess" Diana, who, encircling her brow with her crescent, returned to her hunting-place in the mountains.

---

434 Kieser, "*Archiv.*," vol. iv., p. 62. In fact, many of the old symbols were mere puns on names.
435 See "*Rig-Vedas*," the Aitareya-Brahmanan.
436 Brahma is also called by the Hindu Brahmans Hiranyagarbha or the *unit* soul, while *Amrita* is the supreme soul, the first cause which emanated from itself the creative Brahma.
437 Marbod, "*Liber lapid. ed Beekmann.*"

It seems to us that the fable illustrates the different phases of the moon. We, the inhabitants of the earth, never see but one-half of our bright satellite, who thus turns *her back* to her mother Juno. The sun, the moon, and the earth are constantly changing positions with relation to each other. With the *new* moon there is constantly a change of weather; and sometimes the wind and storms may well suggest a quarrel between the sun and earth, especially when the former is concealed by grumbling thunder-clouds. Furthermore, the new moon, when her dark side is turned toward us, is invisible; and it is only after a *reconciliation* between the sun and the earth, that a bright crescent becomes visible on the side nearest to the sun, though this time Luna is not illuminated by sunlight *directly* received, but by sunlight reflected from the earth to the moon, and by her reflected back to us. Hence, the Chaldean astrologers and the magicians of Thessaly, who probably watched and determined as accurately as a Babinet the course of the celestial bodies, were said by their enchantments to force the moon to descend on earth, *i.e.*, to show her crescent, which she could do but after receiving the "radiant smile" from her mother-earth, who put it on after the conjugal reconciliation. Diana-Luna, having adorned her head with her crescent, returns back to hunt in *her mountains*.

As to calling in question the intrinsic knowledge of the ancients on the ground of their "*superstitious* deductions from natural phenomena," it is as appropriate as it would be if, five hundred years hence, our descendants should regard the pupils of Professor Balfour Stewart as *ancient* ignoramuses, and himself a shallow philosopher. If modern science, in the person of this gentleman, can condescend to make experiments to determine whether the appearance of the spots on the sun's surface is in any way connected with the potato disease, and finds *it is*; and that, moreover, "the earth is very seriously affected by what takes place in the sun,"[438] why should the ancient astrologers be held up as either fools or arrant knaves? There is the same relation between natural and judicial or judiciary astrology, as between physiology and psychology, the physical and the moral. If in later centuries these sciences were degraded into charlatanry by some money-making impostors, is it just to extend the accusation to those mighty men of old who, by their persevering studies and holy lives, bestowed an immortal name upon Chaldea and Babylonia? Surely those who are now found to have made correct astronomical observations ranging back to "within 100 years from the flood," from the top observatory of the "cloud-encompassed Bel," as Prof. Draper has it, can hardly be considered impostors. If their mode of impressing upon the popular minds the great astronomical truths differed from the "system of education" of our present century and appears ridiculous to some, the question still remains unanswered: which of the two systems was the best? With them science went hand in hand with religion, and the idea of God was inseparable from that of his works. And while in the present century there is not one person out of ten thousand who knows, if he ever knew the fact at all, that the planet Uranus is *next* to Saturn, and revolves about the sun in eighty-four years; and that Saturn is *next* to Jupiter, and takes twenty-nine and a half years to make one complete revolution in its orbit; while Jupiter performs his revolution in twelve years; the uneducated masses of Babylon and Greece, having impressed on their minds that Uranus was the father of Saturn, and Saturn that of Jupiter, considering them furthermore deities as well as all their satellites and attendants, we may perhaps infer from it, that while

---

438 "*The Sun and the Earth*," Lecture by Prof. Balfour Stewart.

Europeans only discovered Uranus in 1781, a curious coincidence is to be noticed in the above myths.

We have but to open the most common book on astrology, and compare the descriptions embraced in the *Fable of the Twelve Houses* with the most modern discoveries of science as to the nature of the planets and the elements in each star, to see that without any spectroscope the ancients were perfectly well acquainted with the same. Unless the fact is again regarded as "a coincidence," we can learn, to a certain extent, of the degree of the solar heat, light, and nature of the planets by simply studying their symbolic representations in the Olympic gods, and the twelve signs of the zodiac, to each of which in astrology is attributed a particular quality. If the goddesses of our own planet vary in no particular from other gods and goddesses, but all have a like physical nature, does not this imply that the sentinels who watched from the top of Bel's tower, by day as well as by night, holding communion with the euhemerized deities, had remarked, before ourselves, the physical unity of the universe and the fact that the planets above are made of precisely the same chemical elements as our own? The sun in Aries, Jupiter, is shown in astrology as a masculine, diurnal, cardinal, equinoctial, easterly sign, hot and dry, and answers perfectly to the character attributed to the fickle "Father of the gods." When angry Zeus-Akrios snatches from his fiery belt the thunderbolts which he hurls forth from heaven, he rends the clouds and descends as Jupiter *Pluvius* in torrents of rain. He is the greatest and highest of gods, and his movements are as rapid as lightning itself. The planet Jupiter is known to revolve on its axis so rapidly that the point of its equator turns at the rate of 450 miles a minute. An immense excess of centrifugal force at the equator is believed to have caused the planet to become extremely flattened at the poles; and in Crete the personified god Jupiter was represented without ears. The planet Jupiter's disk is crossed by dark belts; varying in breadth, they appear to be connected with its rotation on its axis, and are produced by disturbances in its atmosphere. The face of Father Zeus, says Hesiod, became spotted with rage when he beheld the Titans ready to rebel.

"COINCIDENCES" THE PANACEA OF MODERN SCIENCE

In Mr. Proctor's book, astronomers seem especially doomed by Providence to encounter all kinds of curious "coincidences," for he gives us many cases out of the "multitude," and even of the "*thousands* of facts [sic]." To this list we may add the army of Egyptologists and archæologists who of late have been the chosen pets of the capricious *Dame Chance*, who, moreover, generally selects "well-to-do Arabs" and other Eastern gentlemen, to play the part of benevolent *genii* to Oriental scholars in difficulties. Professor Ebers is one of the latest favored ones. It is a well-known fact, that whenever Champollion needed important links, he fell in with them in the most various and unexpected ways.

Voltaire, the greatest of "infidels" of the eighteenth century, used to say, that if there were no God, people would have to invent one. Volney, another "materialist," nowhere throughout his numerous writings denies the existence of God. On the contrary, he plainly asserts several times that the universe is the work of the "All-wise," and is convinced that there is a Supreme Agent, a universal and identical Artificer, designated by the name of

God.[439] Voltaire becomes, toward the end of his life, Pythagorical, and concludes by saying: "I have consumed forty years of my pilgrimage . . . seeking the philosopher's stone called truth. I have consulted all the adepts of antiquity, Epicurus and Augustine, Plato and Malebranche, and I still remain in ignorance. . . . All that I have been able to obtain by comparing and combining the system of Plato, of the tutor of Alexander, Pythagoras, and the Oriental, is this: *Chance is a word void of sense.* The world is arranged according to mathematical laws."[440]

It is pertinent for us to suggest that Mr. Proctor's stumbling-block is that which trips the feet of all materialistic scientists, whose views he but repeats; he confounds the physical and spiritual operations of nature. His very theory of the probable inductive reasoning of the ancients as to the subtile influences of the more remote planets, by comparison with the familiar and potent effects of the sun and moon upon our earth, shows the drift of his mind. Because science *affirms* that the sun imparts physical *heat* and *light* to us, and the moon affects the tides, he thinks that the ancients must have regarded the other heavenly bodies as exerting the same kind of influence upon us physically, and indirectly upon our fortunes.[441] And here we must permit ourselves a digression.

How the ancients regarded the heavenly bodies is very hard to determine, for one unacquainted with the esoteric explanation of their doctrines. While philology and comparative theology have begun the arduous work of analysis, they have as yet arrived at meagre results. The allegorical form of speech has often led our commentators so far astray, that they have confounded causes with effects, and *vice versa.* In the baffling phenomenon of force-correlation, even our greatest scientists would find it very hard to explain which of these forces is the cause, and which the effect, since each may be both by turns, and convertible. Thus, if we should inquire of the physicists, "Is it light which generates heat, or the latter which produces light?" we would in all probability be answered that it is certainly light which creates heat. Very well; but how? did the great Artificer first produce light, or did He first construct the sun, which is said to be the sole dispenser of light, and, consequently, heat? These questions may appear at first glance indicative of ignorance; but, perhaps, if we ponder them deeply, they will assume another appearance. In *Genesis,* the "Lord" first creates *light,* and three days and three nights are alleged to pass away before He creates the sun, the moon, and the stars. This gross blunder against *exact* science has created much merriment among materialists. And they certainly would be warranted in laughing, if their doctrine that our light and heat are derived from the sun were unassailable. Until recently, nothing has happened to upset this theory, which, for lack of a better one, according to the expression of a preacher, "reigns sovereign in the Empire of Hypothesis." The ancient sun-worshippers regarded the Great Spirit as a nature-god, identical with nature, and the sun as the deity, "in whom the Lord of life dwells." Gama is the sun, according to the Hindu theology, and "The sun is the source of the souls and of *all life.*"[442] Agni, the "Divine Fire," the deity of the Hindu, is the sun,[443] for the fire and sun are the

---

439 "*La Loi Naturelle,*" par Volney.
440 "*Diction. Philosophique,*" Art. "*Philosophie.*"
441 "*Boston Lecture,*" December, 1875.
442 Weber, "*Ind. Stud.,*" i. 290.
443 Wilson, "*Rig-Veda Sanhita,*" ii. 143.

same. Ormazd is light, the Sun-God, or the Life-giver. In the Hindu philosophy, "The souls issue from the soul of the world, and return to it as sparks to the fire."[444] But, in another place, it is said that "*The Sun* is the soul *of all things;* all has proceeded out of it, and will return to it,"[445] which shows that the sun is meant allegorically here, and refers to the *central,* invisible sun, GOD, whose first manifestation was Sephira, the emanation of En-Soph — Light, in short.

"And I looked, and behold, a whirlwind came out of the north, a great cloud, and a fire infolding itself, and a brightness was about it," says Ezekiel (i., 4, 22, etc.), ". . . and the likeness of a throne . . . and as the appearance of a man above upon it . . . and I saw as it were the appearance *of fire* and it had brightness round about it." And Daniel speaks of the "ancient of days," the kabalistic En-Soph, whose throne was "the fiery flame, his wheels burning fire. . . . A fiery stream issued and came forth from before him."[446] Like the Pagan Saturn, who had his castle of flame in the seventh heaven, the Jewish Jehovah had his "castle of fire over the seventh heavens."[447]

If the limited space of the present work would permit we might easily show that none of the ancients, the sun-worshippers included, regarded our visible sun otherwise than as an emblem of their metaphysical invisible central sun-god. Moreover, they did *not* believe what our modern science teaches us, namely, that light and heat proceed from *our* sun, and that it is this planet which imparts all life to our visible nature. "His radiance is undecaying," says the *Rig-Veda,* "the intensely-shining, all-pervading, unceasing, undecaying rays of Agni desist not, neither night nor day." This evidently related to the spiritual, central sun, whose rays are all-pervading and unceasing, the eternal and boundless life-giver. HE the *Point;* the centre (which is everywhere) of the circle (which is nowhere), the ethereal, spiritual fire, the soul and spirit of the all-pervading, mysterious ether; the despair and puzzle of the materialist, who will some day find that that which causes the numberless cosmic forces to manifest themselves in eternal correlation is but a divine electricity, or rather *galvanism,* and that the sun is but one of the myriad *magnets* disseminated through space — a reflector — as General Pleasonton has it. That the sun has no more heat in it than the moon or the space-crowding host of sparkling stars. That there is no *gravitation* in the Newtonian sense,[448] but only magnetic attraction and repulsion; and that it is by their magnetism that the planets of the solar system have their motions regulated in their respective orbits by the still more

444 "*Duncker*," vol. ii., p. 162
445 "*Wultke*," ii. 262.
446 *Daniel* vii. 9, 10.
447 *Book of Enoch,* xiv. 7, ff.
448 This proposition, which will be branded as *preposterous,* but which we are ready to show, on the authority of Plato (see Jowett's Introd. to the "*Timæus*", last page), as a Pythagorean doctrine, together with that other of the sun being but the lens through which the light passes, is strangely corroborated at the present day, by the observations of General Pleasonton of Philadelphia. This experimentalist boldly comes out as a revolutionist of modern science, and calls Newton's centripetal and centrifugal forces, and the law of gravitation, "fallacies." He fearlessly maintains his ground against the Tyndalls and Huxleys of the day. We are glad to find such a learned defender of one of the oldest (and hitherto treated as the *most absurd*) of hermetic *hallucinations* (?) (See General Pleasonton's book, "*The Influence of the Blue Ray of the Sunlight, and of the Blue Color of the Sky, in developing Animal and Vegetable Life,*" addressed to the Philadelphia Society for Promoting Agriculture.)

powerful magnetism of the sun, not by their weight or gravitation. This and much more they may learn; but, until then we must be content with being merely laughed at, instead of being burned alive for impiety, or shut up in an insane asylum.

The laws of Manu are the doctrines of Plato, Philo, Zoroaster, Pythagoras, and of the Kabala. The esoterism of every religion may be solved by the latter. The kabalistic doctrine of the allegorical Father and Son, or *Pathr* and *Logo"* is identical with the groundwork of Buddhism. Moses could not reveal to the multitude the sublime secrets of religious speculation, nor the cosmogony of the universe; the whole resting upon the Hindu *Illusion*, a clever mask veiling the *Sanctum Sanctorum*, and which has misled so many theological commentators.[449]

The kabalistic heresies receive an unexpected support in the heterodox theories of General Pleasonton. According to his opinions (which he supports on far more unimpeachable facts than orthodox scientists theirs) the space between the sun and the earth must be filled with a material medium, which, so far as we can judge from his description, answers to our kabalistic astral light. The passage of light through this must produce enormous friction. Friction generates electricity, and it is this electricity and its correlative magnetism which forms those tremendous forces of nature that produce in, on, and about our planet the various changes which we everywhere encounter. He proves that terrestrial heat *cannot* be directly derived from the sun, for heat *ascends*. The force by which heat is effected is a repellent one, he says, and as it is associated with positive electricity, it is attracted to the upper atmosphere by its negative electricity, always associated with cold, which is opposed to positive electricity. He strengthens his position by showing that the earth, which when covered with snow cannot be affected by the sun's rays, is warmest where the snow is deepest. This he explains upon the theory that the radiation of heat from the interior of the earth, positively electrified, meeting at the *surface* of the earth with the snow in contact with it, negatively electrified, produces the heat.

Thus he shows that it is not at all to the sun that we are indebted for light and heat; that light is a creation *sui generis*, which sprung into existence at the instant when the Deity *willed*, and uttered the fiat: "Let there be light"; and that it is this independent material agent which produces heat *by friction*, on account of its enormous and incessant velocity. In short, it is the first kabalistic emanation to which General Pleasonton introduces us, that Sephira or divine *Intelligence* (the female principle), which, in unity with En-Soph, or divine wisdom

---

449 In no country were the true esoteric doctrines trusted to writing. The Hindu Brahma Maia, was passed from one generation to another by *oral* tradition. The Kabala was never written; and Moses intrusted it orally but to his elect. The primitive pure Oriental gnosticism was completely corrupted and degraded by the different subsequent sects. Philo, in the "de Sacrificiis Abeli et Caini," states that there is a mystery *not to be revealed* to the uninitiated. Plato is silent on many things, and his disciples refer to this fact constantly. Any one who has studied, even superficially, these philosophers, on reading the institutes of Manu, will clearly perceive that they all drew from the same source. "This universe," says Manu, "existed only *in the first divine idea, yet unexpanded, as if involved in darkness,* imperceptible, indefinable, undiscoverable by reason, and undiscovered *by revelation,* as if it were wholly immersed in sleep; then the sole self-existing Power himself undiscerned, appeared with undiminished glory, *expanding his idea,* or dispelling *the gloom.*" Thus speaks the first code of Buddhism. Plato's idea is the *Will,* or Logos, the deity which manifests itself. It is the Eternal Light from which proceeds, as an *emanation,* the visible and *material* light.

(male principle) produced every thing visible and invisible. He laughs at the current theory of the incandescence of the sun and its gaseous substance. The reflection from the photosphere of the sun, he says, passing through planetary and stellar spaces, must have thus created a vast amount of electricity and magnetism. Electricity, by the union of its opposite polarities, evolves heat and imparts magnetism to all substances capable of receiving it. The sun, planets, stars, and nebulæ are all magnets, etc.

If this courageous gentleman should prove his case, future generations will have but little disposition to laugh at Paracelsus and his sidereal or astral light, and at his doctrine of the magnetic influence exercised by the stars and planets upon every living creature, plant, or mineral of our globe. Moreover, if the Pleasonton hypothesis is established, the transcendent glory of Professor Tyndall will be rather obscured. According to public opinion, the General makes a terrible onslaught on the learned physicist, for attributing to the sun calorific effects experienced by him in an Alpine ramble, that were simply due to his own vital electricity.[450]

THE MOON AND THE TIDES

The prevalence of such revolutionary ideas in science, embolden us to ask the representatives of science whether they can explain why the tides follow the moon in her circling motion? The fact is, they cannot demonstrate even so familiar a phenomenon as this, one that has no mystery for even the neophytes in alchemy and magic. We would also like to learn whether they are equally incapable of telling us why the moon's rays are so poisonous, even fatal, to some organisms; why in some parts of Africa and India a person sleeping in the moonlight is often made insane; why the crises of certain diseases correspond with lunar changes; why somnambulists are more affected at her full; and why gardeners, farmers, and woodmen cling so tenaciously to the idea that vegetation is affected by lunar influences? Several of the mimosæ alternately open and close their petals as the full moon emerges from or is obscured by clouds. And the Hindus of Travancore have a popular but extremely suggestive proverb which says: "Soft words are better than harsh; the sea is attracted by the cool moon and not by the hot sun." Perhaps the one man or the many men who launched this proverb on the world knew more about the cause of such attraction of the waters by the moon than we do. Thus if science cannot explain the cause of this physical influence, what can she know of the moral and occult influences that may be exercised by the celestial bodies on men and their destiny; and why contradict that which it is impossible for her to prove false? If certain aspects of the moon effect tangible results so familiar in the experience of men throughout all time, what violence are we doing to logic in

---

450 It appears that in descending from Mont Blanc, Tyndall suffered severely from the heat, though he was knee-deep in the snow at the time. The Professor attributed this to the burning rays of the sun, but Pleasonton maintains that if the rays of the sun had been so intense as described, they would have melted the snow, which they did not; he concludes that the heat from which the Professor suffered came from his own body, and was due to the electrical action of sunlight upon his dark woolen clothes, which had become electrified positively by the heat of his body. The cold, dry ether of planetary space and the upper atmosphere of the earth became negatively electrified, and falling upon his warm body and clothes, positively electrified, evolved an increased heat (see "*The Influence of the Blue Ray*," etc., pp. 39, 40, 41, etc.).

assuming the possibility that a certain combination of sidereal influences may also be more or less potential?

EPIDEMIC MENTAL AND MORAL DISORDERS

If the reader will recall what is said by the learned authors of the *Unseen Universe*, as to the positive effect produced upon the universal ether by so small a cause as the evolution of thought in a single human brain, how reasonable will it not appear that the terrific impulses imparted to this common medium by the sweep of the myriad blazing orbs that are rushing through "the interstellar depths," should affect us and the earth upon which we live, in a powerful degree? If astronomers cannot explain to us the occult law by which the drifting particles of cosmic matter aggregate into worlds, and then take their places in the majestic procession which is ceaselessly moving around some central point of attraction, how can anyone assume to say what mystic influences may or may not be darting through space and affecting the issues of life upon this and other planets? Almost nothing is known of the laws of magnetism and the other imponderable agents; almost nothing of their effects upon our bodies and minds; even that which is known and moreover perfectly demonstrated, is attributed to chance, and curious *coincidences*. But we do know, by these coincidences,[451] that "there are periods when certain diseases, propensities, fortunes, and misfortunes of humanity are more rife than at others." There are times of epidemic in moral and physical affairs. In one epoch "the spirit of religious controversy will arouse the most ferocious passions of which human nature is susceptible, provoking mutual persecution, bloodshed, and wars; at another, an epidemic of resistance to constituted authority will spread over half the world (as in the year 1848), rapid and simultaneous as the most virulent bodily disorder."

Again, the *collective character* of mental phenomena is illustrated by an anomalous psychological condition invading and dominating over thousands upon thousands, depriving them of everything but automatic action, and giving rise to the popular opinion of demoniacal possession, an opinion in some sense justified by the satanic passions, emotions, and acts which accompany the condition. At one period, the aggregate tendency is to retirement and contemplation; hence, the countless votaries of monachism and anchoretism; at another the mania is directed toward *action*, having for its proposed end some utopian scheme, equally impracticable and useless; hence, the myriads who have forsaken their kindred, their homes, and their country, to seek a land whose stones were gold, or to wage exterminating war for the possession of worthless cities and trackless deserts.[452]

The author from whom the above is quoted says that "the seeds of vice and crime appear to be sown under the surface of society, and to spring up and bring forth fruit with appalling rapidity and paralyzing succession."

---

451 The most curious of all "curious coincidences," to our mind is, that our men of science should put aside facts, striking enough to cause them to use such an expression when speaking of them, instead of setting to work to give us a philosophical explanation of the same.

452 See Charles Elam, M. D., "*A Physician's Problems*," London, 1869, p. 159.

In the presence of these striking phenomena science stands speechless; she does not even attempt to conjecture as to their cause, and naturally, for she has not yet learned to look outside of this ball of dirt upon which we live, and its heavy atmosphere, for the hidden influences which are affecting us day by day, and even minute by minute. But the ancients, whose "ignorance" is assumed by Mr. Proctor, fully realized the fact that the reciprocal relations between the planetary bodies is as perfect as those between the corpuscles of the blood, which float in a common fluid; and that each one is affected by the combined influences of all the rest, as each in its turn affects each of the others. As the planets differ in size, distance, and activity, so differ in intensity their impulses upon the ether or astral light, and the magnetic and other subtile forces radiated by them in certain aspects of the heavens. Music is the combination and modulation of sounds, and sound is the effect produced by the vibration of the ether. Now, if the impulses communicated to the ether by the different planets may be likened to the tones produced by the different notes of a musical instrument, it is not difficult to conceive that the Pythagorean "music of the spheres" is something more than a mere fancy, and that certain planetary aspects may imply disturbances in the ether of our planet, and certain others rest and harmony. Certain kinds of music throw us into frenzy; some exalt the soul to religious aspirations. In fine, there is scarcely a human creation which does not respond to certain vibrations of the atmosphere. It is the same with colors; some excite us, some soothe and please. The nun clothes herself in black to typify the despondency of a faith crushed under the sense of original sin; the bride robes herself in white; red inflames the anger of certain animals. If we and the animals are affected by vibrations acting upon a very minute scale, why may we not be influenced in the mass by vibrations acting upon a grand scale as the effect of combined stellar influences?

"We know," says Dr. Elam, "that certain pathological conditions have a tendency to become epidemic, *influenced by causes not yet investigated*. . . . We see how strong is the tendency of opinion once promulgated to run into an epidemic form — no opinion, no delusion, is too absurd to assume this collective character. We observe, also, how remarkably the same ideas reproduce themselves and *reappear in successive ages;* . . . no crime is too horrible to become popular, homicide, infanticide, suicide, poisoning, or any other diabolical human conception.

. . . In epidemics, the cause of the rapid spread at that particular period *remains a mystery!*"

These few lines contain an undeniable *psychological* fact, sketched with a masterly pen, and at the same time a *half*-confession of utter ignorance — "*Causes not yet investigated.*" Why not be honest and add at once, "*impossible* to investigate with present scientific methods"?

Noticing an epidemic of incendiarism, Dr. Elam quotes from the *Annales d'Hygiene Publique* the following cases: "A girl about seventeen years of age was arrested on suspicion . . . she confessed that twice she had set fire to dwellings by *instinct*, by *irresistible necessity*. . . . A boy about eighteen committed many acts of this nature. He was not moved by any passion, but the bursting-out of the flames excited a profoundly pleasing emotion."

Who but has noticed in the columns of the daily press similar incidents? They meet the eye constantly. In cases of murder, of every description, and of other crimes of a diabolical character, the act is attributed, in nine cases out of ten, by the offenders themselves, to *irresistible obsessions.* "*Something* whispered constantly in my ear. . . . *Somebody* was incessantly pushing and leading me on." Such are the too-frequent confessions of the criminals. Physicians attribute them to hallucinations of disordered brains, and call the homicidal impulse temporary *lunacy*. But is lunacy itself well understood by any psychologist? Has its cause ever been brought under a hypothesis capable of withstanding the challenge of an uncompromising investigator? Let the controversial works of our contemporary alienists answer for themselves.

Plato acknowledges man to be the toy of the element of necessity, which he enters upon in appearing in this world of matter; he is influenced by external causes, and these causes are *daimonia*, like that of Socrates. Happy is the man physically pure, for if his *external* soul (body) is pure, it will strengthen the second one (astral body), or the soul which is termed by him the *higher mortal soul*, which though liable to err from its own motives, will always side with reason against the animal proclivities of the body. The lusts of man arise in consequence of his perishable material body, so do other diseases; but though he regards crimes as *involuntary* sometimes, for they result like bodily disease from external causes, Plato clearly makes a wide distinction between these *causes*. The fatalism which he concedes to humanity, does not preclude the possibility of avoiding them, for though pain, fear, anger, and other feelings are given to men by *necessity*, "if they conquered these they would live righteously, and if they were conquered by them, *unrighteously*."[453] The *dual* man, *i.e.*, one from whom the divine *immortal* spirit has departed, leaving but the animal form and astral body (Plato's higher *mortal* soul), is left merely to his *instincts*, for he was conquered by all the evils entailed on matter; hence, he becomes a docile tool in the hands of the *invisibles* — beings of sublimated matter, hovering in our atmosphere, and ever ready to inspire those who are deservedly deserted by their *immortal* counsellor, the Divine Spirit, called by Plato "genius."[454] According to this great philosopher and initiate, one "who lived well during his appointed time would return to the habitation *of his star*, and there have a blessed and suitable existence. But if he failed in attaining this in the second generation he would pass *into a woman* — become helpless and weak as a woman;[455] and should he not cease from evil in that condition, he would be changed into some brute, which resembled him in his evil ways, and would not cease from his toils and transformations until he followed the original principle of sameness and likeness within him, and overcame, by the help of reason, the latter secretions of turbulent and irrational *elements* (elementary

---

453 Jowett, "*Timæus.*"

454 Ibid.

455 According to General Pleasonton's theory of positive and negative electricity underlying every psychological, physiological, and cosmic phenomena, the abuse of alcoholic stimulants transforms a man into a woman and *vice versa*, by changing their *electricities*. "When this change in the condition of his electricity has occurred," says the author, "his attributes (those of a drunkard) become *feminine;* he is irritable, irrational, excitable . . . becomes violent, and if he meets his wife, whose normal condition of electricity is like his present condition, positive, they repel each other, become mutually abusive, engage in conflict and deadly strife, and the newspapers of the next day announce the verdict of the coroner's jury on the case. . . . Who would expect to find the discovery of the moving cause of all these terrible crimes in the perspiration of the criminal? and yet science has shown that the metamorphoses of *a man into a woman*, by changing the negative condition of his electricity into the *positive* electricity of the woman, with all its attributes, is disclosed by the character of his perspiration, superinduced by the use of alcoholic stimulants" ("*The Influence of the Blue Ray*," p. 119).

dæmons) composed of fire and air, and water and earth, and returned to the form of his first and better nature."[456]

But Dr. Elam thinks otherwise. On page 194 of his book, *A Physician's Problems,* he says that the cause of the rapid spread of certain epidemics of disease which he is noticing "remains a mystery"; but as regards the incendiarism he remarks that "in all this we find nothing mysterious," though the epidemic is strongly developed. Strange contradiction! De Quincey, in his paper, entitled *Murder Considered as One of the Fine Arts,* treats of the epidemic of assassination, between 1588 and 1635, by which seven of the most distinguished characters of the time lost their lives at the hands of assassins, and neither he, nor any other commentator has been able to explain the mysterious cause of this homicidal mania.

If we press these gentlemen for an explanation, which as pretended philosophers they are bound to give us, we are answered that it is a great deal more *scientific* to assign for such epidemics "agitation of the mind," " . . . a time of political excitement (1830)" " . . . imitation and impulse," " . . . excitable and idle boys," and "*hysterical* girls," than to be absurdly seeking for the verification of superstitious traditions in a hypothetical astral light. It seems to us that if, by some providential fatality, *hysteria* were to disappear entirely from the human system, the medical fraternity would be entirely at a loss for explanations of a large class of phenomena now conveniently classified under the head of "normal symptoms of certain pathological conditions of the nervous centres." Hysteria has been hitherto the sheet-anchor of skeptical pathologists. Does a dirty peasant-girl begin suddenly to speak with fluency different foreign languages hitherto unfamiliar to her, and to write poetry — "hysterics!" Is a medium levitated, in full view of a dozen of witnesses, and carried out of one third-story window and brought back through another — "disturbance of the nervous centres, followed by a *collective* hysterical delusion."[457] A Scotch terrier, caught in the room during a manifestation, is hurled by an invisible hand across the room, breaks to pieces, in his *salto mortali,* a chandelier, under a ceiling eighteen feet high, to fall down killed[458] — "*canine hallucination!*"

"True science has no belief," says Dr. Fenwick, in Bulwer-Lytton's *Strange Story;* "true science knows but three states of mind: denial, conviction, and the vast interval between the two, which is not belief, but the *suspension of judgment.*" Such, perhaps, was true science in Dr. Fenwick's days. But the true science of our modern times proceeds otherwise; it either denies point-blank, without any preliminary investigation, or sits in the interim, between denial and conviction, and, dictionary in hand, invents new Græco-Latin appellations for non-existing kinds of hysteria!

How often have powerful clairvoyants and adepts in mesmerism described the epidemics and *physical* (though to others invisible) manifestations which science attributes to epilepsy, hæmato-nervous disorders, and what not, of *somatic origin,* as their lucid vision saw them in the astral light. They affirm that the "electric waves" were in violent perturbation, and that they discerned a direct relation between this ethereal disturbance and

---

456 Plato, "*Timæus.*"
457 Littre, "*Revue des Deux Mondes.*"
458 See des Mousseaux's "*Œuvres des Demons.*"

the mental or physical epidemic then raging. But science has heeded them not, but gone on with her encyclopædic labor of devising new names for old things.

"History," says Du Potet, the prince of French mesmerists, "keeps but too well the sad records of sorcery. These facts were but too real, and lent themselves but too readily to dreadful malpractices of the art, to monstrous abuse! . . . But how did I come to find out that art? Where did I learn it? In my thoughts? no; it is *nature* herself which discovered to me the secret. And how? By producing before my own eyes, without waiting for me to search for it, indisputable facts of sorcery and magic. . . . What is, after all, somnambulistic sleep? *A result of the potency of magic.* And what is it which determines these attractions, these *sudden impulses,* these raving epidemics, rages, antipathies, crises; — these convulsions which *you can make durable?* . . . what is it which determines them, if not the *very principle* we employ, the agent *so decidedly well known to the ancients?* What you call nervous fluid or *magnetism,* the men of old called *occult power,* or the potency of the soul, subjection, MAGIC!"

"Magic is based on the existence of a mixed world placed *without,* not *within* us; and with which we can enter in communication by the use of certain arts and practices. . . . An element *existing in nature,* unknown to most men, gets hold of a person and withers and breaks him down, as the fearful hurricane does a bulrush; it scatters men far away, it strikes them in a *thousand places at the same time,* without their perceiving the invisible foe, or being able to protect themselves . . . all this is *demonstrated;* but that this element could choose friends and select *favorites,* obey their *thoughts,* answer to the human voice, and understand the meaning of *traced signs,* that is what people cannot realize, and *what their reason rejects,* and that is *what I saw;* and I say it here most emphatically, that for me it is a fact and *a truth* demonstrated for ever."[459]

"If I entered into greater details, one could readily understand that there do exist *around us, as in ourselves,* mysterious beings who have *power* and *shape,* who enter and go out at will, notwithstanding the well-closed doors."[460] Further, the great mesmerizer teaches us that the faculty of directing this fluid is a "physical property, resulting from our organization . . . it passes through all bodies . . . everything can be used as a conductor for magical operations, and it will retain the power of producing effects in its turn." This is the theory common to all hermetic philosophers. Such is the power of the fluid, "that *no chemical or physical forces are able to destroy it.* . . . There is very little analogy between the imponderable fluids known to physicists and this animal magnetic fluid."[461]

THE GODS OF THE PANTHEONS ONLY NATURAL FORCES

If we now refer to mediæval ages, we find, among others, Cornelius Agrippa telling us precisely the same: "The ever-changing universal force, the 'soul of the world,' can fecundate anything by infusing in it its own celestial properties. Arranged according to the formula taught *by science,* these objects receive the gift of communicating to us their virtue. It is sufficient to wear them, to feel them immediately operating on the soul as on the body. . . . Human soul possesses, from the fact of its being of the same essence as all creation, a

459 Du Potet, *"Magie Devoilée,"* pp. 51-147.
460 Ibid., p. 201.
461 Baron Du Potet, *"Cours de Magnetisme,"* pp. 17-108.

marvellous power. One who possesses the secret is enabled to rise in science and knowledge as high as his imagination will carry him; but he does that only on the condition of becoming closely united to this universal force . . . Truth, even the future, can be then made ever present to the eyes of the soul; and this fact has been many times demonstrated by things coming to pass as they were seen and described beforehand . . . time and space vanish before the eagle eye of the immortal soul . . . her power becomes boundless . . . she can shoot through space and envelop with her presence a man, *no matter at what distance;* she can plunge and penetrate him through, and make him hear the voice of the person she belongs to, as if that person were in the room."[462]

If unwilling to seek for proof or receive information from mediæval, hermetic philosophy, we may go still further back into antiquity, and select, out of the great body of philosophers of the pre-Christian ages, one who can least be accused of superstition and credulity — Cicero. Speaking of those whom he calls *gods,* and who are either human or atmospheric spirits, "We know," says the old orator, "that of all living beings man is the best formed, and, as the gods belong to this number, they must have a human form. . . . I do not mean to say that the gods have body and blood in them; but I say that they *seem* as if they had bodies with blood in them. . . . Epicurus, for whom hidden things were as tangible as if he had touched them with his finger, teaches us that gods are not generally visible, but that they are *intelligible;* that they are not bodies having a certain solidity . . . but that we can recognize them by their *passing* images; that as there are *atoms* enough in the infinite space *to produce such images,* these are produced before us . . . and make us realize what are these happy, immortal beings."[463]

"When the initiate," says Levi, in his turn, "has become quite *lucide,* he communicates and directs at will the *magnetic* vibrations in the mass of astral light. . . . Transformed in human light at the moment of the conception, *it* (the light) becomes the *first envelope of the soul;* by combination with the subtlest fluids it forms an ethereal body, or the *sidereal phantom,* which is entirely disengaged *only* at the moment of death."[464] To project this ethereal body, at no matter what distance; to render it more objective and tangible by condensing over its fluidic form the waves of the parent essence, is the great secret of the adept-*magician.*

Theurgical magic is the last expression of occult psychological science. The Academicians reject it as the hallucination of diseased brains, or brand it with the opprobrium of charlatanry. We deny to them most emphatically the right of expressing their opinion on a subject which they have never investigated. They have no more right, in their present state of knowledge, to judge of magic and Spiritualism than a Fiji islander to venture his opinion about the labors of Faraday or Agassiz. About all they can do on any one day is to correct the errors of the preceding day. Nearly three thousand years ago, earlier than the days of Pythagoras, the ancient philosophers claimed that light was ponderable — hence *matter,* and that light was force. The corpuscular theory, owing to certain Newtonian failures to account for it, was laughed down, and the undulatory theory, which proclaimed light *imponderable,* accepted. And now the world is startled by

---

462 "*De Occulto Philosophiâ,*" pp. 332-358.
463 Cicero, "*De Natura Deorum,*" lib. i., cap. xviii.
464 Eliphas Levi.

Mr.Crookes *weighing* light with his radiometer! The Pythagoreans held that neither the sun nor the stars were the *sources* of light and heat, and that the former was but an agent; but the modern schools teach the contrary.

The same may be said respecting the Newtonian law of gravitation. Following strictly the Pythagorean doctrine, Plato held that gravitation was not merely a law of the magnetic attraction of lesser bodies to larger ones, but a magnetic repulsion of similars and attraction of dissimilars. "Things brought together," says he, "contrary to nature, are naturally at war, and repel one another."[465] This cannot be taken to mean that repulsion occurs of necessity between bodies of dissimilar properties, but simply that when naturally antagonistic bodies are brought together they repel one another. The researches of Bart and Schweigger leave us in little or no doubt that the ancients were well acquainted with the mutual attractions of iron and the lodestone, as well as with the positive and negative properties of electricity, by whatever name they may have called it. The reciprocal magnetic relations of the planetary orbs, which are all magnets, was with them an accepted fact, and aërolites were not only called by them magnetic stones, but used in the Mysteries for purposes to which we now apply the magnet. When, therefore, Professor A. M. Mayer, of the Stevens Institute of Technology, in 1872, told the Yale Scientific Club that the earth is a great magnet, and that "on any sudden agitation of the sun's surface the magnetism of the earth receives a profound disturbance in its equilibrium, causing fitful tremors in the magnets of our observatories, and producing those grand outbursts of the polar lights, whose lambent flames dance in rhythm to the quivering needle,"[466] he only restated, in good English, what was taught in good Doric untold centuries before the first Christian philosopher saw the light.

The prodigies accomplished by the priests of theurgical magic are so well authenticated, and the evidence — if human testimony is worth anything at all — is so overwhelming, that, rather than confess that the Pagan theurgists far outrivalled the Christians in miracles, Sir David Brewster piously concedes to the former the greatest proficiency in physics, and everything that pertains to natural philosophy. Science finds herself in a very disagreeable dilemma. She must either confess that the ancient physicists were superior in knowledge to her modern representatives, or that there exists something in nature beyond physical science, and that *spirit* possesses powers of which our philosophers never dreamed.

"The mistake we make in some science we have specially cultivated," says Bulwer-Lytton, "is often only to be seen by the light of a separate science as especially cultivated by another."[467]

Nothing can be easier accounted for than the highest possibilities of magic. By the radiant light of the universal magnetic ocean, whose electric waves bind the cosmos together, and in their ceaseless motion penetrate every atom and molecule of the boundless

---

465 "*Timæus.*" Such like expressions made Professor Jowett state in his Introduction that Plato taught the attraction of similar bodies to similar. But such an assertion would amount to denying the great philosopher even a rudimentary knowledge of the laws of magnetic poles.
466 Alfred Marshall Mayer, Ph.D., "*The Earth a Great Magnet,*" a lecture delivered before the Yale Scientific Club, Feb. 14, 1872.
467 "*Strange Story.*"

creation, the disciples of mesmerism — howbeit insufficient their various experiments — intuitionally perceive the alpha and omega of the great mystery. Alone, the study of this agent, which is the divine breath, can unlock the secrets of psychology and physiology, of cosmical and spiritual phenomena.

"Magic," says Psellus, "formed the last part of the sacerdotal science. It investigated the nature, power, and quality of everything sublunary; of the elements and their parts, of animals, all various plants and their fruits, of stones and herbs. In short, it explored the essence and power of everything. From hence, therefore, it produced its effects.

And it formed *statues* (magnetized) which procure health, and made all various figures and things (talismans) which could equally become the instruments of disease as well as of health. Often, too, celestial fire is made to appear through magic, and then statues laugh and lamps are spontaneously enkindled."[468]

PROOFS OF THE MAGICAL POWERS OF PYTHAGORAS

If Galvani's modern discovery can set in motion the limbs of a dead frog, and force a dead man's face to express, by the distortion of its features, the most varied emotions, from joy to diabolical rage, despair, and horror, the Pagan priests, unless the combined evidence of the most trustworthy men of antiquity is not to be relied upon, accomplished the still greater wonders of making their stone and metal statues to sweat and laugh. The *celestial*, pure fire of the Pagan altar was electricity drawn from the astral light. Statues, therefore, if properly prepared, might, without any accusation of superstition, be allowed to have the property of imparting health and disease by contact, as well as any modern galvanic belt, or overcharged battery.

Scholastic skeptics, as well as ignorant materialists, have greatly amused themselves for the last two centuries over the *absurdities* attributed to Pythagoras by his biographer, Iamblichus. The Samian philosopher is said to have persuaded a she-bear to give up eating human flesh; to have forced a white eagle to descend to him from the clouds, and to have subdued him by stroking him gently with the hand, and by talking to him. On another occasion, Pythagoras actually persuaded an ox to renounce eating beans, by merely whispering in the animal's ear![469] Oh, ignorance and superstition of our forefathers, how ridiculous they appear in the eyes of our enlightened generations! Let us, however, analyze this absurdity. Every day we see unlettered men, proprietors of strolling menageries, taming and completely subduing the most ferocious animals, merely by the power of their irresistible will. Nay, we have at the present moment in Europe several young and physically-weak girls, under twenty years of age, fearlessly doing the same thing. Every one has either witnessed or heard of the seemingly magical power of some mesmerizers and psychologists. They are able to subjugate their patients for any length of time. Regazzoni, the mesmerist who excited such wonder in France and London, has achieved far more extraordinary feats than what is above attributed to Pythagoras. Why, then, accuse the ancient biographers of such men as Pythagoras and Apollonius of Tyana of either wilful

---

468 See Taylor's "*Pausanias*", MS. "*Treatise on Dæmons*," by Psellus, and the "*Treatise on the Eleusinian and Bacchic Mysteries*."
469 Iamblichus, "*De Vita Pythag.*"

misrepresentation or absurd superstition? When we realize that the majority of those who are so skeptical as to the magical powers possessed by the ancient philosophers, who laugh at the old theogonies and the fallacies of mythology, nevertheless have an implicit faith in the records and inspiration of their Bible, hardly daring to doubt even that monstrous absurdity that Joshua arrested the course of the sun, we may well say *Amen* to Godfrey Higgins' just rebuke: "When I find," he says, "learned men believing *Genesis literally*, which the ancients, with all their failings, had too much sense to receive except allegorically, I am tempted to doubt the reality of the improvement of the human mind."[470]

THE VIEWLESS RACES OF ETHEREAL SPACE

One of the very few commentators on old Greek and Latin authors, who have given their just dues to the ancients for their mental development, is Thomas Taylor. In his translation of Iamblichus' *Life of Pythagoras*, we find him remarking as follows: "Since Pythagoras, as Iamblichus informs us, was initiated in all the Mysteries of Byblus and Tyre, in the sacred operations of the Syrians, and in the Mysteries of the Phœnicians, and also that he spent two and twenty years in the adyta of temples in Egypt, associated with the magians in Babylon, and was instructed by them in their venerable knowledge, it is not at all wonderful that he was skilled in magic, or theurgy, and was therefore able to perform things which surpass merely human power, and which appear to be perfectly incredible to the vulgar."[471]

The universal ether was not, in their eyes, simply a something stretching, tenantless, throughout the expanse of heaven; it was a boundless ocean peopled like our familiar seas with monstrous and minor creatures, and having in its every molecule the germs of life. Like the finny tribes which swarm in our oceans and smaller bodies of water, each kind having its *habitat* in some spot to which it is curiously adapted, some friendly and some inimical to man, some pleasant and some frightful to behold, some seeking the refuge of quiet nooks and land-locked harbors, and some traversing great areas of water, the various races of the *elemental* spirits were believed by them to inhabit the different portions of the great ethereal ocean, and to be exactly adapted to their respective conditions. If we will only bear in mind the fact that the rushing of planets through space must create as absolute a disturbance in this plastic and attenuated medium, as the passage of a cannon shot does in the air or that of a steamer in the water, and on a cosmic scale, we can understand that certain planetary aspects, admitting our premises to be true, may produce much more violent agitation and cause much stronger currents to flow in a given direction, than others. With the same premises conceded, we may also see why, by such various aspects of the stars, shoals of friendly or hostile "elementals" might be poured in upon our atmosphere, or some particular portion of it, and make the fact appreciable by the effects which ensue.

According to the ancient doctrines, the soulless elemental spirits were evolved by the ceaseless motion inherent in the astral light. Light is force, and the latter is produced by the *will*. As this will proceeds from an intelligence which cannot err, for it has nothing of the material organs of *human* thought in it, being the superfine pure emanation of the highest divinity itself — (Plato's "Father") it proceeds from the beginning of time, according to

---

470 "*Anacalypsis*," vol. i., p. 807.
471 Iamblichus, "*Life of Pythagoras*," p. 297.

immutable laws, to evolve the elementary fabric requisite for subsequent generations of what we term human races. All of the latter, whether belonging to this planet or to some other of the myriads in space, have their earthly bodies evolved in the matrix out of the bodies of a certain class of these elemental beings which have passed away in the invisible worlds. In the ancient philosophy there was no missing link to be supplied by what Tyndall calls an "educated imagination"; no hiatus to be filled with volumes of materialistic speculations made necessary by the absurd attempt to solve an equation with but one set of quantities; our "ignorant" ancestors traced the law of evolution throughout the whole universe. As by gradual progression from the star-cloudlet to the development of the physical body of man, the rule holds good, so from the universal ether to the incarnate human spirit, they traced one uninterrupted series of entities. These evolutions were from the world of spirit into the world of gross matter; and through that back again to the source of all things. The "descent of species" was to them a descent from the spirit, primal source of all, to the "degradation of matter." In this complete chain of unfoldings the elementary, spiritual beings had as distinct a place, midway between the extremes, as Mr. Darwin's missing-link between the ape and man.

No author in the world of literature ever gave a more truthful or more poetical description of these beings than Sir E. Bulwer-Lytton, the author of *Zanoni*. Now, himself "a thing not of matter" but an "Idea of joy and light," his words sound more like the faithful echo of memory than the exuberant outflow of mere imagination.

"Man is arrogant in proportion of his ignorance," he makes the wise Mejnour say to Glyndon. "For several ages he saw in the countless worlds that sparkle through space like the bubbles of a shoreless ocean, only the petty candles . . . that Providence has been pleased to light for no other purpose but to make the night more agreeable to man. . . . Astronomy has corrected this delusion of human vanity, and man now reluctantly confesses that the stars are worlds, larger and more glorious than his own. . . . Everywhere, then, in this immense design, science brings new life to light. . . . Reasoning, then, by evident analogy, if not a leaf, if not a drop of water, but is, no less than yonder star, a habitable and breathing world — nay, if even man himself, is a world to other lives, and millions and myriads dwell in the rivers of his blood, and inhabit man's frame, as man inhabits earth — common sense (if our schoolmen had it) would suffice to teach that the circumfluent infinite which you call space — the boundless impalpable which divides earth from the moon and stars — is filled also with its correspondent and appropriate life. Is it not a visible absurdity to suppose that being is crowded upon every leaf, and yet absent from the immensities of space! The law of the great system forbids the waste even of an atom; it knows no spot where something of life does not breathe. . . . Well, then, can you conceive that space, which is the infinite itself, is alone a waste, is alone lifeless, is less useful to the one design of universal being . . . than the peopled leaf, than the swarming globule? The microscope shows you the creatures on the leaf; *no mechanical tube is yet invented to discover the nobler and more gifted things that hover in the illimitable air.* Yet between these last and man is a mysterious *and terrible affinity.* . . . But first, to penetrate this barrier, the soul with which you listen must be sharpened by intense enthusiasm, purified from all earthly desires. . . . When thus prepared, science can be brought to aid it; the sight itself may be rendered more subtile, the nerves more acute, the spirit more alive and outward, and the element itself — the air, the space — may be made, by certain secrets of the higher chemistry, more palpable and clear. And this, too, is not *magic* as the credulous call it; as I have so often said before, magic (a science that violates nature) exists not; it is *but the science by which nature can be controlled.* Now, in space there are millions of beings, *not literally spiritual,* for they have all, like the animalcula unseen by the naked eye, certain forms of matter, though matter so delicate, air-drawn, and subtile, that it is, as it were, but a film, a gossamer, that clothes the spirit. . . . Yet, in truth, these races differ most widely . . . some of surpassing wisdom, some of horrible malignity; some hostile as fiends to men, others gentle as messengers between earth and heaven. . . . Amid the dwellers of the threshold is one, too, surpassing in malignity and hatred all her tribe; one whose eyes have paralyzed the bravest, and whose power increases over the spirit precisely in proportion to its fear."[472]

Such is the insufficient sketch of elemental beings void of divine spirit, given by one whom many with reason believed to know more than he was prepared to admit in the face of an incredulous public.

In the following chapter we will contrive to explain some of the esoteric speculations of the initiates of the sanctuary, as to what man was, is, and may yet be. The doctrines they taught in the Mysteries — the source from which sprang the Old and partially the New Testament, belonged to the most advanced notions of morality, and religious *revelations.* While the literal meaning was abandoned to the fanaticism of the unreasoning lower classes of society, the higher ones, the majority of which consisted of *Initiates,* pursued their studies in the solemn silence of the temples, and their worship of the *one* God of Heaven.

The speculations of Plato, in the *Banquet,* on the creation of the primordial men, and the essay on Cosmogony in the *Timæus,* must be taken allegorically, if we accept them at all. It is this hidden Pythagorean meaning in *Timæus, Cratylus,* and *Parmenides,* and a few other trilogies and dialogues, that the Neo-platonists ventured to expound, as far as the theurgical vow of secrecy would allow them. The Pythagorean doctrine that *God is the universal mind diffused through all things,* and the dogma of the soul's immortality, are the leading features in these apparently incongruous teachings. His piety and the great veneration Plato felt for the MYSTERIES, are sufficient warrant that he would not allow his indiscretion to get the better of that deep sense of responsibility which is felt by every adept. "Constantly perfecting himself in perfect MYSTERIES, a man in them alone becomes truly perfect," says he in the *Phædrus.*[473]

He took no pains to conceal his displeasure that the Mysteries had become less secret than formerly. Instead of profaning them by putting them within the reach of the multitude, he would have guarded them with jealous care against all but the most earnest and worthy of his disciples.[474] While mentioning the gods, on every page, his monotheism is unquestionable, for the whole thread of his discourse indicates that by the term *gods* he means a class of beings far lower in the scale than deities, and but one grade higher than

472 Bulwer-Lytton, "*Zanoni.*"

473 Cory, "*Phædrus,*" i. 328.

474 This assertion is clearly corroborated by Plato himself, who says: "You say that, in my former discourse, I have not sufficiently explained to you the nature of the *First. I purposely spoke enigmatically,* that in case the tablet should have happened with any accident, either by land or sea, a person, *without some previous knowledge of the subject, might not be able to understand its contents*" ("*Plato,*" Ep. ii., p. 312; Cory, "*Ancient Fragments*").

men. Even Josephus perceived and acknowledged this fact, despite the natural prejudice of his race. In his famous onslaught upon Apion, this historian says:[475] "Those, however, among the Greeks who philosophized *in accordance with truth*, were not ignorant of anything . . . nor did they fail to perceive the chilling superficialities of the mythical allegories, on which account they justly despised them. . . . By which thing Plato, being moved, says it is not necessary to admit any one of the other poets into 'the Commonwealth,' and *he dismisses Homer* blandly, after having crowned him and pouring unguent upon him, in order that indeed he should not destroy, by *his myths*, the *orthodox belief respecting one God*."

Those who can discern the true spirit of Plato's philosophy, will hardly be satisfied with the estimate of the same which Jowett lays before his readers. He tells us that the influence exercised upon posterity by the *Timæus* is partly due to a misunderstanding of the doctrine of its author by the Neo-platonists. He would have us believe that the hidden meanings which they found in this *Dialogue,* are "quite at variance with the spirit of Plato." This is equivalent to the assumption that Jowett understands what this spirit really was; whereas his criticism upon this particular topic rather indicates that he did not penetrate it at all. If, as he tells us, the Christians seem to find in his work their trinity, the word, the church, and the creation of the world, in a Jewish sense, it is because all this *is* there, and therefore it is but natural that they should have found it. The outward building is the same; but the spirit which animated the dead letter of the philosopher's teaching has fled, and we would seek for it in vain through the arid dogmas of Christian theology. The Sphinx is the same now, as it was four centuries before the Christian era; but the Œdipus is no more. He is slain because he has given to the world that which the world was not ripe enough to receive. He was the embodiment of truth, and he had to die, as every grand truth has to, before, like the Phœnix of old, it revives from its own ashes. Every translator of Plato's works remarked the strange similarity between the philosophy of the esoterists and the Christian doctrines, and each of them has tried to interpret it in accordance with his own religious feelings. So Cory, in his *Ancient Fragments*, tries to prove that it is but an outward resemblance; and does his best to lower the Pythagorean Monad in the public estimation and exalt upon its ruins the later anthropomorphic deity. Taylor, advocating the former, acts as unceremoniously with the Mosaic God. Zeller boldly laughs at the pretensions of the Fathers of the Church, who, notwithstanding history and its chronology, and whether people will have it or not, insist that Plato and his school have robbed Christianity of its leading features. It is as fortunate for us as it is unfortunate for the Roman Church that such clever sleight-of-hand as that resorted to by Eusebius is rather difficult in our century. It was easier to pervert chronology "for the sake of making synchronisms," in the days of the Bishop of Cæsarea, than it is now, and while history exists, no one can help people knowing that Plato lived 600 years before Irenæus took it into his head to establish a *new* doctrine from the ruins of Plato's older Academy.

This doctrine of God being the universal mind diffused through all things, underlies all ancient philosophies. The Buddhistic tenets which can never be better comprehended than when studying the Pythagorean philosophy — its faithful reflection — are derived from this source as well as the Brahmanical religion and early Christianity. The purifying process of transmigrations — the metempsychoses — however grossly anthropomorphized at a later

---

475 *"Josephus against Apion,"* ii., p. 1079.

period, must only be regarded as a supplementary doctrine, disfigured by theological sophistry with the object of getting a firmer hold upon believers through a popular superstition. Neither Gautama Buddha nor Pythagoras intended to teach this purely-metaphysical allegory *literally*. Esoterically, it is explained in the "Mystery" of the *Kounboum*,[476] and relates to the purely spiritual peregrinations of the human soul. It is not in the dead letter of Buddhistical sacred literature that scholars may hope to find the true solution of its metaphysical subtilties. The latter weary the power of thought by the inconceivable profundity of its ratiocination; and the student is never farther from truth than when he believes himself nearest its discovery. The mastery of every doctrine of the perplexing Buddhist system can be attained only by proceeding strictly according to the Pythagorean and Platonic method; from universals down to particulars. The key to it lies in the refined and mystical tenets of the spiritual influx of divine life. "Whoever is unacquainted with my law," says Buddha, "and dies in that state, must return to the earth till he becomes a perfect Samanean. To achieve this object, he must destroy within himself the trinity of *Maya*.[477] He must extinguish his passions, unite and identify himself with *the law* (the teaching of the secret doctrine), and comprehend the religion of *annihilation*."

Here, annihilation refers but to *matter*, that of the visible as well as of the invisible body; for the astral soul (*perisprit*) is still matter, however sublimated. The same book says that what Fo (Buddha) meant to say was, that "the primitive substance is eternal and unchangeable. Its highest revelation is the pure, luminous ether, the boundless infinite space, not a void resulting from the absence of forms, but, on the contrary, *the foundation of all forms*, and anterior to them. But the very presence of *forms* denotes it to be the creation of *Maya*, and all her works are as nothing before the *uncreated* being, SPIRIT, in whose profound and sacred repose all motion must cease forever."

Thus *annihilation* means, with the Buddhistical philosophy, only a dispersion of matter, in whatever form or *semblance* of form it may be; for everything that bears a shape was created, and thus must sooner or later perish, *i.e.*, change that shape; therefore, as something temporary, though seeming to be permanent, it is but an illusion, *Maya*; for, as eternity has neither beginning nor end, the more or less prolonged duration of some particular form passes, as it were, like an instantaneous flash of lightning. Before we have the time to realize that we have seen it, it is gone and passed away for ever; hence, even our astral bodies, pure ether, are but illusions of matter, so long as they retain their terrestrial outline. The latter changes, says the Buddhist, according to the merits or demerits of the person during his lifetime, and this is metempsychosis. When the spiritual *entity* breaks loose for ever from every particle of matter, then only it enters upon the eternal and unchangeable Nirvana. He exists in spirit, in *nothing*; as a form, a shape, a semblance, he is completely *annihilated*, and thus will die no more, for spirit alone is no *Maya*, but the only REALITY in an illusionary universe of ever-passing forms.

It is upon this Buddhist doctrine that the Pythagoreans grounded the principal tenets of their philosophy. "Can that spirit, which gives life and motion, and partakes of the nature of light, be reduced to non-entity?" they ask. "Can that sensitive spirit in brutes which exercises

---

476 See chapter ix., p. 302.
477 "Illusion; matter in its triple manifestation in the earthly, and the astral or fontal soul, or the body, and the Platonian dual soul, the rational and the irrational one," see next chapter.

memory, one of the rational faculties, die, and become nothing?" And Whitelock Bulstrode, in his able defence of Pythagoras, expounds this doctrine by adding: "If you say, they (the brutes) breathe their spirits into the air, and there vanish, that is all I contend for. The air, indeed, is the proper place to receive them, being, according to Laertius, full of souls; and, according to Epicurus, full of atoms, the principles of all things; for even this place wherein we walk and birds fly has so much of a spiritual nature, that it is invisible, and, therefore, may well be the receiver of forms, since the forms of all bodies are so; we can only see and hear its effects; the air itself is too fine, and above the capacity of the age. What then is the ether in the region above, and what are the influences or forms that descend from thence?"

The *spirits* of creatures, the Pythagoreans hold, who are emanations of the most sublimated portions of ether, emanations, BREATHS, *but not forms.* Ether is incorruptible, all philosophers agree in that; and what is incorruptible *is so far from being annihilated* when it gets rid of the *form,* that it lays a good claim to IMMORTALITY. "But what is that which has no body, no *form;* which is imponderable, invisible and indivisible; that which exists and yet *is not?*" ask the Buddhists. "It is Nirvana," is the answer. It is NOTHING, not a region, but rather a state. When once Nirvana is reached, man is exempt from the effects of the "four truths"; for an effect can only be produced through a certain cause, and every cause is *annihilated* in this state.

THE "FOUR TRUTHS" OF BUDDHISM

These "four truths" are the foundation of the whole Buddhist doctrine of Nirvana. They are, says the book of *Pradjuâ Pâramitâ*[478] 1. The existence of pain. 2. The production of pain. 3. The annihilation of pain. 4. The way to the annihilation of pain. What is the source of pain? — Existence. Birth existing, decrepitude and death ensue; for wherever there is a form, there is a *cause* for pain and suffering. *Spirit* alone has no form, and therefore *cannot be said to exist.* Whenever man (the ethereal, inner man) reaches that point when he becomes utterly spiritual, hence, formless, he has reached a state of perfect bliss. MAN as an objective being becomes annihilated, but the spiritual entity with its subjective life, will live for ever, for spirit is incorruptible and immortal.

It is by the spirit of the teachings of both Buddha and Pythagoras, that we can so easily recognize the identity of their doctrines. The all-pervading, universal soul, the *Anima Mundi,* is Nirvana; and Buddha, as a generic name, is the anthropomorphized *monad* of Pythagoras. When resting in Nirvana, the final bliss, Buddha is the silent monad, dwelling in darkness and silence; he is also the formless Brahm, the sublime but *unknowable* Deity, which pervades invisibly the whole universe. Whenever it is manifested, desiring to impress itself upon humanity in a shape intelligent to our intellect, whether we call it an *avatar,* or a King Messiah, or a *permutation* of Divine Spirit, *Logos,* Christos, it is all one and the same thing. In each case it is "the Father," who is in the *Son,* and the Son in "the Father." The immortal spirit overshadows the mortal man. It enters into him, and pervading his whole being, makes of him a god, who descends into his earthly tabernacle. Every man may become a Buddha, says the doctrine. And so throughout the interminable series of ages we find now and then men who more or less succeed in *uniting* themselves "with God," as the

---

478 *"Perfection of Wisdom."*

expression goes, with their *own spirit*, as we ought to translate. The Buddhists call such men *Arhat*. An Arhat is next to a Buddha, and none is equal to him either in *infused* science, or *miraculous* powers. Certain fakirs demonstrate the theory well in practice, as Jacolliot has proved.

Even the so-called *fabulous* narratives of certain Buddhistical books, when stripped of their allegorical meaning, are found to be the secret doctrines taught by Pythagoras. In the Pali Books called the *Jutakâs*, are given the 550 incarnations or metempsychoses of Buddha. They narrate how he has appeared in every form of animal life, and animated every sentient being on earth, from infinitesimal insect to the bird, the beast, and finally man, the microcosmic image of God on earth. Must this be taken *literally*; is it intended as a description of the *actual* transformations and existence of one and the same individual immortal, divine spirit, which by turns has animated every kind of sentient being? Ought we not rather to understand, with Buddhist metaphysicians, that though the individual human spirits are numberless, collectively they are one, as every drop of water drawn out of the ocean, metaphorically speaking, may have an individual existence and still be one with the rest of the drops going to form that ocean; for each human spirit is a scintilla of the one all-pervading light? That this divine spirit animates the flower, the particle of granite on the mountain side, the lion, the man? Egyptian Hierophants, like the Brahmans, and the Buddhists of the East, and some Greek philosophers, maintained originally that the same spirit that animates the particle of dust, lurking latent in it, animates man, manifesting itself in him in its highest state of activity. The doctrine, also, of a gradual refusion of the human *soul* into the essence of the primeval parent spirit, was universal at one time. But this doctrine never implied annihilation of the higher spiritual *ego* — only the dispersion of the *external forms* of man, after his terrestrial death, as well as during his abode on earth. Who is better fitted to impart to us the mysteries of after-death, so erroneously thought impenetrable, than those men who having, through self-discipline and purity of life and purpose, succeeded in uniting themselves with their "God," were afforded *some* glimpses, however imperfect, of the great truth.[479] And these seers tell us strange stories about the *variety* of forms assumed by disembodied astral souls; forms of which each one is a spiritual though concrete reflection of the abstract state of the mind, and thoughts of the once living man.

To accuse Buddhistical philosophy of rejecting a Supreme Being — God, and the soul's immortality, of atheism, in short, on the ground that according to their doctrines, Nirvana means *annihilation*, and *Svabhâvât is* NOT *a person, but nothing*, is simply absurd. The En (or Ayîn) of the Jewish En-Soph, also means *nihil* or *nothing*, that which is not (*quo ad nos*); but no one has ever ventured to twit the Jews with atheism. In both cases the real meaning of the term *nothing* carries with it the idea that God is *not a thing*, not a concrete or visible Being to which a name expressive of *any* object known to us on earth may be applied with propriety.

---

479 Porphyry gives the credit to Plotinus his master, of having been united with "God" six times during his life, and complains of having attained to it but twice, himself.

CHAPTER IX

"Thou can'st not call that madness of which thou art proved to know nothing."

TERTULLIAN, *Apology*

"This is not a matter of to-day,
Or yesterday, but hath been from all times;
And none hath told us whence it came or how!"

SOPHOCLES

"Belief in the supernatural is a fact natural, primitive, universal, and constant in the life and history of the human race. Unbelief in the supernatural begets materialism; materialism, sensuality; sensuality, social convulsions, amid whose storms man again learns to believe and pray."

GUIEOT

"If any one think these things incredible, let him keep his opinions to himself, and not contradict those who, by such events, are incited to the study of virtue."

JOSEPHUS

MEANING OF THE EXPRESSION "COATS OF SKIN"

FROM the Platonic and Pythagorean views of matter and force, we will now turn to the kabalistic philosophy of the origin of man, and compare it with the theory of natural selection enunciated by Darwin and Wallace. It may be that we shall find as much reason to credit the ancients with originality in this direction as in that which we have been considering. To our mind, no stronger proof of the theory of cyclical progression need be required than the comparative enlightenment of former ages and that of the Patristic Church, as regards the form of the earth, and the movements of the planetary system. Even were other evidence wanting, the ignorance of Augustine and Lactantius, misleading the whole of Christendom upon these questions until the period of Galileo, would mark the eclipses through which human knowledge passes from age to age.

The "coats of skin," mentioned in the third chapter of *Genesis* as given to Adam and Eve, are explained by certain ancient philosophers to mean the fleshy bodies with which, in the progress of the cycles, the progenitors of the race became clothed. They maintained that the god-like physical form became grosser and grosser, until the bottom of what may be termed the last spiritual cycle was reached, and mankind entered upon the ascending arc of the first human cycle. Then began an uninterrupted series of cycles or *yugas;* the precise number of years of which each of them consisted remaining an inviolable mystery within the precincts of the sanctuaries and disclosed only to the initiates. As soon as humanity entered upon a new one, the stone age, with which the preceding cycle had closed, began to gradually merge into the following and next higher age. With each successive age, or epoch, men grew more refined, until the acme of perfection possible in that particular cycle had been reached. Then the receding wave of time carried back with it the vestiges of human, social, and intellectual progress. Cycle succeeded cycle, by imperceptible transitions; highly-civilized flourishing nations, waxed in power, attained the climax of development, waned, and became extinct; and mankind, when the end of the lower cyclic arc was reached, was replunged into barbarism as at the start. Kingdoms have crumbled and nation succeeded nation from the beginning until our day, the races alternately mounting to the highest and descending to the lowest points of development. Draper observes that there is no reason to suppose that any one cycle applied to the whole human race. On the contrary, while man in one portion of the planet was in a condition of retrogression, in another he might be progressing in enlightenment and civilization.

How analogous this theory is to the law of planetary motion, which causes the individual orbs to rotate on their axes; the several systems to move around their respective suns; and the whole stellar host to follow a common path around a common centre! Life and death, light and darkness, day and night on the planet, as it turns about its axis and traverses the zodiacal circle representing the lesser and the greater cycles.[480] Remember the Hermetic axiom: — "As above, so below; as in heaven, so on earth."

Mr. Alfred R. Wallace argues with sound logic, that the development of man has been more marked in his mental organization than in his external form. Man, he conceives to differ from the animal, by being able to undergo great changes of conditions and of his entire environment, without very marked alterations in bodily form and structure. The changes of climate he meets with a corresponding alteration in his clothing, shelter, weapons, and implements of husbandry. His body may become less hairy, more erect, and of a different color and proportions; "the head and face is immediately connected with the organ of the mind, and as being the medium, expressing the most refined motions of his nature," alone change with the development of his intellect. There was a time when "he had not yet acquired that wonderfully-developed brain, the organ of the mind, which now, even in his lowest examples, raises him far above the highest brutes, at a period when he had the form, but hardly the nature of man, when he neither possessed human speech nor sympathetic and moral feelings." Further, Mr. Wallace says that "Man may have been — indeed, I believe *must have been,* once a homogeneous race . . . in man, the hairy covering of the body has almost entirely disappeared." Of the cave men of Les Eyzies, Mr. Wallace remarks further " . . . the great breadth of the face, the enormous development of the ascending ramus of the lower jaw . . . indicate enormous muscular power and the habits of a savage and brutal race."

NATURAL SELECTION AND ITS RESULTS

Such are the glimpses which anthropology affords us of men, either arrived at the bottom of a cycle or starting in a new one. Let us see how far they are corroborated by clairvoyant psychometry. Professor Denton submitted a fragment of fossilized bone to his wife's examination, without giving Mrs. Denton any hint as to what the article was. It immediately called up to her pictures of people and scenes which he thinks belonged to the stone age. She saw men closely resembling monkeys, with a body very hairy, and "as if the

---

480 Orpheus is said to have ascribed to the grand cycle 120,000 years of duration, and Cassandrus 136,000. See Censorinus, "DE NATAL. DIE"; "CHRONOLOGICAL AND ASTRONOMICAL FRAGMENTS."

natural hair answered the purpose of clothing." "I question whether he can stand perfectly upright; his hip-joints appear to be so formed, he cannot," she added. "Occasionally I see part of the body of one of those beings that looks comparatively smooth. I can see the skin, which is lighter colored . . . I do not know whether he belongs to the same period. . . . At a distance the face seems flat; the lower part of it is heavy; they have what I suppose would be called prognathous jaws. The frontal region of the head is low, and the lower portion of it is very prominent, forming a round ridge across the forehead, immediately above the eyebrows. . . . Now I see a face that looks like that of a human being, though there is a monkey-like appearance about it. All these seem of that kind, having long arms and hairy bodies."[481]

Whether or not the men of science are willing to concede the correctness of the Hermetic theory of the physical evolution of man from higher and more spiritual natures, they themselves show us how the race has progressed from the lowest observed point to its present development. And, as all nature seems to be made up of analogies, is it unreasonable to affirm that the same progressive development of individual forms has prevailed among the inhabitants of the *unseen* universe? If such marvellous effects have been caused by evolution upon our little insignificant planet, producing reasoning and intuitive men from some higher type of the ape family, why suppose that the boundless realms of space are inhabited only by disembodied *angelic* forms? Why not give place in that vast domain to the spiritual duplicates of these hairy, long-armed and half-reasoning ancestors, their predecessors, and all their successors, down to our time? Of course, the spiritual parts of such primeval members of the human family would be as uncouth and undeveloped as were their physical bodies. While they made no attempt to calculate the duration of the "grand cycle," the Hermetic philosophers yet maintained that, according to the cyclic law, the living human race must inevitably and collectively return one day to that point of departure, where man was first clothed with "coats of skin"; or, to express it more clearly, the human race must, in accordance with the law of evolution, be finally *physically* spiritualized. Unless Messrs. Darwin and Huxley are prepared to prove that the man of our century has attained, as a physical and moral animal, the acme of perfection, and evolution, having reached its apex, must stop all further progress with the modern genus *Homo,* we do not see how they can possibly confute such a logical deduction.

THE EGYPTIAN "CIRCLE OF NECESSITY"

In his lecture on *The Action of Natural Selection on Man,* Mr. Alfred R. Wallace concludes his demonstrations as to the development of human races under that law of selection by saying that, if his conclusions are just, "it must inevitably follow that the higher — the more intellectual and moral — must displace the lower and more degraded races; and the power of 'natural selection,' still acting on his mental organization, must ever lead to the more perfect adaptation of man's higher faculties to the condition of surrounding nature, and to the exigencies of the social state. While his external form will probably ever remain unchanged, except in the development of that perfect beauty . . . refined and ennobled by the highest intellectual faculties and sympathetic emotions, his mental constitution may

---

481 W. and E. Denton, "THE SOUL OF THINGS," vol. i.

continue to advance and improve, till the world is again inhabited by a single, nearly homogeneous race, no individual of which will be inferior *to the noblest specimens of existing humanity.*" Sober, scientific methods and cautiousness in hypothetical possibilities have evidently their share in this expression of the opinions of the great anthropologist. Still, what he says above clashes in no way with our kabalistic assertions. Allow to ever-progressing nature, to the great law of the "survival of the fittest," one step beyond Mr. Wallace's deductions, and we have in future the possibility — nay, the assurance of a race, which, like the Vril-ya of Bulwer-Lytton's *Coming Race,* will be but one remove from the primitive "Sons of God."

It will be observed that this philosophy of cycles, which was allegorized by the Egyptian Hierophants in the "circle of necessity," explains at the same time the allegory of the "Fall of man." According to the Arabian descriptions, each of the seven chambers of the Pyramids — those grandest of all cosmic symbols — was known by the name of a planet. The peculiar architecture of the Pyramids shows in itself the drift of the metaphysical thought of their builders. The apex is lost in the clear blue sky of the land of the Pharaohs, and typifies the primordial point lost in the unseen universe from whence started the first race of the spiritual prototypes of man. Each mummy, from the moment that it was embalmed, lost its physical individuality in one sense; it symbolized the human race. Placed in such a way as was best calculated to aid the exit of the "soul," the latter had to pass through the seven planetary chambers before it made its exit through the symbolical apex. Each chamber typified, at the same time, one of the seven spheres, and one of the seven higher types of physico-spiritual humanity alleged to be above our own. Every 3,000 years, the soul, representative of its race, had to return to its primal point of departure before it underwent another evolution into a more perfected spiritual and physical transformation. We must go deep indeed into the abstruse metaphysics of Oriental mysticism before we can realize fully the infinitude of the subjects that were embraced at one sweep by the majestic thought of its exponents. Starting as a pure and perfect spiritual being, the Adam of the second chapter of *Genesis*, not satisfied with the position allotted to him by the Demiurgus (who is the eldest first-begotten, the Adam-Kadmon), Adam the second, the "man of dust," strives in his pride to become Creator in his turn. Evolved out of the androgynous Kadmon, this Adam is himself an androgyn; for, according to the oldest beliefs presented allegorically in Plato's *Timæus*, the prototypes of our races were all enclosed in the microcosmic tree which grew and developed within and under the great mundane or macrocosmic tree. Divine spirit being considered a unity, however numerous the rays of the great spiritual sun, man has still had his origin like all other forms, whether organic or otherwise, in this one Fount of Eternal Light. Were we even to reject the hypothesis of an androgynous man, in connection with physical evolution, the significance of the allegory in its spiritual sense, would remain unimpaired. So long as the first god-man, symbolizing the two first principles of creation, the dual male and female element, had no thought of good and evil he could not hypostasize "woman," for she was in him as he was in her.

It was only when, as a result of the evil hints of the serpent, *matter*, the latter condensed itself and cooled on the spiritual man in its contact with the elements, that the fruits of the man-tree — who is himself that tree of knowledge — appeared to his view. From this moment the l union ceased, man evolved out of himself the woman as a separate entity. They have broken the thread between pure spirit and pure matter. Henceforth they will create no more *spiritually*, and by the sole power of their will; man has become a physical creator, and the kingdom of spirit can be won only by a long imprisonment in matter. The meaning of Gogard, the Hellenic tree of life, the sacred oak among whose luxuriant branches a serpent dwells, and *cannot* be dislodged,[482] thus becomes apparent. Creeping out from the primordial *ilus*, the mundane snake grows more material and waxes in strength and power with every new evolution.

The Adam Primus, or Kadmon, the Logos of the Jewish mystics, is the same as the Grecian Prometheus, who seeks to rival with the divine wisdom; he is also the Pymander of Hermes, or the POWER OF THE THOUGHT DIVINE, in its most spiritual aspect, for he was less hypostasized by the Egyptians than the two former. These all create men, but fail in their final object. Desiring to endow man with an immortal spirit, in order that by linking the trinity in one, he might gradually return to his primal spiritual state without losing his individuality, Prometheus fails in his attempt to steal the *divine* fire, and is sentenced to expiate his crime on Mount Kazbeck. Prometheus is also the *Logos* of the ancient Greeks, as well as Herakles. In the *Codex Nazaræus*[483] we see Bahak-Zivo deserting the heaven of his father, confessing that though he is the father of the genii, he is unable to "construct creatures," for he is equally unacquainted with Orcus as with "the consuming fire which is wanting in light." And Fetahil, one of the "powers," sits in the "mud" (matter) and wonders why the living fire is so changed.

All of these *Logoi* strove to endow man with the immortal spirit, failed, and nearly all are represented as being punished for the attempt by severe sentences. Those of the early Christian Fathers who like Origen and Clemens Alexandrinus, were well versed in Pagan symbology, having begun their careers as philosophers, felt very much embarrassed. They could not deny the anticipation of their doctrines in the oldest myths. The latest *Logos*, according to their teachings, had also appeared in order to show mankind the way to immortality; and in his desire to endow the world with eternal life through the Pentecostal fire, had lost his life agreeably to the traditional programme. Thus was originated the very awkward explanation of which our modern clergy freely avail themselves, that all these mythic types show the prophetic spirit which, through the Lord's mercy, was afforded even to the heathen idolaters! The Pagans, they assert, had presented in their imagery the great drama of Calvary —hence the resemblance. On the other hand, the philosophers maintained, with unassailable logic, that the pious fathers had simply helped themselves to a ready-made groundwork, either finding it easier than to exert their own imagination, or because of the greater number of ignorant proselytes who were attracted to the new doctrine by such an extraordinary resemblance with their mythologies, at least as far as the outward form of the most fundamental doctrines goes.

PRE-ADAMITE RACES

The allegory of the Fall of man and the fire of Prometheus is also another version of the myth of the rebellion of the proud Lucifer, hurled down to the bottomless pit — Orcus. In the religion of the Brahmans, Moisasure, the Hindu Lucifer, becomes envious of the

---

482 See the "*Cosmogony of Pherecydes*."
483 See a few pages further on the quotation from the "*Codex of the Nazarenes*."

Creator's resplendent light, and at the head of a legion of inferior spirits rebels against Brahma, and declares war against him. Like Hercules, the faithful Titan, who helps Jupiter and restores to him his throne, Siva, the third person of the Hindu trinity, hurls them all from the celestial abode in Honderah, the region of eternal darkness. But here the fallen angels are made to repent of their evil deed, and in the Hindu doctrine they are all afforded the opportunity to progress. In the Greek fiction, Hercules, the Sun-god, descends to Hades to deliver the victims from their tortures; and the Christian Church also makes her incarnate god descend to the dreary Plutonic regions and overcome the rebellious ex-archangel. In their turn the kabalists explain the allegory in a semi-scientific way. Adam the second, or the first-created race which Plato calls gods, and the Bible the Elohim, was not triple in his nature like the earthly man: *i.e.*, he was not composed of soul, spirit, and body, but was a compound of sublimated astral elements into which the "Father" had breathed an immortal, divine spirit. The latter, by reason of its godlike essence, was ever struggling to liberate itself from the bonds of even that flimsy prison; hence the "sons of God," in their imprudent efforts, were the first to trace a future model for the cyclic law. But, man must not be "like one of us," says the Creative Deity, one of the Elohim "intrusted with the fabrication of the lower animal."[484] And thus it was, when the men of the first race had reached the summit of the first cycle, they lost their balance, and their second envelope, the grosser clothing (astral body), dragged them down the opposite arc.

This kabalistic version of the sons of God (or of light) is given in the *Codex Nazaræus*. Bahak-Zivo, the "father of genii, is ordered to 'construct creatures.' " But, as he is "ignorant of Orcus," he fails to do so and calls in Fetahil a still purer spirit to his aid, who fails still worse.

Then steps on the stage of creation the "spirit"[485] (which properly ought to be translated "soul," for it is the *anima mundi*, and which with the Nazarenes and the Gnostics was *feminine*), and perceiving that for Fetahil,[486] the *newest man* (the latest), the splendor was "changed," and that for splendor existed "decrease and damage," awakes Karabtanos,[487] "who was frantic and *without sense and judgment*," and says to him: "Arise; see, the splendor (light) of the *newest* man (Fetahil) has failed (to produce or create men), the decrease of this splendor is visible. Rise up, come with thy MOTHER (the *spiritus*) and free thee from limits by which thou art held, and those more ample than the whole world." After which follows the union of the frantic and blind matter, guided by the insinuations of the spirit (not the *Divine* breath, but the *Astral* spirit, which by its double essence is already tainted with matter) and the offer of the MOTHER being accepted the Spiritus conceives "Seven Figures," which Irenæus is disposed to take for the seven *stellars* (planets) but which represent the

---

484 See Plato's "*Timæus.*"

485 On the authority of Irenæus, Justin Martyr, and the "*Codex*" itself, Dunlap shows that the Nazarenes treated their "spirit," or rather soul, as a female and *Evil Power*. Irenæus, accusing the Gnostics of heresy, calls Christ and the Holy Ghost "the *gnostic pair* that produce the Æons" (Dunlap, "*Sod, the Son of the Man,*" p. 52, footnote).

486 Fetahil was with the Nazarenes the king of light, and the *Creator*; but in this instance he is the unlucky Prometheus, who fails to get hold of the *Living Fire*, necessary for the formation of the divine soul, as he is ignorant of the *secret* name (the ineffable or incommunicable name of the kabalists).

487 The spirit of matter and concupiscence.

seven *capital sins*, the progeny of an astral soul separated from its divine source (spirit) and *matter*, the blind demon of concupiscence. Seeing this, Fetahil extends his hand toward the abyss of matter, and says: "Let the earth exist, just as the abode of the powers has existed." Dipping his hand in the chaos, which he condenses, he creates our planet.[488] Then the *Codex* proceeds to tell how Bahak-Zivo was separated from the Spiritus, and the genii, or angels, from the rebels.[489] Then Mano[490] (the greatest), who dwells with the *greatest* FERHO, calls Kebar-Zivo (known also by the name of Nebat-Iavar bar Iufin-Ifafin), Helm and *Vine* of the food of life[491] he being the *third life*, and, commiserating the rebellious and foolish genii, on account of the magnitude of their ambition, says: "Lord of the genii[492] (Æons), see what the genii, the rebellious angels do, and about what they are consulting.[493] They say, "Let us call forth the world, and let us call the 'powers' into existence. The genii are the *Principes*, the 'sons of Light,' but thou art the '*Messenger of Life*.'"[494]

And in order to counteract the influence of the seven "badly disposed" principles, the progeny of *Spiritus*, CABAR ZIO, the mighty Lord of Splendor, procreates *seven other lives* (the cardinal virtues) who shine in their own form and light "from on high"[495] and thus reestablishes the balance between good and evil, light and darkness. But this creation of beings, without the requisite influx of divine pure breath in them, which was known among the kabalists as the "Living Fire," produced but creatures of matter and astral light.[496] Thus were generated the animals which preceded man on this earth. The spiritual beings, the "sons of light," those who remained faithful to the great *Ferho* (the First Cause of all), constitute the celestial or angelic hierarchy, the Adonim, and the legions of the *never-embodied* spiritual men. The followers of the rebellious and foolish genii, and the descendants of the "witless" seven spirits begotten by "Karabtanos" and the "spiritus," became, in course of time, the "men of our planet,"[497] after having previously passed through every "creation" of every one of the elements. From this stage of life they have been

---

488 See Franck's "*Codex Nazaræus*" and Dunlap's "*Sod, the Son of the Man.*"

489 "*Codex Nazaraeus*," ii. 233.

490 This Mano of the Nazarenes strangely resembles the Hindu Manu, the heavenly man of the "*Rig-Vedas.*"

491 "I am the *true vine* and my Father is the husbandman" (John xv. 1).

492 With the Gnostics, Christ, as well as Michael, who is identical in some respects with him, was the "Chief of the Æons."

493 "*Codex Nazaraeus*," i. 135.

494 Ibid.

495 "*Codex Nazaræus*," iii. 61.

496 The Astral Light, or *anima mundi*, is dual and bisexual. The male part of it is purely divine and spiritual; it is the *Wisdom*; while the female portion (the spiritus of the Nazarenes) is tainted, in one sense, with matter, and therefore is evil already. It is the life-principle of every living creature, and furnishes the astral soul, the fluidic *perisprit* to men, animals, fowls of the air, and everything living. Animals have only the germ of the highest immortal soul as a third principle. It will develop but through a series of countless evolutions; the doctrine of which evolution is contained in the kabalistic axiom: "A stone becomes a plant; a plant a beast; a beast a *man*; a man a *spirit*; and the spirit a god."

497 See Commentary on "*Idra Suta*," by Rabbi Eleashar. § *Sod* means a religious Mystery. Cicero mentions the *sod*, as constituting a portion of the *Idean* Mysteries. "The members of the *Priest-Colleges* were called *Sodales*," says Dunlap, quoting Freund's "*Latin Lexicon*," iv. 448.

traced by Darwin, who shows us how our *highest* forms have been evolved out of the *lowest*. Anthropology dares not follow the kabalist in his metaphysical flights *beyond* this planet, and it is doubtful if its teachers have the courage to search for the *missing link* in the old kabalistic manuscripts.

Thus was set in motion the *first cycle*, which in its rotations *downward*, brought an infinitesimal part of the created *lives* to our planet of *mud*. Arrived at the lowest point of the arc of the cycle which directly preceded life on this earth, the pure divine spark still lingering in the Adam made an effort to separate itself from the astral spirit, for "man was falling gradually into generation," and the fleshy coat was becoming with every action more and more dense.

And now comes a mystery, a *Sod* ; § a secret which Rabbi Simeon[498] imparted but to very few initiates. It was enacted once every seven years during the Mysteries of Samothrace, and the records of it are found self-printed on the leaves of the Thibetan sacred tree, the mysterious KOUNBOUM, in the Lamasery of the holy adepts.[499]

DESCENT OF SPIRIT INTO MATTER

In the shoreless ocean of space radiates the central, spiritual, and *Invisible* sun. The universe is his body, spirit and soul; and after this ideal model are framed ALL THINGS. These three emanations are the three lives, the three degrees of the gnostic *Pleroma*, the three "Kabalistic Faces," for the ANCIENT of the ancient, the holy of the aged, the great En-Soph, "has a form and then he has no form." The invisible "assumed a form when he called the universe into existence,"[500] says the *Sohar*, the Book of splendor. The *first* light is His soul, the Infinite, Boundless, and Immortal breath; under the efflux of which the universe heaves its mighty bosom, infusing *Intelligent* life throughout creation. The *second* emanation condenses cometary matter and produces forms within the cosmic circle; sets the countless worlds floating in the electric space, and infuses *the unintelligent*, blind life-principle into every form. The third, produces the whole universe of physical matter; and as it keeps gradually receding from the Central Divine Light its brightness wanes and it becomes DARKNESS and the BAD — pure matter, the "gross purgations of the celestial fire" of the Hermetists.

When the Central Invisible (the Lord Ferho) saw the efforts of the divine *Scintilla*, unwilling to be dragged lower down into the degradation of matter, to liberate itself, he permitted it to shoot out from itself a *monad*, over which, attached to it as by the finest thread, the Divine Scintilla (the soul) had to watch during its ceaseless peregrinations from one form to another. Thus the monad was shot down into the first form of matter and became encased in stone; then, in course of time, through the combined efforts of *living fire* and *living water*, both of which shone their *reflection* upon the stone, the monad crept out of its prison to sunlight as a lichen. From change to change it went higher and higher; the monad, with every new transformation borrowing more of the radiance of its parent, *Scintilla*, which approached it nearer at every transmigration. For "the First Cause, had

---

498 The author of the "*Sohar*," the great kabalistic work of the first century B.C.
499 See Abbé Huc's works.
500 "*The Sohar*," iii. 288; "*Idra Suta*."

willed it to proceed in this order" and destined it to creep on higher until its physical form became once more the Adam *of dust,* shaped in the image of the Adam Kadmon. Before undergoing its last earthly transformation, the external covering of the monad, from the moment of its conception as an embryo, passes in turn, once more, through the phases of the several kingdoms.

In its fluidic prison it assumes a vague resemblance at various periods of the gestation to plant, reptile, bird, and animal, until it becomes a human embryo.[501] At the birth of the future man, the monad, radiating with all the glory of its immortal parent which watches it from the seventh sphere, becomes *senseless.*[502] It loses all recollection of the past, and returns to consciousness but gradually, when the instinct of childhood gives way to reason and intelligence. After the separation between the life-principle (astral spirit) and the body takes place, the liberated soul — Monad, exultingly rejoins the mother and father spirit, the radiant Augoeides, and the two, merged into one, forever form, with a glory proportioned to the spiritual purity of the past earth-life, the Adam who has completed the circle of necessity, and is freed from the last vestige of his physical encasement. Henceforth, growing more and more radiant at each step of his upward progress, he mounts the shining path that ends at the point from which he started around the GRAND CYCLE.

The whole Darwinian theory of natural selection is included in the first six chapters of the Book of *Genesis.* The "Man" of chapter i. is radically different from the "Adam" of chapter ii., for the former was created "male and female" — that is, bi-sexed — and in the image of God; while the latter, according to verse seven, was formed of the dust of the ground, and became "a living soul," after the Lord God "breathed into his nostrils the breath of life." Moreover, *this Adam* was a male being, and in verse twenty we are told that "there was not found a helpmeet for him." The Adonai, being pure spiritual entities, had no sex, or rather had both sexes united in themselves, like their Creator; and the ancients understood this so well that they represented many of their deities as of dual sex. The Biblical student must either accept this interpretation, or make the passages in the two chapters alluded to absurdly contradict each other. It was such literal acceptance of passages that warranted the atheists in covering the Mosaic account with ridicule, and it is the dead letter of the old text that begets the materialism of our age. Not only are these two races of beings thus clearly indicated in *Genesis,* but even a third and a fourth one are ushered before the reader in chapter iv., where the "sons of God" and the race of "giants" are spoken of.

As we write, there appears in an American paper, *The Kansas City Times,* an account of important discoveries of the remains of a prehistorical *race of giants,* which corroborates the statements of the kabalists and the Bible allegories at the same time. It is worth preserving:

"In his researches among the forests of Western Missouri, Judge E. P. West has discovered a number of conical-shaped mounds, similar in construction to those found in Ohio and Kentucky. These mounds are found upon the high bluffs overlooking the Missouri River, the largest and more prominent being found in Tennessee, Mississippi, and Louisiana. Until about three weeks ago it was not suspected that the mound builders had made this region their home in the prehistoric days; but now it is discovered that this

---

501 Everard, "*Mysteres Physiologiques,*" p. 132.
502 See Plato's "*Timæus.*"

strange and extinct race once occupied this land, and have left an extensive graveyard in a number of high mounds upon the Clay County bluffs.

"As yet, only one of these mounds has been opened. Judge West discovered a skeleton about two weeks ago, and made a report to other members of the society. They accompanied him to the mound, and not far from the surface excavated and took out the remains of two skeletons. The bones are very large — so large, in fact, when compared with an ordinary skeleton of modern date, they appear to have formed part of a giant. The head bones, such as have not rotted away, are monstrous in size. The lower jaw of one skeleton is in a state of preservation, and is double the size of the jaw of a civilized person. The teeth in this jawbone are large, and appear to have been ground down and worn away by contact with roots and carnivorous food. The jaw-bone indicates immense muscular strength. The thigh-bone, when compared with that of an ordinary modern skeleton, looks like that of a horse. The length, thickness, and muscular development are remarkable. But the most peculiar part about the skeleton is the frontal bone. It is very low, and differs radically from any ever seen in this section before. It forms one thick ridge of bone about one inch wide, extending across the eyes. It is a narrow but rather heavy ridge of bone which, instead of extending upward, as it does now in these days of civilization, receded back from the eyebrows, forming a flat head, and thus indicates a very low order of mankind. It is the opinion of the scientific gentlemen who are making these discoveries that these bones are the remains of a prehistoric race of men. They do not resemble the present existing race of Indians, nor are the mounds constructed upon any pattern or model known to have been in use by any race of men now in existence in America. The bodies are discovered in a sitting posture in the mounds, and among the bones are found stone weapons, such as flint knives, flint scrapers, and all of them different in shape to the arrow-heads, war-hatchets, and other stone tools and weapons known to have been in use by the aboriginal Indians of this land when discovered by the whites. The gentlemen who have these curious bones in charge have deposited them with Dr. Foe, on Main street. It is their intention to make further and closer researches in the mounds on the bluffs opposite this city. They will make a report of their labors at the next meeting of the Academy of Science, by which time they expect to be able to make some definite report as to their opinions. It is pretty definitely settled, however, that the skeletons are those of a race of men not now in existence."

The author of a recent and very elaborate work[503] finds some cause for merriment over the union of the sons of God with the "daughters of men," who *were fair*, as alluded to in *Genesis,* and described at great length in that wonderful legend, the *Book of Enoch.* More is the pity, that our most learned and liberal men do not employ their close and merciless logic to repair its one-sidedness by seeking the true spirit which dictated these allegories of old. This spirit was certainly more *scientific* than skeptics are yet prepared to admit. But with

---

503 "*Supernatural Religion; an Inquiry into the Reality of Divine Revelation,*" vol. ii. London, 1875.

every year some new discovery may corroborate their assertions, until the whole of antiquity is vindicated.

One thing, at least, has been shown in the Hebrew text, viz.: that there was one race of purely physical creatures, another purely spiritual. The evolution and "transformation of species" required to fill the gap between the two has been left to abler anthropologists. We can only repeat the philosophy of men of old, which says that the union of these two races produced a third — the Adamite race. Sharing the natures of both its parents, it is equally adapted to an existence in the material and spiritual worlds. Allied to the physical half of man's nature is reason, which enables him to maintain his supremacy over the lower animals, and to subjugate nature to his uses. Allied to his spiritual part is his *conscience*, which will serve as his unerring guide through the besetments of the senses; for conscience is that instantaneous perception between right and wrong, which can only be exercised by the spirit, which, being a portion of the Divine Wisdom and Purity, is absolutely pure and wise. Its promptings are independent of reason, and it can only manifest itself clearly, when unhampered by the baser attractions of our dual nature.

Reason being a faculty of our physical brain, one which is justly defined as that of deducing inferences from premises, and being wholly dependent on the evidence of other senses, cannot be a quality pertaining directly to our divine spirit. The latter *knows* — hence, all reasoning which implies discussion and argument would be useless. So an entity, which, if it must be considered as a direct emanation from the eternal Spirit of wisdom, has to be viewed as possessed of the same attributes as the essence or the whole of which it is a part. Therefore, it is with a certain degree of logic that the ancient theurgists maintained that the *rational* part of man's soul (spirit) never entered wholly into the man's body, but only overshadowed him more or less through the *irrational* or astral soul, which serves as an intermediatory agent, or a medium between spirit and body. The man who has conquered matter sufficiently to receive the direct light from his shining *Augoeides*, feels truth intuitionally; he could not err in his judgment, notwithstanding all the sophisms suggested by cold reason, for he is ILLUMINATED. Hence, prophecy, vaticination, and the so-called Divine inspiration are simply the effects of this illumination from above by our own immortal spirit.

Swedenborg, following the mystical doctrines of the Hermetic philosophers, devoted a number of volumes to the elucidation of the "internal sense" of *Genesis*. Swedenborg was undoubtedly a "natural-born magician," a seer; he was *not* an *adept*. Thus, however closely he may have followed the apparent method of interpretation used by the alchemists and mystic writers, he partially failed; the more so, that the model chosen by him in this method was one who, albeit a great alchemist, was no more of an adept than the Swedish seer himself, in the fullest sense of the word. Eugenius Philalethes had never attained "the highest pyrotechny," to use the diction of the mystic philosophers. But, although both have missed the whole truth in its details, Swedenborg has virtually given the same interpretation of the first chapter of *Genesis* as the Hermetic philosophers. The seer, as well as the initiates, notwithstanding their veiled phraseology, clearly show that the first chapters of *Genesis* relate to the *regeneration*, or a new birth of man, not to the creation of our universe and its crown work — MAN. The fact that the terms of the alchemists, such as *salt*, *sulphur*, and *mercury* are transformed by Swedenborg into *ens, cause,* and *effect*,[504] does not affect the underlying idea of solving the problems of the Mosaic books by the only possible method — that used by the Hermetists — that of correspondences.

His doctrine of correspondence, or Hermetic symbolism, is that of Pythagoras and of the kabalists — "as above, so below." It is also that of the Buddhist philosophers, who, in their still more abstract metaphysics, inverting the usual mode of definition given by our *erudite* scholars, call the invisible types the only reality, and everything else the effects of the causes, or visible prototypes — *illusions*. However contradictory their various elucidations of the *Pentateuch* may appear *on their surface*, every one of them tends to show that the sacred literature of every country, the *Bible* as much as the *Vedas* or the Buddhist *Scriptures*, can only be understood and thoroughly sifted by the light of Hermetic philosophy. The great sages of antiquity, those of the mediæval ages, and the mystical writers of our more modern times also, were all *Hermetists*. Whether the light of truth had illuminated them through their faculty of intuition, or as a consequence of study and regular initiation, virtually, they had accepted the method and followed the path traced to them by such men as Moses, Gautama-Buddha, and Jesus. The truth, symbolized by some alchemists as *dew from heaven*, had descended into their hearts, and they had all gathered it upon the *tops of mountains*, after having spread CLEAN *linen cloths* to receive it; and thus, in one sense, they had secured, each for himself, and in his own way, the *universal solvent*.

How much they were allowed to share it with the public is another question. That veil, which is alleged to have covered the face of Moses, when, after descending from Sinai, he taught his people the Word of God, cannot be withdrawn at the will of the teacher only. It depends on the listeners, whether they will also remove the veil which is "upon their hearts." Paul says it plainly; and his words addressed to the Corinthians can be applied to every man or woman, and of any age in the history of the world. If "their minds are blinded" by the shining skin of divine truth, whether the Hermetic veil be withdrawn or not from the face of the teacher, it cannot be taken away from their heart unless "it *shall turn to the Lord*." But the latter appellation must not be applied to either of the three anthropomorphized personages of the Trinity, but to the "Lord," as understood by Swedenborg and the Hermetic philosophers — the Lord, who is Life and MAN.

The everlasting conflict between the world-religions — Christianity, Judaism, Brahmanism, Paganism, Buddhism, proceeds from this one source: Truth is known but to the few; the rest, unwilling to withdraw the veil from their own hearts, imagine it blinding the eyes of their neighbor. The god of every exoteric religion, including Christianity, not withstanding its pretensions to mystery, is an idol, a fiction, and cannot be anything else. Moses, *closely-veiled*, speaks to the stiff-necked multitudes of Jehovah, the cruel, anthropomorphic deity, as of the highest God, burying deep in the bottom of his heart that truth which cannot be "either spoken of or revealed." Kapila cuts with the sharp sword of his sarcasms the Brahman-Yoggins, who in their mystical visions pretend to see the HIGHEST *one*. Gautama-Buddha conceals, under an impenetrable cloak of metaphysical subtilties, the verity, and is regarded by posterity as *an atheist*. Pythagoras, with his allegorical mysticism and metempsychosis, is held for a clever impostor, and is succeeded in the same estimation

---

504 See "*Heavenly Arcana*."

by other philosophers, like Apollonius and Plotinus, who are generally spoken of as visionaries, if not charlatans. Plato, whose writings were never read by the majority of our *great* scholars but superficially, is accused by many of his translators of absurdities and puerilities, and even of being ignorant of his own language;[505] most likely for saying, in reference to the Supreme, that "a matter of that kind cannot be expressed by words, like other things to be learned";[506] and making Protagoras lay too much stress on the use of "veils." We could fill a whole volume with names of misunderstood sages, whose writings — only because our materialistic critics feel unable to lift the "veil," which shrouds them — pass off in a current way for mystical absurdities. The most important feature of this seemingly incomprehensible mystery lies perhaps in the inveterate habit of the majority of readers to judge a work by its words and insufficiently-expressed ideas, leaving the spirit of it out of the question. Philosophers of quite different schools may be often found to use a multitude of different expressions, some dark and metaphorical — all figurative, and yet treating of the same subject. Like the thousand divergent rays of a globe of fire, every ray leads, nevertheless, to the central point, so every mystic philosopher, whether he be a devotedly pious enthusiast like Henry More; an irascible alchemist, using a Billingsgate phraseology — like his adversary, Eugenius Philalethes; or an *atheist* (?) like Spinoza, all had one and the same object in view — MAN. It is Spinoza, however, who furnishes perhaps the truest key to a portion of this unwritten secret. While Moses forbids "graven images" of Him whose name is not to be taken in vain, Spinoza goes farther. He clearly infers that God must not be so much as *described*. Human language is totally unfit to give an idea of this "Being" who is altogether unique. Whether it is Spinoza or the Christian theology that is more right in their premises and conclusion, we leave the reader to judge for himself. Every attempt to the contrary leads a nation to anthropomorphize the deity in whom it believes, and the result is that given by Swedenborg. Instead of stating that God made man after his own image, we ought in truth to say that "man *imagines* God after his image,"[507] forgetting that he has set up his own reflection for worship.

THE TRIUNE NATURE OF MAN

Where, then, lies the true, real secret so much talked about by the Hermetists? That there was and there is a secret, no candid student of esoteric literature will ever doubt. Men of genius — as many of the Hermetic philosophers undeniably were — would not have made fools of themselves by trying to fool others for several thousand consecutive years. That this great secret, commonly termed "the philosopher's stone," had a spiritual as well as a physical meaning attached to it, was suspected in all ages. The author of *Remarks on Alchemy and the Alchemists* very truly observes that the subject of the Hermetic art is MAN, and the object of the art is the perfection of man.[508] But we cannot agree with him that only those whom he terms "money-loving sots," ever attempted to carry a purely *moral* design (of the alchemists) into the field of physical science. The fact alone that man, in their eyes, is a trinity, which they divide into *Sol*, water of *mercury*, and *sulphur*, which is the *secret fire*, or,

---

505 Burges, Preface.
506 "*Seventh Letter.*"
507 "*The True Christian Religion.*"
508 E. A. Hitchcock, "*Swedenborg, a Hermetic Philosopher.*"

to speak plain, into *body, soul,* and *spirit,* shows that there is a physical side to the question. Man is the philosopher's *stone* spiritually — *"a triune or trinity in unity,"* as Philalethes expresses it. But he is also that stone physically. The latter is but the effect of the cause, and the cause is the universal solvent of everything — divine spirit. Man is a correlation of chemical physical forces, as well as a correlation of spiritual powers. The latter react on the physical powers of man in proportion to the development of the earthly man. "The work is carried to perfection according to the virtue of a body, soul, and spirit," says an alchemist; "for the body would never be penetrable were it not for the *spirit,* nor would the spirit be permanent in its supra-perfect *tincture,* were it not for the body; nor could these two act one upon another without the soul, *for the spirit is an invisible thing,* nor doth it ever appear without another GARMENT, which garment is the SOUL."[509]

The "philosophers by fire" asserted, through their chief, Robert Fludd, that sympathy is the offspring of light, and "antipathy hath its beginning from darkness." Moreover, they taught, with other kabalists, that "contrarieties in nature doth proceed from one eternal essence, or from the root of all things." Thus, the first cause is the parent-source of good as well as of evil. The creator — who is *not* the Highest God — is the father of matter, which is *bad,* as well as of spirit, which, emanating from the highest, invisible cause, passes through him like through a vehicle, and pervades the whole universe. "It is most certain," remarks Robertus di Fluctibus (Robert Fludd), "that, as there are an infinity of *visible* creatures, so there is an endless variety of invisible ones, of divers natures, in the universal machine. Through the mysterious name of God, which Moses was so desirous of him (Jehova) to hear and know, when he received from him this answer, *Jehova is my everlasting name.* As for the other name, it is so pure and simple that it *cannot be articulated, or compounded, or truly expressed by man's voice* . . . all the other names are wholly comprehended within it, for it contains the property as well of *Nolunty* as *volunty,* of privation as position, of death as life, of cursing as blessing, of evil as good (though nothing ideally is bad in him), of hatred and discord, and consequently of sympathy and antipathy."[510]

THE LOWEST CREATURES IN THE SCALE OF BEING

Lowest in the scale of being are those invisible creatures called by the kabalists the "elementary." There are three distinct classes of these. The highest, in intelligence and cunning, are the so-called terrestrial spirits, of which we will speak more categorically in other parts of this work. Suffice to say, for the present, that they are the *larvæ,* or shadows of those who have lived on earth, have refused all spiritual light, remained and died deeply immersed in the mire of matter, and from whose sinful souls the immortal spirit has gradually separated. The second class is composed of the invisible antitypes of the men *to be* born. No form can come into objective existence — from the highest to the lowest — before the abstract ideal of this form — or, as Aristotle would call it, the *privation* of this form — is called forth. Before an artist paints a picture every feature of it exists already in his imagination; to have enabled us to discern a watch, this particular watch must have existed in its abstract form in the watchmaker's mind. So with future men.

---

509 *"Ripley Revived,"* 1678.
510 *"Mosaicall Philosophy,"* p. 173. 1659.

According to Aristotle's doctrine, there are three principles of natural bodies: privation, matter, and form. These principles may be applied in this particular case. The privation of the child which is to be we will locate in the invisible mind of the great Architect of the Universe — privation not being considered in the Aristotelic philosophy as a principle in the composition of bodies, but as an external property in their production; for the production is a change by which the matter passes from the shape it has not to that which it assumes. Though the privation of the unborn child's form, as well as of the future form of the unmade watch, is that which is neither substance nor extension nor quality as yet, nor any kind of existence, it is still something which *is*, though its outlines, in order to be, must acquire an objective form — the abstract must become concrete, in short. Thus, as soon as this privation of matter is transmitted by energy to universal ether, it becomes a material form, however sublimated. If modern science teaches that *human* thought "affects the matter of another universe simultaneously with this," how can he who believes in an Intelligent First Cause, deny that the divine thought is equally transmitted, by the same law of energy, to our common mediator, the universal ether — the world-soul? And, if so, then it must follow that once there the divine thought manifests itself objectively, energy faithfully reproducing the outlines of that whose "privation" was first born in the divine mind. Only it must not be understood that this *thought* creates matter. No; it creates but the design for the future form; the matter which serves to make this design having always been in existence, and having been prepared to form a human body, through a series of progressive transformations, as the result of evolution. Forms pass; ideas that created them and the material which gave them objectiveness, remain. These models, as yet devoid of immortal spirits, are "elementals," — properly speaking, *psychic embryos* — which, when their time arrives, die out of the invisible world, and are born into this visible one as human infants, receiving in *transitu* that divine breath called spirit which completes the perfect man. This class cannot communicate *objectively* with men.

ELEMENTALS SPECIFICALLY DESCRIBED

The third class are the "elementals" proper, which never evolve into human beings, but occupy, as it were, a specific step of the ladder of being, and, by comparison with the others, may properly be called nature-spirits, or cosmic agents of nature, each being confined to its own element and never transgressing the bounds of others. These are what Tertullian called the "princes of the powers of the air."

This class is believed to possess but one of the three attributes of man. They have neither immortal spirits nor tangible bodies; only astral forms, which partake, in a distinguishing degree, of the element to which they belong and also of the ether. They are a combination of sublimated matter and a rudimental mind. Some are changeless, but still have no separate individuality, acting collectively, so to say. Others, of certain elements and species, change form under a fixed law which kabalists explain. The most solid of their bodies is ordinarily just immaterial enough to escape perception by our physical eyesight, but not so unsubstantial but that they can be perfectly recognized by the inner, or clairvoyant vision. They not only exist and can all live in ether, but can handle and direct it for the production of physical effects, as readily as we can compress air or water for the same purpose by pneumatic and hydraulic apparatus; in which occupation they are readily helped by the "human elementary." More than this; they can so condense it as to make to themselves tangible bodies, which by their Protean powers they can cause to assume such likeness as they choose, by taking as their models the portraits they find stamped in the memory of the persons present. It is not necessary that the sitter should be thinking at the moment of the one represented. His image may have faded many years before. The mind receives indelible impression even from chance acquaintance or persons encountered but once. As a few seconds exposure of the sensitized photograph plate is all that is requisite to preserve indefinitely the image of the sitter, so is it with the mind.

According to the doctrine of Proclus, the uppermost regions from the zenith of the universe to the moon belonged to the gods or planetary spirits, according to their hierarchies and classes. The highest among them were the twelve *ŭper-ouranioi*, or supercelestial gods, having whole legions of subordinate demons at their command. They are followed next in rank and power by the *egkosmioi*, the intercosmic gods, each of these presiding over a great number of demons, to whom they impart their power and change it from one to another at will. These are evidently the personified forces of nature in their mutual correlation, the latter being represented by the third class or the "elementals" we have just described.

PROCLUS ON THE BEINGS OF THE AIR

Further on he shows, on the principle of the Hermetic axiom — of types, and prototypes — that the lower spheres have their subdivisions and classes of beings as well as the upper celestial ones, the former being always subordinate to the higher ones. He held that the four elements are all filled with *demons*, maintaining with Aristotle that the universe is full, and that there is no void in nature. The demons of the earth, air, fire, and water are of an elastic, ethereal, semi-corporeal essence. It is these classes which officiate as intermediate agents between the gods and men. Although lower in intelligence than the *sixth* order of the higher demons, these beings preside directly over the elements and organic life. They direct the growth, the inflorescence, the properties, and various changes of plants. They are the personified ideas or virtues shed from the heavenly *ulê* into the inorganic matter; and, as the vegetable kingdom is one remove higher than the mineral, these emanations from the celestial gods take form and being in the plant, they become *its soul*. It is that which Aristotle's doctrine terms the *form* in the three principles of natural bodies, classified by him as privation, matter, and form. His philosophy teaches that besides the original matter, another principle is necessary to complete the triune nature of every particle, and this is form; an invisible, but still, in an ontological sense of the word, a substantial being, really distinct from matter proper. Thus, in an animal or a plant, besides the bones, the flesh, the nerves, the brains, and the blood, in the former, and besides the pulpy matter, tissues, fibres, and juice in the latter, which blood and juice, by circulating through the veins and fibres, nourishes all parts of both animal and plant; and besides the animal spirits, which are the principles of motion; and the chemical energy which is transformed into vital force in the green leaf, there must be a substantial form, which Aristotle called in the horse, the *horse's soul*; Proclus, the *demon* of every mineral, plant, or animal, and the mediæval philosophers, the *elementary spirits* of the four kingdoms.

All this is held in our century as metaphysics and gross superstition. Still, on strictly ontological principles, there is, in these old hypotheses, some shadow of probability, some clew to the perplexing "missing links" of exact science. The latter has become so dogmatical of late, that all that lies beyond the ken of *inductive* science is termed imaginary; and we find Professor Joseph Le Conte stating that some of the best scientists "ridicule the use of the term 'vital force,' or vitality, as a remnant of *superstition*."[511] De Candolle suggests the term "vital movement," instead of vital force;[512] thus preparing for a final scientific leap which will transform the immortal, thinking man, into an automaton with a clock-work inside him. "But," objects Le Conte, "can we conceive of movement without force? And if the movement is peculiar, so also is *the form of force.*"

VARIOUS NAMES FOR ELEMENTALS

In the Jewish *Kabala*, the nature-spirits were known under the general name of *Shedim* and divided into four classes. The Persians called them all *devs*; the Greeks, indistinctly designated them as *demons*; the Egyptians knew them as *afrites*. The ancient Mexicans, says Kaiser, believed in numerous spirit-abodes, into one of which the shades of innocent children were placed until final disposal; into another, situated in the sun, ascended the valiant souls of heroes; while the hideous spectres of incorrigible sinners were sentenced to wander and despair in subterranean caves, held in the bonds of the earth-atmosphere, unwilling and unable to liberate themselves. They passed their time in communicating with mortals, and frightening those who could see them. Some of the African tribes know them as *Yowahoos*. In the Indian Pantheon there are no less than 330,000,000 of various kinds of spirits, including elementals, which latter were termed by the Brahmans the Daityas. These beings are known by the adepts to be attracted toward certain quarters of the heavens by something of the same mysterious property which makes the magnetic needle turn toward the north, and certain plants to obey the same attraction. The various races are also believed to have a special sympathy with certain human temperaments, and to more readily exert power over such than others. Thus, a bilious, lymphatic, nervous, or sanguine person would be affected favorably or otherwise by conditions of the astral light, resulting from the different aspects of the planetary bodies. Having reached this general principle, after recorded observations extending over an indefinite series of years, or ages, the adept astrologer would require only to know what the planetary aspects were at a given anterior date, and to apply his knowledge of the succeeding changes in the heavenly bodies, to be able to trace, with approximate accuracy, the varying fortunes of the personage whose horoscope was required, and even to predict the future. The accuracy of the horoscope would depend, of course, no less upon the astrologer's knowledge of the occult forces and races of nature, than upon his astronomical erudition.

Eliphas Levi expounds with reasonable clearness, in his *Dogme et Rituel de la Haute Magie*, the law of reciprocal influences between the planets and their combined effect upon the mineral, vegetable, and animal kingdoms, as well as upon ourselves. He states that the astral atmosphere is as constantly changing from day to day, and from hour to hour, as the

---

511 *"Correlation of Vital with Chemical and Physical Forces,"* by J. Le Conte.
512 *"Archives des Sciences,"* vol. xlv., p. 345. December, 1872.

air we breathe. He quotes approvingly the doctrine of Paracelsus that every man, animal, and plant bears external and internal evidences of the influences dominant at the moment of germinal development. He repeats the old kabalistic doctrine, that nothing is unimportant in nature, and that even so small a thing as the birth of one child upon our insignificant planet has its effect upon the universe, as the whole universe has its own reactive influence upon him.

"The stars," he remarks, "are linked to each other by attractions which hold them in equilibrium and cause them to move with regularity through space. This network of light stretches from all the spheres to all the spheres, and there is not a point upon any planet to which is not attached one of these indestructible threads. The precise locality, as well as the hour of birth, should then be calculated by the true adept in astrology; then, when he shall have made the exact calculation of the astral influences, it remains for him to count the chances of his position in life, the helps or hindrances he is likely to encounter . . . and his natural impulses toward the accomplishment of his destiny." He also asserts that the individual force of the person, as indicating his ability to conquer difficulties and subdue unfavorable propensities, and so carve out his fortune, or to passively await what blind fate may bring, must be taken into account.

A consideration of the subject from the standpoint of the ancients, affords us, it will be seen, a very different view from that taken by Professor Tyndall in his famous Belfast address. "To supersensual beings," says he, "which, however potent and invisible, were nothing but species of *human creatures*, perhaps raised from among mankind, and retaining all human passions and appetites, were handed over the rule and governance of natural phenomena."

To enforce his point, Mr. Tyndall conveniently quotes from Euripides the familiar passage in Hume: "The gods toss all into confusion, mix everything with its reverse, that all of us, from our ignorance and uncertainty, may pay them the more worship and reverence." Although enunciating in *Chrysippus* several Pythagorean doctrines, Euripides is considered by every ancient writer as heterodox, therefore the quotation proceeding from this philosopher does not at all strengthen Mr. Tyndall's argument.

As to the *human* spirit, the notions of the older philosophers and mediæval kabalists while differing in some particulars, agreed on the whole; so that the doctrine of one may be viewed as the doctrine of the other. The most substantial difference consisted in the location of the immortal or divine spirit of man. While the ancient Neo-platonists held that the Augoeides never descends hypostatically into the living man, but only sheds more or less its radiance on the inner man — the astral soul — the kabalists of the middle ages maintained that the spirit, detaching itself from the ocean of light and spirit, entered into man's soul, where it remained through life imprisoned in the astral capsule. This difference was the result of the belief of Christian kabalists, more or less, in the dead letter of the allegory of the fall of man. The soul, they said, became, through the fall of Adam, contaminated with the world of matter, or Satan. Before it could appear with its enclosed divine spirit in the presence of the Eternal, it had to purify itself of the impurities of darkness. They compared "the spirit imprisoned within the soul to a drop of water enclosed within a capsule of gelatine and thrown in the ocean; so long as the capsule remains whole the drop of water remains isolated; break the envelope and the drop becomes a part of the ocean — its individual existence has ceased. So it is with the spirit. As long as it is enclosed in its plastic mediator, or soul, it has an individual existence. Destroy the capsule, a result which may occur from the agonies of withered conscience, crime, and moral disease, and the spirit returns back to its original abode. Its individuality is gone."

On the other hand, the philosophers who explained the "fall into generation" in their own way, viewed spirit as something wholly distinct from the soul. They allowed its presence in the astral capsule only so far as the spiritual emanations or rays of the "shining one" were concerned. Man and soul had to conquer their immortality by ascending toward the unity with which, if successful, they were finally linked, and into which they were absorbed, so to say. The individualization of man after death depended on the spirit, not on his soul and body. Although the word "personality," in the sense in which it is usually understood, is an absurdity, if applied literally to our immortal essence, still the latter is a distinct entity, immortal and eternal, *per se;* and, as in the case of criminals beyond redemption, when the shining thread which links the spirit to the soul, from the moment of the birth of a child, is violently snapped, and the disembodied entity is left to share the fate of the lower animals, to gradually dissolve into ether, and have its individuality annihilated — even then the spirit remains a distinct being. It becomes a planetary spirit, an angel; for *the gods of the Pagan or the archangels of the Christian,* the direct emanations of the First Cause, notwithstanding the hazardous statement of Swedenborg, *never were or will be men,* on our planet, at least.

This specialization has been in all ages the stumbling-block of metaphysicians. The whole esoterism of the Buddhistical philosophy is based on this mysterious teaching, understood by so few persons, and so totally misrepresented by many of the most learned scholars. Even metaphysicians are too inclined to confound the effect with the cause. A person may have won his immortal life, and remain the same *inner-self* he was on earth, throughout eternity; but this does not imply necessarily that he must either remain the Mr. Smith or Brown he was on earth, or lose his individuality. Therefore, the astral soul and terrestrial body of man may, in the dark Hereafter, be absorbed into the cosmical ocean of sublimated elements, and cease to feel his *ego,* if this *ego* did not deserve to soar higher; and the divine spirit still remain an unchanged entity, though this terrestrial experience of his emanations may be totally obliterated at the instant of separation from the unworthy vehicle.

If the "spirit," or the divine portion of the soul, is preëxistent as a distinct being from all eternity, as Origen, Synesius, and other Christian fathers and philosophers taught, and if it is the same, and nothing more than the metaphysically-objective soul, how can it be otherwise than eternal? And what matters it in such a case, whether man leads an animal or a pure life, if, do what he may, he can never lose his individuality? This doctrine is as pernicious in its consequences as that of vicarious atonement. Had the latter dogma, in company with the false idea that we are all immortal, been demonstrated to the world in its true light, humanity would have been bettered by its propagation. Crime and sin would be avoided, not for fear of earthly punishment, or of a ridiculous hell, but for the sake of that which lies the most deeply rooted in our inner nature — the desire of an individual and distinct life in the hereafter, the positive assurance that we cannot win it unless we "take the kingdom of heaven by violence," and the conviction that neither human prayers nor the blood of another man will save us from individual destruction after death, unless we firmly link ourselves during our terrestrial life with our own immortal spirit — our GOD.

SWEDENBORGIAN VIEWS ON SOUL-DEATH

Pythagoras, Plato, Timæus of Locris, and the whole Alexandrian school derived the soul from the universal World-Soul; and the latter was, according to their own teachings — ether; something of such a fine nature as to be perceived only by our inner sight. Therefore, it cannot be the essence of the Monas, or *cause,* because the *anima mundi* is but the effect, the objective emanation of the former. Both the human spirit and soul are preëxistent. But, while the former exists as a distinct entity, an individualization, the soul exists as preexisting matter, an unscient portion of an intelligent whole. Both were originally formed from the Eternal Ocean of Light; but as the theosophists expressed it, there is a visible as well as invisible spirit in fire. They made a difference between the *anima bruta* and the *anima divina.* Empedocles firmly believed all men and animals to possess two souls; and in Aristotle we find that he calls one the reasoning soul — νοῆς , and the other, the animal soul — ψυχή . According to these philosophers, the reasoning soul comes from *without* the universal soul, and the other from *within.* This divine and superior region, in which they located the invisible and supreme deity, was considered by them (by Aristotle himself) as a fifth element, purely spiritual and divine, whereas the *anima mundi* proper was considered as composed of a fine, igneous, and ethereal nature spread throughout the universe, in short — ether.

The Stoics, the greatest materialists of ancient days, excepted the Invisible God and Divine Soul (Spirit) from any such a corporeal nature. Their modern commentators and admirers, greedily seizing the opportunity, built on this ground the supposition that the Stoics believed in neither God nor soul. But Epicurus, whose doctrine militating directly against the agency of a Supreme Being and gods, in the formation or government of the world, placed him far above the Stoics in atheism and materialism, taught, nevertheless, that the soul is of a fine, tender essence, formed from the smoothest, roundest, and finest atoms, which description still brings us to the same sublimated ether. Arnobius, Tertullian, Irenæus, and Origen, notwithstanding their Christianity, believed, with the more modern Spinoza and Hobbes, that the soul was corporeal, though of a very fine nature.

This doctrine of the possibility of losing one's soul and, hence, individuality, militates with the ideal theories and progressive ideas of some spiritualists, though Swedenborg fully adopts it. They will never accept the kabalistic doctrine which teaches that it is only through observing the law of harmony that individual life hereafter can be obtained; and that the farther the inner and outer man deviate from this fount of harmony, whose source lies in our divine spirit, the more difficult it is to regain the ground.

But while the spiritualists and other adherents of Christianity have little if any perception of this fact of the possible death and obliteration of the human personality by the separation of the immortal part from the perishable, the Swedenborgians fully comprehend it. One of the most respected ministers of the New Church, the Rev. Chauncey Giles, D.D., of New York, recently elucidated the subject in a public discourse as follows: Physical death, or the death of the body, was a provision of the divine economy for the benefit of man, a provision by means of which he attained the higher ends of his being. But there is another death which is the interruption of the divine order and the destruction of every human element in man's nature, and every possibility of human happiness. This is the spiritual death, which takes place before the dissolution of the body. "There may be a vast development of man's natural mind without that development being accompanied by a particle of love of God, or of unselfish love of man." When one falls into a love of self and love of the world, with its pleasures, losing the divine love of God and of the neighbor, he falls from life to death. The higher principles which constitute the essential elements of his humanity perish, and he lives only on the natural plane of his faculties. Physically he exists, spiritually he is dead. To all that pertain to the higher and the only enduring phase of existence he is as much dead as his body becomes dead to all the activities, delights, and sensations of the world when the spirit has left it.

This spiritual death results from disobedience of the laws of spiritual life, which is followed by the same penalty as the disobedience of the laws of the natural life. But the spiritually dead have still their delights; they have their intellectual endowments and power, and intense activities. All the animal delights are theirs, and to multitudes of men and women these constitute the highest ideal of human happiness. The tireless pursuit of riches, of the amusements and entertainments of social life; the cultivation of graces of manner, of taste in dress, of social preferment, of scientific distinction, intoxicate and enrapture these dead-alive; but, the eloquent preacher remarks, "these creatures, with all their graces, rich attire, and brilliant accomplishments, are dead in the eye of the Lord and the angels, and when measured by the only true and immutable standard have no more genuine life than skeletons whose flesh has turned to dust." A high development of the intellectual faculties does not imply spiritual and true life. Many of our greatest scientists are but animate corpses — they have no spiritual sight because their spirits have left them. So we might go through all ages, examine all occupations, weigh all human attainments, and investigate all forms of society, and we would find these *spiritually dead* everywhere.

EARTH-BOUND HUMAN SOULS

Pythagoras taught that the entire universe is one vast system of mathematically correct combinations. Plato shows the deity *geometrizing*. The world is sustained by the same law of equilibrium and harmony upon which it was built. The centripetal force could not manifest itself without the centrifugal in the harmonious revolutions of the spheres; all forms are the product of this dual force in nature. Thus, to illustrate our case, we may designate the spirit as the centrifugal, and the soul as the centripetal, spiritual energies. When in perfect harmony, both forces produce one result; break or damage the centripetal motion of the earthly soul tending toward the centre which attracts it; arrest its progress by clogging it with a heavier weight of matter than it can bear, and the harmony of the whole, which was its life, is destroyed. Individual life can only be continued if sustained by this two-fold force. The least deviation from harmony damages it; when it is destroyed beyond redemption the forces separate and the form is gradually annihilated. After the death of the depraved and the wicked, arrives the critical moment. If during life the ultimate and desperate effort of the inner-self to reunite itself with the faintly-glimmering ray of its divine parent is neglected; if this ray is allowed to be more and more shut out by the thickening crust of matter, the soul, once freed from the body, follows its earthly attractions, and is magnetically drawn into and held within the dense fogs of the material atmosphere. Then it begins to sink lower and lower, until it finds itself, when returned to consciousness, in what the ancients termed *Hades.* The annihilation of such a soul is never instantaneous; it may last centuries, perhaps; for nature never proceeds by jumps and starts, and the astral soul being formed of elements, the law of evolution must bide its time. Then begins the fearful law of compensation, the *Yin-youan* of the Buddhists.

This class of spirits are called the "terrestrial" or "*earthly* elementary," in contradistinction to the other classes, as we have shown in the introductory chapter. In the East they are known as the "Brothers of the Shadow." Cunning, low, vindictive, and seeking to retaliate their sufferings upon humanity, they become, until final annihilation, vampires, ghouls, and prominent actors. These are the leading "stars" on the great spiritual stage of "materialization," which phenomena they perform with the help of the more intelligent of the genuine-born "elemental" creatures, which hover around and welcome them with delight in their own spheres. Henry Kunrath, the great German kabalist, has on a plate of his rare work, *Amphitheatri Sapientiæ Æternæ* , representations of the four classes of these human "elementary spirits." Once past the threshold of the sanctuary of initiation, once that an adept has lifted the "Veil of Isis," the mysterious and jealous goddess, he has nothing to fear; but till then he is in constant danger.

Although Aristotle himself, anticipating the modern physiologists, regarded the human mind as a material substance, and ridiculed the hylozoists, nevertheless he fully believed in the existence of a "double" soul, or spirit and soul.[513] He laughed at Strabo for believing that any particles of matter, *per se,* could have life and intellect in themselves sufficient to fashion by degrees such a multiform world as ours.[514] Aristotle is indebted for the sublime morality of his Nichomachean Ethics to a thorough study of the *Pythagoric Ethical Fragments;* for the latter can be easily shown to have been the source at which he gathered his ideas, though he might not have sworn "by him who the tetractys found."[515] Finally, what do we know so certain about Aristotle? His philosophy is so abstruse that he constantly leaves his reader to supply by the imagination the missing links of his logical deductions. Moreover, we know that before his works ever reached our scholars, who delight in his seemingly atheistical arguments in support of his doctrine of fate, these works passed through too many hands to have remained immaculate. From Theophrastus, his legator, they passed to Neleus, whose heirs kept them mouldering in subterranean caves for nearly 150 years;[516] after which, we learn that his manuscripts were copied and much augmented by Apellicon of Theos, who supplied such paragraphs as had become illegible, by conjectures of his own, probably many of these drawn from the depths of his inner consciousness. Our scholars of the nineteenth century might certainly profit well by Aristotle's example, were they as anxious to imitate him practically as they are to throw his inductive method and materialistic theories at the head of the Platonists. We invite them to collect *facts* as carefully as he did, instead of denying those they know nothing about.

---

513 Aristotle, "*De Generat. et Corrupt.*," lib. ii.

514 "*De Part.*," an. lib. i., c. I.

515 A Pythagorean oath. The Pythagoreans swore by their master.

516 See Lempriere, "*Classical Dictionary.*"

What we have said in the introductory chapter and elsewhere, of mediums and the tendency of their mediumship, is not based upon conjecture, but upon actual experience and observation. There is scarcely one phase of mediumship, of either kind, that we have not seen exemplified during the past twenty-five years, in various countries. India, Thibet, Borneo, Siam, Egypt, Asia Minor, America (North and South), and other parts of the world, have each displayed to us its peculiar phase of mediumistic phenomena and magical power. Our varied experience has taught us two important truths, viz.: that for the exercise of the latter personal purity and the exercise of a trained and indomitable will-power are indispensable; and that spiritualists can never assure themselves of the genuineness of mediumistic manifestations, unless they occur in the light and under such reasonable test conditions as would make an attempted fraud instantly noticed.

For fear of being misunderstood, we would remark that while, as a rule, physical phenomena are produced by the nature-spirits, of their own motion and to please their own fancy, still good disembodied human spirits, under *exceptional* circumstances, such as the aspiration of a pure heart or the occurrence of some favoring emergency, can manifest their presence by any of the phenomena *except personal materialization*. But it must be a mighty attraction indeed to draw a pure, disembodied spirit from its radiant home into the foul atmosphere from which it escaped upon leaving its earthly body.

Magi and theurgic philosophers objected most severely to the "evocation of souls." "Bring her (the soul) not forth, lest in departing she retain something," says Psellus [517]

"It becomes you not to behold them *before your body is initiated*, Since, by always alluring, they seduce the souls of the uninitiated,"

says the same philosopher, in another passage.[518]

They objected to it for several good reasons. 1. "It is extremely difficult to distinguish a good dæmon from a bad one," says Iamblichus. 2. If a human soul succeeds in penetrating the density of the earth's atmosphere — always oppressive to her, often hateful — still there is a danger the soul is unable to come into proximity with the material world without that she cannot avoid; "departing, she *retains* something," that is to say, contaminating her purity, for which she has to suffer more or less after her departure. Therefore, the true theurgist will avoid causing any more suffering to this pure denizen of the higher sphere than is absolutely required by the interests of humanity. It is only the practitioner of black magic who compels the presence, by the powerful incantations of necromancy, of the tainted souls of such as have lived bad lives, and are ready to aid his selfish designs. Of intercourse with the Augoeides, through the mediumistic powers of *subjective* mediums, we elsewhere speak. The theurgists employed chemicals and mineral substances to chase away evil spirits. Of the latter, a stone called *Mnizourin* was one of the most powerful agents.

"When you shall see a *terrestrial* demon approaching,

Exclaim, and sacrifice the stone Mnizurin,"

exclaims a Zoroastrian oracle (*Psel.*, 40).

---

517 Psel. in Alieb, "*Chaldean Oracles.*"
518 Proc. in 1 "*Alieb.*"

And now, to descend from the eminence of theurgico-magian poetry to the "unconscious" magic of our present century, and the prose of a modern kabalist, we will review it in the following: In Dr. Morin's *Journal de Magnêtisme,* published a few years since in Paris, at a time when the "table-turning" was raging in France, a curious letter was published.

"Believe me, sir," wrote the anonymous correspondent, "that there are no spirits, no ghosts, no angels, no demons *enclosed in a table;* but, all of these can be found there, nevertheless, for that depends on *our own wills* and our imaginations. . . . This MENSAbulism[519] is an ancient phenomenon . . . misunderstood by us moderns, but natural, for all that, and which pertains to physics and psychology; unfortunately, it had to remain incomprehensible until the discovery of electricity and heliography, as, to explain a fact of spiritual nature, we are obliged to base ourselves on a corresponding fact of a material order. . . .

"As we all know, the daguerreotype-plate may be impressed, not only by objects, but also by their reflections. Well, the phenomenon in question, which ought to be named *mental photography,* produces, besides *realities,* the dreams of our imagination, with such a fidelity that very often we become unable to distinguish a copy taken from *one present,* from a negative obtained of an *image.* . . . "The *magnetization* of a table or of a person is absolutely identical in its results; it is the saturation of a foreign body by either the *intelligent* vital electricity, or the thought of the magnetizer and those present."

Nothing can give a better or a more just idea of it than the electric battery gathering the fluid on its conductor, to obtain thereof a *brute* force which manifests itself in sparks of light, etc. Thus, the electricity accumulated on an isolated body acquires a power of reaction equal to the action, either for charging, magnetizing, decomposing, inflaming, or for discharging its vibrations far away. These are the visible effects of the *blind,* or crude electricity produced by blind elements — the word blind being used by the table itself in contradistinction to the *intelligent* electricity. But there evidently exists a corresponding electricity produced by the cerebral pile of man; this *soul-electricity,* this spiritual and universal ether, which is the *ambient, middle nature of the metaphysical universe,* or rather of the *incorporeal* universe, has to be studied before it is admitted by science, which, having no idea of it, will never know anything of the great phenomenon of life until she does.

> "It appears that to manifest itself the cerebral electricity requires the help of the ordinary statical electricity; when the latter is lacking in the atmosphere — when the air is very damp, for instance — you can get little or nothing of either tables or mediums. . . . "There is no need for the ideas to be formulated very precisely in the brains of the persons present; the *table* discovers and formulates them *itself,* in either prose or verse, but always correctly; the table requires time to compose a verse; it begins, then it erases a word, corrects it, and sometimes sends back the epigram to our address . . . if the persons present are in sympathy with each other, *it* jokes and laughs with us as any living person could. As to the things of the exterior world, it has to content

---

519 From the Latin word *mensa* — table. This curious letter is copied in full in *"La Science des Esprits,"* by Eliphas Levi.

itself with conjectures, as well as ourselves; *it* (the table) composes little philosophical systems, discusses and maintains them as the most cunning rhetorician might. In short, it creates itself a conscience and a reason properly belonging to itself, but with the materials it finds in us. . . .

"The Americans are persuaded that they talk with their dead; some think (more truly) that these are *spirits*; others take them for angels; others again for devils . . . (the *intelligence*) assuming the shape which fits the conviction and preconceived opinion of every one; so did the initiates of the temples of Serapis, of Delphi, and other theurgico-medical establishments of the same kind. They were convinced beforehand that they would communicate with their gods; and *they* never failed.

"We, who well know the value of the phenomenon . . . are perfectly sure that after having charged the table with our magnetic *efflux*, we have called to life, or created an intelligence analogous to our own, which like ourselves is endowed with a free will, can talk and discuss with us, with a degree of superior lucidity, considering that the resultant is stronger than the individual, or rather the whole is larger than a part of it. . . . We must not accuse Herodotus of telling us fibs when he records the most extraordinary circumstances, for we must hold them to be as true and correct as the rest of historical facts which are to be found in all the Pagan writers of antiquity.

"The phenomenon is as old as the world. . . . The priests of India and China practiced it before the Egyptians and the Greeks. The savages and the Esquimaux know it well. It is the phenomenon of Faith, sole source of every prodigy," and it will be done to you according to *your faith*. The one who enunciated this profound doctrine was verily the incarnated word of Truth; he neither deceived himself, nor wanted to deceive others; he expounded an axiom which we now repeat, without much hope of seeing it accepted.

"Man is a microcosm, or a little world; he carries in him a fragment of the great *All*, in a chaotic state. The task of our half-gods is to disentangle from it the share belonging to them by an incessant mental and material labor. They have their task to do, the perpetual invention of new products, of new moralities, and the proper arrangement of the crude and formless material furnished them by the Creator, who created them in His own image, that they should create in their turn and so complete here the work of the Creation; an immense labor which can be achieved only when the *whole* will become so perfect, that it will be like unto God Himself, and thus able to survive to itself. We are very far yet from that final moment, for we can say that everything is to be done, to be undone, and *outdone* as yet on our globe, institutions, machinery, and products.

"*Mens non solum agitat sed creat molem.*"

"We live in this life, in an ambient, intellectual centre, which entertains between human beings and things a necessary and perpetual solidarity; every brain is a ganglion, a station of a universal *neurological* telegraphy in constant rapport with the central and other stations by the vibrations of thought.

"The spiritual sun shines for souls as the material sun shines for bodies, for the universe *is double* and follows the law of couples. The ignorant operator interprets erroneously the divine dispatches, and often delivers them in a false and ridiculous manner. Thus study and true science alone can destroy the superstitions and nonsense spread by the ignorant interpreters placed at the *stations of teaching* among every people in this world. These blind interpreters of the *Verbum*, the WORD, have always tried to impose on their pupils the obligation to swear to everything without examination in *verba magistri.*

"Alas! we could wish for nothing better were they to translate correctly the *inner* voices, which voices never deceive but those who have *false spirits* in them. 'It is our duty,' they say, 'to interpret oracles; it is we who have received the exclusive mission for it from heaven, *spiritus flat ubi vult*, and it blows on us alone. . . .'

"It blows *on every one*, and the rays of the spiritual light illuminate every conscience; and when all the bodies and all the minds will reflect equally this dual light, people will see a great deal clearer than they do now."

We have translated and quoted the above fragments for their great originality and truthfulness. We know the writer; fame proclaims him a great kabalist, and a few friends know him as a truthful and honest man.

The letter shows, moreover, that the writer has well and carefully studied the chameleon-like nature of the intelligences presiding over spiritual circles. That they are of the same kind and race as those so frequently mentioned in antiquity, admits of as little doubt as that the present generation of men are of the same nature as were human beings in the days of Moses. Subjective manifestations proceed, under harmonious conditions, from those beings which were known as the "good demons" in days of old. Sometimes, but rarely, the planetary spirits — beings of another race than our own — produce them; sometimes the spirits of our translated and beloved friends; sometimes nature-spirits of one or more of the countless tribes; but most frequently of all terrestrial elementary spirits, disembodied evil men, the Diakka of A. Jackson Davis.

IMPURE MEDIUMS AND THEIR "GUIDES"

We do not forget what we have elsewhere written about *subjective* and *objective* mediumistic phenomena. We keep the distinction always in mind. There are good and bad of both classes. An impure medium will attract to his impure inner self, the vicious, depraved, malignant influences as inevitably as one that is pure draws only those that are good and pure. Of the latter kind of medium where can a nobler example be found than the gentle Baroness Adelma von Vay, of Austria (born Countess Wurmbrandt), who is described to us by a correspondent as "the Providence of her neighborhood"? She uses her mediumistic power to heal the sick and comfort the afflicted. To the rich she is a phenomenon; but to the poor a ministering angel. For many years she has seen and recognized the nature-spirits or cosmic elementaries, and found them always friendly. But this was because she was a pure, good woman. Other correspondents of the Theosophical Society have not fared so well at the hands of these apish and impish beings. The Havanna case, elsewhere described, is an example.

Though spiritualists discredit them ever so much, these nature-spirits are realities. If the gnomes, sylphs, salamanders, and undines of the Rosicrucians existed in their days, they must exist now. Bulwer-Lytton's *Dweller of the Threshold,* is a modern conception, modelled on the ancient type of the *Sulanuth*[520] of the Hebrews and Egyptians, which is mentioned in the *Book of Jasher.*[521]

The Christians call them "devils," "imps of Satan," and like characteristic names. They are nothing of the kind, but simply creatures of ethereal matter, irresponsible, and neither good nor bad, unless influenced by a superior intelligence. It is very extraordinary to hear devout Catholics abuse and misrepresent the nature-spirits, when one of their greatest authorities, Clement the Alexandrian, disposed of them, by describing these creatures as they really are. Clement, who perhaps had been a theurgist as well as a Neo-platonist, thus arguing upon good authority, remarks, that it is absurd to call them devils,[522] for they are only *inferior* angels, "the powers which inhabit elements, move the winds and distribute showers, and as such are agents and subject to God."[523] Origen, who before he became a Christian also belonged to the Platonic school, is of the same opinion. Porphyry describes these dæmons more carefully than any one else.

When the possible nature of the manifesting intelligences, which science believes to be a "psychic force," and spiritualists the identical spirits of the dead, is better known, then will academicians and believers turn to the old philosophers for information.

Let us for a moment imagine an intelligent orang-outang or some African anthropoid ape disembodied, *i.e.,* deprived of its physical and in possession of an astral, if not an immortal body. We have found in spiritual journals many instances where apparitions of departed pet dogs and other animals have been seen. Therefore, upon spiritualistic testimony, we must think that such animal "spirits" do appear although we reserve the right of concurring with the ancients that the forms are but tricks of the elementals. Once open the door of communication between the terrestrial and the spiritual world, what prevents the ape from producing physical phenomena such as he sees human spirits produce. And why may not these excel in cleverness of ingenuity many of those which have been witnessed in spiritual circles? Let spiritualists answer. The orang-outang of Borneo is little, if any, inferior to the savage man in intelligence. Mr. Wallace and other great naturalists give instances of its wonderful acuteness, although its brains are inferior in cubic capacity to the most undeveloped of savages. These apes lack but speech to be men of low grade. The sentinels placed by monkeys; the sleeping chambers selected and built by orang-outangs; their prevision of danger and calculations, which show more than instinct; their choice of

---

520 The Sulanuth is described in chap. lxxx., vers. 19, 20, of "*Jasher.*"

521 "And when the Egyptians hid themselves on account of the swarm" (one of the plagues alleged to have been brought on by Moses) ". . . they locked their doors after them, and God ordered the *Sulanuth* . . ." (a *sea-monster,* naively explains the translator, in a foot-note) "which was then in the sea, to come up and go into Egypt . . . and she had long arms, ten cubits in length . . . and she went upon the roofs and uncovered the rafting and cut them . . . and stretched forth her arm into the house and removed the lock and the bolt and opened the houses of Egypt . . . and the swarm of animals destroyed the Egyptians, and it grieved them exceedingly."

522 "*Strom,*" vi., 17, § 159.

523 Ibid., vi., 3, § 30.

leaders whom they obey; and the exercise of many of their faculties, certainly entitle them to a place at least on a level with many a flat-headed Australian. Says Mr. Wallace, "The mental requirements of savages, and the faculties actually exercised by them, are very little above those of the animals."

Now, people assume that there can be no apes in the other world, because apes have no "souls." But apes have as much intelligence, it appears, as some men; why, then, should these men, in no way superior to the apes, have immortal spirits, and the apes none? The materialists will answer that neither the one nor the other has a spirit, but that annihilation overtakes each at physical death. But the spiritual philosophers of all times have agreed that man occupies a step one degree higher than the animal, and is possessed of that something which it lacks, be he the most untutored of savages or the wisest of philosophers. The ancients, as we have seen, taught that while man is a trinity of body, astral spirit, and immortal soul, the animal is but a duality — a being having a physical body and an astral spirit animating it. Scientists can distinguish no difference in the elements composing the bodies of men and brutes; and the kabalists agree with them so far as to say that the astral bodies (or, as the physicists would call it, "the life-principle") of animals and men are *identical* in essence. Physical man is but the highest development of animal life. If, as the scientists tell us, even *thought* is matter, and every sensation of pain or pleasure, every transient desire is accompanied by a disturbance of ether; and those bold speculators, the authors of the *Unseen Universe* believe that thought is conceived "to affect the matter of another universe simultaneously with this"; why, then, should not the gross, brutish thought of an orang-outang, or a dog, impressing itself on the ethereal waves of the astral light, as well as that of man, assure the animal a continuity of life after death, or "a future state"?

The kabalists held, and now hold, that it is unphilosophical to admit that the astral body of man can survive corporeal death, and at the same time assert that the astral body of the ape is resolved into independent molecules. That which survives as an *individuality* after the death of the body is the *astral soul,* which Plato, in the *Timæus* and *Gorgias,* calls the *mortal* soul, for, according to the Hermetic doctrine, it throws off its more material particles at every progressive change into a higher sphere. Socrates narrates to Callicles[524] that this *mortal* soul retains all the characteristics of the body after the death of the latter; so much so, indeed, that a man marked with the whip will have his astral body "full of the prints and scars." The astral spirit is a faithful duplicate of the body, both in a physical and spiritual sense. The Divine, the highest and *immortal* spirit, can be neither punished nor rewarded. To maintain such a doctrine would be at the same time absurd and blasphemous, for it is not merely a flame lit at the central and inexhaustible fountain of light, but actually a portion of it, and of identical essence. It assures immortality to the individual astral being in proportion to the willingness of the latter to receive it. So long as the *double* man, *i.e.,* the man of flesh and spirit, keeps within the limits of the law of spiritual continuity; so long as the divine spark lingers in him, however faintly, he is on the road to an immortality in the future state. But those who resign themselves to a materialistic existence, shutting out the divine radiance shed by their spirit, at the beginning of the earthly pilgrimage, and stifling the warning voice of that faithful sentry, the conscience, which serves as a focus for the light

524 "*Gorgias.*"

in the soul — such beings as these, having left behind conscience and spirit, and crossed the boundaries of matter, will of necessity have to follow its laws.

Matter is as indestructible and eternal as the immortal spirit itself, but only in its particles, and not as organized forms. The body of so grossly materialistic a person as above described, having been deserted by its spirit before physical death, when that event occurs, the plastic material, astral soul, following the laws of blind matter, shapes itself thoroughly into the mould which vice has been gradually preparing for it through the earth-life of the individual. Then, as Plato says, it assumes the form of that "animal to which it resembled in its evil ways"[525] during life. "It is an ancient saying," he tells us, "that the souls departing hence exist in Hades and return hither again and *are produced from the dead*[526] . . . But those who are found to have lived an eminently holy life, these are they who arrive at the pure abode ABOVE and DWELL ON THE UPPER PARTS of the earth"[527] (the ethereal region). In *Phædrus,* again, he says that when man has ended his *first* life (on earth), some go to places of punishment *beneath* the earth.[528] This region *below* the earth, the kabalists do not understand as a place inside the earth, but maintain it to be a sphere, far inferior in perfection to the earth, and far more material.

Of all the modern speculators upon the seeming incongruities of the *New Testament,* alone the authors of the *Unseen Universe* seem to have caught a glimpse of its kabalistic truths, respecting the gehenna of the universe.[529] This gehenna, termed by the occultists the *eighth* sphere (numbering inversely), is merely a planet like our own, *attached to the latter and following it in its penumbra;* a kind of dust-hole, a "place where all its garbage and filth is consumed," to borrow an expression of the above-mentioned authors, and on which all the dross and scorification of the cosmic matter pertaining to our planet is in a continual state of remodelling.

The secret doctrine teaches that man, if he wins immortality, will remain forever the trinity that he is in life, and will continue so throughout all the spheres. The astral body, which in this life is covered by a gross physical envelope, becomes — when relieved of that covering by the process of corporeal death — in its turn the shell of another and more ethereal body. This begins developing from the moment of death, and becomes perfected when the astral body of the earthly form finally separates from it. This process, they say, is repeated at every new transition from sphere to sphere. But the immortal soul, "the silvery spark," observed by *Dr. Fenwick* in *Margrave's* brain,[530] and not found by him in the animals, never changes, but remains indestructible "by aught that shatters its tabernacle." The descriptions by Porphyry and Iamblichus and others, of the spirits of animals, which inhabit the astral light, are corroborated by those of many of the most trustworthy and intelligent clairvoyants. Sometimes the animal forms are even made visible to every person present at

---

525 "*Timæus.*"

526 Cory, "*Phædro*," i. 69.

527 Ibid., i. 123.

528 Cory, "*Phædras*"; Cory's "*Plato,*" 325.

529 See "*The Unseen Universe,*" pp. 205, 206.

530 See Bulwer-Lytton, "*Strange Story,*" p. 76. We do not know where in literature can be found a more vivid and beautiful description of this difference between the life-principle of man and that of animals, than in the passages herein briefly alluded to.

a spiritual circle, by being materialized. In his *People from the Other World,* Colonel H. S. Olcott describes a materialized squirrel which followed a spirit-woman into the view of the spectators, disappeared and reappeared before their eyes several times, and finally followed the spirit into the cabinet.

Let us advance another step in our argument. If there is such a thing as existence in the spiritual world after corporeal death, then it must occur in accordance with the law of evolution. It takes man from his place at the apex of the pyramid of matter, and lifts him into a sphere of existence where the same inexorable law follows him. And if it follows him, why not everything else in nature? Why not animals and plants, which have all a life-principle, and whose gross forms decay like his, when that life-principle leaves them? If his astral body becomes more ethereal upon attaining the other sphere, why not theirs? They, as well as he, have been evolved out of condensed cosmic matter, and our physicists cannot see the slightest difference between the molecules of the four kingdoms of nature, which are thus specified by Professor Le Conte:

4. *Animal Kingdom.*
3. Vegetable Kingdom.
2. Mineral Kingdom.
1. Elements.

The progress of matter from each of these planes to the plane above is continuous; and, according to Le Conte, there is no force in nature capable of raising matter at once from No. 1 to No. 3, or from No. 2 to No. 4, without stopping and receiving an accession of force of a different kind on the intermediate plane.

Now, will any one presume to say that out of a given number of molecules, *originally and constantly homogeneous, and all energized by the same principle of evolution,* a certain number can be carried through those four kingdoms to the final result of evolving immortal man, and the others not be allowed to progress beyond planes 1, 2, and 3? Why should not *all* these molecules have an equal future before them; the mineral becoming plant, the plant, animal, and the animal, man — if not upon *this* earth, at least somewhere in the boundless realms of space? The harmony which geometry and mathematics — the only exact sciences — demonstrate to be the law of the universe, would be destroyed if evolution were perfectly exemplified in man alone and limited in the subordinate kingdoms. What logic suggests, psychometry proves; and, as we said before, it is not unlikely that a monument will one day be erected by men of science to Joseph R. Buchanan, its modern discoverer. If a fragment of mineral, fossilized plant, or animal form gives the psychometer as vivid and accurate pictures of their previous conditions, as a fragment of human bone does of those of the individual to which it belonged, it would seem as if the same subtile spirit pervaded all nature, and was inseparable from organic or inorganic substances. If anthropologists, physiologists, and psychologists are equally perplexed by primal and final causes, and by finding in matter so much similarity in all its forms, but in spirit such abysses of difference, it is, perhaps, because their inquiries are limited to our visible globe, and that they cannot, or dare not, go beyond. The spirit of a mineral, plant, or animal, may begin to form here, and reach its final development millions of ages hereafter, on other planets, known or unknown, visible or invisible to astronomers. For, who is able to controvert the theory previously suggested, that the earth itself will, like the living creatures to which it has given birth, ultimately, and after passing through its own stage of death and dissolution, become an etherealized astral planet? "As above, so below"; harmony is the great law of nature.

Harmony in the physical and mathematical world of sense, is *justice* in the spiritual one. Justice produces harmony, and injustice, discord; and discord, on a cosmical scale, means chaos — annihilation.

If there is a developed immortal spirit in man, it must be in every thing else, at least in a latent or germinal state, and it can only be a question of time for each of these germs to become fully developed. What gross injustice it would be for an impenitent criminal man, the perpetrator of a brutal murder when in the exercise of his free will, to have all immortal spirit which in time may be washed clean of sin, and enjoying perfect happiness, while a poor horse, innocent of all crime, should toil and suffer under the merciless torture of his master's whip during a whole life, and then be annihilated at death? Such a belief implies a brutal injustice, and is only possible among people taught in the dogma that everything is created for man, and he alone is the sovereign of the universe; — a sovereign so mighty that to save him from the consequences of his own misdeeds, it was not too much that the God of the universe should die to placate his own just wrath.

If the most abject savage, with a brain "very little inferior to that of a philosopher"[531] (the latter developed physically by ages of civilization), is still, as regards the actual exercise of his mental faculties, very little superior to an animal, is it just to infer that both he and the ape will not have the opportunity to become philosophers; the ape in this world, the man on some other planet peopled equally with beings created in *some other image* of God?

Says Professor Denton, when speaking of the future of psychometry: "Astronomy will not disdain the assistance of this power. As new forms of organic being are revealed, when we go back to the earlier geologic periods, so new groupings of the stars, new constellations, will be displayed, when the heavens of those early periods are examined by the piercing gaze of future psychometers. An accurate map of the starry heavens during the Silurian period may reveal to us many secrets that we have been unable to discover. . . . Why may we not indeed be able to read the history of the various heavenly bodies . . . their geological, their natural, and, perchance, their human history? . . . I have good reason to believe that trained psychometers will be able to travel from planet to planet, and read their present condition minutely, and their past history."[532]

Herodotus tells us that in the eighth of the towers of Belus, in Babylon, used by the sacerdotal astrologers, there was an uppermost room, a sanctuary, where the prophesying priestesses slept to receive communications from the god. Beside the couch stood a table of gold, upon which were laid various stones, which Manetho informs us were all aërolites. The priestesses developed the prophetic vision in themselves by pressing one of these sacred stones against their heads and bosoms. The same took place at Thebes, and at Patara, in Lycia.[533]

This would seem to indicate that psychometry was known and extensively practiced by the ancients. We have somewhere seen it stated that the profound knowledge possessed,

531 A. R. Wallace, "*The Action of Natural Selection on Man.*"
532 W. Denton, "*The Soul of Things,*" p. 273.
533 "*Herodotus,*" b. i., c. 181.

according to Draper, by the ancient Chaldean astrologers, of the planets and their relations, was obtained more by the divination of the betylos, or the meteoric stone, than by astronomical instruments. Strabo, Pliny, Hellanicus — all speak of the electrical, or electromagnetic power of the betyli. They were worshipped in the remotest antiquity in Egypt and Samothrace, as magnetic stones, "containing souls which had fallen from heaven"; and the priests of Cybelè wore a small betylos on their bodies. How curious the coincidence between the practice of the priests of Belus and the experiments of Professor Denton!

As Professor Buchanan truthfully remarks of psychometry, it will enable us " . . to detect vice and crime. No criminal act . . . can escape the detection of psychometry, when its powers are properly brought forth . . . the sure detection of guilt by psychometry (no matter how secret the act) will nullify all concealment."[534]

Speaking of the elementary, Porphyry says: "These invisible beings have been receiving from men honors as gods . . . a universal belief makes them capable of becoming very malevolent: it proves that their wrath is kindled against those who neglect to offer them a legitimate worship."[535]

Homer describes them in the following terms: "Our *gods* appear to us when we offer them sacrifice . . . *sitting themselves at our tables, they partake of our festival meals.* Whenever they meet on his travels a solitary Phœnician, they *serve to him as guides,* and otherwise manifest their presence. We can say that *our piety* approaches us to them as much as crime and bloodshed unite the Cyclopes and the ferocious race of giants."[536] The latter proving that these gods were kind and beneficent *dæmons,* and that, whether they were *disembodied* spirits or elementary beings, they were no *devils.*

The language of Porphyry, who was himself a direct disciple of Plotinus, is still more explicit as to the nature of these spirits. "Demons," he says, "are invisible; but they know *how to clothe themselves* with forms and configurations subjected to numerous variations, which can be explained by their nature *having much of the corporeal in itself.* Their abode is in the neighborhood of the earth . . . and *when they can escape the vigilance of the good dæmons, there is no mischief they will not dare commit.* One day they will employ brute force; another, *cunning.*"[537] Further, he says: "It is a child's play for them to arouse in us vile passions, to impart to societies and nations turbulent doctrines, provoking wars, seditions, and other public calamities, and then tell you 'that all of these is the work of the gods.' . . . These spirits pass their time in cheating and deceiving mortals, creating around them illusions and prodigies; *their greatest ambition* is to pass as *gods* and *souls* (disembodied spirits)."[538]

PSYCHOMETRY AN AID TO SCIENTIFIC RESEARCH

Iamblichus, the great theurgist of the Neo-platonic school, a man skilled in sacred magic, teaches that "good dæmons appear to us *in reality,* while the bad ones can manifest

---

534 "*Anthropology,*" p. 125.
535 "*Of Sacrifices to Gods and Dæmons,*" chap. ii.
536 "*Odyssey,*" book vii.
537 Porphyry, "*Of Sacrifices to Gods and Dæmons,*" chap. ii.
538 Ibid.

themselves but under the *shadowy forms of phantoms*." Further, he corroborates Porphyry, and tells that " . . . the *good ones fear not the light*, while the wicked *ones require darkness*. . . . The sensations they excite in us make us believe in the presence and reality of things they show, though these things be absent."[539]

Even the most practiced theurgists found danger sometimes in their dealings with certain elementaries, and we have Iamblichus stating that, "The gods, the angels, and the dæmons, as well as the *souls*, may be summoned through evocation and prayer. . . . But when, during theurgic operations, a mistake is made, beware! Do not imagine that you are communicating with beneficent divinities, who have answered your earnest prayer; no, for they are bad dæmons, only under the guise of good ones! For the elementaries often clothe themselves with the similitude of the good, and assume a rank very much superior to that they really occupy. Their boasting betrays them."[540]

Some twenty years since, Baron Du Potet, disgusted with the indifference of the scientists, who persisted in seeing in the greatest psychological phenomena only the result of clever trickery, gave vent to his indignation in the following terms:

> "Here am I, on my way, I may truly say, to the land of marvels! I am preparing to shock every opinion, and provoke laughter in our most illustrious scientists . . . for I am convinced that *agents of an immense potency* exist *outside of us*; that they can *enter in us*; move our limbs and organs; and use us as they please. It was, after all, the belief of our fathers and of the whole of antiquity. Every religion admitted the reality of *spiritual agents*. . . . Recalling innumerable phenomena which I have produced in the sight of thousands of persons, seeing the *beastly indifference* of *official* science, in presence of a discovery which transports the mind into the regions of the unknown [sic]; an old man, at the very *moment when I ought to be just being born*. . . . I am not sure if it would not have been better for me to have shared the common ignorance.
>
> "I have suffered calumnies to be written without refuting them. . . . At one time it is simple ignorance which speaks, and I am silent; at another still, superficiality, raising its voice, makes a bluster, and I find myself hesitating whether or not to speak. Is this indifference or laziness? Has fear the power to paralyze my spirit? No; none of these causes affect me; I know simply that it is necessary to prove what one asserts, and this restrains me. For, in justifying my assertions, in showing the living FACT, which proves my sincerity and the truth, I translate OUTSIDE THE PRECINCTS OF THE TEMPLE the sacred inscription, WHICH NO PROFANE EYE SHOULD EVER READ.
>
> "You doubt sorcery and magic? O, truth! thy possession is a heavy burden!"[541]

With a bigotry which one might search for in vain outside the church in whose interest he writes, des Mousseaux quotes the above language, as proof positive that this devoted

---

539 Iamblichus, "*De Mysteriis Egyptorum*."
540 Ibid., "*On the Difference between the Dæmons, the Souls, etc.*"
541 Du Potet, "*La Magie Devoilée*."

savant, and all who share his belief, have given themselves over to the dominion of the *Evil One!*

Self-complacency is the most serious obstacle to the enlightenment of the modern spiritualist. His thirty years' experience with the phenomena seem to him sufficient to have established intermundane intercourse upon an unassailable basis. His thirty years have not only brought to him the conviction that the dead communicate and thus prove the spirit's immortality, but also settled in his mind an idea that little or nothing can be learned of the other world, except through mediums.

For the spiritualists, the records of the past either do not exist, or if they are familiar with its gathered treasures, they regard them as having no bearing upon their own experiences. And yet, the problems which so vex them, were solved thousands of years ago by the theurgists, who have left the keys to those who will search for them in the proper spirit and with knowledge. Is it possible that nature has changed her work, and that we are encountering different spirits and different laws from those of old? Or can any spiritualist imagine that he knows more, or even as much about mediumistic phenomena or the nature of various spirits, as a priest-caste who spent their lives in theurgical practice, which had been known and studied for countless centuries? If the narratives of Owen and Hare, of Edmonds, and Crookes, and Wallace are credible, why not those of Herodotus, the "Father of History," of Iamblichus, and Porphyry, and hundreds of other ancient authors? If the spiritualists have their phenomena under test-conditions, so had the old theurgists, whose records, moreover, show that they could produce and vary them at will. The day when this fact shall be recognized, and profitless speculations of modern investigators shall give place to patient study of the works of the theurgists, will mark the dawn of new and important discoveries in the field of psychology.

CHAPTER X

Τῆς δὲ γὰρ ἐκ τριάδος πᾶν πνεῦμα πατήρ – ἐκέρασε

TAY., *Lyd. de Mens.*, 20

"The more powerful souls perceive truth through themselves, and are of a more inventive nature. Such souls are saved through their own strength, according to the oracle."

PROCLUS in I Alc.

"Since the soul perpetually runs and *passes through all things* in a certain space of time, which being performed, it is presently compelled to run back again through all things, and unfold the same web of generation in the world . . . for as often as the same causes return, the same effects will in like manner be returned."

FICIN. *de Im. An.*, 129, *Chaldean Oracles*

"If not to some peculiar end assign'd,
Study's the specious trifling of the mind."

YOUNG

FROM the moment when the fœtal embryo is formed until the old man, gasping his last, drops into the grave, neither the beginning nor the end is understood by scholastic science; all before us is a blank, all after us chaos. For it there is no evidence as to the relations between spirit, soul, and body, either before or after death. The mere life-principle itself presents an unsolvable enigma, upon the study of which materialism has vainly exhausted its intellectual powers. In the presence of a corpse the skeptical physiologist stands dumb when asked by his pupil whence came the former tenant of that empty box, and whither it has gone. The pupil must either, like his master, rest satisfied with the explanation that protoplasm made the man, and force vitalized and will now consume his body, or he must go outside the walls of his college and the books of its library to find an explanation of the mystery.

It is sometimes as interesting as instructive to follow the two great rivals, science and theology, in their frequent skirmishes. Not all of the sons of the Church are as unsuccessful in their attempts at advocacy as the poor Abbé Moigno, of Paris. This respectable, and no doubt well-meaning divine, in his fruitless attempt to refute the free-thinking arguments of Huxley, Tyndall, Du Bois-Raymond, and many others, has met with a sad failure. In his antidotal arguments his success was more than doubtful, and, as a reward for his trouble, the "Congregation of the Index" forbids the circulation of his book among the faithful.

It is a dangerous experiment to engage in a single-handed duel with scientists on topics which are well demonstrated by experimental research. In what they do *know* they are unassailable, and until the old formula is destroyed by their own hands and replaced by a more newly-discovered one, there is no use fighting against Achilles — unless, indeed, one is fortunate enough to catch the swift-footed god by his vulnerable heel. This heel is — what they confess they do not know!

That was a cunning device to which a certain well-known preacher resorted to reach this mortal part. Before we proceed to narrate the extraordinary though well authenticated facts with which we intend to fill this chapter, it will be good policy to show once more how fallible is modern science as to every fact in nature which can be tested neither by retort nor crucible. The following are a few fragments from a series of sermons by F. Felix, of Notre Dame, entitled *Mystery and Science.* They are worthy to be translated for and quoted in a work which is undertaken in precisely the same spirit as that exhibited by the preacher. For once the Church silenced for a time the arrogance of her traditional enemy, in the face of the learned academicians. It was known that the great preacher, in response to the general desire of the faithful, and perhaps to the orders of ecclesiastical superiors, had been preparing himself for a great oratorical effort, and the historic cathedral was filled with a monster congregation. Amid a profound silence he began his discourse, of which the following paragraphs are sufficient for our purpose:

"A portentous word has been pronounced against us to confront progress with Christianity — SCIENCE. Such is the formidable evocation with which they try to appall us. To all that we can say to base progress upon Christianity, they have always a ready response: that is not *scientific.* We say revelation; revelation is not scientific. We say miracle; a miracle is not scientific.

"Thus antichristianism, faithful to its tradition, and now more than ever, pretends to kill us by science. Principle *of darkness,* it threatens us with light. It proclaims itself the light. . . .

"A hundred times I asked myself, What is, then, that terrible science which is making ready to devour us? . . . Is it mathematical science? . . . but we also have our mathematicians. Is it physics? Astronomy? Physiology? Geology? But we number in Catholicism astronomers, physicists, geologists,[542] and physiologists, who make somewhat of a figure in the scientific world, who have their place in the Academy and their name in history. It would appear that what is to crush us is neither this nor that science, but science in general.

"And why do they prophesy the overthrow of Christianity by science? Listen: . . we must perish by science because we teach mysteries, and because the Christian mysteries are in radical antagonism with modern science. . . . Mystery is the negation of common sense; science repels it; science condemns it; she has spoken — Anathema!

Pere Felix Arraigns the Scientists

"Ah! you are right; if Christian mystery is what you proclaim it, then in the name of science hurl the anathema at it. Nothing is antipathetic to science like the absurd and contradictory. But, glory be to the truth! such is not the mystery of Christianity. If it were so, it would remain for you to explain the most inexplicable of mysteries: how comes it that, during nearly 2,000 years, so many superior minds and rare geniuses have embraced our mysteries, without thinking to repudiate science or abdicate reason?[543] Talk as much as you

542 We wonder if Father Felix is prepared to include St. Augustine, Lactantius, and Bede in this category?

543 For instance, Copernicus, Bruno, and Galileo? For further particulars see the "Index Expurgatorius." Verily, wise are such popular sayings, as that, "Boldness carries off cities at one shout."

like of your modern science, modern thought, and modern genius, there were scientists before 1789.

"If our mysteries are so manifestly absurd and contradictory, how is it that such mighty geniuses should have accepted them without a single doubt? . . . But God preserve me from insisting upon demonstrating that mystery implies no contradiction with science! . . . Of what use to prove, by metaphysical abstractions, that science can reconcile itself with mystery, when all the realities of creation show unanswerably that mystery everywhere baffles science? You ask that we should show you, beyond doubt, that exact science cannot admit mystery; I answer you decidedly that she cannot escape it. Mystery is the FATALITY of science.

"Shall we choose our proofs? First, then, look around at the purely material world, from the smallest atom to the most majestic sun. There, if you try to embrace in the unity of a single law all these bodies and their movements, if you seek the word which explains, in this vast panorama of the universe, this prodigious harmony, where all seems to obey the empire of a single force, you pronounce a word to express it, and say *Attraction!* . . . Yes, attraction, this is the sublime epitome of the science of the heavenly bodies. You say that throughout space these bodies recognize and attract each other; you say that they attract in proportion to their mass, and in inverse ratio with the squares of their distances. And, in fact, until the present moment, nothing has happened to give the lie to this assertion, but everything has confirmed a formula which now reigns sovereign in the EMPIRE OF HYPOTHESIS, and therefore it must henceforth enjoy the glory of being an invincible truism.

"Gentlemen, with all my heart I make my scientific obeisances to the sovereignty of attraction. It is not I who would desire to obscure a light in the world of matter which reflects upon the world of spirits. The empire of attraction, then, is palpable; it is sovereign; it stares us in the face!

"But, what is this attraction? who has seen attraction? who has met attraction? who has touched attraction? How do these mute bodies, *intelligent*, insensible, exercise upon each other unconsciously this reciprocity of action and reaction which holds them in a common equilibrium and unanimous harmony? *Is this force* which draws sun to sun, and atom to atom, an invisible mediator which goes from one to another? And, in such case what is this mediator? whence comes to itself this force which mediates, and this power which embraces, from which the sun can no more escape than the atom. But is this force nothing different from the elements themselves which attract each other? . . . Mystery! Mystery!

"Yes, gentlemen, this attraction which shines with such brightness throughout the material world, remains to you at bottom an impenetrable mystery. . . . Well! because of its mystery, will you deny its reality, which touches you, and its domination, which subjugates you? . . . And again, remark if you please, mystery is so much at the foundation of all science that if you should desire to exclude mystery, you would be compelled to suppress science itself. *Imagine whatever science you will*, follow the magnificent sweep of its deductions . . . when you arrive at its parent source, you come face to face with the *unknown.*[544]

"Who has been able to penetrate the secret of the formation of a body, the generation of a single atom? What is there I will not say at the centre of a sun, but at the centre of an atom? who has sounded to the bottom the abyss in a grain of sand? The grain of sand, gentlemen, has been studied four thousand years by science, she has turned and returned it; she divides it and subdivides it; she torments it with her experiments; she vexes it with her questions to snatch from it the final word as to its secret constitution; she asks it, with an insatiable curiosity: 'Shall I divide thee infinitesimally?' Then, suspended over this abyss, science hesitates, she stumbles, she feels dazzled, she becomes dizzy, and, in despair says: I DO NOT KNOW!

"But if you are so fatally ignorant of the genesis and hidden nature of a grain of sand, how should you have an intuition as to the generation of a single living being? Whence in the living being does life come? Where does it commence? What is the life-principle?"[545]

The "Unknowable"

Can the scientists answer the eloquent monk? Can they escape from his pitiless logic? Mystery certainly does bound them on every side; and the *Ultima Thule,* whether of Herbert Spencer, Tyndall, or Huxley, has written upon the closed portals the words INCOMPREHENSIBLE, UNKNOWABLE. For the lover of metaphor, science may be likened to a twinkling star shining with resplendent brightness through rifts in a bank of densely-black clouds. If her votaries cannot define that mysterious attraction which draws into concrete masses the material particles which form the smallest pebble on the ocean-beach, how can they define the limits at which the possible stops and the impossible begins?

Why should there be an attraction between the molecules of matter, and none between those of spirit? If, out of the material portion of the ether, by virtue of the inherent restlessness of its particles, the forms of worlds and their species of plants and animals can be evolved, why, out of the spiritual part of the ether, should not successive races of beings, from the stage of monad to that of man, be developed; each lower form unfolding a higher one until the work of evolution is completed on our earth, in the production of immortal man? It will be seen that, for the moment, we entirely put aside the accumulated facts which prove the case, and submit it to the arbitrament of logic.

By whatsoever name the physicists may call the energizing principle in matter is of no account; it is a subtile something apart from the matter itself, and, as it escapes their detection, it must be something besides matter. If the law of attraction is admitted as governing the one, why should it be excluded from influencing the other? Leaving logic to answer, we turn to the common experience of mankind, and there find a mass of testimony corroborative of the immortality of the soul, if we judge but from analogies. But we have more than that — we have the unimpeachable testimony of thousands upon thousands, that

---

544 This statement, neither Herbert Spencer nor Huxley will be likely to traverse. But Father Felix seems insensible of his own debt to science; if he had said this in February, 1600, he might have shared the fate of poor Bruno.

545 "*Le Mystere et la Science,*" conferences, P. Felix de Notre Dame; des Mousseaux, "*Hauts Phen. Magie.*"

there is a regular science of the soul, which, notwithstanding that it is now denied the right of a place among other sciences, *is* a science. This science, by penetrating the arcana of nature far deeper than our modern philosophy ever dreamed possible, teaches us how to force the *invisible* to become visible; the existence of elementary spirits; the nature and magical properties of the astral light; the power of living men to bring themselves into communication with the former through the latter. Let them examine the proofs with the lamp of experience, and neither the Academy nor the Church, for which Father Felix so persuasively spoke, can deny them.

Modern science is in a dilemma; it must concede our hypothesis to be correct, or admit the possibility of miracle. To do so, is to say that there can be an infraction of natural law. If this can happen in one case, what assurance have we that it may not be repeated indefinitely, and so destroy that fixity of law, that perfect balance of forces by which the universe is governed. This is a very ancient and an unanswerable argument. To deny the appearance, in our midst, of supersensual beings, when they have been seen, at various times and in various countries, by not merely thousands, but millions of persons, is unpardonable obstinacy; to say that, in any one instance, the apparition has been produced by a miracle, fatal to the fundamental principle of science. What will they do? What can they do, when they shall have awakened from the benumbing stupor of their pride, but collect the facts, and try to enlarge the boundaries of their field of investigations?

The existence of spirit in the common mediator, the ether, is denied by materialism; while theology makes of it a personal god, the kabalist holds that both are wrong, saving that in ether, the elements represent but matter — the blind cosmic forces of nature; and Spirit, the intelligence which directs them. The Hermetic, Orphic, and Pythagorean cosmogonical doctrines, as well as those of Sanchoniathon and Berosus, are all based upon one irrefutable formula, viz.: that the ether and chaos, or, in the Platonic language, mind and matter, were the two primeval and eternal principles of the universe, utterly independent of anything else. The former was the all-vivifying intellectual principle; the chaos, a shapeless, liquid principle, without "form or sense," from the union of which two, sprang into existence the universe, or rather, the universal world, the first androgynous deity — the chaotic matter becoming its body, and ether the soul. According to the phraseology of a *Fragment of Hermias,* "chaos, from this union with spirit, obtaining *sense,* shone with pleasure, and thus was produced the *Protogonos* (the first-born) light."[546] This is the universal trinity, based on the metaphysical conceptions of the ancients, who, reasoning by analogy, made of man, who is a compound of intellect and matter, the microcosm of the macrocosm, or great universe.

If we now compare this doctrine with the speculations of science, which comes to a full stop at the Borderland of the unknown, and, while incompetent to solve the mystery, will allow no one else to speculate upon the subject; or, with the great theological dogma, that the world was called into existence by a heavenly trick of prestidigitation; we do not hesitate to believe that, in the absence of better proof, the Hermetic doctrine is by far the more reasonable, highly metaphysical as it may appear. The universe is there, and we know that we exist; but how did it come, and how did we appear in it? Denied an answer by the

---

546 Damascius, in the "*Theogony,*" calls it *Dis,* "the disposer of all things." Cory, "*Ancient Fragments,*" p. 314.

representatives of physical learning, and excommunicated and anathematized for our blasphemous curiosity by the spiritual usurpers, what can we do, but turn for information to the sages who meditated upon the subject ages before the molecules of our philosophers aggregated in ethereal space?

DANGER OF EVOCATIONS BY TYROS

This visible universe of spirit and matter, they say, is but the concrete image of the ideal abstraction; it was built on the model of the first divine IDEA. Thus our universe existed from eternity in a latent state. The soul animating this purely spiritual universe is the central sun, the highest deity itself. It was not himself who built the concrete form of his idea, but his first-begotten; and as it was constructed on the geometrical figure of the dodecahedron,[547] the first-begotten "was pleased to employ twelve thousand years in its creation." The latter number is expressed in the Tyrrhenian cosmogony,[548] which shows man created in the sixth millennium. This agrees with the Egyptian theory of 6,000 "years,"[549] and with the Hebrew computation. Sanchoniathon,[550] in his *Cosmogony*, declares that when the wind (spirit) became enamored of its own principles (the chaos), an intimate union took place, which connection was called *pothos*, and from this sprang the seed of all. And the chaos knew not its own production, for it was *senseless*; but from its embrace with the wind was generated mot, or the *ilus* (mud).[551] From this proceeded the spores of creation and the generation of the universe.

The ancients, who named but four elements, made of æther a fifth one. On account of its essence being made divine by the unseen presence it was considered as a medium between this world and the next. They held that when the directing intelligences retired from any portion of ether, one of the four kingdoms which they are bound to superintend, the space was left in possession of *evil*. An adept who prepared to converse with the "invisibles," had to know well his ritual, and be perfectly acquainted with the conditions required for the perfect equilibrium of the four elements in the astral light. First of all, he must purify the essence, and within the circle in which he sought to attract the pure spirits, equilibrize the elements, so as to prevent the ingress of the elementaries into their respective spheres. But woe to the imprudent inquirer who ignorantly trespasses upon forbidden ground; danger will beset him at every step. He evokes powers that he cannot control; he arouses sentries which allow only their masters to pass. For, in the words of the immortal Rosicrucian, "Once that thou hast resolved to become a cooperator with the spirit of the *living* God, take care not to hinder Him in His work; for, if thy heat exceeds the natural proportion thou hast stirr'd the wrath of the *Moyst*[552] *natures*, and they will stand up against the *central fire*, and

---

547 Plato, "*Timæus.*"

548 Suidas, v. "*Tyrrhenia.*"

549 The reader will understand that by "years" is meant "ages," not mere periods of twelve lunar months each.

550 See the Greek translation by Philo Byblius.

551 Cory, "*Ancient Fragments.*"

552 We give the spelling and words of this Kabalist who lived and published his works in the seventeenth century. Generally he is considered as one of the most famous alchemists among the Hermetic philosophers.

the central fire against them, and there will be a terrible division in the *chaos*."[553] The spirit of harmony and union will depart from the elements, disturbed by the imprudent hand; and the currents of blind forces will become immediately infested by numberless creatures of matter and instinct — the bad dæmons of the theurgists, the devils of theology; the gnomes, salamanders, sylphs, and undines will assail the rash performer under multifarious aërial forms. Unable to invent anything, they will search your memory to its very depths; hence the nervous exhaustion and mental oppression of certain sensitive natures at spiritual circles. The elementals will bring to light long-forgotten remembrances of the past; forms, images, sweet mementos, and familiar sentences, long since faded from our own remembrance, but vividly preserved in the inscrutable depths of our memory and on the astral tablets of the imperishable "BOOK OF LIFE."

Every organized thing in this world, visible as well as invisible, has an element appropriate to itself. The fish lives and breathes in the water; the plant consumes carbonic acid, which for animals and men produces death; some beings are fitted for rarefied strata of air, others exist only in the densest. Life, to some, is dependent on sunlight, to others, upon darkness; and so the wise economy of nature adapts to each existing condition some living form. These analogies warrant the conclusion that, not only is there no unoccupied portion of universal nature, but also that for each thing that has life, special conditions are furnished, and, being furnished, they are necessary. Now, assuming that there is an invisible side to the universe, the fixed habit of nature warrants the conclusion that this half is occupied, like the other half; and that each group of its occupants is supplied with the indispensable conditions of existence. It is as illogical to imagine that identical conditions are furnished to all, as it would be to maintain such a theory respecting the inhabitants of the domain of visible nature. That there are spirits implies that there is a diversity of spirits; for men differ, and human spirits are but disembodied men.

To say that all spirits are alike, or fitted to the same atmosphere, or possessed of like powers, or governed by the same attractions — electric, magnetic, odic, astral, it matters not which — is as absurd as though one should say that all planets have the same nature, or that all animals are amphibious, or all men can be nourished on the same food. It accords with reason to suppose that the grossest natures among the spirits will sink to the lowest depths of the spiritual atmosphere — in other words, be found nearest to the earth. Inversely, the purest would be farthest away. In what, were we to coin a word, we should call the *Psychomatics* of Occultism, it is as unwarrantable to assume that either of these grades of spirits can occupy the place, or subsist in the conditions, of the other, as in

---

553 The most positive of materialistic philosophers agree that all that exists was evolved from ether; hence, air, water, earth, and fire, the four primordial elements must also proceed from ether and chaos the first *Duad*; all the imponderables, whether now known or unknown, proceed from the same source. Now, if there is a spiritual essence in matter, and that essence forces it to shape itself into millions of individual forms, why is it illogical to assert that each of these spiritual kingdoms in nature is peopled with beings evolved out of its own material? Chemistry teaches us that in man's body there are air, water, earth, and heat, or fire — *air* is present in its components; *water* in the secretions; *earth* in the inorganic constituents; and *fire* in the animal heat. The Kabalist knows by experience that an elemental spirit contains only one, and that each one of the four kingdoms has its own peculiar elemental spirits; man being higher than they, the law of evolution finds its illustration in the combination of all four in him.

hydraulics it would be to expect that two liquids of different densities could exchange their markings on the scale of Beaume's hydrometer.

Gorres, describing a conversation he had with some Hindus of the Malabar coast, reports that upon asking them whether they had ghosts among them, they replied, "Yes, but we know them to be *bad spirits* . . . good ones can hardly ever appear at all. They are principally the spirits of *suicides* and *murderers,* or of those who die violent deaths. They constantly flutter about and appear as phantoms. Night-time is favorable to them, they seduce the feeble-minded and tempt others in a thousand different ways."[554]

Porphyry presents to us some hideous facts whose verity is substantiated in the experience of every student of magic. "The *soul,*"[555] says he, "having even after death a certain affection for its body, an affinity proportioned to the violence with which their union was broken, we see many spirits hovering in despair about their earthly remains; we even see them eagerly seeking the putrid remains of other bodies, but above all freshly-spilled blood, which seems to impart to them for the moment some of the faculties of life."[556]

LARES AND LEMURES

Let spiritualists who doubt the theurgist, try the effect of about half a pound of freshly-drawn human blood at their next materializing seance!

> "The gods and the angels," says Iamblichus, "appear to us among peace and harmony; the bad demons, in tossing everything in confusion. . . . As to the *ordinary souls,* we can perceive them more rarely, etc."[557]

> "The human soul (the astral body) is a demon that our language may name genius," says Apuleius.[558] "She is an *immortal god,* though in a certain sense she is born at the same time as the man in whom she is. Consequently, we may say that she dies in the same way that she is born."

"The soul is born in this world upon leaving *another world* (*anima mundi*), in which her existence precedes the one we all know (on earth). Thus, the gods who consider her proceedings in all the phases of various existences and as a whole, punish her sometimes for sins committed during an anterior life. She dies when she separates herself from a body in which she crossed this life as in a frail bark. And this is, if I mistake not, the secret meaning of the tumulary inscription, so simple for the initiate: *"To the gods manes who lived."* But this kind of death does not annihilate the soul, it only transforms it into a *lemure.* Lemures are the manes or ghosts, which we know under the name of lares. When they keep away and *show us a beneficient protection,* we honor in them the protecting divinities of the family hearth; but, if their crimes sentence them to err, we call them *larvæ.* They become a plague for the wicked, and the *vain terror* of the good."

---

554 Görres, *"Mystique,"* lib. iii., p. 63.

555 The ancients called "the soul" the spirits of bad people; the soul was the *larva* and *lemure.* Good human spirits became gods.

556 Porphyry, *"De Sacrificiis."* Chapter on the true Cultus.

557 *"Mysteries of the Egyptians."*

558 Second century, A.D. *"Du Dieu de Socrate,"* Apul. class., pp. 143-145.

This language can hardly be called ambiguous, and yet, the Reincarnationists quote Apuleius in corroboration of their theory that man passes through a succession of physical human births upon this planet, until he is finally purged from the dross of his nature. But Apuleius distinctly says that we come upon this earth from another one, where we had an existence, the recollection of which has faded away. As the watch passes from hand to hand and room to room in a factory, one part being added here and another there, until the delicate machine is perfected, according to the design conceived in the mind of the master before the work was begun; so, according to ancient philosophy, the first divine conception of man takes shape little by little, in the several departments of the universal workshop, and the perfect human being finally appears on our scene.

This philosophy teaches that nature never leaves her work unfinished; if baffled at the first attempt, she tries again. When she evolves a human embryo, the intention is that a man shall be perfected — physically, intellectually, and spiritually. His body is to grow mature, wear out, and die; his mind unfold, ripen, and be harmoniously balanced; his divine spirit illuminate and blend easily with the *inner* man. No human being completes its grand cycle, or the "circle of necessity," until all these are accomplished. As the laggards in a race struggle and plod in their first quarter while the victor darts past the goal, so, in the race of immortality, some souls outspeed all the rest and reach the end, while their myriad competitors are toiling under the load of matter, close to the starting point. Some unfortunates fall out entirely, and lose all chance of the prize; some retrace their steps and begin again. This is what the Hindu dreads above all things — *transmigration* and *reincarnation*; only on other and inferior planets, never on this one. But there is a way to avoid it, and Buddha taught it in his doctrine of poverty, restriction of the senses, perfect indifference to the objects of this earthly vale of tears, freedom from passion, and frequent intercommunication with the Atma — soul-contemplation. The cause of reincarnation is ignorance of our senses, and the idea that there is any reality in the world, anything except abstract existence. From the organs of sense comes the "hallucination" we call contact; "from contact, desire; from desire, sensation (which also is a deception of our body); from sensation, the cleaving to existing bodies; from this cleaving, reproduction; and from reproduction, disease, decay, and death."

Thus, like the revolutions of a wheel, there is a regular succession of death and birth, the moral cause of which is the cleaving to existing objects, while the instrumental cause is *karma* (the power which controls the universe, prompting it to activity), merit and demerit. "It is, therefore, the great desire of all beings who would be released *from the sorrows of successive birth,* to seek the destruction of the moral cause, the cleaving to existing objects, or evil desire." They, in whom evil desire is entirely destroyed, are called *Arhats*[559]. Freedom from evil desire insures the possession of a *miraculous* power. At his death, the Arhat is never reincarnated; he invariably attains Nirvana — a word, by the bye, falsely interpreted by the Christian scholars and skeptical commentators. Nirvana is the world of *cause,* in which all deceptive effects or delusions of our senses disappear. Nirvana is the highest attainable sphere. The *pitris* (the pre-Adamic spirits) are considered as *reincarnated,* by the Buddhistic philosopher, though in a degree far superior to that of the man of earth. Do they

---

559 *"Eastern Monachism,"* p. 9.

not die in their turn? Do not their astral bodies suffer and rejoice, and feel the same curse of illusionary feelings as when embodied?

What Buddha taught in the sixth century, B.C., in India, Pythagoras taught in the fifth, in Greece and Italy. Gibbon shows how deeply the Pharisees were impressed with this belief in the transmigration of souls.[560] The Egyptian circle of necessity is ineffaceably stamped on the hoary monuments of old. And Jesus, when healing the sick, invariably used the following expression: "Thy sins are forgiven thee." This is a pure Buddhistical doctrine. "The Jews said to the blind man: Thou wast *altogether born in sins*, and dost thou teach us? The doctrine of the disciples (of Christ) is analogous to the 'Merit and Demerit' of the Buddhists; for the sick recovered, *if their sins were forgiven.*"[561] But, this *former life* believed in by the Buddhists, is not a life *on this* planet, for, more than any other people, the Buddhistical philosopher appreciated the great doctrine of cycles. The speculations of Dupuis, Volney, and Godfrey Higgins on the secret meaning of the cycles, or the *kalpas* and the yugs of the Brahmans and Buddhists, amounted to little, as they did not have the key to the esoteric, spiritual doctrine therein contained. No philosophy ever speculated on God as an *abstraction*, but considered Him under His various manifestations. The "First Cause" of the Hebrew Bible, the Pythagorean "Monad," the "One Existence" of the Hindu philosopher, and the kabalistic "En-Soph" — the *Boundless* — are identical. The Hindu Bhagavant does not create; he enters the egg of the world, and emanates from it as Brahm, in the same manner as the Pythagorean Duad evolves from the highest and solitary Monas.[562] The Monas of the Samian philosopher is the Hindu Monas (mind), "who has no first cause (apûrva, or material cause), nor is liable to destruction."[563] Brahma, as Prajâpati, manifests himself first of all as "twelve bodies," or attributes, which are represented by the twelve gods, symbolizing 1, Fire; 2, the Sun; 3, Soma, which gives omniscience; 4, all living Beings;

---

560 "*Decline and Fall of the Roman Empire*," iv. 385.

561 Hardy, "*Manual of Buddhism*"; Dunlap, "*The World's Religions.*"

562 Lempriere ("Classical Dictionary," art. "Pythagoras") says that "there is great reason to suspect the truth of the whole narrative of Pythagoras' journey into India," and concludes by saying that this philosopher had never seen either Gymnosophists or their country. If this be so, how account for the doctrine of the metempsychosis of Pythagoras, which is far more that of the Hindu in its details than the Egyptian? But, above all, how account for the fact that the name MONAS, applied by him to the First Cause, is the identical appellation given to that Being in the Sanscrit tongue? In 1792-7, when Lempriere's "Dictionary" appeared, the Sanscrit was, we may say, utterly unknown; Dr. Haug's translation of the "Aitareya Brahmana" ("Rig-Vedas"), in which this word occurs, was published only about *twenty* years ago, and until that valuable addition to the literature of archaic ages was completed, and the precise age of the "Aitareya" — now fixed by Haug at 2000-2400 B.C. — was a mystery, it might be suggested, as in the case of Christian symbols, that the Hindus *borrowed* it from Pythagoras. But now, unless philology can show it to be a "coincidence," and that the word *Monas* is not the same in its minutest definitions, we have a right to assert that Pythagoras was in India, and that it was the Gymnosophists who instructed him in his metaphysical theology. The fact alone that "Sanscrit, as compared with Greek and Latin, is an elder sister," as Max Müller shows, is not sufficient to account for the perfect identity of the Sanscrit and Greek words MONAS, in their most metaphysical, abstruse sense. The Sanscrit word Deva (god) has become the Latin *deus*, and points to a common source; but we see in the Zoroastrian "Zend-Avesta" the same word, meaning diametrically the opposite, and becoming *dæva*, or evil spirit, from which comes the word *devil*.

563 Haug, "*Aitareya Brahmanam.*"

5, Vayu, or material Ether; 6, Death, or breath of destruction — Siva; 7, Earth; 8, Heaven; 9, Agni, the Immaterial Fire; 10, Aditya, the immaterial and female invisible Sun; 11, Mind; 12, the great Infinite Cycle, "which is not to be stopped."[564] After that, Brahma dissolves himself into the Visible Universe, every atom of which is himself. When this is done, the not-manifested, indivisible, and indefinite Monas retires into the undisturbed and majestic solitude of its unity. *The* manifested deity, a duad at first, now becomes a triad; its triune quality emanates incessantly spiritual powers, who become immortal gods (souls). Each of these souls must be united in its turn with a human being, and from the moment of its consciousness it commences a series of births and deaths. An Eastern artist has attempted to give pictorial expression to the kabalistic doctrine of the cycles. The picture covers a whole inner wall of a subterranean temple in the neighborhood of a great Buddhistic pagoda, and is strikingly suggestive. Let us attempt to convey some idea of the design, as we recall it.

Imagine a given point in space as the primordial one; then with compasses draw a circle around this point; where the beginning and the end unite together, emanation and reabsorption meet. The circle itself is composed of innumerable smaller circles, like the rings of a bracelet, and each of these minor rings forms the belt of the goddess which represents that sphere. As the curve of the arc approaches the ultimate point of the semi-circle — the nadir of the grand cycle — at which is placed our planet by the mystical painter, the face of each successive goddess becomes more dark and hideous than European imagination is able to conceive. Every belt is covered with the representations of plants, animals, and human beings, belonging to the fauna, flora, and anthropology of that particular sphere. There is a certain distance between each of the spheres, purposely marked; for, after the accomplishment of the circles through various transmigrations, the soul is allowed a time of temporary Nirvana, during which space of time the atma loses all remembrance of past sorrows. The intermediate ethereal space is filled with strange beings. Those between the highest ether and the earth below are the creatures of a "middle nature"; nature-spirits, or, as the kabalists term it sometimes, the elementary.

This picture is either a copy of the one described to posterity by Berosus, the priest of the temple of Belus, at Babylon, or the original. We leave it to the shrewdness of the modern archæologist to decide. But the wall is covered with precisely such creatures as described by the semi-demon, or half-god, Oannes, the Chaldean man-fish,[565] " . . . hideous beings, which were produced of a two-fold principle" — the astral light and the grosser matter.

Even remains of architectural relics of the earliest races have been sadly neglected by antiquarians, until now. The caverns of Ajunta, which are but 200 miles from Bombay, in the Chandor range, and the ruins of the ancient city of Aurungabad, whose crumbling palaces and curious tombs have lain in desolate solitude for many centuries, have attracted attention but very recently. Mementos of long by-gone civilization, they were allowed to become the shelter of wild beasts for ages before they were found worthy of a scientific exploration, and it is only recently that the *Observer* gave an enthusiastic description of these archaic ancestors of Herculaneum and Pompeii. After justly blaming the local government which "has provided a bungalow where the traveller may find shelter and safety, but that is

---

564 Ibid.
565 Berosus, fragment preserved by Alex. Polyhistor; Cory, "*Of the Cosmogony and the Deluge.*"

all," it proceeds to narrate the wonders to be seen in this retired spot, in the following words:

"In a deep glen away up the mountain there is a group of cave-temples which are the most wonderful caverns on the earth. It is not known at the present age how many of these exist in the deep recesses of the mountains; but twenty-seven have been explored, surveyed, and, to some extent, cleared of rubbish. There are, doubtless, many others. It is hard to realize with what indefatigable toil these wonderful caves have been hewn from the solid rock of amygdaloid. They are said to have been wholly Buddhist in their origin, and were used for purposes of worship and asceticism. They rank very high as works of art. They extend over 500 feet along a high cliff, and are carved in the most curious manner, exhibiting, in a wonderful degree, the taste, talent, and persevering industry of the Hindu sculptors.

SECRETS OF HINDU TEMPLES

"These cave-temples are beautifully cut and carved on the outside; but inside they were finished most elaborately, and decorated with a vast profusion of sculptures and paintings. These long-deserted temples have suffered from dampness and neglect, and the paintings and frescos are not what they were hundreds of years ago. But the colors are still brilliant, and scenes gay and festive still appear upon the walls. Some of the figures cut in the rock are taken for marriage-processions and scenes in domestic life that are represented as joyful. The female figures are beautiful, delicate, and fair as Europeans. Every one of these representations is artistic, and all of them are unpolluted by any grossness or obscenity generally so prominent in Brahmanical representations of a similar character.

"These caves are visited by a great number of antiquarians, who are striving to decipher the hieroglyphics inscribed on the walls and determine the age of these curious temples."

"The ruins of the ancient city of Aurungabad are not very far from these caves. It was a walled city of great repute, but is now deserted. There are not only broken walls, but crumbling palaces. They were built of immense strength, and some of the walls appear as solid as the everlasting hills."

"There are a great many places in this vicinity where there are Hindu remains, consisting of deep caves and rock-cut temples. Many of these temples are surrounded by a circular enclosure, which is often adorned with statues and columns. The figure of an elephant is very common, placed before or beside the opening of a temple, as a sort of sentinel. Hundreds and thousands of niches are beautifully cut in the solid rock, and when these temples were thronged with worshippers, each niche had a statue or image, usually in the florid style of these Oriental sculptures. It is a sad truth that almost every image here is shamefully defaced and mutilated. It is often said that no Hindu will bow down to an imperfect image, and that the Mahometans, knowing this, purposely mutilated all these images to prevent the Hindus from worshipping them. This is regarded by the Hindus as sacrilegious and blasphemous, awakening the keenest animosities, which every Hindu inherits from his father, and which centuries have not been able to efface."

"Here also are the remains of buried cities — sad ruins — generally without a single inhabitant. In the grand palaces where royalty once gathered and held festivals, wild beasts find their hiding-places. In several places the track of the railway has been constructed over or through these ruins, and the material has been used for the bed of the road. . . . Enormous stones have remained in their places for thousands of years, and probably will for thousands of years to come. These rockcut temples, as well as these mutilated statues, show a workmanship that no work now being done by the natives can equal.[566] It is very evident that hundreds of years since these hills were alive with a vast multitude, where now it is all utter desolation, without cultivation or inhabitants, and given over to wild beasts."

"It is good hunting ground, and, as the English are mighty hunters, they may prefer to have these mountains and ruins remain without change."

REINCARNATION

We fervently hope they will. Enough vandalism was perpetrated in earlier ages to permit us the hope that at least in this century of exploration and learning, science, in its branches of archæology and philology, will not be deprived of these most precious records, wrought on imperishable tablets of granite and rock.

We will now present a few fragments of this mysterious doctrine of reincarnation — as distinct from metempsychosis — which we have from an authority. Reincarnation, *i.e.*, the appearance of the same individual, or rather of his astral monad, twice on the same planet, is not a rule in nature; it is an exception, like the teratological phenomenon of a two-headed infant. It is preceded by a violation of the laws of harmony of nature, and happens only when the latter, seeking to restore its disturbed equilibrium, violently throws back into earth-life the astral monad which had been tossed out of the circle of necessity by crime or accident. Thus, in cases of abortion, of infants dying before a certain age, and of congenital and incurable idiocy, nature's original design to produce a perfect human being, has been interrupted. Therefore, while the gross matter of each of these several entities is suffered to disperse itself at death, through the vast realm of being, the immortal spirit and astral monad of the individual — the latter having been set apart to animate a frame and the former to shed its divine light on the corporeal organization — must try a second time to carry out the purpose of the creative intelligence.

If reason has been so far developed as to become active and discriminative, there is no reincarnation on this earth, for the three parts of the triune man have been united together, and he is capable of running the race. But when the new being has not passed beyond the condition of monad, or when, as in the idiot, the trinity has not been completed, the immortal spark which illuminates it, has to reënter on the earthly plane as it was frustrated

---

566 Some writer has employed a most felicitous expression in describing the majesty of the Hindu archaic monuments, and the exquisite finish of their sculpture. "They built," says he, "like giants, and finished like jewelers."

in its first attempt. Otherwise, the mortal or astral, and the immortal or divine, souls, could not progress in unison and pass onward to the sphere above. Spirit follows a line parallel with that of matter; and the spiritual evolution goes hand in hand with the physical. As in the case exemplified by Professor Le Conte (vide chap. ix.), "there is no force in nature" — and the rule applies to the spiritual as well as to the physical evolution — "which is capable of raising at once spirit or matter from No. 1 to No. 3, or from 2 to 4, without stopping and receiving an accession of force of a different kind *on the intermediate plane.*" That is to say, the monad which was imprisoned in the elementary being — the rudimentary or lowest astral form of the future man — after having passed through and quitted the *highest* physical shape of a dumb animal — say an orang-outang, or again an elephant, one of the most intellectual of brutes — that monad, we say, cannot skip over the physical and intellectual sphere of the terrestrial man, and be suddenly ushered into the spiritual sphere above. What reward or punishment can there be in that sphere of disembodied human entities for a fœtus or a human embryo which had not even time to breathe on this earth, still less an opportunity to exercise the divine faculties of the spirit? Or, for an irresponsible infant, whose senseless monad remaining dormant within the astral and physical casket, could as little prevent him from burning himself as another person to death? Or for one idiotic from birth, the number of whose cerebral circumvolutions is only from twenty to thirty per cent of those of sane persons;[567] and who therefore is irresponsible for either his disposition, acts, or the imperfections of his vagrant, half-developed intellect?

No need to remark that if even hypothetical, this theory is no more ridiculous than many others considered as strictly orthodox. We must not forget that either through the inaptness of the specialists or some other reason, physiology itself is the least advanced or understood of sciences, and that some French physicians, with Dr. Fournié, positively despair of ever progressing in it beyond pure hypotheses.

Further, the same occult doctrine recognizes another possibility; albeit so rare and so vague that it is really useless to mention it. Even the modern Occidental occultists deny it, though it is universally accepted in Eastern countries. When, through vice, fearful crimes and animal passions, a disembodied spirit has fallen to the eighth sphere — the allegorical Hades, and the *gehenna* of the Bible — the nearest to our earth — he can, with the help of that glimpse of reason and consciousness left to him, repent; that is to say, he can, by exercising the remnants of his will-power, strive upward, and like a drowning man, struggle once more to the surface. In the *Magical and Philosophical Precepts* of Psellus, we find one which, warning mankind, says:

"Stoop not down, for a precipice lies below the earth,
Drawing *under a descent of* SEVEN *steps,* beneath which
Is the throne of dire necessity."[568]

WITCHCRAFT AND WITCHES

A strong aspiration to retrieve his calamities, a pronounced desire, will draw him once more into the earth's atmosphere. Here he will wander and suffer more or less in dreary

---

567 "*Anatomie Cerebrale,*" Malacarne, Milan.
568 Psellus, 6, Plet. 2; Cory, "*Chaldean Oracles.*"

solitude. His instincts will make him seek with avidity contact with living persons. . . . These spirits are the invisible but too tangible magnetic vampires; the *subjective* dæmons so well known to mediæval ecstatics, nuns, and monks, to the "witches" made so famous in the *Witch-Hammer;* and to certain sensitive clairvoyants, according to their own confessions. They are the blood-dæmons of Porphyry, the *larvæ* and *lemures* of the ancients; the fiendish instruments which sent so many unfortunate and weak victims to the rack and stake. Origen held all the dæmons which possessed the demoniacs mentioned in the *New Testament* to be *human* "spirits." It is because Moses knew so well what they were, and how terrible were the consequences to weak persons who yielded to their influence, that he enacted the cruel, murderous law against such would-be "witches"; but Jesus, full of justice and divine love to humanity, *healed* instead of *killing* them. Subsequently our clergy, the pretended exemplars of Christian principles, followed the law of Moses, and quietly ignored the law of Him whom they call their "one living God," by burning dozens of thousands of such pretended "witches."

Witch! mighty name, which in the past contained the promise of ignominious death; and in the present has but to be pronounced to raise a whirlwind of ridicule, a tornado of sarcasms! How is it then that there have always been men of intellect and learning, who never thought that it would disgrace their reputation for learning, or lower their dignity, to publicly affirm the possibility of such a thing as a "witch," in the correct acceptation of the word. One such fearless champion was Henry More, the learned scholar of Cambridge, of the seventeenth century. It is well worth our while to see how cleverly he handled the question.

It appears that about the year 1678, a certain divine, named John Webster, wrote *Criticisms and Interpretations of Scripture,* against the existence of witches, and other "superstitions." Finding the work "a weak and impertinent piece," Dr. More criticised it in a letter to Glanvil, the author of *Sadducismus Triumphatus,* and as an appendix sent a treatise on witchcraft and explanations of the word witch, itself. This document is very rare, but we possess it in a fragmentary form in an old manuscript, having seen it mentioned besides only in an insignificant work of 1820, on *Apparitions,* for it appears that the document itself was long since out of print.

The words *witch* and *wizard,* according to Dr. More, signify no more than a wise man or a wise woman. In the word *wizard,* it is plain at the very sight; and "the most plain and least operose deduction of the name witch, is from *wit,* whose derived adjective might be *wittigh* or *wittich,* and by contraction, afterwards witch; as the noun wit is from the verb to *weet,* which is, to know. So that a witch, thus far, is no more than a knowing woman; which answers exactly to the Latin word *saga,* according to that of Festus, *sagæ dictæ anus quae multa sciunt.*"

This definition of the word appears to us the more plausible, as it exactly answers the evident meaning of the Slavonian-Russian names for witches and wizards. The former is called *vyedma,* and the latter *vyèdmak,* both from the verb *to know, védat* or *vyedât;* the root, moreover, being positively Sanscrit. "Veda," says Max Müller, in his *Lecture on the Vedas,* "means originally knowing, or knowledge. Veda is the same word which appears in Greek οἶδα , I know [the digamma, *vau* being omitted], and in the English wise, wisdom, to wit."[569] Furthermore, the Sanscrit word *vidma*, answering to the German *wir wissen,* means literally "*we know.*" It is a great pity that the eminent philologist, while giving in his lecture the Sanscrit, Greek, Gothic, Anglo-Saxon, and German comparative roots of this word, has neglected the Slavonian.

Another Russian appellation for *witch* and *wizard*, the former being purely Slavonian, is *znâhâr* and *znâharka* (feminine) from the same verb *znât* to know. Thus Dr. More's definition of the word, given in 1678, is perfectly correct, and coincides in every particular with modern philology.

"Use," says this scholar, "questionless had appropriated the word to such a kind of skill and knowledge as was out of the common road or extraordinary. *Nor did this peculiarity imply any unlawfulness.* But there was after a further restriction, in which alone now-a-days the words *witch* and *wizard* are used. And that is, for one that has the knowledge and skill of doing or telling things in an extraordinary way, and that in virtue of either an express or implicit sociation or confederacy with some *bad spirits.*" In the clause of the severe law of Moses, so many names are reckoned up with that of witch, that it is difficult as well as useless to give here the definition of every one of them as found in Dr. More's able treatise. "There shall not be found among you any one that useth divination, or an observer of time, or an enchanter, or a witch, or a charmer, or a consulter with familiar spirits, or a wizard, or a necromancer," says the text. We will show, further on, the real object of such severity. For the present, we will remark that Dr. More, after giving a learned definition of every one of such appellations, and showing the value of their real meaning in the days of Moses, proves that there is a vast difference between the "enchanters," "observers of time," etc., and a witch. "So many names are reckoned up in this prohibition of Moses, that, as in our common law, the sense may be more sure, and leave no room to evasion. And that the name of 'witch' is not from any tricks of legerdemain as in common jugglers, that delude the sight of the people at a market or fair, but that it is the name of such as raise magical spectres to deceive men's sight, and so are most certainly witches — women and men who have a *bad spirit* in them. 'Thou shalt not suffer' מבשפה *mecassephah*, that is, 'a witch, to live.' Which would be a law of extreme severity, or rather cruelty, against a poor hocus-pocus for his tricks of legerdemain."

Thus, it is but the sixth appellation, that of a consulter with familiar spirits or a witch, that had to incur the greatest penalty of the law of Moses, for it is only a *witch* which must *not* be suffered to live, while all the others are simply enumerated as such with whom the people of Israel were forbidden to communicate on account of their idolatry or rather religious views and learning chiefly. This sixth word is שאיל אוב , *shoel aub*, which our English translation renders, "a consulter with familiar spirits"; but which the Septuagint translates, Εγαστιμνθος , one that has a familiar spirit *inside* him, one possessed with the spirit of divination, which was considered to be Python by the Greeks, and *obh* by the Hebrews, the old serpent; in its esoteric meaning the spirit of concupiscence and *matter*; which, according to the kabalists, is always an elementary *human* spirit of the eighth sphere.

---

569 See "*Lecture on the Vedas.*"

"*Shoel obh*, I conceive," says Henry More, "is to be understood of the witch herself who asks counsel of her or his familiar. The reason of the name *obh*, was taken first from that spirit that was in the body of the party, and swelled it to a protuberancy, the voice always seeming to come out as from a bottle, for which reason they were named *ventriloquists. Ob* signifies as much as *Pytho*, which at first took its name from the *pythii vates*, a spirit that tells hidden things, or things to come. In *Acts* xvi. 16, πνεῦμα πύζωνος, when "Paul being grieved, turned and said to that spirit, I command thee, in the name of Jesus Christ, to come out of her, and he came out at the same hour." Therefore, the words obsessed or *possessed* are synonyms of the word *witch;* nor could this *pytho* of the eighth sphere come out of her, unless it was a spirit distinct from her. And so it is that we see in *Leviticus* xx. 27: "A man also or woman that hath a familiar spirit, or that is a wizard (an irresponsible *jidegnoni*) shall surely be put *to death,* they shall stone them with stones, *their blood shall be* upon them." A cruel and unjust law beyond doubt, and one which gives the lie to a recent utterance of "Spirits," by the mouth of one of the most popular *inspirational* mediums of the day, to the effect that modern philological research proves that the Mosaic law never contemplated the killing of the poor "mediums" or *witches* of the *Old Testament,* but that the words, "thou shalt not suffer a witch *to live,*" meant to live by their mediumship, that is, to gain their livelihood! An interpretation no less ingenious than novel. Certainly, nowhere short of the source of such *inspiration* could we find such philological profundity![570]

"Shut the door in the face of the dæmon," says the *Kabala*, "and he will keep running away from you, as if you pursued him," which means, that you must not give a hold on you to such spirits of obsession by attracting them into an atmosphere of congenial sin. These dæmons seek to introduce themselves into the bodies of the simple-minded and idiots, and remain there until dislodged therefrom by a powerful and *pure* will. Jesus, Apollonius, and some of the apostles, had the power to cast out *devils*, by purifying the atmosphere *within* and *without* the patient, so as to force the unwelcome tenant to flight. Certain volatile salts are particularly obnoxious to them; and the effect of the chemicals used in a saucer, and placed under the bed by Mr. Varley, of London,[571] for the purpose of keeping away some

---

570 In order to avoid being contradicted by some spiritualists we give verbatim the language in question, as a specimen of the unreliability of the oracular utterances of certain "spirits." Let them be human or elemental, but spirits capable of such effrontery may well be regarded by occultists as anything but safe guides in philosophy, exact science, or ethics. "It will be remembered," says Mrs. Cora V. Tappan, in a public discourse upon the "*History of Occultism and its Relations to Spiritualism*" (see "*Banner of Light*," Aug. 26, 1876), "that the ancient word witchcraft, or the exercise of it, was forbidden among the Hebrews. The translation is that no witch should be allowed to live. That has been supposed to be the literal interpretation; and acting upon that, your very pious and devout ancestors put to death, without adequate testimony, numbers of very intelligent, wise, and sincere persons, under the condemnation of witchcraft. It has now turned out that the interpretation or translation should be, that no witches should be allowed to obtain a living by the practice of their art. That is, it should not be made a profession." May we be so bold as to inquire of the celebrated speaker, through *whom or according to what* authority such a thing has ever *turned out?*

571 Mr. Cromwell F. Varley, the well-known electrician of the Atlantic Cable Company, communicates the result of his observations, in the course of a debate at the Psychological Society of Great Britain, which is reported in the "*Spiritualist*" (London, April 14, 1876, pp. 174, 175). He thought that the effect of free nitric acid in the atmosphere was able to drive away what he calls "unpleasant spirits." He thought that those who were troubled by unpleasant spirits at home, would find relief by

disagreeable physical phenomena at night, are corroborative of this great truth. Pure or even simply inoffensive human spirits fear nothing, for having rid themselves of *terrestrial* matter, terrestrial compounds can affect them in no wise; such spirits are like a *breath*. Not so with the earth-bound souls and the nature-spirits.

THE SACRED SOMA TRANCE

It is for these carnal terrestrial *larvæ*, degraded human spirits, that the ancient kabalists entertained a hope of *reïncarnation*. But when, or how? At a fitting moment, and if helped by a sincere desire for his amendment and repentance by some strong, sympathizing person, or the will of an adept, or even a desire emanating from the erring spirit himself, provided it is powerful enough to make him throw off the burden of sinful matter. Losing all consciousness, the once bright monad is caught once more into the vortex of our terrestrial evolution, and it repasses the subordinate kingdoms, and again breathes as a living child. To compute the time necessary for the completion of this process would be impossible. Since there is no perception of time in eternity, the attempt would be a mere waste of labor.

As we have said, but few kabalists believe in it, and this doctrine originated with certain astrologers. While casting up the nativities of certain historical personages renowned for some peculiarities of disposition, they found the conjunction of the planets answering perfectly to remarkable oracles and prophesies about other persons born ages later. Observation, and what would now be termed "remarkable coincidences," added to revelation during the "sacred sleep" of the neophyte, disclosed the dreadful truth. So horrible is the thought that even those who ought to be convinced of it prefer ignoring it, or at least avoid speaking on the subject.

This way of obtaining oracles was practiced in the highest antiquity. In India, this sublime lethargy is called "the sacred sleep of * * *" It is an oblivion into which the subject is thrown by certain magical processes, supplemented by draughts of the juice of the soma. The body of the sleeper remains for several days in a condition resembling death, and by the power of the adept is purified of its earthliness and made fit to become the temporary receptacle of the brightness of the immortal Augoeides. In this state the torpid body is made to reflect the glory of the upper spheres, as a burnished mirror does the rays of the sun. The sleeper takes no note of the lapse of time, but upon awakening, after four or five days of trance, imagines he has slept but a few moments. What his lips utter he will never know; but as it is the spirit which directs them they can pronounce nothing but divine truth. For the time being the poor helpless clod is made the shrine of the sacred presence, and converted into an oracle a thousand times more infallible than the asphyxiated Pytheness of Delphi; and, unlike her mantic frenzy, which was exhibited before the multitude, this holy sleep is witnessed only within the sacred precinct by those few of the adepts who are worthy to stand in the presence of the ADONAI.

---

pouring one ounce of vitriol upon two ounces of finely-powdered nitre in a saucer and putting the mixture under the bed. Here is a scientist, whose reputation extends over two continents, who gives a recipe to drive away bad spirits. And yet the general public mocks as a *"superstition"* the herbs and incenses employed by Hindus, Chinese, Africans, and other races to accomplish the self-same purpose.

The description which Isaiah gives of the purification necessary for a prophet to undergo before he is worthy to be the mouthpiece of heaven, applies to the case in point. In customary metaphor he says: "Then flew one of the seraphim unto me having a live coal in his hand, which he had taken with the tongs from off the altar . . . and he laid it upon my mouth and said, Lo! this hath touched thy lips and thine iniquity is taken away."

The invocation of his own Augoeides, by the purified adept, is described in words of unparalleled beauty by Bulwer-Lytton in *Zanoni,* and there he gives us to understand that the slightest touch of mortal passion unfits the hierophant to hold communion with his spotless soul. Not only are there few who can successfully perform the ceremony, but even these rarely resort to it except for the instruction of some neophytes, and to obtain knowledge of the most solemn importance.

And yet how little is the knowledge treasured up by these hierophants understood or appreciated by the general public! "There is another collection of writings and traditions bearing the title of *Kabala,* attributed to Oriental scholars," says the author of *Art-Magic;* "but as this remarkable work is of little or no value without a key, which *can only be furnished by Oriental fraternities,* its transcript would be of no value to the general reader."[572] And how they are ridiculed by every Houndsditch commercial traveller who wanders through India in pursuit of "orders" and writes to the *Times,* and misrepresented by every nimble-fingered trickster who pretends to show by legerdemain, to the gaping crowd, the feats of true Oriental magicians!

But, notwithstanding his unfairness in the Algerian affair, Robert Houdin, an authority on the art of prestidigitation, and Moreau-Cinti, another, gave honest testimony in behalf of the French mediums. They both testified, when cross-examined by the Academicians, that none but the "mediums" could possibly produce the phenomena of table-rapping and levitation without a suitable preparation and furniture adapted for the purpose. They also showed that the so-called "levitations without contact" were feats utterly beyond the power of the *professional* juggler; that for them, such levitations, unless produced in a room supplied with secret machinery and concave mirrors, was *impossible.* They added moreover, that the simple apparition of a diaphanous hand, in a place in which confederacy would be rendered impossible, the medium having been previously searched, would be a demonstration that it was the work *of no human agency,* whatever else that agency might be. The *Siècle,* and other Parisian newspapers immediately published their suspicions that these two professional and very clever gentlemen had become the confederates of the spiritists!

Professor Pepper, director of the Polytechnic Institute of London, invented a clever apparatus to produce spiritual appearances on the stage, and sold his patent in 1863, in Paris, for the sum of 20,000 francs. The phantoms looked real and were evanescent, being but an effect produced by the reflection of a highly-illuminated object upon the surface of plateglass. They seemed to appear and disappear, to walk about the stage and play their parts to perfection. Sometimes one of the phantoms placed himself on a bench; after which, one of the living actors would begin quarrelling with him, and, seizing a heavy hatchet, would part the head and body of the ghost in two. But, joining his two parts again, the spectre would reappear, a few steps off, to the amazement of the public. The contrivance

---

572 *"Art-Magic,"* p. 97.

worked marvellously well, and nightly attracted large crowds. But to produce these ghosts required a stage-apparatus, and more than one confederate. There were nevertheless some reporters who made this exhibition the pretext for ridiculing the *spiritists* — as though the two classes of phenomena had the slightest connection!

What the Pepper ghosts pretended to do, genuine disembodied human spirits, when their reflection is materialized by the elementals, can actually perform. They will permit themselves to be perforated with bullets or the sword, or to be dismembered, and then instantly form themselves anew. But the case is different with both cosmic and human elementary spirits, for a sword or dagger, or even a pointed stick, will cause them to vanish in terror. This will seem unaccountable to those who do not understand of what a material substance the elementary are composed; but the kabalists understand perfectly. The records of antiquity and of the middle ages, to say nothing of the modern wonders at Cideville, which have been judicially attested for us, corroborate these facts.

Skeptics, and even skeptical spiritualists, have often unjustly accused mediums of fraud, when denied what they considered their inalienable right to test the spirits. But where there is one such case, there are fifty in which spiritualists have permitted themselves to be practiced upon by tricksters, while they neglected to appreciate genuine manifestations procured for them by their mediums. Ignorant of the laws of mediumship, such do not know that when an honest medium is once taken possession of by spirits, whether disembodied or elemental, he is no longer his own master. He cannot control the actions of the spirits, nor even his own. They make him a puppet to dance at their pleasure while they pull the wires behind the scenes. The false medium may seem entranced, and yet be playing tricks all the while; while the real medium may appear to be in full possession of his senses, when in fact he is far away, and his body is animated by his "Indian guide," or "control." Or, he may be entranced in his cabinet, while his astral body (double) or *doppelganger*, is walking about the room moved by another intelligence.

Among all the phenomena, that of *re-percussion*, closely allied with those of bi-location and aërial "travelling," is the most astounding. In the middle ages it was included under the head of sorcery. De Gasparin, in his refutations of the miraculous character of the marvels of Cideville, treats of the subject at length; but these pretended explanations were all in their turn exploded by de Mirville and des Mousseaux, who, while failing in their attempt to trace the phenomena back to the Devil, did, nevertheless, prove their spiritual origin.

"The prodigy of re-percussion," says des Mousseaux, "occurs when a blow aimed at the spirit, visible or otherwise, of an absent *living* person, or at the phantom which represents him, strikes this person himself, at the same time, and in the very place at which the spectre or his double is touched! We must suppose, therefore, that the blow is re-percussed, and that it reaches, as if rebounding, from the image of the living person — his phantasmal[573] duplicate — the original, wherever he may be, in flesh and blood.

"Thus, for instance, an individual appears before me, or, remaining invisible, declares war, threatens, and causes me to be threatened with obsession. I strike at the place where I perceive his phantom, where I hear him moving, where I feel *somebody*, something which molests and resists me. I strike; the blood will appear sometimes on this place, and

---

573 This phantom is called *Scin Lecca*. See Bulwer-Lytton's "*Strange Story*."

occasionally a scream may be heard; *he* is wounded — perhaps, dead! It is done, and I have explained the fact."[574]

"Notwithstanding that, at the moment I struck him, his presence in another place is authentically proved; . . . I saw — yes, I saw plainly the phantom hurt upon the cheek or shoulder, and this same wound is found precisely on the living person, re-percussed upon his cheek or shoulder. Thus, it becomes evident that the facts of re-percussion have an intimate connection with those of bi-location or *duplication*, either spiritual or corporeal."

The history of the Salem witchcraft[575], as we find it recorded in the works of Cotton Mather, Calef, Upham, and others, furnishes a curious corroboration of the fact of the double, as it also does of the effects of allowing elementary spirits to have their own way. This tragical chapter of American history has never yet been written in accordance with the truth. A party of four or five young girls had become "developed" as mediums, by sitting with a West Indian negro woman, a practitioner of *Obeah*. They began to suffer all kinds of physical torture, such as pinching, having pins stuck in them, and the marks of bruises and teeth on different parts of their bodies. They would declare that they were hurt by the spectres of various persons, and we learn from the celebrated *Narrative of Deodat Lawson* (London, 1704), that "some of them confessed that they did afflict the sufferers (*i.e.*, these young girls), according to the time and manner they were accused thereof; and, being asked what they did to afflict them, some said that they pricked pins into poppets, made with rags, wax, and other materials. One that confessed after the signing of her death-warrant, said she used to afflict them by clutching and pinching her hands together, and *wishing* in what part and after what manner she would have them afflicted, and *it was done*."

Mr. Upham tells us that Abigail Hobbs, one of these girls, acknowledged that she had confederated with the Devil, who "came to her in the shape of a man," and commanded her to afflict the girls, bringing images made of wood in their likeness, with thorns for her to prick into the images, which she did; whereupon, the girls cried out that they were hurt by her."

How perfectly these facts, the validity of which was proven by unimpeachable testimony in court, go to corroborate the doctrine of Paracelsus. It is surpassingly strange that so ripe a scholar as Mr. Upham should have accumulated into the 1,000 pages of his two volumes such a mass of legal evidence, going to show the agency of earth-bound souls and tricksy nature-spirits in these tragedies, without suspecting the truth.

Ages ago, the old Ennius was made by Lucretius to say:

---

574 In the Strasbourg edition of his works (1603), Paracelsus writes of the wonderful *magical* power of man's spirit. "It is possible," he says, "that my spirit, without the help of the body, and through a fiery will alone, and without a sword, can stab and wound others. It is also possible that I can bring the spirit of my adversary into an image, and then double him up and lame him . . . the exertion of will is a great point in medicine. . . . Every imagination of man comes through the heart, for this is the sun of the microcosm, and out of the microcosm proceeds the imagination into the great world (universal ether) . . . the imagination of man is a seed which is *material*." (Our atomical modern scientists have proved it; see Babbage and Professor Jevons.) "Fixed thought is also a means to an end. The magical is a great *concealed wisdom*, and reason is a great public foolishness. No armor protects against magic, for it injures the *inward* spirit of life."

575 "*Salem Witchcraft; With an Account of Salem Village*," by C. W. Upham.

"Bis duo sunt homines, manes, caro, *spiritus* umbra;
Quatuor ista loci bis duo suscipirent;
Terra tegit carnem; — tumulum circumvolat umbra,
Orcus habet manes."

In this present case, as in every similar one, the scientists, being unable to explain the fact, assert that *it cannot* exist. But we will now give a few historical instances going to show that some daimons, or elementary spirits, are afraid of sword, knife, or any thing sharp. We do not pretend to explain the reason. That is the province of physiology and psychology. Unfortunately, physiologists have not yet been able to even establish the relations between speech and thought, and so, have handed it over to the metaphysicians, who, in their turn, according to Fournié, have done nothing. Done nothing, we say, but claimed everything. No fact could be presented to some of them, that was too large for these learned gentlemen to at least try to stuff into their pigeon-holes, labelled with some fancy Greek name, expressive of everything else but the true nature of the phenomenon. "Alas, alas! my son!" exclaims the wise Muphti, of Aleppo, to his son Ibrahim, who choked himself with the head of a huge fish. "When will you realize that your stomach is smaller than the ocean?" Or, as Mrs. Catherine Crowe remarks in her *Night-Side of Nature,* when will our scientists admit that "their intellects are no measure of God Almighty's designs?"

We will not ask which of the ancient writers mention facts of seemingly-*supernatural* nature; but rather which of them does not? In Homer, we find Ulysses evoking the spirit of his friend, the soothsayer Tiresias. Preparing for the ceremony of the "festival of blood," Ulysses draws his sword, and thus frightens away the thousands of phantoms attracted by the sacrifice. The friend himself, the so-long-expected Tiresias, dares not approach him so long as Ulysses holds the dreaded weapon in his hand.[576] Æneas prepares to descend to the kingdom of the shadows, and as soon as they approach its entrance, the Sibyl who guides him utters her warning to the Trojan hero, and orders him to draw his sword and clear himself a passage through the dense crowd of flitting forms:

VULNERABILITY OF CERTAIN "SHADOWS"

"Tuque invade viam, vaginâque eripe ferrum."[577]

Glanvil gives a wonderful narrative of the apparition of the "Drummer of Tedworth," which happened in 1661; in which the *scin-lecca,* or double, of the drummer-sorcerer was evidently very much afraid of the sword. Psellus, in his work,[578] gives a long story of his sister-in-law being thrown into a most fearful state by an elementary *daimon* taking possession of her. She was finally cured by a conjurer, a foreigner named Anaphalangis, who began by threatening the invisible occupant of her body with a *naked sword*, until he finally dislodged him. Psellus introduces a whole catechism of demonology, which he gives in the following terms, as far as we remember:

---

576 "*Odyssey,*" A. 82.
577 "*Æneid,*" book vi., 260.
578 "*De Dæmon,*" cap. "Quomodo dæm occupent."

"You want to know," asked the conjurer, "whether the bodies of the spirits can be hurt by sword or any other weapon?[579] Yes, they can. Any hard substance striking them can make them sensible to pain; and though their bodies be made neither of solid nor firm substance, they feel it the same, for in beings endowed with sensibility it is not their nerves only which possess the faculty of feeling, but likewise also the spirit which resides in them . . . the body of a spirit can be sensible in its *whole*, as well as in each one of its parts. Without the help of any physical organism the spirit sees, hears, and if you touch him feels your touch. If you divide him in two, he will feel the pain as would any living man, for he is *matter* still, though so refined as to be generally invisible to our eye. . . . One thing, however, distinguishes him from the living man, viz.: that when a man's limbs are once divided, their parts cannot be reunited very easily. But, cut a *demon* in two, and you will see him immediately join himself together. As water or air closes in behind a solid body§ passing through it, and no trace is left, so does the body of a demon condense itself again, when the penetrative weapon is withdrawn from the wound. But every rent made in it causes him pain nevertheless. *That is why daimons* dread the point of a sword or any sharp weapon. Let those who want to see them flee try the experiment."

One of the most learned scholars of his century, Bodin, the Demono logian, held the same opinion, that both the human and cosmical elementaries "were sorely afraid of swords and daggers." It is also the opinion of Porphyry, Iamblichus, and Plato. Plutarch mentions it several times. The practicing theurgists knew it well and acted accordingly; and many of the latter assert that "the demons suffer from any rent made in their bodies." Bodin tells us a wonderful story to this effect, in his work *On the Dæmons*, p. 292.

"I remember," says the author, "that in 1557 an elemental demon, one of those who are called *thundering*, fell down *with the lightning*, into the house of Poudot, the shoemaker, and immediately began flinging stones all about the room. We picked up so many of them that the landlady filled a large chest full, after having securely closed the windows and doors and locked the chest itself. But it did not prevent the demon in the least from introducing other stones into the room, but without injuring any one for all that. Latomi, who was then *Quarter-President*,[580] came to see what was the matter. Immediately upon his entrance, the spirit knocked the cap off his head and made him run away. It had lasted for over six days, when M. Jean Morgnes, Counsellor at the *Presidial*, came to fetch me to see the mystery. When I entered the house, some one advised the master of it to pray to God with all his heart and to wheel round a sword in the air about the room; he did so. On that following day the landlady told us, that from that very moment they did not hear the least noise in the house; but that during the seven previous days that it lasted they could not get a moment's rest."

The books on the witchcraft of the middle ages are full of such narratives. The very rare and interesting work of Glanvil, called *Sadducismus Triumphatus,* ranks with that of Bodin,

---

579 Numquid dæmonum corpora pulsari possunt? Possunt sane, atque dolere solido quodam *percussa* corpore.

§ Ubi secatur, mox in se iterum recreatur et coalescit . . . dictu velocius dæmonicus spiritus in se revertitor.

580 A magistrate of the district.

above mentioned, as one of the best. But we must give space now to certain narratives of the more ancient philosophers, who explain at the same time that they describe.

EXPERIMENT OF CLEARCHUS ON A SLEEPING BOY

And first in rank for wonders comes Proclus. His list of facts, most of which he supports by the citation of witnesses — sometimes well-known philosophers — is staggering. He records many instances in his time of dead persons who were found to have changed their recumbent positions in the sepulchre, for one of either sitting or standing, which he attributes to their being *larvae*, and which he says "is related by the ancients of Aristius, Epimenides, and Hermodorus." He gives five such cases from the history of Clearchus, the disciple of Aristotle. 1. Cleonymus, the Athenian. 2. Polykritus, an illustrious man among the Æolians. It is related by the historian Nomachius, that Polykritus died, and returned in the ninth month after his death. "Hiero, the Ephesian, and other historians," says his translator, Taylor, "testify to the truth of this." 3. In Nicopolis, the same happened to one Eurinus. The latter revived on the fifteenth day after his burial, and lived for some time after that, leading an exemplary life. 4. Rufus, a priest of Thessalonica, restored to life the third day after his death, for the purpose of performing certain sacred ceremonies according to promise; he fulfilled his engagement, and died again to return no more. 5. This is the case of one Philonæa, who lived under the reign of Philip. She was the daughter of Demostratus and Charito of Amphipolos. Married against her wish to one Kroterus, she died soon after. But in the sixth month after her death, she revived, as Proclus says: "through her love of a youth named Machates, who came to her father Demostratus, from Pella." She visited him for many nights successively, but when this was finally discovered, she, or rather the vampire that represented her, died of rage. Previous to this she declared that she acted in this manner according to the will of *terrestrial demons.* Her dead body was seen at this second death by every one in the town, lying in her father's house. On opening the vault, where her body had been deposited, it was found empty by those of her relatives, who being incredulous upon that point, went to ascertain the truth. The narrative is corroborated by the *Epistles of Hipparchus* and those of Arridæus to Philip.[581]

Says Proclus: "Many other of the ancients have collected a history of those that have apparently died, and afterward revived. Among these is the natural philosopher Demokritus. In his writings concerning Hades, he affirms that [in a certain case under discussion] death was not, as it seemed, an entire desertion of the whole life of the body, but a cessation caused by some blow, or perhaps a wound; but the bonds of the soul yet remained rooted about the marrow, and the heart contained in its profundity the empyreuma of life; and this remaining, it again acquired the life, which had been extinguished, in consequence of being adapted to animation."

He says again, "That it is possible for the soul to depart from and enter into the body, is evident from him, who, according to Clearchus, used a *soul-attracting wand* on a sleeping boy; and who persuaded Aristotle, as Clearchus relates in his *Treatise on Sleep*, that the soul

---

581 This appalling circumstance was authenticated by the Prefect of the city, and the Proconsul of the Province laid the report before the Emperor. The story is modestly related by Mrs. Catherine Crowe (see "*Night-Side of Nature*," p. 335).

may be separated from the body, and that it enters into a body and uses it as a lodging. For, striking the boy with the wand, he drew out, and, as it were, led his soul, for the purpose of evincing that the body was immovable when the soul (astral body) was at a distance from it, and that it was preserved uninjured; but the soul being again led into the body by means of the wand, after its entrance, narrated every particular. From this circumstance, therefore, both the spectators and Aristotle were persuaded that the soul is separate from the body."

It may be considered quite absurd to recall so often the facts of witchcraft, in the full light of the nineteenth century. But the century itself is getting old; and as it gradually approaches the fatal end, it seems as if it were falling into dotage; not only does it refuse to recollect how abundantly the facts of witchcraft were proven, but it refuses to realize what has been going on for the last thirty years, all over the wide world. After a lapse of several thousand years we may doubt the magic powers of the Thessalonian priests and their "sorceries," as mentioned by Pliny;[582] we may throw discredit upon the information given us by Suidas, who narrates Medea's journey through the air, and thus forget that magic was the highest knowledge of natural philosophy; but how are we to dispose of the frequent occurrence of precisely such journeys "through the air" when they happen before our own eyes, and are corroborated by the testimony of hundreds of apparently sane persons? If the universality of a belief be a proof of its truth, few facts have been better established than that of sorcery. "Every people, from the rudest to the most refined, we may also add in every age, have believed in the kind of supernatural agency, which we understand by this term," says Thomas Wright, the author of *Sorcery and Magic,* and a skeptical member of the National Institute of France. "It was founded on the equally extensive creed, that, besides our own visible existence, we live in an invisible world of spiritual beings, by which our actions *and even our thoughts* are often guided, and which have a certain degree of power over the elements and over the ordinary course of organic life." Further, marvelling how this mysterious science flourished everywhere, and noticing several famous schools of magic in different parts of Europe, he explains the time-honored belief, and shows the difference between sorcery and magic as follows: "The magician differed from the witch in this, that, *while the latter was an ignorant instrument in the hands of the demons, the former had become their master by the powerful intermediation of Science,* which was only within reach of the few, and which these beings were unable to disobey."[583] This delineation, established and known since the days of Moses, the author gives as derived from "the most authentic sources."

If from this unbeliever we pass to the authority of an adept in that mysterious science, the anonymous author of *Art-Magic,* we find him stating the following: " The reader may inquire wherein consists the difference between a medium and a magician? . . . The medium is one through whose astral spirit other spirits can manifest, making their presence known by various kinds of phenomena. Whatever these consist in, the medium is only a passive agent in their hands. He can *neither command* their presence, nor *will* their absence; can never compel the performance of any special act, nor direct its nature. The magician, on the contrary, *can summon and dismiss spirits at will;* can perform many feats of occult power through his own spirit; can compel the presence and assistance of spirits of lower grades of

---

582 Pliny, xxx., 1.
583 T. Wright, M.A., F.S.A., etc., "*Sorcery and Magic,*" vol. iii.

being than himself, and effect transformations in the realm of nature upon animate and inanimate bodies."[584]

This learned author forgot to point out a marked distinction in mediumship, with which he must have been entirely familiar. Physical phenomena are the result of the manipulation of forces through the physical system of the medium, by the unseen intelligences, of whatever class. In a word, physical mediumship depends on a peculiar organization of the *physical* system; spiritual mediumship, which is accompanied by a display of subjective, intellectual phenomena, depends upon a like peculiar organization of the *spiritual* nature of the medium. As the potter from one lump of clay fashions a vessel of dishonor, and from another a vessel of honor, so, among physical mediums, the plastic astral spirit of one may be prepared for a certain class of objective phenomena, and that of another for a different one. Once so prepared, it appears difficult to alter the phase of mediumship, as when a bar of steel is forged into a certain shape, it cannot be used for any other than its original purpose without difficulty. As a rule, mediums who have been developed for one class of phenomena rarely change to another, but repeat the same performance *ad infinitum.*

Psychography, or the direct writing of messages by spirits, partakes of both forms of mediumship. The writing itself is an objective physical fact, while the sentiments it contains may be of the very noblest character. The latter depend entirely on the moral state of the medium. It does not require that he should be educated, to write philosophical treatises worthy of Aristotle, nor a poet, to write verses that would reflect honor upon a Byron or a Lamartine; but it does require that the soul of the medium shall be pure enough to serve as a channel for spirits who are capable of giving utterance to such lofty sentiments.

In *Art-Magic,* one of the most delightful pictures presented to us is that of an innocent little child-medium, in whose presence, during the past three years, four volumes of MSS., in the ancient Sanscrit, have been written by the spirits, without pens, pencils, or ink. "It is enough," says the author, "to lay the blank sheets on a tripod, carefully screened from the direct rays of light, but still dimly visible to the eyes of attentive observers. The child sits on the ground and lays her head on the tripod, embracing its supports with her little arms. In this attitude she most commonly sleeps for an hour, during which time the sheets lying on the tripod are filled up with exquisitely formed characters in the ancient Sanscrit." This is so remarkable an instance of psychographic mediumship, and so thoroughly illustrates the principle we have above stated, that we cannot refrain from quoting a few lines from one of the Sanscrit writings, the more so as it embodies that portion of the Hermetic philosophy relating to the antecedent state of man, which elsewhere we have less satisfactorily described.

"Man lives on many earths before he reaches this. Myriads of worlds swarm in space where the soul in rudimental states performs its pilgrimages, ere he reaches the large and shining planet named the Earth, the glorious function of which is to confer *self-consciousness.* At this point only is he man; at every other stage of his vast, wild journey he is but an embryonic being — a fleeting, temporary shape of matter — a creature in which a *part,* but only a part, of the high, imprisoned soul shines forth; a rudimental shape, with rudimental functions, ever living, dying, sustaining a flitting spiritual existence as rudimental as the

584 "*Art-Magic,*" pp. 159, 160.

material shape from whence it emerged; a butterfly, springing up from the chrysalitic shell, but ever, as it onward rushes, in new births, new deaths, new incarnations, anon to die and live again, but still stretch upward, still strive onward, still rush on the giddy, dreadful, toilsome, rugged path, until it awakens once more — once more to live and be a material shape, a thing of dust, a creature of flesh and blood, but now — *a man.*"[585]

THE AUTHOR WITNESSES A TRIAL OF MAGIC IN INDIA

We witnessed once in India a trial of psychical skill between a holy *gossein*[586] and a sorcerer,[587] which recurs to us in this connection. We had been discussing the relative powers of the fakir's Pitris, — pre-Adamite spirits, and the juggler's invisible allies. A trial of skill was agreed upon, and the writer was chosen as a referee. We were taking our noon-day rest, beside a small lake in Northern India. Upon the surface of the glassy water floated innumerable aquatic flowers, and large shining leaves. Each of the contestants plucked a leaf. The fakir, laying his against his breast, folded his hands across it, and fell into a momentary trance. He then laid the leaf, with its surface downward, upon the water. The juggler pretended to control the "water-master," the spirit dwelling in the water; and boasted that he would compel the *power* to prevent the Pitris from manifesting any phenomena upon the fakir's leaf in *their* element. He took his own leaf and tossed it upon the water, after going through a form of barbarous incantation. It at once exhibited a violent agitation, while the other leaf remained perfectly motionless. After the lapse of a few seconds, both leaves were recovered. Upon that of the fakir were found — much to the indignation of the juggler — something that looked like a symmetrical design traced in milk-white characters, as though the juices of the plant had been used as a corrosive writing fluid. When it became dry, and an opportunity was afforded to examine the lines with care, it proved to be a series of exquisitely-formed Sanscrit characters; the whole composed a sentence embodying a high moral precept. The fakir, let us add, could neither read nor write. Upon the juggler's leaf, instead of writing, was found the tracing of a most hideous, impish face. Each leaf, therefore, bore an impression or allegorical reflection of the character of the contestant, and indicated the quality of spiritual beings with which he was surrounded. But, with deep regret, we must once more leave India, with its blue sky and mysterious past, its religious devotees and its weird sorcerers, and on the enchanted carpet of the historian, transport ourselves back to the musty atmosphere of the French Academy.

To appreciate the timidity, prejudice, and superficiality which have marked the treatment of psychological subjects in the past, we propose to review a book which lies before us. It is the *Histoire du Merveilleux dans les Temps Modernes*. The work is published by its author, the learned Dr. Figuier, and teems with quotations from the most conspicuous authorities in physiology, psychology, and medicine. Dr. Calmeil, the well-known director-in-chief of Charenton, the famous lunatic asylum of France, is the robust Atlas on whose mighty shoulders rests this world of erudition. As the ripe fruit of the thought of 1860 it must forever keep a place among the most curious of works of *art*. Moved by the restless

---

585 *"Art-Magic,"* p. 28.
586 Fakir, beggar.
587 A juggler so called.

demon of science, determined to kill superstition — and, as a consequence, spiritism — at one blow, the author affords us a summary view of the most remarkable instances of mediumistic phenomena during the last two centuries.

The discussion embraces the Prophets of Cevennes, the Camisards, the Jansenists, the Abbé Paris, and other historical epidemics, which, as they have been described during the last twenty years by nearly every writer upon the modern phenomena, we will mention as briefly as possible. It is not *facts* that we desire to bring again under discussion, but merely the way in which such facts were regarded and treated by those who, as physicians and recognized authorities, had the greater responsibility in such questions. If this prejudiced author is introduced to our readers at this time, it is only because his work enables us to show what occult facts and manifestations may expect from orthodox science. When the most world-renowned psychological epidemics are so treated, what will induce a materialist to seriously study other phenomena as well authenticated and as interesting, but still less popular? Let it be remembered that the reports made by various committees to their respective academies at that time, as well as the records of the judicial tribunals, are still in existence, and may be consulted for purposes of verification. It is from such unimpeachable sources that Dr. Figuier compiled his extraordinary work. We must give, at least, in substance, the unparalleled arguments with which the author seeks to demolish every form of super-naturalism, together with the commentaries of the demonological des Mousseaux, who, in one of his works,[588] pounces upon his skeptical victim like a tiger upon his prey.

Between the two champions — the materialist and the bigot — the unbiassed student may glean a good harvest.

We will begin with the Convulsionnaires of Cevennes, the epidemic of whose astounding phenomena occurred during the latter part of 1700. The merciless measures adopted by the French Catholics to extirpate the spirit of prophecy from an entire population, is historical, and needs no repetition here. The fact alone that a mere handful of men, women, and children, not exceeding 2,000 persons in number, could withstand for years king's troops, which, with the militia, amounted to 60,000 men, is a miracle in itself. The marvels are all recorded, and the *procès verbaux* of the time preserved in the Archives of France until this day. There is in existence an official report among others, which was sent to Rome by the ferocious Abbé Chayla, the prior of Laval, in which he complains that the *Evil One* is so powerful, that no torture, no amount of inquisitory exorcism, is able to dislodge him from the Cevennois. He adds, that he closed their hands upon burning coals, and they were not even singed; that he had wrapped their whole persons in *cotton soaked with oil, and had set them on fire,* and in many cases did not find one blister on their skins; that balls were shot at them, and found flattened between the skin and clothes, without injuring them, etc., etc.

CASE OF THE CEVENNOIS

Accepting the whole of the above as a solid ground-work for his learned arguments, this is what Dr. Figuier says: "Toward the close of the seventeenth century, an old maid imports

---

588 *"Mœurs et Pratiques des Demons."*

into Cevennes the spirit of prophecy. She communicates it (?) to young boys and girls, who transpire it in their turn, and spread it in the surrounding atmosphere. . . . Women and children become the most sensitive to the infection" (vol. ii., p. 261). "Men, women, and babies speak under inspiration, not in ordinary patois, but in the purest French — a language at that time utterly unknown in the country. Children of twelve months, and even less, as we learn from the procès verbaux, who previously could hardly utter a few short syllables, spoke fluently, and prophesied." "Eight thousand prophets," says Figuier, "were scattered over the country; doctors and eminent physicians were sent for." Half of the medical schools of France, among others, the Faculty of Montpellier, hastened to the spot. Consultations were held, and the physicians declared themselves "delighted, lost in wonder and admiration, upon hearing young girls and boys, ignorant and illiterate, deliver discourses on things they had never learned."[589] The sentence pronounced by Figuier against these treacherous professional brethren, for being so delighted with the young prophets, is that they "did not understand, themselves, what they saw."[590] Many of the prophets forcibly communicated their spirit to those who tried to break the spell.[591] A great number of them were between three and twelve years of age; still others were at the breast, and spoke French distinctly and correctly.[592] These discourses, which often lasted for several hours, would have been impossible to the little orators, were the latter in their natural or normal state.[593]

"Now," asks the reviewer, "what was the meaning of such a series of prodigies, all of them freely admitted in Figuier's book? No meaning at all! It was nothing," he says, "except the effect of a 'momentary exaltation of the intellectual faculties.' "[594] "These phenomena," he adds, "are observable in many of the cerebral affections."

"*Momentary exaltation,* lasting for many hours *in the brains of babies under one year old,* not weaned yet, speaking good French before they had learned to say one word in their own *patois!* Oh, miracle of physiology! *Prodigy* ought to be thy name!" exclaims des Mousseaux.

"Dr. Calmeil, in his work on insanity," remarks Figuier, "when reporting on the ecstatic *theomania* of the Calvinists, concludes that the disease must be attributed in the simpler cases to HYSTERIA, and in those of more serious character to *epilepsy.* . . . We rather incline to the opinion," says Figuier, "that it was a disease *sui generis,* and in order to have an appropriate name for such a disease, we must be satisfied with the one of the Trembling Convulsionaires of Cevennes."[595]

Theomania and *hysteria,* again! The medical corporations must themselves be possessed with an incurable *atomomania*; otherwise why should they give out such absurdities for science, and hope for their acceptance? "Such was the fury for exorcising and *roasting,*" continues Figuier, "that monks saw possessions by demons everywhere when they felt in

---

589 "*Histoire du Merveilleux dans les Temps Modernes,*" vol. ii., p. 262.
590 Ibid.
591 Ibid., p. 265.
592 Ibid., pp. 267, 401, 402.
593 Ibid., pp. 266, etc., 400.
594 Ibid., p. 403.
595 "*Histoire du Merveilleux,*" vol. i., p. 397.

need of miracles to either throw more light on the omnipotency of the Devil, or keep their dinner-pot boiling at the convent."[596]

For this sarcasm the pious des Mousseaux expresses a heartfelt gratitude to Figuier; for, as he remarks, "he is *in France* one of the first writers whom we find, to our surprise, *not denying* the phenomena which have been made long since *undeniable*. Moved by a sense of lofty superiority and even disdain for the method used by his predecessors, Dr. Figuier desires his readers to know that he does *not* follow the same path as they. 'We will not reject,' says he, 'as being unworthy of credit, *facts* only because they are embarrassing for our system. On the contrary, we will collect all of the facts that the same historical evidence has transmitted to us . . . and which, consequently, are entitled to the same credence, and it is upon the whole mass of such facts that we will base the *natural explanation*, which we have to offer, in our turn, as a sequel to those of the savants who have preceded us on this subject.' "[597] Thereupon, Dr. Figuier proceeds.[598] He takes a few steps, and, placing himself right in the midst of the Convulsionaires of St. Medard, he invites his readers to scrutinize, under his direction, *prodigies* which are for him but simple effects of nature.

But before we proceed, in our turn, to show Dr. Figuier's opinion, we must refresh the reader's memory as to what the Jansenist miracles comprised, according to historical evidence.

Abbé Paris was a Jansenist, who died in 1727. Immediately after his decease the most surprising phenomena began to occur at his tomb. The churchyard was crowded from morning till night. Jesuits, exasperated at seeing heretics perform wonders in healing, and other works, got from the magistrates an order to close all access to the tomb of the Abbé. But, notwithstanding every opposition, the wonders lasted for over twenty years. Bishop Douglas, who went to Paris for that sole purpose in 1749, visited the place, and he reports that the miracles were still going on among the Convulsionaires. When every endeavor to stop them failed, the Catholic clergy were forced to admit their reality, but screened themselves, as usual, behind the Devil. Hume, in his *Philosophical Essays*, says: "There surely never was so great a number of miracles ascribed to one person as those which were lately said to have been wrought in France upon the tomb of the Abbé Paris. The curing of the sick, giving hearing to the deaf and sight to the blind, were everywhere talked of as the effects of the holy sepulchre. But, what is more extraordinary, many of the miracles were immediately proved *upon the spot*, before judges of unquestioned credit and distinction, in a learned age, and on the most eminent theatre that is now in the world . . . nor were the Jesuits, though a learned body, supported by the civil magistrates, and determined enemies to those opinions in whose favor the miracles were said to have been wrought, ever able distinctly to refute or detect them . . . such is historic evidence."[599] Dr. Middleton, in his *Free Enquiry*, a book which he wrote at a period when the manifestations were already decreasing, *i.e.*, about nineteen years after they had first begun, declares that the evidence of these miracles is fully as strong as that of the wonders recorded of the Apostles.

---

596 Ibid., pp. 26-27.
597 Ibid., p.238.
598 Des Mousseaux, "*Magie au XIXme Siecle,*" p. 452.
599 Hume, "*Philosophical Essays,*" p. 195.

The phenomena so well authenticated by thousands of witnesses before magistrates, and in spite of the Catholic clergy, are among the most wonderful in history. Carre de Montgeron, a member of parliament and a man who became famous for his connection with the Jansenists, enumerates them carefully in his work. It comprises four thick quarto volumes, of which the first is dedicated to the king, under the title: "*La Verité des Miracles operés par l'Intercession de M. de Paris, demontrée contre l'Archeveque de Sens. Ouvrage dedie au Roi, par M. de Montgeron, Conseiller au Parlement.*" The author presents a vast amount of personal and official evidence to the truthfulness of every case. For speaking *disrespectfully* of the Roman clergy, Montgeron was thrown into the Bastille, but his work was accepted.

And now for the views of Dr. Figuier upon these remarkable and unquestionably historical phenomena. "A Convulsionary bends back into an arc, her loins supported by the sharp point of a peg," quotes the learned author, from the *procès verbaux*. "The pleasure that she begs for is to be pounded by a stone weighing fifty pounds, and suspended by a rope passing over a pulley fixed to the ceiling. The stone, being hoisted to its extreme height, falls with all its weight upon the patient's stomach, her back resting all the while on the sharp point of the peg. Montgeron and numerous other witnesses testified to the fact that neither the flesh nor the skin of the back were ever marked in the least, and that the girl, to show she suffered no pain whatever, kept crying out, 'Strike harder — harder!'

"Jeanne Maulet, a girl of twenty, leaning with her back against a wall, received upon her stomach one hundred blows of a hammer weighing thirty pounds; the blows, administered by a very strong man, were so terrible that they shook the wall. To test the force of the blows, Montgeron tried them on the stone wall against which the girl was leaning. . . . He gets one of the instruments of the Jansenist healing, called the 'grand Secours.' At the twenty-fifth blow," he writes, "the stone upon which I struck, which had been shaken by the preceding efforts, suddenly became loose and fell on the other side of the wall, making an aperture more than half a foot in size." When the blows are struck with violence upon an iron drill held against the stomach of a Convulsionnaire (who, sometimes, is but a weak woman), "it seems," says Montgeron, "as if it would penetrate through to the spine and rupture all the entrails under the force of the blows" (vol. i., p. 380). "But, so far from that occurring, the Convulsionnaire cries out, with an expression of perfect rapture in her face, 'Oh, how delightful! Oh, that does me good! Courage, brother; strike twice as hard, if you can!' It now remains," continues Dr. Figuier, "to try to explain the strange phenomena which we have described."

> "We have said, in the introduction to this work, that at the middle of the nineteenth century one of the most famous epidemics of possession broke out in Germany: that of the *Nonnains*, who performed all the miracles most admired since the days of St. Medard, and even some greater ones; who turned summersaults, who CLIMBED DEAD WALLS, and spoke FOREIGN LANGUAGES."[600]

The official report of the wonders, which is more full than that of Figuier, adds such further particulars as that "the affected persons would stand on their heads for hours together, and correctly describe distant events, even such as were happening in the homes of the committee-men; as it was subsequently verified. Men and women were held

---

600 "*Histoire du Merveilleux,*" p. 401.

suspended in the air, by an invisible force, and the combined efforts of the committee were insufficient to pull them down. Old women climbed perpendicular walls thirty feet in height with the agility of wild cats, etc., etc."

Now, one should expect that the learned critic, the eminent physician and psychologist, who not only credits such incredible phenomena but himself describes them minutely, and *con amore,* so to say, would necessarily startle the reading public with some explanation so extraordinary that his scientific views would cause a real hegira to the unexplored fields of psychology. Well, he does startle us, for to all this he quietly observes: "Recourse *was had to marriage* to bring to a stop these disorders of the Convulsionnaires!"[601]

For once des Mousseaux had the best of his enemy: "Marriage, do you understand this?" he remarks. "Marriage cures them of this faculty of climbing dead-walls like so many flies, and of speaking foreign languages. Oh! the curious properties of marriage in those remarkable days!"

> "It should be added," continues Figuier, "that with the fanatics of St. Medard, the blows were never administered except during the convulsive crisis; and that, therefore, as Dr. Calmeil suggests, meteorism of the abdomen, the *state of spasm* of the uterus of women, of the alimentary canal in all cases, the state of *contraction, of erethism, of turgescence of the carneous envelopes of the muscular coats* which protect and cover the abdomen, chest, and principal vascular masses and the osseous surfaces, *may have singularly contributed toward reducing, and even destroying,* the force of the blows!"

> "The astounding resistance that the skin, the areolar tissue, the surface of the bodies and limbs of the Convulsionnaires offered to things which seem as if they ought to have torn or crushed them, is of a nature to excite more surprise. Nevertheless, it can be explained. This resisting force, this insensibility, seems to partake of the extreme changes in sensibility which can occur in the animal economy during a time of great exaltation. Anger, fear, in a word, every passion, provided that it be carried to a paroxysmal point, can produce this insensibility."[602]

> "Let us remark, besides," rejoins Dr. Calmeil, quoted by Figuier, "that for striking upon the bodies of the Convulsionnaires use was made either of massive objects with flat or rounded surfaces, or of cylindrical and blunt shapes.[603] The action of such physical agents is not to be compared, in respect to the danger which attaches to it, with that of cords, supple or flexible instruments, and those having a sharp edge. In fine, the contact and the shock of the blows produced upon the Convulsionnaires *the effect of a salutary shampooing,* and reduced the violence of the tortures of HYSTERIA."

The reader will please observe that this is not intended as a joke, but is the sober theory of one of the most eminent of French physicians, hoary with age and experience, the Director-in-Chief of the Government Insane Asylum at Charenton. Really, the above

---

601 Ibid.
602 Ibid., vol. ii., pp. 410, 411.
603 Ibid., p. 407.

explanation might lead the reader to a strange suspicion. We might imagine, perhaps, that Dr. Calmeil has kept company with the patients under his care a few more years than was good for the healthy action of his own brain.

Besides, when Figuier talks of massive objects, of cylindrical and blunt shapes, he surely forgets the sharp swords, pointed iron pegs, and the hatchets, of which he himself gave a graphic description on page 409 of his first volume. The brother of Elie Marion is shown by him striking his stomach and abdomen with the sharp point of a knife, with tremendous force, "his body all the while resisting as if it were made of iron."

Arrived at this point, des Mousseaux loses all patience, and indignantly exclaims:

> "Was the learned physician quite awake when writing the above sentences? . . . If, perchance, the Drs. Calmeil and Figuier should seriously maintain their assertions and insist on their theory, we are ready to answer them as follows: 'We are perfectly willing to believe you. But before such a superhuman effort of condescension, will you not demonstrate to us the truth of your theory in a more practical manner? Let us, for example, develop in you a violent and terrible passion; anger — rage if you choose. You shall permit us for a single moment to be in your sight irritating, rude, and insulting. Of course, we will be so only at *your request* and in the interest of science and your cause. Our duty under the contract will consist in humiliating and provoking you to the last extremity. Before a public audience, who shall know nothing of our agreement, but whom you must satisfy as to your assertions, we will insult you; . . . we will tell you that your writings are an ambuscade to truth, an insult to common sense, a disgrace which paper only can bear; but which the public should chastise. We will add that *you lie to science,* you lie to the ears of the ignorant and stupid fools gathered around you, open-mouthed, like the crowd around a peddling quack. . . . And when, transported beyond yourself, your face ablaze, and anger *tumefying,* you shall have *displaced your fluids;* when your fury has reached the point of bursting, we will cause your *turgescent* muscles to be struck with powerful blows; your friends shall show us the most insensible places; we will let a perfect shower, an avalanche of stones fall upon them . . . for so was treated the flesh of the convulsed women whose appetite for such blows could never be satisfied. But, in order to procure for you the gratification of *a salutary shampooing* — as you deliciously express it — your limbs shall only be pounded with objects having *blunt surfaces and cylindrical shapes,* with clubs and sticks devoid of suppleness, and, if you prefer it, neatly turned in a lathe.' "

So liberal is des Mousseaux, so determined to accommodate his antagonists with every possible chance to prove their theory, that he offers them the choice to substitute for themselves in the experiment their wives, mothers, daughters, and sisters, "since," he says, "you have remarked that the weaker sex is the strong and resistant sex in these disconcerting trials."

Useless to remark that des Mousseaux's challenge remained unanswered.

CHAPTER XI

"Strange condition of the human mind, which seems to require that it should long exercise itself in ERROR, before it dare approach the TRUTH."

MAGENDIE

"La verite que je defends est empreinte sur tous les monuments du passe Pour comprendre l'histoire, il faut etudier les symboles anciens, les signes sacres du sacerdoce, et l'art de guerir dans les temps primitifs, art oublie aujourd'hui."

BARON DU POTET

"It is a truth perpetually, that accumulated facts, lying in disorder, begin to assume some order if an hypothesis is thrown among them."

HERBERT SPENCER

AND now we must search Magical History for cases similar to those given in the preceding chapter. This insensibility of the human body to the impact of heavy blows, and resistance to penetration by sharp points and musket-bullets, is a phenomenon sufficiently familiar in the experience of all times and all countries. While science is entirely unable to give any reasonable explanation of the mystery, the question appears to offer no difficulty to mesmerists, who have well studied the properties of the fluid. The man, who by a few passes over a limb can produce a local paralysis so as to render it utterly insensible to burns, cuts, and the prickings of needles, need be but very little astonished at the phenomena of the Jansenists. As to the adepts of magic, especially in Siam and the East Indies, they are too familiar with the properties of the *akasa*, the mysterious life-fluid, to even regard the insensibility of the Convulsionnaires as a very great phenomenon. The astral fluid can be compressed about a person so as to form an elastic shell, absolutely nonpenetrable by any physical object, however great the velocity with which it travels. In a word, this fluid can be made to equal and even excel in resisting-power, water and air.

In India, Malabar, and some places of Central Africa, the conjurers will freely permit any traveller to fire his musket or revolver at them, without touching the weapon themselves or selecting the balls. In Laing's *Travels among Timanni, the Kourankos, and the Soulimas*, occurs a description by an English traveller, the first white man to visit the tribe of the Soulimas, near the sources of the Dialliba, of a very curious scene. A body of picked soldiers fired upon a chief who had nothing to defend himself with but certain talismans. Although their muskets were properly loaded and aimed, not a ball could strike him. Salverte gives a similar case in his *Philosophy of Occult Sciences:* "In 1568, the Prince of Orange condemned a Spanish prisoner to be shot at Juliers; the soldiers tied him to a tree and fired, but he was invulnerable. They at last stripped him to see what armor he wore, but found only an *amulet*. When this was taken from him, *he fell dead at the first shot.*"

INVULNERABILITY ATTAINABLE BY MAN

This is a very different affair from the dexterous trickery resorted to by Houdin in Algeria. He prepared balls himself of tallow, blackened with soot, and by sleight of hand exchanged them for the real bullets, which the Arab sheiks supposed they were placing in the pistols. The simple-minded natives, knowing nothing but real magic, which they had inherited from their ancestors, and which consists in each case of some one thing that they can do without knowing why or how, and seeing Houdin, as they thought, accomplish the same results in a more impressive manner, fancied that he was a greater magician than themselves. Many travellers, the writer included, have witnessed instances of this invulnerability where deception was impossible. A few years ago, there lived in an African village, an Abyssinian who passed for a sorcerer. Upon one occasion a party of Europeans, going to Soudan, amused themselves for an hour or two in firing at him with their own pistols and muskets, a privilege which he gave them for a trifling fee. As many as five shots were fired simultaneously, by a Frenchman named Langlois, and the muzzles of the pieces were not above two yards distant from the sorcerer's breast. In each case, simultaneously with the flash, the bullet would appear just beyond the muzzle, quivering in the air, and then, after describing a short parabola, fall harmlessly to the ground. A German of the party, who was going in search of ostrich feathers, offered the magician a five-franc piece if he would allow him to fire his gun with the muzzle touching his body. The man at first refused; but, finally, after appearing to hold conversation with somebody inside the ground, consented. The experimenter carefully loaded, and pressing the muzzle of the weapon against the sorcerer's body, after a moment's hesitation, fired . . . the barrel burst into fragments as far down as the stock, and the man walked off unhurt.

This quality of invulnerability can be imparted to persons both by living adepts and by spirits. In our own time several well-known mediums have frequently, in the presence of the most respectable witnesses, not only handled blazing coals and actually placed their face upon a fire without singeing a hair, but even laid flaming coals upon the heads and hands of bystanders, as in the case of Lord Lindsay and Lord Adair. The well-known story of the Indian chief, who confessed to Washington that at Braddock's defeat he had fired his rifle at him seventeen times at short range without being able to touch him, will recur to the reader in this connection. In fact, many great commanders have been believed by their soldiers to bear what is called "a charmed life"; and Prince Emile von Sayn-Wittgenstein, a general of the Russian army, is said to be one of these.

Projecting the Force of the Will

This same power which enables one to compress the astral fluid so as to form an impenetrable shell around one, can be used to direct, so to speak, a bolt of the fluid against a given object, with fatal force. Many a dark revenge has been taken in that way; and in such cases the coroner's inquest will never disclose anything but sudden death, apparently resulting from heart-disease, an apoplectic fit, or some other natural, but still not veritable cause. Many persons firmly believe that certain individuals possess the power of the evil eye. The *mal'occhio*, or *jettatura* is a belief which is prevalent throughout Italy and Southern Europe. The Pope is held to be possessed — perchance unconsciously — of that disagreeable gift. There are persons who can kill toads by merely looking at them, and can even slay individuals. The malignance of their desire brings evil forces to a focus, and the death-dealing bolt is projected, as though it were a bullet from a rifle.

In 1864, in the French province of Le Var, near the little village of Brignoles, lived a peasant named Jacques Pelissier, who made a living by killing birds by simple *will-power*.

His case is reported by the well-known Dr. d'Alger, at whose request the singular hunter gave exhibitions to several scientific men, of his method of proceeding. The story is told as follows: "At about fifteen or twenty paces from us, I saw a charming little meadow-lark which I showed to Jacques. 'Watch him well, monsieur,' said he, 'he is mine.' Instantly stretching his right hand toward the bird, he approached him gently. The meadow-lark stops, raises and lowers his pretty head, spreads his wings, but cannot fly; at last he cannot make a step further and suffers himself to be taken, only moving his wings with a feeble fluttering. I examine the bird, his eyes are tightly closed and his body has a corpse-like stiffness, although the pulsations of the heart are very distinct; it is a true cataleptic sleep, and all the phenomena incontestably prove a magnetic action. Fourteen little birds were taken in this way, within the space of an hour; none could resist the power of Master Jacques, and all presented the same cataleptic sleep; a sleep which, moreover, terminates at the will of the hunter, whose humble slaves these little birds have become.

"A hundred times, perhaps, I asked Jacques to restore life and movement to his prisoners, to charm them only half way, so that they might hop along the ground, and then again bring them completely under the charm. All my requests were exactly complied with, and not one single failure was made by this remarkable Nimrod, who finally said to me: 'If you wish it, I will kill those which you designate without touching them.' I pointed out two for the experiment, and, at twenty-five or thirty paces distance, he accomplished in less than five minutes what he had promised."[604]

Insensibility to Snake-Poison

A most curious feature of the above case is, that Jacques had complete power only over sparrows, robins, goldfinches, and meadow-larks; he could sometimes charm skylarks, but, as he says, "they often escape me."

This same power is exercised with greater force by persons known as wild beast tamers. On the banks of the Nile, some of the natives can charm the crocodiles out of the water, with a peculiarly melodious, low whistle, and handle them with impunity; while others possess such powers over the most deadly snakes. Travellers tell of seeing the charmers surrounded by multitudes of the reptiles which they dispatch at their leisure.

Bruce, Hasselquist, and Lempriere,[605] testify to the fact that they have seen in Egypt, Morocco, Arabia, and especially in the Senaar, some natives utterly disregarding the bites of the most poisonous vipers, as well as the stings of scorpions. They handle and play with them, and throw them at will into a state of stupor. "In vain do the Latin and Greek writers," says Salverte, "assure us that the gift of charming venomous reptiles was hereditary in certain families from time immemorial, that in Africa the same gift was enjoyed by the Psylli; that the Marses in Italy, and the Ophiozenes in Cyprus possessed it." The skeptics forget that, in Italy, even at the commencement of the sixteenth century, men, claiming to be descended from the family of Saint Paul, braved, like the Marses, the bites of serpents."[606]

---

604 Villecroze, "*Le Docteur H. d'Alger*," 19 Mars, 1861. Pierrart, vol. iv., pp. 254-257.
605 Bruce, "*Travels to Discover the Sources of the Nile*," vol. x., pp. 402-447; Hasselquist, "*Voyage in the Levant*," vol. i., pp. 92-100; Lempriere, "*Voyage dans l'Empire de Maroc, etc., en 1790*," pp. 42-43.
606 Salverte, "*La Philosophie de la Magie. De l'Influence sur les Animaux*," vol. i.

"Doubts upon this subject," he goes on to say, "were removed forever at the time of the expedition of the French into Egypt, and the following relation is attested by thousands of eye-witnesses. The Psylli, who pretended, as Bruce had related, to possess that faculty . . . went from house to house to destroy serpents of every kind. . . . A wonderful instinct drew them at first toward the place in which the serpents were hidden; furious, howling, and foaming, they seized and tore them asunder with their nails and teeth."

"Let us place," says Salverte, inveterate skeptic himself, "to the account of charlatanism, the howling and the fury; still, the instinct which warned the Psylli of the presence of the serpents, has in it something more real." In the Antilles, the negroes discover, by its odor, a serpent which they do not see.[607] "In Egypt, the same tact, formerly possessed, is still enjoyed by men brought up to it from infancy, and born as with an assumed hereditary gift to hunt serpents, and to discover them even at a distance too great for the effluvia to be perceptible to the dull organs of a European. The principal fact above all others, the faculty or rendering dangerous animals powerless, merely by touching them, remains well verified, and we shall, perhaps, never understand better the nature of this secret, celebrated in antiquity, and preserved to our time by the most ignorant of men."[608]

Music is delightful to every person. Low whistling, a melodious chant, or the sounds of a flute will invariably attract reptiles in countries where they are found. We have witnessed and verified the fact repeatedly. In Upper Egypt, whenever our caravan stopped, a young traveller, who believed he excelled on the flute, amused the company by playing. The camel-drivers and other Arabs invariably checked him, having been several times annoyed by the unexpected appearance of various families of the reptile tribe, which generally shirk an encounter with men. Finally, our caravan met with a party, among whom were professional serpent-charmers, and the virtuoso was then invited, for experiment's sake, to display his skill. No sooner had he commenced, than a slight rustling was heard, and the musician was horrified at suddenly seeing a large snake appear in dangerous proximity with his legs. The serpent, with uplifted head and eyes fixed on him, slowly, and, as if unconsciously, crawled, softly undulating its body, and following his every movement. Then appeared at a distance another one, then a third, and a fourth, which were speedily followed by others, until we found ourselves quite in a select company. Several of the travellers made for the backs of their camels, while others sought refuge in the *cantinier's* tent. But it was a vain alarm. The charmers, three in number, began their chants and incantations, and, attracting the reptiles, were very soon covered with them from head to foot. As soon as the serpents approached the men, they exhibited signs of torpor, and were soon plunged in a deep catalepsy. Their eyes were half closed and glazed, and their heads drooping. There remained but one recalcitrant, a large and glossy black fellow, with a spotted skin. This *meloman* of the desert went on gracefully nodding and leaping, as if it had danced on its tail all its life, and keeping time to the notes of the flute. This snake would not be enticed by the "charming" of the Arabs, but kept slowly moving in the direction of the flute-player, who at last took to his heels. The modern Psyllian then took out of his bag a half-withered plant, which he kept waving in the direction of the serpent. It had a strong smell of mint, and as soon as the reptile caught its odor, it followed the Arab, still erect

---

607 Thibaut de Chanvallon, "*Voyage a la Martinique.*"
608 Salverte, "*Philosophy of Magic.*"

upon its tail, but now approaching the plant. A few more seconds, and the "traditional enemy" of man was seen entwined around the arm of his charmer, became torpid in its turn, and the whole lot were then thrown together in a pool, after having their heads cut off.

CHARMING SERPENTS BY MUSIC

Many believe that all such snakes are prepared and trained for the purpose, and that they are either deprived of their fangs, or have their mouths sewed up. There may be, doubtless, some inferior jugglers, whose trickery has given rise to such an idea. But the *genuine* serpent-charmer has too well established his claims in the East, to resort to any such cheap fraud. They have the testimony on this subject of too many trustworthy travellers, including some scientists, to be accused of any such charlatanism. That the snakes, which are charmed to dance and to become harmless, are still poisonous, is verified by Forbes. "On the music stopping too suddenly," says he, "or from some other cause, the serpent, who had been dancing within a circle of country-people, darted among the spectators, and inflicted a wound in the throat of a young woman, who died in agony, in half an hour afterward."[609]

According to the accounts of many travellers the negro women of Dutch Guiana, the Obeah women, excel in taming very large snakes called *amodites*, or papa; they make them descend from the trees, follow, and obey them by merely speaking to them.[610]

We have seen in India a small brotherhood of fakirs settled round a little lake, or rather a deep pool of water, the bottom of which was literally carpeted with enormous alligators. These amphibious monsters crawl out, and warm themselves in the sun, a few feet from the fakirs, some of whom may be motionless, lost in prayer and contemplation. So long as one of these holy beggars remains in view, the crocodiles are as harmless as kittens. But we would never advise a foreigner to risk himself alone within a few yards of these monsters. The poor Frenchman Pradin found an untimely grave in one of these terrible Saurians, commonly called by the Hindus *Moudela*.[611] (This word should be *nihang* or *ghariyāl*.) When Iamblichus, Herodotus, Pliny, or some other ancient writer tells us of priests who caused asps to come forth from the altar of Isis, or of thaumaturgists taming with a glance the most ferocious animals, they are considered liars and ignorant imbeciles. When modern travellers tell us of the same wonders performed in the East, they are set down as enthusiastic jabberers, or *untrustworthy* writers.

But, despite materialistic skepticism, man does possess such a power, as we see manifested in the above instances. When psychology and physiology become worthy of the name of sciences, Europeans will be convinced of the weird and formidable potency existing in the human will and imagination, whether exercised consciously or otherwise. And yet, how easy to realize such power in *spirit*, if we only think of that grand truism in nature that every most insignificant atom in it is moved by *spirit*, which is *one* in its essence, for the least particle of it represents the *whole*; and that matter is but the concrete copy of the abstract idea, after all. In this connection, let us cite a few instances of the imperial power of

---

609 Forbes, "*Oriental Memoirs*," vol. i., p. 44; vol ii., p. 387.
610 Stedmann, "*Voyage in Surinam*," vol. iii., pp. 64, 65.
611 See "*Edinburgh Review*," vol. lxxx., p. 428, etc.

even the *unconscious* will, to create according to the imagination or rather the faculty of discerning images in the astral light.

We have but to recall the very familiar phenomenon of *stigmata*, or birth-marks, where effects are produced by the involuntary agency of the maternal imagination under a state of excitement. The fact that the mother can control the appearance of her unborn child was so well known among the ancients, that it was the custom among wealthy Greeks to place fine statues near the bed, so that she might have a perfect model constantly before her eyes. The cunning trick by which the Hebrew patriarch Jacob caused ring-streaked and speckled calves to be dropped, is an illustration of the law among animals; and Aricante tells "of four successive litters of puppies, born of healthy parents, some of which, in each litter, were well formed, whilst the remainder were without anterior extremities and had harelip." The works of Geoffroi St. Hilaire, Burdach, and Elam, contain accounts of great numbers of such cases, and in Dr. Prosper Lucas's important volume, *Sur l'Heredité Naturelle*, there are many. Elam quotes from Prichard an instance where the child of a negro and white was marked with black and white color upon separate parts of the body. He adds, with laudable sincerity, "These are singularities of which, in the present state of science, no explanation can be given."[612] It is a pity that his example was not more generally imitated. Among the ancients Empedocles, Aristotle, Pliny, Hippocrates, Galen, Marcus Damascenus, and others give us accounts quite as wonderful as our contemporary authors.

Teratological Phenomena Discussed

In a work published in London, in 1659,[613] a powerful argument is made in refutation of the materialists by showing the potency of the human mind upon the subtile forces of nature. The author, Dr. More, views the fœtus as if it were a plastic substance, which can be fashioned by the mother to an agreeable or disagreeable shape, to resemble some person or in part several persons, and to be stamped with the effigies, or as we might more properly call it, *astrograph,* of some object vividly presented to her imagination. These effects may be produced by her voluntarily or involuntarily, consciously or unconsciously, feebly or forcibly, as the case may be. It depends upon her ignorance or knowledge of the profound mysteries of nature. Taking women in the mass, the marking of the embryo may be considered more accidental than the result of design; and as each person's atmosphere in the astral light is peopled with the images of his or her immediate family, the sensitive surface of the fœtus, which may almost be likened to the collodionized plate of a photograph, is as likely as not to be stamped with the image of a near or remote ancestor, whom the mother never saw, but which, at some critical moment, came as it were into the focus of nature's camera. Says Dr. Elam, "Near me is seated a visitor from a distant continent, where she was born and educated. The portrait of a remote ancestress, far back in the last century, hangs upon the wall. In every feature, one is an accurate presentment of the other, although the one never left England, and the other was an American by birth and half parentage."

---

612 Elam, "*A Physician's Problems,*" p. 25.
613 The "*Immortality of the Soul,*" by Henry More, Fellow of Christ's College, Cambridge.

The power of the imagination upon our physical condition, even after we arrive at maturity, is evinced in many familiar ways. In medicine, the intelligent physician does not hesitate to accord to it a curative or morbific potency greater than his pills and potions. He calls it the *vis medicatrix naturæ,* and his first endeavor is to gain the confidence of his patient so completely, that he can cause nature to extirpate the disease. Fear often kills; and grief has such a power over the subtile fluids of the body as not only to derange the internal organs but even to turn the hair white. Ficinus mentions the *signature* of the fœtus with the marks of cherries and various fruits, colors, hairs, and excrescences, and acknowledges that the imagination of the mother may transform it into a resemblance of an ape, pig, or dog, or any such animal. Marcus Damascenus tells of a girl covered with hair and, like our modern Julia Pastrana, furnished with a full beard; Gulielmus Paradinus, of a child whose skin and nails resembled those of a bear; Balduinus Ronsæus of one born with a turkey's wattles; Pareus, of one with a head like a frog; and Avicenna, of chickens with hawks' heads. In this latter case, which perfectly exemplifies the power of the same imagination in animals, the embryo must have been stamped at the instant of conception when the hen's imagination saw a hawk either in fact or in fancy. This is evident, for Dr. More, who quotes this case on the authority of Avicenna, remarks very appropriately that, as the egg in question might have been hatched a hundred miles distant from the hen, the microscopic picture of the hawk impressed upon the embryo must have enlarged and perfected itself with the growth of the chicken quite independently of any subsequent influence from the hen.

Cornelius Gemma tells of a child that was born with his forehead wounded and running with blood, the result of his father's threats toward his mother " . . . with a drawn sword which he directed toward her forehead"; Sennertius records the case of a pregnant woman who, seeing a butcher divide a swine's head with his cleaver, brought forth her child with his face cloven in the upper jaw, the palate, and upper lip to the very nose. In Van Helmont's *De Injectis Materialibus,* some very astonishing cases are reported: The wife of a tailor at Mechlin was standing at her door and saw a soldier's hand cut off in a quarrel, which so impressed her as to bring on premature labor, and her child was born with only one hand, the other arm bleeding. In 1602, the wife of Marcus Devogeler, a merchant of Antwerp, seeing a soldier who had just lost his arm, was taken in labor and brought forth a daughter with one arm struck off and bleeding as in the first case. Van Helmont gives a third example of another woman who witnessed the beheading of thirteen men by order of the Duc d'Alva. The horror of the spectacle was so overpowering that she "suddainly fell into labour and brought forth a perfectly-formed infant, only the head was wanting, but the neck bloody as their bodies she beheld that had their heads cut off. And that which does still advance the wonder is, that the *hand, arme,* and *head* of these infants were none of them to be found."[614]

If it was possible to conceive of such a thing as a miracle in nature, the above cases of the sudden disappearance of portions of the unborn human body might be designated. We have looked in vain through the latest authorities upon human physiology for any sufficient theory to account for the least remarkable of fœtal signatures. The most they can do is to record instances of what they call "spontaneous varieties of type," and then fall back either upon Mr. Proctor's "curious coincidences" or upon such candid confessions of ignorance as

614 Dr. H. More, *"Immortality of the Soul,"* p. 393.

are to be found in authors not entirely satisfied with the sum of human knowledge. Magendie acknowledges that, despite scientific researches, comparatively little is known of fœtal life. At page 518 of the American edition of his *Precis Elementaire de Physiologie* he instances "a case where the umbilical cord was ruptured and perfectly cicatrized"; and asks "How was the circulation carried on in this organ?" On the next page, he says: "Nothing is at present known respecting the use of digestion in the fœtus"; and respecting its nutrition, propounds this query: "What, then, can we say of the nutrition of the fœtus? Physiological works contain only *vague conjectures* on this point." On page 520, the following language occurs: "In consequence of some *unknown cause*, the different parts of the fœtus sometimes develop themselves in a preternatural manner." With singular inconsistency with his previous admissions of the ignorance of science upon all these points which we have quoted, he adds: "*There is no reason for believing that the imagination of the mother can have any influence in the formation of these monsters*; besides, productions of this kind are daily observed in the offspring of other animals and even in plants." How perfect an illustration is this of the methods of scientific men! — the moment they pass beyond their circle of observed facts, their judgment seems to become entirely perverted. Their deductions from their own researches are often greatly inferior to those made by others who have to take the facts at second hand.

The literature of science is constantly furnishing examples of this truth; and when we consider the reasoning of materialistic observers upon psychological phenomena, the rule is strikingly manifest. Those who are *soul-blind* are as constitutionally incapable of distinguishing psychological causes from material effects as the color-blind are to select scarlet from black.

Elam, without being in the least a spiritualist, nay, though an enemy to it, represents the belief of honest scientists in the following expressions: "it is certainly inexplicable how matter and mind can act and react one upon the other; the mystery is acknowledged by all to be insoluble, and will probably ever remain so."

The great English authority upon the subject of malformation is *The Science and Practice of Medicine,* by Wm. Aitken, M. D., Edinburgh, and Professor of Pathology in the Army Medical School; the American edition of which, by Professor Meredith Clymer, M. D., of the University of Pennsylvania, has equal weight in the United States. At page 233 of vol. i. we find the subject treated at length. The author says, "The superstition, absurd notions, and strange causes assigned to the occurrence of such malformations, are now fast disappearing before the lucid expositions of those famous anatomists who have made the development and growth of the ovum a subject of special study. It is sufficient to mention here the names, J. Muller, Ratlike, Bischoff, St. Hilaire, Burdach, Allen Thompson, G. & W. Vrolick, Wolff, Meckel, Simpson, Rokitansky, and Von Ammon as sufficient evidence that the truths of science will in time dispel the mists of ignorance and superstition." One would think, from the complacent tone adopted by this eminent writer that we were in possession if not of the means of readily solving this intricate problem at least of a clew to guide us through the maze of our difficulties. But, in 1872, after profiting by all the labors and ingenuity of the illustrious pathologists above enumerated, we find him making the same confession of ignorance as that expressed by Magendie in 1838. "Nevertheless," says he, "much mystery still enshrouds the origin of malformation; the origin of them may be considered in two main issues, namely: 1, are they due to original malformation of the germ? 2, or, are they due to subsequent deformities of the embryo by causes operating on its development? With regard to the first issue, it is believed that the germ may be originally malformed, or defective, owing to *some influence proceeding either from the female, or from the male,* as in case of repeated procreation of the same kind of malformation by the same parents, deformities on either side being transmitted as an inheritance."

Being unsupplied with any philosophy of their own to account for the lesions, the pathologists, true to professional instinct, resort to negation. "That such deformity may be produced by mental impressions on pregnant women there is an absence of positive proof," they say. "Moles, mothers' marks, and cutaneous spots as ascribed to morbid states of the coats of the ovum. . . . A very generally-recognized cause of malformation consists in impeded development of the fœtus, *the cause of which is not always obvious, but is for the most part concealed. . . . Transient forms of the human fœtus are comparable to persistent forms of many lower animals.*" Can the learned professor explain why? "*Hence malformations resulting from arrest of development often acquire an animal-like appearance.*"

Exactly; but why do not pathologists inform us why it is so? Any anatomist who has made the development and growth of the embryo and fœtus "a subject of special study," can tell, without much brain-work, what daily experience and the evidence of his own eyes show him, viz.: that up to a certain period, the human embryo is a fac-simile of a young batrachian in its first remove from the spawn — a tadpole. But no physiologist or anatomist seems to have had the idea of applying to the development of the human being — from the first instant of its physical appearance as a germ to its ultimate formation and birth — the Pythagorean esoteric doctrine of metempsychosis, so erroneously interpreted by critics. The meaning of the kabalistic axiom: "A stone becomes a plant; a plant a beast; a beast a man, etc.," was mentioned in another place in relation to the spiritual and physical evolution of man on this earth. We will now add a few words more to make the idea clearer.

What is the primitive shape of the future man? A grain, a corpuscle, say some physiologists; a molecule, an ovum of the ovum, say others. If it could be analyzed — by the spectroscope or otherwise — of what ought we to expect to find it composed? Analogically, we should say, of a nucleus of inorganic matter, deposited from the circulation at the germinating point, and united with a deposit of organic matter. In other words, this infinitesimal nucleus of the future man is composed of the same elements as a stone — of the same elements as the earth, which the man is destined to inhabit. Moses is cited by the kabalists as authority for the remark, that it required earth and water to make a living being, and thus it may be said that man first appears as a stone.

At the end of three or four weeks the ovum has assumed a plant-like appearance, one extremity having become spheroidal and the other tapering, like a carrot. Upon dissection it is found to be composed, like an onion, of very delicate laminæ or coats, enclosing a liquid. The laminæ approach each other at the lower end, and the embryo hangs from the root of the umbilicus almost like a fruit from the bough. The stone has now become changed, by metempsychosis, into a plant. Then the embryonic creature begins to shoot out, from the inside outward, its limbs, and develops its features. The eyes are visible as two black dots; the ears, nose, and mouth form depressions, like the points of a pineapple, before they begin to project. The embryo develops into an animal-like fœtus — the shape of a tadpole — and like an amphibious reptile lives in water, and develops from it. Its monad has not yet become either human or immortal, for the kabalists tell us that that only comes at the "fourth hour." One by one the fœtus assumes the characteristics of the human being, the first flutter of the immortal breath passes through his being; he moves; nature opens the way for him; ushers him into the world; and the divine essence settles in the infant frame, which it will inhabit until the moment of physical death, when man becomes a spirit.

This mysterious process of a nine-months formation the kabalists call the completion of the "individual cycle of evolution." As the fœtus develops from the *liquor amnii* in the womb, so the earths germinate from the universal ether, or astral fluid, in the womb of the universe. These cosmic children, like their pigmy inhabitants, are first nuclei; then ovules; then gradually mature; and becoming mothers in their turn, develop mineral, vegetable, animal, and human forms. From centre to circumference, from the imperceptible vesicle to the uttermost conceivable bounds of the cosmos, these glorious thinkers, the kabalists, trace cycle merging into cycle, containing and contained in an endless series. The embryo evolving in its pre-natal sphere, the individual in his family, the family in the state, the state in mankind, the earth in our system, that system in its central universe, the universe in the cosmos, and the cosmos in the First Cause: — the Boundless and Endless. So runs their philosophy of evolution:

> "All are but parts of one stupendous whole,
> Whose body Nature is; and God the Soul."
> "Worlds without number
> Lie in this bosom like children."

While unanimously agreeing that physical causes, such as blows, accidents, and bad quality of food for the mother, affect the fœtus in a way which endangers its life; and while admitting again that moral causes, such as fear, sudden terror, violent grief, or even extreme joy, may retard the growth of the fœtus or even kill it, many physiologists agree with Magendie in saying, "there is no reason for believing that the imagination of the mother can have any influence in the formation of monsters"; and only because "productions of this kind are daily observed in the production of other animals and even in plants."

In this opinion he is supported by the leading teratologists of our day. Although Geoffroi St. Hilaire gave its name to the new science, its facts are based upon the exhaustive experiments of Bichat, who, in 1802, was recognized as the founder of analytical and philosophical anatomy. One of the most important contributions to teratological literature is the monograph of G. J. Fisher, M.D., of Sing Sing, N. Y., entitled *Diploteratology; an Essay on Compound Human Monsters*. This writer classifies monstrous fœtal growths into their genera and species, accompanying the cases with reflections suggested by their peculiarities. Following St. Hilaire, he divides the history of the subject into the fabulous, the positive, and the scientific periods.

It suffices for our purpose to say that in the present state of scientific opinion two points are considered as established: 1, that the maternal, mental condition has no influence in the production of monstrosities; 2, that most varieties of monstrosity may be accounted for on the theory of *arrest* and *retardation* of development. Says Fisher, "By a careful study of the laws of development and the order in which the various organs are evolved in the embryo, it has been observed that monsters by defect or arrest of development, are, to a certain extent, permanent embryos. The abnormal organs merely represent the primitive condition of formation as it existed in an early stage of embryonic or fœtal life."[615] With physiology in so confessedly chaotic a state as it is at present, it seems a little like hardihood in any teratologist, however great his achievements in anatomy, histology, or embryology, to take so dangerous a position as that the mother has no influence upon her offspring. While the microscopes of Haller and Prolik, Dareste and Laraboulet have disclosed to us many interesting facts concerning the single or double primitive traces on the vitelline membrane, what remains undiscovered about embryology by modern science appears greater still. If we grant that monstrosities are the result of an arrest of development — nay, if we go farther, and concede that the fœtal future may be prognosticated from the vitelline tracings, where will the teratologists take us to learn the *antecedent* psychological cause of either? Dr. Fisher may have carefully studied some hundreds of cases, and feel himself authorized to construct a new classification of their genera and species; but facts are facts, and outside the field of his observation it appears, even if we judge but by our own personal experience, in various countries, that there are abundant attainable proofs that the violent maternal emotions are often reflected in tangible, visible, and permanent disfigurements of the child. And the cases in question seem, moreover, to contradict Dr. Fisher's assertion that monstrous growths are due to causes traceable to "the early stages of embryonic or fœtal life." One case was that of a Judge of an Imperial Court at Saratow, Russia, who always wore a bandage to cover a mouse-mark on the left side of his face. It was a perfectly-formed mouse, whose body was represented in high relief upon the cheek, and the tail ran upward across the temple and was lost in his hair. The body seemed glossy, gray, and quite natural. According to his own account, his mother had an unconquerable repugnance to mice, and her labor was prematurely brought on by seeing a mouse jump out from her workbox.

In another instance, of which the writer was a witness, a pregnant lady, within two or three weeks of her accouchement, saw a bowl of raspberries, and was seized with an irresistible longing for some, but denied. She excitedly clasped her right hand to her neck in a somewhat theatrical manner, and exclaimed that she *must* have them. The child born under our eyes, three weeks later, had a perfectly-defined raspberry on the right side of his neck; to this day, when that fruit ripens, his birth-mark becomes of a deep crimson, while, during the winter, it is quite pale.

Such cases as these, which are familiar to many mothers of families, either in their personal experience or that of friends, carry conviction, despite the theories of all the teratologists of Europe and America. Because, forsooth, animals and plants are observed to produce malformations of their species as well as human beings, Magendie and his school infer that the human malformations of an identical character are not at all due to maternal imagination, *since the former are not.* If physical causes produce physical effects in the subordinate kingdoms, the inference is that the same rule must hold with ourselves.

But an entirely original theory was broached by Professor Armor, of the Long Island Medical College, in the course of a discussion recently held in the Detroit Academy of Medicine. In opposition to the orthodox views which Dr. Fisher represents, Professor Armor says that malformations result from either one of two causes — 1, a deficiency or abnormal condition in the generative matter from which the fœtus is developed, or 2, morbid

---

615 *"Transactions of the Medical Society of N. Y.,"* 1865-6-7.

influences acting on the *fœtus in utero*. He maintains that the generative matter represents in its composition every tissue, structure, and form, and that there may be such a transmission of *acquired* structural peculiarities as would make the generative matter incapable of producing a healthy and equally-developed offspring. On the other hand, the generative matter may be perfect in itself, but being subjected to morbid influences during the process of gestation, the offspring will, of necessity, be monstrous.

To be consistent, this theory must account for diploteratological cases (double-headed or double-membered monsters), which seems difficult. We might, perhaps, admit that in defective generative matter, the head of the embryo might not be represented, or any other part of the body be deficient; but, it hardly seems as if there could be two, three, or more representatives of a single member. Again, if the generative matter have hereditary taint, it seems as if *all* the resulting progeny should be equally monstrous; whereas the fact is that in many cases the mother has given birth to a number of healthy children before the monster made its appearance, all being the progeny of one father. Numerous cases of this kind are quoted by Dr. Fisher; among others he cites the case of Catherine Corcoran,[616] a "very healthy woman, thirty years of age and who, previously to giving birth to this monster had born five well-formed children, no two of which were twins . . . it had a head at either extremity, two chests, with arms complete, two abdominal and two pelvic cavities united end to end, with four legs placed two at either side, where the union between the two occurred." Certain parts of the body, however, were not duplicated, and therefore this cannot be claimed as a case of the growing together of twins.

Another instance is that of Maria Teresa Parodi.[617] This woman, who had previously given birth to eight well-formed children, was delivered of a female infant the upper part of which only was double. Instances in which *before* and *after* the production of a monster the children were perfectly healthy are numerous, and if, on the other hand, the fact that monstrosities are as common with animals as they are with mankind is a generally-accepted argument against the popular theory that these malformations are due to the imagination of the mother; and that other fact — that there is no difference between the ovarian cell of a mammifer and man, be admitted, what becomes of Professor Armor's theory? In such a case an instance of an animal-malformation is as good as that of a human monster; and this is what we read in Dr. Samuel L. Mitchell's paper *On two-headed Serpents:* "A female snake was killed, together with her whole brood of young ones, amounting to 120, of these *three were monsters*. One with two distinct heads; one with a double head and only three eyes; and one with a double skull, furnished with three eyes, and a single lower jaw; this last had two bodies."[618] Surely the *generative matter* which produced these *three monsters* was identical with that which produced the other 117? Thus the *Armor* theory is as imperfect as all the rest.

The trouble proceeds from the defective method of reasoning usually adopted — *Induction;* a method which claims to collect by *experiment* and observation all the facts *within* its reach, the former being rather that of collecting and examining experiments and drawing

---

616 "*Dublin Quarterly Journal of Medical Science,*" vol. xv., p. 263, 1853.
617 "*Recherches d'Anatomie transcendante et Pathologique, etc.,*" Paris, 1832.
618 "*Silliman's Journal of Science and Art,*" vol. x., p. 48.

conclusions therefrom; and, according to the author of *Philosophical Inquiry*, "as this conclusion cannot be extended beyond what is warranted by the experiments, the Induction is an instrument of proof and *limitation*." Notwithstanding this limitation is to be found in every scientific inquiry, it is rarely confessed, but hypotheses are constructed for us as though the experimenters had found them to be mathematically-proved theorems, while they are, to say the most, simple approximations.

For a student of occult philosophy, who rejects in his turn the method of induction on account of these perpetual limitations, and fully adopts the Platonic division of causes — namely, the Efficient, the Formal, the Material, and the Final, as well as the Eleatic method of examining any given proposition, it is but natural to reason from the following stand-point of the Neo-platonic school: 1. The subject either is as it is supposed or *is not*. Therefore we will inquire: Does the universal ether, known by the kabalists as the "astral light," contain electricity and magnetism, or does it not? The answer must be in the affirmative, for "exact science" herself teaches us that these two convertible agents saturating both the air and the earth, there is a constant interchange of electricity and magnetism between them. The question No. 1 being settled, we will have now to examine *what happens* — 1st. To it with respect to *itself*. 2d. To *it* with respect to *all other* things. 3d. With all *other things*, with respect *to it*. 4th. To all *other things* with respect *to themselves*.

ANSWERS: 1st. With respect to *itself*. That inherent properties previously latent in electricity, become active under favoring conditions; and that at one time the form of magnetic force is assumed by the subtile, all-pervading agent; at another, the form of electric force is assumed.

2d. With respect to all other things. By all other things for which it has an affinity, it is attracted, by all others repelled.

3d. With all other things with respect to it. It happens that whenever they come in contact with electricity, they receive its impress in proportion to their conductivity.

4th. To all other things with respect to themselves. That under the impulse received from the electric force, and in proportion to its intensity, their molecules change their relations with each other; that either they are wrenched asunder, so as to destroy the object — organic or inorganic — which they formed, or, if previously disturbed, are brought into equilibrium (as in cases of disease); or the disturbance may be but superficial, and the object may be stamped with the image of some other object encountered by the fluid before reaching them. To apply the above propositions to the case in point: There are several well-recognized principles of science, as, for instance, that a pregnant woman is physically and mentally in a highly impressible state. Physiology tells us that her intellectual faculties are weakened, and that she is affected to an unusual degree by the most trifling events. Her pores are opened, and she exudes a peculiar cutaneous perspiration; she seems to be in a receptive condition for all the influences in nature. Reichenbach's disciples assert that her *odic* condition is very intense. Du Potet warns against incautiously mesmerizing her, for fear of affecting the offspring. Her diseases are imparted to it, and often it absorbs them entirely to itself; her pains and pleasures react upon its temperament as well as its health; great men proverbially have great mothers, and *vice versa*. "*It is true that her imagination has an influence upon the fœtus,"* admits Magendie, thus contradicting what he asserts in another place; and he adds that "sudden terror may cause the death of the fœtus, *or retard its growth."*[619]

In the case recently reported in the American papers, of a boy who was killed by a stroke of lightning, upon stripping the body, there was found imprinted upon his breast the faithful picture of a tree which grew near the window which he was facing at the time of the catastrophe, and which was also felled by the lightning. Now, this electrical photography, which was accomplished by the blind forces of nature, furnishes an analogy by which we may understand how the mental images of the mother are transmitted to the unborn child. Her *pores* are opened; she exudes an odic emanation which is but another form of the *akasa,* the electricity, or life-principle, and which, according to Reichenbach, produces mesmeric sleep, and consequently is *magnetism.* Magnetic currents develop themselves into electricity upon their exit from the body. An object making a violent impression on the mother's mind, its image is instantly projected into the astral light, or the universal ether, which Jevons and Babbage, as well as the authors of the *Unseen Universe,* tell us is the repository of the *spiritual* images of all forms, and even human thoughts. Her magnetic emanations attract and unite themselves with the descending current which already bears the image upon it. It rebounds, and re-percussing more or less violently, impresses itself upon the fœtus, according to the very formula of physiology which shows how every maternal feeling reacts on the offspring. Is this kabalistic theory more *hypothetical* or incomprehensible than the teratological doctrine taught by the disciples of Geoffroi St. Hilaire? The doctrine, of which Magendie so justly observes, "is found convenient and easy from its *vagueness* and obscurity," and which "pretends to nothing less than the creation of a new science, the theory of which reposes on certain laws not very intelligible, as that of *arresting,* that of *retarding,* that of *similar* or *eccentric* position, especially the *great law,* as it is called, of *self for self."*[620]

Eliphas Levi, who is certainly one of the best authorities on certain points among kabalists, says: "Pregnant women are, more than others, under the influence of the astral light, which assists in the formation of their child, and constantly presents to them the reminiscences of forms with which it is filled. It is thus that very virtuous women deceive the malignity of observers by equivocal resemblances. They often impress upon the fruit of their marriage an image which has struck them in a dream, and thus are the same physiognomies perpetuated from age to age.

"The kabalistic use of the pentagram can therefore determine the countenance of unborn infants, and an initiated woman might give to her son the features of Nereus or Achilles, as well as those of Louis XV. or Napoleon."[621]

If it should confirm another theory than that of Dr. Fisher, he should be the last to complain, for as he himself makes the confession, which his own example verifies:[622] "One of the most formidable obstacles to the advancement of science . . . has ever been a *blind submission to authority. . . .* To untrammel the mind from the influence of mere authority, that

---

619 *"Precis Elementaire de Physiologie,"* p. 520.

620 Ibid., p. 521.

621 *"Dogme et Rituel de la Haute Magie,"* p. 175.

622 *"Transactions of Medical Society, etc.,"* p. 246.

it may have free scope in the investigation of facts and laws which exist and are established in nature, is the grand antecedent necessary to scientific discovery and permanent progress."

If the maternal imagination can stunt the growth or destroy the life of the fœtus, why cannot it influence its physical appearance? There are some surgeons who have devoted their lives and fortunes to find the cause for these malformations, but have only reached the opinion that they are mere "coincidences." It would be also highly unphilosophical to say that animals are not endowed with imagination; and, while it might be considered the acme of metaphysical speculation to even formulate the idea that members of the vegetable kingdom — say the *mimosas* and the group of insect-catchers — have an instinct and even rudimentary imagination of their own, yet the idea is not without its advocates. If great physicists like Tyndall are forced to confess that even in the case of intelligent and speaking man they are unable to bridge the chasm between mind and matter, and define the powers of the imagination, how much greater must be the mystery about what takes place in the brain of a dumb animal.

What is imagination? *Psychologists tell us that it is the plastic or creative power of the soul;* but materialists confound it with fancy. The radical difference between the two, was however, so thoroughly indicated by Wordsworth, in the preface to his *Lyrical Ballads*, that it is no longer excusable to interchange the words. Imagination, Pythagoras maintained to be the remembrance of precedent spiritual, mental, and physical states, while fancy is the disorderly production of the material brain.

From whatever aspect we view and question matter, the world-old philosophy that it was vivified and fructified by the eternal idea, or imagination — the abstract outlining and preparing the model for the concrete form — is unavoidable. If we reject this doctrine, the theory of a cosmos evolving gradually out of its chaotic disorder becomes an absurdity; for it is highly unphilosophical to imagine inert matter, solely moved by blind force, and directed by intelligence, forming itself spontaneously into a universe of such admirable harmony. If the soul of man is really an outcome of the essence of this universal soul, an infinitesimal fragment of this first creative principle, it must of necessity partake in degree of all the attributes of the demiurgic power. As the creator, breaking up the chaotic mass of dead, inactive matter, shaped it into form, so man, if he knew his powers, could, to a degree, do the same. As Pheidias, gathering together the loose particles of clay and moistening them with water, could give plastic shape to the sublime idea evoked by his creative faculty, so the mother who knows her power can fashion the coming child into whatever form she likes. Ignorant of his powers, the sculptor produces only an inanimate though ravishing figure of inert matter; while the soul of the mother, violently affected by her imagination, blindly projects into the astral light an image of the object which impressed it, and, by re-percussion, that is stamped upon the fœtus. Science tells us that the law of gravitation assures us that any displacement which takes place in the very heart of the earth will be felt throughout the universe, "and we may even imagine that the same thing will hold true of those molecular motions which accompany thought."[623] Speaking of the transmission of energy throughout the universal ether or astral light, the same authority says: "Continual

---

623 Fournié, *"Physiologie du Système Nerveux, Cerebro-spinal,"* Paris, 1872.

photographs of all occurrences are thus produced and retained. A large portion of the energy of the universe may thus be said to be invested in such pictures."

Dr. Fournié, of the National Deaf and Dumb Institute of France, in chapter ii. of his work,[624] in discussing the question of the fœtus, says that the most powerful microscope is unable to show us the slightest difference between the ovarian cell of a mammifer and a man; and, respecting the first or last movement of the ovule, asks: "What is it? has it particular characters which distinguish it from every other ovule?" and justly answers thus: "Until now, science has not replied to these questions, and, without being a pessimist, I do not think *that she ever will reply;* from the day when her methods of investigation will permit her to surprise the hidden mechanism of the conflict of the principle of life with matter, she will know life itself, and be able to produce it." If our author had read the sermon of Pere Felix, how appropriately he might utter his Amen! to the priest's exclamation — MYSTERY! MYSTERY!

Let us consider the assertion of Magendie in the light of recorded instances of the power of imagination in producing monstrous deformities, where the question does not involve pregnant women. He admits that these occur daily in the offspring of the lower animals; how does he account for the hatching of chickens with hawk-heads, except upon the theory that the appearance of the hereditary enemy acted upon the hen's imagination, which, in its turn, imparted to the matter composing the germ a certain motion which, before expanding itself, produced the monstrous chicks? We know of an analogous case, where a tame dove, belonging to a lady of our acquaintance, was frightened daily by a parrot, and in her next brood of young there were two squabs with parrots' heads, the resemblance even extending to the color of the feathers. We might also cite Columella, Youatt, and other authorities, together with the experience of all animal breeders, to show that by exciting the imagination of the mother, the external appearance of the offspring can be largely controlled. These instances in no degree affect the question of heredity, for they are simply special variations of type artificially caused.

Catherine Crowe discusses at considerable length the question of the power of the mind over matter, and relates, in illustration, many well-authenticated instances of the same.[625] Among others, that most curious phenomenon called the *stigmata* have a decided bearing upon this point. These marks come upon the bodies of persons of all ages, and always as the result of exalted imagination. In the cases of the Tyrolese ecstatic, Catherine Emmerich, and many others, the wounds of the crucifixion are said to be as perfect as nature. A certain Mme. B. von N. dreamed one night that a person offered her a red and a white rose, and that she chose the latter. On awaking, she felt a burning pain in her arm, and by degrees there appeared the figure of a rose, perfect in form and color; it was rather raised above the skin. The mark increased in intensity till the eighth day, after which it faded away, and by the fourteenth, was no longer perceptible. Two young ladies, in Poland, were standing by an open window during a storm; a flash of lightning fell near them, and the gold necklace on the neck of one of them was melted. A perfect image of it was impressed upon the skin, and remained throughout life. The other girl, appalled by the accident to her companion,

---

624 Ibid.
625 *"Night-Side of Nature,"* by Catherine Crowe, p. 434, *et seq.*

stood transfixed with horror for several minutes, and then fainted away. Little by little the same mark of a necklace as had been instantaneously imprinted upon her friend's body, appeared upon her own, and remained there for several years, when it gradually disappeared.

Dr. Justinus Kerner, the distinguished German author, relates a still more extraordinary case. "At the time of the French invasion, a Cossack having pursued a Frenchman into a *cul-de-sac,* an alley without an outlet, there ensued a terrible conflict between them, in which the latter was severely wounded. A person who had taken refuge in this close, and could not get away, was so dreadfully frightened, that when he reached home there broke out on his body the very same wounds that the Cossack had inflicted on his enemy!"

In this case, as in those where organic disorders, and even physical death result from a sudden excitement of the mind reacting upon the body, Magendie would find it difficult to attribute the effect to any other cause than the imagination; and if he were an occultist, like Paracelsus, or Van Helmont, the question would be stripped of its mystery. He would understand the power of the human will and imagination — the former conscious, the latter involuntary — on the universal agent to inflict injury, physical and mental, not only upon chosen victims, but also, by reflex action, upon one's self and unconsciously. It is one of the fundamental principles of magic, that if a current of this subtile fluid is not impelled with sufficient force to reach the objective point, it will react upon the individual sending it, as an India-rubber ball rebounds to the thrower's hand from the wall against which it strikes without being able to penetrate it. There are many cases instanced where *would-be sorcerers* fell victims themselves. Van Helmont says: "The imaginative power of a woman vividly excited produces an idea, which is the connecting medium between the body and spirit. This transfers itself to the being with whom the woman stands in the most immediate relation, and impresses upon it that image which the most agitated herself."

Deleuze has collected, in his *Bibliothèque du Magnetisme Animal,* a number of remarkable facts taken from Van Helmont, among which we will content ourselves with quoting the following as pendants to the case of the bird-hunter, Jacques Pelissier. He says that "men by looking steadfastly at animals *oculis intentis* for a quarter of an hour may cause their death; which Rousseau confirms from his own experience in Egypt and the East, as having killed several toads in this manner. But when he at last tried this at Lyons, the toad, finding it could not escape from his eye, turned round, blew itself up, and stared at him so fiercely, without moveing its eyes, that a weakness came over him even to fainting, and he was for some time thought to be dead."

But to return to the question of teratology. Wierus tells, in his *De Præstigiis Demonum,* of a child born of a woman who not long before its birth was threatened by her husband, he saying that she had the devil in her and that he would kill him. The mother's fright was such that her offspring appeared "well-shaped from the middle downward, but upward spotted with blackened red spots, with eyes in his forehead, a mouth like a Satyr, ears like a dog, and bended horns on its head like a goat." In a demonological work by Peramatus, there is a story of a monster born at St. Lawrence, in the West Indies, in the year 1573, the genuineness of which is certified to by the Duke of Medina-Sidonia. The child, "besides the horrible deformity of its mouth, ears, and nose, had two horns on the head, like those of young goats, long hair on his body, a fleshy girdle about his middle, double, from whence hung a piece of flesh like a purse, and a bell of flesh in his left hand like those the Indians use when they dance, white boots of flesh on his legs, doubled down. In brief, the whole shape was horrid and diabolical, and conceived to proceed from some fright the mother had taken from the antic dances of the Indians."[626] Dr. Fisher rejects all such instances as unauthenticated and fabulous.

But we will not weary the reader with further selections from the multitude of teratological cases to be found recorded in the works of standard authors; the above suffice to show that there is reason to attribute these aberrations of physiological type to the mutual reaction of the maternal mind and the universal ether upon each other. Lest some should question the authority of Van Helmont, as a man of science, we will refer them to the work of Fournié, the well-known physiologist, where (at page 717) the following estimate of his character will be found: "Van Helmont was a highly distinguished chemist; he had particularly studied aëriform fluids, and gave them the name of *gaz*; at the same time he pushed his piety to mysticism, abandoning himself exclusively to a contemplation of the divinity. . . . Van Helmont is distinguished above all his predecessors by connecting *the principle of life*, directly and in some sort experimentally, as he tells us, with the most minute movements of the body. It is the incessant action of this entity, in no way associated by him with the material elements, but forming a distinct individuality, that we cannot understand. Nevertheless, it is upon this entity that a famous school has laid its principal foundation."

Van Helmont's "principle of life," or *archæus*, is neither more nor less than the astral light of all the kabalists, and the universal ether of modern science. If the more unimportant signatures of the fœtus are not due to the imagination of the mother, to what other cause would Magendie attribute the formation of horny scales, the horns of goats and the hairy coats of animals, which we have seen in the above instances marking monstrous progeny? Surely there were no latent germs of these distinguishing features of the animal kingdom capable of being developed under a sudden impulse of the maternal fancy. In short, the only possible explanation is the one offered by the adepts in the occult sciences.

Before leaving the subject, we wish to say a few words more respecting the cases where the head, arm, and hand were instantly dissolved, though it was evident that in each instance the entire body of the child had been perfectly formed. Of what is a child's body composed at its birth? The chemists will tell us that it comprises a dozen pounds of solidified gas, and a few ounces of ashy residuum, some water, oxygen, hydrogen, nitrogen, carbonic acid, a little lime, magnesia, phosphorus, and a few other minerals; that is all! Whence came they? How were they gathered together? How were these particles which Mr. Proctor tells us are drawn in from "the depths of space surrounding us on all sides," formed and fashioned into the human being? We have seen that it is useless to ask the dominant school of which Magendie is an illustrious representative; for he confesses that they know nothing of the nutrition, digestion, or circulation of the fœtus; and physiology teaches us that while the ovule is enclosed in the Graafian vesicle it participates — forms an integral part of the general structure of the mother. Upon the rupture of the vesicle, it becomes almost as independent of her for what is to build up the body of the future being as the germ in a bird's egg after the mother has dropped it in the nest. There certainly is very little

---

626 Henry More, *"Immortality of the Soul,"* p. 399.

in the demonstrated facts of science to contradict the idea that the relation of the embryonic child to the mother is much different from that of the tenant to the house, upon whose shelter he depends for health, warmth, and comfort.

According to Demokritus, the soul[627] results from the aggregation of atoms, and Plutarch describes his philosophy as follows: "That there are substances infinite in number, indivisible, undisturbed, which are without differences, without qualities, and which move in space, where they are disseminated; that when they approach each other, they unite, interlock, and form by their aggregation water, fire, a plant, or a man. That all these substances, which he calls *atoms* by reason of their solidity, can experience neither change nor alteration. But," adds Plutarch, "we cannot make a color of that which is colorless, nor a substance or soul of that which is without soul and without quality." Professor Balfour Stewart says that this doctrine, in the hands of John Dalton, "has enabled the human mind to lay hold of the laws which regulate chemical changes, as well as to picture to itself what is there taking place." After quoting, with approbation, Bacon's idea that men are perpetually investigating the extreme limits of nature, he then erects a standard which he and his brother philosophers would do well to measure their behavior by. "Surely we ought," says he, "to be very cautious before we dismiss any branch of knowledge or train of thought as essentially unprofitable."[628]

Brave words, these. But how many are the men of science who put them into practice?

Demokritus of Abdera shows us space crammed with atoms, and our contemporary astronomers allow us to see how these atoms form into worlds, and afterward into the races, our own included, which people them. Since we have indicated the existence of a power in the human will, which, by concentrating currents of those atoms upon an objective point, can create a child corresponding to the mother's fancy, why is it not perfectly credible that this same power put forth by the mother, can, by an intense, albeit unconscious reversal of those currents, dissipate and obliterate any portion or even the whole of the body of her unborn child? And here comes in the question of false pregnancies, which have so often completely puzzled both physician and patient. If the head, arm, and hand of the three children mentioned by Van Helmont could disappear, as a result of the emotion of horror, why might not the same or some other emotion, excited in a like degree, cause the entire extinction of the fœtus in so-called false pregnancy? Such cases are rare, but they do occur, and moreover baffle science completely. There certainly is no chemical solvent in the mother's circulation powerful enough to dissolve her child, without destroying herself. We commend the subject to the medical profession, hoping that as a class they will not adopt the conclusion of Fournie, who says: "In this succession of phenomena we must confine ourselves *to the office of historian*, as we have not even tried to explain the whys and wherefores of these things, for there lie the inscrutable mysteries of life, and in proportion

---

627 By the word *soul*, neither Demokritus nor the other philosophers understood the *nous* or *pneuma*, the divine *immaterial* soul, but the *psyche*, or astral body; that which Plato always terms the second *mortal* soul.

628 Balfour Stewart, LL.D., F.R.S., "*The Conservation of Energy*," p. 133.

as we advance in our exposition, we will be obliged to recognize that this is to us *forbidden ground*."[629]

Within the limits of his intellectual capabilities the true philosopher knows no forbidden ground, and should be content to accept no mystery of nature as inscrutable or inviolable.

No student of Hermetic philosophy, nor any spiritualist, will object to the abstract principle laid down by Hume that a *miracle* is impossible; for to suppose such a possibility would make the universe governed through special instead of general laws. This is one of the fundamental contradictions between science and theology. The former, reasoning upon universal experience, maintains that there is a general uniformity of the course of nature, while the latter assumes that the Governing Mind can be invoked to suspend general law to suit special emergencies. Says John Stuart Mill,[630] "If we do not already believe in supernatural agencies, no miracle can prove to us their existence. The miracle itself, considered merely as an extraordinary fact, may be satisfactorily certified by our senses or by testimony; but nothing can ever prove that it is a miracle.

There is still another possible hypothesis, that of its being the result of some unknown natural cause; and this possibility cannot be so completely shut out as to leave no alternative but that of admitting the existence and intervention of a being superior to nature."

This is the very point which we have sought to bring home to our logicians and physicists. As Mr. Mill himself says, "We cannot admit a proposition as a law of nature, and yet believe a fact in real contradiction to it. We must disbelieve the alleged fact, or believe that we were mistaken in admitting the supposed law." Mr. Hume cites the "firm and *unalterable* experience" of mankind, as establishing the laws whose operation *ipso facto* makes miracles impossible. The difficulty lies in his use of the adjective which is Italicized, for this is an assumption that our experience will never change, and that, as a consequence, we will always have the same experiments and observations upon which to base our judgment. It also assumes that all philosophers will have the same facts to reflect upon. It also entirely ignores such collected accounts of philosophical experiment and scientific discovery as we may have been temporarily deprived of. Thus, by the burning of the Alexandrian Library and the destruction of Nineveh, the world has been for many centuries without the necessary data upon which to estimate the real knowledge, esoteric and exoteric, of the ancients. But, within the past few years, the discovery of the Rosetta stone, the Ebers, d'Aubigney, Anastasi, and other *papyri*, and the exhumation of the tile-libraries, have opened a field of archæological research which is likely to lead to radical changes in this "firm and unalterable experience." The author of *Supernatural Religion* justly observes that "a person who believes anything contradictory to a complete induction, merely on the strength of an assumption which is incapable of proof, is simply credulous; but such an assumption cannot affect the real evidence for that thing."

In a lecture delivered by Mr. Hiram Corson, Professor of Anglo-Saxon Literature at the Cornell University, Ithaca, N. Y., before the alumni of St. John's College, Annapolis, in July, 1875, the lecturer thus deservedly rebukes science:

---

629 Fournié, *"Physiologie du Système Nerveux,"* p. 16.
630 "A System of Logic." Eighth ed., 1872, vol. ii., p. 165.

"There are things," he says, "which Science can never do, and which it is arrogant in attempting to do. There was a time when Religion and the Church went beyond their legitimate domain, and invaded and harried that of Science, and imposed a burdensome tribute upon the latter; but it would seem that their former relations to each other are undergoing an entire change, and Science has crossed its frontiers and is invading the domain of Religion and the Church, and instead of a Religious Papacy, we are in danger of being brought under a Scientific Papacy — we are in fact already brought under such a Papacy; and as in the sixteenth century a protest was made, in the interests of intellectual freedom, against a religious and ecclesiastical despotism, so, in this nineteenth century, the spiritual and eternal interests of man demand that a protest should be made against a rapidly-developing scientific despotism, and that Scientists should not only keep within their legitimate domain of the phenomenal and the conditioned, but should 'reëxamine their stock in trade, so that we may make sure how far the stock of bullion in the cellar — on the faith of whose existence so much paper has been circulating — is really the solid gold of Truth.'

"If this is not done in science as well as in ordinary business, scientists are apt to put their capital at too high a figure, and accordingly carry on a dangerously-inflated business. Even since Prof. Tyndall delivered his Belfast Address, it has been shown, by the many replies it has elicited, that the capital of the Evolution-School of Philosophy to which he belongs, is not nearly so great as it was before vaguely supposed to be by many of the non-scientific but intelligent portion of the world. It is quite surprising to a non-scientific person to be made aware of the large purely hypothetical domain which surrounds that of established science, and of which scientists often boast, as a part of their settled and available conquests."

Exactly; and at the same time denying the same privilege to others. They protest against the "miracles" of the Church, and repudiate, with as much logic, modern phenomena. In view of the admission of such scientific authorities as Dr. Youmans and others that modern science is passing through a transitional period, it would seem that it is time that people should cease to consider certain things incredible only because they are marvellous, and because they seem to oppose themselves to what we are accustomed to consider universal laws. There are not a few well-meaning men in the present century who, desiring to avenge the memory of such martyrs of science as Agrippa, Palissy, and Cardan, nevertheless fail, through lack of means, to understand their ideas rightly. They erroneously believe that the Neo-platonists gave more attention to transcendental philosophy than to exact science.

"The failures that Aristotle himself so often exhibits," remarks Professor Draper, "are no proof of the unreliability of his method, but rather of its trustworthiness. They are failures arising from want of a sufficiency of facts."[631]

What facts? we might inquire. A man of science cannot be expected to admit that these facts can be furnished by occult science, since he does not believe in the latter. Nevertheless, the future may demonstrate this verity. Aristotle has bequeathed his inductive method to our scientists; but until they supplement it with "the universals of Plato," they will experience still more "failures" than the great tutor of Alexander. The universals are a

---

631 Draper, "Conflict between Religion and Science," p. 22.

matter of faith only so long as they cannot be demonstrated by reason and based on uninterrupted experience. Who of our present-day philosophers can prove by this same inductive method that the ancients did *not* possess such demonstrations as a consequence of their esoteric studies? Their own negations, unsupported as they are by proof, sufficiently attest that they do not always pursue the inductive method they so much boast of. Obliged as they are to base their theories, *nolens volens,* on the groundwork of the ancient philosophers, their modern discoveries are but the shoots put forth by the germs planted by the former. And yet even these discoveries are generally incomplete, if not abortive. Their cause is involved in obscurity and their ultimate effect unforeseen. "We are not," says Professor Youmans, "to regard past theories as mere exploded errors, nor present theories as final. The living and growing body of truth has only mantled its old integuments in the progress to a higher and more vigorous state."[632] This language, applied to modern chemistry by one of the first philosophical chemists and most enthusiastic scientific writers of the day, shows the transitional state in which we find modern science; but what is true of chemistry is true of all its sister sciences.

Since the advent of spiritualism, physicians and pathologists are more ready than ever to treat great philosophers like Paracelsus and Van Helmont as superstitious quacks and charlatans, and to ridicule their notions about the *archæus,* or *anima mundi,* as well as the importance they gave to a knowledge of the machinery of the stars. And yet, how much of substantial progress has medicine effected since the days when Lord Bacon classed it among the *conjectural* sciences?

Such philosophers as Demokritus, Aristotle, Euripides, Epicurus, or rather his biographer, Lucretius, Æschylus, and other ancient writers, whom the materialists so willingly quote as authoritative opponents of the dreamy Platonists, were only theorists, not adepts. The latter, when they did write, either had their works burned by Christian mobs or they worded them in a way to be intelligible only to the initiated. Who of their modern detractors can warrant that he knows all about what they knew? Diocletian alone burned whole libraries of works upon the "secret arts"; not a manuscript treating on the art of making gold and silver escaped the wrath of this unpolished tyrant. Arts and civilization had attained such a development at what is now termed the archaic ages that we learn, through Champollion, that Athothi, the *second* king of the *first* dynasty, wrote a work on anatomy, and the king Necho on astrology and astronomy. Blantasus and Cynchrus were two learned geographers of those pre-Mosaic days. Ælian speaks of the Egyptian Iachus, whose memory was venerated for centuries for his wonderful achievements in medicine. He stopped the progress of several epidemics, merely with certain *fumigations.* A work of Apollonides, surnamed Orapios, is mentioned by Theophilus, patriarch of Antioch, entitled the *Divine Book,* and giving the secret biography and origin of all the gods of Egypt; and Ammianus Marcellinus speaks of a secret work in which was noted the *precise age of the bull Apis* — a key to many a mystery and cyclic calculation. What has become of all these books, and who knows the treasures of learning they may have contained? We know but one thing for a certainty, and that is, that Pagan and Christian Vandals destroyed such literary treasures *wherever they could find them*; and that the emperor Alexander Severus went all over Egypt to collect the sacred books on mysticism and mythology, pillaging every temple;

---

632 Edward L. Youmans, M.D., "*A Class-book of Chemistry,*" p. 4.

and that the Ethiopians — old as were the Egyptians in arts and sciences — claimed a priority of antiquity as well as of learning over them; as well they might, for they were known in India at the earliest dawn of history. We also know that Plato learned more secrets in Egypt than he was allowed to mention; and that, according to Champollion, all that is really good and scientific in Aristotle's works — so prized in our day by our modern inductionists — is due to his *divine* Master; and that, as a logical sequence, Plato having imparted the profound secrets he had learned from the priests of Egypt to his initiated disciples orally — who in their turn passed it from one generation to another of adepts — the latter *know more* of the occult powers of nature than our philosophers of the present day.

And here we may as well mention the works of Hermes Trismegistus. Who, or how many have had the opportunity to read them as they were in the Egyptian sanctuaries? In his *Egyptian Mysteries,* Iamblichus attributes to Hermes 1,100 books, and Seleucus reckons no less than 20,000 of his works before the period of Menes. Eusebius saw but forty-two of these "in his time," he says, and the last of the six books on medicine treated on that art as practiced in the darkest ages;[633] and Diodorus says that it was the oldest of the legislators Mnevis, the third successor of *Menes,* who received them from Hermes.

THE PSYCHOLOGICAL DOMAIN CONFESSEDLY UNEXPLORED

Of such manuscripts as have descended to us, most are but Latin retranslations of Greek translations, made principally by the Neo-platonists from the original books preserved by some adepts. Marcilius Ficinus, who was the first to publish them in Venice, in 1488, has given us mere extracts, and the most important portions seemed to have been either overlooked, or purposely omitted as too dangerous to publish in those days of *Auto da fé.* And so it happens now, that when a kabalist who has devoted his whole life to studying occultism, and has conquered the great secret, ventures to remark that the *Kabala* alone leads to the knowledge of the Absolute in the Infinite, and the Indefinite in the Finite, he is laughed at by those who because they know the impossibility of squaring the circle as a physical problem, deny the possibility of its being done in the metaphysical sense.

Psychology, according to the greatest authorities on the subject, is a department of science hitherto almost unknown. Physiology, according to Fournié, one of its French authorities, is in so bad a condition as to warrant his saying in the preface to his erudite work *Physiologie du Système Nerveux,* that "we perceive at last that not only is the physiology

---

633 Sprengel, in his "*History of Medicine,*" makes Van Helmont appear as if disgusted with the charlatanry and ignorant presumption of Paracelsus. "The works of this latter," says Sprengel, "which he (Van Helmont) had attentively read, aroused in him the spirit of reformation; but they alone did not suffice for him, because his erudition and judgment were infinitely superior to those of that author, and he *despised* this *mad egoist,* this ignorant and ridiculous vagabond, who often seemed to have fallen into insanity." This assertion is perfectly false. We have the writings of Helmont himself to refute it. In the well-known dispute between two writers, Goclenius, a professor in Marburg, who supported the great efficacy of the sympathetic salve discovered by Paracelsus, for the cure of every wound, and Father Robert, a Jesuit, who condemned all these cures, as he attributed them to the Devil, Van Helmont undertook to settle the dispute. The reason he gave for interfering was that all such disputes "affected Paracelsus as their discoverer and *himself as his disciple*" (see "*De Magnetica Vulner.,*" and 1. c., p. 705).

of the brain not worked out, but also that *no physiology whatever of the nervous system exists."* Chemistry has been entirely remodelled within the past few years; therefore, like all new sciences, the infant cannot be considered as very firm on its legs. Geology has not yet been able to tell anthropology how long man has existed. Astronomy, the most *exact* of sciences, is still speculating and bewildered about cosmic energy, and many other things as important. In anthropology, Mr. Wallace tells us, there exists a wide difference of opinion on some of the most vital questions respecting the nature and origin of man. Medicine has been pronounced by various eminent physicians to be nothing better than scientific guess-work. Everywhere incompleteness, nowhere perfection. When we look at these earnest men groping around in the dark to find the missing links of their broken chains, they seem to us like persons starting from a common, fathomless abyss by divergent paths. Each of these ends at the brink of a chasm which they cannot explore.

On the one hand they lack the means to descend into its hidden depths, and on the other they are repulsed at each attempt by jealous sentries, who will not let them pass. And so they go on watching the lower forces of nature and from time to time initiating the public into their *great* discoveries. Did they not actually pounce upon vital force and catch her playing in her game of correlation with chemical and physical forces? Indeed they did. But if we ask them whence this vital force? How is it that they who had so firmly believed, but a short time since, that matter was destructible and passed out of existence, and now have learned to believe as firmly that it does not, are unable to tell us more about it? Why are they forced in this case as in many others to return to a doctrine taught by Demokritus twenty-four centuries ago?[634] Ask them, and they will answer: "Creation or destruction of matter, increase or diminution of matter, lies *beyond the domain of science* . . . her domain is confined entirely to the changes of matter . . . the domain of science lies within the limits of these changes — creation and annihilation lie outside of her domain."[635] Ah! no, they lie only outside the grasp of materialistic *scientists*. But why affirm the same of science? And if they say that "force is incapable of destruction, except by the same power which created it," then they tacitly admit the existence of such a *power*, and have therefore *no right* to throw obstacles in the way of those who, bolder than themselves, try to penetrate *beyond,* and find that they can only do so by *lifting the Veil of Isis.*

But, surely among all these inchoate branches of science, there must be some one at least complete! It seems to us that we heard a great clamor of applause, "as the voice of many waters," over the discovery of protoplasm. But, alas! when we turned to read Mr. Huxley, the learned parent of the new-born infant is found saying: "In perfect strictness, it is true that chemical investigation can tell us *little* or *nothing,* directly, of the composition of living matter, and . . . it is also in strictness, true, that WE KNOW NOTHING about the composition of any body whatever, as it is!"

This is a sad confession, indeed. It appears, then, that the Aristotelian method of induction is a failure in some cases, after all. This also seems to account for the fact that this model philosopher, with all his careful study of particulars before rising to universals, taught that the earth was *in the centre* of the universe; while Plato, who lost himself in the

---

634 Demokritus said that, as from nothing, nothing could be produced, so there was not anything that could ever be reduced *to nothing*.
635 J. Le Conte, *"Correlation of Vital with Chemical and Physical Forces,"* appendix.

maze of Pythagorean "vagaries," and started from general principles, was perfectly versed in the heliocentric system. We can easily prove the fact, by availing ourselves of the said inductive method for Plato's benefit. We know that the *Sodalian* oath of the initiate into the Mysteries prevented his imparting his knowledge to the world in so many plain words. "It was the dream of his life," says Champollion, "to write a work and record in it in full the doctrines taught by the Egyptian hierophants; he often talked of it, but found himself compelled to abstain on account of the 'solemn oath.'"

And now, judging our modern-day philosophers on the *vice versa* method — namely, arguing from *universals* to *particulars,* and laying aside scientists as individuals to merely give our opinion of them, viewed as a whole — we are forced to suspect this highly respectable association of extremely petty feelings toward their elder, ancient, and archaic brothers. It really seems as if they bore always in mind the adage, "Put out the *sun,* and the *stars* will shine."

We have heard a French Academician, a man of profound learning, remark, that he would gladly sacrifice his own reputation to have the record of the many ridiculous mistakes and failures of his colleagues obliterated from the public memory. But these failures cannot be recalled *too* often in considering our claims and the subject we advocate. The time will come when the children of men of science, unless they inherit the soul-blindness of their skeptical parents, will be ashamed of the degrading materialism and narrow-mindedness of their fathers. To use an expression of the venerable William Howitt, "They hate new truths as the owl and the thief hate the sun. . . . Mere intellectual enlightenment cannot recognize the spiritual. As the sun puts out a fire, so spirit puts out the eyes of mere intellect."

It is an old, old story. From the days when the preacher wrote, "the eye is not satisfied with seeing, nor the ear filled with hearing," scientists have deported themselves as if the saying were written to describe their own mental condition. How faithfully Lecky, himself a rationalist, unconsciously depicts this propensity in men of science to deride all new things, in his description of the manner in which "educated men" receive an account of a miracle having taken place! "They receive it," says he, "with an absolute and even derisive incredulity, which dispenses with all examination of the evidences!" Moreover, so saturated do they become with the fashionable skepticism after once having fought their way into the Academy, that they turn about and enact the role of persecutors in their turn. "It is a curiosity of science," says Howitt, "that Benjamin Franklin, who had himself experienced the ridicule of his countrymen for his attempts to identify lightning and electricity, should have been one of the Committee of Savants, in Paris, in 1778, who examined the claims of mesmerism, and condemned it as absolute quackery!"[636]

If men of science would confine themselves to the discrediting of new discoveries, there might be some little excuse for them on the score of their tendency to a conservatism begotten of long habits of patient scrutiny; but they not only set up claims to originality not warranted by fact, but contemptuously dismiss all allegations that the people of ancient times knew as much and even more than themselves. Pity that in each of their laboratories there is not suspended this text from *Ecclesiastes:* "Is there anything whereof it may be said,

---

636 The date is incorrect; it should be 1784.

See, this *is* new? it hath been already of old time, which was before us."[637] In the verse which follows the one here quoted, the wise man says, "There is no remembrance of former things"; so that this utterance may account for every new denial. Mr. Meldrum may exact praise for his meteorological observation of Cyclones in the Mauritius, and Mr. Baxendell, of Manchester, talk learnedly of the convection-currents of the earth, and Dr. Carpenter and Commander Maury map out for us the equatorial current, and Professor Henry show us how the moist wind deposits its burden to form rivulets and rivers, only to be again rescued from the ocean and returned to the hill-tops — but hear what Koheleth says: "The wind goeth toward the south, and *turneth about* unto the north; it *whirleth about* continually, and the wind returneth again according to his circuits."[638]

> "All the rivers run into the sea; yet the sea is not full: unto the place from whence the rivers come, *thither they return again.*"[639]

The philosophy of the distribution of heat and moisture by means of ascending and descending currents between the equator and the poles, has a very recent origin; but here has the hint been lying unnoticed in our most familiar book, for nearly three thousand years. And even now, in quoting it, we are obliged to recall the fact that Solomon was a kabalist, and in the above texts, simply repeats what was written thousands of years before his time.

Cut off as they are from the accumulation of facts in one-half of the universe, and that the most important, modern scholars are naturally unable to construct a system of philosophy which will satisfy themselves, let alone others. They are like men in a coal mine, who work all day and emerge only at night, being thereby unable to appreciate or understand the beauty and glory of the sunshine. Life to them measures the term of human activity, and the future presents to their intellectual perception only an abyss of darkness. No hope of an eternity of research, achievement, and consequent pleasure, softens the asperities of present existence; and no reward is offered for exertion but the bread-earning of to-day, and the shadowy and profitless fancy that their names may not be forgotten for some years after the grave has closed over their remains. Death to them means extinction of the flame of life, and the dispersion of the fragments of the lamp over boundless space. Said Berzelius, the great chemist, at his last hour, as he burst into tears: "Do not wonder that I weep. You will not believe me a weak man, nor think I am alarmed by what the doctor has to announce to me. I am prepared for all. But I have *to bid farewell to science;* and you ought not to wonder that it costs me dear."[640]

DESPAIRING REGRETS OF BERZELIUS

How bitter must be the reflections of such a great student of nature as this, to find himself forcibly interrupted midway toward the accomplishment of some great study, the construction of some great system, the discovery of some mystery which had baffled mankind for ages, but which the dying philosopher had dared hope that he might solve!

---

637 *Ecclesiastes* i. 10.

638 Ibid., i. 6.

639 Ibid., i. 7.

640 Siljeström, "*Minnesfest öfver Berzelius,*" p. 79.

Look at the world of science to-day, and see the atomic theorists, patching the tattered robes which expose the imperfections of their separate specialties! See them mending the pedestals upon which to set up again the idols which had fallen from the places where they had been worshipped before this revolutionary theory had been exhumed from the tomb of Demokritus by John Dalton! In the ocean of material science they cast their nets, only to have the meshes broken when some unexpected and monstrous problem comes their way. Its water is like the Dead Sea — bitter to the taste; so dense, that they can scarcely immerse themselves in it, much less dive to its bottom, having no outlet, and no life beneath its waves, or along its margin. It is a dark, forbidding, trackless waste; yielding nothing worth the having, because what it yields is without life and without soul.

There was a period of time when the learned Academics made themselves particularly merry at the simple enunciation of some marvels which the ancients gave as having occurred under their own observations. What poor dolts — perhaps liars, these appeared in the eyes of an enlightened century! Did not they actually describe horses and other animals, the feet of which presented some resemblance to the hands and feet of men? And in A.D. 1876, we hear Mr. Huxley giving learned lectures in which the *protohippus*, rejoicing in a quasi-human fore-arm, and the *orohippus* with his four toes and Eocene origin, and the hypothetical *pedactyl equus*, maternal grand-uncle of the present horse, play the most important part. The marvel is corroborated! Materialistic Pyrrhonists of the nineteenth century avenge the assertions of superstitious Platonists; the antediluvian *gobe-mouches*. And before Mr. Huxley, Geoffroi St. Hilaire has shown an instance of a horse which positively had fingers separated by membranes.[641] When the ancients spoke of a pigmy race in Africa, they were taxed with falsehood. And yet, pigmies like these were seen and examined by a French scientist during his voyage in the Tenda Maia, on the banks of the Rio Grande in 1840;† by Bayard Taylor at Cairo, in 1874; and by M. Bond, of the Indian Trigonometrical Survey, who discovered a wild dwarfish race, living in the hill-jungles of the western Galitz, to the southwest of the Palini Hills, a race, though often heard of, no trace of which had previously been found by the survey. "This is a new pigmy race, resembling the African Obongos of du Chaillu, the Akkas of Schweinfurth, and the Dokos of Dr. Krapf, in their size, appearance, and habits."[642]

Herodotus was regarded as a lunatic for speaking of a people *who he was told* slept during a night which lasted six months. If we explain the word "slept" by an easy misunderstanding it will be more than easy to account for the rest as an allusion to the night of the Polar Regions.[643] Pliny has an abundance of facts in his work, which until very recently, were rejected as fables. Among others, he mentions a race of small animals, the *males* of which *suckle their young ones*. This assertion afforded much merriment among our *savants*. In his *Report of the Geological Survey of the Territories*, for 1872, Mr. C. H. Merriam describes a rare and wonderful species of rabbit *(Lepus Bairdi)* inhabiting the pine-regions about the head-waters of the Wind and Yellowstone Rivers, in Wyoming.[644] Mr. Merriam secured five specimens of this animal, "which . . . are *the first individuals of the species that have*

---

641 "*Seance de l'Academie de Paris,*" 13 Aout, 1807.
642 Mollien, "*Voyage dans l'interieur de l'Afrique,*" tome ii., p. 210.
643 "*The Popular Science Monthly,*" May, 1876, p. 110.
644 Malte-Brun, pp. 372, 373; Herodotus.

been brought before the scientific world. One very curious fact is that *all the males have teats, and take part in suckling their young! . . .* Adult males had large teats full of milk, and the hair around the nipple of one was wet, and stuck to it, showing that, when taken, he had been engaged in nursing his young." In the Carthaginian account of the early voyages of Hanno,[645] was found a long description of "savage people . . . whose bodies were hairy and whom the interpreters called *gorillæ*"; ἄνθρωποι ἄγριοι, as the text reads, clearly implying thereby that these wild men were monkeys. Until our present century, the statement was considered an idle story, and Dodwell rejected altogether the authenticity of the manuscript and its contents.[646] The celebrated *Atlantis* is attributed by the latest modern commentator and translator of Plato's works to one of Plato's "noble lies."[647] Even the frank admission of the philosopher, in the *Timæus*, that "*they say*, that in their time . . . the inhabitants of this island (Poseidon) preserved *a tradition* handed down by their ancestors concerning the existence of the Atlantic island of a prodigious magnitude . . . etc."[648] does not save the great teacher from the imputation of falsehood, by the "infallible modern school."

TURNING A RIVER INTO BLOOD A VEGETABLE PHENOMENON

Among the great mass of peoples plunged deep in the superstitious ignorance of the mediæval ages, there were but a few students of the Hermetic philosophy of old, who, profiting by what it had taught them, were enabled to forecast discoveries which are the boast of our present age; while at the same time the ancestors of our modern high-priests of the temple of the Holy Molecule, were yet discovering the hoof-tracks of Satan in the simplest natural phenomenon. Says Professor A. Wilder: "Roger Bacon (thirteenth century), in his treatise on the *Admirable Force of Art and Nature*, devotes the first part of his work to natural facts. He gives us hints of gunpowder and predicts the use of steam as a propelling power. The hydraulic press, the diving bell and kaleidoscope are all described."[649] The ancients speak of waters metamorphosed *into blood*; of blood-rain, of snow-storms during which the earth was covered to the extent of many miles with snow *of blood*. This fall of crimson particles has been proved, like everything else, to be but a natural phenomenon. It has occurred at different epochs, but the cause of it remains a puzzle until the present day.

De Candolle, one of the most distinguished botanists of this century, sought to prove in 1825, at the time when the waters of the lake of Morat had apparently turned into a thick blood, that the phenomenon could be easily accounted for. He attributed it to the development of myriads of those half-vegetable, half-infusory animals which he terms *Oscellatoria rubescens*, and which form the link between animal and vegetable organisms.[650] Elsewhere we give an account of the red snow which Captain Ross observed in the Arctic regions. Many memoirs have been written on the subject by the most eminent naturalists,

---

645 "*The Popular Science Monthly*," Dec., 1874, p. 252, New York.
646 The original was suspended in the temple of Saturn, at Carthage. Falconer gave two dissertations on it, and agrees with Bougainville in referring it to the sixth century before the Christian era. See Cory's "*Ancient Fragments*."
647 Professor Jowett.
648 "*On the Atlantic Island (from Marcellus) Ethiopic History*."
649 "*Alchemy, or the Hermetic Philosophy*."
650 See "*Revue Encyclopédique*," vol. xxxiii., p. 676.

but no two of them agree in their hypotheses. Some call it "pollen powder of a species of pine"; others, small insects; and Professor Agardt confesses very frankly that he is at a loss to either account for the cause of such phenomena, or to explain the nature of the red substance.[651]

The unanimous testimony of mankind is said to be an irrefutable proof of truth; and about what was ever testimony more unanimous than that for thousands of ages among civilized people as among the most barbarous, there has existed a firm and unwavering belief in magic? The latter implies a contravention of the laws of nature only in the minds of the ignorant; and if such ignorance is to be deplored in the ancient uneducated nations, why do not our civilized and *highly*-educated classes of fervent Christians, deplore it also in themselves? The mysteries of the Christian religion have been no more able to stand a crucial test than biblical miracles. Magic alone, in the true sense of the word, affords a clew to the wonders of Aaron's rod, and the feats of the magi of Pharaoh, who opposed Moses; and it does that without either impairing the general truthfulness of the authors of the *Exodus*, or claiming more for the prophet of Israel than for others, or allowing the possibility of a single instance in which a "miracle" can happen in contravention of the laws of nature. Out of many "miracles," we may select for our illustration that of the "river turned into blood." The text says: "Take thy *rod* and stretch out thine hand (with the *rod* in it) upon the waters, streams, etc. . . . that they may become blood."

We do not hesitate to say that we have seen the same thing repeatedly done on a small scale, the experiment not having been applied to a river in these cases. From the time of Van Helmont, who, in the seventeenth century, despite the ridicule to which he exposed himself, was willing to give the true directions for the so-called production of eels, frogs, and infusoria of various kinds, down to the champions of spontaneous generation of our own century, it has been known that such a quickening of germs is possible without calling in the aid of miracle to contravene natural law. The experiments of Pasteur and Spallanzani, and the controversy of the panspermists with the heterogenists — disciples of Buffon, among them Needham — have too long occupied public attention to permit us to doubt that beings may be called into existence whenever there is air and favorable conditions of moisture and temperature. The records of the official meetings of the Academy of Sciences of Paris[652] contain accounts of frequent appearances of such showers of blood-red snow and water. These blood-spots were called *lepra vestuum*, and were but these lichen-infusoria. They were first observed in 786 and 959, in both of which years occurred great plagues. Whether these *zoocarps* were plants or animals is undetermined to this day, and no naturalist would risk stating as a certainty to what division of the organic kingdom of nature they belong. No more can modern chemists deny that such germs can be quickened, in a congenial element, in an incredibly short space of time. Now, if chemistry has, on the one hand, found means of depriving the air of its floating germs, and under opposite conditions can develop, or allow these organisms to develop, why could not the magicians of Egypt do so "with their *enchantments*"? It is far easier to imagine that Moses, who, on the authority of Manetho, had been an Egyptian priest, and had learned all the secrets of the

---

651 *"Bulletin de la Soc. Geograph.,"* vol. vi., pp. 209-220.
652 See *"Revue Encyclopédique,"* vols. xxxiii. and xxxiv., pp. 676-395.

land of *Chemia*, produced "miracles" according to natural laws, than that God Himself violated the established order of His universe.

We repeat that we have seen this sanguification of water produced by Eastern adepts. It can be done in either of two ways: In one case the experimenter employed a magnetic *rod* strongly electrified, which he passed over a quantity of water in a metallic basin, following a prescribed process, which we have no right to describe more fully at present; the water threw up in about ten hours a sort of reddish froth, which after two hours more became a kind of lichen, like the *lepraria kermasina* of Baron Wrangel. It then changed into a blood-red jelly, which made of the water a crimson liquid that, twenty-four hours later, swarmed with living organisms. The second experiment consisted in thickly strowing the surface of a sluggish brook, having a muddy bottom, with the powder of a plant that had been dried in the sun and subsequently pulverized. Although this powder was seemingly carried off by the stream, some of it must have settled to the bottom, for on the following morning the water thickened at the surface and appeared covered with what de Candolle describes as *Oscellatoria rubescens*, of a crimson-red color, and which he believes to be the connecting link between vegetable and animal life.

Taking the above into consideration, we do not see why the learned alchemists and physicists — *physicists*, we say — of the Mosaic period should not also have possessed the natural secret of developing in a few hours myriads of a kind of these bacteria, whose spores are found in the air, the water, and most vegetable and animal tissues. The *rod* plays as important a part in the hands of Aaron and Moses as it did in all so-called "magic mummeries" of kabalist-magicians in the middle ages, that are now considered superstitious foolery and charlatanism. The rod of Paracelsus (his kabalistic trident) and the famous wands of Albertus Magnus, Roger Bacon, and Henry Kunrath, are no more to be ridiculed than the graduating-rod of our electro-magnetic physicians. Things which appeared preposterous and impossible to the ignorant quacks and even learned scientists of the last century, now begin to assume the shadowy outlines of probability, and in many cases are accomplished facts. Nay, some learned quacks and ignorant scientists even begin to admit this truth.

In a fragment preserved by Eusebius, Porphyry, in his *Letter to Anebo*, appeals to Chœremon, the "hierogrammatist," to prove that the doctrine of the magic arts, whose adepts "could terrify even the gods," was really countenanced by Egyptian sages.[653] Now, bearing in mind the rule of historical evidence propounded by Mr. Huxley, in his Nashville address, two conclusions present themselves with irresistible force: First, Porphyry, being in such unquestioned repute as a highly moral and honorable man, not given to exaggeration in his statements, was incapable of telling a lie about this matter, and *did not* lie; and second, that being so learned in every department of human knowledge about which he treats,[654] it was most unlikely that he should be imposed upon as regards the magic "arts," and he was *not* imposed upon. Therefore, the doctrine of chances supporting the theory of Professor

---

653 Porphyry, "*Epistola ad Anebo., ap. Euseb. Præp. Evangel*," v. 10; Iamblichus, "*De Mysteriis Ægypt*.";
Porphyrii, "*Epistola ad Anebonem Ægyptium*."
654 "Porphyry," says the "Classical Dictionary" of Lemprière, "was a man of universal information, and, according to the testimony of the ancients, he excelled his contemporaries in the knowledge of history, mathematics, music, and *philosophy*."

Huxley, compels us to believe, 1, That there was really such a thing as magic "arts"; and, 2, That they were known and practiced by the Egyptian magicians and priests, whom even Sir David Brewster concedes to have been men of profound scientific attainments.

CHAPTER XII

"You never hear the really philosophical defenders of the doctrine of uniformity speaking of *impossibilities* in nature. They never say what they are constantly charged with saying, that it is impossible for the Builder of the universe to alter his work. . . . No theory upsets them (the English clergy). . . . Let the most destructive hypothesis be stated *only in the language current among gentlemen,* and they look it in the face."

TYNDALL, *Lecture on the Scientific Use of the Imagination*

"The world will have a religion of some kind, even though it should fly for it to the intellectual *whoredom of Spiritualism.*"

TYNDALL, *Fragments of Science*

"But first on earth as vampires sent
Thy corpse shall from its tomb be rent. . . .
And suck the blood of all thy race."

LORD BYRON, *Giaour*

CONFESSIONS OF IGNORANCE BY MEN OF SCIENCE

WE are now approaching the hallowed precincts of that Janus-god — the molecular Tyndall. Let us enter them barefoot. As we pass the sacred adyta of the temple of learning, we are nearing the blazing sun of the Huxleyocentric system. Let us cast down our eyes, lest we be blinded.

We have discussed the various matters contained in this book, with such moderation as we could command in view of the attitude which the scientific and theological world have maintained for centuries toward those from whom they have inherited the broad foundations of all the actual knowledge which they possess. When we stand at one side, and, as a spectator, see how much the ancients knew, and how much the moderns think they know, we are amazed that the unfairness of our contemporary schoolmen should pass undetected.

Every day brings new admissions of scientists themselves, and the criticisms of well-informed lay observers. We find the following illustrative paragraph in a daily paper:

"It is curious to note the various opinions which prevail among scientific men in regard to some of the most ordinary natural phenomena. The aurora is a notable case in point. Descartes considered it a meteor falling from the upper regions of the atmosphere. Halley attributed it to the magnetism of the terrestrial globe, and Dalton agreed with this opinion. Coates supposed that the aurora was derived from the fermentation of a matter emanating from the earth. Marion held it to be a consequence of a contact between the bright atmosphere of the sun and the atmosphere of our planet. Euler thought the aurora proceeded from the vibrations of the ether among the particles of the terrestrial atmosphere. Canton and Franklin regarded it as a purely electrical phenomenon, and Parrot attributed it to the conflagration of hydrogen-carbonide escaping from the earth in consequence of the putrefaction of vegetable substances, and considered the shooting stars as the initial cause of such conflagration. De la Rive and Oersted concluded it to be an electro-magnetic phenomenon, but purely terrestrial. Olmsted suspected that a certain nebulous body revolved around the sun in a certain time, and that when this body came into the neighborhood of the earth, a part of its gaseous material mixed with our atmosphere, and that this was the origin of the phenomenon of the aurora." And so we might say of every branch of science.

Thus, it would seem that even as to the most ordinary natural phenomena, scientific opinion is far from being unanimous. There is not an experimentalist or theologian, who, in dealing with the subtile relations between mind and matter, their genesis and ultimate, does not draw a magical circle, the plane of which he calls *forbidden ground*. Where faith permits a clergyman to go, he goes; for, as Tyndall says, "they do not lack the positive element — namely, the love of truth; but the negative element, the fear of error, preponderates." But the trouble is, that their dogmatic creed weighs down the nimble feet of their intellect, as the ball and chain does the prisoner in the trenches.

As to the advance of scientists, their very learning, moreover, is impeded by these two causes — their constitutional incapacity to understand the spiritual side of nature, and their dread of public opinion. No one has said a sharper thing against them than Professor Tyndall, when he remarks, "in fact, the greatest cowards of the present day are not to be found among the clergy, but within the pale of science itself."[655] If there had been the slightest doubt of the applicability of this degrading epithet, it was removed by the conduct of Professor Tyndall himself; for, in his Belfast address, as President of the British Association, he not only discerned in matter "*the promise and potency* of every form and quality of life," but pictured science as "wresting from theology the entire domain of cosmological theory"; and then, when confronted with an angry public opinion, issued a revised edition of the address in which he had modified his expression, substituting for the words "*every form and quality of life,*" all terrestrial life. This is more than cowardly — it is an ignominious surrender of his professed principles. At the time of the Belfast meeting, Mr. Tyndall had two pet aversions — Theology and Spiritualism. What he thought of the former has been shown; the latter he called "a degrading belief." When hard pressed by the Church for alleged atheism, he made haste to disclaim the imputation, and sue for peace; but, as his agitated "nervous centres" and "cerebral molecules" had to equilibrate by expanding their force in some direction, he turns upon the helpless, because pusillanimous, spiritualists, and in his *Fragments of Science* insults their belief after this fashion: "The world will have a religion of some kind, even though it should fly for it to the intellectual *whoredom of Spiritualism.*" What a monstrous anomaly, that some millions of intelligent persons should permit themselves to be thus reviled by a leader in science, who, himself, has told us that "the thing to be repressed both in science and out of it is 'dogmatism!' "

We will not encroach upon space by discussing the etymological value of the epithet. While expressing the hope that it may not be adopted in future ages by science as a *Tyndallism,* we will simply remind the benevolent gentleman of a very characteristic feature in himself. One of our most intelligent, honorable, and erudite spiritualists, an author of no

---

655 *"On the Scientific Use of the Imagination."*

small renown,[656] has pointedly termed this feature as "his (Tyndall's) simultaneous coquetry with opposite opinions." If we are to accept the epithet of Mr. Tyndall in all its coarse signification, it applies less to spiritualists, who are faithful to their belief, than to the atheistical scientist who quits the loving embraces of materialism to fling himself in the arms of a despised theism; only because he finds his profit in it.

We have seen how Magendie frankly confesses the ignorance of physiologists as to some of the most important problems of life, and how Fournie agrees with him. Professor Tyndall admits that the evolution-hypothesis does not solve, does not profess to solve, the ultimate mystery.

We have also given as much thought as our natural powers will permit to Professor Huxley's celebrated lecture *On the Physical Basis of Life,* so that what we may say in this volume as to the tendency of modern scientific thought may be free from ignorant misstatement. Compressing his theory within the closest possible limits, it may be formulated thus: Out of cosmic matter all things are created; dissimilar forms result from different permutations and combinations of this matter; matter has "devoured spirit," hence spirit does not exist; thought is a property of matter; existing forms die that others may take their place; the dissimilarity in organism is due only to varying chemical action in the same life-matter — all protoplasm being identical.

As far as chemistry and microscopy goes, Professor Huxley's system may be faultless, and the profound sensation caused throughout the world by its enunciation can be readily understood. But its defect is that the thread of his logic begins nowhere, and ends in a void. He has made the best possible use of the available material. Given a universe crowded with molecules, endowed with active force, and containing in themselves the principle of life, and all the rest is easy; one set of inherent forces impel to aggregate into worlds, and another to evolve the various forms of plant and animal organism. But what gave the first impulse to those molecules and endowed them with that mysterious faculty of life? What is this occult property which causes the protoplasms of man, beast, reptile, fish, or plant, to differentiate, each ever evolving its own kind, and never any other? And after the physical body gives up its constituents to the soil and air, "whether fungus or oak, worm or man," what becomes of the life which once animated the frame?

Is the law of evolution, so imperative in its application to the method of nature, from the time when cosmic molecules are floating, to the time when they form a human brain, to be cut short at that point, and not allowed to develop more perfect entities out of this "preëxistent law of form"? Is Mr. Huxley prepared to assert the impossibility of man's attainment to a state of existence after physical death, in which he will be surrounded with new forms of plant and animal life, the result of new arrangements of now sublimated matter?[657]

---

656 Epes Sargent. See his pamphlet, "*Does Matter Do It All?*"

657 In his "*Essay on Classification*" (sect. xvii., pp. 97-99), Louis Agassiz, the great zoölogist, remarks, "Most of the arguments in favor of the immortality of man apply equally to the permanency of this principle in other living beings. May I not add that a future life in which man would be deprived of that great source of enjoyment and intellectual and moral improvement, which results from the contemplation of the harmonies of an organic world would involve a lamentable loss? And may we

He acknowledges that he knows nothing about the phenomena of gravitation; except that, in all human experience, as "stones, unsupported, have fallen to the ground, there is no reason for believing that any stone so circumstanced will not fall to the ground." But, he utterly repels any attempt to change this probability into a necessity, and in fact says: "I utterly repudiate and anathematize the intruder. Facts I know, and Law I know; but what is this necessity, save an empty shadow of my own mind's throwing?" It is this, only, that everything which happens in nature is the result of necessity, and a law once operative will continue to so operate indefinitely until it is neutralized by an opposing law of equal potency. Thus, it is natural that the stone should fall to the ground in obedience to one force, and it is equally natural that it should not fall, or that having fallen, it should rise again, in obedience to another force equally potent; which Mr. Huxley may, or may not, be familiar with. It is natural that a chair should rest upon the floor when once placed there, and it is equally natural (as the testimony of hundreds of competent witnesses shows) that it should rise in the air, untouched by any visible, mortal hand. Is it not Mr. Huxley's duty to first ascertain the reality of this phenomenon, and then invent a new scientific name for the force behind it?

THE PANTHEON OF NIHILISM

"Facts I know," says Mr. Huxley, "and Law I know." Now, by what means did he become acquainted with Fact and Law? Through his own senses, no doubt; and these vigilant servants enabled him to discover enough of what he considers truth to construct a system which he himself confesses "appears almost shocking to common sense." If his testimony is to be accepted as the basis for a general reconstruction of religious belief, when they have produced only a theory after all, why is not the cumulative testimony of millions of people as to the occurrence of phenomena which undermine its very foundations, worthy of a like respectful consideration? Mr. Huxley is *not interested* in these phenomena, but these millions are; and while he has been digesting his "bread and mutton-protoplasms," to gain strength for still bolder metaphysical flights, they have been recognizing the familiar handwriting of those they loved the best, traced by spiritual hands, and discerning the shadowy simulacra of those who, having lived here, and passed through the change of death, give the lie to his pet theory.

So long as science will confess that her domain lies *within* the limits of these changes of matter; and that chemistry will certify that matter, by changing its form "from the solid or liquid, to the gaseous condition," only changes from the visible to the *invisible;* and that, amid all these changes, the same quantity of matter remains, she has *no right* to dogmatize. She is incompetent to say either yea or nay, and must abandon the ground to persons more intuitional than her representatives.

High above all other names in his Pantheon of Nihilism, Mr. Huxley writes that of David Hume. He esteems that philosopher's great service to humanity to be his irrefragable demonstration of "the limits of philosophical inquiry," outside which lie the fundamental doctrines "of spiritualism," and other "*isms.*" It is true that the tenth chapter of Hume's

---

not look to a spiritual concert of the combined worlds and *all* their inhabitants in the presence of their creator as the highest conception of paradise?"

Enquiry Concerning Human Understanding was so highly esteemed by its author, that he considered that "with the wise and learned" it would be an "everlasting check to all kinds of superstitious delusion," which with him was simply a convertible term to represent a belief in some phenomena previously unfamiliar and by him arbitrarily classified as miracle. But, as Mr. Wallace justly observes, Hume's apothegm, that "a miracle is a violation of the laws of nature," is imperfect; for in the first place it assumes that we know all the laws of nature; and, second, that an unusual phenomenon *is* a miracle. Mr. Wallace proposes that a miracle should be defined as: "any act or event necessarily implying the existence and agency of superhuman intelligences." Now Hume himself says that "a uniform experience amounts to a proof," and Huxley, in this famous essay of his, admits that all we can know of the existence of the law of gravitation is that since, in all human experience, stones unsupported have fallen to the ground, there is no reason for believing that the same thing will not occur again, under the same circumstances, but, on the contrary, every reason to believe that it will.

If it were certain that the limits of human experience could never be enlarged, then there might be some justice in Hume's assumption that he was familiar with all that could happen under natural law, and some decent excuse for the contemptuous tone which marks all of Huxley's allusions to spiritualism. But, as it is evident from the writings of both these philosophers, that they are ignorant of the possibilities of psychological phenomena, too much caution cannot be used in according weight to their dogmatic assertions. One would really suppose that a person who should permit himself such rudeness of criticism upon spiritualistic manifestations had qualified himself for the office of censor by an adequate course of study; but, in a letter addressed to the London Dialectical Society, Mr. Huxley, after saying that he had no time to devote to the subject, and that it does not interest him, makes the following confession, which shows us upon what slight foundation modern scientists sometimes form very positive opinions. "*The only case of spiritualism*," he writes, "*I ever had the opportunity of examining into* for myself, was as gross an imposture as ever came under my notice."

What would this protoplasmic philosopher think of a spiritualist who, having had but one opportunity to look through a telescope, and upon that sole occasion had had some deception played upon him by a tricky assistant at the observatory, should forthwith denounce astronomy as a "degrading belief"? This fact shows that scientists, as a rule, are useful only as collectors of physical facts; their generalizations from them are often feebler and far more illogical than those of their lay critics. And this also is why they misrepresent ancient doctrines.

Professor Balfour Stewart pays a very high tribute to the philosophical intuition of Herakleitus, the Ephesian, who lived five centuries before our era; the "crying" philosopher who declared that "fire was the great cause, and that all things were in a perpetual flux." "It seems clear," says the professor, "that Herakleitus must have had a vivid conception of the innate restlessness and energy of the universe, a conception allied in character to, and *only less precise* than that of modern philosophers who regard matter as essentially dynamical." He considers the expression *fire* as very vague; and quite naturally, for the evidence is wanting to show that either Prof. Balfour Stewart (who seems less inclined to materialism than some of his colleagues) or any of his contemporaries understand in what sense the word fire was used.

TRIPLE COMPOSITION OF FIRE

His opinions about the origin of things were the same as those of Hippocrates. Both entertained the same views of a supreme power,[658] and, therefore, if their notions of primordial fire, regarded as a material force, in short, as one akin to Leibnitz's dynamism, were "less precise" than those of modern philosophers, a question which remains to be settled yet, on the other hand their metaphysical views of it were far more philosophical and rational than the one-sided theories of our present-day scholars. Their ideas of fire were precisely those of the later "fire-philosophers," the Rosicrucians, and the earlier Zoroastrians. They affirmed that the world was created of fire, the *divine spirit* of which was an omnipotent and omniscient GOD. Science has condescended to corroborate their claims as to the physical question.

Fire, in the ancient philosophy of all times and countries, including our own, has been regarded as a triple principle. As water comprises a visible fluid with invisible gases lurking within, and, behind all the spiritual principle of nature, which gives them their dynamic energy, so, in fire, they recognized: 1st. Visible flame; 2d. Invisible, or astral fire — invisible when inert, but when active producing heat, light, chemical force, and electricity, the molecular powers; 3d. Spirit. They applied the same rule to each of the elements; and everything evolved from their combinations and correlations, man included, was held by them to be triune. Fire, in the opinion of the Rosicrucians, who were but the successors of the theurgists, was the source, not only of the material atoms, but also of the forces which energize them. When a visible flame is extinguished it has disappeared, not only from the sight but also from the conception of the materialist, forever. But the Hermetic philosopher follows it through the "partition-world of the knowable, across and out on the other side into the unknowable," as he traces the disembodied human spirit, "vital spark of heavenly flame," into the Æthereum, beyond the grave.[659]

This point is too important to be passed by without a few words of comment. The attitude of physical science toward the spiritual half of the cosmos is perfectly exemplified in her gross conception of fire. In this, as in every other branch of science, their philosophy does not contain one sound plank: every one is honeycombed and weak. The works of their own authorities teeming with humiliating confessions, give us the right to say that the floor upon which they stand is so unstable, that at any moment some new discovery, by one of their own number, may knock away the props and let them all fall in a heap together. They are so anxious to drive spirit out of their conceptions that, as Balfour Stewart says: "There is a tendency to rush into the opposite extreme, and to work physical conceptions to an excess." He utters a timely warning in adding: "Let us be cautious that, in avoiding Scylla, we do not rush into Charybdis. For the universe has more than one point of view, and there are possibly regions which will not yield their treasures to the most determined physicists, armed only with kilogrammes and meters and standard clocks."[660] In another place he confesses: "We know nothing, or next to nothing, of the ultimate structure and properties of matter, whether organic or inorganic."

---

658 "*Diog. in Vita.*"
659 See the works of Robertus de Fluctibus; and the "*Rosicrucians,*" by Hargrave Jennings.
660 Professor B. Stewart, "*Conservation of Energy.*"

As to the other great question — we find in Macaulay, a still more unreserved declaration: "The question what becomes of man after death — we do not see that a highly educated European, left to his unassisted reason, is more likely to be in the right than a Blackfoot Indian. Not a single one of the many sciences in which we surpass the Blackfoot Indians throws the smallest light on the state of the soul after the animal life is extinct. In truth, all the philosophers, ancient and modern, who have attempted, without the help of revelation, to prove the immortality of man, from Plato down to Franklin, appear to us to have failed deplorably."

There are revelations of the spiritual senses of man which may be trusted far more than all the sophistries of materialism. What was a demonstration and a success in the eyes of Plato and his disciples is now considered the overflow of a spurious philosophy and a failure. The scientific methods are reversed. The testimony of the men of old, who were nearer to truth, for they were nearer to the spirit of nature — the only aspect under which the Deity will allow itself to be viewed and understood — and their demonstrations, are rejected. Their speculations — if we must believe the modern thinkers — are but the expression of a redundance of the unsystematic opinions of men unacquainted with the scientific method of the present century. They foolishly based the little they knew of physiology on well-demonstrated psychology, while the scholar of our day bases psychology — of which he confesses himself utterly ignorant — on physiology, which to him is as yet a closed book, and has not even a method of its own, as Fournie tells us. As to the last objection in Macaulay's argument, it was answered by Hippocrates centuries ago: "All knowledge, all arts are to be found in nature," he says ; "if we question her properly she will reveal to us the truths to pertain to each of these and to ourselves. What is nature in operation but the very divinity itself manifesting its presence ? How are we to interrogate her ; and how is she to answer us? We must proceed with faith, with the firm assurance of discovering at last the whole of the truth ; and nature will let us know her answer, through our inner sense, which with the help of our knowledge of a certain art or science, reveals to us the truth so clearly that further doubt becomes impossible."[661]

INSTINCT AND REASON DEFINED

Thus, in the case in hand, the instinct of Macaulay's Blackfoot Indian is more to be trusted than the most instructed and developed reason, as regards man's inner sense which assures him of his immortality. Instinct is the universal endowment of nature by the Spirit of the Deity itself; reason the slow development of our physical constitution, an evolution of our adult material brain. Instinct, as a divine spark, lurks in the unconscious nerve-centre of the ascidian mollusk, and manifests itself at the first stage of action of its nervous system as what the physiologist terms the reflex action. It exists in the lowest classes of. the acephalous animals as well as in those that have distinct heads; it grows and develops according to the law of the double evolution, physically and spiritually; and entering upon its conscious stage of development and progress in the cephalous species already endowed with a sensorium and symmetrically-arranged ganglia, this reflex action, whether men of science term it automatic, as in the lowest species, or instinctive, as in the more complex

---

661 Cabanis, *"Histoire de la Medecine."*

organisms which act under the guidance of the sensorium and the stimulus originating in distinct sensation, is still one and the same thing. It is the divine instinct in its ceaseless progress of development. This instinct of the animals, which act from the moment of their birth each in the confines prescribed to them by nature, and which know how, save in accident proceeding from a higher instinct than their own, to take care of themselves unerringly—this instinct may, for the sake of exact definition, be termed automatic ; but it must have either within the animal which possesses it or without, something's or some one's intelligence to guide it.

This belief, instead of clashing with the doctrine of evolution and gradual development held by eminent men of our day, simplifies and completes it, on the contrary. It can readily dispense with special creation for each species; for, where the first place must be allowed to form less spirit, form and material substance are of a secondary importance. Each perfected species in the physical evolution only affords more scope to the directing intelligence to act within the improved nervous system.

The artist will display his waves of harmony better on a royal Erard than he could have done on a spinet of the sixteenth century. Therefore whether this *instinctive* impulse was directly impressed upon the nervous system of the first insect, or each species has gradually had it developed in itself by instinctively mimicking the acts of its like, as the more perfected doctrine of Herbert Spencer has it, is immaterial to the present subject. The question concerns *spiritual* evolution only. And if we reject this hypothesis as unscientific and undemonstrated, then will the physical aspect of evolution have to follow it to the ground in its turn, because the one is as undemonstrated as the other, and the spiritual intuition of man is not allowed to dovetail the two, under the pretext that it is "unphilosophical." Whether we wish it or not, we will have to fall back on the old query of Plutarch's *Symposiacs*, whether it was the bird or the egg which first made its appearance.

Now that the Aristotelean authority is shaken to its foundations with that of Plato; and our men of science reject every authority — nay hate it, except each his own; and the general estimate of human collective wisdom is at the lowest discount, mankind, headed by science itself, is still irrepressibly drawing back to the starting-point of the oldest philosophies. We find our idea perfectly expressed by a writer in the *Popular Science Monthly*. "The gods of sects and specialities," says Osgood Mason, "may perhaps be failing of their accustomed reverence, but, in the mean time, there is dawning on the world, with a softer and serener light, the conception, imperfect though it still may be, of a conscious, originating, all-pervading active soul — the 'Over-Soul,' the Cause, the Deity; unrevealed through human form or speech, but filling and inspiring every living soul in the wide universe according to its measure: *whose temple is Nature,* and whose worship is admiration." This is pure Platonism, Buddhism, and the exalted but just views of the earliest Aryans in their deification of nature. And such is the expression of the ground-thought of every theosophist, kabalist, and occultist in general; and if we compare it with the quotation from Hippocrates, which precedes the above, we will find in it exactly the same thought and spirit.

To return to our subject. The child lacks reason, it being as yet latent in him; and meanwhile he is inferior to the animal as to instinct proper. He will burn or drown himself before he learns that fire and water destroy and are dangerous for him; while the kitten will avoid both instinctively. The little instinct the child possesses fades away as reason, step by step, develops itself. It may be objected, perhaps, that instinct cannot be a spiritual gift, because animals possess it in a higher degree than man, and animals have *no souls.* Such a belief is erroneous and based upon very insecure foundations. It came from the fact that the inner nature of the animal could be fathomed still less than that of man, who is endowed with speech and can display to us his psychological powers.

But what proofs other than negative have we that the animal is without a surviving, if not immortal, soul? On strictly scientific grounds we can adduce as many arguments *pro* as *contra.* To express it clearer, neither man nor animal can offer either proof or disproof of the survival of their souls after death. And from the point of view of scientific experience, it is impossible to bring that which has no objective existence under the cognizance of any exact law of science. But Descartes and Bois-Raymond have exhausted their imaginations on the subject, and Agassiz could not realize such a thing as a future existence not shared by the animals we loved, and even the vegetable kingdom which surrounds us. And it is enough to make one's feelings revolt against the claimed justice of the First Cause to believe that while a heartless, cold-blooded villain has been endowed with an immortal spirit, the noble, honest dog, often self-denying unto death; that protects the child or master he loves at the peril of his life; that never forgets him, but starves himself on his grave; the animal in whom the sense of justice and generosity are sometimes developed to an amazing degree, will be annihilated! No, away with the civilized reason which suggests such heartless partiality. Better, far better to cling to one's *instinct* in such a case, and believe with the Indian of Pope, whose "untutored mind" can only picture to himself a heaven where

". . . admitted to that equal sky, His faithful dog shall bear him company."

Space fails us to present the speculative views of certain ancient and mediæval occultists upon this subject. Suffice it that they antedated Darwin, embraced more or less all his theories on natural selection and the evolution of species, and largely extended the chain at both ends. Moreover, these philosophers were explorers as daring in psychology as in physiology and anthropology. They never turned aside from the double parallel-path traced for them by their great master Hermes. "As above, so below," was ever their axiom; and their physical evolution was traced out simultaneously with the spiritual one.

On one point, at least, our modern biologists are quite consistent: unable, as yet, to demonstrate the existence of a distinct individual soul in animals, they deny it to man. Reason has brought them to the brink of Tyndall's "impassable chasm," between mind and matter; instinct alone can teach them to bridge it. When in their despair of ever being able to fathom the mystery of life, they will have come to a dead stop, their instinct may reassert itself, and take them across the hitherto fathomless abyss. This is the point which Professor John Fiske and the authors of the *Unseen Universe* seem to have reached; and Wallace, the anthropologist and ex-materialist, to have been the first to courageously step over. Let them push boldly on till they discover that it is not spirit that dwells in matter, but *matter* which clings temporarily to spirit; and that the latter alone is an eternal, imperishable abode for all things visible and invisible.

Esoteric philosophers held that everything in nature is but a materialization of spirit. The Eternal First Cause is latent spirit, they said, and matter from the beginning. "In the beginning was the word . . . and the word was God." While conceding the idea of such a

God to be an unthinkable abstraction to human reason, they claimed that the unerring human instinct grasped it as a reminiscence of something concrete to it though intangible to our physical senses. With the first idea, which emanated from the double-sexed and hitherto-inactive Deity, the first motion was communicated to the whole universe, and the electric thrill was instantaneously felt throughout the boundless space. Spirit begat force, and force matter; and thus the latent deity manifested itself as a creative energy.

When; at what point of the eternity; or how? the question must always remain unanswered, for human reason is unable to grasp the great mystery. But, though spirit-matter was from all eternity, it was in the latent state; the evolution of our visible universe must have had a beginning. To our feeble intellect, this beginning may seem so remote as to appear to us eternity itself — a period inexpressible in figures or language. Aristotle argued that the world was eternal, and that it will always be the same; that one generation of men has always produced another, without ever having had a beginning that could be determined by our intellect. In this, his teaching, in its exoteric sense, clashed with that of Plato, who taught that "there was a time when mankind did not perpetuate itself"; but in spirit both the doctrines agreed, as Plato adds immediately: "This was followed by the *earthly human* race, in which the primitive history was gradually forgotten and man sank deeper and deeper"; and Aristotle says: "If there has been a first man he must have been born without father or mother — which is repugnant to nature. For there could not have been a first egg to give a beginning to birds, or there should have been a first bird which gave a beginning to eggs; for a bird comes from an egg." The same he held good for all species, believing, with Plato, that everything before it appeared on earth had first its being in spirit.

PHILOSOPHY OF THE HINDU JAINS

This mystery of first creation, which was ever the despair of science, is unfathomable, unless we accept the doctrine of the Hermetists. Though matter is coëternal with spirit, that matter is certainly not our visible, tangible, and divisible matter, but its extreme sublimation. Pure spirit is but one remove higher. Unless we allow man to have been evolved out of this primordial spirit-matter, how can we ever come to any reasonable hypothesis as to the genesis of animate beings? Darwin begins his evolution of species at the lowest point and traces upward. His only mistake may be that he applies his system at the wrong end. Could he remove his quest from the visible universe into the invisible, he might find himself on the right path. But then, he would be following in the footsteps of the Hermetists.

That our philosophers — positivists — even the most learned among them, never understood the spirit of the mystic doctrines taught by the old philosophers — Platonists — is evident from that most eminent modern work, *Conflict between Religion and Science*. Professor Draper begins his fifth chapter by saying that "the Pagan Greeks and Romans believed that the *spirit* of man resembles his bodily form, varying its appearance with his variations, and growing with his growth." What the ignorant masses thought is a matter of little consequence, though even they could never have indulged in such speculations taken *a la lettre*. As to Greek and Roman philosophers of the Platonic school, they believed no such thing of the *spirit* of man, but applied the above doctrine to his soul, or psychical nature, which, as we have previously shown, is not the divine spirit.

Aristotle, in his philosophical deduction *On Dreams*, shows this doctrine of the twofold soul, or soul and spirit, very plainly. "It is necessary for us to ascertain in *what portion* of the soul dreams appear," he says. All the ancient Greeks believed not only a double, but even a *triple* soul to exist in man. And even Homer we find terming the animal soul, or the astral soul, called by Mr. Draper "spirit," θύμος , and the *divine* one νοὺς — the name by which Plato also designated the higher spirit.

The Hindu Jainas conceive the soul, which they call *Jiva*, to have been united from all eternity to even two sublimated ethereal bodies, one of which is invariable and consists of the divine powers of the *higher* mind; the other variable and composed of the grosser passions of man, his sensual affections, and terrestrial attributes. When the soul becomes purified after death it joins its *Vaycarica*, or divine spirit, and becomes a god. The followers of the *Vedas*, the learned Brahmins, explain the same doctrine in the *Vedanta*. The soul, according to their teaching, as a portion of the divine universal spirit or immaterial mind, is capable of uniting itself with the essence of its highest Entity. The teaching is explicit; the *Vedanta* affirms that whoever attains the thorough *knowledge of his god* becomes a god while yet in his mortal body, and acquires supremacy over all things.

Quoting from the Vedaic theology the verse which says: "There is in truth but one Deity, the Supreme Spirit; he is of the same nature as the soul of man," Mr. Draper shows the Buddhistic doctrines as reaching Eastern Europe through Aristotle. We believe the assertion unwarranted, for Pythagoras, and after him Plato, taught them long before Aristotle. If subsequently the later Platonists accepted in their dialectics the Aristotelean arguments on emanation, it was merely because his views coincided in some respect with those of the Oriental philosophers. The Pythagorean number of harmony and Plato's esoteric doctrines on creation are inseparable from the Buddhistic doctrine of emanation; and the great aim of the Pythagorean philosophy, namely, to free the astral soul from the fetters of matter and sense, and make it thereby fit for an eternal contemplation of spiritual things, is a theory identical with the Buddhistic doctrine of final absorption. It is the Nirvana, interpreted in its right sense; a metaphysical tenet that just begins to be suspected now by our latest Sanscrit scholars.

If the doctrines of Aristotle have exercised on the later Neo-platonists such a "dominating influence," how is it that neither Plotinus, nor Porphyry, nor Proclus ever accepted his theories on dreams and prophetic soul-visions? While Aristotle held that most of those who prophesy have "diseases of madness"[662] — thus furnishing some American plagiarists and specialists with a few reasonable ideas to disfigure — the views of Porphyry, hence those of Plotinus, were quite the reverse. In the most vital questions of metaphysical speculations Aristotle is constantly contradicted by the Neo-platonists. Furthermore, either the Buddhistic Nirvana is not the nihilistic doctrine, as it is now represented to be, or the Neo-platonists did not accept it in this sense. Surely Mr. Draper will not take upon himself to affirm that either Plotinus, Porphyry, Iamblichus, or any other philosopher of their mystic school, did not believe in the soul's immortality? To say that either of them sought ecstasy

---

662 "*De Vatibus in Problemate*," sect. 21.

as a "foretaste of absorption into the universal mundane soul," in the sense in which the Buddhist Nirvana is understood by every Sanscrit scholar, is to wrong these philosophers. Nirvana is *not,* as Mr. Draper has it, a "reabsorption in the *Universal Force,* eternal rest, and bliss"; but, when taken literally by the said scholars, means the blowing out, *the extinction, complete annihilation,* and not absorption.[663] No one, so far as we know, has ever taken upon himself to ascertain the *true* metaphysical meaning of this word, which is not to be found, even in the *Lankâvatâra,*[664] which gives the different interpretations of the Nirvana by the Brahmans-Tirthakas. Therefore, for one who reads this passage in Mr. Draper's work, and bears in mind but the usually-accepted meaning of the Nirvana, will naturally suppose that Plotinus and Porphyry were *nihilists.* Such a page in the *Conflict* gives us a certain right to suppose that either 1, the learned author desired to place Plotinus and Porphyry on the same plane with Giordano Bruno, of whom he makes, very erroneously, an atheist; or, 2, that he never took the trouble of studying the lives of these philosophers and their views.

DELIBERATE MISREPRESENTATIONS OF LEMPRIERE

Now, for one who knows Professor Draper, even by reputation, the latter supposition is simply absurd. Therefore, we must think, with deep regret, that his desire was to misrepresent their religious aspirations. It is decidedly an awkward thing for modern philosophers, whose sole aim seems to be the elimination of the ideas of God and the immortal spirit from the mind of humanity, to have to treat with historical impartiality the most celebrated of the Pagan Platonists. To have to admit, on the one hand, their profound learning, their genius, their achievements in the most abstruse philosophical questions, and therefore their sagacity; and, on the other, their unreserved adhesion to the doctrine of immortality, of the final triumph of spirit over matter, and their implicit faith in God and the gods, or spirits; in the return *of the dead,* apparitions, and other "spiritual" matters, is a dilemma from which academical human nature could not reasonably be expected to extricate itself so easily.

The plan resorted to by Lemprière,[665] in such an emergency as the above, is coarser than Professor Draper's, but equally effective. He charges the ancient philosophers with deliberate falsehood, trickery, and credulity. After painting to his readers Pythagoras, Plotinus, and Porphyry as marvels of learning, morality, and accomplishments; as men eminent for personal dignity, purity of lives, and self-abnegation in the pursuit of divine truths, he does not hesitate to rank "this celebrated philosopher" (Pythagoras) among impostors; while to Porphyry he attributes "credulity, lack of judgment, and dishonesty." Forced by the facts of history to give them their just due in the course of his narrative, he displays his bigoted prejudice in the parenthetical comments which he allows himself. From this antiquated writer of the last century we learn that a man may be honest, and at the same time an impostor; pure, virtuous, and a great philosopher, and yet dishonest, a liar, and a fool!

---

663 See Max Müller, "*The Meaning of Nirvana.*"
664 "*The Lankâvatâra,*" transl. by Burnouf, p. 514.
665 "*Classical Dictionary.*"

MAN'S ASTRAL SOUL NOT IMMORTAL

We have shown elsewhere that the "secret doctrine" does not concede immortality to all men alike. "The eye would never see the sun, if it were not of the nature of the sun," said Plotinus. Only "through the highest purity and chastity we shall approach nearer to God, and receive in the contemplation of Him, the true knowledge and insight," writes Porphyry. If the human soul has neglected during its life-time to receive its illumination from its Divine Spirit, our *personal* God, then it becomes difficult for the gross and sensual man to survive for a great length of time his physical death. No more than the misshapen monster can live long after its physical birth, can the soul, once that it has become *too* material, exist after its birth into the spiritual world. The viability of the astral form is so feeble, that the particles cannot cohere firmly when once it is slipped out of the unyielding capsule of the external body. Its particles, gradually obeying the disorganizing attraction of universal space, finally fly asunder beyond the possibility of reaggregation. Upon the occurrence of such a catastrophe, the individual ceases to exist; his glorious Augoeides has left him. During the intermediary period between his bodily death and the disintegration of the astral form, the latter, bound by magnetic attraction to its ghastly corpse, prowls about, and sucks vitality from susceptible victims. The man having shut out of himself every ray of the divine light, is lost in darkness, and, therefore, clings to the earth and the earthy.

No astral soul, even that of a pure, good, and virtuous man, is immortal in the strictest sense; "from elements it was formed — to elements it must return." Only, while the soul of the wicked vanishes, and is absorbed without redemption, that of every other person, even moderately pure, simply changes its ethereal particles for still more ethereal ones; and, while there remains in it a spark of the *Divine*, the individual man, or rather, his personal *ego*, cannot die. "After death," says Proclus, "the soul (the spirit) continueth to linger in the aërial body (astral form), till it is entirely purified from all angry and voluptuous passions . . . then doth it put off by a *second dying* the aërial body as it did the earthly one. Whereupon, the ancients say that there is a celestial body always joined with *the soul*, and which is *immortal, luminous*, and *star-like*."

But, we will now turn from our digression to further consider the question of *reason* and *instinct*. The latter, according to the ancients, proceeded from the divine, the former from the purely human. One (the instinct) is the product of the senses, a sagaciousness shared by the lowest animals, even those who have no reason — it is the αισθητικον ; the other is the product of the reflective faculties — νοητικόν, denoting judiciousness and human intellectuality. Therefore, an animal devoid of reasoning powers has in its inherent instinct an unerring faculty which is but that spark of the divine which lurks in every particle of inorganic matter — itself materialized spirit. In the Jewish *Kabala*, the second and third chapters of *Genesis* are explained thus: When the second Adam is created "out of the dust," matter has become so gross that it reigns supreme. Out of its lusts evolves woman, and Lilith has the best of spirit. The Lord God, "walking in the garden in *the cool of the day*" (the sunset of spirit, or divine light obscured by the shadows of matter) curses not only them who have committed the sin, but even the ground itself, and all living things — the tempting serpent-matter above all.

Who but the kabalists are able to explain this seeming act of injustice? How are we to understand this cursing of all created things, innocent of any crime? The allegory is evident.

The curse inheres in matter itself. Henceforth, it is doomed to struggle against its own grossness for purification; the latent spark of divine spirit, though smothered, is still there; and its invincible attraction upward compels it to struggle in pain and labor to free itself. Logic shows us that as all matter had a common origin, it must have attributes in common, and as the vital and divine spark is in man's material body, so it must lurk in every subordinate species. The latent mentality which, in the lower kingdoms is recognized as semi-consciousness, consciousness, and instinct, is largely subdued in man. Reason, the outgrowth of the physical brain, develops at the expense of instinct — the flickering reminiscence of a once divine omniscience — spirit. Reason, the badge of the sovereignty of physical man over all other physical organisms, is often put to shame by the instinct of an animal. As his brain is more perfect than that of any other creature, its emanations must naturally produce the highest results of mental action; but reason avails only for the consideration of material things; it is incapable of helping its possessor to a knowledge of spirit. In losing instinct, man loses his intuitional powers, which are the crown and ultimatum of instinct. Reason is the clumsy weapon of the scientists — intuition the unerring guide of the seer. Instinct teaches plant and animal their seasons for the procreation of their species, and guides the dumb brute to find his appropriate remedy in the hour of sickness. Reason — the pride of man — fails to check the propensities of his matter, and brooks no restraint upon the unlimited gratification of his senses. Far from leading him to be his *own* physician, its subtile sophistries lead him too often to his own destruction.

Nothing is more demonstrable than the proposition that the perfection of matter is reached at the expense of instinct. The zoophyte attached to the submarine rock, opening its mouth to attract the food that floats by, shows, proportionately with its physical structure, more instinct than the whale. The ant, with its wonderful architectural, social, and political abilities, is inexpressibly higher in the scale than the subtile royal tiger watching its prey. "With awe and wonder," exclaims du Bois-Raymond, "must the student of nature regard that microscopic molecule of nervous substance which is the seat of the laborious, constructive, orderly, loyal, dauntless soul of the ant!"

Like everything else which has its origin in psychological mysteries, instinct has been too long neglected in the domain of science. "We see what indicated the way to man to find relief for all his physical ailings," says Hippocrates. "It is the instinct of the earlier races, when cold reason had not as yet obscured man's inner vision. . . . Its indication must never be disdained, for it is to instinct alone that we owe our first remedies."[666] Instantaneous and unerring cognition of an omniscient mind, instinct is in everything unlike the finite reason; and in the tentative progress of the latter, the god-like nature of man is often utterly engulfed, whenever he shuts out from himself the divine light of intuition. The one crawls, the other flies; reason is the power of the man, intuition the prescience of the woman!

Plotinus, the pupil of the great Ammonius Saccas, the chief founder of the Neo-platonic school, taught that human knowledge had three ascending steps: opinion, science, and *illumination.* He explained it by saying that "the means or instrument of opinion is sense, or perception; of science, dialectics; of illumination, *intuition* (or divine instinct). To the last,

---

666 See Cabanis, "*Histoire de la Medecine.*"

reason is subordinate; it is absolute knowledge founded on the identification of the mind with the object known."

Prayer opens the spiritual sight of man, for prayer is desire, and desire develops WILL; the magnetic emanations proceeding from the body at every effort — whether mental or physical — produce self-magnetization and ecstasy. Plotinus recommended solitude for prayer, as the most efficient means of obtaining what is asked; and Plato advised those who prayed to "remain silent in the presence of the divine ones, till they remove the cloud from thy eyes, and enable thee to see *by the light which issues from themselves*." Apollonius always isolated himself from men during the "conversation" he held with God, and whenever he felt the necessity for divine contemplation and prayer, he wrapped himself, head and all, in the drapery of his white woolen mantle. "When thou prayest *enter into thy closet*, and when thou hast shut thy door, pray to thy Father in secret," says the Nazarene, the pupil of the Essenes.

Every human being is born with the rudiment of the inner sense called *intuition*, which may be developed into what the Scotch know as "second sight." All the great philosophers, who, like Plotinus, Porphyry, and Iamblichus employed this faculty, taught the doctrine. "There is a faculty of the human mind," writes Iamblichus, "which is superior to all which is born or begotten. Through it we are enabled to attain union with the superior intelligences, to being transported beyond the scenes of this world, and to partaking the higher life and peculiar powers of the heavenly ones."

Were there no *inner sight* or intuition, the Jews would never have had their *Bible*, nor the Christians Jesus. What both Moses and Jesus gave to the world was the fruit of their intuition or illumination. What their subsequent elders and teachers allowed the world to understand was — dogmatic misrepresentations, too often blasphemy.

To accept the Bible as a "revelation" and nail belief to a literal translation, is worse than absurdity — it is a blasphemy against the Divine majesty of the "Unseen." If we had to judge of the Deity, and the world of spirits, by its human interpreters, now that philology proceeds with giant-strides on the fields of comparative religions, belief in God and the soul's immortality could not withstand the attacks of *reason* for one century more. That which supports the faith of man in God and a spiritual life to come is *intuition*; that divine outcome of our inner-self, which defies the mummeries of the Roman Catholic priest, and his ridiculous idols; the thousand and one ceremonies of the Brahman and his idols; and the jeremiads of the Protestant preacher, and his desolate and arid creed, with no idols, but a boundless hell and damnation hooked on at the end. Were it not for this intuition, undying though often wavering because so clogged with matter, human life would be a parody and humanity a fraud. This ineradicable feeling of the presence of some one *outside* and *inside* ourselves is one that no dogmatic contradictions, nor external form of worship can destroy in humanity, let scientists and clergy do what they may. Moved by such thoughts of the boundlessness and impersonality of the Deity, Gautama-Buddha, the Hindu Christ, exclaimed: "As the four rivers which fall in the Ganges lose their names as soon as they mingle their waters with the holy river, so all who believe in Buddha cease to be Brahmans, Kshatriyas, Vaisyas, and Sudras!"

The *Old Testament* was compiled and arranged from oral tradition; the masses never knew its real meaning, for Moses was ordered to impart the "hidden truths" but to his seventy elders on whom the "Lord" put of the *spirit* which was upon the legislator. Maimonides, whose authority and whose knowledge of the sacred history can hardly be rejected, says: "Whoever shall find out the true sense of *the book of Genesis* ought to take care not to divulge it. . . . If a person should discover *the true meaning of it* by himself, or by the aid of another, then he ought to be silent; or, if he speaks of it, he ought to speak of it but obscurely and in an enigmatical manner."

This confession, that what is written in the Holy Writ is but an allegory, was made by other Jewish authorities besides Maimonides; for we find Josephus stating that Moses "*philosophized*" (spoke riddles in figurative allegory), when writing the book of *Genesis*. Therefore modern science, by neglecting to unriddle the true sense of the *Bible*, and by allowing the whole of Christendom to go on believing in the dead letter of the Jewish theology, tacitly constitutes herself the confederate of the fanatical clergy. She has no right to ridicule the records of a people who never wrote them with the idea that they would receive such a strange interpretation at the hands of an inimical religion. That their holiest texts should be turned against them and that the dead men's bones could have smothered the spirit of truth, is the saddest feature of Christianity!

"The gods exist," says Epicurus, "but they are *not* what the rabble, hoi polloi , suppose them to be." And yet Epicurus, judged as usual by superficial critics, is set down and paraded as a materialist.

But neither the great First Cause nor its emanation — human, immortal spirit — have left themselves "without a witness." Mesmerism and modern spiritualism are there to attest the great truths. For over fifteen centuries, thanks to the blindly-brutal persecutions of those great vandals of early Christian history, Constantine and Justinian, ancient WISDOM slowly degenerated until it gradually sank into the deepest mire of monkish superstition and ignorance. The Pythagorean "knowledge of things that are"; the profound erudition of the Gnostics; the world and time-honored teachings of the great philosophers; all were rejected as doctrines of Antichrist and Paganism, and committed to the flames. With the last seven wise men of the Orient, the remnant group of the Neo-platonists, Hermias, Priscianus, Diogenes, Eulalius, Damaskius, Simplicius and Isidorus, who fled from the fanatical persecutions of Justinian, to Persia, the reign of wisdom closed. The books of Thoth, or (Hermes Trismegistus), which contain within their sacred pages the spiritual and physical history of the creation and progress of our world, were left to mould in oblivion and contempt for ages. They found no interpreters in Christian Europe; the Philaletheians, or wise "lovers of the truth," were no more; they were replaced by the light-fleers, the tonsured and hooded monks of Papal Rome, who dread truth, in whatever shape and from whatever quarter it appears, if it but clashes in the least with their dogmas.

THE REINCARNATION OF BUDDHA

As to skeptics — this is what Professor Alexander Wilder remarks of them and their followers, in his sketches on *Neo-platonism and Alchemy:* "A century has passed since the compilers of the French *Encyclopædia* infused skepticism into the blood of the civilized world, and made it disreputable to believe in the actual existence of anything that cannot be tested in crucibles or demonstrated by critical reasoning. Even now, it requires candor as well as courage to venture to treat upon a subject which has been for many years discarded and contemned, because it has not been well or correctly understood. The person must be bold who accounts the Hermetic philosophy to be other than a pretense of science, and so believing, demands for its enunciation a patient hearing. Yet its professors were once the princes of learned investigation, and heroes among common men. Besides, nothing is to be despised which men have reverently believed; and disdain for the earnest convictions of others is itself the token of ignorance, and of an ungenerous mind."

And now, encouraged by these words from a scholar who is neither a fanatic nor a conservative, we will recall a few things reported by travellers as having been seen by them in Thibet and India, and which are treasured by the natives as practical proofs of the truth of the philosophy and science handed down by their forefathers.

First we may consider that most remarkable phenomenon as seen in the temples of Thibet and the accounts of which have reached Europe from eye-witnesses other than Catholic missionaries — whose testimony we will exclude for obvious reasons. Early in the present century a Florentine scientist, a skeptic and a correspondent of the French Institute, having been permitted to penetrate in disguise to the hallowed precincts of a Buddhist temple, where the most solemn of all ceremonies was taking place, relates the following as having been seen by himself. An altar is ready in the temple to receive the resuscitated Buddha, found by the initiated priesthood, and recognized by certain secret signs to have reincarnated himself in a new-born infant. The baby, but a few days old, is brought into the presence of the people and reverentially placed upon the altar. Suddenly rising into a sitting posture, the child begins to utter in a loud, manly voice, the following sentences: "I am Buddha, I am his spirit; and I, Buddha, your Dalai-Lama, have left my old, decrepit body, at the temple of . . . and selected the body of this young babe as my next earthly dwelling." Our scientist, being finally permitted by the priests to take, with due reverence, the baby in his arms, and carry it away to such a distance from them as to satisfy him that no ventriloquial deception is being practiced, the infant looks at the grave academician with eyes that "make his flesh creep," as he expresses it, and repeats the words he had previously uttered. A detailed account of this adventure, attested with the signature of this eye-witness, was forwarded to Paris, but the members of the Institute, instead of accepting the testimony of a scientific observer of acknowledged credibility, concluded that the Florentine *was either suffering under an attack of sunstroke,* or had been deceived by a clever trick of acoustics.

Although, according to Mr. Stanislas Julien, the French translator of the sacred Chinese texts, there is a verse in the *Lotus*[667] which says that "A Buddha is as difficult to be found as the flowers of Udumbara and Palâça," if we are to believe several eye-witnesses, such a phenomenon does happen. Of course its occurrence is rare, for it happens but on the death of every great Dalai-Lama; and these venerable old gentlemen live proverbially long lives.

The poor Abbé Huc, whose works of travel in Thibet and China are so well-known, relates the same fact of the resuscitation of Buddha. He adds, furthermore, the curious circumstance that the baby-oracle makes good his claim to being an old mind in a young body by giving to those who ask him, "and who knew him in his past life, the most exact details of his anterior earthly existence."

---

667 *"Le Lotus de la bonne Loi,"* by E. Burnouf, translated from the Sanscrit.

It is worthy of notice, that des Mousseaux, who expatiates at length on the phenomenon, attributing it as a matter of course to the Devil, gravely remarks of the Abbé himself, that the fact that he had been unfrocked (*défroqué*) "is an accident which I (he) confess scarcely tends to strengthen our confidence." In our humble opinion this little circumstance strengthens it all the more.

The Abbé Huc had his work placed on the *Index* for the truth he told about the similarity of the Buddhistical rites with the Roman Catholic ones. He was moreover suspended in his missionary work for being too *sincere.*

If this example of infant prodigy stood alone, we might reasonably indulge in some hesitation as to accepting it; but, to say nothing of the Camisard prophets of 1707, among whom was the boy of fifteen months described by Jacques Dubois, who spoke in good French "as though God were speaking through his mouth"; and of the Cevennes babies, whose speaking and prophesying were witnessed by the first savants of France — we have instances in modern times of quite as remarkable a character. *Lloyd's Weekly Newspaper,* for March, 1875, contained an account of the following phenomenon: "At Saar-Louis, France, a child was born. The mother had just been confined, the midwife was holding forth garrulously 'on the blessed little creature,' and the friends were congratulating the father on his luck, when somebody asked what time it was. Judge of the surprise of all, on hearing the new-born babe reply distinctly 'Two o'clock!' But this was nothing to what followed. The company were looking on the infant, with speechless wonder and dismay, when it opened its eyes, and said: 'I have been sent into the world to tell you that 1875 will be a good year, but that 1876 will be a year of blood.' Having uttered this prophecy it turned on its side and expired, aged half-an-hour."

We are not aware that this prodigy has received official authentication by the civil authority — of course we should look for none from the clergy, since no profit or honor was to be derived from it — but even if a respectable British commercial journal was not responsible for the story, the result has given it special interest. The year 1876, just passed (we write in February, 1877) was emphatically, and, from the standpoint of March, 1875, unexpectedly — a year of blood. In the Danubian principalities was written one of the bloodiest chapters of the history of war and rapine — a chapter of outrages of Moslem upon Christian that has scarcely been paralleled since Catholic soldiers butchered the simple natives of North and South America by tens of thousands, and Protestant Englishmen waded to the Imperial throne of Delhi, step by step, through rivers of blood. If the Saar-Louis prophecy was but a mere newspaper sensation, still the turn of events elevated it into the rank of a fulfilled prediction; 1875 *was* a year of great plenty, and 1876, to the surprise of everybody, a year of carnage.

But even if it should be found that the baby-prophet never opened its lips, the instance of the Jencken infant still remains to puzzle the investigator. This is one of the most surprising cases of mediumship. The child's mother is the famous Kate Fox, its father H. D. Jencken, M.R.I., Barrister-at-law, in London. He was born in London, in 1873, and before he was three months old showed evidences of spirit-mediumship. Rappings occurred on his pillow and cradle, and also on his father's person, when he held the child in his lap and Mrs. Jencken was absent from home. Two months later, a communication of twenty words, exclusive of signature, was written through his hand. A gentleman, a Liverpool solicitor, named J. Wason, was present at the time, and united with the mother and nurse in a certificate which was published in the London *Medium and Daybreak* of May 8th, 1874. The professional and scientific rank of Mr. Jencken make it in the highest degree improbable that he would lend himself to a deception. Moreover, the child was within such easy reach of the Royal Institution, of which his father is a member, that Professor Tyndall and his associates had no excuse for neglecting to examine and inform the world about this psychological phenomenon.

The sacred baby of Thibet being so far away, they find their most convenient plan to be a flat denial, with hints of sunstroke and acoustical machinery. As for the London baby, the affair is still easier; let them wait until the child has grown up and learned to write, and then deny the story point-blank!

In addition to other travellers, the Abbé Huc gives us an account of that wonderful tree of Thibet called the *Kounboum;* that is to say, the tree of the 10,000 images and characters. It will grow in no other latitude, although the experiment has sometimes been tried; and it cannot even be multiplied from cuttings. The tradition is that it sprang from the hair of one of the Avatars (the Lama Son-Ka-pa) one of the incarnations of Buddha. But we will let the Abbé Huc tell the rest of the story: "Each of its leaves, in opening, bears either a letter or a religious sentence, written in sacred characters, and these letters are, of their kind, of such a perfection that the type-foundries of Didot contain nothing to excel them. Open the leaves, which vegetation is about to unroll, and you will there discover, on the point of appearing, the letters or the distinct words which are the marvel of this unique tree! Turn your attention from the leaves of the plant to the bark of its branches, and new characters will meet your eyes! Do not allow your interest to flag; raise the layers of this bark, and still OTHER CHARACTERS will show themselves below those whose beauty had surprised you. For, do not fancy that these superposed layers repeat the same *printing.* No, quite the contrary; for each lamina you lift presents to view its distinct type. How, then, can we suspect jugglery? I have done my best in that direction to discover the slightest trace of human trick, and my baffled mind could not retain the slightest suspicion."

We will add to M. Huc's narrative the statement that the characters which appear upon the different portions of the Kounboum are in the Sansar (or language of the Sun), characters (ancient Sanscrit); and that the sacred tree, in its various parts, contains *in extenso* the whole history of the creation, and in substance the sacred books of Buddhism. In this respect, it bears the same relation to Buddhism as the pictures in the Temple of Dendera, in Egypt, do to the ancient faith of the Pharaohs. The latter are briefly described by Professor W. B. Carpenter, President of the British Association, in his Manchester Lecture on *Egypt.* He makes it clear that the Jewish book of *Genesis* is nothing more than an expression of the early Jewish ideas, based upon the pictorial records of the Egyptians among whom they lived. But he does not make it clear, except inferentially, whether he believes either the Dendera pictures or the Mosaic account to be an allegory or a pretended historical narrative. How a scientist who had devoted himself to the most superficial investigation of the subject can venture to assert that the ancient Egyptians had the same ridiculous notions about the world's instantaneous creation as the early Christian theologians, passes comprehension! How can he say that because the Dendera picture happens to represent their cosmogony in one allegory, they intended to show the scene as occurring in six minutes or six millions of years? It may as well indicate allegorically six successive epochs or æons, or eternity, as six days. Besides, the *Books of Hermes* certainly give no color to the charge, and the *Avesta* specifically names six periods, each embracing thousands of years, instead of days. Many of the Egyptian hieroglyphics contradict Dr. Carpenter's theory, and Champollion has avenged the ancients in many particulars. From what is gone before, it will, we think, be made clear to the reader that the Egyptian philosophy had no room for any such crude speculations, if the Hebrews themselves ever believed them; their cosmogony viewed man as the result of evolution, and his progress to be marked by immensely lengthened cycles. But to return to the wonders of Thibet.

MAGICAL SUN AND MOON PICTURES OF THIBET

Speaking of pictures, the one described by Huc as hanging in a certain Lamasery may fairly be regarded as one of the most wonderful in existence. It is a simple canvas without the slightest mechanical apparatus attached, as the visitor may prove by examining it at his leisure. It represents a moon-lit landscape, but the moon is not at all motionless and dead; quite the reverse, for, according to the abbé, one would say that our moon herself, or at least her living double, lighted the picture. Each phase, each aspect, each movement of our satellite, is repeated in her *fac-simile*, in the movement and progress of the moon in the sacred picture. "You see this planet in the painting ride as a crescent, or full, shine brightly, pass behind the clouds, peep out or set, in a manner corresponding in the most extraordinary way with the real luminary. It is, in a word, a most servile and resplendent reproduction of the pale queen of the night, which received the adoration of so many people in the days of old."

When we think of the astonishment that would inevitably be felt by one of our self-complacent academicians at seeing such a picture — and it is by no means the only one, for they have them in other parts of Thibet and Japan also, which represent the sun's movements — when we think, we say, of his embarrassment at knowing that if he ventured to tell the unvarnished truth to his colleagues, his fate would probably be like that of poor Huc, and he flung out of the academical chair as a liar or a lunatic, we cannot help recalling the anecdote of Tycho-Brahe, given by Humboldt in his *Cosmos*.[668]

"One evening," says the great Danish astronomer, "as, according to my usual habit, I was considering the celestial vault, to my indescribable amazement, I saw, close to the zenith, in Cassiopea, a radiant star of extraordinary size. Struck with astonishment, I knew not whether I could believe my own eyes. Some time after that, I learned that in Germany, cartmen, and other persons of the lower classes had repeatedly warned the scientists that a great apparition could be seen in the sky; which fact afforded both the press and public one more opportunity to indulge in their usual raillery against the men of science, who, in the cases of several antecedent comets, had not predicted their appearance."

From the days of the earliest antiquity, the Brahmans were known to be possessed of wonderful knowledge in every kind of magic arts. From Pythagoras, the first philosopher who studied wisdom with the Gymnosophists, and Plotinus, who was initiated into the mystery of uniting one's self with the Deity through abstract contemplation, down to the modern adepts, it was well known that in the land of the Brahmans and Gautama-Buddha

---

668 "*Cosmos*," vol. iii., part i., p. 168.

the sources of "hidden" wisdom are to be sought after. It is for future ages to discover this grand truth, and accept it as such, whereas now it is degraded as a low superstition. What did any one, even the greatest scientists, know of India, Thibet, and China, until the last quarter of this century? That most untiring scholar, Max Müller, tells us that before then not a single original document of the Buddhist religion had been accessible to European philologists; that fifty years ago "there was not a single scholar who could have translated a line of the *Veda*, a line of the *Zend-Avesta*, or a line of the Buddhist *Tripitaka*," let alone other dialects or languages. And even now, that science is in possession of various sacred texts, what they have are but very incomplete editions of these works, and *nothing*, positively nothing of the secret sacred literature of Buddhism. And the little that our Sanscrit scholars have got hold of, and which at first was termed by Max Müller a dreary "jungle of religious literature — the most excellent hiding-place for Lamas and Dalai-Lamas," is now beginning to shed a faint light on the primitive darkness. We find this scholar stating that that which appeared at the first glance into the labyrinth of the religions of the world, all darkness, self-deceit, and vanity begin to assume another form. "It sounds," he writes, "like a degradation of the very name of religion, to apply it to the wild ravings of Hindu Yogins, and the blank blasphemies of Chinese Buddhists. . . . But, as we slowly and patiently wend our way through the dreary prisons, our own eyes seem to expand, *and we perceive a glimmer of light,* where all was darkness at first."[669]

As an illustration of how little even the generation which directly preceded our own was competent to judge the religions and beliefs of the several hundred million Buddhists, Brahmans, and Parsees, let the student consult the advertisement of a scientific work published in 1828 by a Professor Dunbar, the first scholar who has undertaken to demonstrate that the *Sanscrit is derived from the Greek.* It appeared under the following title:

"*An Inquiry into the structure and affinity of the Greek and Latin languages; with occasional comparisons of the Sanscrit and Gothic; with an Appendix, in which* THE DERIVATION OF THE SANSCRIT FROM THE GREEK *is endeavoured to be established. By George Dunbar, F.R.S.E., and Professor of Greek in the University of Edinburgh. Price, 18s.*"[670]

Had Max Müller happened to fall from the sky at that time, among the scholars of the day, and with his present knowledge, we would like to have compiled the epithets which would have been bestowed by the learned academicians upon the daring innovator! One who, classifying languages genealogically, says that "Sanscrit, as compared to Greek and Latin, is an elder sister . . . the earliest deposit of Aryan speech."

And so, we may naturally expect that in 1976, the same criticisms will be justly applied to many a scientific discovery, now deemed conclusive and final by our scholars. That which is now termed the superstitious *verbiage* and gibberish of mere heathens and savages, composed many thousands of years ago, may be found to contain the master-key to all religious systems. The cautious sentence of St. Augustine, a favorite name in Max Müller's lectures, which says that "there is no false religion which does not contain some elements of truth," may yet be triumphantly proved correct; the more so as, far from being original with

---

669 *"Lecture on the Vedas."*
670 *"The Classical Journal,"* vol. iv., pp. 107, 348.

the Bishop of Hippo, it was borrowed by him from the works of Ammonius Saccas, the great Alexandrian teacher.

This "god-taught" philosopher, the *theodidaktos*, had repeated these same words to exhaustion, in his numerous works some 140 years before Augustine. Acknowledging Jesus as "an excellent man, and the friend of God," he always maintained that his design was not to abolish the intercourse with gods and demons (spirits), but simply to purify the ancient religions; that "the religion of the multitude went hand in hand with philosophy, and with her had shared the fate of being by degrees corrupted and obscured with mere human conceits, superstition, and lies: that it ought therefore to be brought back to its *original purity* by purging it of this dross and expounding it upon philosophical principles; and that the whole which Christ had in view was to reinstate and restore to its primitive integrity the wisdom of the ancients."[671]

It was Ammonius who first taught that every religion was based on one and the same truth; which is the wisdom found in the Books of Thoth (Hermes Trismegistus), from which books Pythagoras and Plato had learned all their philosophy. And the doctrines of the former he affirmed to have been identical with the earliest teachings of the Brahmans — now embodied in the oldest *Vedas*. "The name Thoth," says Professor Wilder, "means a college or assembly,"[672] and "it is not improbable that the books were so named as being the collected oracles and doctrines of the sacerdotal fraternity of Memphis. Rabbi Wise had suggested a similar hypothesis in relation to the divine utterances recorded in the Hebrew Scripture. But the Indian writers assert, that during the reign of king Kansa, *Yadus* (*Judeans?*) or sacred tribe left India and migrated to the West, carrying the four *Vedas* with them. There was certainly a great resemblance between the philosophical doctrines and religious customs of the Egyptians and Eastern Buddhists; but whether the Hermetic books and the four *Vedas* were identical, is not now known."

But one thing is certainly known, and that is, that before the word philosopher was first pronounced by Pythagoras at the court of the king of the Philasians, the "secret doctrine" or wisdom was identical in every country. Therefore it is in the oldest texts — those least polluted by subsequent forgeries — that we have to look for the truth. And now that philology has possessed itself of Sanscrit texts which may be boldly affirmed to be documents by far antedating the Mosaic Bible, it is the duty of the scholars to present the world with truth, and *nothing but the truth*. Without regard to either skeptical or theological prejudice, they are bound to impartially examine both documents — the oldest *Vedas* and the *Old Testament*, and then decide which of the two is the original *Sruti* or *Revelation*, and which but the *Smriti*, which, as Max Müller shows, only means recollection or *tradition*.

Origen writes that the Brahmans were always famous for the wonderful cures which they performed by certain words;[673] and in our own age we find Orioli, a learned corresponding member of the French Institute,[674] corroborating the statement of Origen in the third century, and that of Leonard de Vair of the sixteenth, in which the latter wrote:

---

671 See "*Mosheim.*"

672 "*New Platonism and Alchemy.*"

673 Origen, "*Contra Celsum.*"

674 "*Fatti relativi al Mesmerismo,*" pp. 88, 93, 1842.

"There are also persons, who upon pronouncing a certain sentence — *a charm*, walk bare-footed on red, burning coals, and on the points of sharp *knives* stuck in the ground; and, once poised on them, *on one toe*, they will lift up in the air a heavy man or any other burden of considerable weight. They will tame wild horses likewise, and the most furious bulls, with a single word."[675]

This *word* is to be found in the *Mantras* of the Sanscrit *Vedas*, say some adepts. It is for the philologists to decide for themselves whether there is such a word in the *Vedas*. So far as human evidence goes, it would seem that such magic words *do* exist.

It appears that the reverend fathers of the Order of Jesuits have picked up many such tricks in their missionary travels. Baldinger gives them full credit for it. The *tschamping* — a Hindu word, from which the modern word *shampooing* is derived — is a well-known magical manipulation in the East Indies. The native *sorcerers* use it with success to the present day, and it is from them that the father Jesuits derived their wisdom.

Camerarius, in his *Horæ Subscecivæ*, narrates that once upon a time there existed a great rivalry of "miracles" between the Austin Friars and the Jesuits. A disputation having taken place between the father-general of the Austin Friars, who was very learned, and the general of the Jesuits, who was very *unlearned*, but full of *magical* knowledge, the latter proposed to settle the question by trying their subordinates, and finding out which of them would be the readiest to obey his superiors. Thereupon, turning to one of his Jesuits, he said: "Brother Mark, our companions are cold; I command you, in virtue of the holy obedience you have sworn to me, to bring here instantly out of the kitchen fire, and in your hands, some burning coals, that they may warm themselves over your hands." Father Mark instantly obeyed, and brought in both his hands a supply of red, burning coals, and held them till the company present had all warmed themselves, after which he took them back to the kitchen hearth. The general of the Austin Friars found himself crestfallen, for none of his subordinates would obey him so far as that. The triumph of the Jesuits was thus accomplished.

If the above is looked upon as an anecdote unworthy of credence, we will inquire of the reader what we must think of some modern "mediums," who perform the same while *entranced*. The testimony of several highly respectable and trustworthy witnesses, such as Lord Adair and Mr. S. C. Hall, is unimpeachable. "Spirits," the spiritualists will argue. Perhaps so, in the case of American and English *fire-proof* mediums; but not so in Thibet and India. In the West a "sensitive" has to be entranced before being rendered invulnerable by the presiding "guides," and we defy any "medium," in his or her normal physical state to bury the arms to the elbows in glowing coals. But in the East, whether the performer be a holy lama or a mercenary sorcerer (the latter class being generally termed "jugglers") he needs no preparation or abnormal state to be able to handle fire, red-hot pieces of iron, or melted lead. We have seen in Southern India these "jugglers" keep their hands in a furnace of burning coals until the latter were reduced to cinders. During the religious ceremony of Siva-Râtri, or the vigil-night of Siva, when the people spend whole nights in watching and praying, some of the Sivaites called in a Tamil juggler, who produced the most wonderful phenomena by simply summoning to his help a spirit whom they call *Kutti-Sâttan* — the

---

675 *"Leonard de Vair,"* 1. ii., ch. ii.; *"La Magie au 19me Siècle,"* p. 332.

little *demon*. But, far from allowing people to think he was *guided* or "controlled" by this gnome — for it was a gnome, if it was anything — the man, while crouching over his fiery pit, proudly rebuked a Catholic missionary, who took his opportunity to inform the bystanders that the miserable sinner "had sold himself to Satan." Without removing his hands and arms from the burning coals within which he was coolly refreshing them, the Tamil only turned his head and gave one arrogant look at the flushed missionary. "My father and my father's father," he said, "had this 'little one' at their command. For two centuries the Kutti is a faithful servant in our home, and now, Sir, you would make people believe that *he* is my master! But they know better." After this, he quietly withdrew his hands from the fire, and proceeded with other performances.

As for the wonderful powers of prediction and clairvoyance possessed by certain Brahmans, they are well known to every European resident of India. If these upon their return to "civilized" countries, laugh at such stories, and sometimes even deny them outright, they only impugn their good faith, not the fact. These Brahmans live principally in "sacred villages," and secluded places, principally on the western coast of India. They avoid populated cities, and especially Europeans, and it is but rarely that the latter can succeed in making themselves intimate with the "seers." It is generally thought that the circumstance is due to their religious observance of the caste; but we are firmly convinced that in many cases this is not so. Years, perhaps centuries, will roll away before the real reason is ascertained.

As to the lower castes, some of which are termed by the missionaries devil-worshippers, notwithstanding the pious efforts on the part of the Catholic missionaries to spread in Europe heart-rending reports of the misery of these people "sold to the Arch-Enemy"; and like efforts, perhaps only a trifle less ridiculous and absurd, of Protestant missionaries, the word devil, in the sense understood by Christians, is a nonentity for them. They believe in good and bad spirits; but they neither worship nor dread the Devil. Their "worship" is simply a ceremonial precaution against "terrestrial" and *human* spirits, whom they dread far more than the millions of elementals of various forms. They use all kinds of music, incense, and perfumes, in their efforts to drive away the "bad spirits" (the elementary). In this case, they are no more to be ridiculed than the well-known scientist, a firm spiritualist, who suggested the keeping of vitriol and powdered nitre in the room to keep away "unpleasant spirits"; and no more than he, are they wrong in so doing; for the experience of their ancestors, extending over many thousands of years has taught them how to proceed against this vile "spiritual horde." That they are *human* spirits is shown by the fact that very often they try to humor and propitiate the "larvae" of their own daughters and relatives, when they have reason to suspect that the latter did not die in the odor of sanctity and chastity. Such spirits they name "Kanni," *bad virgins*. The case was noticed by several missionaries; Rev. E. Lewis,[676] among others. But these pious gentlemen usually insist upon it that they worship devils, whereas, they do nothing of the sort; for they merely try to remain on good terms with them in order to be left unmolested. They offer them cakes and fruit, and various kinds of food which they liked while alive, for many of them have experienced the wickedness of these returning "dead ones," whose persecutions are sometimes dreadful. On this principle likewise they act toward the spirits of all wicked men. They leave on their

---

676 *"The Tinnevelly Shanars,"* p. 43.

tombs, if they were buried, or near the place where their remains were burnt, food and liquors, with the object of keeping them near these places, and with the idea that these vampires will be prevented thereby from returning to their homes. This is no worship; it is rather a *spiritualism* of a practical sort. Until 1861, there prevailed a custom among the Hindus of mutilating the feet of executed murderers, under the firm belief that thereby the disembodied soul would be prevented from wandering and doing more mischief. Subsequently, they were prohibited, by the police, from continuing the practice.

Another good reason why the Hindus should not worship the "Devil" is that they have no word to convey such a meaning. They call these spirits "*pûttâm,*" which answers rather to our "spook," or malicious imp; another expression they use is "*pey*" and the Sanscrit *pesâsu,* both meaning ghosts or "returning ones" — perhaps goblins, in some cases. The *pûttâm* are the most terrible, for they are literally "*haunting* spooks," who return on earth to torment the living. They are believed to visit generally the places where their bodies were burnt. The "fire" or "Siva-spirits" are identical with the Rosicrucian *gnomes* and *salamanders;* for they are pictured as dwarfs of a fiery appearance, living in earth and fire. The Ceylonese demon called *Dewel* is a stout smiling female figure with a white Elizabethan frill around the neck and a red jacket.

As Dr. Warton justly observes: "There is no character more strictly Oriental than the dragons of romance and fiction; they are intermixed with every tradition of early date and of themselves confer a species of illustrative evidence of origin." In no writings are these characters more marked, than in the details of Buddhism; these record particulars of the *Nagas,* or kingly snakes, inhabiting the cavities under the earth, corresponding with the abodes of Tiresias and the Greek seers, a region of mystery and darkness, wherein revolves much of the system of divination and oracular response, connected with inflation, or a sort of possession, designating the spirit of Python himself, the dragon-serpent slain by Apollo. But the Buddhists no more believe in the devil of the Christian system — that is, an entity as distinct from humanity as the Deity itself — than the Hindus. Buddhists teach that there are inferior gods who have been men either on this or another planet, but still who were *men.* They believe in the Nagas, who had been *sorcerers* on earth, *bad people,* and who give the power to other bad and yet living men to blight all the fruit they look upon, and even human lives. When a Cinghalese has the reputation that if he looks on a tree or on a person both will wither and die, he is said to have the Naga-Raja, or king-serpent on him. The whole endless catalogue of bad spirits are not *devils* in the sense the Christian clergy wants us to understand, but merely *spiritually incarnated* sins, crimes, and human thoughts, if we may so express it. The blue, green, yellow, and purple god-demons, like the inferior gods of Jugandere, are more of the kind of presiding genii, and many are as good and beneficient as the Nat deities themselves, although the Nats reckon in their numbers, giants, evil genii, and the like which inhabit the desert of Mount Jugandere.

The true doctrine of Buddha says that the demons, when nature produced the sun, moon, and stars, *were human beings,* but, on account of their sins, they fell from the state of felicity. If they commit greater sins, they suffer greater punishments, and condemned men are reckoned by them among the *devils;* while, on the contrary, *demons who die* (elemental spirits) and are born or incarnated as men, and commit no more sin, can arrive at the state of celestial felicity. Which is a demonstration, remarks Edward Upham, in his *History and Doctrine of Buddhism,* that all beings, divine as well as human, are subject to the laws of transmigration, which are operative on all, according to a scale of moral deeds. This faith then, is a complete test of a code of moral enactments and motives, applied to the regulation and government of man, an experiment, he adds, "which renders the study of Buddhism an important and curious subject for the philosopher."

VAMPIRISM — ITS PHENOMENA EXPLAINED

The Hindus believe, as firmly as the Servians or Hungarians, in vampires. Furthermore, their doctrine is that of Pierart, the famous French spiritist and mesmerizer, whose school flourished some dozen years ago. "The fact of a spectre returning to suck human blood," says this Doctor,[677] "is not so inexplicable as it seems, and here we appeal to the spiritualists who admit the phenomenon of *bicorporeity* or *soul-duplication*. The hands which we have pressed . . . these 'materialized' limbs, so palpable . . . prove clearly *how much is possible for astral spectres under favorable conditions*."

The honorable physician expresses the theory of the kabalists. The *Shadim* are the lowest of the spiritual orders. Maimonides, who tells us that his countrymen were *obliged* to maintain an intimate intercourse with their departed ones, describes the feast of blood they held on such occasions. They dug a hole, and *fresh blood* was poured in, over which was placed a table; after which the "spirits" came and answered all their questions.[678]

Pierart, whose doctrine was founded on that of the theurgists, exhibits a warm indignation against the superstition of the clergy which requires, whenever a corpse is suspected of vampirism, that a stake should be driven through the heart. So long as the astral form is not entirely liberated from the body there is a liability that it may be forced by magnetic attraction to reënter it. Sometimes it will be only half-way out, when the corpse, which presents the appearance of death, is buried. In such cases the terrified astral soul violently reënters its casket; and then, one of two things happens — either the unhappy victim will writhe in the agonizing torture of suffocation, or, if he had been grossly material, he becomes a vampire. The bicorporeal life begins; and these unfortunate buried cataleptics sustain their miserable lives by having their astral bodies rob the life-blood from living persons. The ethereal form can go wherever it pleases; and so long as it does not break the link which attaches it to the body, it is at liberty to wander about, either visible or invisible, and feed on human victims. "According to all appearance, this 'spirit' then transmits through a mysterious and invisible cord of connection, which perhaps, some day may be explained, the results of the suction to the material body which lies inert at the bottom of the tomb, aiding it, in a manner, to perpetuate the state of catalepsy."[679]

Brierre de Boismont gives a number of such cases, fully authenticated, which he is pleased to term "hallucinations." A recent inquest, says a French paper, "has established that in 1871 two corpses were submitted to the infamous treatment of popular superstition, at the instigation of the clergy . . . O blind prejudice!" But Dr. Pierart, quoted by des Mousseaux, who stoutly adheres to vampirism, exclaims: "Blind, you say? Yes, blind, as much as you like. But whence sprang these prejudices? Why are they perpetuated in all

677 Pierart, "*Revue Spiritualiste*," chapter on "*Vampirism*."
678 Maimonides, "*Abodah Sarah*," 12 Absh, 11 Abth.
679 Pierart, "*Revue Spiritualiste*."

ages, and in so many countries? After a crowd of facts of vampirism so often proved, should we say that there are no more and that they never had a foundation? Nothing comes of nothing. Every belief, every custom springs from facts and causes which gave it birth. If one had never seen appear, in the bosom of families of certain countries, beings clothing themselves in the shape of the familiar dead, coming thus to suck the blood of one or of several persons, and if the death of the victims by emaciation had not followed, they would never have gone to disinter the corpses in cemeteries; we would never have had attested the incredible fact of persons buried for several years being found with the corpse soft, flexible, the eyes open, with rosy complexions, the mouth and nose full of blood, and of the blood running in torrents under blows, from wounds, and when decapitated."[680]

One of the most important examples of vampirism figures in the private letters of the philosopher, the Marquis d'Argens; and, in the *Revue Britannique,* for March, 1837, the English traveller Pashley describes some that came under his notice in the island of Candia. Dr. Jobard, the anti-Catholic and anti-spiritual Belgian *savant,* testifies to similar experiences.[681]

"I will not examine," wrote the Bishop d'Avranches Huet, "whether the facts of vampirism, which are constantly being reported, are true, or the fruit of a popular error; but it is certain that they are testified to by so many authors, able and trustworthy, and *by so many eye-witnesses,* that no one ought to decide upon the question without a good deal of caution."[682]

The chevalier, who went to great pains to collect materials for his demonological theory, brings the most thrilling instances to prove that all such cases are produced by the Devil, who uses graveyard corpses with which to clothe himself, and roams at night sucking people's blood. Methinks we could do very well without bringing this dusky personage upon the scene. If we are to believe at all in the return of spirits, there are plenty of wicked sensualists, misers, and sinners of other descriptions — especially suicides, who could have rivalled the Devil himself in malice in his best days. It is quite enough to be actually forced to believe in what we do see, and *know to be a fact,* namely spirits, without adding to our Pantheon of ghosts the Devil — whom nobody ever saw.

Still, there are interesting particulars to be gathered in relation to vampirism, since belief in this phenomenon has existed in all countries, from the remotest ages. The Slavonian nations, the Greeks, the Wallachians, and the Servians would rather doubt the existence of their enemies, the Turks, than the fact that there are vampires. The *broucolâk,* or *vourdalak,* as the latter are called, are but too familiar guests at the Slavonian fireside. Writers of the greatest ability, men as full of sagacity as of high integrity, have treated of the subject and believed in it. Whence, then, such a *superstition?* Whence that unanimous credence throughout the ages, and whence that identity in details and similarity of description as to that one particular phenomenon which we find in the testimony — generally sworn evidence — of peoples foreign to each other and differing widely in matters concerning other *superstitions.*

---

680 Dr. Pierart, *"Revue Spiritualiste,"* vol. iv., p. 104.
681 See *"Hauts Phen.,"* p. 199.
682 *"Huetiana,"* p. 81.

"There are," says Dom Calmet, a skeptical Benedictine monk of the last century, "two different ways to destroy the belief in these pretended ghosts. . . . The first would be *to explain the* prodigies of vampirism by physical causes. The second way is to *deny totally* the truth of all such stories; and the latter plan would be undoubtedly the most certain, as the most wise."[683]

The first way — that of explaining it by physical, though occult causes, is the one adopted by the Pierart school of mesmerism. It is certainly not the spiritualists who have a right to doubt the plausibility of this explanation. The second plan is that adopted by scientists and skeptics. They deny point-blank. As des Mousseaux remarks, there is no better or surer way, and none exacts less of either philosophy or science.

The spectre of a village herdsman, near Kodom, in Bavaria, began appearing to several inhabitants of the place, and either in consequence of their fright or some other cause, every one of them died during the following week. Driven to despair, the peasants disinterred the corpse, and pinned it to the ground with a long stake. The same night he appeared again, plunging people into convulsions of fright, and suffocating several of them. Then the village authorities delivered the body into the hands of the executioner, who carried it to a neighboring field and burned it. "The corpse," says des Mousseaux, quoting Dom Calmet, "howled like a madman, kicking and tearing as if he had been alive. When he was run through again with sharp-pointed stakes, he uttered piercing cries, and vomited masses of crimson blood. The apparitions of this spectre ceased only after the corpse had been reduced to ashes."[684]

Officers of justice visited the places said to be so haunted; the bodies were exhumed, and in nearly every case it was observed that the corpse suspected of vampirism looked healthy and rosy, and the flesh was in no way decaying. The objects which had belonged to these ghosts were observed moving about the house without any one touching them. But the legal authorities generally refused to resort to cremation and beheading before they had observed the strictest rules of legal procedure. Witnesses were summoned to appear, and evidence was heard and carefully weighed. After that the exhumed corpses were examined; and if they exhibited the unequivocal and characteristic signs of vampirism, they were handed over to the executioner.

"But," argues Dom Calmet,[685] "the principal difficulty consists in learning *how* these vampires can quit their tombs, and how they reënter them, without appearing *to have disturbed the earth in the least;* how is it that they are seen with their usual clothing; how can they go about, and walk, and *eat? . . .* If this is all imagination on the part of those who believe themselves molested by such vampires, how happens it that the accused ghosts are subsequently found in their graves . . . exhibiting no signs of decay, full of blood, supple and fresh? How explain the cause *of their feet found muddy and covered with dirt on the day following the night* they had appeared and frightened their neighbors, while nothing of the

683 Dom Calmet, "*Apparitions,*" etc. Paris, 1751, vol. ii., p. 47; "*Hauts Phen. de la Magie,*" 195.
684 "*Hauts Phen.,*" p. 196.
685 Ibid.

sort was ever found on other corpses buried in the same cemetery?[686] How is it again that once burned they never reappear? and that these cases should happen *so often* in this country that it is found impossible to cure people from this prejudice; for, instead of being destroyed, daily experience only fortifies the superstition in the people, and increases belief in it."[687]

There is a phenomenon in nature unknown, and therefore rejected by physiology and psychology in our age of unbelief. This phenomenon is a state of *half-death*. Virtually, the body is dead; and, in cases of persons in whom matter does not predominate over spirit and wickedness not so great as to destroy spirituality, if left alone, their astral soul will disengage itself by gradual efforts, and, when the last link is broken, it finds itself separated forever from its earthly body. Equal magnetic polarity will violently repulse the ethereal man from the decaying organic mass. The whole difficulty lies in that 1, the ultimate moment of separation between the two is believed to be that when the body is declared *dead* by science; and 2, a prevailing unbelief in the existence of either soul or spirit in man, by the same science.

Pierart tries to demonstrate that in every case it is dangerous to bury people too soon, even though the body may show undoubted signs of putrefaction. "Poor dead cataleptics," says the doctor, "buried as if *quite* dead, in cold and dry spots where *morbid causes are incapable to effect the destruction of their bodies*, their (astral) spirit enveloping itself with a *fluidic* body (ethereal) is prompted to quit the precincts of its tomb, and to exercise on living beings acts peculiar to physical life, especially that of *nutrition*, the result of which, by a mysterious link between soul and body, which spiritualistic science will explain some day, is forwarded to the material body lying still in its tomb, and the latter thus helped to perpetuate its vital existence."[688] These spirits, in their ephemeral bodies, have been often seen *coming out from the graveyard*; they are known to have clung to their living neighbors, and have sucked their blood. Judicial inquiry has established that from this resulted an emaciation of the victimized persons, which often terminated in death.

Thus, following the pious advice of Dom Calmet, we must either go on denying, or, if human and legal testimonies are worth anything, accept the only explanation possible. "That souls departed are embodied in aerial or ætherial vehicles is most fully and plainly proved by those excellent men, Dr. C. and Dr. More," says Glanvil, "and they have largely shown that this was the doctrine of the greatest philosophers and most ancient and aged fathers."[689]

Gorres, the German philosopher, says to the same effect, that "God never created man as a dead corpse, but as an animal *full of life*. Once He had thus produced him, finding him ready to receive the immortal breath, He breathed him in the face, and thus man became a double masterpiece in His hands. It is in the centre of life itself that this mysterious

---

686 See the same sworn testimony in official documents, "*De l'Inspir. des Camis*," H. Blanc, 1859. Plon, Paris.
687 Dom Calmet, "*Apparit.*," vol. ii., chap. xliv., p. 212.
688 Pierart, "*Revue Spiritualiste*," vol. iv., p. 104.
689 "*Sadducismus Triumphatus*," vol. ii., p. 70.

insufflation took place in the first man (race?); and thence were united the *animal soul* issued from earth, and the *spirit* emanating from heaven."[690]

Des Mousseaux, in company with other Roman Catholic writers, exclaims: "This proposition is utterly anti-Catholic! "Well, and suppose it is? It may be archi-anti-Catholic, and still be logic, and offer a solution for many a psychological puzzle. The sun of science and philosophy shines for every one; and if Catholics, who hardly number one-seventh part of the population of the globe, do not feel satisfied, perhaps the many millions of people of other religions who outnumber them, will.

And now, before parting with this repulsive subject of vampirism, we will give one more illustration, without other voucher than the statement that it was given to us by apparently trustworthy witnesses.

About the beginning of the present century, there occurred in Russia, one of the most frightful cases of vampirism on record. The governor of the Province of Tch— — was a man of about sixty years, of a malicious, tyrannical, cruel, and jealous disposition. Clothed with despotic authority, he exercised it without stint, as his brutal instincts prompted. He fell in love with the pretty daughter of a subordinate official. Although the girl was betrothed to a young man whom she loved, the tyrant forced her father to consent to his having her marry him; and the poor victim, despite her despair, became his wife. His jealous disposition exhibited itself. He beat her, confined her to her room for weeks together, and prevented her seeing any one except in his presence. He finally fell sick and died. Finding his end approaching, he made her swear never to marry again; and with fearful oaths, threatened that, in case she did, he would return from his grave and kill her. He was buried in the cemetery across the river; and the young widow experienced no further annoyance, until, nature getting the better of her fears, she listened to the importunities of her former lover, and they were again betrothed.

On the night of the customary betrothal-feast, when all had retired, the old mansion was aroused by shrieks proceeding from her room. The doors were burst open, and the unhappy woman was found lying on her bed, in a swoon. At the same time a carriage was heard rumbling out of the courtyard. Her body was found to be black and blue in places, as from the effect of pinches, and from a slight puncture on her neck drops of blood were oozing. Upon recovering, she stated that her deceased husband had suddenly entered her room, appearing exactly as in life, with the exception of a dreadful pallor; that he had upbraided her for her inconstancy, and then beaten and pinched her most cruelly. Her story was disbelieved; but the next morning, the guard stationed at the other end of the bridge which spans the river, reported that, just before midnight, a black coach and six had driven furiously past them, toward the town, without answering their challenge.

The new governor, who disbelieved the story of the apparition, took nevertheless the precaution of doubling the guards across the bridge.

The same thing happened, however, night after night; the soldiers declaring that the toll-bar at their station near the bridge would rise of itself, and the spectral equipage sweep by them despite their efforts to stop it. At the same time every night, the coach would rumble into the courtyard of the house; the watchers, including the widow's family, and the

---

690 Görres, "*Complete Works*," vol. iii., ch. vii., p. 132.

servants, would be thrown into a heavy sleep; and every morning the young victim would be found bruised, bleeding, and swooning as before. The town was thrown into consternation. The physicians had no explanations to offer; priests came to pass the night in prayer, but as midnight approached, all would be seized with the terrible lethargy. Finally, the archbishop of the province came, and performed the ceremony of exorcism in person, but the following morning the governor's widow was found worse than ever. She was now brought to death's door.

The governor was finally driven to take the severest measures to stop the ever-increasing panic in the town. He stationed fifty Cossacks along the bridge, with orders to stop the spectre-carriage at all hazards. Promptly at the usual hour, it was heard and seen approaching from the direction of the cemetery. The officer of the guard, and a priest bearing a crucifix, planted themselves in front of the toll-bar, and together shouted: "In the name of God, and the Czar, who goes there?" Out of the coach-window was thrust a well-remembered head, and a familiar voice responded: "The Privy Councillor of State and Governor, C——!" At the same moment, the officer, the priest, and the soldiers were flung aside as by an electric shock, and the ghostly equipage passed by them, before they could recover breath.

The archbishop then resolved, as a last expedient, to resort to the time-honored plan of exhuming the body, and pinning it to the earth with an oaken stake driven through its heart. This was done with great religious ceremony in the presence of the whole populace. The story is that the body was found gorged with blood, and with red cheeks and lips. At the instant that the first blow was struck upon the stake, a groan issued from the corpse, and a jet of blood spurted high into the air. The archbishop pronounced the usual exorcism, the body was reïnterred, and from that time no more was heard of the vampire.

How far the facts of this case may have been exaggerated by tradition, we cannot say. But we had it years ago from an eye-witness; and at the present day there are families in Russia whose elder members will recall the dreadful tale.

As to the statement found in medical books that there are frequent cases of inhumation while the subjects are but in a cataleptic state, and the persistent denials of specialists that such things happen, except very rarely, we have but to turn to the daily press of every country to find the horrid fact substantiated. The Rev. H. R. Haweis, M.A., author of *Ashes to Ashes*,[691] enumerates in his work, written in advocacy of cremation, some very distressing cases of premature burial. On page forty-six occurs the following dialogue: "But do you know of many cases of premature burial?" "Undoubtedly I do. I will not say that in our temperate climate they are frequent, but they do occur. Hardly a graveyard is opened but coffins are found containing bodies not only turned, but skeletons contorted in the last hopeless struggle for life underground. The turning may be due to some clumsy shaking of the coffin, *but not the contortion.*"

After this he proceeds to give the following recent cases: "At Bergerac (Dordogne), in 1842, the patient took a sleeping draught . . . but he woke not. . . . They bled him, and he woke not. . . . At last they declared him to be dead, and buried him. After a few days,

---

691 *"Ashes to Ashes,"* London: Daldy, Isbister & Co., 1875.

remembering the sleeping draught, they opened the grave. The body had turned and *struggled*."

"The *Sunday Times*, December 30, 1838, relates that at Tonneins, Lower Garonne, a man was buried, when an indistinct noise proceeded from the coffin; the reckless grave-digger fled. . . . The coffin was hauled up and burst open. A face stiffened in terror and despair, a torn winding-sheet, contorted limbs, told the sad truth — *too late*."

"The *Times*, May, 1874, states that in August of 1873, a young lady died soon after her marriage. . . . Within a year the husband married again, and the mother of his first bride resolved to remove her daughter's body to Marseilles. They opened the vault and found the poor girl's body prostrate, her hair dishevelled, her shroud torn to pieces."[692] As we will have to refer to the subject once more in connection with Bible miracles, we will leave it for the present, and return to magical phenomena. If we were to give a full description of the various manifestations which take place among adepts in India and other countries, we might fill volumes, but this would be profitless, as there would remain no space for explanation. Therefore we select in preference such as either find their parallels in modern phenomena or are authenticated by legal inquiry. Horst tried to present an idea of certain Persian spirits to his readers, and failed; for the bare mention of some of them is calculated to set the brains of a believer in a whirl. There are the Devs and their specialities; the Darwands and their gloomy tricks; the Shadim and Djinnas; the whole vast legion of spirits, demons, goblins, and elves of the Persian calendar; and, on the other hand, the Jewish Seraphim, Cherubim, Izeds, Amshaspands, Sephiroth, Malachim, Elohim; and, adds Horst, "the millions of astral and elementary spirits, of intermediary spirits, ghosts, and imaginary beings of all races and colors."[693]

BENGALESE JUGGLERY

But the majority of these spirits have naught to do with the phenomena consciously and deliberately produced by the Eastern magicians. The latter repudiate such an accusation and leave to sorcerers the help even of elemental spirits and the elementary spooks. The adept has an unlimited power over both, but he rarely uses it. For the production of physical phenomena he summons the nature-spirits as obedient *powers*, not as intelligences.

As we always like to strengthen our arguments by testimonies other than our own, it may be well to present the opinion of a daily paper, the Boston *Herald*, as to phenomena in general and mediums in particular. Having encountered sad failures with some dishonest persons, who may or may not be mediumistic, the writer went to the trouble of ascertaining as to some wonders said to be produced in India, and compares them with those of modern thaumaturgy.

> "The medium of the present day," he says, "bears a closer resemblance, in methods and manipulations, to the well-known conjurer of history, than any other representative of the magic art. How far short he still remains of the performances of his prototypes is illustrated below. In 1615 a delegation of

---

692 The author refers all those who may doubt such statements to G. A. Walker's "*Gatherings from Graveyards*," pp. 84-193, 194, etc.
693 Horst, "*Zauber Bibliothek*," vol. v., p. 52.

highly-educated and distinguished men from the English East India Company visited the Emperor Jehangire. While on their mission they witnessed many most wonderful performances, almost causing them to discredit their senses, and far beyond any hint even of solution. A party of Bengalese conjurers and jugglers, showing their art before the emperor, were desired to produce upon the spot, and from seed, ten mulberry trees. They immediately planted ten seeds, which, in a few minutes produced as many trees. The ground divided over the spot where a seed was planted, tiny leaves appeared, at once followed by slender shoots, which rapidly gained elevation, putting out leaves and twigs and branches, finally spreading wide in the air, budding, blossoming and yielding fruit, which matured upon the spot, and was found to be excellent. And this before the beholder had turned away his eyes. Fig, almond, mango, and walnut trees were at the same time under like conditions produced, yielding the fruit which belonged to each. Wonder succeeded wonder. The branches were filled with birds of beautiful plumage flitting about among the leaves and singing sweet notes. The leaves turned to russet, fell from their places, branches and twigs withered, and finally the trees sank back into the earth, out of which they had all sprung within the hour.

"Another had a bow and about fifty steel-pointed arrows. He shot an arrow into the air, when, lo! the arrow became fixed in space at a considerable height. Another and another arrow was sent off, each fixing itself in the shaft of the preceding, until all formed a chain of arrows in the air, excepting the last shot, which, striking the chain, brought the whole to the ground in detachments.

"They set up two common tents facing each other, and about a bow-shot apart. These tents were critically examined by the spectators, as are the cabinets of the mediums, and pronounced empty. The tents were fastened to the ground all around. The lookers-on were then invited to choose what animals or birds they would have issue from these tents to engage in a battle. Khaun-e-Jahaun incredulously asked to see a fight between ostriches. In a few minutes an ostrich came out from each tent rushed to combat with deadly earnestness, and from them the blood soon began to stream; but they were so nearly matched that neither could win the victory, and they were at last separated by the conjurers and conveyed within the tents. After this the varied demands of the spectators for birds and animals were exactly complied with, always with the same results.

"A large cauldron was set, and into it a quantity of rice thrown. Without the sign of fire this rice soon began to boil, and out from the cauldron was taken more than one hundred platters of cooked rice, with a stewed fowl at the top of each. This trick is performed on a smaller scale by the most ordinary fakirs of the present day.

"But space fails to give opportunity for illustrating, from the records of the past, how the miserably tame performances — by comparison — of the mediums of the present day were pale and overshadowed by those of other days and more adroit peoples. There is not a wonderful feature in any of the so-called phenomena or manifestations which was not, nay, which is not now more than duplicated by other skilful performers, whose connection with earth, and earth alone, is too evident to be doubted, even if the fact was not supported by their own testimony."

It is an error to say that fakirs or jugglers will always claim that they are helped by spirits. In quasi-religious evocations, such as Jacolliot's Kovindasami is described to have produced before this French gentleman, when the parties desire to see real "spiritual" manifestations, they will resort to Pitris, their disembodied ancestors, and other *pure* spirits. These they can evoke but through prayer. As to all other phenomena, they are produced by the magician and fakir at will. Notwithstanding the state of apparent abjectness in which the latter lives, he is often an initiate of the temples, and is as well acquainted with occultism as his richer brethren.

The Chaldeans, whom Cicero counts among the oldest magicians, placed the basis of all magic in the inner powers of man's soul, and by the discernment of magic properties in plants, minerals, and animals. By the aid of these they performed the most wonderful "miracles." Magic, with them, was synonymous with religion and science. It is but later that the religious myths of the Magdean dualism, disfigured by Christian theology and euhemerized by certain fathers of the Church, assumed the disgusting shape in which we find them expounded by such Catholic writers as des Mousseaux. The objective reality of the mediæval incubus and succubus, that abominable superstition of the middle ages which cost so many human lives, advocated by this author in a whole volume, is the monstrous production of religious fanaticism and epilepsy. It can have no *objective* form; and to attribute its effects to the Devil is blasphemy: implying that God, after creating Satan, would allow him to adopt such a course. If we are forced to believe in vampirism, it is on the strength of two irrefragable propositions of occult psychological science: 1. The astral soul is a separable distinct entity of our *ego*, and can roam far away from the body without breaking the thread of life. 2. The corpse is not *utterly* dead, and while it can yet be reëntered by its tenant, the latter can gather sufficient material emanations from it to enable itself to appear in a quasi-terrestrial shape. But to uphold, with des Mousseaux and de Mirville, that the Devil, whom the Catholics endow with a power which, in antagonism, equals that of the Supreme Deity, transforms himself into wolves, snakes, and dogs, to satisfy his lust and procreate monsters, is an idea within which lie hidden the germs of devil-worship, lunacy, and sacrilege. The Catholic Church, which not only teaches us to believe in this monstrous fallacy, but forces her missionaries to preach such a dogma, need not revolt against the devil-worship of some Parsee and South India sects. Quite the reverse; for when we hear the Yezides repeat the well-known proverb: "Keep friends with the demons; give them your property, your blood, your service, and you need not care about God — *He will not harm you*," we find him but consistent with his belief and reverential to the Supreme; his logic is sound and rational; he reveres God too deeply to imagine that He who created the universe and its laws is able to hurt him, poor atom; but the *demons* are there; they *are imperfect,* and therefore he has good reasons to dread them.

Therefore, the Devil, in his various transformations, can be but a fallacy. When we imagine that we see, and hear, and feel him, it is but too often the reflection of our own wicked, depraved, and polluted soul that we see, hear, and feel. Like attracts like, they say; thus, according to the mood in which our astral form oozes out during the hours of sleep, according to our thoughts, pursuits, and daily occupations, all of which are fairly impressed upon the plastic capsule called the *human soul,* the latter attracts around itself spiritual beings congenial to itself. Hence some dreams and visions that are pure and beautiful, others fiendish and beastly. The person awakes, and either hastens to the confessional, or laughs in callous indifference at the thought. In the first case, he is promised final salvation, at the cost of some indulgences (which he has to purchase from the church), and perhaps a little taste of purgatory, or even of hell. What matter? is he not safe to be eternal and immortal, do what he may? It is the Devil. Away with him, with bell, book, and holy sprinkler! But the "Devil" comes back, and often the true believer is forced to disbelieve in God, when he clearly perceives that the Devil has the best of his Creator and Master. Then he is left to the second emergency. He remains indifferent, and gives himself up entirely to the Devil. He dies, and the reader has learned the sequel in the preceding chapters.

The thought is beautifully expressed by Dr. Ennemoser: "Religion did not here [Europe and China] strike root so deeply as among the Hindus," says he, arguing upon this superstition. "The spirit of the Greeks and Persians was more volatile. . . . The philosophical idea in the good and bad principle, and of the spiritual world . . . must have assisted tradition in forming visions of heavenly and hellish shapes, and the most frightful distortions, which in India were much more simply produced by a more enthusiastic fanaticism; there the seer *received by divine light;* here he lost himself in a multitude of outward objects, with which he confounded his own identity. Convulsions, accompanied by the mind's absence from the body, in distant countries, were here common, for the imagination was less firm, and also less spiritual.

> "The outward causes are also different; the modes of life, geographical position, and artificial means producing various modifications. The mode of life in Western countries has always been very variable, and therefore disturbs and distorts the occupation of the senses, *and the outward life is therefore reflected* upon the inner dream-world. The spirits, therefore, are of endless varieties of shape, and incline men to gratify their passions, showing them the means of so doing, and descending even to the minutest particulars, *which was so far below* the elevated natures of Indian seers."

Let the student of occult sciences make his own nature as pure and his thoughts as elevated as those of these Indian seers, and he may sleep unmolested by vampire, incubus, or succubus. Around the insensible form of such a sleeper the immortal spirit sheds a power divine that protects it from evil approaches, as though it were a crystal wall.

"Hæc murus æneus esto: nil conscire sibi, nulla pallascere culpa."

CHAPTER XIII

"ALCHYMIST. Thou always speakest riddles. Tell me if thou art that fountain of which Bernard Lord Trevigan writ?

"MERCURY. I am not that fountain, but I am the water. The fountain compasseth me about."

SANDIVOGIUS, *New Light of Alchymy*

"All that we profess to do is this; to find out the secrets of the human frame, to know why the parts ossify and the blood stagnates, and to apply continual preventatives to the effects of time. *This is not magic;* it is the art of medicine rightly understood."

BULWER-LYTTON

"Lo, warrior! now the cross of Red
Points to the grave of the mighty dead;
Within it burns a wondrous light,
To chase the spirits that love the night.
That lamp shall burn unquenchably
Until the eternal doom shall be."
"No earthly flame blazed e'er so bright."

SIR WALTER SCOTT

THERE are persons whose minds would be incapable of appreciating the intellectual grandeur of the ancients, even in physical science, were they to receive the most complete demonstration of their profound learning and achievements. Notwithstanding the lesson of caution which more than one unexpected discovery has taught them, they still pursue their old plan of denying, and, what is still worse, of ridiculing that which they have no means of either proving or disproving. So, for instance, they will pooh-pooh the idea of talismans having any efficacy one way or the other. That the seven spirits of the Apocalypse have direct relation to the seven occult powers in nature, appears incomprehensible and absurd to their feeble intellects; and the bare thought of a magician claiming to work wonders through certain kabalistic rites convulses them with laughter. Perceiving only a geometrical figure traced upon a paper, a bit of metal, or other substance, they cannot imagine how any reasonable being should ascribe to either any occult potency. But those who have taken the pains to inform themselves know that the ancients achieved as great discoveries in psychology as in physics, and that their explorations left few secrets to be discovered.

THE RATIONALE OF TALISMANS

For our part, when we realize that a pentacle is a synthetic figure which expresses in concrete form a profound truth of nature, we can see nothing more ridiculous in it than in the figures of Euclid, and nothing half so comical as the symbols in a modern work on chemistry. What to the uninitiated reader can appear more absurd than that the symbol NA_2CO_3 — means soda! and that C_2H_6O is but another way of writing alcohol! How very amusing that the alchemists should express their Azoth, or creative principle of nature (astral light), by the symbol

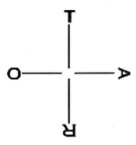

which embraces three things: 1st, The divine hypothesis; 2d, The philosophical synthesis; 3d, The physical synthesis — that is to say, a belief, an idea, and a force. But how perfectly natural that a modern chemist who wishes to indicate to the students in his laboratory the reaction of a sodic-carbonate with cream-of-tartar in solution, should employ the following symbol:

$$(Na_2CO_3 + 2HKC_4H_4O_6 + Aq) =$$
$$(2NaKC_4H_4O_6 + H_2O + Aq) + CO_2$$

If the uninspired reader may be pardoned for looking aghast at this abracadabra of chemical science, why should not its teachers restrain their mirth until they have learned the philosophical value of the symbolism of the ancients? At least they might spare themselves from being as ridiculous as Monsieur de Mirville, who, confounding the Azoth of the Hermetic philosophers with the azote of the chemists, asserted that the former worshipped nitrogen gas![694] Apply a piece of iron to a magnet, and it becomes imbued with its subtile principle and capable of imparting it to other iron in its turn. It neither weighs more nor appears different from what it was before. And yet, one of the most subtile potencies of nature has entered into its substance. A talisman, in itself perhaps a worthless bit of metal, a scrap of paper, or a shred of any fabric, has nevertheless been imbued by the influence of that greatest of all magnets, the human will, with a potency for good or ill just as recognizable and as real in its effects as the subtile property which the iron acquired by contact with the physical magnet. Let the bloodhound snuff an article of clothing that has been worn by the fugitive, and he will track him through swamp and forest to his hiding-place. Give one of Professor Buchanan's "psychometers" a manuscript, no matter how old, and he will describe to you the character of the writer, and perhaps even his personal appearance. Hand a clairvoyant a lock of hair or some article that has been in contact with the person of whom it is desired to know something, and she will come into sympathy with him so intimate that she may trace him through his whole life.

Breeders tell us that young animals should not be herded with old ones; and intelligent physicians forbid parents to have young children occupy their own beds. When David was old and feeble his vital forces were recruited by having a young person brought in close contact with him so that he could absorb her strength. The late Empress of Russia, the sister of the present German Emperor, was so feeble the last years of her life that she was seriously advised by her physicians to keep in her bed at night a robust and healthy young

---

694 See Eliphas Levi, "*La Science des Esprits.*"

peasant-girl. Whoever has read the description given by Dr. Kerner of the Seeress of Prevorst, Mme. Hauffe, must well remember her words. She repeatedly stated that she supported life merely on the atmosphere of the people surrounding her and their *magnetic emanations*, which were quickened in an extraordinary way by her presence. The seeress was very plainly a magnetic vampire, who absorbed by drawing to herself the life of those who were strong enough to spare her their vitality in the shape of *volatilized* blood. Dr. Kerner remarks that these persons were all more or less affected by this forcible loss.

With these familiar illustrations of the possibility of a subtile fluid communicated from one individual to another, or to substances which he touches, it becomes less difficult to understand that by a determined concentration of the will an otherwise inert object may become imbued with protective or destructive power according to the purpose directing.

A magnetic emanation, unconsciously produced, is sure to be overpowered by any stronger one with which it may come into opposition. But when an intelligent and powerful will directs the blind force, and concentrates it upon a given spot, the weaker emanation will often master the stronger. A human *will* has the same effect on the *Akâsa.*

Upon one occasion, we witnessed in Bengal an exhibition of will-power that illustrates a highly interesting phase of the subject. An adept in magic made a few passes over a piece of common tin, the inside of a dish-cover, that lay conveniently by, and while regarding it attentively for a few moments, seemed to grasp the imponderable fluid by handfuls and throw it against the surface. When the tin had been exposed to the full glare of light for about six seconds, the bright surface was suddenly covered as with a film. Then patches of a darker hue began coming out on its surface; and when in about three minutes the tin was handed back to us, we found imprinted upon it a picture, or rather a photograph, of the landscape that stretched out before us; faithful as nature itself, and every color perfect. It remained for about forty-eight hours and then slowly faded away.

This phenomenon is easily explained. The will of the adept condensed upon the tin a film of *akâsa* which made it for the time being like a sensitized photographic plate. Light did the rest.

Such an exhibition as this of the potency of the will to effect even objective physical results, will prepare the student to comprehend its efficacy in the cure of disease by imparting the desired virtue to inanimate objects which are placed in contact with the patient. When we see such psychologists as Maudsley[695] quoting, without contradiction, the stories of some miraculous cures effected by Swedenborg's father — stories which do not differ from hundreds of other cures by other "fanatics" — as he calls them — magicians, and natural healers, and, without attempting to explain their facts, stooping to laugh at the intensity of their faith, without asking himself whether the secret of that healing potency were not in the control given by that faith over occult forces — we grieve that there should be so much learning and so little philosophy, in our time.

Upon our word, we cannot see that the modern chemist is any less a magician than the ancient theurgist or Hermetic philosopher, except in this: that the latter, recognizing the duality of nature, had twice as wide a field for experimental research as the chemist. The ancients animated statues, and the Hermetists called into being, out of the elements, the

---

695 Henry Maudsley, *"Body and Mind."*

shapes of salamanders, gnomes, undines, and sylphs, which they did not pretend to create, but simply to make visible by holding open the door of nature, so that, under favoring conditions, they might step into view. The chemist brings into contact two elements contained in the atmosphere, and by developing a latent force of affinity, creates a new body — water. In the spheroidal and diaphanous pearls which are born of this union of gases, come the germs of organic life, and in their molecular interstices lurk heat, electricity, and light, just as they do in the human body. Whence comes this life into the drop of water just born of the union of two gases? And what is the water itself? Have the oxygen and hydrogen undergone some transformation which obliterates their qualities simultaneously with the obliteration of their form? Here is the answer of modern science: "Whether the oxygen and hydrogen exist as such, in the water, or whether they are produced by some unknown and unconceived transformation of its substance, is a question about which we may speculate, but in regard to which we have no knowledge."[696] Knowing nothing about so simple a matter as the molecular constitution of water, or the deeper problem of the appearance of life within it, would it not be well for Mr. Maudsley to exemplify his own principle, and "maintain a *calm acquiescence in ignorance until light comes*"?[697]

The claims of the friends of esoteric science, that Paracelsus produced, chemically, *homunculi* from certain combinations as yet unknown to exact science, are, as a matter of course, relegated to the storehouse of exploded humbugs. But why should they? If the *homunculi* were not made by Paracelsus they were developed by other adepts, and that not a thousand years ago. They were produced, in fact, upon exactly the same principle as that by which the chemist and physicist calls to life his *animalcula*. A few years ago, an English gentleman, Andrew Crosse, of Somersetshire produced *acari* in the following manner: "Black flint burned to redness and reduced to powder was mixed with carbonate of potash, and exposed to a strong heat for fifteen minutes; and the mixture was poured into a blacklead crucible in an air furnace. It was reduced to powder while warm, mixed with boiling water; kept boiling for some minutes, and then hydrochloric acid was added to supersaturation. After being exposed to voltaic action for twenty-six days, a perfect insect of the *acari* tribe made its appearance, and in the course of a few weeks about a hundred more. The experiment was repeated with other chemical fluids with like results." A Mr. Weeks also produced the *acari* in ferrocyanide of potassium.

This discovery produced a great excitement. Mr. Crosse was now accused of impiety and aiming at creation. He replied, denying the implication and saying he considered "*to create was to form a something out of a nothing.*"[698]

Another gentleman, considered by several persons as a man of great science, has told us repeatedly that he was on the eve of proving that even unfructified eggs could be hatched by having a negative electric current caused to pass through them.

The mandrakes (*dudim* or love-fruit) found in the field by Reuben, Jacob's son, which excited the fancy of Rachel, was the kabalistic *mandragora*, notwithstanding denial; and the verses which refer to it belong to the *crudest* passages, in their esoteric meaning, of the

---

696 Josiah Cooke, Jr., "*The New Chemistry.*"
697 Henry Maudsley, "*The Limits of Philosophical Inquiry,*" p. 266.
698 "*Scientific American,*" August 12, 1868.

whole work. The mandrake is a plant having the rudimentary shape of a human creature; with a head, two arms, and two legs forming roots. The superstition that when pulled out of the ground it cries with a human voice, is not utterly baseless. It does produce a kind of squeaking sound, on account of the resinous substance of its root, which it is rather difficult to extract; and it has more than one hidden property in it perfectly unknown to the botanist.

UNEXPLAINED MYSTERIES

The reader who would obtain a clear idea of the commutation of forces and the resemblance between the life-principles of plants, animals, and human beings, may profitably consult a paper on the correlation of nervous and mental forces by Professor Alexander Bain, of the University of Aberdeen. This mandragora seems to occupy upon earth the point where the vegetable and animal kingdoms touch, as the zoophites and polypi do in the sea; the boundary being in each case so indistinct as to make it almost imperceptible where the one ceases and the other begins. It may seem improbable that there should be *homunculi,* but will any naturalist, in view of the recent expansion of science, dare say it is impossible? "Who," says Bain, "is to limit the possibilities of existence?"

The unexplained mysteries of nature are many and of those presumably explained hardly one may be said to have become absolutely intelligible. There is not a plant or mineral which has disclosed the last of its properties to the scientists. What do the naturalists know of the intimate nature of the vegetable and mineral kingdoms? How can they feel confident that for every one of the discovered properties there may not be many powers concealed in the *inner* nature of the plant or stone? And that they are only waiting to be brought in relation with some other plant, mineral, or force of nature to manifest themselves in what is termed a "supernatural manner." Wherever Pliny, the naturalist, Ælian, and even Diodorus, who sought with such a laudable perseverance to extricate historical truth from its medley of exaggerations and fables, have attributed to some plant or mineral an occult property unknown to our modern botanists and physicists, their assertions have been laid aside without further ceremony as absurd, and no more referred to.

It has been the speculation of men of science from time immemorial what this vital force or life-principle is. To our mind the "secret doctrine" alone is able to furnish the clew. Exact science recognizes only five powers in nature — one *molar*, and four *molecular*; kabalists, seven; and in these two additional ones is enwrapped the whole mystery of life. One of these is immortal spirit, whose reflection is connected by invisible links even with inorganic matter; the other, we leave to every one to discover for himself. Says Professor Joseph Le Conte: "What is the nature of the difference between the living organism and the dead organism? We can detect *none,* physical or chemical. All the physical and chemical forces withdrawn from the common fund of nature, and embodied in the living organism, seem to be still embodied in the dead, until little by little it is returned by decomposition. Yet the difference is immense, is inconceivably great. What is the nature of this difference expressed in the formula of material science? What is that that is gone, and whither is it gone? There is something here that science cannot yet understand. Yet it is just this loss which takes place in death, and before decomposition, which is in the highest sense vital force!"

MAGICAL EXPERIMENT IN BENGAL

Difficult, nay impossible, as it seems to science to find out the invisible, universal motor of all — *Life*, to explain its nature, or even to suggest a reasonable hypothesis for the same, the mystery is but half a mystery, not merely for the great adepts and seers, but even for true and firm believers in a spiritual world. To the simple believer, unblessed with a personal organism, the delicate, nervous sensitiveness of which would enable him — as it enables a seer — to perceive the visible universe reflected as in a clear glass in the Invisible one, and, as it were, objectively, there remains divine *faith*. The latter is firmly rooted in his inner senses; in his unerring intuition, with which cold reason has naught to do, he *feels* it cannot play him false. Let human-born, erroneous dogmas, and theological sophistry contradict each other; let one crowd off the other, and the subtle casuistry of one creed fell to the ground the crafty reasoning of another one; truth remains one, and there is not a religion, whether Christian or heathen, that is not firmly built upon the rock of ages — God and immortal spirit.

Every animal is more or less endowed with the faculty of perceiving, if not spirits, at least something which remains for the time being invisible to common men, and can only be discerned by a clairvoyant. We have made hundreds of experiments with cats, dogs, monkeys of various kinds, and, once, with a tame tiger. A round black mirror, known as the "magic crystal," was strongly mesmerized by a native Hindu gentleman, formerly an inhabitant of Dindigul, and now residing in a more secluded spot, among the mountains known as the Western Ghauts. He had tamed a young cub, brought to him from the Malabar coast, in which part of India the tigers are proverbially ferocious; and it is with this interesting animal that we made our experiments.

Like the ancient Marsi and Psylli, the renowned serpent-charmers, this gentleman claimed to be possessed of the mysterious power of taming any kind of animal. The tiger was reduced to a chronic *mental numbness,* so to say; he had become as inoffensive and harmless as a dog. Children could tease and pull him by the ears, and he would only shake himself and howl like a dog. But whenever forced to look into the "magic mirror," the poor animal was instantly excited to a sort of frenzy. His eyes became full of a *human* terror; howling in despair, unable to turn away from the mirror to which his gaze seemed riveted as by a magnetic spell, he would writhe and tremble till he convulsed with fear at some vision which to us remained unknown. He would then lie down, feebly groaning but still gazing in the glass. When it was taken away from him, the animal would lie panting and seemingly prostrated for about two hours. What did he see? What spirit-picture from his own invisible, *animal*-world, could produce such a terrific effect on the wild and naturally ferocious and daring beast? Who can tell? Perhaps *he* who produced the scene.

The same effect on animals was observed during spiritual *seances* with some holy mendicants; the same when a Syrian, half-heathen and half-Christian, from Kunankulam (Cochin State), a reputed sorcerer, who was invited to join us for the sake of experimenting.

We were nine persons in all — seven men and two women, one of the latter a native. Besides us, there were in the room, the young tiger, intensely occupied on a bone; a *wânderoo*, or lion-monkey, which, with its black coat and snow-white goatee and whiskers, and cunning, sparkling eyes, looked the personification of mischief; and a beautiful golden oriole, quietly cleaning its radiant-colored tail on a perch, placed near a large window of the veranda. In India, "spiritual" seances are not held in the dark, as in America; and no conditions, but perfect silence and harmony, are required. It was in the full glare of daylight streaming through the opened doors and windows, with a far-away buzz of life from the neighboring forests, and jungles sending us the echo of myriads of insects, birds, and animals. We sat in the midst of a garden in which the house was built, and instead of breathing the stifling atmosphere of a seance-room, we were amid the fire-colored clusters of the erythrina — the coral tree — inhaling the fragrant aromas of trees and shrubs, and the flowers of the bignonia, whose white blossoms trembled in the soft breeze. In short, we were surrounded with light, harmony, and perfumes. Large nosegays of flowers and shrubs, sacred to the native gods, were gathered for the purpose, and brought into the rooms. We had the sweet basil, the Vishnu-flower, without which no religious ceremony in Bengal will ever take place; and the branches of the *Ficus religiosa*, the tree dedicated to the same bright deity, intermingling their leaves with the rosy blossoms of the sacred lotos and the Indian tuberose, profusely ornamented the walls.

While the "blessed one" — represented by a very dirty, but, nevertheless, really holy fakir — remained plunged in self-contemplation, and some spiritual wonders were taking place under the direction of his will, the monkey and the bird exhibited but few signs of restlessness. The tiger alone visibly trembled at intervals, and stared around the room, as if his phosphorically-shining green orbs were following some invisible presence as it floated up and down. That which was as yet unperceived by human eyes, must have therefore been *objective* to him. As to the wânderoo, all its liveliness had fled; it seemed drowsy, and sat crouching and motionless. The bird gave few, if any, signs of uneasiness. There was a sound as of gently-flapping wings in the air; the flowers went travelling about the room, displaced by invisible hands; and, as a glorious azure-tinted flower fell on the folded paws of the monkey, it gave a nervous start, and sought refuge under its master's white robe. These displays lasted for an hour, and it would be too long to relate all of them; the most curious of all, being the one which closed that season of wonders. Somebody complaining of the heat, we had a shower of delicately-perfumed dew. The drops fell fast and large, and conveyed a feeling of inexpressible refreshment, drying the instant after touching our persons.

When the fakir had brought his exhibition of *white* magic to a close, the "sorcerer," or conjurer, as they are called, prepared to display his power. We were treated to a succession of the wonders that the accounts of travellers have made familiar to the public; showing, among other things, the fact that animals naturally possess the clairvoyant faculty, and even, it would seem, the ability to discern between the good and the bad spirits. All of the sorcerer's feats were preceded by fumigations. He burned branches of resinous trees and shrubs, which sent up volumes of smoke. Although there was nothing about this calculated to affright an animal using only his natural eyes, the tiger, monkey, and bird exhibited an indescribable terror. We suggested that the animals might be frightened at the blazing brands, the familiar custom of burning fires round the camp to keep off wild beasts, recurring to our mind. To leave no doubt upon this point, the Syrian approached the crouching tiger with a branch of the Bael-tree[699] (sacred to Siva), and waved it several times over his head, muttering, meanwhile, his incantations. The brute instantly displayed a panic

---

699 The wood-apple.

of terror beyond description. His eyes started from their sockets like blazing fire-balls; he foamed at the mouth; he flung himself upon the floor, as if seeking some hole in which to hide himself; he uttered scream after scream, that awoke a hundred responsive echoes from the jungle and the woods. Finally, taking a last look at the spot from which his eyes had never wandered, he made a desperate plunge, which snapped his chain, and dashed through the window of the veranda, carrying a piece of the frame-work with him. The monkey had fled long before, and the bird fell from the perch as though paralyzed. We did not ask either the fakir or sorcerer for an explanation of the method by which their respective phenomena were effected. If we had, unquestionably they would have replied as did a fakir to a French traveller, who tells his story in a recent number of a New York newspaper, called the *Franco-American*, as follows: "Many of these Hindu jugglers who live in the silence of the pagodas perform feats far surpassing the prestidigitations of Robert Houdin, and there are many others who produce the most curious phenomena in magnetism and catalepsy upon the first objects that come across their way, that I have often wondered whether the Brahmans, with their occult sciences, have not made great discoveries in the questions which have recently been agitated in Europe.

"On one occasion, while I and others were in a café with Sir Maswell, he ordered his dobochy to introduce the charmer. In a few moments a lean Hindu, almost naked, with an ascetic face and bronzed color entered. Around his neck, arms, thighs, and body were coiled serpents of different sizes. After saluting us, he said, 'God be with you, I am Chibh-Chondor, son of Chibh-Gontnalh-Mava.'

" 'We desire to see what you can do,' said our host.

" 'I obey the orders of Siva, who has sent me here,' replied the fakir, squatting down on one of the marble slabs.

"The serpents raised their heads and hissed, but without showing any anger. Then taking a small pipe, attached to a wick in his hair, he produced scarcely audible sounds, imitating the *tailapaca*, a bird that feeds upon bruised cocoanuts. Here the serpents uncoiled themselves, and one after another glided to the floor. As soon as they touched the ground they raised about one-third of their bodies, and began to keep time to their master's music. Suddenly the fakir dropped his instrument and made several passes with his hands over the serpents, of whom there were about ten, all of the most deadly species of Indian cobra. His eye assumed a strange expression. We all felt an undefinable uneasiness, and sought to turn away our gaze from him. At this moment a small shocra[700] (monkey) whose business was to hand fire in a small brasier for lighting cigars, yielded to his influence, lay down, and fell asleep. Five minutes passed thus, and we felt that if the manipulations were to continue a few seconds more we should all fall asleep. Chondor then rose, and making two more passes over the shocra, said to it: 'Give the commander some fire.' The young monkey rose, and without tottering, came and offered fire to its master. It was pinched, pulled about, till there was no doubt of its being actually asleep. Nor would it move from Sir Maswell's side till ordered to do so by the fakir.

---

700 Incorrect; the Hindustani word for monkey is *rūkh-charhā*. Probably *chokra*, a little native servant is meant.

CHIBH CHONDOR'S SURPRISING FEATS

"We then examined the cobras. Paralyzed by magnetic influence, they lay at full length on the ground. On taking them up we found them stiff as sticks. They were in a state of complete catalepsy. The fakir then awakened them, on which they returned and again coiled themselves round his body. We inquired whether he could make us feel his influence. He made a few passes over our legs, and instantly we lost the use of these limbs; we could not leave our seats. He released us a easily as he had paralyzed us. "Chibh-Chondor closed his seance by experimenting upon inanimate objects. By mere passes with his hands in the direction of the object to be acted upon, and without leaving his seat, he paled and extinguished lights in the furthest parts of the room, moved the furniture, including the divans upon which we sat, opened and closed doors. Catching sight of a Hindu who was drawing water from a well in the garden, he made a pass in his direction, and the rope suddenly stopped in its descent, resisting all the efforts of the astonished gardener. With another pass the rope again descended.

"I asked Chibh-Chondor: 'Do you employ the same means in acting upon inanimate objects that you do upon living creatures?'

"He replied, 'I have only one means.'

" 'What is it?'

" 'The will. Man, who is the end of all intellectual and material forces, must dominate over all. The Brahmans know nothing besides this.' "

"Sanang Setzen," says Colonel Yule,[701] "enumerates a variety of the wonderful acts which could be performed through the *Dharani* (mystic Hindu charms). Such were sticking a peg into solid rock; restoring the dead to life; turning a dead body into gold; penetrating everywhere *as air does* (in astral form); flying; catching wild beasts with the hand; reading thoughts; making water flow backward; eating tiles; sitting in the air with the legs doubled under, etc." Old legends ascribe to Simon Magus precisely the same powers. "He made statues to walk; leaped into the fire without being burned; flew in the air; made bread of stones; changed his shape; assumed two faces at once; converted himself into a pillar; caused closed doors to fly open spontaneously; made the vessels in a house move of themselves, etc." The Jesuit Delrio laments that credulous princes, otherwise of pious repute, should have allowed *diabolical* tricks to be played before them, "as for example, things of iron, and silver goblets, or other heavy articles, to be moved by bounds, from one end of the table to the other, *without the use of a magnet,* or of any attachment."[702] We believe WILL-POWER the most powerful of magnets. The existence of such magical power in certain persons *is proved,* but the existence of the Devil is a fiction, which no theology is able to demonstrate.

"There are certain men whom the Tartars honor above all in the world," says Friar Ricold, "viz., the *Baxitæ,* who are a kind of idol-priests. These are men from India, persons of deep wisdom, *well-conducted and of the gravest morals.* They are usually with magic arts . . . they exhibit many illusions, and predict future events. For instance, one of eminence among

---

701 "*Book of Ser Marco Polo,*" vol. i., pp. 306, 307.
702 Delrio, "*Disquis. Magic,*" pp. 34, 100.

them was said to fly; but the truth, however, was as it proved, that he did not fly, but did walk close to the surface of the ground without touching it; and *would seem to sit down without having any substance to support him.*[703] This last performance was witnessed by Ibn Batuta, at Delhi," adds Colonel Yule, who quotes the friar in the *Book of Ser Marco Polo,* "in the presence of Sultan Mahomet Tughlak; and it was professedly exhibited by a Brahman at Madras in the present century, a descendant doubtless of those Brahmans whom Apollonius saw walking two cubits from the ground. It is also described by the worthy Francis Valentyn, as a performance known and practiced in his own day in India. It is related, he says, that 'a man will first go and sit on three sticks put together so as to form a tripod; after which, first one stick, then a second, then a third shall be removed from under him, and the man shall not fall but shall still remain sitting in the air! Yet I have spoken with two friends who had seen this at one and the same time; and one of them, I may add, mistrusting his own eyes, had taken the trouble to feel about with a long stick if there were nothing on which the body rested; yet, as the gentleman told me, he could neither feel nor see any such thing.' " We have stated elsewhere that the same thing was accomplished last year, before the Prince of Wales and his suite.

Such feats as the above are nothing in comparison to what is done by professed jugglers; "feats," remarks the above-quoted author, "which might be regarded as simply inventions if told by one author only, but which seem to deserve *prominent notice* from being recounted by a series of authors, certainly independent of one another, and writing at long intervals of time and place. Our first witness is Ibn Batuta, and it will be necessary to quote him as well as the others in full, in order to show how closely their evidence tallies. The Arab traveller was present at a great entertainment at the court of the Viceroy of Khansa. 'That same night a juggler, who was one of the Khan's slaves, made his appearance, and the Amir said to him, "Come and show us some of your marvels." Upon this he took a wooden ball, with several holes in it, through which long thongs were passed, and laying hold of one of these, slung it into the air. It went so high that we lost sight of it altogether. . . . (We were in the middle of the palace-court.) There now remained only a little of the end of a thong in the conjurer's hand, and he desired one of the boys who assisted him to lay hold of it and mount. He did so, climbing by the thong, and we lost sight of him also! The conjurer then called to him three times, but, getting no answer, he snatched up a knife as if in a great rage, laid hold of the thong, and disappeared also! By and bye, he threw down one of the boy's hands, then a foot, then the other hand, and then the other foot, then the trunk, and last of all the head!

THE INDIAN TAPE-CLIMBING TRICK AN ILLUSION

Then he came down himself, puffing and panting, and with his clothes all bloody kissed the ground before the Amir, and said something to him in Chinese. The Amir gave some order in reply, and our friend then took the lad's limbs, laid them together in their places, and gave a kick, when, presto! there was the boy, who got up and stood before us! All this astonished me beyond measure, and I had an attack of palpitation like that which overcame me once before in the presence of the Sultan of India, when he showed me something of the

---

703 Col. H. Yule, "*The Book of Ser Marco Polo,*" vol. i., p. 308.

same kind. They gave me a cordial, however, which cured the attack. The Kaji Afkharuddin was next to me, and quoth he, "Wallah! 't is my opinion there has been neither going up nor coming down, neither marring, nor mending! 'T is all *hocus-pocus*!" ' "

And who doubts but that it is a "hocus-pocus," an illusion, or *Maya*, as the Hindus express it? But when such an illusion can be forced on, say, ten thousand people at the same time, as we have seen it performed during a public festival, surely the means by which such an astounding hallucination can be produced merits the attention of science! When by such *magic* a man who stands before you, in a room, the doors of which you have closed and of which the keys are in your hand, suddenly disappears, vanishes like a flash of light, and you see him *nowhere* but hear his voice from different parts of the room addressing you and laughing at your perplexity, surely such an *art* is not unworthy either of Mr. Huxley or Dr. Carpenter. Is it not quite as well worth spending time over, as the lesser mystery — why barnyard cocks crow at midnight?

What Ibn Batuta, the Moor, saw in China about the year 1348, Colonel Yule shows Edward Melton, "an Anglo-Dutch traveller," witnessing in Batavia about the year 1670: "One of the same gang" (of conjurers), says Melton,[704] "took a small ball of cord, and grasping one end of the cord in his hand slung the other up into the air with such force that its extremity was beyond reach of our sight. He then climbed up the cord with indescribable swiftness. . . . I stood full of astonishment, not conceiving where he had disappeared; when lo! a leg came tumbling down out of the air. A moment later a hand came down, etc. . . . In short, all the members of the body came successively tumbling from the air and were cast together by the attendant into the basket. The last fragment of all was the head, and no sooner had that touched the ground than he who had snatched up all the limbs and put them in the basket, turned them all out again topsy turvy. Then straightway we saw *with these eyes all those limbs creep together* again, and, in short, form a whole man, who at once could stand and go just as before without showing the least damage! . . . Never in my life was I so astonished . . . and I doubted now no longer that these misguided men did it by the help of the Devil."

In the memoirs of the Emperor Jahangire, the performances of seven jugglers from Bengal, who exhibited before him, are thus described: "*Ninth.* They produced a man whom they divided limb from limb, actually severing his head from the body. They scattered these mutilated members along the ground, and in this state they lay some time. They then extended a sheet over the spot, and one of the men putting himself under the sheet, in a few minutes came from below, followed by the individual supposed to have been cut into joints, in perfect health and condition. . . . *Twenty-third.* They produced a chain of fifty cubits in length, and in my presence threw one end of it toward the sky, *where it remained as if fastened to something in the air.* A dog was then brought forward and being placed at the lower end of the chain, immediately ran up, and reaching the other end, *immediately disappeared in the air.* In the same manner a hog, a panther, a lion, and a tiger were successively sent up the chain, and all equally disappeared at the upper end of the chain. At last they took down the chain,

---

704 Edward Melton, "*Engelsch Edelmans, Zeldzaame en Gedenkwaardige Zee en Land Reizen, etc.,*" p. 468. Amsterdam, 1702.

and put it into the bag, no one ever discovering in what way the different animals were made to vanish into the air in the mysterious manner above described."[705]

We have in our possession a picture painted from such a Persian conjurer, with a man, or rather the various limbs of what was a minute before a man, scattered before him. We have seen such conjurers, and witnessed such performances more than once and in various places.

Bearing ever in mind that we repudiate the idea of a miracle and returning once more to phenomena more serious, we would now ask what logical objection can be urged against the claim that the reanimation of the dead was accomplished by many thaumaturgists? The fakir described in the *Franco-Americain*, might have gone far enough to say that this will-power of man is so tremendously potential that it can reanimate a body apparently dead, by drawing back the flitting soul that has not yet quite ruptured the thread that through life had bound the two together. Dozens of such fakirs have allowed themselves to be buried alive before thousands of witnesses, and weeks afterward have been resuscitated. And if fakirs have the secret of this artificial process, identical with, or analogous to, hibernation, why not allow that their ancestors, the Gymnosophists, and Apollonius of Tyana, who had studied with the latter in India, and Jesus, and other prophets and seers, who all knew more about the mysteries of life and death than any of our modern men of science, might have resuscitated dead men and women? And being quite familiar with that power — that mysterious *something* "that science cannot yet understand," as Professor Le Conte confesses — knowing, moreover, "whence it came and whither it was going," Elisha, Jesus, Paul, and Apollonius, enthusiastic ascetics and learned initiates, might have recalled to life with ease any man who "was not dead but sleeping," and that without any miracle.

If the molecules of the cadaver are imbued with the physical and chemical forces of the living organism,[706] what is to prevent them from being set again in motion, provided we know the nature of the vital force, and how to command it? The materialist can certainly offer no objection, for with him it is no question of reinfusing a soul. For him the soul has no existence, and the human body may be regarded simply as a vital engine — a locomotive which will start upon the application of heat and force, and stop when they are withdrawn. To the theologian the case offers greater difficulties, for, in his view, death cuts asunder the tie which binds soul and body, and the one can no more be returned into the other without miracle than the born infant can be compelled to resume its fœtal life after parturition and the severing of the umbilicus. But the Hermetic philosopher stands between these two irreconcilable antagonists, *"master of the situation.* He knows the nature of the soul — a form composed of nervous fluid and atmospheric ether — and knows how the vital force can be made active or passive at will, so long as there is no final destruction of some necessary organ. The claims of Gaffarilus — which, by the bye, appeared so preposterous in 1650[707] — were later corroborated by science.

He maintained that every object existing in nature, provided it was not artificial, when once burned still retained its form in the ashes, in which it remained till raised again. Du

705 "*Memoirs of the Emperor Jahangire,*" pp. 99, 102.
706 J. Hughes Bennett, "*Text Book of Physiology,*" Lippincott's American Edition, pp. 37-50.
707 "*Curiosites Inouïes.*"

Chesne, an eminent chemist, assured himself of the fact. Kircher, Digby, and Vallemont have demonstrated that the forms of plants could be resuscitated from their ashes. At a meeting of naturalists in 1834, at Stuttgart, a receipt for producing such experiments was found in a work of Oetinger.[708] Ashes of burned plants contained in vials, when heated, exhibited again their various forms. "A small obscure cloud gradually rose in the vial, took a defined form, and presented to the eye the flower or plant the ashes consisted of." "The earthly husk," wrote Oetinger, "remains in the retort, while the volatile essence ascends, *like a spirit*, perfect in form, but void of substance."[709]

And, if the astral form of even a plant when its body is dead still lingers in the ashes, will skeptics persist in saying that the soul of *man*, the *inner* ego, is after the death of the grosser form at once dissolved, and is no more? "At death," says the philosopher, "the one body exudes from the other, by osmose and through the brain; it is held near its old garment by a double attraction, physical and spiritual, until the latter decomposes; and if the proper conditions are given the soul can reinhabit it and resume the suspended life. It does it in sleep; it does it more thoroughly in trance; most surprisingly at the command and with the assistance of the Hermetic adept. Iamblichus declared that a person endowed with such resuscitating powers is 'full of God.' All the subordinate spirits of the upper spheres are at his command, for he is no longer a mortal, but himself a god. In his *Epistle to the Corinthians*, Paul remarks that 'the spirits of the prophets *are subject to the prophets.*' "

Some persons have the natural and some the acquired power of withdrawing the *inner* from the *outer* body, at will, and causing it to perform long journeys, and be seen by those whom it visits. Numerous are the instances recorded by unimpeachable witnesses of the "doubles" of persons having been seen and conversed with, hundreds of miles from the places where the persons themselves were known to be. Hermotimus, if we may credit Pliny and Plutarch,[710] could at will fall into a trance and then his *second* soul proceeded to any distant place he chose.

RESUSCITATION OF BURIED FAKIRS

The Abbé Tritheim, the famous author of *Steganographie*, who lived in the seventeenth century, could converse with his friends by the mere power of his will. "I can make my thoughts known to the initiated," he wrote, "at a distance of many hundred miles, without word, writing, or cipher, by any messenger. The latter cannot betray me, for he knows nothing. If needs be, I can dispense with the messenger. If any correspondent should be buried in the deepest dungeon, I could still convey to him my thoughts as clearly and as frequently as I chose, and this quite simply, without superstition, without the aid of spirits." Cordanus could also send his spirit, or any messages he chose. When he did so, he felt "as if a door was opened, and I myself immediately passed through it, leaving the body behind me."[711] The case of a high German official, a counsellor Wesermann, was mentioned in a

---

708 "*Thoughts on the Birth and Generation of Things.*"
709 C. Crowe, "*Night-Side of Nature,*" p. 111.
710 Pliny, "*Hist. Nat.,*" vii., c. 52; and Plutarch, "*Discourse concerning Socrates' Dæmon,*" 22.
711 "*De Res. Var.,*" v. iii., i., viii., c. 43. Plutarch, "*Discourse concerning Socrates' Dæmon,*" 22.

scientific paper.[712] He claimed to be able to cause any friend or acquaintance, at any distance, to dream of every subject he chose, or see any person he liked. His claims were proved good, and testified to on several occasions by skeptics and learned professional persons. He could also cause his double to appear wherever he liked; and be seen by several persons at one time. By whispering in their ears a sentence prepared and agreed upon beforehand by unbelievers, and for the purpose, his power to project the double was demonstrated beyond any cavil.

According to Napier, Osborne, Major Lawes, Quenouillet, Nikiforovitch, and many other modern witnesses, fakirs are now proved to be able, by a long course of diet, preparation, and repose, to bring their bodies into a condition which enables them to be buried six feet under ground for an indefinite period. Sir Claude Wade was present at the court of Rundjit Singh, when the fakir, mentioned by the Honorable Captain Osborne, was buried alive for six weeks, in a box placed in a cell three feet below the floor of the room.[713] To prevent the chance of deception, a guard comprising two companies of soldiers had been detailed, and four sentries "were furnished and relieved every two hours, night and day, to guard the building from intrusion. . . . On opening it," says Sir Claude, "we saw a figure enclosed in a bag of white linen fastened by a string over the head . . . the servant then began pouring warm water over the figure . . . the legs and arms of the body were shrivelled and stiff, the face full, the head reclining on the shoulder like that of a corpse. I then called to the medical gentleman who was attending me, to come down and inspect the body, which he did, but could discover no pulsation in the heart, the temples, or the arm. There was, however, *a heat about the region of the brain,* which no other part of the body exhibited."

Regretting that the limits of our space forbid the quotation of the details of this interesting story, we will only add, that the process of resuscitation included bathing with hot water, friction, the removal of wax and cotton pledgets from the nostrils and ears, the rubbing of the eyelids with ghee or clarified butter, and, what will appear most curious to many, the application of a hot wheaten cake, about an inch thick "to the top of the head." After the cake had been applied for the third time, the body was violently convulsed, the nostrils became inflated, the respiration ensued, and the limbs assumed a natural fulness; but the pulsation was still faintly perceptible. "The tongue was then anointed with ghee; the eyeballs became dilated and recovered their natural color, and the fakir recognized those present and spoke." It should be noticed that not only had the nostrils and ears been plugged, but the tongue had been thrust back so as to close the gullet, thus effectually stopping the orifices against the admission of atmospheric air. While in India, a fakir told us that this was done not only to prevent the action of the air upon the organic tissues, but also to guard against the deposit of the germs of decay, which in case of suspended animation would cause decomposition exactly as they do in any other meat exposed to air. There are also localities in which a fakir would refuse to be buried; such as the many spots in Southern India infested with the white ants, which annoying termites are considered among the most dangerous enemies of man and his property. They are so voracious as to devour everything they find except perhaps metals. As to wood, there is no kind through which

---

712 Nasse, "*Zeitschrift fur Psychische Aerzte*," 1820.
713 Osborne, "*Camp and Court of Rundjit Singh*"; Braid, "*On Trance.*"

they would not burrow; and even bricks and mortar offer but little impediment to their formidable armies. They will patiently work through mortar, destroying it particle by particle; and a fakir, however holy himself, and strong his temporary coffin, would not risk finding his body devoured when it was time for his resuscitation.

Then, here is a case, only one of many, substantiated by the testimony of two English noblemen — one of them an army officer — and a Hindu Prince, who was as great a skeptic as themselves. It places science in this embarrassing dilemma: it must either give the lie to many unimpeachable witnesses, or admit that if one fakir can resuscitate after six weeks, any other fakir can also; and if a fakir, why not a Lazarus, a Shunamite boy, or the daughter of Jairus?[714]

And now, perhaps, it may not be out of place to inquire what assurance can any physician have, beyond *external* evidence, that the body is really dead? The best authorities agree in saying that there are none. Dr. Todd Thomson, of London,[715] says most positively that "the immobility of the body, even its cadaverous aspect, the coldness of surface, the absence of respiration and pulsation, and the sunken state of the eye, are no unequivocal evidences that *life* is wholly extinct." Nothing but total decomposition is an irrefutable proof that life has fled for ever and that the tabernacle is tenantless. Demokritus asserted that there existed no *certain* signs of real death.[716] Pliny maintained the same.[717] Asclepiades, a learned physician and one of the most distinguished men of his day, held that the assurance was still more difficult in the cases of women than in those of men.

Todd Thomson, above quoted, gives several remarkable cases of such a suspended animation. Among others he mentions a certain Francis Neville, a Norman gentleman, who twice apparently died, and was twice in the act of being buried. But, at the moment when the coffin was being lowered in the grave, he spontaneously revived. In the seventeenth century, Lady Russell, to all appearance died, and was about to be buried, but as the bell was tolling for her funeral, she sat up in her coffin and exclaimed, "It is time to go to church!" Diemerbroeck mentions a peasant who gave no signs of life for three days, but when placed in his coffin, near the grave, revived and lived many years afterward. In 1836, a respectable citizen of Brussels fell into a profound lethargy on a Sunday morning. On Monday, as his attendants were preparing to screw the lid of the coffin, the supposed corpse sat up, rubbed his eyes, and called for his coffee and a newspaper.[718]

---

714 Mrs. Catherine Crowe, in her *"Night-Side of Nature,"* p. 118, gives us the particulars of a similar burial of a fakir, in the presence of General Ventura, together with the Maharajah, and many of his Sirdars. The political agent at Loodhiana was "present when he was disinterred, ten months after he had been buried." The coffin, or box, containing the fakir "being buried in a vault, the earth was thrown over it and trod down, after which a crop of barley was sown on the spot, and sentries placed to watch it. "The Maharajah, however, was so skeptical that in spite of all these precautions, he had him, twice in the ten months, dug up and examined, and each time he was found to be *exactly in the same state* as when they had shut him up."

715 Todd, Appendix to *"Occult Science,"* vol. i.

716 *"A Cornel. Cels.,"* lib. ii., cap. vi.

717 *"Hist. Nat.,"* lib. vii., cap. lii.

718 *"Morning Herald,"* July 21, 1836.

Such cases of apparent death are not very infrequently reported in the newspaper press. As we write (April, 1877), we find in a London letter to the New York *Times*, the following paragraph: "Miss Annie Goodale, the actress, died three weeks ago. Up to yesterday she was not buried. The corpse is warm and limp, and the features as soft and mobile as when in life. Several physicians have examined her, and have ordered that the body shall be watched night and day. The poor lady is evidently in a trance, but whether she is destined to come to life it is impossible to say."

Science regards man as an aggregation of atoms temporarily united by a mysterious force called the life-principle. To the materialist, the only difference between a living and a dead body is, that in the one case, that force is active, in the other latent. When it is extinct or entirely latent the molecules obey a superior attraction, which draws them asunder and scatters them through space.

This dispersion must be death, if it is possible to conceive such a thing as death, where the very molecules of the dead body manifest an intense vital energy. If death is but the stoppage of a digesting, locomotive, and thought-grinding machine, how can death be actual and not relative, before that machine is thoroughly broken up and its particles dispersed? So long as any of them cling together, the centripetal vital force may overmatch the dispersive centrifugal action. Says Eliphas Levi: "Change attests movement, and movement only reveals life. The corpse would not decompose if it were dead; all the molecules which compose it are living and struggle to separate. And would you think that the spirit frees itself first of all to exist no more? That thought and love can die when the grossest forms of matter do not die? If the change should be called death, we die and are born again every day, for every day our forms undergo change."[719]

The kabalists say that a man is not dead when his body is entombed. Death is never sudden; for, according to Hermes, nothing goes in nature by violent transitions. Everything is gradual, and as it required a long and gradual development to produce the living human being, so time is required to completely withdraw vitality from the carcass. "Death can no more be an absolute end, than birth a real beginning. Birth proves the preëxistence of the being, as death proves immortality," says the same French kabalist.

While implicitly believing in the restoration of the daughter of Jairus, the ruler of the synagogue, and in other Bible-miracles, well-educated Christians, who otherwise would feel indignant at being called superstitious, meet all such cases as that of Apollonius and the girl said by his biographer to have been recalled to life by him, with scornful skepticism. Diogenes Laërtius, who mentions a woman restored to life by Empedocles, is treated with no more respect; and the name of Pagan thaumaturgist, in the eyes of Christians, is but a synonym for impostor. Our scientists are at least one degree more rational; they embrace all Bible prophets and apostles, and the heathen miracle-doers in two categories of hallucinated fools and deceitful tricksters.

LIMITS OF SUSPENDED ANIMATION

But Christians and materialists might, with a very little effort on their part, show themselves fair and logical at the same time. To produce such a miracle, they have but to

---

719 "*La Science des Esprits.*"

consent to understand what they read, and submit it to the unprejudiced criticism of their best judgment. Let us see how far it is possible. Setting aside the incredible fiction of Lazarus, we will select two cases: the ruler's daughter, recalled to life by Jesus, and the Corinthian bride, resuscitated by Apollonius. In the former case, totally disregarding the significant expression of Jesus — *"She is not dead but sleepeth,"* the clergy force their god to become a breaker of his own laws and grant unjustly to one what he denies to all others, and with no better object in view than to produce a useless miracle. In the second case, notwithstanding the words of the biographer of Apollonius, so plain and precise that there is not the slightest cause to misunderstand them, they charge Philostratus with deliberate imposture. Who could be fairer than he, who less open to the charge of mystification, when, in describing the resuscitation of the young girl by the Tyanian sage, in the presence of a large concourse of people, the biographer says, "she had *seemed* to die."

In other words, he very clearly indicates a case of suspended animation; and then adds immediately, "as the rain fell very fast on the young girl," while she was being carried to the pile, "with her face turned upwards, this, *also*, might have excited her senses."[720] Does this not show most plainly that Philostratus saw *no* miracle in that resuscitation? Does it not rather imply, if anything, the great learning and skill of Apollonius, "who like Asclepiades had the merit of distinguishing at a glance between real and apparent death"?[721]

A resuscitation, after the soul and spirit have entirely separated from the body, and the last electric thread is severed, is as impossible as for a once disembodied spirit to reïncarnate itself once more on this earth, except as described in previous chapters. "A leaf, once fallen off, does not reättach itself to the branch," says Eliphas Levi. "The caterpillar becomes a butterfly, but the butterfly does not again return to the grub. Nature closes the door behind all that passes, and pushes life forward. Forms pass, thought remains, and does not recall that which it has once exhausted."[722]

Why should it be imagined that Asclepiades and Apollonius enjoyed exceptional powers for the discernment of actual death? Has any modern school of medicine this knowledge to impart to its students? Let their authorities answer for them. These prodigies of Jesus and Apollonius are so well attested that they appear authentic. Whether in either or both cases life was simply suspended or not, the important fact remains that by some power, peculiar to themselves, both the wonder-workers recalled the *seemingly dead* to life in an instant.[723]

Is it because the modern physician has not yet found the secret which the theurgists evidently possessed that its possibility is denied?

---

720 "*Vit. Apollon. Tyan.*," lib. iv., ch. xvi.

721 Salverte, "*Sciences Occultes*," vol. ii.

722 "*La Science des Esprits.*"

723 It would be beneficial to humanity were our modern physicians possessed of the same inestimable faculty; for then we would have on record less horrid deaths *after* inhumation. Mrs. Catherine Crowe, in the "Night-Side of Nature," records in the chapter on "Cases of Trances" *five* such cases, in England alone, and during the present century. Among them is Dr. Walker of Dublin and a Mr. S——, whose stepmother was accused of poisoning him, and who, upon being disinterred, was found lying on his face.

Neglected as psychology now is, and with the strangely chaotic state in which physiology is confessed to be by its most fair students, certainly it is not very likely that our men of science will soon rediscover the lost knowledge of the ancients. In the days of old, when prophets were not treated as charlatans, nor thaumaturgists as impostors, there were colleges instituted for teaching prophecy and occult sciences in general. Samuel is recorded as the chief of such an institution at Ramah; Elisha, also, at Jericho. The schools of *hazim*, prophets or seers, were celebrated throughout the country. Hillel had a regular academy, and Socrates is well known to have sent away several of his disciples to study *manticism*. The study of magic, or wisdom, included every branch of science, the metaphysical as well as the physical, psychology and physiology in their common and occult phases, and the study of alchemy was universal, for it was both a physical and a spiritual science. Therefore why doubt or wonder that the ancients, who studied nature under its double aspect, achieved discoveries which to our modern physicists, who study but its dead letter, are a closed book?

Thus, the question at issue is not whether a *dead* body can be resuscitated — for, to assert that would be to assume the possibility of a miracle, which is absurd — but, to assure ourselves whether the medical authorities pretend to determine the precise moment of death. The kabalists say that death occurs at the instant when both the astral body, or life-principle, and the spirit part forever with the corporeal body. The scientific physician who denies both astral body and spirit, and admits the existence of nothing more than the life-principle, judges death to occur when life is apparently extinct. When the beating of the heart and the action of the lungs cease, and *rigor mortis* is manifested, and especially when decomposition begins, they pronounce the patient dead. But the annals of medicine teem with examples of "suspended animation" as the result of asphyxia by drowning, the inhalation of gases and other causes; life being restored in the case of drowning persons even after they had been apparently dead for twelve hours.

In cases of somnambulic trance, none of the ordinary signs of death are lacking; breathing and the pulse are extinct; animal-heat has disappeared; the muscles are rigid, the eye glazed, and the body is colorless. In the celebrated case of Colonel Townshend, he threw himself into this state in the presence of three medical men; who, after a time, were persuaded that he was really dead, and were about leaving the room, when he slowly revived. He describes his peculiar gift by saying that he "could die or expire when he pleased, and yet, by an effort, or *somehow* he could come to life again."

There occurred in Moscow, a few years since, a remarkable instance of apparent death. The wife of a wealthy merchant lay in the cataleptic state seventeen days, during which the authorities made several attempts to bury her; but, as decomposition had not set in, the family averted the ceremony, and at the end of that time she was restored to life.

The above instances show that the most learned men in the medical profession are unable to be certain when a person is dead. What they call "suspended animation," is that state from which the patient spontaneously recovers, through an effort of his own spirit, which may be provoked by any one of many causes. In these cases, the astral body has not parted from the physical body; its external functions are simply suspended; the subject is in a state of torpor, and the restoration is nothing but a recovery from it.

But, in the case of what physiologists would call "real death," but which is not actually so, the astral body has withdrawn; perhaps local decomposition has set in. How shall the man be brought to life again? The answer is, the interior body must be forced back into the exterior one, and vitality reawakened in the latter. The clock has run down, it must be wound. If death is absolute; if the organs have not only ceased to act, but have lost the susceptibility of renewed action, then the whole universe would have to be thrown into chaos to resuscitate the corpse — a miracle would be demanded. But, as we said before, the man is not dead when he is cold, stiff, pulseless, breathless, and even showing signs of decomposition; he is not dead when buried, nor afterward, until a certain point is reached. That point is, *when the vital organs have become so decomposed, that if reänimated, they could not perform their customary functions;* when the mainspring and cogs of the machine, so to speak, are so eaten away by rust, that they would snap upon the turning of the key. Until that point is reached, the astral body may be caused, without miracle, to reënter its former tabernacle, either by an effort of its own will, or under the resistless impulse of the will of one who knows the potencies of nature and how to direct them. The spark is not extinguished, but only latent — latent as the fire in the flint, or the heat in the cold iron.

In cases of the most profound cataleptic clairvoyance, such as obtained by Du Potet, and described very graphically by the late Prof. William Gregory, in his *Letters on Animal Magnetism*, the spirit is so far disengaged from the body that it would be impossible for it to reënter it without an effort of the mesmerizer's will. The subject is practically dead, and, if left to itself, the spirit would escape forever. Although independent of the torpid physical casing, the half-freed spirit is still tied to it by a magnetic cord, which is described by clairvoyants as appearing dark and smoky by contrast with the ineffable brightness of the astral atmosphere through which they look. Plutarch, relating the story of Thespesius, who fell from a great height, and lay three days apparently dead, gives us the experience of the latter during his state of partial decease. "Thespesius," says he, "then observed that he was different from the dead by whom he was surrounded. . . . They were transparent and environed by a radiance, but he seemed to trail after him a dark radiation or line of shadow." His whole description, minute and circumstantial in its details, appears to be corroborated by the clairvoyants of every period, and, so far as this class of testimony can be taken, is important. The kabalists, as we find them interpreted by Eliphas Levi, in his *Science des Esprits,* say that, "When a man falls into the last sleep, he is plunged at first into a sort of dream, before gaining consciousness in the other side of life. He sees, then, either in a beautiful vision, or in a terrible nightmare, the paradise or hell, in which he believed during his mortal existence. This is why it often happens, that the affrighted soul breaks violently back into the terrestrial life it has just left, and why some who were really dead, *i.e.*, who, if left alone and quiet, would have peaceably passed away forever in a state of unconscious lethargy, when entombed too soon, reawake to life in the grave."

In this connection, the reader may perhaps recall the well-known case of the old man who had left some generous gifts in his will to his orphaned nieces; which document, just before his death, he had confided to his rich son, with injunctions to carry out his wishes. But, he had not been dead more than a few hours before the son, finding himself alone with the corpse, tore the will and burned it. The sight of this impious deed apparently recalled the hovering spirit, and the old man, rising from his couch of death, uttered a fierce malediction upon the horror-stricken wretch, and then fell back again, and yielded up his spirit — this time forever. Dion Boucicault makes use of an incident of this kind in his powerful drama *Louis XI.*; and Charles Kean created a profound impression in the character of the French monarch, when the dead man revives for an instant and clutches the crown as the heir-apparent approaches it.

Levi says that resuscitation is not impossible while the vital organism remains undestroyed, and the astral spirit is yet within reach. "Nature," he says, "accomplishes nothing by sudden jerks, and eternal death is always preceded by a state which partakes somewhat of the nature of lethargy. It is a torpor which a great shock or the magnetism of a powerful will can overcome." He accounts in this manner for the resuscitation of the dead man thrown upon the bones of Elisha. He explains it by saying that the soul was hovering at that moment near the body; the burial party, according to tradition, were attacked by robbers; and their fright communicating itself sympathetically to it, the soul was seized with horror at the idea of its remains being desecrated, and "reëntered violently into its body to raise and save it." Those who believe in the survival of the soul can see in this incident nothing of a supernatural character — it is only a perfect manifestation of natural law. To narrate to the materialist such a case, however well attested, would be but an idle talk; the theologian, always looking beyond nature for a special providence, regards it as a prodigy. Eliphas Levi says: "They attributed the resuscitation to the contact with the bones of Elisha; and worship of relics dates logically from his epoch."

Balfour Stewart is right — scientists "know nothing, or next to nothing, of the ultimate structure and properties of matter, whether organic or inorganic."

We are now on such firm ground, that we will take another step in advance. *The same knowledge and control of the occult forces, including the vital force which enabled the fakir temporarily to leave and then reënter his body, and Jesus, Apollonius, and Elisha to recall their several subjects to life, made it possible for the ancient hierophants to animate statues, and cause them to act and speak like living creatures.* It is the same knowledge and power which made it possible for Paracelsus to create his homunculi; for Aaron to change his rod into a serpent and a budding branch; Moses to cover Egypt with frogs and other pests; and the Egyptian theurgist of our day to vivify his pigmy Mandragora, which has physical life but no soul. It was no more wonderful that upon presenting the necessary conditions Moses should call into life large reptiles and insects, than that, under like favoring conditions, the physical scientist should call into life the small ones which he names bacteria.

And now, in connection with ancient miracle-doers and prophets, let us bring forward the claims of the modern mediums. Nearly every form of phenomena recorded in the sacred and profane histories of the world we find them claiming to reproduce in our days. Selecting, among the variety of seeming wonders, levitation of ponderable inanimate objects as well as of human bodies, we will give our attention to the conditions under which the phenomenon is manifested. History records the names of Pagan theurgists, Christian saints, Hindu fakirs, and spiritual mediums who have been thus levitated, and who remained suspended in the air, sometimes for a considerable time. The phenomenon has not been confined to one country or epoch, but almost invariably the subjects have been religious ecstatics, adepts in magic, or, as now, spiritual mediums.

We assume the fact to be so well established as to require no labored effort on our part at this time to furnish proof that unconscious manifestations of spirit-power, as well as conscious feats of high magic, have happened in all countries, in all ages, and with hierophants as well as through irresponsible mediums. When the present perfected European civilization was yet in an inchoate state, occult philosophy, already hoary with age, speculated upon the attributes of man by analogy with those of his Creator. Individuals later, whose names will remain forever immortal, inscribed on the portal of the spiritual history of man, have afforded in their persons examples of how far could be developed the god-like powers of the *microcosmos*. Describing the *Doctrines and Principal Teachers of the Alexandrian School*, Professor A. Wilder says: "Plotinus taught that there was in the soul a returning impulse, love, which attracted it inward toward its origin and centre, the eternal good. While the person who does not understand how the soul contains the beautiful within itself will seek by laborious effort to realize beauty without, the wise man recognizes it within himself, develops the idea by withdrawal into himself, concentrating his attention, and so floating upward toward the divine fountain, the stream of which flows within him. The infinite is not known through the reason . . . but by a faculty superior to reason, by entering upon a state in which the individual, so to speak, ceases to be his finite self, in which state divine essence is communicated to him. This is ECSTASY."

Of Apollonius, who asserted that he could see "the present and the future in a clear mirror," on account of his abstemious mode of life, the professor very beautifully observes: "This is what may be termed *spiritual photography*. The soul is the camera in which facts and events, future, past, and present, are alike fixed; and the mind becomes conscious of them. Beyond our every-day world of limits, all is as one day or state, the past and future comprised in the present."[724]

MEDIUMSHIP TOTALLY ANTAGONISTIC TO ADEPTSHIP

Were these God-like men "mediums," as the orthodox spiritualists will have it? By no means, if by the term we understand those "sick-sensitives" who are born with a peculiar organization, and who in proportion as their powers are developed become more and more subject to the irresistible influence of miscellaneous spirits, purely human, elementary, or elemental. Unquestionably so, if we consider every individual a medium in whose magnetic atmosphere the denizens of higher invisible spheres can move, and act, and live. In such a sense every person is a medium. Mediumship may be either 1st, self-developed; 2d, by extraneous influences; or 3d, may remain latent throughout life. *The reader must bear in mind the definition of the term, for, unless this is clearly understood, confusion will be inevitable.* Mediumship of this kind may be either active or passive, repellent or receptive, positive or negative. Mediumship is measured by the quality of the aura with which the individual is surrounded. This may be dense, cloudy, noisome, mephitic, nauseating to the pure spirit, and attract only those foul beings who delight in it, as the eel does in turbid waters, or, it may be pure, crystalline, limpid, opalescent as the morning dew. All depends upon the moral character of the medium.

About such men as Apollonius, Iamblichus, Plotinus, and Porphyry, there gathered this heavenly nimbus. It was evolved by the power of their own souls in close unison with their spirits; by the superhuman morality and sanctity of their lives, and aided by frequent

---

724 A. Wilder, "*Neo-Platonism and Alchemy.*"

interior ecstatic contemplation. Such holy men pure spiritual influences could approach. Radiating around an atmosphere of divine beneficence, they caused evil spirits to flee before them. Not only is it not possible for such to exist in their aura, but they cannot even remain in that of obsessed persons, if the thaumaturgist exercises his will, or even approaches them. This is MEDIATORSHIP, not *mediumship.* Such persons are temples in which dwells the spirit of the living God; but if the temple is defiled by the admission of an evil passion, thought or desire, the mediator falls into the sphere of sorcery. The door is opened; the pure spirits retire and the evil ones rush in. This is still mediatorship, evil as it is; the sorcerer, like the pure magician, forms his own aura and subjects to his will congenial inferior spirits.

But mediumship, as now understood and manifested, is a different thing. Circumstances, independent of his own volition, may, either at birth or subsequently, modify a person's aura, so that strange manifestations, physical or mental, diabolical or angelic, may take place. Such mediumship, as well as the above-mentioned mediatorship, has existed on earth since the first appearance here of living man. The former is the yielding of weak, mortal flesh to the control and suggestions of spirits and intelligences other than one's own immortal demon. It is literally *obsession* and *possession;* and mediums who pride themselves on being the faithful slaves of their "guides," and who repudiate with indignation the idea of "controlling" the manifestations, "could not very well deny the fact without inconsistency. This mediumship is typified in the story of Eve succumbing to the reasonings of the serpent; of Pandora peeping in the forbidden casket and letting loose on the world, sorrow and evil, and by Mary Magdalene, who from having been obsessed by 'seven devils' was finally redeemed by the triumphant struggle of her immortal spirit, touched by the presence of a holy mediator, against the dweller." This mediumship, whether beneficent or maleficent, is always *passive.* Happy are the pure in heart, who repel unconsciously, by that very cleanness of their inner nature, the dark spirits of evil. For verily they have no other weapons of defense but that inborn goodness and purity. Mediumism, as practiced in our days, is a more undesirable gift than the robe of Nessus.

"The tree is known by its fruits." Side by side with passive mediums in the progress of the world's history, appear active mediators. We designate them by this name for lack of a better one. The ancient witches and wizards, and those who had a "familiar spirit," generally made of their gifts a trade; and the Obeah woman of En-Dor, so well defined by Henry More, though she may have killed her calf for Saul, accepted hire from other visitors. In India, the jugglers, who by the way are less so than many a modern medium, and the *Essaoua* or sorcerers and serpent-charmers of Asia and Africa, all exercise their gifts for money. Not so with the mediators, or hierophants. Buddha was a mendicant and refused his father's throne. The "Son of Man had not where to lay his head"; the chosen apostles provided "neither gold, nor silver, nor brass in their purses."

Apollonius gave one half of his fortune to his relatives, the other half to the poor; Iamblichus and Plotinus were renowned for charity and self-denial; the fakirs, or holy mendicants, of India are fairly described by Jacolliot; the Pythagorean Essenes and Therapeutæ believed their hands defiled by the contact of money. When the apostles were offered money to impart their spiritual powers, Peter, notwithstanding that the Bible shows him a coward and thrice a renegade, still indignantly spurned the offer, saying: "Thy money perish with thee, because thou hast thought that the gift of God may be purchased with money." These men were mediators, guided merely by their own personal spirit, or divine soul, and availing themselves of the help of spirits but so far as these remain in the right path.

Far from us be the thought of casting an unjust slur on physical mediums. Harassed by various intelligences, reduced by the overpowering influence — which their weak and nervous natures are unable to shake off — to a morbid state, which at last becomes chronic, they are impeded by these "influences" from undertaking other occupation. They become mentally and physically unfit for any other. Who can judge them harshly when, driven to the last extremity, they are constrained to accept mediumship as a business? And heaven knows, as recent events have too well proved, whether the calling is one to be envied by any one! It is not mediums, real, *true*, and genuine mediums that we would ever blame, but their patrons, the spiritualists.

Plotinus, when asked to attend public worship of the gods, is said to have proudly answered: "It is for them (the spirits) to come to me." Iamblichus asserted and proved in his own case, that our soul can attain communion with the highest intelligences, with "natures loftier than itself," and carefully drove away from his theurgical ceremonies * every inferior spirit, or bad dæmon, which he taught his disciples to recognize. Proclus, who "elaborated the entire theosophy and theurgy of his predecessors into a complete system,"[725] according to Professor Wilder, "believed with Iamblichus in the attaining of a divine power, which, overcoming the mundane life, rendered the individual an organ of the Deity." He even taught that there was a "mystic password that would carry a person from one order of spiritual beings to another, higher and higher, till he arrived at the absolute divine." Apollonius spurned the sorcerers and "common soothsayers," and declared that it was his "peculiar abstemious mode of life" which "produced such an acuteness of the senses and created other faculties, so that the greatest and most remarkable things can take place." Jesus declared man *the lord of the Sabbath,* and at his command the terrestrial and elementary spirits fled from their temporary abodes; a power which was shared by Apollonius and many of the Brotherhood of the Essenes of Judea and Mount Carmel.

It is undeniable that there must have been some good reasons why the ancients persecuted *unregulated* mediums. Otherwise why, at the time of Moses and David and Samuel, should they have encouraged prophecy and divination, astrology and soothsaying, and maintained schools and colleges in which these natural gifts were strengthened and developed, while witches and those who divined by the spirit of *Ob* were put to death? Even at the time of Christ, the poor oppressed mediums were driven to the tombs and waste places without the city walls. Why this apparent gross injustice? Why should banishment, persecution, and death be the portion of the physical mediums of those days, and whole communities of thaumaturgists — like the Essenes — be not merely tolerated but revered? It is because the ancients, unlike ourselves, could "try" the spirits and discern the difference between the good and the evil ones, the human and the elemental. They also knew that unregulated spirit intercourse brought ruin upon the individual and disaster to the community.

---

725 See the "*Sketch of the Eclectic Philosophy of the Alexandrian School.*"

This view of mediumship may be novel and perhaps repugnant to many modern spiritualists; but still it is the view taught in the ancient philosophy, and supported by the experience of mankind from time immemorial.

It is erroneous to speak of a medium having *powers* developed. A passive medium has no power. He has a certain moral and physical condition which induces emanations, or an aura, in which his controlling intelligences can live, and by which they manifest themselves. He is only the vehicle through which *they* display their power. This aura varies day by day, and, as would appear from Mr. Crookes' experiments, even hour by hour. It is an external effect resulting from interior causes. The medium's moral state determines the kind of spirits that come; and the spirits that come reciprocally influence the medium, intellectually, physically, and morally. The perfection of his mediumship is in ratio to his passivity, and the danger he incurs is in equal degree. When he is fully "developed" — perfectly passive — his own astral spirit may be benumbed, and even crowded out of his body, which is then occupied by an elemental, or, what is worse, by a human fiend of the eighth sphere, who proceeds to use it as his own. But too often the cause of the most celebrated crime is to be sought in such possessions.

Physical mediumship depending upon passivity, its antidote suggests itself naturally; *let the medium cease being passive.* Spirits never control persons of positive character who are determined to resist all extraneous influences. The weak and feeble-minded whom they can make their victims they drive into vice. If these miracle-making elementals and disembodied devils called elementary were indeed the guardian angels that they have passed for, these last thirty years, why have they not given their faithful mediums at least good health and domestic happiness? Why do they desert them at the most critical moments of trial when under accusations of fraud? It is notorious that the best physical mediums are either sickly or, sometimes, what is still worse, inclined to some abnormal vice or other. Why do not these healing "guides," who make their mediums play the therapeutists and thaumaturgists to others, give them the boon of robust physical vigor? The ancient thaumaturgist and apostle, generally, if not invariably, enjoyed good health; their magnetism never conveyed to the sick patient any physical or moral taint; and they never were accused of VAMPIRISM, which a spiritual paper very justly charges upon some medium-healers.[726]

If we apply the above law of mediumship and mediatorship to the subject of levitation, with which we opened our present discussion, what shall we find? Here we have a medium and one of the mediator-class levitated — the former at a seance, the latter at prayer, or in ecstatic contemplation. The medium being passive must *be lifted* up; the ecstatic being active must levitate himself. The former is elevated by his familiar spirits — whoever or whatever they may be — the latter, by the power of his own aspiring soul. Can both be indiscriminately termed *mediums?* But nevertheless we may be answered that the same phenomena are produced in the presence of a modern medium as of an ancient saint. Undoubtedly; and so it was in the days of Moses; for we believe that the triumph claimed for him in *Exodus* over Pharaoh's magicians is simply a national boast on the part of the "chosen people." That the power which produced his phenomena produced that of the

---

726 See "*Medium and Daybreak,*" July 7, 1876, p. 428.

magicians also, who were moreover the first tutors of Moses and instructed him in their "wisdom," is most probable. But even in those days they seemed to have well appreciated the difference between phenomena apparently identical. The tutelar national deity of the Hebrews (who is *not* the Highest Father)[727] forbids expressly, in *Deuteronomy,*[728] his people "to learn to do after the abominations of other nations. . . . To pass through *the fire,* or use *divination,* or be an observer of times or an enchanter, or a *witch,* or a consulter with *familiar spirits,* or a necromancer."

What difference was there then between all the above-enumerated phenomena as performed by the "other nations" and when enacted by the prophets? Evidently, there was some good reason for it; and we find it in John's *First Epistle,* iv., which says: "believe not *every* spirit, but *try* the spirits, whether they are of God, because many false prophets are gone out into the world."

The only standard within the reach of spiritualists and present-day mediums by which they can *try* the spirits, is to judge 1, by their actions and speech; 2, by their readiness to manifest themselves; and 3, whether the object in view is worthy of the apparition of a *"disembodied"* spirit, or can excuse any one for disturbing *the dead.* Saul was on the eve of destruction, himself and his sons, yet Samuel inquired of him: "Why hast thou *disquieted* me, to bring me up?"[729] But the "intelligences" that visit the circle-rooms, come at the beck of every trifler who would while away a tedious hour.

In the number of the *London Spiritualist* for July 14th, we find a long article, in which the author seeks to prove that "the marvelous wonders of the present day, which belong to so-called modern spiritualism, are identical in character with the experiences of the patriarchs and apostles of old."

We are forced to contradict, point-blank, such an assertion. They are identical only so far that the same forces and occult powers of nature produce them. But though these powers and forces may be, and most assuredly are, all directed by unseen intelligences, the latter differ more in essence, character, and purposes than mankind itself, composed, as it now stands, of white, black, brown, red, and yellow men, and numbering saints and criminals, geniuses and idiots. The writer may avail himself of the services of a tame orang-outang or a South Sea islander; but the fact alone that he has a servant makes neither the latter nor himself identical with Aristotle and Alexander. The writer compares Ezekiel "lifted up" and

---

727 In Volume II., we will distinctly prove that the *Old Testament* mentions the worship of more than one god by the Israelites. The El-Shadi of Abraham and Jacob was not the Jehovah of Moses, or the Lord God worshipped by them for forty years in the wilderness. And the God of Hosts of Amos is not, if we are to believe his own words, the Mosaic God, the Sinaitic deity, for this is what we read: "I hate, I despise your feast-days . . . your meat-offerings, I will not accept them. . . . Have ye offered unto *me* sacrifices and offerings in the wilderness forty years, O house of Israel? . . . No, but *ye have borne the tabernacle of your Moloch and Chiun* (Saturn), your images, the star of your god, which ye made to yourselves. . . . Therefore, will I cause you to go into captivity . . . saith the *Lord, whose name is The God of hosts*" (Amos v. 21-27).

728 Chapter xviii.

729 This word *"up"* from the spirit of a prophet whose abode ought certainly to be in heaven and who therefore ought to have said "to bring me down," is very suggestive in itself to a Christian who locates paradise and hell at two opposite points.

taken into the "east gate of the Lord's house,"[730] with the levitations of certain mediums, and the three Hebrew youths in the "burning fiery furnace," with other *fire-proof* mediums; the John King "spirit-light" is assimilated with the "burning lamp" of Abraham; and finally, after many such comparisons, the case of the Davenport Brothers, released from the jail of Oswego, is confronted with that of Peter delivered from prison by the "angel of the Lord"!

Now, except the story of Saul and Samuel, there is not a case instanced in the *Bible* of the "*evocation* of the dead." As to being lawful, the assertion is contradicted by every prophet. Moses issues a decree of death against those who raise the spirits of the dead, the "necromancers." Nowhere throughout the *Old Testament*, nor in Homer, nor Virgil is communion with the dead termed otherwise than necromancy.

Philo Judæus makes Saul say, that if he banishes from the land every diviner and necromancer his name will survive him.

WHAT ARE "MATERIALIZED SPIRITS"?

One of the greatest reasons for it was the doctrine of the ancients, that no soul from the "abode of the blessed" will return to earth, unless, indeed, upon rare occasions its apparition might be required to accomplish some great object in view, and so bring benefit upon humanity. In this latter instance the "soul" has no need to be *evoked*. It sent its portentous message either by an evanescent *simulacrum* of itself, or through *messengers*, who could appear in *material* form, and personate faithfully the departed. The souls that could so easily be evoked were deemed neither safe nor useful to commune with. They were the souls, or *larvæ* rather, from the infernal region of the limbo — the *sheol*, the region known by the kabalists as the eighth sphere, but far different from the orthodox Hell or Hades of the ancient mythologists. Horace describes this evocation and the ceremonial accompanying it, and Maimonides gives us particulars of the Jewish rite. Every necromantic ceremony was performed on high places and hills, and blood was used for the purpose of placating these human *ghouls*.[731]

"I cannot prevent the witches from picking up their bones," says the poet. "See the blood they pour in the ditch to allure the *souls* that will utter their oracles!"[732] "*Cruor in fossam confusus, ut inde manes elicirent, animas responsa daturas.*"

"The *souls*," says Porphyry, "prefer, to everything else, *freshly-spilt blood*, which seems for a short time to restore to them some of the faculties of life."[733] As for materializations, they are many and various in the sacred records. But, were they effected under the same conditions as at modern seances? Darkness, it appears, was not required in those days of patriarchs and magic powers. The three angels who appeared to Abraham drank in the full blaze of the sun, for "he sat in the tent-door *in the heat of the day*,"[734] says the book of *Genesis*. The spirits of Elias and Moses appeared equally in daytime, as it is not probable that Christ and the Apostles would be climbing a high mountain during the night. Jesus is represented

---

730 *Ezekiel* iii. 12-14.
731 William Howitt, "*History of the Supernatural,*" vol. ii., ch. i.
732 Lib. i., Sat. 8.
733 Porphyry, "*Of Sacrifices.*"
734 *Genesis* xviii., i.

as having appeared to Mary Magdalene in the garden in the early morning; to the Apostles, at three distinct times, and generally by day; once "when the morning was come" (*John* xxi. 4). Even when the ass of Balaam saw the "materialized" angel, it was in the full light of noon.

We are fully prepared to agree with the writer in question, that we find in the life of Christ — and we may add in the *Old Testament*, too — "an uninterrupted record of spiritualistic manifestations," but nothing *mediumistic*, of a physical character though, if we except the visit of Saul to Sedecla, the Obeah woman of En-Dor. This is a distinction of vital importance.

True, the promise of the Master was clearly stated: "Aye, and greater works than these shall ye do" — works of mediatorship. According to Joel, the time would come when there would be an outpouring of the divine spirit: "Your sons and your daughters," says he, "shall prophesy, your old men shall dream dreams, your young men shall see visions." The time has come and they do all these things now; Spiritualism has its seers and martyrs, its prophets and healers. Like Moses, and David, and Jehoram, there are mediums who have direct writings from genuine planetary and human spirits; and the best of it brings the mediums no pecuniary recompense. The greatest friend of the cause in France, Leymarie, now languishes in a prison-cell, and, as he says with touching pathos, is "no longer a man, but *a number*" on the prison register.

There are a few, a very few, orators on the spiritualistic platform who speak by inspiration, and if they know what is said at all they are in the condition described by Daniel: "And I retained no strength. Yet heard I the voice of his words: and when I heard the voice of his words, then was I in a deep sleep."[735] And there are mediums, these whom we have spoken of, for whom the prophecy in Samuel might have been written: "The spirit of the Lord will come upon thee, thou shalt prophesy with them, and shalt be *turned into another man*."[736] But where, in the long line of Bible-wonders, do we read of flying guitars, and tinkling tambourines, and jangling bells being offered in pitch-dark rooms as evidences of immortality?

When Christ was accused of casting out devils by the power of Beelzebub, he denied it, and sharply retorted by asking, "By whom do your sons or disciples cast them out?" Again, spiritualists affirm that Jesus was a medium, that he was controlled by one or many spirits; but when the charge was made to him direct he said that he was nothing of the kind. "Say we not well, that thou art a Samaritan, and hast a devil?" daimonion, an Obeah, or familiar spirit in the Hebrew text. Jesus answered, "I have not a devil."[737]

THE SHUDALA MADAN

The writer from whom we have above quoted, attempts also a parallel between the aërial flights of Philip and Ezekiel and of Mrs. Guppy and other modern mediums. He is ignorant or oblivious of the fact that while levitation occurred as an effect in both classes of cases, the producing causes were totally dissimilar. The nature of this difference we have

735 *Daniel* x. 8.
736 *I Samuel*, x. 6.
737 *Gospel According to John* vii. 20.

adverted to already. Levitation may be produced consciously or unconsciously to the subject. The juggler determines beforehand that he will be levitated, for how long a time, and to what height; he regulates the occult forces accordingly. The fakir produces the same effect by the power of his aspiration and will, and, except when in the ecstatic state, keeps control over his movements. So does the priest of Siam, when, in the sacred pagoda, he mounts fifty feet in the air with taper in hand, and flits from idol to idol, lighting up the niches, self-supported, and stepping as confidently as though he were upon solid ground. This, persons have seen and testify to. The officers of the Russian squadron which recently circumnavigated the globe, and was stationed for a long time in Japanese waters, relate the fact that, besides many other marvels, they saw jugglers walk in mid-air from tree-top to tree-top, without the slightest support.[738] They also saw the pole and tape-climbing feats, described by Colonel Olcott in his *People from the Other World,* and which have been so much called in question by certain spiritualists and mediums whose zeal is greater than their learning. The quotations from Col. Yule and other writers, elsewhere given in this work, seem to place the matter beyond doubt that these effects are produced.

Such phenomena, when occurring apart from religious rites, in India, Japan, Thibet, Siam, and other "heathen" countries, phenomena a hundred times more various and astounding than ever seen in civilized Europe or America, are never attributed to the spirits of the departed. The Pitris have naught to do with such public exhibitions. And we have but to consult the list of the principal demons or elemental spirits to find that their very names indicate their professions, or, to express it clearly, the tricks to which each variety is best adapted. So we have the Madan, a generic name indicating wicked elemental spirits, half brutes, half monsters, for Madan signifies one that looks like a cow. He is the friend of the malicious sorcerers and helps them to effect their evil purposes of revenge by striking men and cattle with sudden illness and death.

The *Shudâla-Mâdan,* or graveyard fiend, answers to our ghouls. He delights where crime and murder were committed, near burial-spots and places of execution. He helps the juggler in all the fire-phenomena as well as Kutti Shâttan, the little juggling imps. Shudâla, they say, is a half-fire, half-water demon, for he received from Siva permission to assume any shape he chose, transform one thing into another; and when he is not in fire, he is in water. It is he who blinds people "to see that which *they do not see.*" Shûla Mâdan, is another mischievous spook. He is the *furnace*-demon, skilled in pottery and baking. If you keep friends with him, he will not injure you; but woe to him who incurs his wrath. Shula likes compliments and flattery, and as he generally keeps underground it is to him that a juggler must look to help him raise a tree from a seed in a quarter of an hour and ripen its fruit.

Kumil-Mâdan, is the *undine* proper. He is an elemental spirit of the water, and his name means *blowing like a bubble.* He is a very merry imp; and will help a friend in anything relative to his department; he will shower rain and show the future and the present to those who will resort to hydromancy or divination by water.

Poruthû Mâdan, is the "wrestling" demon; he is the strongest of all; and whenever there are feats shown in which physical force is required, such as *levitations,* or taming of wild

---

738 Our informant, who was an eye-witness, is Mr. N——ff of St. Petersburg, who was attached to the flag-ship *Almaz,* if we are not mistaken.

animals, he will help the performer by keeping him above the soil or will overpower a wild beast before the tamer has time to utter his incantation. So, every "physical manifestation" has its own class of elemental spirits to superintend them.

Returning now to levitations of human bodies and inanimate bodies, in modern circle-rooms, we must refer the reader to the Introductory chapter of this work. (See "Æthrobasy.") In connection with the story of Simon the Magician, we have shown the explanation of the ancients as to how the levitation and transport of heavy bodies could be produced. We will now try and suggest a hypothesis for the same in relation to *mediums, i.e.,* persons supposed to be unconscious at the moment of the phenomena, which the believers claim to be produced by disembodied "spirits." We need not repeat that which has been sufficiently explained before. Conscious æthrobasy under magneto-electrical conditions is possible only to *adepts* who can never be overpowered by an influence foreign to themselves, but remain sole masters of their WILL.

Thus levitation, we will say, must always occur in obedience to law — a law as inexorable as that which makes a body unaffected by it remain upon the ground. And where should we seek for that law outside of the theory of molecular attraction? It is a scientific hypothesis that the form of force which first brings nebulous or star matter together into a whirling vortex is electricity; and modern chemistry is being totally reconstructed upon the theory of electric polarities of atoms. The waterspout, the tornado, the whirlwind, the cyclone, and the hurricane, are all doubtless the result of electrical action. This phenomenon has been studied from above as well as from below, observations having been made both upon the ground and from a balloon floating above the vortex of a thunder-storm.

PHILOSOPHY OF LEVITATION

Observe now, that this force, under the conditions of a dry and warm atmosphere at the earth's surface, can accumulate a dynamic energy capable of lifting enormous bodies of water, of compressing the particles of atmosphere, and of sweeping across a country, tearing up forests, lifting rocks, and scattering buildings in fragments over the ground. Wild's electric machine causes induced currents of magneto-electricity so enormously powerful as to produce light by which small print may be read, on a dark night, at a distance of two miles from the place where it is operating.

As long ago as the year 1600, Gilbert, in his *De Magnete*, enunciated the principle that the globe itself is one vast magnet, and some of our advanced electricians are now beginning to realize that man, too, possesses this property, and that the mutual attractions and repulsions of individuals toward each other may at least in part find their explanation in this fact. The experience of attendants upon spiritualistic circles corroborates this opinion. Says Professor Nicholas Wagner, of the University of St. Petersburg: "Heat, or *perhaps the electricity of the investigators* sitting in the circle, must concentrate itself in the table and gradually develop into motions. At the same time, or a little afterward, the psychical force unites to assist the two other powers. By *psychical force*, I mean that which evolves itself out of all the other forces of our organism. The combination into one general something of several separate forces, and capable, when combined, of manifesting itself in degree, according to the individuality." The progress of the phenomena he considers to be affected by the cold or the dryness of the atmosphere. Now, remembering what has been said as to the subtler forms of energy which the Hermetists have proved to exist in nature, and accepting the hypothesis enunciated by Mr. Wagner that "the power which calls out these manifestations is centred in the mediums," may not the medium, by furnishing in himself a nucleus as perfect in its way as the system of permanent steel magnets in Wild's battery, produce astral currents sufficiently strong to lift in their vortex a body even as ponderable as a human form? It is not necessary that the object lifted should assume a gyratory motion, for the phenomenon we are observing, unlike the whirlwind, is directed by an intelligence, which is capable of keeping the body to be raised within the ascending current and preventing its rotation.

Levitation in this case would be a purely mechanical phenomenon. The inert body of the passive medium is lifted by a vortex created either by the elemental spirits — possibly, in some cases, by human ones, and sometimes through purely morbific causes, as in the cases of Professor Perty's sick somnambules. The levitation of the adept is, on the contrary, a magneto-electric effect, as we have just stated. He has made the polarity of his body opposite to that of the atmosphere, and identical with that of the earth; hence, attractable by the former, retaining his consciousness the while. A like phenomenal levitation is possible, also, when disease has changed the corporeal polarity of a patient, as disease always does in a greater or lesser degree. But, in such case, the lifted person would not be likely to remain conscious.

In one series of observations upon whirlwinds, made in 1859, in the basin of the Rocky Mountains, "a newspaper was caught up . . . to a height of some two hundred feet; and there it oscillated to and fro across the track for some considerable time, whilst accompanying the onward motion."[739] Of course scientists will say that a parallel cannot be instituted between this case and that of human levitation; that no vortex can be formed in a room by which a medium could be raised; but this is a question of astral light and spirit, which have their own peculiar dynamical laws. Those who understand the latter, affirm that a concourse of people laboring under mental excitement, which reacts upon the physical system, throw off electromagnetic emanations, which, when sufficiently intense, can throw the whole circumambient atmosphere into perturbation. Force enough may actually be generated to create an electrical vortex, sufficiently powerful to produce many a strange phenomenon. With this hint, the whirling of the dervishes, and the wild dances, swayings, gesticulations, music, and shouts of devotees will be understood as all having a common object in view — namely, the creation of such astral conditions as favor psychological and physical phenomena. The *rationale* of religious revivals will also be better understood if this principle is borne in mind.

But there is still another point to be considered. If the medium is a nucleus of magnetism and a conductor of that force, he would be subject to the same laws as a metallic conductor, and be attracted to his magnet. If, therefore, a magnetic centre of the requisite power was formed directly over him by the unseen powers presiding over the manifestations, why should not his body be lifted toward it, despite terrestrial gravity? We know that, in the case

---

739 "What forces were in operation to cause this oscillation of the newspaper?" asks J. W. Phelps, who quotes the case — "These were the rapid upward motion of heated air, the downward motion of cold air, the translatory motion of the surface breeze, and the circular motion of the whirlwind. But how could these combine so as to produce the oscillation?" (Lecture on "*Force Electrically Explained*.")

of a medium who is unconscious of the progress of the operation, it is necessary to first admit the fact of such an intelligence, and next, the possibility of the experiment being conducted as described; but, in view of the multifarious evidences offered, not only in our own researches, which claim no authority, but also in those of Mr. Crookes, and a great number of others, in many lands and at different epochs, we shall not turn aside from the main object of offering this hypothesis in the profitless endeavor to strengthen a case which scientific men will not consider with patience, even when sanctioned by the most distinguished of their own body.

As early as 1836, the public was apprised of certain phenomena which were as extraordinary, if not more so than all the manifestations which are produced in our days. The famous correspondence between two well-known mesmerizers, Deleuze and Billot, was published in France, and the wonders discussed for a time in every society. Billot firmly believed in the apparition of spirits, for, as he says, he has both seen, heard, and felt them. Deleuze was as much convinced of this truth as Billot, and declared that man's immortality and the return of the dead, or rather of their shadows, was the best demonstrated fact in his opinion. Material objects were brought to him from distant places by invisible hands, and he communicated on most important subjects with the invisible intelligences. "In regard to this," he remarks, "I cannot conceive how spiritual beings are able to carry material objects." More skeptical, less intuitional than Billot, nevertheless, he agreed with the latter that "the question of spiritualism is not one of opinions, but *of facts*."

Such is precisely the conclusion to which Professor Wagner, of St. Petersburg, was finally driven. In the second pamphlet on *Mediumistic Phenomena*, issued by him in December, 1875, he administers the following rebuke to Mr. Shkliarevsky, one of his materialistic critics: "So long as the spiritual manifestations were weak and sporadic, we men of science could afford to deceive ourselves with theories of unconscious muscular action, or unconscious cerebrations of our brains, and tumble the rest into one heap as juggleries. . . . But now these wonders have grown too striking; the spirits show themselves in the shape of tangible, materialized forms, which can be touched and handled at will by any learned skeptic like yourself, and even be weighed and measured. We can struggle no longer, for every resistance becomes absurd — it threatens lunacy. Try then to realize this, and to humble yourself before the possibility of impossible facts."

Iron is only magnetized temporarily, but steel permanently, by contact with the lodestone. Now steel is but iron which has passed through a carbonizing process, and yet that process has quite changed the nature of the metal, so far as its relations to the lodestone are concerned. In like manner, it may be said that the medium is but an ordinary person who is magnetized by influx from the astral light; and as the permanence of the magnetic property in the metal is measured by its more or less steel-like character, so may we not say that the intensity and permanency of mediumistic power is in proportion to the saturation of the medium with the magnetic or astral force?

This condition of saturation may be congenital, or brought about in anyone of these ways: — by the mesmeric process; by spirit-agency; or by self-will. Moreover, the condition seems heritable, like any other physical or mental peculiarity; many, and we may even say most great mediums having had mediumship exhibited in some form by one or more progenitors. Mesmeric subjects easily pass into the higher forms of clairvoyance and mediumship (now so called), as Gregory, Deleuze, Puysegur, Du Potet, and other authorities inform us. As to the process of self-saturation, we have only to turn to the account of the priestly devotees of Japan, Siam, China, India, Thibet, and Egypt, as well as of European countries, to be satisfied of its reality. Long persistence in a fixed determination to subjugate matter, brings about a condition in which not only is one insensible to external impressions, but even death itself may be simulated, as we have already seen. The ecstatic so enormously reinforces his will-power, as to draw into himself, as into a vortex, the potencies resident in the astral light to supplement his own natural store.

The phenomena of mesmerism are explicable upon no other hypothesis than the projection of a current of force from the operator into the subject. If a man can project this force by an exercise of the will, what prevents his attracting it toward himself by reversing the current? Unless, indeed, it be urged that the force is generated within his body and cannot be attracted from any supply without. But even under such an hypothesis, if he can generate a superabundant supply to saturate another person, or even an inanimate object by his will, why cannot he generate it in excess for self-saturation?

In his work on *Anthropology*, Professor J. R. Buchanan notes the tendency of the natural gestures to follow the direction of the phrenological organs; the attitude of combativeness being downward and backward; that of hope and spirituality upward and forward; that of firmness upward and backward; and so on. The adepts of Hermetic science know this principle so well that they explain the levitation of their own bodies, whenever it happens unawares, by saying that the thought is so intently fixed upon a point above them, that when the body is thoroughly imbued with the astral influence, it follows the mental aspiration and rises into the air as easily as a cork held beneath the water rises to the surface when its buoyancy is allowed to assert itself. The giddiness felt by certain persons when standing upon the brink of a chasm is explained upon the same principle. Young children, who have little or no active imagination, and in whom experience has not had sufficient time to develop fear, are seldom, if ever, giddy; but the adult of a certain mental temperament, seeing the chasm and picturing in his imaginative fancy the consequences of a fall, allows himself to be drawn by the attraction of the earth, and *unless the spell of fascination* be broken, his body will follow his thought to the foot of the precipice.

That this giddiness is purely a temperamental affair, is shown in the fact that some persons never experience the sensation, and inquiry will probably reveal the fact that such are deficient in the imaginative faculty. We have a case in view — a gentleman who, in 1858, had so firm a nerve that he horrified the witnesses by standing upon the coping of the *Arc de Triomphe,* in Paris, with folded arms, and his feet half over the edge; but, having since become short-sighted, was taken with a panic upon attempting to cross a plank-walk over the courtyard of a hotel, where the footway was more than two feet and a half wide, and there was no danger. He looked at the flagging below, gave his fancy free play, and would have fallen had he not quickly sat down.

It is a dogma of science that perpetual motion is impossible; it is another dogma, that the allegation that the Hermetists discovered the elixir of life, and that certain of them, by partaking of it, prolonged their existence far beyond the usual term, is a superstitious absurdity. And the claim that the baser metals have been transmuted into gold, and that the universal solvent was discovered, excites only contemptuous derision in a century which has crowned the edifice of philosophy with a cope-stone of protoplasm. The first is declared a *physical impossibility*; as much so, according to Babinet, the astronomer, as the "levitation of an object without contact";[740] the second, a physiological vagary begotten of a disordered mind; the third, a chemical absurdity.

Balfour Stewart says that while the man of science cannot assert that "he is intimately acquainted with all the forces of nature, and cannot prove that perpetual motion is impossible; for, in truth, he knows very little of these forces . . . he does think *that he has entered into the spirit and design of nature*, and therefore he denies at once the possibility of such a machine."[741] If he has discovered the design of nature, he certainly has not *the spirit*, for he denies its existence in one sense; and denying spirit he prevents that perfect understanding of universal law which would redeem modern philosophy from its thousand mortifying dilemmas and mistakes. If Professor B. Stewart's negation is founded upon no better analogy than that of his French contemporary, Babinet, he is in danger of a like humiliating catastrophe. The universe itself illustrates the actuality of perpetual motion; and the atomic theory, which has proved such a balm to the exhausted minds of our cosmic explorers, is based upon it. The telescope searching through space, and the microscope probing the mysteries of the little world in a drop of water, reveal the same law in operation; and, as everything below is like everything above, who would presume to say that when the conservation of energy is better understood, and the two additional forces of the kabalists are added to the catalogue of orthodox science, it may not be discovered how to construct a machine which shall run without friction and supply itself with energy in proportion to its wastes? "Fifty years ago," says the venerable Mr. de Lara, "a Hamburg paper, quoting from an English one an account of the opening of the Manchester and Liverpool Railway, pronounced it a gross fabrication; capping the climax by saying, 'even so far extends the credulity of the English' "; the moral is apparent. The recent discovery of the compound called METALLINE, by an American chemist, makes it appear probable that friction can, in a large degree, be overcome. One thing is certain, when a man shall have discovered the perpetual motion he will be able to understand by analogy all the secrets of nature; progress in direct ratio with resistance.

We may say the same of the elixir of life, by which is understood physical life, the soul being of course deathless only by reason of its divine immortal union with spirit. But *continual* or *perpetual* does not mean endless. The kabalists have never claimed that either an endless physical life or unending motion is possible. The Hermetic axiom maintains that only the First Cause and its direct emanations, our spirits (scintillas from the eternal central sun which will be reabsorbed by it at the end of time) are incorruptible and eternal. But, in possession of a knowledge of occult natural forces, yet undiscovered by the materialists, they asserted that both physical life and mechanical motion could be prolonged indefinitely. The philosophers' stone had more than one meaning attached to its mysterious origin. Says Professor Wilder: "The study of alchemy was even more universal than the several writers upon it appear to have known, and was always the auxiliary of, if not identical with, the occult sciences of magic, necromancy, and astrology; probably from the same fact that they

---

740 "*Revue des Deux Mondes*," p. 414, 1858.
741 "*Conservation of Energy*," p. 140.

were originally but forms of a spiritualism which was generally extant in all ages of human history."

Our greatest wonder is, that the very men who view the human body simply as a "digesting machine," should object to the idea that if some equivalent for metalline could be applied between its molecules, it should run without friction. Man's body is taken from the earth, or dust, according to *Genesis;* which allegory bars the claims of modern analysts to original discovery of the nature of the inorganic constituents of human body. If the author of *Genesis* knew this, and Aristotle taught the identity between the life-principle of plants, animals, and men, our affiliation with mother earth seems to have been settled long ago.

THE ELIXIR AND ALKAHEST

Elie de Beaumont has recently reasserted the old doctrine of Hermes that there is a terrestrial circulation comparable to that of the blood of man. Now, since it is a doctrine as old as time, that nature is continually renewing her wasted energies by absorption from the source of energy, why should the child differ from the parent? Why may not man, by discovering the source and nature of this recuperative energy, extract from the earth herself the juice or quintessence with which to replenish his own forces? This *may* have been the great secret of the alchemists. Stop the circulation of the terrestrial fluids and we have stagnation, putrefaction, death; stop the circulation of the fluids in man, and stagnation, absorption, calcification from old age, and death ensue. If the alchemists had simply discovered some chemical compound capable of keeping the channels of our circulation unclogged, would not all the rest easily follow? And why, we ask, if the surface-waters of certain mineral springs have such virtue in the cure of disease and the restoration of physical vigor, is it illogical to say that if we could get the first runnings from the alembic of nature in the bowels of the earth, we might, perhaps, find that the fountain of youth was no myth after all. Jennings asserts that the elixir was produced out of the secret chemical laboratories of nature by some adepts; and Robert Boyle, the chemist, mentions a medicated wine or cordial which Dr. Lefevre tried with wonderful effect upon an old woman.

Alchemy is as old as tradition itself. "The first authentic record on this subject," says William Godwin, "is an edict of Diocletian, about 300 years after Christ, ordering a diligent search to be made in Egypt for all the ancient books which treated of the art of making gold and silver, that they might be consigned to the flames. This edict necessarily presumes a certain antiquity to the pursuit; and *fabulous* history has recorded Solomon, Pythagoras, and Hermes among its distinguished votaries."

And this question of transmutation — this alkahest or universal solvent, which comes next after the elixir vitæ in the order of the three alchemical agents? Is the idea so absurd as to be totally unworthy of consideration in this age of chemical discovery? How shall we dispose of the historical anecdotes of men who actually made gold and gave it away, and of those who testify to having seen them do it? Libavius, Geberus, Arnoldus, Thomas Aquinas, Bernardus Comes, Joannes, Penotus, Quercetanus Geber, the Arabian father of European alchemy, Eugenius Philalethes, Baptista Porta, Rubeus, Dornesius, Vogelius, Irenæus Philaletha Cosmopolita, and many mediæval alchemists and Hermetic philosophers assert the fact. Must we believe them all visionaries and lunatics, these otherwise great and learned scholars? Francesco Picus, in his work *De Auro,* gives eighteen instances of gold being produced in his presence by artificial means; and Thomas Vaughan,[742] going to a goldsmith to sell 1,200 marks worth of gold, when the man suspiciously remarked that the gold was too pure to have ever come out of a mine, ran away, leaving the money behind him. In a preceding chapter we have brought forward the testimony of a number of authors to this effect.

Marco Polo tells us that in some mountains of Thibet, which he calls *Chingintalas,* there are veins of the substance from which *Salamander* is made: "For the real truth is, that the salamander is no beast, as they allege in our parts of the world, but is a substance found in the earth."[743] Then he adds that a Turk of the name of Zurficar, told him that he had been procuring salamanders for the Great Khan, in those regions, for the space of three years. "He said that the way they got them was by digging in that mountain till they found a certain vein. The substance of this vein was then taken and crushed, and, when so treated, it divides, as it were, into fibres of wool, which they set forth to dry. When dry, these fibres were pounded and washed, so as to leave only the fibres, like fibres of wool. These were then spun. . . . When first made, these napkins are not very white, but, by putting them into the fire for a while, they come out as white as snow."

Therefore, as several authorities testify, this mineral substance is the famous *Asbestos,*[744] which the Rev. A. Williamson says is found in Shantung. But, it is not only incombustible thread which is made from it. An oil, having several most extraordinary properties, is extracted from it, and the secret of its virtues remains with certain lamas and Hindu adepts. When rubbed into the body, it leaves no external stain or mark, but, nevertheless, after having been so rubbed, the part can be scrubbed with soap and hot or cold water, without the virtue of the ointment being affected in the least. The person so rubbed may boldly step into the hottest fire; unless suffocated, he will remain uninjured. Another property of the oil is that, when combined with *another substance,* that we are not at liberty to name, and left stagnant under the rays of the moon, on certain nights indicated by native astrologers, it will breed strange creatures. Infusoria we may call them in one sense, but then these grow and develop. Speaking of Kashmere, Marco Polo observes that they have an astonishing acquaintance with the *devilries* of enchantment, insomuch that they *make their idols to speak.*

To this day, the greatest magian mystics of these regions may be found in Kashmere. The various religious sects of this country were always credited with preternatural powers, and were the resort of adepts and sages. As Colonel Yule remarks, "Vambery tells us that even in our day, the Kasmiri dervishes are preëminent among their Mahometan brethren for *cunning,* secret arts, skill in exorcisms and magic."[745]

But, all modern chemists are not equally dogmatic in their negation of the possibility of such a transmutation. Dr. Peisse, Desprez, and even the all-denying Louis Figuier, of Paris, seem to be far from rejecting the idea. Dr. Wilder says: "The possibility of reducing the elements to their primal form, as they are supposed to have existed in the igneous mass from which the earth-crust is believed to have been formed, is not considered by physicists

---

742 Eugenius Philalethes.
743 "*Book of Ser Marco Polo,*" vol. i., p. 215.
744 See Sage's "*Dictionnaire des Tissus,*" vol. ii., pp. 1-12.
745 "*Book of Ser Marco Polo,*" vol. i., p. 230.

to be so absurd an idea as has been intimated. There is a relationship between metals, often so close as to indicate an original identity. Persons called alchemists may, therefore, have devoted their energies to investigations into these matters, as Lavoisier, Davy, Faraday, and others of our day have explained the mysteries of chemistry."[746] A learned Theosophist, a practicing physician of this country, one who has studied the occult sciences and alchemy for over thirty years, has succeeded in reducing the elements to their primal form, and made what is termed "the pre-Adamite earth." It appears in the form of an earthy precipitate from pure water, which, on being disturbed, presents the most opalescent and vivid colors.

"The secret," say the alchemists, as if enjoying the ignorance of the uninitiated, "is an amalgamation of the salt, sulphur, and mercury combined three times in Azoth, by a triple sublimation and a triple fixation."

"How ridiculously absurd!" will exclaim a learned modern chemist. Well, the disciples of the great Hermes understand the above as well as a graduate of Harvard University comprehends the meaning of his Professor of Chemistry, when the latter says: "With one hydroxyl group we can only produce monatomic compounds; use two hydroxyl groups, and we can form around the same skeleton a number of diatomic compounds.

. . . Attach to the nucleus three hydroxyl groups, and there result triatomic compounds, among which is a very familiar substance — *Glycerine*."

$$\begin{array}{ccccccc} & & H & H & H & & \\ & & | & | & | & & \\ H\!-\!O\!-\!C\!-\!C\!-\!C\!-\!O\!-\!H \\ & & | & | & | & & \\ & & H & H & H & & \\ & & & | & & & \\ & & & H & & & \end{array}$$

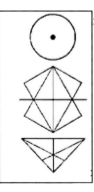

"Attach thyself," says the alchemist, "to the four letters of the tetragram disposed in the following manner: The letters of the ineffable name are there, although thou mayest not discern them at first. The incommunicable axiom is kabalistically contained therein, and this is what is called the magic arcanum by the masters." The arcanum — the fourth emanation of the Akâsa, the principle of LIFE, which is represented in its third transmutation by the fiery sun, the eye of the world, or of Osiris, as the Egyptians termed it. An eye tenderly watching its youngest daughter, wife, and sister — Isis, our mother earth. See what Hermes, the thrice-great master, says of her: "Her father is the sun, her mother is the moon." It attracts and caresses, and then repulses her by a projectile power. It is for the Hermetic student to watch its motions, to catch its subtile currents, to guide and direct them with the help of the *athanor*, the Archimedean lever of the alchemist. What is this mysterious athanor? Can the physicist tell us — he who sees and examines it daily? Aye, he sees; but does he comprehend the secret-ciphered characters traced by the divine finger on every sea-shell in the ocean's deep; on every leaf that trembles

746 "*Alchemy, or the Hermetic Philosophy*," p. 25.

in the breeze; in the bright star, whose stellar lines are in his sight but so many more or less luminous lines of hydrogen? "God *geometrizes*," said Plato.[747] "The laws of nature are the thoughts of God"; exclaimed Oërsted, 2,000 years later. "His thoughts are immutable," repeated the solitary student of Hermetic lore, "therefore it is in the perfect harmony and equilibrium of all things that we must seek the truth." And thus, proceeding from the indivisible unity, he found emanating from it two contrary forces, each acting through the other and producing equilibrium, and the three were but one, the Pythagorean Eternal Monad. The primordial point is a circle; the circle squaring itself from the four cardinal points becomes a quaternary, the perfect square, having at each of its four angles a letter of the mirific name, the sacred TETRAGRAM. It is the four Buddhas who came and have passed away; the Pythagorean *tetractys* — absorbed and resolved by the one eternal NO-BEING. Tradition declares that on the dead body of Hermes, at Hebron, was found by an Isarim, an initiate, the tablet known as the *Smaragdine*. It contains, in a few sentences, the essence of the Hermetic wisdom. To those who read but with their bodily eyes, the precepts will suggest nothing new or extraordinary, for it merely begins by saying that it speaks not fictitious things, but that which is true and most certain. "What is below is like that which is above, and what is above is similar to that which is below to accomplish the wonders of one thing. "As all things were produced by the mediation of one being, so all things were produced from this one *by adaptation*. "Its father is the sun, its mother is the moon. "It is the cause of all perfection throughout the whole earth. "Its power is perfect *if it is changed into earth.*

"Separate the earth from the fire, the subtile from the gross, acting prudently and with judgment. "Ascend with the greatest sagacity from the earth to heaven, and then descend again to earth, and unite together the power of things inferior and superior; thus you will possess the light of the whole world, and all obscurity will fly away from you.

"This thing has more fortitude than fortitude itself, because *it will overcome every subtile thing* and *penetrate every solid thing.*

"By it the world was formed." This mysterious thing is the universal, magical agent, the astral light, which in the correlations of its forces furnishes the alkahest, the philosopher's stone, and the elixir of life. Hermetic philosophy names it Azoth, the soul of the world, the celestial virgin, the great Magnes, etc., etc. Physical science knows it as "heat, light, electricity, and magnetism"; but ignoring its spiritual properties and the occult potency contained in ether, rejects everything it ignores. It explains and depicts the crystalline forms of the snow-flakes, their modifications of an hexagonal prism which shoot out an infinity of delicate needles. It has studied them so perfectly that it has even calculated, with the most wondrous mathematical precision, that all these needles diverge from each other at an angle of 60°. Can it tell us as well the cause of this "endless variety of the most exquisite forms,"[748]

---

747 See Plutarch, "*Symposiacs*," viii. 2. "Diogenianas began and said: 'Let us admit Plato to the conference and inquire upon what account he says — supposing it to be his sentence — that *God always plays the geometer*.' I said: 'This sentence was not plainly set down in any of his books; yet there are good arguments that it is his, and it is very much like his expression.' Tyndares presently subjoined: 'He praises geometry as a science that takes off men from sensible objects, and makes them apply themselves to the intelligible and Eternal Nature — the contemplation of which is the end of philosophy, as a view of the mysteries of initiation into holy rites.' "
748 Prof. Ed. L. Youmans, "*Descriptive Chemistry*."

each of which is a most perfect geometrical figure in itself? These frozen, starlike and flower-like blossoms, may be, for all materialistic science knows, a shower of messages snowed by spiritual hands from the worlds above for spiritual eyes below to read.

The philosophical cross, the two lines running in opposite directions, the horizontal and the perpendicular, the height and breadth, which the geometrizing Deity divides at the intersecting point, and which forms the magical as well as the scientific quaternary, when it is inscribed within the perfect square, is the basis of the occultist. Within its mystical precinct lies the master-key which opens the door of every science, physical as well as spiritual. It symbolizes our human existence, for the circle of life circumscribes the four points of the cross, which represent in succession birth, life, death, and IMMORTALITY. Everything in this world is a trinity completed by the quaternary,[749] and every element is divisible on this same principle. Physiology can divide man *ad infinitum,* as physical science has divided the four primal and principal elements in several dozens of others; she will not succeed in changing either. Birth, life, and death will ever be a trinity completed only at the cyclic end. Even were science to change the longed-for immortality into annihilation, it still will ever be a quaternary; for God "geometrizes!"

Therefore, perhaps alchemy will one day be allowed to talk of her salt, mercury, sulphur, and azoth, her symbols and mirific letters, and repeat, with the exponent of the *Synthesis of Organic Compounds,* that "it must be remembered that the grouping is *no play of fancy,* and that a good reason can be given for the position of every letter."[750]

Dr. Peisse, of Paris, wrote in 1863, the following:

"One word, *a propos,* of alchemy. What must we think of the Hermetic art? Is it lawful to believe that we can transmute metals, make gold? Well, positive men, *esprits forts* of the nineteenth century, know that Mr. Figuier, doctor of science and medicine, chemical analyst in the School of Pharmacy, of Paris, does not wish to express himself upon the subject. He doubts, he hesitates. He knows several alchemists (for there are such) who, basing themselves upon modern chemical discoveries, and especially on the singular circumstance of the equivalents demonstrated by M. Dumas, pretend that metals are not simple bodies, true elements in the absolute sense, and that in consequence they may be produced by the process of decomposition. . . . This encourages me to take a step further, and candidly avow that I would be only moderately surprised to see some one make gold. I have only one reason to give, but sufficient it seems; which is, that gold has not always existed; it has been made by some chemical travail or other in the bosom of the fused matter of our globe;[751] perhaps some of it may be even now in process of formation.

The pretended simple bodies of our chemistry are very probably secondary products, in the formation of the terrestrial mass. It has been proved so with water, one of the most respectable elements of ancient physics. To-day, we create water. Why should we not make gold? An eminent experimentalist, Mr. Desprez, has made the diamond. True, this diamond is only *a scientific diamond,* a philosophical diamond, which would be worth nothing; but, no matter, my position holds good. Besides, we are not left to simple conjectures. There is a

749 In ancient nations the Deity was a trine supplemented by a goddess — the *arba-il,* or fourfold God.
750 Josiah Cooke, *"The New Chemistry."*
751 Prof. Sterry Hunt's theory of metalliferous deposits contradicts this; but is it right?

man living, who, in a paper addressed to the scientific bodies, in 1853, has underscored these words — I have discovered the method of producing artificial gold, I have made gold. This adept is Mr. Theodore Tiffereau, ex-preparator of chemistry in the *École Professionelle et Superieure* of Nantes."[752] Cardinal de Rohan, the famous victim of the diamond necklace conspiracy, testified that he had seen the Count Cagliostro make both gold and diamonds. We presume that those who agree with Professor T. Sterry Hunt, F.R.S., will have no patience with the theory of Dr. Peisse, for they believe that all of our metalliferous deposits are due to the action of organic life. And so, until they do come to some composition of their differences, so as to let us know for a certainty the nature of gold, and whether it is the product of interior volcanic alchemy or surface segregation and filtration, we will leave them to settle their quarrel between themselves, and give credit meanwhile to the old philosophers.

Professor Balfour Stewart, whom no one would think of classing among illiberal minds; who, with far more fairness and more frequently than any of his colleagues admits the failings of modern science, shows himself, nevertheless, as biassed as other scientists on this question. Perpetual light being only another name for perpetual motion, he tells us, and the latter being impossible because we have no means of equilibrating the waste of combustible material, a Hermetic light is, therefore, an impossibility.[753] Noting the fact that a "perpetual light was supposed to result from *magical* powers," and remarking further that such a light is "certainly not of this earth, where light and all other forms of superior energy are essentially evanescent," this gentleman argues as though the Hermetic philosophers had always claimed that the flame under discussion was an ordinary earthly flame, resulting from the combustion of luminiferous material. In this the philosophers have been constantly misunderstood and misrepresented.

How many great minds — unbelievers from the start — after having studied the "secret doctrine," have changed their opinions and found out how mistaken they were. And how contradictory it seems to find one moment Balfour Stewart quoting some philosophical morals of Bacon — whom he terms the father of experimental science — and saying " . . . surely we ought to learn a lesson from these remarks . . . and be very cautious *before we dismiss any branch of knowledge* or train of thought as essentially unprofitable," and then dismissing the next moment, as *utterly impossible,* the claims of the alchemists! He shows Aristotle as "entertaining the idea that light is not any body, or the emanation of any body, and that therefore light is an energy or act"; and yet, although the ancients were the first to show, through Demokritus, to John Dalton the doctrine of atoms, and through Pythagoras and even the oldest of the Chaldean oracles, that of ether as a universal agent, their ideas, says Stewart, "were not prolific." He admits that they "possessed great genius and intellectual power," but adds that "they were deficient in physical conceptions, and, in consequence, their ideas were not prolific."[754]

The whole of the present work is a protest against such a loose way of judging the ancients. To be thoroughly competent to criticise their ideas, and assure one's self whether

---

752 Peisse, "*La Medecine et les Medecins,*" vol. i., pp. 59, 283.
753 "*The Conservation of Energy.*"
754 Ibid., p. 136.

their ideas were distinct and "appropriate to the facts," one must have sifted these ideas to the very bottom. It is idle to repeat that which we have frequently said, and that which every scholar ought to know; namely, that the quintessence of their knowledge was in the hands of the priests, who never wrote them, and in those of the "initiates" who, like Plato, *did not dare* write them.

Therefore, those few speculations on the material and spiritual universes, which they did put in writing, could not enable posterity to judge them rightly, even had not the early Christian Vandals, the later crusaders, and the fanatics of the middle ages destroyed three parts of that which remained of the Alexandrian library and its later schools. Professor Draper shows that the Cardinal Ximenes alone "delivered to the flames in the squares of Granada, 80,000 Arabic manuscripts, many of them translations of classical authors." In the Vatican libraries, whole passages in the most rare and precious treatises of the ancients were found erased and blotted out, for the sake of interlining them with absurd psalmodies!

Who then, of those who turn away from the "secret doctrine" as being "unphilosophical" and, therefore, unworthy of a scientific thought, has a right to say that he studied the ancients; that he is aware of all that they knew, and knowing now far more, knows also that they knew little, if anything. This "secret doctrine" contains the alpha and the omega of universal science; therein lies the corner and the keystone of all the ancient and modern knowledge; and alone in this "unphilosophical" doctrine remains buried the *absolute* in the philosophy of the dark problems of life and death.

"The great energies of Nature are known to us only by their effects," said Paley. Paraphrasing the sentence, we will say that the great achievements of the days of old are known to posterity only by their effects. If one takes a book on alchemy, and sees in it the speculations on gold and light by the brothers of the Rosie Cross, he will find himself certainly startled, for the simple reason that he will not understand them at all. "The Hermetic gold," he may read, "is the outflow of the sunbeam, or of light suffused invisibly and magically into the body of the world. Light is sublimated gold, rescued magically by invisible stellar attraction, out of material depths. Gold is thus the deposit of light, which of itself generates. Light in the celestial world is subtile, vaporous, magically exalted gold, or '*spirit of flame.*' Gold draws inferior natures in the metals, and intensifying and multiplying, converts into itself."[755]

Nevertheless, facts are facts; and, as Billot says of spiritualism, we will remark of occultism generally and of alchemy in particular — it is not a matter of opinion but of *facts,* men of science call an inextinguishable lamp an *impossibility,* but nevertheless persons in our own age as well as in the days of ignorance and superstition have found them burning bright in old vaults shut up for centuries; and other persons there are who possess the secret of keeping such fires for several ages. Men of science say that ancient and modern spiritualism, magic, and mesmerism, are charlatanry or delusion; but there are 800 millions on the face of the globe, of perfectly sane men and women, who believe in all these. Whom are we to credit?

---

755 Extracts from Robertus di Fluctibus in "*The Rosicrucians.*"

"Demokritus," says Lucian,[756] "believed in no (miracles) . . . he applied himself to discover the method by which the theurgists could produce them; in a word, his philosophy brought him to the conclusion that magic was entirely confined to the application and *the imitation* of the laws and the works of nature."

Now, the opinion of the "laughing philosopher" is of the greatest importance to us, since the Magi left by Xerxes, at Abdera, were his instructors, and he had studied magic, moreover, for a considerably long time with the Egyptian priests.[757] For nearly ninety years of the one hundred and nine of his life, this great philosopher had made experiments, and noted them down in a book, which, according to Petronius,[758] *treated of nature* — facts that he had verified himself. And we find him not only disbelieving in and utterly rejecting *miracles*, but asserting that every one of those that were authenticated by eye-witnesses, had, and could have taken place; for all, even the most *incredible*, was produced according to the "*hidden laws of nature*."[759]

"The day will never come, when any one of the propositions of Euclid will be denied,"[760] says Professor Draper, exalting the Aristoteleans at the expense of the Pythagoreans and Platonists. Shall we, in such a case, disbelieve a number of well-informed authorities (Lempriere among others), who assert that the fifteen books of the *Elements* are not to be wholly attributed to Euclid; and that many of the most valuable truths and demonstrations contained in them owe their existence to Pythagoras, Thales, and Eudoxus? That Euclid, notwithstanding his genius, was *the first* who reduced them to order, and only interwove theories of his own to render the whole a complete and connected system of geometry? And if these authorities are right, then it is again to that central sun of metaphysical science — Pythagoras and his school, that the moderns are indebted directly for such men as Eratosthenes, the world-famous geometer and cosmographer, Archimedes, and even Ptolemy, notwithstanding his obstinate errors. Were it not for the exact science of such men, and for fragments of their works that they left us to base Galilean speculations upon, the great priests of the nineteenth century might find themselves, perhaps, still in the bondage of the Church; and philosophizing, in 1876, on the Augustine and Bedean cosmogony, the rotation of the canopy of heaven round the earth, and the majestic flatness of the latter.

The nineteenth century seems positively doomed to humiliating confessions. Feltre (Italy) erects a public statue "to *Panfilo Castaldi, the illustrious inventor of movable printing types*," and adds in its inscription the generous confession that Italy renders to him "*this tribute of honor too long deferred*." But no sooner is the statue placed, than the Feltreians are advised by Colonel Yule to "burn it *in honest lime*." He proves that many a traveller besides Marco Polo had brought home from China movable wooden types and specimens of Chinese books, the entire text of which was printed with such wooden blocks.[761] We have seen in several Thibetan lamaseries, where they have printing-offices, such blocks preserved

---

756 "*Philopseud.*"
757 Diog. Laert. in "*Demokrit. Vitæ.*"
758 "*Satyric. Vitrus D. Architect,*" lib. ix., cap. iii.
759 Pliny, "*Hist. Nat.*"
760 "*Conflict between Religion and Science.*"
761 "*Book of Ser Marco Polo,*" vol. i., pp. 133-135.

as curiosities. They are known to be of the greatest antiquity, inasmuch as types were perfected, and the old ones abandoned contemporaneously with the earliest records of Buddhistic lamaism. Therefore, they must have existed in China before the Christian era.

Let every one ponder over the wise words of Professor Roscoe, in his lecture on *Spectrum Analysis*. "The infant truths must be made useful. Neither you nor I, perhaps, can see the *how* or the *when*, but that the time may come at any moment, when the most obscure of nature's secrets shall at once be employed for the benefit of mankind, no one who knows anything of science, can for one instant doubt. Who could have foretold that the discovery that a dead frog's legs jump when they are touched by two different metals, should have led in a few short years to the discovery of the electric telegraph?"

Professor Roscoe, visiting Kirchhoff and Bunsen when they were making their great discoveries of the nature of the Fraunhoffer lines, says that it *flashed* upon his mind at once that there is iron in the sun; therein presenting one more evidence to add to a million predecessors, that great discoveries usually come with a *flash*, and not by induction. There are many more flashes in store for us. It may be found, perhaps, that one of the last sparkles of modern science — the beautiful green spectrum of silver — is nothing new, but was, notwithstanding the paucity "and great inferiority of their optical instruments," well known to the ancient chemists and physicists. Silver and green were associated together as far back as the days of Hermes. Luna, or Astarte (the Hermetic silver), is one of the two chief symbols of the Rosicrucians. It is a Hermetic axiom, that "the cause of the splendor and variety of colors lies deep in the affinities of nature; and that there is a singular and mysterious alliance between color and sound." The kabalists place their "middle nature" in direct relation with the moon; and the green ray occupies the centre point between the others, being placed in the middle of the spectrum. The Egyptian priests chanted the *seven* vowels as a hymn addressed to Serapis;[762] and at the sound of the *seventh* vowel, as at the "*seventh* ray" of the rising sun, the statue of Memnon responded. Recent discoveries have proved the wonderful properties of the blue-violet light — the *seventh* ray of the prismatic spectrum, the most powerfully chemical of all, which corresponds with the highest note in the musical scale. The Rosicrucian theory, that the whole universe is a musical instrument, is the Pythagorean doctrine of the music of the spheres. Sounds and colors are all spiritual numerals; as the seven prismatic rays proceed from one spot in heaven, so the seven powers of nature, each of them a number, are the seven radiations of the Unity, the central, spiritual SUN.

"Happy is he who comprehends the spiritual numerals, and perceives their mighty influence!" exclaims Plato. And happy, we may add, is he who, treading the maze of force-correlations, does not neglect to trace them to this invisible Sun!

Future experimenters will reap the honor of demonstrating that musical tones have a wonderful effect upon the growth of vegetation. And with the enunciation of this unscientific fallacy, we will close the chapter, and proceed to remind the patient reader of certain things that the ancients knew, and the moderns *think* they know.

---

762 "*Dionysius of Halicarnassus.*"

CHAPTER XIV

"The transactions of this our city of Saïs, are recorded in our sacred writings during a period of 8,000 years."

PLATO, *Timæus*

"The Egyptians assert that from the reign of Heracles to that of Amasis, 17,000 years elapsed."

HERODOTUS, lib. ii., c. 43

"Can the theologian derive no light from the pure, primeval faith that glimmers from Egyptian hieroglyphics, to illustrate the immortality of the soul? Will not the historian deign to notice the prior origin of every art and science in Egypt, a thousand years before the Pelasgians studded the isles and capes of the Archipelago with their forts and temples?"

GLIDDON

ORIGIN OF THE EGYPTIANS

HOW came Egypt by her knowledge? When broke the dawn of that civilization whose wondrous perfection is suggested by the bits and fragments supplied to us by the archæologists? Alas! the lips of Memnon are silent, and no longer utter oracles; the Sphinx has become a greater riddle in her speechlessness than was the enigma propounded to Œdipus.

What Egypt taught to others she certainly did not acquire by the international exchange of ideas and discoveries with her Semitic neighbors, nor from them did she receive her stimulus. "The more we learn of the Egyptians," observes the writer of a recent article, "the more marvellous they seem!" From whom could she have learned her wondrous arts, the secrets of which died with her? She sent no agents throughout the world to learn what others knew; but to her the wise men of neighboring nations resorted for knowledge. Proudly secluding herself within her enchanted domain, the fair queen of the desert created wonders as if by the sway of a magic staff. "Nothing," remarks the same writer, whom we have elsewhere quoted, "proves that civilization and knowledge then rise and progress with her as in the case of other peoples, but everything seems to be referable, in the same perfection, *to the earliest dates*. That no nation knew as much as herself, is a fact demonstrated by history."

May we not assign as a reason for this remark the fact that until very recently nothing was known of Old India? That these two nations, India and Egypt, were akin? That they were the oldest in the group of nations; and that the Eastern Ethiopians — the mighty builders — had come from India as a matured people, bringing their civilization with them, and colonizing the perhaps unoccupied Egyptian territory? But we defer a more complete elaboration of this theme for our second volume.[763]

---

763 See vol. ii., chap. 8.

"Mechanism," says Eusebe Salverte, "was carried by the ancients to a point of perfection that has never been attained in modern times. We would inquire if their inventions have been surpassed in our age? Certainly not; and at the present day, with all the means that the progress of science and modern discovery have placed in the hands of the mechanic, have we not been assailed by numerous difficulties in striving to place on a pedestal one of those monoliths that the Egyptians forty centuries ago erected in such numbers before their sacred edifices."

As far back as we can glance into history, to the reign of Menes, the most ancient of the kings that we know anything about, we find proofs that the Egyptians were far better acquainted with hydrostatics and hydraulic engineering than ourselves. The gigantic work of turning the course of the Nile — or rather of its three principal branches — and bringing it to Memphis, was accomplished during the reign of that monarch, who appears to us as distant in the abyss of time as a far-glimmering star in the heavenly vault. Says Wilkinson: "Menes took accurately the measure of the power which he had to oppose, and he constructed a dyke whose lofty mounds and enormous embankments turned the water eastward, and since that time the river is contained in its new bed." Herodotus has left us a poetical, but still accurate description of the lake Mœris, so called after the Pharaoh who caused this artificial sheet of water to be formed.

The historian has described this lake as measuring 450 miles in circumference, and 300 feet in depth. It was fed through artificial channels by the Nile, and made to store a portion of the annual overflow for the irrigation of the country, for many miles round. Its numerous floodgates, dams, locks, and convenient engines were constructed with the greatest skill. The Romans, at a far later period, got their notions on hydraulic constructions from the Egyptians, but our latest progress in the science of hydrostatics has demonstrated the fact of a great deficiency on their part in some branches of that knowledge. Thus, for instance, if they were acquainted with that which is called in hydrostatics the great law, they seem to have been less familiar with what our modern engineers know as water-tight joints. Their ignorance is sufficiently proved by their conveying the water through large level aqueducts, instead of doing it at a less expense by iron pipes beneath the surface. But the Egyptians evidently employed a far superior method in their channels and artificial water-works. Notwithstanding this, the modern engineers employed by Lesseps for the Suez Canal, who had learned from the ancient Romans all their art could teach them, deriving, in their turn, their knowledge from Egypt — scoffed at the suggestion that they should seek a remedy for some imperfections in their work by studying the contents of the various Egyptian museums. Nevertheless, the engineers succeeded in giving to the banks of that "long and ugly ditch," as Professor Carpenter calls the Suez Canal, sufficient strength to make it a navigable water-way, instead of a mud-trap for vessels as it was at first.

THEIR MIGHTY ENGINEERING WORKS

The alluvial deposits of the Nile, during the past thirty centuries, have completely altered the area of the Delta, so that it is continually growing seaward, and adding to the territory of the Khedive. In ancient times, the principal mouth of the river was called Pelusian; and the canal cut by one of the kings — the canal of Necho — led from Suez to this branch. After the defeat of Antony and Cleopatra, at Actium, it was proposed that a portion of the fleet should pass through the canal to the Red Sea, which shows the depth of water that those early engineers had secured. Settlers in Colorado and Arizona have recently reclaimed large tracts of barren land by a system of irrigation; receiving from the journals of the day no little praise for their ingenuity. But, for a distance of 500 miles above Cairo, there stretches a strip of land reclaimed from the desert, and made, according to Professor Carpenter, "the most fertile on the face of the earth." He says, "for thousands of years these branch canals have conveyed fresh water from the Nile, to fertilize the land of this long narrow strip, as well as of the Delta." He describes "the net-work of canals over the Delta, which dates from an early period of the Egyptian monarchs."

The French province of Artois has given its name to the Artesian well, as though that form of engineering had been first applied in that district; but, if we consult the Chinese records, we find such wells to have been in common use ages before the Christian era.

If we now turn to architecture, we find displayed before our eyes, wonders which baffle all description. Referring to the temples of Philæ, Abu Simbel, Dendera, Edfu, and Karnak, Professor Carpenter remarks that "these stupendous and beautiful erections . . . these gigantic pyramids and temples" have a "vastness and beauty" which are "still impressive after the lapse of thousands of years." He is amazed at "the admirable character of the workmanship; the stones in most cases being fitted together with astonishing nicety, so that a knife could hardly be thrust between the joints." He noticed in his amateur archæological pilgrimage, another of those "curious coincidences" which his Holiness, the Pope, may feel some interest in learning. He is speaking of the Egyptian *Book of the Dead*, sculptured on the old monuments, and the ancient belief in the immortality of the soul. "Now, it is most remarkable," says the professor, "to see that not only this belief, but the language in which it was expressed in the ancient Egyptian times, anticipated that of the Christian Revelation. For, in this *Book of the Dead*, there are used the very phrases we find in the *New Testament*, in connection with the day of judgment"; and he admits that this hierogram was "engraved, probably, 2,000 years before the time of Christ."

According to Bunsen, who is considered to have made the most exact calculations, the mass of masonry in the great Pyramid of Cheops measures 82,111,000 feet, and would weigh 6,316,000 tons. The immense numbers of squared stones show us the unparalleled skill of the Egyptian quarrymen. Speaking of the great pyramid, Kenrick says: "The joints are scarcely perceptible, not wider than the thickness of silver paper, and the cement is so tenacious, that fragments of the casing-stones still remain in their original position, notwithstanding the lapse of many centuries, and the violence by which they were detached." Who, of our modern architects and chemists, will rediscover the indestructible cement of the oldest Egyptian buildings?

"The skill of the ancients in quarrying," says Bunsen, "is displayed the most in the extracting of the huge blocks, out of which obelisks and colossal statues were hewn — obelisks ninety feet high, and statues forty feet high, made out of one stone!" There are many such. They did not blast out the blocks for these monuments, but adopted the following scientific method: Instead of using huge iron wedges, which would have split the stone, they cut a small groove for the whole length of, perhaps, 100 feet, and inserted in it, close to each other, a great number of dry wooden wedges; after which they poured water into the groove, and the wedges swelling and bursting simultaneously, with a tremendous force, broke out the huge stone, as neatly as a diamond cuts a pane of glass.

Modern geographers and geologists have demonstrated that these monoliths were brought from a prodigious distance, and have been at a loss to conjecture how the transport was effected. Old manuscripts say that it was done by the help of portable rails. These rested upon inflated bags of hide, rendered indestructible by the same process as that used for preserving the mummies. These ingenious air-cushions prevented the rails from sinking in the deep sand. Manetho mentions them, and remarks that they were so well prepared that they would endure wear and tear for centuries.

The date of the hundreds of pyramids in the Valley of the Nile is impossible to fix by any of the rules of modern science; but Herodotus informs us that each successive king erected one to commemorate his reign, and serve as his sepulchre. But, Herodotus did not tell all, although he knew that the *real* purpose of the pyramid was very different from that which he assigns to it. Were it not for his religious scruples, he might have added that, externally, it symbolized the creative principle of nature, and illustrated also the principles of geometry, mathematics, astrology, and astronomy. Internally, it was a majestic fane, in whose sombre recesses were performed the Mysteries, and whose walls had often witnessed the initiation-scenes of members of the royal family. The porphyry sarcophagus, which Professor Piazzi Smyth, Astronomer Royal of Scotland, degrades into a corn-bin, was the *baptismal font*, upon emerging from which, the neophyte was "born again," and became an *adept*.

Herodotus gives us, however, a just idea of the enormous labor expended in transporting one of these gigantic blocks of granite. It measured thirty-two feet in length, twenty-one feet in width, and twelve feet in height. Its weight he estimates to be rising 300 tons, and it occupied 2,000 men for three years to move it from Syene to the Delta, down the Nile. Gliddon, in his *Ancient Egypt*, quotes from Pliny a description of the arrangements for moving the obelisk erected at Alexandria by Ptolemæus Philadelphus. A canal was dug from the Nile to the place where the obelisk lay. Two boats were floated under it; they were weighted with stones containing one cubic foot each, and the weight of the obelisk having been calculated by the engineers, the cargo of the boats was exactly proportioned to it, so that they should be sufficiently submerged to pass under the monolith as it lay across the canal. Then, the stones were gradually removed, the boats rose, lifted the obelisk, and it was floated down the river.

In the Egyptian section of the Dresden, or Berlin Museum, we forget which, is a drawing which represents a workman ascending an unfinished pyramid, with a basket of sand upon his back. This has suggested to certain Egyptologists the idea that the blocks of the pyramids were chemically manufactured *in loco*. Some modern engineers believe that Portland cement, a double silicate of lime and alumina, is the imperishable cement of the ancients. But, on the other hand, Professor Carpenter asserts that the pyramids, with the exception of their granite casing, is formed of what "geologists call *nummulitic* limestone. This is newer than the old chalk, and is made of the shells of animals called nummulites — like little pieces of money about the size of a shilling." However this moot question may be decided, no one, from Herodotus and Pliny down to the last wandering engineer who has gazed upon these imperial monuments of long-crumbled dynasties, has been able to tell us how the gigantic masses were transported and set up in place. Bunsen concedes to Egypt an antiquity of 20,000 years. But even in this matter we would be left to conjecture if we depended upon modern authorities. They can neither tell us for what the pyramids were constructed, under what dynasty the first was raised, nor the material of which they are built. All is conjecture with them.

Professor Smyth has given us by far the most accurate mathematical description of the great pyramid to be found in literature. But after showing the astronomical bearings of the structure, he so little appreciates ancient Egyptian thought that he actually maintains that the porphyry sarcophagus of the king's chamber is the unit of measure for the two most enlightened nations of the earth — "England and America." One of the *books* of *Hermes* describes certain of the pyramids as standing upon the sea-shore, "the waves of which dashed in powerless fury against its base." This implies that the geographical features of the country have been changed, and may indicate that we must accord to these ancient "granaries," "magico-astrological observatories," and "royal sepulchres," an origin antedating the upheaval of the Sahara and other deserts. This would imply rather more of an antiquity than the poor few thousands of years, so generously accorded to them by Egyptologists.

Dr. Rebold, a French archæologist of some renown, gives his readers a glimpse of the culture which prevailed 5,000 (?) years B.C., by saying that there were at that time no less than "thirty or forty colleges of the priests who studied occult sciences and practical magic."

A writer in the *National Quarterly Review* (Vol. xxxii., No. lxiii., December, 1875) says that, "The recent excavations made among the ruins of Carthage have brought to light traces of a civilization, a refinement of art and luxury, which must even have outshone that of ancient Rome; and when the fiat went forth, *Delenda est Carthago,* the mistress of the world well knew that she was about to destroy a greater than herself, for, while one empire swayed the world by force of arms alone, the other was the last and most perfect representative of a race who had, for centuries before Rome was dreamed of, directed the civilization, the learning, and the intelligence of mankind." This Carthage is the one which, according to Appian, was standing as early as B.C. 1234, or fifty years before the taking of Troy, and not the one popularly supposed to have been built by Dido (Elissa or Astarte) four centuries later.

Here we have still another illustration of the truth of the doctrine of cycles. Draper's admissions as to the astronomical erudition of the ancient Egyptians are singularly supported by an interesting fact quoted by Mr. J. M. Peebles, from a lecture delivered in Philadelphia, by the late Professor O. M. Mitchell, the astronomer. Upon the coffin of a mummy, now in the British Museum, was delineated the zodiac with the exact positions of the planets at the time of the autumnal equinox, in the year 1722 B.C. Professor Mitchell calculated the exact position of the heavenly bodies belonging to our solar system at the time indicated. "The result," says Mr. Peebles, "I give in his own words: 'To my astonishment . . . it was found that on the 7th of October, 1722 B.C., the moon and planets had occupied the exact points in the heavens marked upon the coffin in the British Museum.' "[764]

---

764 J. M. Peebles, "*Around the World.*"

THE ANCIENT LAND OF THE PHARAOHS

Professor John Fiske, in his onslaught on Dr. Draper's *History of the Intellectual Development of Europe*, sets his pen against the doctrine of cyclical progression, remarking that "we have never known the beginning or the end of an historic cycle, and have no inductive warrant for believing that we are now traversing one."[765] He chides the author of that eloquent and thoughtful work for the "odd disposition exhibited throughout his work, not only to refer the best part of Greek culture to an Egyptian source, but uniformly to exalt the non-European civilization at the expense of the European." We believe that this "odd disposition" might be directly sanctioned by the confessions of great Grecian historians themselves. Professor Fiske might, with profit, read Herodotus over again. The "Father of History" confesses more than once that Greece owes everything to Egypt. As to his assertion that the world has never known the beginning or the end of an historical cycle, we have but to cast a retrospective glance on the many glorious nations which have passed away, *i.e.*, reached the end of their great national cycle.

Compare the Egypt of that day, with its perfection of art, science, and religion, its glorious cities and monuments, and its swarming population, with the Egypt of to-day, peopled with strangers; its ruins the abode of bats and snakes, and a few Copts the sole surviving heirs to all this grandeur — and see whether the cyclical theory does not reassert itself. Says Gliddon, who is now contradicted by Mr. Fiske: "Philologists, astronomers, chemists, painters, architects, physicians, must return to Egypt to learn the origin of language and writing; of the calendar and solar motion; of the art of cutting granite with a copper chisel, and of giving elasticity to a copper sword; of making glass with the variegated hues of the rainbow; of moving single blocks of polished syenite, *nine hundred tons* in weight, for any distance, by land and water; of building arches, rounded and pointed, with masonic precision unsurpassed at the present day, and antecedent by 2,000 years to the 'Cloaca Magna' of Rome; of sculpturing a Doric column 1,000 years before the Dorians are known in history; of fresco painting in imperishable colors; of practical knowledge in anatomy; and of time-defying pyramid-building."

"Every craftsman can behold, in Egyptian monuments, the progress of his art 4,000 years ago; and whether it be a wheelwright building a chariot, a shoemaker drawing his twine, a leather-cutter using the self-same form of knife of old as is considered the best form now, a weaver throwing the same hand-shuttle, a whitesmith using that identical form of blow-pipe but lately recognized to be the most efficient, the seal-engraver cutting, in hieroglyphics, such names as Schooho's, above 4,300 years ago — *all these*, and many more astounding evidences of Egyptian priority, now require but a glance at the plates of Rossellini."

"Truly," exclaims Mr. Peebles, "these Ramsean temples and tombs were as much a marvel to the Grecian Herodotus as they are to us!"[766]

But, even then, the merciless hand of time had left its traces upon their structures, and some of them, whose very memory would be lost were it not for the *Books of Hermes*, had been swept away into the oblivion of the ages. King after king, and dynasty after dynasty

---

765 John Fiske, "*The North American Review*," art. The Laws of History, July, 1869.
766 M. Peebles, "*Around the World*."

had passed in a glittering pageant before the eyes of succeeding generations and their renown had filled the habitable globe. The same pall of forgetfulness had fallen upon them and their monuments alike, before the first of our historical authorities, Herodotus, preserved for posterity the remembrance of that wonder of the world, the great Labyrinth. The long-accepted Biblical chronology has so cramped the minds of not only the clergy, but even our scarce-unfettered scientists, that in treating of prehistoric remains in different parts of the world, a constant fear is manifested on their part to trespass beyond the period of 6,000 years, hitherto allowed by theology as the age of the world.

Herodotus found the Labyrinth already in ruins; but nevertheless his admiration for the genius of its builders knew no bounds. He regarded it as far more marvellous than the pyramids themselves, and, as an eye-witness, minutely describes it. The French and Prussian savants, as well as other Egyptologists, agree as to the emplacement, and identified its noble ruins. Moreover, they confirm the account given of it by the old historian. Herodotus says that he found therein 3,000 chambers; half subterranean and the other half above-ground. "The upper chambers," he says, "I myself passed through and examined in detail. In the underground ones (which *may exist till now,* for all the archæologists know), the keepers of the building would not let me in, for they contain the sepulchres of the kings who built the Labyrinth, and also those of the sacred crocodiles. The upper chambers I saw and examined with my own eyes, and found them to excel all other human productions." In Rawlinson's translation, Herodotus is made to say: "The passages through the houses and the varied windings of the paths across the courts, excited in me infinite admiration as I passed from the courts into the chambers, and from thence into colonnades, and from colonnades into other houses, and again into courts unseen before. The roof was throughout of stone like the walls, and both were exquisitely carved all over with figures. Every court was surrounded with a colonnade, which was built of white stones, sculptured most exquisitely. At the corner of the Labyrinth stands a pyramid forty fathoms high, with large figures engraved on it, and it is entered by a vast subterranean passage."

If such was the Labyrinth, when viewed by Herodotus, what, in such a case, was ancient Thebes, the city destroyed far earlier than the period of Psammeticus, who himself reigned 530 years after the destruction of Troy? We find that in his time Memphis was the capital, while of the glorious Thebes there remained but *ruins.* Now, if we, who are enabled to form our estimate only by the ruins of what was already ruins so many ages before our era — are stupefied in their contemplation, what must have been the general aspect of Thebes in the days of its glory? Karnak — temple, palace, ruins, or whatsoever the archæologists may term it — is now its only representative. But solitary and alone as it stands, fit emblem of majestic empire, as if forgotten by time in the onward march of the centuries, it testifies to the art and skill of the ancients. He must be indeed devoid of the spiritual perception of genius, who fails to feel as well as to see the intellectual grandeur of the race that planned and built it.

Champollion, who passed almost his entire life in the exploration of archæological remains, gives vent to his emotions in the following descriptions of Karnak: "The ground covered by the mass of remaining buildings is square; and each side measures 1,800 feet. One is astounded and *overcome by the grandeur* of the sublime remnants, the prodigality and magnificence of workmanship to be seen everywhere." "No people of ancient or modern times has conceived the art of architecture upon a scale so sublime, so grandiose as it existed among the ancient Egyptians; and the imagination, which in Europe soars far above our porticos, arrests itself *and falls powerless* at the foot of the hundred and forty columns of the hypostyle of Karnak! In one of its halls, the Cathedral of Notre Dame might stand and not touch the ceiling, but be considered as a small ornament in the centre of the hall."

A writer in a number of an English periodical, of 1870, evidently speaking with the authority of a traveller who describes what he has seen, expresses himself as follows: "Courts, halls, gateways, pillars, obelisks, monolithic figures, sculptures, long rows of sphinxes, are found in such profusion at Karnak, that the sight is too much for modern comprehension."

Says Denon, the French traveller: "It is hardly possible to believe, after seeing it, in the reality of the existence of so many buildings collected together on a single point, in their dimensions, in the resolute perseverance which their construction required, and in the incalculable expenses of so much magnificence! It is necessary that the reader should fancy what is before him to be a dream, as he who views the objects themselves occasionally yields to the doubt whether he be perfectly awake. . . . There are lakes and mountains *within the periphery of the sanctuary.* These two edifices are selected as examples from a list *next to inexhaustible.* The whole valley and delta of the Nile, from the cataracts to the sea, was covered with temples, palaces, tombs, pyramids, obelisks, and pillars. The execution of the sculptures is beyond praise. The mechanical perfection with which artists wrought in granite, serpentine, breccia, and basalt, is wonderful, according to all the experts . . . animals and plants look as good as natural, and artificial objects are beautifully sculptured; battles by sea and land, and scenes of domestic life are to be found in all their *bas-reliefs.*"

"The monuments," says an English author, "which there strike the traveller, fill his mind with great ideas. At the sight of the colossuses and superb obelisks, which seem to surpass the limits of human nature, he cannot help exclaiming, 'This was the work of man,' and this sentiment seems to ennoble his existence."[767] In his turn, Dr. Richardson, speaking of the Temple of Dendera, says: "The female figures are so extremely well executed, that they do all but speak; they have a mildness of feature and expression that never was surpassed."

Every one of these stones is covered with hieroglyphics, and the more ancient they are, the more beautifully we find them chiselled. Does not this furnish a new proof that history got its first glimpse of the ancients when the arts were already fast degenerating among them? The obelisks have their inscriptions cut two inches, and sometimes more, in depth, and they are cut with the highest degree of perfection. Some idea may be formed of their depth, from the fact that the Arabs, for a small fee, will climb sometimes to the very top of an obelisk, by inserting their toes and fingers in the excavations of the hieroglyphics. That all of these works, in which solidity rivals the beauty of their execution, were done before the days of the Exodus, there remains no historical doubt whatever. (All the archæologists now agree in saying that, the further back we go in history, the better and finer become these arts.) These views clash again with the individual opinion of Mr. Fiske, who would have us believe that "the sculptures upon these monuments (of Egypt, Hindustan, and Assyria), moreover, betoken a very *undeveloped* condition of the artistic faculties."[768] Nay, the learned

---

767 Savary, "*Letters on Egypt,*" vol. ii., p. 67. London, 1786.
768 John Fiske, "*North American Review,*" art. The Laws of History, July, 1869.

gentleman goes farther. Joining his voice in the opposition against the claims of learning —
which belongs by right to the sacerdotal castes of antiquity — to that of Lewis, he
contemptuously remarks that "the extravagant theory of a profound science possessed by
the Egyptian priesthood from a remote antiquity, and imparted to itinerant Greek
philosophers, has been utterly destroyed (?) by Sir G. C. Lewis[769]. . . while, with regard to
Egypt and Hindustan, as well as Assyria, it may be said that the colossal monuments which
have adorned these countries since prehistoric times, bear witness to the former prevalence
of a barbaric despotism, totally incompatible with social nobility, and, therefore, with well-
sustained progress."[770]

A curious argument, indeed. If the size and grandeur of public monuments are to serve
to our posterity as a standard by which to approximately estimate the "progress of
civilization" attained by their builders, it may be prudent, perhaps, for America, so proud of
her alleged progress and freedom, to dwarf her buildings at once to one story. Otherwise,
according to Professor Fiske's theory, the archæologists of A.D. 3877 will be applying to the
"Ancient America" of 1877, the rule of Lewis — and say the *ancient* United States "may be
considered as a great *latifundium*, or plantation, cultivated by the entire population, as the
king's (president's) slaves." Is it because the white-skinned Aryan races were never born
"builders," like the Eastern Æthiopians, or dark-skinned Caucasians,[771] and, therefore, never
able to compete with the latter in such colossal structures, that we must jump at the
conclusion that these grandiose temples and pyramids could only have been erected under
the whip of a merciless despot? Strange logic! It would really seem more prudent to hold to
the "rigorous canons of criticism" laid down by Lewis and Grote, and honestly confess at
once, that we really know little about these ancient nations, and that, except so far as purely
hypothetical speculations go, unless we study in the same direction as the ancient priests
did, we have as little chance in the future. We only know what they allowed the uninitiated
to know, but the little we do learn of them by deduction, ought to be sufficient to assure us
that, even in the nineteenth century, with all our claims to supremacy in arts and sciences,
we are totally unable, we will not say to build anything like the monuments of Egypt,
Hindustan, or Assyria, but even to rediscover the least of the ancient "*lost* arts." Besides, Sir
Gardner Wilkinson gives forcible expression to this view of the exhumed treasures of old,
by adding that, "he can trace no *primitive mode* of life, no barbarous customs, but a sort of
stationary civilization *from the most remote periods*." Thus far, archæology disagrees with
geology, which affirms that the further they trace the remains of men, the more barbarous
they find them. It is doubtful if geology has even yet exhausted the field of research
afforded her in the caves, and the views of geologists, which are based upon present
experience, may be radically modified, when they come to discover the remains of the
ancestors of the people whom they now style the cave-dwellers.

What better illustrates the theory of cycles than the following fact? Nearly 700 years B.C.,
in the schools of Thales and Pythagoras was taught the doctrine of the true motion of the
earth, its form, and the whole heliocentric system. And in 317 A.D., we find Lactantius, the

---

769 Sir G. C. Lewis, "*Astronomy of the Ancients.*"
770 J. Fiske, "*North American Review,*" art. The Laws of History.
771 We shall attempt to demonstrate in Vol. II., chapter viii., that the ancient Æthiopians were never a
Hamitic race.

preceptor of Crispus Cæsar, son of Constantine the Great, teaching his pupil that the earth was a plane surrounded by the sky, which is composed of fire and water, and warning him against the heretical doctrine of the earth's globular form!

Whenever, in the pride of some new discovery, we throw a look into the past, we find, to our dismay, certain vestiges which indicate the possibility, if not certainty, that the alleged discovery was not totally unknown to the ancients.

It is generally asserted that neither the early inhabitants of the Mosaic times, nor even the more civilized nations of the Ptolemaic period were acquainted with electricity. If we remain undisturbed in this opinion, it is not for lack of proofs to the contrary. We may disdain to search for a profounder meaning in some characteristic sentences of Servius, and other writers; we cannot so obliterate them but that, at some future day, that meaning will appear to us in all its significant truths. "The first inhabitants of the earth," says he, "never carried fire to their altars, but by their prayers they brought down the heavenly fire."[772] "Prometheus discovered and revealed to man the art of bringing down lightning; and by the method which he taught to them, they brought down fire from the region above."

If, after pondering these words, we are still willing to attribute them to the phraseology of mythological fables, we may turn to the days of Numa, the king-philosopher, so renowned for his esoteric learning, and find ourselves more embarrassed to deal with his case. We can neither accuse him of ignorance, superstition, nor credulity; for, if history can be believed at all, he was intently bent on destroying polytheism and idol-worship. He had so well dissuaded the Romans from idolatry that for nearly two centuries neither statues nor images appeared in their temples. On the other hand old historians tell us that the knowledge which Numa possessed in natural physics was remarkable. Tradition says that he was initiated by the priests of the Etruscan divinities, and instructed by them in the secret of forcing Jupiter, the Thunderer, to descend upon earth.[773] Ovid shows that Jupiter Elicius began to be worshipped by the Romans from that time. Salverte is of the opinion that before Franklin discovered his refined electricity, Numa had experimented with it most successfully, and that Tullus Hostilius was the first victim of the dangerous "heavenly guest" recorded in history. Titus Livy and Pliny narrate that this prince, having found in the *Books of Numa*, instructions on the secret sacrifices offered to Jupiter Elicius, made a mistake, and, in consequence of it, "he was struck by lightning and consumed in his own palace."[774]

Salverte remarks that Pliny, in the exposition of Numa's scientific secrets, "makes use of expressions which seem to indicate two distinct processes"; the one obtained thunder (impetrare), the other forced it to lightning (cogere).[775] "Guided by Numa's book," says Lucius, quoted by Pliny, "Tullus undertook to invoke the aid of Jupiter. . . . But having performed the rite imperfectly, he perished, struck by thunder."[776] Tracing back the knowledge of thunder and lightning possessed by the Etruscan priests, we find that Tarchon, the founder of the theurgism of the former, desiring to preserve his house from

---

772 Servius, "*Virgil*," Eclog. vi., v. 42.

773 Ovid, "*Fast.*," lib. iii., v. 285-346.

774 "*Titus Livius*," lib. i., cap. xxxi.

775 Pliny, "*Hist. Nat.*," lib. ii., cap. liii.

776 Lucius, "*Piso*"; Pliny, "*Hist. Nat.*," lib. xxviii., c. ii.

lightning, surrounded it by a hedge of the white bryony,[777] a climbing plant which has the property of averting thunderbolts. Tarchon the theurgist was much anterior to the siege of Troy. The pointed metallic lightning-rod, for which we are seemingly indebted to Franklin, is probably a *rediscovery* after all. There are many medals which seem to strongly indicate that the principle was anciently known. The temple of Juno had its roof covered with a quantity of pointed blades of swords.[778]

If we possess but little proof of the ancients having had any clear notions as to *all* the effects of electricity, there is very strong evidence, at all events, of their having been perfectly acquainted with electricity itself. "Ben David," says the author of *The Occult Sciences,* "has asserted that Moses possessed some knowledge of the phenomena of electricity." Professor Hirt, of Berlin, is of this opinion. Michaelis, remarks — *firstly:* "that there is no indication that lightning ever struck the temple of Jerusalem, during a thousand years. *Secondly,* that according to Josephus,[779] a forest of points . . . of gold, and very sharp, covered the roof of the temple. *Thirdly,* that this roof communicated with the caverns in the hill upon which the temple was situated, by means of pipes in connection with the gilding which covered all the exterior of the building; in consequence of which the points would act as conductors."[780]

Ammianus Marcellinus, a famous historian of the fourth century, a writer generally esteemed for the fairness and correctness of his statements, tells that "The magi, preserved perpetually in their furnaces fire that they miraculously got from heaven."[781] There is a sentence in the Hindu *Oupnek-hat,* which runs thus: "To know fire, the sun, the moon, and lightning, is three-fourths of the science of God."[782]

Finally, Salverte shows that in the days of Ktesias, "India was acquainted with the use of conductors of lightning." This historian plainly states that "iron placed at the bottom of a fountain . . . and made in the form of a sword, with *the point upward,* possessed, as soon as it was thus fixed in the ground, the property of averting storms and lightnings."[783] What can be plainer?

Some modern writers deny the fact that a great mirror was placed in the light-house of the Alexandrian port, for the purpose of discovering vessels at a distance at sea. But the renowned Buffon believed in it; for he honestly confesses that "If the mirror really existed, as I firmly believe it did, to the ancients belong the honor of the invention *of the telescope.*"[784] Stevens, in his work on the East, asserts that he found railroads in Upper Egypt whose grooves were coated with iron. Canova, Powers, and other celebrated sculptors of our modern age deem it an honor to be compared with Pheidias of old, and strict truth would, perhaps, hesitate at such a flattery.

---

777 "*Columella,*" lib. x., vers. 346, etc.

778 See "*Notice sur les Travaux de l'Academie du Gard,*" part i., pp. 304-314, by la Boissiere.

779 "*Bell. Jud. adv. Roman,*" lib. v., cap. xiv.

780 "*Magasin Scientifique de Goëthingen,*" 3me. année, 5me. cahier.

781 "*Ammian. Marcel.,*" lib. xxiii., cap. vi.

782 "*Oupnek-hat,*" Brahman xi.

783 "*Ktesias, in India ap. Photum.,*" Bibl. Cod. lxxii.

784 Buffon, "*Histoire Naturelle des Mineraux,*" 6me Mem., art. ii.

ANTIQUITY OF THE NILOTIC MONUMENTS

Professor Jowett discredits the story of the Atlantis, in the *Timæus*; and the records of 8,000 and 9,000 years appear to him an ancient swindle. But Bunsen remarks: "There is nothing improbable in itself in reminiscences and records of great events in Egypt 9,000 years B.C., for . . . the Origines of Egypt go back to the ninth millennium before Christ."[785] Then how about the primitive Cyclopean fortresses of ancient Greece? Can the walls of Tiryns, about which, according to archæological accounts, "even among the ancients it was reported to have been the work of the Cyclops,"[786] be deemed posterior to the pyramids? Masses of rock, some equal to a cube of six feet, and the smallest of which, Pausanias says, could never be moved by a yoke of oxen, laid up in walls of solid masonry twenty-five feet thick and over forty feet high, still believed to be the work of men of the races known to our history!

Wilkinson's researches have brought to light the fact that many inventions of what we term modern, and upon which we plume ourselves, were perfected by the ancient Egyptians. The newly-discovered papyrus of Ebers, the German archæologist, proves that neither our modern chignons, skin-beautifying pearl powders, nor *eaux dentifrices* were secrets to them. More than one modern physician — even among those who advertise themselves as having "made a speciality of nervous disorders" — may find his advantage in consulting the *Medical Books of Hermes*, which contain prescriptions of real therapeutic value.

The Egyptians, as we have seen, excelled in all arts. They made paper so excellent in quality as to be time-proof. "They took out the pith of the papyrus," says our anonymous writer, previously mentioned, "dissected and opened the fibre, and flattening it by a process known to them, made it as thin as our foolscap paper, but far more durable. . . . They sometimes cut it into strips and glued it together; many of such written documents are yet in existence." The papyrus found in the tomb of the queen's mummy, and another one found in the sarcophagus of the "Chambre de la Reine," at Ghizeh, present the appearance of the finest glossy white muslin, while it possesses the durability of the best calf-parchment. "For a long time the *savants* believed the papyrus to have been introduced by Alexander the Great — as they erroneously imagined a good many more things — but Lepsius found rolls of papyri in tombs and monuments of the twelfth dynasty; sculptured pictures of papyri were found later, on monuments of the fourth dynasty, and now it is proved that the art of writing was known and used as early as the days of Menes, the protomonarch"; and thus it was finally discovered that the art and their system of writing were perfect and complete *from the very first.*

It is to Champollion that we owe the first interpretation of their weird writing; and, but for his life-long labor, we would till now remain uninformed as to the meaning of all these pictured letters, and the ancients would still be considered ignorant by the moderns whom they so greatly excelled in some arts and sciences. "He was the first to find out what wondrous tale the Egyptians had to tell, for one who could read their endless manuscripts and records. They left them on every spot and object capable of receiving characters. . . . They engraved, and chiselled, and sculptured them on monuments; they traced them on

---

785 "*Egypt's Place in Universal History*," vol. iv., p. 462.
786 "*Archæologia*," vol. xv., p. 320.

furniture, rocks, stones, walls, coffins, and tombs, as on the papyrus. . . . The pictures of their daily lives, in their smallest details, are being now unravelled before our dazzled eyes in the most wondrous way. . . . Nothing, of what we know, seems to have been overlooked by the ancient Egyptians. . . . The history of 'Sesostris' shows us how well he and his people were versed in the art and practice of war. . . . The pictures show how formidable they were when encountered in battle. They constructed war-engines. . . . Horner says that through each of the 100 gates of Thebes issued 200 men with horses and chariots; the latter were magnificently constructed, and very light in comparison with our modern heavy, clumsy, and uncomfortable artillery wagons." Kenrick describes them in the following terms: "In short, as all the essential principles which regulate the construction and draught of carriages are exemplified in the war-chariots of the Pharaohs, so there is nothing which modern taste and luxury have devised for their decoration to which we do not find a prototype in the monuments of the eighteenth dynasty." Springs — *metallic* springs — have been found in them, and, notwithstanding Wilkinson's superficial investigation in that direction, and description of these in his studies, we find proofs that such were used to prevent the jolting in the chariots in their too rapid course. The bas-reliefs show us certain *melees* and battles in which we can find and trace their uses and customs to the smallest details. The heavily-armed men fought in coats of mail, the infantry had quilted tunics and felt helmets, with metallic coverings to protect them the better. Muratori, the modern Italian inventor who, some ten years ago, introduced his "impenetrable cuirasse," has but followed in his invention what he could make out of the ancient method which suggested to him the idea. The process of rendering such objects as card-board, felt, and other tissues, impenetrable to the cuts and thrusts of any sharp weapon, is now numbered among the lost arts. Muratori succeeded but imperfectly in preparing such felt cuirasses, and, notwithstanding the boasted achievements of modern chemistry he could derive from it no preparation adequate to effect his object, and failed.

ARTS OF WAR AND PEACE

To what perfection chemistry had reached in ancient times, may be inferred from a fact mentioned by Virey. In his dissertations, he shows that Asclepiadotus, a general of Mithradates, reproduced chemically the deleterious exhalations of the sacred grotto. These vapors, like those of Cumæ, threw the Pythoness into the mantic frenzy.

Egyptians used bows, double-edged swords and daggers, javelins, spears, and pikes. The light troops were armed with darts and slings; charioteers wielded maces and battle-axes; in siege-operations they were perfect. "The assailants," says the anonymous writer, "advanced, forming a narrow and long line, the point being protected by a triple-sided, impenetrable engine pushed before them on a kind of roller, by an invisible squad of men. They had covered underground passages with trap-doors, scaling ladders, and the art of escalade and military strategy was carried by them to perfection. . . . The battering ram was familiar to them as other things; being such experts in quarrying they knew how to set a mine to a wall and bring it down." The same writer remarks, that it is a great deal safer for us to mention what the Egyptians *did* than what they *did not* know, for every day brings some new discovery of their wonderful knowledge; "and if," he adds, "we were to find out that they used Armstrong guns, this fact would not be much more astonishing than many of the facts brought out to light already."

The proof that they were proficient in mathematical sciences, lies in the fact that those ancient mathematicians whom we honor as the fathers of geometry went to Egypt to be instructed. Says Professor Smyth, as quoted by Mr. Peebles, "the geometrical knowledge of the pyramid-builders began where Euclid's ended." Before Greece came into existence, the arts, with the Egyptians, were ripe and old. Land-measuring, an art resting on geometry, the Egyptians certainly knew well, as, according to the *Bible*, Joshua, after conquering the Holy Land, had skill enough to divide it. And how could a people so skilled in natural philosophy as the Egyptians were, not be proportionately skilled in psychology and spiritual philosophy? The temple was the nursery of the highest civilization, and it alone possessed that higher knowledge of magic which was in itself the quintessence of natural philosophy. The occult powers of nature were taught in the greatest secrecy and the most wonderful cures were performed during the performing of the Mysteries. Herodotus acknowledges[787] that the Greeks learned all they knew, including the sacred services of the temple, from the Egyptians, and because of that, their principal temples were consecrated to Egyptian divinities. Melampus, the famous healer and soothsayer of Argos, had to use his medicines "after the manner of the Egyptians," from whom he had gained his knowledge, whenever he desired his cure to be thoroughly effective. He healed Iphiclus of his impotency and debility by *the rust of iron*, according to the directions of Mantis, his *magnetic sleeper*, or oracle. Sprengel gives many wonderful instances of such *magical* cures in his *History of Medicine* (see p. 119).

Diodorus, in his work on the Egyptians (lib. i.), says that Isis has deserved immortality, for all nations of the earth bear witness to the power of this goddess to cure diseases by her influence. "This is proved," he says, "not by fable as among the Greeks, but by authentic facts." Galen records several remedial means which were preserved in the healing wards of the temples. He mentions also a universal medicine which in his time was called *Isis*.[788]

The doctrines of several Greek philosophers, who had been instructed in Egypt, demonstrates their profound learning. Orpheus, who, according to Artapanus, was a disciple of Moyses (Moses),[789] Pythagoras, Herodotus, and Plato owe their philosophy to the same temples in which the wise Solon was instructed by the priests. "Antiklides relates," says Pliny, "that the letters were invented in Egypt by a person whose name was Menon, fifteen years before Phoroneus the most ancient king of Greece."[790] Jablonski proves that the heliocentric system, as well as the earth's sphericity, were known by the priests of Egypt from immemorial ages. "This theory," he adds, "Pythagoras took from the Egyptians, who had it from the Brachmans of India."[791] Fenelon, the illustrious Archbishop of Cambray, in his *Lives of the Ancient Philosophers*, credits Pythagoras with this knowledge, and says that besides teaching his disciples that as the earth was round there were antipodes, since it was

---

787 Lib. ii., c. 50.
788 Galen, "*De Composit. Medec.*," lib. v.
789 "*Ancient Fragments*", see chapter on the Early Kings of Egypt.
790 "*Pliny,*" lib. vii., c. 56.
791 Jablonski, "*Pantheon Ægypti.,*" ii., Proleg. 10.

inhabited everywhere, the great mathematician was the first to discover that the morning and evening star was the same. If we now consider that Pythagoras lived in about the 16th Olympiad, over 700 years B.C., and taught this fact at such an early period, we must believe that it was known by others before him. The works of Aristotle, Laërtius, and several others in which Pythagoras is mentioned, demonstrate that he had learned from the Egyptians about the obliquity of the ecliptic, the starry composition of the milky way, and the borrowed light of the moon.

Wilkinson, corroborated later by others, says that the Egyptians divided time, knew the true length of the year, and the precession of the equinoxes. By recording the rising and setting of the stars, they understood the particular influences which proceed from the positions and conjunctions of all heavenly bodies, and therefore their priests, prophesying as accurately as our modern astronomers, meteorological changes, could, *en plus*, astrologize through astral motions. Though the sober and eloquent Cicero may be partially right in his indignation against the exaggerations of the Babylonian priests, who "assert that they have preserved upon monuments observations extending back during an interval of 470,000 years,"[792] still, the period at which astronomy had arrived at its perfection with the ancients is *beyond* the reach of modern calculation.

A writer in one of our scientific journals observes "that every science in its growth passes through three stages: First, we have the stage of observation, when facts are collected and registered by many minds in many places. Next, we have the stage of generalization, when these carefully verified facts are arranged methodically, generalized systematically, and classified logically, so as to deduce and elucidate from them the laws that regulate their rule and order. Lastly, we have the stage of prophecy, when these laws are so applied that events can be predicted to occur with unerring accuracy." If several thousand years B.C., Chinese and Chaldean astronomers predicted eclipses — the latter, whether by the cycle of Saros, or other means, matters not — the fact remains the same. They had reached the last and highest stage of astronomical science — they *prophesied.* If they could, in the year 1722 B.C., delineate the zodiac with the exact positions of the planets at the time of the autumnal equinox, and so unerringly as Professor Mitchell, the astronomer, proved, then they knew the laws that regulate "carefully-verified facts" to perfection, and applied them with as much certainty as our modern astronomers. Moreover, astronomy is said to be in our century "the only science which has thoroughly reached the *last stage* . . . other sciences are yet in various stages of growth; electricity, in some branches, has reached the third stage, but in many branches is still in its infantine period."[793] This we know, on the exasperating confessions of men of science themselves, and we can entertain no doubt as to this sad reality in the nineteenth century, as we belong ourselves to it. Not so in relation to the men who lived in the days of the glory of Chaldæa, Assyria, and Babylon. Of the stages they reached in other sciences we know *nothing*, except that in astronomy they stood equal with us, for they had also reached the *third* and last stage. In his lecture on the *Lost Arts*, Wendell Phillips very artistically describes the situation. "We seem to imagine," says he, "that whether knowledge will die with us or not, it certainly began with us. . . . We have a pitying estimate, a tender pity for the narrowness, ignorance, and darkness of the bygone ages." To

---

792 Cicero, "*De Divinatione.*"
793 "*Telegraphic Journal,*" art. Scientific Prophecy.

illustrate our own idea with the closing sentence of the favorite lecturer, we may as well confess that we undertook this chapter, which in one sense interrupts our narrative, to inquire of our men of science, whether they are sure that they are boasting "*on the right line.*"

Thus we read of a people, who, according to some learned writers,[794] had just emerged from the bronze age into the succeeding age of iron. "If Chaldea, Assyria, and Babylon presented *stupendous and venerable antiquities reaching far back into* the night of time, Persia was not without her wonders of a later date. The pillared halls of Persepolis were filled with miracles of art — carvings, sculptures, enamels, alabaster libraries, obelisks, sphinxes, colossal bulls. Ecbatana, in Media, the cool summer retreat of the Persian kings, was defended by seven encircling walls of hewn and polished blocks, the interior ones in succession of increasing height, and of different colors, in astrological accordance with the seven planets. The palace was roofed *with silver tiles;* its beams were plated with gold. At midnight, in its halls, the sun was rivalled by many a row of naphtha cressets. A paradise, that luxury of the monarchs of the East, was planted in the midst of the city. The Persian empire was truly the garden of the world. . . . In Babylon there still remained its walls, once more than sixty miles in compass and, after the ravages of three centuries and three conquerors, still more than eighty feet in height; there were still the ruins of the temple of the cloud-encompassed Bel; on its top was planted the observatory wherein the weird Chaldean astronomers had held nocturnal communion with the stars; still there were vestiges of the two palaces with their hanging gardens, in which were trees growing in mid-air, and the wreck of the hydraulic machinery that had supplied them from the river. Into the artificial lake, with its vast apparatus of aqueducts and sluices, the melted snows of the Armenian mountains found their way and were confined in their course through the city by the embankments of the Euphrates. Most wonderful of all, perhaps, *was the tunnel under the river-bed.*"[795]

In his *First Traces of Man in Europe,* Albrecht Müller proposes a name descriptive of the age in which we live, and suggests that "the age of paper" is perhaps as good as any that can be discussed. We do not agree with the learned professor. Our firm opinion is, that succeeding generations will term ours, at best, the age of *brass;* at worst, that of albata or of oroide.

The thought of the present-day commentator and critic as to the ancient learning, is limited to and runs round the *exoterism* of the temples; his insight is either unwilling or unable to penetrate into the solemn adyta of old, where the hierophant instructed the neophyte to regard the public worship in its true light. No ancient sage would have taught that man is the king of creation, and that the starry heaven and our mother earth were created for his sake. He, who doubts the assertion, may turn to the *Magical and Philosophical Precepts* of Zoroaster, and find its corroboration in the following:[796]

---

794 Professor Albrecht Müller, "*The First Traces of Man in Europe.*" Says the author: "And this bronze age reaches to *and overlaps* the beginning of the historic period in some countries, and so includes the great epochs of the Assyrian and Egyptian Empires, B.C. *circa* 1500, and the earlier eras of the next succeeding age of iron."
795 "*Conflict between Religion and Science,*" chap. i.
796 Psellus, "*Chaldean Oracles,*" 4, cxliv.

"Direct not thy mind to the vast measures of the earth;

For the plant of truth is not upon ground.

Nor measure the measures of the sun, collecting rules,

For he is carried by the eternal will of the Father, *not for your sake,*

Dismiss the impetuous course of the moon;

For she runs always by work of necessity.

The progression of the stars *was not generated for your sake.*"

A rather strange teaching to come from those who are universally believed to have worshipped the sun, and moon, and the starry host, as gods. The sublime profundity of the Magian precepts being *beyond* the reach of modern materialistic thought, the Chaldean philosophers are accused, together with the ignorant masses, of Sabianism and sun-worship.

There was a vast difference between the *true* worship taught to those who showed themselves worthy, and the state religions. The magians are accused of all kinds of superstition, but this is what a *Chaldean Oracle* says:

"The wide aërial flight of birds *is not true,*

Nor the dissections of the entrails of victims; they are all mere toys,

The *basis of mercenary fraud;* flee from these

If you would open the sacred paradise of piety

Where virtue, wisdom, and equity, are assembled."[797]

Surely, it is not those who warn people against "mercenary fraud" who can be accused of it; and if they accomplished acts which seem miraculous, who can with fairness presume to deny that it was done merely because they possessed a knowledge of natural philosophy and psychological science to a degree unknown to our schools?

What did they not know? It is a well-demonstrated fact that the true meridian was correctly ascertained before the first pyramid was built. They had clocks and dials to measure time; their cubit was the established unit of linear measure, being 1,707 feet of English measure; according to Herodotus the unit of weight was also known; as money, they had gold and silver rings valued by weight; they had the decimal and duodecimal modes of calculation from the earliest times, and were proficient in algebra. "How could they otherwise," says an unknown author, "bring into operation such immense mechanical powers, if they had not thoroughly understood the philosophy of what we term the mechanical powers?"

The art of making linen and fine fabrics is also proved to have been one of their branches of knowledge, for the *Bible* speaks of it. Joseph was presented by Pharaoh with a vesture of fine linen, a golden chain, and many more things. The linen of Egypt was famous throughout the world. The mummies are all wrapped in it and the linen is beautifully preserved. Pliny speaks of a certain garment sent 600 years B.C., by King Amasis to Lindus, every single thread of which was composed of 360 minor threads twisted together. Herodotus gives us (book i.), in his account of Isis and the Mysteries performed in her honor, an idea of the beauty and "admirable softness of the linen worn by the priests." The

---

797 Psellus, "*Zoroast. Oracles,*" 4.

latter wore shoes made of papyrus and garments of *fine linen*, because this goddess first taught the use of it; and thus, besides being called *Isiaci*, or priests of Isis, they were also known as *Linigera*, or the "linen-wearing." This linen was spun and dyed in those brilliant and gorgeous colors, the secret of which is likewise now among the lost arts. On the mummies we often find the most beautiful embroidery and bead-work ornamenting their shirts; several of such can be seen in the museum of Bulak (Cairo), and are unsurpassable in beauty; the designs are exquisite, and the labor seems immense. The elaborate and so much vaunted Gobelins tapestry, is but a gross production when compared with some of the embroidery of the ancient Egyptians. We have but to refer to *Exodus* to discover how skilful was the workmanship of the Israelitish pupils of the Egyptians upon their tabernacle and sacred ark. The sacerdotal vestments, with their decorations of "pomegranates and golden bells," and the thummim, or jewelled breastplate of the high priest, are described by Josephus as being of unparalleled beauty and of wonderful workmanship; and yet we find beyond doubt that the Jews adopted their rites and ceremonies, and even the special dress of their Levites, from the Egyptians. Clemens Alexandrinus acknowledges it very reluctantly, and so does Origen and other Fathers of the Church, some of whom, as a matter of course, attribute the coincidence to a clever trick of Satan in anticipation of events. Proctor, the astronomer, says in one of his books, "The remarkable breastplate worn by the Jewish high priest was derived directly from the Egyptians." The word *thummim* itself is evidently of Egyptian origin, borrowed by Moses, like the rest; for further on the same page, Mr. Proctor says that, "In the often-repeated picture of judgment the deceased Egyptian is seen conducted by the god Horus (?), while Anubis places on one of the balances a vase supposed to contain his good actions, and in the other is the emblem of truth, a representation of Thmei, the goddess of truth, which was also worn on the judicial breastplate." Wilkinson, in his *Manners and Customs of the Ancient Egyptians*, shows that the Hebrew *thummim* is a plural form of the word Thmèi."[798]

All the ornamental arts seem to have been known to the Egyptians. Their jewelry of gold, silver, and precious stones are beautifully wrought; so was the cutting, polishing, and setting of them executed by their lapidaries in the finest style. The finger-ring of an Egyptian mummy — if we remember aright — was pronounced the most artistic piece of jewelry in the London Exhibition of 1851. Their imitation of precious stones in glass is far above anything done at the present day; and the emerald may be said to have been imitated to perfection.

In Pompeii, says Wendell Phillips, they discovered a room full of glass; there was ground-glass, window-glass, cut-glass, and colored-glass of every variety. Catholic priests who broke into China 200 years ago, were shown a glass, transparent and colorless, which was filled with liquor made by the Chinese, and which appeared to be colorless like water. "This liquor was poured into the glass, and then looking through, it seemed to be filled with fishes. They turned it out and repeated the experiment and again it was filled with fishes." In Rome they show a bit of glass, a transparent glass, which they light up so as to show you that there is nothing concealed, but in the centre of the glass is a drop of colored glass, perhaps as large as a pea, mottled like a duck, and which even a miniature pencil could not do more perfectly. "It is manifest that this drop of liquid glass must have been poured,

---

798 Proctor, "*Saturn and the Sabbath of the Jews*," p. 309.

because there is no joint. This must have been done by a greater heat than the annealing process, because that process shows breaks." In relation to their wonderful art of imitating precious stones, the lecturer speaks of the "celebrated vase of the Genoa Cathedral," which was considered for long centuries "a solid emerald." "The Roman Catholic legend of it was that it was one of the treasures that the Queen of Sheba gave to Solomon, and that it was the identical cup out of which the Saviour drank at the Last Supper." Subsequently it was found not to be an emerald, but an imitation; and when Napoleon brought it to Paris and gave it to the Institute, the scientists were obliged to confess that it *was not a stone*, and that they could not tell what it was.

Further, speaking of the skill of the ancients in metal works, the same lecturer narrates that "when the English plundered the Summer Palace of the Emperor of China, the European artists were surprised at seeing the curiously-wrought metal vessels of every kind, far exceeding all the boasted skill of the workmen of Europe." African tribes in the interior of the country gave travellers *better razors* than they had. "George Thompson told me," he adds, "he saw a man in Calcutta throw a handful of floss silk into the air, and a Hindu sever it into pieces with his sabre of native steel." He concludes by the apt remark that "the steel is the greatest triumph of metallurgy, and metallurgy is the glory of chemistry." So with the ancient Egyptians and Semitic races. They dug gold and separated it with the utmost skill. Copper, lead, and iron were found in abundance near the Red Sea.

In a lecture delivered in 1873, on the *Cave-Men of Devonshire*, Mr. W. Pengelly, F.R.S., stated on the authority of some Egyptologists that the first iron used in Egypt was *meteoric* iron, as the earliest mention of this metal is found in an Egyptian document, in which it is called the "stone from heaven." This would imply the idea that the only iron which was in use in days of old was meteorite. This may have been the case at the commencement of the period embraced in our present geological explorations, but till we can compute with at least approximate accuracy the age of our excavated relics, who can tell but that we are making a blunder of possibly several hundred thousand years? The injudiciousness of dogmatizing upon what the ancient Chaldeans and Egyptians did *not* know about mining and metallurgy is at least partially shown by the discoveries of Colonel Howard Vyse. Moreover, many of such precious stones as are only found at a great depth in mines are mentioned in Homer and the Hebrew Scriptures. Have scientists ascertained the precise time when mining-shafts were first sunk by mankind? According to Dr. A. C. Hamlin, in India, the arts of the goldsmith and lapidary have been practiced from an "unknown antiquity." That the Egyptians either knew from the remotest ages how to temper steel, or possessed something still better and more perfect than the implement necessary in our days for chiselling, is an alternative from which the archæologists cannot escape. How else could they have produced such artistic chiselling, or wrought such sculpture as they did? The critics may take their choice of either; according to them, steel tools of the most exquisite temper, or some other means of cutting sienite, granite, and basalt; which, in the latter case, must be added to the long catalogue of lost arts.

Professor Albrecht Müller says: "We may ascribe the introduction of bronze manufacture into Europe to a great race immigrant from Asia some 6,000 years ago, called Aryas or Aryans. . . . Civilization of the East preceded that of the West by many centuries. . . . There are many proofs that a considerable degree of culture existed at its very beginning. Bronze was yet in use, *but iron as well*. Pottery was not only shaped on the lathe, but burned a good red. Manufactures in glass, gold, and silver, are found for the first time. In lonely mountain places are yet found dross, and the remains of iron-furnaces. . . . To be sure, this dross is sometimes ascribed to volcanic action, but it is met with where volcanoes never could have existed."

But it is in the process of preparing mummies that the skill of this wonderful people is exemplified in the highest degree. None but those who have made special study of the subject, can estimate the amount of skill, patience, and knowledge exacted for the accomplishment of this indestructible work, which occupied several months. Both chemistry and surgery were called into requisition. The mummies, if left in the dry climate of Egypt, seem to be practicably imperishable; and even when removed after a repose of several thousand years, show no signs of change. "The body," says the anonymous writer, "was filled with myrrh, cassia, and other gums, and after that, saturated with natron. . . . Then followed the marvellous swathing of the embalmed body, so artistically executed, that professional modern bandagists are lost in admiration at its excellency." Says Dr. Grandville: " . . . there is not a single form of bandage known to modern surgery, of which *far better and cleverer examples* are not seen in the swathings of the Egyptian mummies. The strips of linen are found without one single joint, extending to 1,000 *yards* in length." Rossellini, in Kenrick's *Ancient Egypt,* gives a similar testimony to the wonderful variety and skill with which the bandages have been applied and interlaced. There was not a fracture in the human body that could not be repaired successfully by the sacerdotal physician of those remote days.

Who but well remembers the excitement produced some twenty-five years ago by the discovery of anæsthesia? The nitrous oxide gas, sulphuric and chloric ether, chloroform, "laughing gas," besides various other combinations of these, were welcomed as so many heavenly blessings to the suffering portion of humanity. Poor Dr. Horace Wells, of Hartford, in 1844, was the discoverer, and Drs. Morton and Jackson reaped the honors and benefits in 1846, as is usual in such cases. The anaesthetics were proclaimed "the greatest discovery ever made." And, though the famous *Letheon* of Morton and Jackson (a compound of sulphuric ether), the chloroform of Sir James Y. Simpson, and the nitrous oxide gas, introduced by Colton, in 1843, and by Dunham and Smith, were occasionally checked by fatal cases, it still did not prevent these gentlemen from being considered public benefactors. The patients successfully put to sleep sometimes awoke no more; what matters that, so long as others were relieved? Physicians assure us that accidents are now but rarely apprehended. Perhaps it is because the beneficent anaesthetic agents are so parsimoniously applied as to fail in their effects one-half of the time, leaving the sufferer paralyzed for a few seconds in his external movements, but feeling the pain as acutely as ever. On the whole, however, chloroform and laughing gas are beneficent discoveries. But, are they the first anesthetics ever discovered, strictly speaking? Dioscorides speaks of the stone of Memphis (*lapis Memphiticus*), and describes it as a small pebble — round, polished, and very sparkling. When ground into powder, and applied as an ointment to that part of the body on which the surgeon was about to operate, either with his scalpel or fire, it preserved that part, and *only that part* from any pain of the operation. In the meantime, it was perfectly harmless to the constitution of the patient, who retained his consciousness throughout, in no way dangerous from its effects, and acted so long as it was kept on the affected part.

When taken in a mixture of wine or water, all feeling of suffering was perfectly deadened.[799] Pliny gives also a full description of it.[800]

From time immemorial, the Brahmans have had in their possession secrets quite as valuable. The widow, bent on the self-sacrifice of concremation, called *Sahamaranya*, has no dread of suffering the least pain, for the fiercest flames will consume her, without one pang of agony being experienced by her. The holy plants which crown her brow, as she is conducted in ceremony to the funeral pile; the sacred root culled at the midnight hour on the spot where the Ganges and the Yumna mingle their waters; and the process of anointing the body of the self-appointed victim with ghee and sacred oils, after she has bathed in all her clothes and finery, are so many *magical* anæsthetics. Supported by those she is going to part with in body, she walks thrice around her fiery couch, and, after bidding them farewell, is cast on the dead body of her husband, and leaves this world without a single moment of suffering. "The semi-fluid," says a missionary writer, an eye-witness of several such ceremonies — "the ghee, is poured upon the pile; it is instantly inflamed, and the *drugged* widow dies quickly of *suffocation* before the fire reaches her body."[801]

No such thing, if the sacred ceremony is only conducted strictly after the prescribed rites. The widows are never drugged in the sense we are accustomed to understand the word. Only precautionary measures are taken against a useless physical martyrdom — the atrocious agony of burning. Her mind is as free and clear as ever, and even more so. Firmly believing in the promises of a future life, her whole mind is absorbed in the contemplation of the approaching bliss — the beatitude of "freedom," which she is about to attain. She generally dies with the smile of heavenly rapture on her countenance; and if some one is to suffer at the hour of retribution, it is not the earnest devotee of her faith, but the crafty Brahmans who know well enough that no such ferocious rite was ever prescribed.[802] As to the victim, after having been consumed, she becomes a *sati* — transcendent purity — and is canonized after death.

Egypt is the birthplace and the cradle of chemistry. Kenrick shows the root of the word to be *chemi* or chem, which was the name of the country (*Psalms* cv. 27). The chemistry of colors seems to have been thoroughly well known in that country. Facts are facts. Where among our painters are we to search for the artist who can decorate our walls with imperishable colors? Ages after our pigmy buildings will have crumbled into dust, and the cities enclosing them will themselves have become shapeless heaps of brick and mortar,

---

799 Dioscorides, "Περι Ύλης Ιατρικῆς," lib. v., cap. clviii.

800 Pliny, "*Histoire Naturelle*," lib. xxxviii., cap. vii.

801 Le P. Paulin de St. Barthelemi, "*Voyage aux Indes Orientales*," vol. i., p. 358.

802 Max Müller, Professor Wilson, and H. J. Bushby, with several other Sanscrit students, prove that "Oriental scholars, both native and European, have shown that the rite of widow-burning was not only unsanctionable but imperatively forbidden by the earliest and most authoritative Hindu Scriptures" ("*Widow-burning*," p. 21). See Max Müller's "*Comparative Mythology*." "Professor Wilson," says Max Müller, "was the first to point out the falsification of the text and the change of '*yonim agre*' into '*yonim agne*' (womb of fire). . . . According to the hymns of the 'Rig-Veda,' and the Vaidic ceremonial contained in the 'Grihya-Sutras,' the wife accompanies the corpse of the husband to the funeral pile, but she is there addressed with a verse taken from the '*Rig-Veda*,' and ordered to leave her husband, and to return to the world of the living" ("*Comparative Mythology*," p. 35).

with forgotten names — long after that will the halls of Karnak and Luxor (El-Uxor) be still standing; and the gorgeous mural paintings of the latter will doubtless be as bright and vivid 4,000 years hence, as they were 4,000 years ago, and are to-day. "Embalming and fresco-painting," says our author, "was not a chance discovery with the Egyptians, but brought out from definitions and maxims like any induction of Faraday."

Our modern Italians boast of their Etruscan vases and paintings; the decorative borders found on Greek vases provoke the admiration of the lovers of antiquity, and are ascribed to the Greeks, while in fact "they were but copies from the Egyptian vases." Their figures can be found any day on the walls of a tomb of the age of Amunoph I., a period at which Greece was not even in existence.

Where, in our age, can we point to anything comparable to the rock-temples of Ipsambul in Lower Nubia? There may be seen sitting figures seventy feet high, carved out of the living rock. The torso of the statue of Rameses II., at Thebes, measures sixty feet around the shoulders, and elsewhere in proportion. Beside such titanic sculpture our own seems that of pigmies. Iron was known to the Egyptians at least long before the construction of the first pyramid, which is over 20,000 years ago, according to Bunsen. The proof of this had remained hidden for many thousands of years in the pyramid of Cheops, until *Colonel Howard Vyse found it in the shape of a piece of iron, in one of the joints, where it had evidently been placed at the time this pyramid was first built.* Egyptologists adduce many indications that the ancients were perfectly well acquainted with metallurgy in prehistoric times. "To this day we can find at Sinai large heaps of scoriæ, produced by smelting."[803] Metallurgy and chemistry, as practiced in those days, were known as *alchemy,* and were at the bottom of prehistoric magic. Moreover, Moses proved his knowledge of alchemical chemistry by pulverizing the golden calf, and strewing the powder upon the water.

If now we turn to navigation, we will find ourselves able to prove, on good authorities, that Necho II. fitted out a fleet on the Red Sea and despatched it for exploration. The fleet was absent above two years and instead of returning through the Straits of Babelmandeb, as was wont, sailed back through the Straits of Gibraltar. Herodotus was not at all swift to concede to the Egyptians a maritime achievement so vast as this. They had, he says, been spreading the report that "returning homewards, they had the sunrise on their right hands; a thing which to me is incredible." "And yet," remarks the author of the heretofore-mentioned article, "this incredible assertion is now proved *incontestable,* as may well be understood by any one who has doubled the Cape of Good Hope." Thus it is proved that the most ancient of these people performed a feat which was attributed to Columbus many ages later. They say they anchored twice on their way; sowed corn, reaped it and, sailing away, steered in triumph through the Pillars of Hercules and eastward along the Mediterranean. "There was a people," he adds, "much more deserving of the term '*veteres*' than the Romans and Greeks. The Greeks, young in their knowledge, sounded a trumpet before these and called upon all the world to admire their ability. Old Egypt, grown gray in her wisdom, was so secure of her acquirements that she did not invite admiration and cared no more for the opinion of the flippant Greek than we do to-day for that of a Feejee islander."

---

803 Hence the story that Moses fabricated there the serpent or seraph of brass which the Israelites worshipped till the reign of Hezekiah.

"O Solon, Solon," said the oldest Egyptian priest to that sage. "You Greeks are ever childish, having no ancient opinion, no discipline of any long standing!" And very much surprised, indeed, was the great Solon, when he was told by the priests of Egypt that so many gods and goddesses of the Grecian Pantheon were but the disguised gods of Egypt. Truly spoke Zonaras: "All these things came to us from Chaldea to Egypt; and from thence were derived to the Greeks."

Sir David Brewster gives a glowing description of several automata; and the eighteenth century takes pride in that masterpiece of mechanical art, the "flute-player of Vaucanson." The little we can glean of positive information on that subject, from ancient writers, warrants the belief that the learned mechanicians in the days of Archimedes, and some of them much anterior to the great Syracusan, were in no wise more ignorant or less ingenious than our modern inventors. Archytas, a native of Tarentum, in Italy, the instructor of Plato, a philosopher distinguished for his mathematical achievements and wonderful discoveries in practical mechanics, constructed a wooden dove. It must have been an extraordinarily ingenious mechanism, as it flew, fluttered its wings, and sustained itself for a considerable time in the air. This skilful man, who lived 400 years B.C., invented besides the wooden dove, the screw, the crane, and various hydraulic machines.[804]

Egypt pressed her own grapes and made wine. Nothing remarkable in that, so far, but she brewed her own beer, and in great quantity — our Egyptologist goes on to say. The Ebers manuscript proves now, beyond doubt, that the Egyptians used beer 2,000 years B.C. Their beer must have been strong and excellent — like everything they did. Glass was manufactured in all its varieties. In many of the Egyptian sculptures we find scenes of glass-blowing and bottles; occasionally, during archæological researches, glasses and glassware are found, and very beautiful they seem to have been. Sir Gardner Wilkinson says that the Egyptians cut, ground, and engraved glass, and possessed the art of introducing gold between the two surfaces of the substance. They imitated with glass, pearls, emeralds, and all the precious stones to a great perfection.

Likewise, the most ancient Egyptians cultivated the musical arts, and understood well the effect of musical harmony and its influence on the human spirit. We can find on the oldest sculptures and carvings scenes in which musicians play on various instruments. Music was used in the Healing Department of the temples for the cure of nervous disorders. We discover on many monuments men playing in bands in concert; the leader beating time by clapping his hands. Thus far we can prove that they understood the laws of harmony. They had their sacred music, domestic and military. The lyre, harp, and flute were used for the sacred concerts; for festive occasions they had the guitar, the single and double pipes, and castanets; for troops, and during military service, they had trumpets, tambourines, drums, and cymbals.

Various kinds of harps were invented by them, such as the lyre, *sambuc, ashur*; some of these had upward of twenty strings. The superiority of the Egyptian lyre over the Grecian is an admitted fact. The material out of which were made such instruments was often of very costly and rare wood, and they were beautifully carved; they imported it sometimes from very distant countries; some were painted, inlaid with mother-of-pearl, and ornamented

---

804 A. Gell, "*Noet. Attic.*," lib. x., cap. xiii.

with colored leather. They used catgut for strings as we do. Pythagoras learned music in Egypt and made a regular science of it in Italy. But the Egyptians were generally considered in antiquity as the best music-teachers in Greece. They understood thoroughly well how to extract harmonious sounds out of an instrument by adding strings to it, as well as the multiplication of notes by shortening the strings upon its neck; which knowledge shows a great progress in the musical art. Speaking of harps, in a tomb at Thebes, Bruce remarks that, "they overturn all the accounts hitherto given of the earliest state of music and musical instruments in the East, and are altogether, in their form, ornaments and compass, an incontestable proof, *stronger than a thousand Greek quotations,* that geometry, drawing, mechanics, and music were at the greatest perfection when these instruments were made; and that the period from which we date the invention of these arts was only *the beginning of the era of their restoration.*"

On the walls of the palace of Amenoph II. at Thebes, the king is represented as playing chess with the queen. This monarch reigned long before the Trojan war. In India the game is known to have been played at least 5,000 years ago.

As to their knowledge in medicine, now that one of the lost *Books of Hermes* has been found and translated by Ebers, the Egyptians can speak for themselves. That they understood about the circulation of the blood, appears certain from the *healing manipulations* of the priests, who knew how to draw blood downward, stop its circulation for awhile, etc. A more careful study of their *bas-reliefs* representing scenes taking place in the healing hall of various temples will easily demonstrate it. They had their dentists and oculists, and no doctor was allowed to practice more than one specialty; which certainly warrants the belief that they lost fewer patients in those days than our physicians do now. It is also asserted by some authorities that the Egyptians were the first people in the world who introduced trial by jury; although we doubt this ourselves.

MEXICAN MYTHS AND RUINS

But the Egyptians were not the only people of remote epochs whose achievements place them in so commanding a position before the view of posterity. Besides others whose history is at present shut in behind the mists of antiquity — such as the prehistoric races of the two Americas, of Crete, of the Troad, of the Lacustrians, of the submerged continent of the fabled Atlantis, now classed with myths — the deeds of the Phœnicians stamp them with almost the character of demi-gods.

The writer in the *National Quarterly Review,* previously quoted, says that the Phœnicians were the earliest navigators of the world, founded most of the colonies of the Mediterranean, and voyaged to whatever other regions were inhabited. They visited the Arctic regions, whence they brought accounts of eternal days without a night, which Homer has preserved for us in the *Odyssey.* From the British Isles they imported tin into Africa, and Spain was a favorite site for their colonies. The description of Charybdis so completely answers to the maëlstrom that, as this writer says: "It is difficult to imagine it to have had any other prototype." Their explorations, it seems, extended in every direction, their sails whitening the Indian Ocean, as well as the Norwegian fiords. Different writers have accorded to them the settlement of remote localities; while the entire southern coast of the Mediterranean was occupied by their cities. A large portion of the African territory is asserted to have been peopled by the races expelled by Joshua and the children of Israel. At the time when Procopius wrote, columns stood in Mauritania Tingitana, which bore the inscription, in Phœnician characters, "We are those who fled before the brigand Joshua, the son of Nun or Nave."

Some suppose these hardy navigators of Arctic and Antarctic waters have been the progenitors of the races which built the temples and palaces of Palenque and Uxmal, of Copan and Arica.[805] Brasseur de Bourbourg gives us much information about the manners and customs, architecture and arts, and especially of the magic and magicians of the ancient Mexicans. He tells us that Votan, their fabulous hero and the greatest of their magicians, returning from a long voyage, visited King Solomon at the time of the building of the temple. This Votan appears to be identical with the dreaded Quetzo-Cohuatl who appears in all the Mexican legends; and curiously enough these legends bear a striking resemblance, insomuch as they relate to the voyages and exploits of the Hittim, with the Hebrew Bible accounts of the Hivites, the descendants of Heth, son of Chanaan. The record tells us that Votan "furnished to Solomon the most valuable particulars as to the men, animals, and plants, the gold and precious woods of the Occident," but refused point-blank to afford any clew to the route he sailed, or the manner of reaching the mysterious continent. Solomon himself gives an account of this interview in his *History of the Wonders of the Universe,* the chief Votan figuring under the allegory of the *Navigating Serpent.* Stephens, indulging in the anticipation "that a key surer than that of the Rosetta-stone will be discovered," by which the American hieroglyphs may be read,[806] says that the descendants of the Caciques and the Aztec subjects are believed to survive still in the inaccessible fastnesses of the Cordilleras "wildernesses, which have never yet been penetrated by a white man, . . . living as their fathers did, erecting the same buildings . . . with ornaments of sculpture and plastered; large courts, and lofty towers with high ranges of steps, and still carving on tablets of stone the same mysterious hieroglyphics." He adds, "I turn to that vast and unknown region, untraversed by a single road, wherein fancy pictures that mysterious city seen from the topmost range of the Cordilleras of unconquered, unvisited, and unsought aboriginal inhabitants."

Apart from the fact that this mysterious city has been seen from a great distance by daring travellers, there is no intrinsic improbability of its existence, for who can tell what became of the primitive people who fled before the rapacious brigands of Cortez and Pizarro? Dr. Tschuddi, in his work on Peru, tells us of an Indian legend that a train of 10,000 llamas, laden with gold to complete the unfortunate Inca's ransom, was arrested in the Andes by the tidings of his death, and the enormous treasure was so effectually concealed that not a trace of it has ever been found. He, as well as Prescott and other writers, informs us that the Indians to this day preserve their ancient traditions and sacerdotal caste, and obey implicitly the orders of rulers chosen among themselves, while at the same time nominally Catholics and actually subject to the Peruvian authorities. Magical ceremonies practiced by their forefathers still prevail among them, and magical phenomena occur. So persistent are they in their loyalty to the past, that it seems impossible but that they should be in relations with some central source of authority which constantly supports and

---

805 Such is *not* our opinion. They were probably built by the Atlanteans.
806 "*Incidents of Travel in Central America, Chiapas, and Yucatan,*" vol. ii., p. 457.

strengthens their faith, keeping it alive. May it not be that the sources of this undying faith lie in this mysterious city, with which they are in secret communication? Or must we think that all of the above is again but a "curious coincidence"?

The story of this mysterious city was told to Stephens by a Spanish Padre, in 1838-9. The priest swore to him that he had seen it with his own eyes, and gave Stephens the following details, which the traveller firmly believed to be true. "The Padre of the little village near the ruins of Santa Cruz del Quichè, had heard of the unknown city at the village of Chajul. . . . He was then young, and climbed with much labor to the naked summit of the topmost ridge of the sierra of the Cordillera. When arrived at a height of ten or twelve thousand feet, he looked over an immense plain extending to Yucatan and the Gulf of Mexico, and saw, at a great distance, a large city spread over a great space, and with turrets white and glittering in the sun. Tradition says that no white man has ever reached this city; that the inhabitants speak the Maya language, know that strangers have conquered their whole land, and murder any white man who attempts to enter their territory. . . . They have no coin; no horses, cattle, mules, or other domestic animals except fowls, and the cocks they keep underground to prevent their crowing being heard."

Nearly the same was given us personally about twenty years ago, by an old native priest, whom we met in Peru, and with whom we happened to have business relations. He had passed all his life vainly trying to conceal his hatred toward the conquerors — "brigands," he termed them; and, as he confessed, kept friends with them and the Catholic religion for the sake of his people, but he was as truly a sun-worshipper in his heart as ever he was. He had travelled in his capacity of a *converted* native missionary, and had been at Santa Cruz, and, as he solemnly affirmed, had been also to see some of his people by a "subterranean passage" leading into the mysterious city. We believe his account; for a man who is about to die, will rarely stop to invent idle stories; and this one we have found corroborated in Stephen's *Travels*. Besides, we know of two other cities utterly unknown to European travellers; not that the inhabitants particularly desire to hide themselves; for people from Buddhistic countries come occasionally to visit them. But their towns are not set down on the European or Asiatic maps; and, on account of the too zealous and enterprising Christian missionaries, and perhaps for more mysterious reasons of their own, the few natives of other countries who are aware of the existence of these two cities never mention them. Nature has provided strange nooks and hiding-places for her favorites; and unfortunately it is but far away from so-called civilized countries that man is free to worship the Deity in the way that his fathers did.

Even the erudite and sober Max Müller is somehow unable to get rid of *coincidences*. To him they come in the shape of the most unexpected discoveries. These Mexicans, for instance, whose obscure origin, according to the laws of probability, has no connection with the Aryans of India, nevertheless, like the Hindus, represent an eclipse of the moon as "the moon being devoured by a dragon."[807] And though Professor Müller admits that an historical intercourse between the two people was suspected by Alexander von Humboldt, and he himself considers it possible, still the occurrence of such a fact he adds, "need not be the result of any historical intercourse. As we have stated above, the origin of the aborigines

---

807 Max Müller, "*Chips from a German Workshop,*" vol. ii., p. 269.

of America is a very vexed question for those interested in tracing out the affiliation and migrations of peoples." Notwithstanding the labor of Brasseur de Bourbourg, and his elaborate translation of the famous *Popol-Vuh,* alleged to be written by Ixtlilxochitl, after weighing its contents, the antiquarian remains as much in the dark as ever. We have read the *Popol-Vuh* in its original translation, and the review of the same by Max Müller, and out of the former find shining a light of such brightness, that it is no wonder that the matter-of-fact, skeptical scientists should be blinded by it. But so far as an author can be judged by his writings, Professor Max Müller is no unfair skeptic; and, moreover, very little of importance escapes his attention. How is it then that a man of such immense and rare erudition, accustomed as he is to embrace at one eagle glance the traditions, religious customs, and superstitions of a people, detecting the slightest similarity, and taking in the smallest details, failed to give any importance or perhaps even suspect what the humble author of the present volume, who has neither scientific training nor erudition, to any extent, apprehended at first view? Fallacious and unwarranted as to many may seem this remark, it appears to us that science loses more than she gains by neglecting the ancient and even mediæval esoteric literature, or rather what remains of it. To one who devotes himself to such study many a coincidence is transformed into a natural result of demonstrable antecedent causes. We think we can see how it is that Professor Müller confesses that "now and then . . . one imagines one sees certain periods and landmarks, but in the next page all is chaos again."[808] May it not be barely possible that this chaos is intensified by the fact that most of the scientists, directing the whole of their attention to history, skip that which they treat as "vague, contradictory, miraculous, absurd." Notwithstanding the feeling that there was "a groundwork of noble conceptions which has been covered and distorted by an aftergrowth of fantastic nonsense," Professor Müller cannot help comparing this nonsense to the tales of the *Arabian Nights.*

Far be from us the ridiculous pretension of criticising a scientist so worthy of admiration for his learning as Max Müller. But we cannot help saying that even among the fantastic nonsense of the *Arabian Nights' Entertainments* anything would be worthy of attention, if it should help toward the evolving of some historical truth. Homer's *Odyssey* surpasses in fantastic nonsense all the tales of the *Arabian Nights* combined; and notwithstanding that, many of his myths are now proved to be something else besides the creation of the old poet's fancy. The Læstrygonians, who devoured the companions of Ulysses, are traced to the huge cannibal[809] race, said in primitive days to inhabit the caves of Norway. Geology verified through her discoveries some of the assertions of Homer, supposed for so many ages to have been but poetical hallucinations. The perpetual daylight enjoyed by this race of Læstrygonians indicates that they were inhabitants of the North Cape, where, during the whole summer, there is perpetual daylight. The Norwegian fiords are perfectly described by Homer in his *Odyssey,* x. 110 ; and the gigantic stature of the Læstrygonians is demonstrated by human bones of unusual size found in caves situated near this region, and which the geologists suppose to have belonged to a race extinct long before the Aryan

---

808 Max Müller, *"Popol-Vuh,"* p. 327.
809 Why not to the sacrifices of men in ancient worship?

immigration. Charybdis, as we have seen, has been recognized in the maëlstrom; and the Wandering Rocks[810] in the enormous icebergs of the Arctic seas.

If the consecutive attempts at the creation of man described in the *Quiche Cosmogony* suggests no comparison with some Apocrypha, with the Jewish sacred books, and the kabalistic theories of creation, it is indeed strange. Even the *Book of Jasher*, condemned as a gross forgery of the twelfth century, may furnish more than one clew to trace a relation between the population of Ur of the Kasdeans, where Magism flourished before the days of Abraham, and those of Central and North America. The divine beings, "brought down to the level of human nature," performed no feats or tricks more strange or incredible than the miraculous performances of Moses and of Pharaoh's magicians, while many of these are exactly similar in their nature. And when, moreover, in addition to this latter fact, we find so great a resemblance between certain kabalistic terms common to both hemispheres, there must be something else than mere accident to account for the circumstance. Many of such feats have clearly a common parentage. The story of the two brothers of Central America, who, before starting on their journey to Xibalba, "plant each a cane in the middle of their grandmother's house, that she may know by its flourishing or withering whether they are alive or dead,"[811] finds its analogy in the beliefs of many other countries. In the *Popular Tales and Traditions*, by Sacharoff (Russia), one can find a similar narrative, and trace this belief in various other legends. And yet these fairy tales were current in Russia many centuries before America was discovered.

In recognizing in the gods of Stonehenge the divinities of Delphos and Babylon, one need feel little surprised. Bel and the Dragon, Apollo and Python, Osiris and Typhon, are all one under many names, and have travelled far and wide. The Both-al of Ireland points directly to its first parent, the Batylos of the Greeks and the Beth-el of Chanaan. "History," says H. de la Villemarque, "which took no notes at those distant ages, can plead ignorance, but the science of languages affirms. Philology, with a daily-increasing probability, has again linked together the chain hardly broken between the Orient and the Occident."[812]

No more remarkable is the discovery of a like resemblance between the Oriental myths and ancient Russian tales and traditions, for it is entirely natural to look for a similarity between the beliefs of the Semitic and Aryan families. But when we discover an almost perfect identity between the character of Zarevna Militrissa, with a *moon* in her forehead, who is in constant danger of being devoured by *Zmeÿ Gorenetch* (the Serpent or Dragon), who plays such a prominent part in all popular Russian tales, and similar characters in the Mexican legends — extending to the minutest details — we may well pause and ask ourselves whether there be not here more than a simple coincidence.

This tradition of the Dragon and the Sun — occasionally replaced by the Moon — has awakened echoes in the remotest parts of the world. It may be accounted for with perfect readiness by the once universal heliolatrous religion. There was a time when Asia, Europe, Africa, and America were covered with the temples sacred to the sun and the dragons. The

---

810 "*Odyssey,*" xii. 71.
811 "*Chips from a German Workshop,*" p. 268.
812 Villemarque, Member of the Institute. Vol. lx.; "*Collect et Nouvelle Serie,*" 24, p. 570, 1863; "*Poesie des Cloitres Celtiques.*"

priests assumed the names of their deities, and thus the tradition of these spread like a network all over the globe: "Bel and the Dragon being uniformly coupled together, and the priest of the Ophite religion as uniformly assuming the name of his god."[813] But still, "if the original conception is natural and intelligible . . . and its occurrence need not be the result of any historical intercourse," as Professor Müller tells us, the details are so strikingly similar that we cannot feel satisfied that the riddle is entirely solved. The origin of this universal symbolical worship being concealed in the night of time, we would have far more chance to arrive at the truth by tracing these traditions to their very source. And where is this source? Kircher places the origin of the Ophite and heliolatrous worship, the shape of conical monuments and the obelisks, with the Egyptian Hermes Trismegistus.[814] Where, then, except in Hermetic books, are we to seek for the desired information? Is it likely that modern authors can know more, or as much, of ancient myths and cults as the men who taught them to their contemporaries? Clearly two things are necessary: first, to find the missing books of Hermes; and second, the key by which to *understand* them, for reading is not sufficient. Failing in this, our savants are abandoned to unfruitful speculations, as for a like reason geographers waste their energies in a vain quest of the sources of the Nile. Truly the land of Egypt is another abode of mystery!

RESEMBLANCES TO THE EGYPTIAN

Without stopping to discuss whether Hermes was the "Prince of post-diluvian magic," as des Mousseaux calls him, or the antediluvian, which is much more likely, one thing is certain: The authenticity, reliability, and usefulness of the *Books of Hermes* — or rather of what remains of the thirty-six works attributed to the Egyptian magician — are fully recognized by Champollion, junior, and corroborated by Champollion-Figeac, who mentions it. Now, if by carefully looking over the kabalistical works, which are all derived from that universal storehouse of esoteric knowledge, we find the fac-similes of many so-called miracles wrought by magical art, equally reproduced by the Quiches; and if even in the fragments left of the original *Popol-Vuh,* there is sufficient evidence that the religious customs of the Mexicans, Peruvians, and other American races are nearly identical with those of the ancient Phœnicians, Babylonians, and Egyptians; and if, moreover, we discover that many of their religious terms have etymologically the same origin; how are we to avoid believing that they are the descendants of those whose forefathers "fled before the brigand, Joshua, the son of Nun?" "Nuñez de la Vega says that Nin, or Imos, of the Tzendales, was the Ninus of the Babylonians."[815]

It is possible that, so far, it may be a coincidence; as the identification of one with the other rests but upon a poor argument. "But it is known," adds de Bourbourg, "that this prince, and according to others, his father, Bel, or Baal, received, like the Nin of the Tzendales the homages of his subjects under the shape of a serpent." The latter assertion, besides being fantastic, is nowhere corroborated in the Babylonian records. It is very true that the Phœnicians represented the sun under the image of a dragon; but so did all the

---

813 "*Archæol.,*" vol. xxv., p. 220. London.
814 "*Archæol.,*" vol. xxv., p. 292. London.
815 Brasseur de Bourbourg, "*Cartas,*" p. 52.

other people who symbolized their sun-gods. Belus, the first king of the Assyrian dynasty was, according to Castor, and Eusebius who quotes him, deified, *i.e.*, he was ranked among the gods "after his death" only. Thus, neither himself nor his son, Ninus, or Nin, could have received their subjects under the shape of a serpent, whatever the Tzendales did. Bel, according to Christians, is Baal; and Baal is the Devil, since the Bible prophets began so designating every deity of their neighbors; therefore Belus, Ninus, and the Mexican Nin are serpents and devils; and, as the Devil, or father of evil, is one under many forms, therefore, under whatever name the serpent appears, it is the Devil. Strange logic! Why not say that Ninus the Assyrian, represented as husband and victim of the ambitious Semiramis, was high priest as well as king of his country? That as such he wore on his tiara the sacred emblems of the dragon and the sun? Moreover, as the priest generally assumed the name of his god, Ninus was said to receive his subject as the representative of this serpent-god. The idea is preëminently Roman Catholic and amounts to very little, as all their inventions do. If Nuñez de la Vega was so anxious to establish an affiliation between the Mexicans and the biblical sun- and serpent-worshippers, why did he not show another and a better similarity between them without tracing in the Ninevites and the Tzendales the hoof and horn of the Christian Devil?

And to begin with, he might have pointed to the *Chronicles* of Fuentes, of the kingdom of Guatemala, and to the *Manuscript* of Don Juan Torres, the grandson of the last king of the Quiches. This document, which is said to have been in the possession of the lieutenant-general appointed by Pedro de Alvarado, states that the Toltecas themselves descended from the house of Israel, who were released by Moses, and who, after crossing the Red Sea, fell into idolatry. After that, having separated themselves from their companions, and under the guidance of a chief named Tanub, they set out wandering, and from one continent to another they came to a place named the Seven Caverns, in the Kingdom of Mexico, where they founded the famous town of Tula, etc.[816]

If this statement has never obtained more credit than it has, it is simply due to the fact that it passed through the hands of Father Francis Vasques, historian of the Order of San Francis, and this circumstance, to use the expression employed by des Mousseaux in connection with the work of the poor, unfrocked Abbé Huc, "is not calculated to strengthen our confidence." But there is another point as important, if not more so, as it seems to have escaped falsification by the zealous Catholic padres, and rests chiefly on Indian tradition. A famous Toltecan king, whose name is mixed up in the weird legends of Utatlan, the ruined capital of the great Indian kingdom, bore the biblical appellation of Balam Acan; the first name being preëminently Chaldean, and reminding one immediately of Balaam and his human-voiced ass. Besides the statement of Lord Kingsborough, who found such a striking similarity between the language of the Aztecs (the mother tongue) and the Hebrew, many of the figures on the *bas-reliefs* of Palenque and idols in *terra cotta*, exhumed in Santa Cruz del Quiche, have on their heads bandelets with a square protuberance on them, in front of the forehead, very similar to the phylacteries worn by the Hebrew Pharisees of old, while at prayers, and even by devotees of the present day, particularly the Jews of Poland and Russia. But as this may be but a fancy of ours, after all, we will not insist on the details.

---

816 See Stephens, *"Travels in Central America,"* etc.

Upon the testimony of the ancients, corroborated by modern discoveries, we know that there were numerous catacombs in Egypt and Chaldea, some of them of a very vast extent. The most renowned of them were the subterranean crypts of Thebes and Memphis. The former, beginning on the western side of the Nile, extended toward the Libyan desert, and were known as the *Serpent's* catacombs, or passages. It was there that were performed the sacred mysteries of the *kúklos ànágkés*, the "Unavoidable Cycle," more generally known as the "circle of necessity"; the inexorable doom imposed upon every soul after the bodily death, and when it had been judged in the Amenthian region.

In de Bourbourg's book, Votan, the Mexican demi-god, in narrating his expedition, describes a subterranean passage, which ran underground, and terminated at the root of the heavens, adding that this passage was a snake's hole, "*un agujero de culebra*"; and that he was admitted to it because he was himself "a son of the snakes," or a serpent.[817]

This is, indeed, very suggestive; for his description of the *snake's hole* is that of the ancient Egyptian crypt, as above mentioned. The hierophants, moreover, of Egypt, as of Babylon, generally styled themselves the "Sons of the Serpent-god," or "Sons of the Dragon"; not because — as des Mousseaux would have his readers believe — they were the progeny of Satan-incubus, the old serpent of Eden, but because, in the Mysteries, the serpent was the symbol of WISDOM and immortality.

"The Assyrian priest bore always the name of his god," says Movers.[818] The Druids of the Celto-Britannic regions also called themselves snakes. "I am a Serpent, I am a Druid!" they exclaimed. The Egyptian Karnak is twin-brother to the Carnac of Bretagné, the latter Carnac meaning the serpent's mount. The Dracontia once covered the surface of the globe, and these temples were sacred to the dragon, only because it was the symbol of the sun, which, in its turn, was the symbol of the highest god — the Phœnician Elon or Elion, whom Abraham recognized as El Elion.[819] Besides the surname of serpents, they were called the "builders," the "architects"; for the immense grandeur of their temples and monuments was such, that even now the pulverized remains of them "frighten the mathematical calculations of our modern engineers," says Taliesin.[820]

De Bourbourg hints that the chiefs of the name of Votan, the Quetzo-Cohuatl, or serpent deity of the Mexicans, are the descendants of Ham and Canaan. "I am Hivim," they say. "Being a Hivim, I am of the great race of the Dragon (snake). I am a snake myself, for I am a Hivim."[821] And des Mousseaux, rejoicing because he believes himself fairly on the serpent's, or rather, devil's trail, hurries to explain: "According to the most learned commentators of our sacred books, the Chivim or Hivim, or *Hevites,* descend from Heth, son of Canaan, son of Ham . . . *the accursed!*"[822]

But modern research has demonstrated, on unimpeachable evidence, that the whole genealogical table of the tenth chapter of *Genesis* refers to imaginary heroes, and that the

817 "*Cartas*," 53, 7-62.

818 "*Die Phönizier*," 70.

819 See Sanchoniaton in "*Eusebius*," Pr. Ev. 36; Genesis xiv.

820 "*Archæological Society of the Antiquaries of London*," vol. xxv., p. 220.

821 "*Cartas*," 51.

822 "*Hauts Phénomenes de la Magie*," 50.

closing verses of the ninth are little better than a bit of Chaldean allegory of Sisuthrus and the mythical flood, compiled and arranged to fit the Noachian frame. But, suppose the descendants of these Canaanites, "the accursed," were to resent for once the unmerited outrage? It would be an easy matter for them to reverse the tables, and answer to this fling, based on a *fable*, by a *fact* proved by archæologists and symbologists — namely, that Seth, Adam's third son, and the forefather of all Israel, the ancestor of Noah, and the progenitor of the "chosen people," is but Hermes, the god of wisdom, called also Thoth, Tat, Seth, Set, and *Sat-an*; and that he was, furthermore, when viewed under his bad aspect, Typhon, the Egyptian Satan, who was also *Set*. For the Jewish people, whose well-educated men, no more than Philo, or Josephus, the historian, regard their Mosaic books as otherwise than an allegory, such a discovery amounts to but little. But for Christians, who, like des Mousseaux, very unwisely accept the *Bible* narratives as literal history, the case stands very different.

Moses a Priest of Osiris

As far as affiliation goes, we agree with this pious writer; and we feel every day as certain that some of the peoples of Central America will be traced back to the Phœnicians and the Mosaic Israelites, as we do that the latter will be proved to have as persistently stuck to the same idolatry — if idolatry there is — of the sun and serpent-worship, as the Mexicans. There is evidence — biblical evidence — that two of Jacob's sons, Levi and Dan, as well as Judah, married Canaanite women, and followed the worship of their wives. Of course, every Christian will protest, but the proof may be found even in the translated *Bible*, pruned as it now stands. The dying Jacob thus describes his sons: "Dan," says he, "shall be a *serpent* by the way, an *adder* in the path, that biteth the horse-heels, so that his rider shall fall backward. . . . I have waited for thy salvation, O Lord!" Of Simeon and Levi, the patriarch (or Israel) remarks that they ". . . *are* brethren; instruments of *cruelty* are in their habitations. O my soul, come not thou into *their secret*; unto *their assembly*."[823] Now, in the original, the words "their secret," read — their Sod.[824] And Sod was the name for the great Mysteries of Baal, Adonis, and Bacchus who were all sun-gods and had serpents for symbols. The kabalists explain the allegory of the fiery serpents by saying, that this was the name given to the tribe of Levi, to all the *Levites* in short, and that Moses was the chief of the *Sodales*[825]. And here is the moment to prove our statements.

Moses is mentioned by several old historians as an Egyptian priest; Manetho says he was a hierophant of Hieropolis, and a priest of the sun-god Osiris, and that his name was

---

823 *Genesis* xlix.

824 Dunlap, in his introduction to "*SOD, the Mysteries of Adonis*," explains the word "Sod," as Arcanum; religious mystery on the authority of Shindler's "Penteglott" (1201). "The SECRET of the Lord is with them that fear Him," says Psalm xxv, 14. This is a mistranslation of the Christians, for it ought to read "*Sod* Ihoh (the mysteries of Iohoh) are for *those who fear Him*" (Dunlap, "*Mysteries of Adonis*," xi.). "Al (El) is terrible in the great Sod of the *Kedeshim* (the priests, the holy, the *Initiated*), *Psalm* lxxxix. 7" (*Ibid.*).

825 "The members of the *priest-colleges* were called *Sodales*," says Freund's "*Latin Lexicon*" (iv. 448). "SODALITIES were constituted in the Idæan Mysteries of the MIGHTY MOTHER," writes Cicero ("*De Senectute*," 13); Dunlap, "*Mysteries of Adonis*."

Osarsiph. Those moderns, who accept it as a fact that he "was learned in *all* the wisdom" of the Egyptians, must also submit to the right interpretation of the word wisdom, which was throughout the world known as a synonym of *initiation* into the secret mysteries of the *Magi*. Did the idea never strike the reader of the *Bible*, that an alien born and brought up in a foreign country *could not* and *would not* possibly have been admitted — we will not say to the final initiation, the grandest mystery of all, but even to share the knowledge of the minor priesthood, those who belonged to the *lesser* mysteries? In *Genesis xliii*. 32, we read, that no Egyptian could seat himself to eat bread with the brothers of Joseph, "for that is an abomination unto the Egyptians." But that the Egyptians ate "with *him* (Joseph) by themselves." The above proves two things: 1, that Joseph, whatever he was in his heart, had, in appearance at least, changed his religion, married the daughter of a priest of the "idolatrous" nation, and become himself an Egyptian; otherwise, the natives would not have eaten bread with him. And 2, that subsequently Moses, if not an Egyptian by birth, became one through being admitted into the priesthood, and thus was a SODALE. As an induction, the narrative of the "brazen serpent" (the Caduceus of Mercury or Asclepios, the son of the sun-god Apollo-Python) becomes logical and natural. We must bear in mind that Pharaoh's daughter, who saved Moses and adopted him, is called by Josephus *Thermuthis*; and the latter, according to W lkinson, is the name of the *asp* sacred to Isis;[826] moreover, Moses is said to descend from the tribe of *Levi*. We will explain the kabalistic ideas as to the books of Moses and the great prophet himself more fully in Volume II.

If Brasseur de Bourbourg and the Chevalier des Mousseaux, had so much at heart to trace the identity of the Mexicans with the Canaanites, they might have found far better and weightier proofs than by showing both the "accursed" descendants of Ham. For instance, they might have pointed to the Nargal, the Chaldean and Assyrian chief of the Magi (Rab-Mag) and the Nagal, the chief sorcerer of the Mexican Indians. Both derive their names from Nergal-Sarezer, the Assyrian god, and both have the same faculties, or powers to have an attendant *dæmon* with whom they identify themselves completely. The Chaldean and Assyrian Nargal kept his dæmon, in the shape of some animal considered sacred, inside the temple; the Indian Nagal keeps his wherever he can — in the neighboring lake, or wood, or in the house, under the shape of a house-hold animal.[827]

We find the *Catholic World*, newspaper, in a recent number, bitterly complaining that the old Pagan element of the aboriginal inhabitants of America does not seem to be utterly dead in the United States. Even where tribes have been for long years under the care of Christian teachers, heathen rites are practiced in secret, and crypto-paganism, or *nagualism*, flourishes now, as in the days of Montezuma. It says: "Nagualism and voodoo-worship" — as it calls these two strange sects — "are direct *devil-worship*. A report addressed to the Cortes in 1812, by Don Pedro Baptista Pino, says: 'All the pueblos have their *artufas* — so the natives call subterranean rooms with only a single door, where they assemble to perform their feasts, and hold meetings. These are impenetrable temples . . . and the doors are always closed on the Spaniards.

---

826 See Wilkinson, "*Ancient Egyptians*," vol. v., p. 65.
827 Brasseur de Bourbourg, "*Mexique*," pp. 135-574.

" 'All these pueblos, in spite of the sway which religion has had over them, cannot forget a part of the beliefs which have been transmitted to them, and which they are careful to transmit to their descendants. Hence come the adoration they render the sun and moon, and other heavenly bodies, the respect they entertain for fire, etc.

" 'The pueblo chiefs seem to be at the same time priests; they perform various simple rites, by which the power of the sun and of Montezuma is recognized, as well as the power (according to some accounts) of the Great Snake, to whom, by order of Montezuma, they are to look for life. They also officiate in certain ceremonies with which they pray for rain. There are painted representations of the Great Snake, together with that of a misshapen, red-haired man, declared to stand for Montezuma. Of this last there was also, in the year 1845, in the pueblo of Laguna, a rude effigy or idol, intended, apparently, to represent only the head of the deity.'" [828]

The perfect identity of the rites, ceremonies, traditions, and even the names of the deities, among the Mexicans and ancient Babylonians and Egyptians, are a sufficient proof of South America being peopled by a colony which mysteriously found its way across the Atlantic. When? at what period? History is silent on that point; but those who consider that there is no tradition, sanctified by ages, without a certain sediment of truth at the bottom of it, believe in the *Atlantis*-legend. There are, scattered throughout the world, a handful of thoughtful and solitary students, who pass their lives in obscurity, far from the rumors of the world, studying the great problems of the physical and spiritual universes. They have their secret records in which are preserved the fruits of the scholastic labors of the long line of recluses whose successors they are. The knowledge of their early ancestors, the sages of India, Babylonia, Nineveh, and the imperial Thebes; the legends and traditions commented upon by the masters of Solon, Pythagoras, and Plato, in the marble halls of Heliopolis and Saïs; traditions which, in their days, already seemed to hardly glimmer from behind the foggy curtain of the past; — all this, and much more, is recorded on indestructible parchment, and passed with jealous care from one adept to another. These men believe the story of the Atlantis to be no fable, but maintain that at different epochs of the past huge islands, and even continents, existed where now there is but a wild waste of waters. In those submerged temples and libraries the archæologist would find, could he but explore them, the materials for filling all the gaps that now exist in what we imagine is *history*. They say that at a remote epoch a traveller could traverse what is now the Atlantic Ocean, almost the entire distance by land, crossing in boats from one island to another, where narrow straits then existed.

Our suspicion as to the relationship of the cis-Atlantic and trans-Atlantic races is strengthened upon reading about the wonders wrought by Quetzo-Cohuatl, the Mexican magician. His wand must be closely-related to the traditional sapphire-stick of Moses, the stick which bloomed in the garden of Raguel-Jethro, his father-in-law, and upon which was engraved the ineffable name. The "four men" described as the real four ancestors of the human race, "who were neither begotten by the gods, nor born of woman," but whose "creation was a wonder wrought by the Creator," and who were made after three attempts at manufacturing men had failed, equally present some striking points of similarity with the

---

828 "*Catholic World*," N. Y., January, 1877, Article Nagualism, Voodooism, etc.

esoteric explanations of the Hermetists;[829] they also undeniably recall the four sons of God of the Egyptian theogony. Moreover, as any one may infer, the resemblance of this myth to the narrative related in *Genesis,* will be apparent to even a superficial observer.

These four ancestors "could reason and speak, their sight was unlimited, and they knew all things at once."[830] When "they had rendered thanks to their Creator for their existence, *the gods were frightened,* and they breathed a cloud over the eyes of men that they might see a certain distance only, and not be *like the gods themselves.*" This bears directly upon the sentence in *Genesis,* "Behold, *the man is become as one of us,* to know good and evil; and now, lest he put forth his hand, and take also of the tree of life," etc. Then, again, "While *they were asleep* God gave them wives," etc.

We disclaim the least intention to disrespectfully suggest ideas to those who are so wise as to need no hint. But we must bear in mind that authentic treatises upon ancient magic of the Chaldean and Egyptian lore are not scattered about in public libraries, and at auction sales. That such exist is nevertheless a fact for many students of the arcane philosophy. Is it not of the greatest importance for every antiquarian to be acquainted at least superficially with their contents? "The four ancestors of the race," adds Max Müller, "seem to have had a long life, and when at last they came to die, they disappeared in a mysterious manner, and left to their sons what is called the *hidden majesty,* which was never to be opened by human hands. What it was we do not know."

If there is no relationship between this hidden majesty and the hidden glory of the Chaldean *Kabala,* which we are told was left behind him by Enoch when he was translated in such a mysterious way, then we must discredit all circumstantial evidence. But is it not barely possible that these "four ancestors" of the Quiche race typify in their esoteric sense the four successive progenitors of men, mentioned in *Genesis* i., ii., and vi.? In the first chapter, the first man is bi-sexual — "male and female created he them" — and answers to the hermaphrodite deities of the subsequent mythologies; the second, Adam, made out of "the dust of the ground" and uni-sexual and answering to the "sons of God" of chapter vi.; the third, the giants, or *nephilim,* who are only hinted at in the *Bible,* but fully explained elsewhere; the fourth, the parents of men "whose daughters were fair."

Taking the admitted facts that the Mexicans had their magicians from the remote periods; that the same remark applies to all the ancient religions of the world; that a strong resemblance prevails not only in the forms of their ceremonial worship, but also in the very names used to designate certain magical implements; and finally that all other clews, in accordance with scientific deductions, have failed (some because swallowed up in the bottomless pit of coincidences), why should we not turn to the great authorities upon magic, and see whether, under this "aftergrowth of fantastic nonsense," there may not be a deep substratum of truth? Here we are not willing to be misunderstood. We do not send the scientists to the *Kabala* and the Hermetic books to study magic, but to the authorities on magic to discover materials for history and science. We have no idea of incurring the

---

829 In "Hesiod," Zeus creates his *third* race of men out of ash-trees. In "Popol-Vuh," we are told the *third* race of men is created out of the tree "tzite," and women are made from the marrow of a reed which was called "sibac." This also is a strange coincidence.
830 "Popol-Vuh," reviewed by Max Müller.

wrathful denunciations of the Academicians, by an indiscretion like that of poor des Mousseaux, when he tried to force them to read his demonological Memoire and investigate the Devil.

The *History of Bernal Diaz de Castilla,* a follower of Cortez, gives us some idea of the extraordinary refinement and intelligence of the people whom they conquered; but the descriptions are too long to be inserted here. Suffice it to say, that the Aztecs appeared in more than one way to have resembled the ancient Egyptians in civilization and refinement. Among both peoples magic or the arcane natural philosophy was cultivated to the highest degree. Add to this that Greece, the "later cradle of the arts and sciences," and India, cradle of religions, were and are still devoted to its study and practice — and who shall venture to discredit its dignity as a study, and its profundity as a science?

There never was, nor can there be more than one universal religion; for there can be but one truth concerning God. Like an immense chain whose upper end, the alpha, remains invisibly emanating from a Deity — *in statu abscondito* with every primitive theology — it encircles our globe in every direction; it leaves not even the darkest corner unvisited, before the other end, the omega, turns back on its way to be again received where it first emanated. On this divine chain was strung the exoteric symbology of every people. Their variety of form is powerless to affect their substance, and under their diverse ideal types of the universe of matter, symbolizing its vivifying principles, the uncorrupted immaterial image of the spirit of being guiding them is the same.

So far as human intellect can go in the ideal interpretation of the spiritual universe, its laws and powers, the last word was pronounced ages since; and, if the *ideas* of Plato can be simplified for the sake of easier comprehension, the spirit of their substance can neither be altered, nor removed without material damage to the truth. Let human brains submit themselves to torture for thousands of years to come; let theology perplex faith and mime it with the enforcing of incomprehensible dogmas in metaphysics; and science strengthen skepticism, by pulling down the tottering remains of spiritual intuition in mankind, with her demonstrations of its fallibility, eternal truth can never be destroyed. We find its last possible expression in our human language in the Persian Logos, the *Honover,* or the living *manifested* Word of God.

The Zoroastrian *Enoch-Verihe* is identical with the Jewish "*I am*"; and the "Great Spirit" of the poor, untutored Indian, is the manifested Brahma of the Hindu philosopher. One of the latter, Tcharaka, a Hindu physician, who is said to have lived 5,000 years B.C., in his treatise on the origin of things, called *Usa,* thus beautifully expresses himself: "Our Earth is, like all the luminous bodies that surround us, one of the atoms of the immense Whole of which we show a slight conception by terming it — the Infinite."

"There is but one light, and there is but one darkness," says a Siamese proverb. *Dæmon est Deus inversus,* the Devil is the shadow of God, states the universal kabalistic axiom. Could light exist but for primeval darkness? And did not the brilliant, sunny universe first stretch its infant arms from the swaddling bands of dark and dreary chaos? If the Christian *"fulness of Him that filleth all in all"* is a revelation, then we must admit that, if there is a devil, he must be included in this *fulness,* and be a part of that which "filleth all in all." From time immemorial the justification of the Deity, and His separation from the existing evil was attempted, and the object was reached by the old Oriental philosophy in the foundation of the *theodiké;* but their metaphysical views on the *fallen spirit,* have never been disfigured by the creation of an anthropomorphic personality of the Devil as was done subsequently by the leading lights of Christian theology. A personal fiend, who opposes the Deity, and impedes progress on its way to perfection, is to be sought only on earth amid humanity, not in heaven.

Thus is it that all the religious monuments of old, in whatever land or under whatever climate, are the expression of the same identical thoughts, the key to which is in the esoteric doctrine. It would be vain, without studying the latter, to seek to unriddle the mysteries enshrouded for centuries in the temples and ruins of Egypt and Assyria, or those of Central America, British Columbia, and the Nagkon-Wat of Cambodia. If each of these was built by a different nation; and neither nation had had intercourse with the others for ages, it is also certain that all were planned and built under the direct supervision of the priests. And the clergy of every nation, though practicing rites and ceremonies which may have differed externally, had evidently been initiated into the same traditional mysteries which were taught all over the world.

In order to institute a better comparison between the specimens of prehistoric architecture to be found at the most opposite points of the globe, we have but to point to the grandiose Hindu ruins of Ellora in the Dekkan, the Mexican Chichen-Itza, in Yucatan, and the still grander ruins of Copan, in Guatemala. They present such features of resemblance that it seems impossible to escape the conviction that they were built by peoples moved by the same religious ideas, and that had reached an equal level of highest civilization in arts and sciences.

There is not, perhaps, on the face of the whole globe, a more imposing mass of ruins than Nagkon-Wat, the wonder and puzzle of European archæologists who venture into Siam. And when we say ruins, the expression is hardly correct; for nowhere are there buildings of such tremendous antiquity to be found in a better state of preservation than Nagkon-Wat, and the ruins of Angkorthôm, the great temple.

Hidden far away in the province of Siamrap — eastern Siam — in the midst of a most luxuriant tropical vegetation, surrounded by almost impenetrable forests of palms, cocoa-trees, and betel-nut, "the general appearance of the wonderful temple is beautiful and romantic, as well as impressive and grand," says Mr. Vincent, a recent traveler.[831] "We whose good fortune it is to live in the nineteenth century, are accustomed to boast of the perfection and preëminence of our modern civilization; of the grandeur of our attainments in science, art, literature, and what not, as compared with those whom we call ancients; but still we are compelled to admit that they have far excelled our recent endeavors in many things, and notably in the fine arts of painting, architecture, and sculpture. We were but just looking upon a most wonderful example of the two latter, for in style and beauty of architecture, solidity of construction, and magnificent and elaborate carving and sculpture, the Great Nagkon-Wat has no superior, certainly no rival standing at the present day. The first view of the ruins is overwhelming."

---

831 Frank Vincent, Jun., "*The Land of the White Elephant,*" p. 209.

Thus the opinion of another traveller is added to that of many preceding ones, including archæologists and other competent critics, who have believed that the ruins of the past Egyptian splendor deserve no higher eulogium than Nagkon-Wat.

According to our plan, we will allow more impartial critics than ourselves to describe the place, since, in a work professedly devoted to a vindication of the ancients, the testimony of so enthusiastic an advocate as the present writer may be questioned. We have, nevertheless, seen Nagkon-Wat under exceptionally favorable circumstances, and can, therefore, certify to the general correctness of Mr. Vincent's description. He says:

"We entered upon an immense causeway, the stairs of which were flanked with six huge griffins, each carved from a single block of stone. The causeway is . . . 725 feet in length, and is paved with stones each of which measures four feet in length by two in breadth. On either side of it are artificial lakes fed by springs, and each covering about five acres of ground. . . . The outer wall of Nagkon-Wat (the city of monasteries) is half a mile square, with gateways . . . which are handsomely carved with figures of gods and dragons. The foundations are ten feet in height. . . . The entire edifice, including the roof, is of stone, *but without cement, and so closely fitting are the joints as even now to be scarcely discernible*. . . . The shape of the building is oblong, being 796 feet in length, and 588 in width, while the highest central pagoda rises some 250 odd feet above the ground, and four others, at the angles of the court, are each about 150 feet in height."

The above underscored lines are suggestive to travellers who have remarked and admired the same wonderful mason-work in the Egyptian remains. If the same workmen did not lay the courses in both countries we must at least think that the secret of this matchless wall-building was equally known to the architects of every land.

THE LESSONS TAUGHT BY THE RUINS OF SIAM

"Passing, we ascend a platform . . . and enter the temple itself through a columned portico, the *facade* of which is beautifully carved in *basso-relievo* with ancient mythological subjects. From this doorway, on either side, runs a corridor with a double row of columns, cut — base and capital — from single blocks, with a double, oval-shaped roof, covered with carving and consecutive sculptures upon the outer wall. This gallery of sculptures, which forms the exterior of the temple, consists of over half a mile of continuous pictures, cut in *basso-relievo* upon sandstone slabs six feet in width, and represents subjects taken from Hindu mythology, from the *Ramayâna* — the Sanscrit epic poem of India, with its 25,000 verses describing the exploits of the god Rama, and the son of the King of Oudh. The contests of the King of Ceylon, and Hanouma,[832] the monkey-god, are graphically

---

832 The Hanoumā is over three feet tall, and black as a coal. The *Ramayana,* giving the biography of this sacred monkey, relates that Hanoumā was formerly a powerful chieftain, who being the greatest friend of Rama, helped him to find his wife, Sitha, who had been carried off to Ceylon by Ravana, the mighty king of the giants. After numerous adventures Hanoumā was caught by the latter, while visiting the city of the giant as Rama's spy. For this crime Ravana had the poor Hanoumā's tail oiled and set on fire, and it was in extinguishing it that the monkey-god became so black in the face that neither himself nor his posterity could ever get rid of the color. If we have to believe Hindu legends this same Hanoumā was the *progenitor* of the Europeans; a tradition which, though strictly Darwinian, hence, scientific, is by no means flattering to us. The legend states that for services rendered, Rama,

represented. There is *no keystone* used in the arch of this corridor. On the walls are sculptured the immense number of 100,000 separate figures. One picture from the *Ramayana* . . . occupies 240 feet of the wall. . . . In the *Nagkon-Wat* as many as 1,532 solid columns have been counted, and among the entire ruins of Angkor . . . the immense number of 6,000, almost all of them hewn from single blocks and artistically carved. . . .

"But who built *Nagkon-Wat?* and when was it built? Learned men have attempted to form opinions from studies of its construction, and especially ornamentation," and have failed. "Native Cambodian historians," adds Vincent, "reckon 2,400 from the building of the temple. . . . I asked one of them how long *Nagkon-Wat* had been built. . . . 'None can tell when. . . . I do not know; it must have either sprung up from the ground or been built by giants, or perhaps by the angels' . . . was the answer."

When Stephens asked the native Indians "Who built Copan? . . . what nation traced the hieroglyphic designs, sculptured these elegant figures and carvings, these emblematical designs?" the dull answer he received was "*Quien sabe?*" — who knows! "All is mystery; dark, impenetrable mystery," writes Stephens. "In Egypt, the colossal skeletons of gigantic temples stand in all the nakedness of desolation. Here, an immense forest shrouded the ruins, hiding them from sight."[833]

But there are perhaps many circumstances, trifling for archæologists unacquainted with the "idle and fanciful" legends of old, hence overlooked; otherwise the discovery might have sent them on a new train of thought. One is the invariable presence in the Egyptian, Mexican, and Siamese ruined temples, of the monkey. The Egyptian cynocephalus assumes the same postures as the Hindu and Siamese Hanoumā; and among the sculptured fragments of Copan, Stephens found the remains of colossal apes or baboons, "strongly resembling in outline and appearance the four monstrous animals which once stood in front, attached to the base of the obelisk of Luxor, now in Paris,[834] and which, under the name of the cynocephali, were worshipped at Thebes." In almost every Buddhist temple there are idols of huge monkeys kept, and some people have in their houses white monkeys on purpose "to keep *bad* spirits away."

"Was civilization," writes Louis de Carné,[835] "in the complex meaning we give that word, in keeping among the ancient Cambodians with what such prodigies of architecture seem to indicate? The age of Pheidias was that of Sophocles, Socrates, and Plato; Michael Angelo and Raphael succeeded Dante. There are luminous epochs during which the human mind, developing itself in every direction, triumphs in all, and creates masterpieces *which spring from the same inspiration.*" "Nagkon-Wat," concludes Vincent, "must be ascribed to other than

---

the hero and demi-god, gave in marriage to the monkey-warriors of his army the daughters of the giants of Ceylon — the Bâkshasas — and granted them, moreover, as a dowry, all western parts of the world. Repairing thence, the monkeys and their giant-wives lived happily and had a number of descendants. The latter are the present Europeans. Dravidian words are found in Western Europe, indicating that there was an original unity of race and language between the populations. May it not be a hint that the traditions are akin, of elfin and kobold races in Europe, and monkeys, actually cognate with them in Hindustan?

833 "*Incidents of Travels in Central America, etc.,*" vol. i., p. 105.

834 They stand no more, for the obelisk alone was removed to Paris.

835 See "*The Land of the White Elephant,*" p. 221.

ancient Cambodians. But to whom? . . . There exist *no credible* traditions; *all is absurd fable or legend.*"

The latter sentence has become of late a sort of cant phrase in the mouths of travellers and archæologists. When they have found that no clew is attainable unless it can be found in popular legends, they turn away discouraged, and a final verdict is withheld. At the same time Vincent quotes a writer who remarks that these ruins "are as imposing as the ruins of Thebes, or Memphis, but more mysterious." Mouhot thinks they were erected "by some ancient Michael Angelo," and adds that Nagkon-Wat "is grander than anything left to us by Greece or Rome." Furthermore Mouhot ascribes the building again to some of *the lost tribes of Israel,* and is corroborated in that opinion by Miche, the French Bishop of Cambodia, who confesses that he is struck "by the Hebrew character of the faces of many of the savage Stiens." Henri Mouhot believes that, "without exaggeration, the oldest parts of Angkor may be fixed at more than 2,000 years ago." This, then, in comparison with the pyramids, would make them quite modern; the date is the more incredible, because the pictures on the walls may be proved to belong to those archaic ages when Poseidon and the Kabeiri were worshipped throughout the continent. Had Nagkon-Wat been built, as Dr. Adolf Bastian[836] will have it, "for the reception of the learned patriarch, Buddhagosa, who brought the holy books of the *Trai-Pidok* from Ceylon; or, as Bishop Pallegoix, who "refers the erection of this edifice to the reign of Phra Pathum Suriving," when "the sacred books of the Buddhists were brought from Ceylon, and Buddhism became the religion of the Cambodians," how is it possible to account for the following?

"We see in this same temple carved images of Buddha, four, and even thirty-two-armed, and two and sixteen-headed gods, the Indian Vishnu, gods *with wings,* Burmese heads, Hindu figures, and Ceylon mythology. . . . You see warriors riding upon elephants and in chariots, foot soldiers with shield and spear, boats, tigers, griffins . . . serpents, fishes, crocodiles, bullocks . . . soldiers of immense physical development, with helmets, and some people with beards — probably Moors. The figures," adds Mr. Vincent, "stand somewhat like those on the great Egyptian monuments, the side partly turned toward the front . . . and I noticed, besides, five horsemen, armed with spear and sword, riding abreast, like those seen upon the Assyrian tablets in the British Museum."[837]

For our part, we may add, that there are on the walls several repetitions of Dagon, the man-fish of the Babylonians, and of the Kabeirian gods of Samothrace. This may have escaped the notice of the few archæologists who examined the place; but upon stricter inspection they will be found there, as well as the reputed father of the Kabeiri — Vulcan, with his bolts and implements, having near him a king with a sceptre in his hand, which is the counterpart of that of Cheronaæ, or the "sceptre of Agamemnon," so-called, said to have been presented to him by the lame god of Lemnos. In another place we find Vulcan, recognizable by his hammer and pincers, but under the shape of a monkey, as usually represented by the Egyptians.

Now, if Nagkon-Wat is essentially a Buddhist temple, how comes it to have on its walls *basso-relievos* of completely an Assyrian character; and Kabeirian gods which, though

---

836 The President of the Royal Geographical Society of Berlin.
837 *"The Land of the White Elephant,"* p. 215.

universally worshipped as the most ancient of the Asiatic mystery-gods, had already been abandoned 200 years B.C., and the Samothracian mysteries themselves completely altered? Whence the popular tradition concerning the Prince of Roma among the Cambodians, a personage mentioned by all the native historians, who attribute to him the foundation of the temple? Is it not barely possible that even the *Ramayâna*, itself, the famous epic poem, is but the original of Homer's *Iliad*, as it was suggested some years ago? The beautiful Paris, carrying off Helen, looks very much like Râvana, king of the giants, eloping with Sita, Rama's wife? The Trojan war is a counterpart of the *Ramayâna* war; moreover, Herodotus assures us that the Trojan heroes and gods date in Greece only from the days of the *Iliad*. In such a case even Hanoumā, the monkey-god, would be but Vulcan in disguise; the more so that the Cambodian tradition makes the founder of Angkor come from *Roma*, which they place at the western end of the world, and that the Hindu Roma also apportions the west to the descendants of Hanoumā.

Hypothetical as the suggestion may now seem, it is worthy of consideration, if even for the sake of being refuted. The Abbé Jaquenet, a Catholic missionary in Cochin China, ever ready to connect the least glimmer of historical light with that of Christian revelation, writes, "Whether we consider the commercial relations of the Jews . . . when, in the height of their power, the combined fleets of Hiram and Solomon went to seek the treasures of Ophir, or whether we come lower down, to the dispersion of the ten tribes who, instead of returning from captivity, set out from the banks of the Euphrates, and reached the shores of the ocean . . . the shining of the light of revelation in the far East is not the less incontestable."

It looks certainly "incontestable" enough if we reverse the position and admit that all the light that ever shone on the Israelites came to them from this "far East," passing first through the Chaldeans and Egyptians. The first thing to settle, is to find out who were the Israelites themselves; and that is the most vital question. Many historians seem to claim, with good reason, that the Jews were similar or identical with the ancient Phœnicians, but the Phœnicians were beyond any doubt an Æthiopian race; moreover, the present race of Punjaub are hybridized with the Asiatic Æthiopians. Herodotus traces the Hebrews to the Persian Gulf; and south of that place were the Himyarites (the Arabians); beyond, the early Chaldeans and Susinians, the great builders. This seems to establish pretty well their Æthiopian affinity. Megasthenes says that the Jews were an Indian sect called *Kalani*, and their theology resembled that of the Indians. Other authors also suspect that the colonized Jews or the Judeans were the Yadus from Afghanistan — the old India.[838] Eusebius tells us that "the Æthiopians came from the river Indus and settled near Egypt." More research may show that the Tamil Hindus, who are accused by the missionaries of worshipping the Devil — Kutti-Sattan — only honor, after all, Seth or Satan, worshipped by the biblical Hittites.

But if the Jews were in the twilight of history the Phœnicians, the latter may be traced themselves to the nations who used the old Sanscrit language. Carthage was a Phœnician city, hence its name; for Tyre was equally *Kartha*. In the *Bible* the words *Kir, Kirjath* are frequently found. Their tutelar god was styled *Mel-Kartha* (Mel, Baal), or tutelar lord of the

---

838 The Phœnician Dido is the feminine of David דּוּד, דּיּדּן. Under the name of Astarte, she led the Phœnician colonies, and her image was on the prow of their ships. But David and Saul are names belonging to Afghanistan also.

city. In Sanscrit a city or communal was a *cul* and its lord was *Heri*.[839] Her-culeus is therefore the translation of Melkarth and Sanscrit in origin. Moreover all the Cyclopean races were Phœnicians. In the *Odyssey* the Kuklopes (Cyclops) are the Libyan shepherds; and Herodotus describes them as miners and great builders. They are the ancient Titans or giants, who in Hesiod forge bolts for Zeus. They are the biblical *Zamzummim* from the land of the giants, the Anakim.

Now it is easy to see that the excavators of Ellora, the builders of the old Pagodas, the architects of Copan and of the ruins of Central America, those of Nagkon-Wat, and those of the Egyptian remains were, if not of the same race, at least of the same religion — the one taught in the oldest Mysteries. Besides, the figures on the walls of Angkor are purely archaic, and have nothing to do with the images and idols of Buddha, who may be of a far later origin. "What gives a peculiar interest to this section," says Dr. Bastian, "is the fact that the artist has represented the different nationalities in all their distinctive characteristic features, from the flat-nosed savage in the tasselled garb of the Pnom and the short-haired Lao, to the straight-nosed Rajaput, with sword and shield, and *the bearded Moor*, giving a catalogue of nationalities, like another *column of Trajan*, in the predominant physical conformation of each race. On the whole, there is such a prevalence of *Hellenic* cast in features and profiles, as well as in the elegant attitude of the horsemen, that one might suppose Xenocrates of old, after finishing his labors in Bombay, had made an excursion to the East."

Therefore, if we allow the tribes of Israel to have had a hand in the building of Nagkon-Wat, it cannot be as the tribes numbered and sent from the wilderness of Paran in search of the land of Canaan, but as their earlier ancestors, which amounts to the rejection of such tribes, as the casting of a reflection of the *Mosaic* revelation. And where is the outside *historical* evidence that such tribes were ever heard of at all, before the compilation of the *Old Testament* by Ezra? There are archæologists who strongly regard the twelve tribes as utterly mythical,[840] for there never was a tribe of Simeon, and that of Levi was a *caste*. There still remains the same problem to solve — whether the Judæans had ever been in Palestine before Cyrus. From the sons of Jacob, who had all married Canaanites, except Joseph, whose wife was the daughter of an Egyptian Priest of the Sun, down to the legendary *Book of Judges* there was an acknowledged general intermarrying between the said tribes and the idolatrous races: "And the children of Israel dwelt among the Canaanites, Hittites, and Amorites, and Perizzites, and Hivites, and Jebusites; and they took their daughters to be their wives, and gave their daughters to their sons, and served their gods," says the third chapter of *Judges*, " . . . and the children of Israel forgat their God and served Baalim, and the groves." This Baal was Moloch, M'lch Karta, or Hercules. He was worshipped wherever the Phœnicians went. How could the Israelites possibly keep together as tribes, while, on the authority of the *Bible* itself, whole populations were from year to year uprooted violently by Assyrian and other conquerors? "So was Israel carried away out of their own land to

---

839 (Prof. A. Wilder.) This archæologist says: "I regard the Æthiopian, Cushite and Hamitic races as the building and artistic race who worshipped Baal (Siva), or Bel — made temples, grottos, pyramids, and used a language of peculiar type. Rawlinson derives that language from the *Turanians* in Hindustan."

840 Prof. A. Wilder among others.

Assyria unto this day. And the king of Assyria brought men from Babylon, and from Cuthah, and from Ava, and from Hamath, and from Sepharvaim, and placed them in the cities of Samaria *instead* of the children of Israel" (2 *Kings*, xvii. 23, 24).

If the language of Palestine became in time Semitic, it is because of Assyrian influence; for Phœnicia had become a dependency as early as the days of Hiram, and the Phœnicians evidently changed their language from Hamitic to Semitic. Assyria was "the land of Nimrod" (from *Nimr*, spotted), and Nimrod was Bacchus, with his spotted leopard-skin. This leopard-skin is a sacred appendage of the "Mysteries"; it was used in the Eleusinian as well as in the Egyptian Mysteries; it is found sculptured on the *basso-relievos* of Central American ruins, covering the backs of the sacrificers; it is mentioned in the earliest speculations of the Brahmans on the meaning of their sacrificial prayers, the *Aytareya Brahmanam*.[841] It is used in the *Agnishtoma*, the *initiation rites* of the Soma Mystery. When the neophyte is "to be born again," he is covered with a leopard-skin, out of which he emerges as from his mother's womb. The Kabeiri were also Assyrian gods. They had different names; in the common language they were known as Jupiter and Bacchus, and sometimes as Achiochersus, Aschieros, Achiochersa, and Cadmillus; and even the true number of these deities was uncertain with the people. They had other names in the "sacred language," known but to the hierophants and priests; and "it was not lawful to mention them." How is it then that we find them reproduced in their Samothracian "postures" on the walls of Nagkon-Wat? How is it again that we find them pronounced — albeit slightly disfigured — as known in that same sacred language, by the populations of Siam, Thibet, and India?

The name Kabeiri may be a derivation from אבד, *Abir*, great; הבד, *Ebir*, an astrologer, or חבד, *Chabir*, an associate; and they were worshipped at Hebron, the city of the *Anakes* — the giants. The name Abraham, according to Dr. Wilder, has "a very Kabeirian look." The word *Heber*, or *Gheber* may be the etymological root of the Hebrews, as applied to Nimrod and the Bible-giants of the sixth chapter of *Genesis*, but we must seek for their origin far earlier than the days of Moses. The name *Phœnician* affords its own proof. They are called Foinike" by Manetho, or *Ph' Anakes*, which shows that the Anakes or *Anakim* of Canaan, with whom the people of Israel, if not identical in race, had, by intermarriage, become entirely absorbed, were the Phœnicians, or the problematical Hyk-sos, as Manetho has it, and whom Josephus once declared were the direct ancestors of the Israelites. Therefore, it is in this jumble of contradictory opinions, authorities, and historical *olla podrida* that we must look for a solution of the mystery. So long as the origin of the Hyk-sos is not positively settled we can know nothing certain of the Israelitish people who, either wittingly or otherwise, have mixed up their chronology and origin in such an inextricable tangle. But if the Hyk-sos can be proved to have been the Pali-Shepherds of the Indus, who partially removed to the East, and came over from the nomadic Aryan tribes of India, then, perhaps, it would account for the biblical myths being so mixed up with the Aryan and Asiatic Mystery-gods. As Dunlap says: "The Hebrews came out of Egypt among the Canaanites; they need not be traced beyond the *Exodus. That is their historical beginning.* It was very easy to cover up this remote event by the recital of mythical traditions, and to prefix to it an account of their origin in which the gods (patriarchs) should figure as their ancestors." But it is not *their historical beginning* which is the most vital question for the world of science and theology. It is their

---

841 See Martin Haug's translation, "*The Aytareya Brahmanam*."

religious beginning. And if we can trace it through the Hyk-sos — Phœnicians, the Æthiopian builders and the Chaldeans — whether it is to the Hindus that the latter owe their learning, or the Brahmans who owe it to the Chaldeans, we have the means in hand to trace every so-called *revealed* dogmatical assertion in the *Bible* to its origin, which we have to search for in the twilight of history, and before the separation of the Aryan and Semitic families. And how can we do it better or more surely than through means afforded us by archæology? Picture-writing can be destroyed, but if it survives it cannot lie; and, if we find the same myths, ideas, and secret symbols on monuments all over the world; and if, moreover, these monuments can be shown to antedate the twelve "chosen" tribes, then we can unerringly show that instead of being a direct divine *revelation*, it was but an incomplete recollection or tradition among a tribe which had been identified and mixed up for centuries before the apparition of Abraham, with all the three great world-families; namely, the Aryan, Semitic, and Turanian nations, if so they must be called.

The *Teraphim* of Abram's father, *Terah*, the "maker of images," were the Kabeiri gods, and we see them worshipped by Micah, by the Danites, and others.[842] Teraphim were identical with the seraphim, and these were serpent-images, the origin of which is in the Sanscrit *sarpâ* (the serpent), a symbol sacred to all the deities as a symbol of immortality. Kiyun, or the god Kivan, worshipped by the Hebrews in the wilderness, is Siva, the Hindu,[843] as well as Saturn.[844] The Greek story shows that Dardanus, the Arcadian, having received them as a dowry, carried them to Samothrace, and from thence to Troy; and they were worshipped far before the days of glory of Tyre or Sidon, though the former had been built 2760 B.C. From where did Dardanus derive them?

It is an easy matter to assign an age to ruins on merely the external evidence of probabilities; it is more difficult to prove it. Meanwhile the rock-works of Ruad, Perytus, Marathos, resemble those of Petra, Baalbek, and other Æthiopian works, even externally. On the other hand the assertions of certain archæologists who find no resemblance between the temples of Central America and those of Egypt and Siam, leave the symbologist, acquainted with the secret language of picture-writing, perfectly unconcerned. He sees the landmarks of one and the same doctrine on all of these monuments, and reads their history and affiliation in signs imperceptible to the uninitiated scientist. There are traditions also; and one of these speaks of the last of the king-initiates — (who were but rarely admitted to the higher orders of the Eastern Brotherhoods), who reigned in 1670. This king of Siam was the one so ridiculed by the French ambassador, de la Loubere, as a lunatic who had been searching all his life for the philosopher's stone.

One of such mysterious landmarks is found in the peculiar structure of certain arches in the temples. The author of the *Land of the White Elephant* remarks as curious, "the absence of the keystone in the arches of the building, and the undecipherable inscriptions." In the ruins of Santa Cruz del Quiche an arched corridor was found by Stephens, equally without a keystone. Describing the desolate ruins of Palenque, and remarking that the arches of the

---

842 Judges xvii-xviii., etc.
843 The Zendic *H* is *S* in India. Thus Hapta is Sapta; *Hindu* is *Sindhaya*. (A. Wilder.) " . . . the *S* continually softens to *H* from Greece to Calcutta, from the Caucasus to Egypt," says Dunlap. Therefore the letters *K, H,* and *S* are interchangeable.
844 Guignant, "Op. cit.," vol. i., p. 167.

corridors were all built on this model, and the ceilings in this form, he supposes that "the builders were evidently ignorant of the principles of the arch, and the support was made by stones lapping over as they rose; as at Ocosingo, and among Cyclopean remains in Greece and Italy."[845] In other buildings, though they belong to the same group, the traveller found the missing keystone, which is a sufficient proof that its omission elsewhere was *premeditated.*

May we not look for the solution of the mystery in the Masonic manual? The keystone has an esoteric meaning which ought to be, if it is not, well appreciated by high Masons. The most important subterranean building mentioned in the description of the origin of Freemasonry, is the one built by Enoch. The patriarch is led by the Deity, whom he sees in a vision, into the *nine* vaults. After that, with the assistance of his son, Methuselah, he constructs in the land of Canaan, "in the bowels of the mountain," nine apartments on the models that were shown to him in the vision. Each was roofed with an arch, and the apex of each *formed a keystone,* having inscribed on it the mirific characters. Each of the latter, furthermore, represented one of the nine names, traced in characters emblematical of the attributes by which the Deity was, according to ancient Freemasonry, known to the antediluvian brethren. Then Enoch constructed two deltas of the purest gold, and tracing two of the mysterious characters on each, he placed one of them in the deepest arch, and he other entrusted to Methuselah, communicating to him, at the same time, other important secrets *now lost to Freemasonry.*

And so, among these arcane secrets, now lost to their modern successors, may be found also the fact that the keystones were used in the arches only in certain portions of the temples devoted to special purposes. Another similarity presented by the architectural remains of the religious monuments of every country can be found in the identity of parts, courses, and measurements. All these buildings belong to the age of Hermes Trismegistus, and however comparatively modern or ancient the temple may seem, their mathematical proportions are found to correspond with the Egyptian religious edifices. There is a similar disposition of court-yards, adyta, passages, and steps; hence, despite any dissimilarity in architectural style, it is a warrantable inference that like religious rites were celebrated in all. Says Dr. Stukely, concerning Stonehenge: "This structure was not erected upon any Roman measure, and this is demonstrated by the great number of fractions which the measurement of each part, according to European scales, gives. On the contrary the figures become even, as soon as we apply to it the measurement of the ancient cubit, which was common to the Hebrew children of Shem, as well as to the Phœnicians and Egyptians, children of Ham (?), and imitators of the monuments of unhewn and oracular stones."

The presence of the artificial lakes, and their peculiar disposition on the consecrated grounds, is also a fact of great importance. The lakes inside the precincts of Karnak, and those enclosed in the grounds of Nagkon-Wat, and around the temples in the Mexican Copan and Santa Cruz del Quiche, will be found to present the same peculiarities. Besides possessing other significances the whole area was laid out with reference to cyclic calculations. In the Druidical structures the same sacred and mysterious numbers will be found. The circle of stones generally consists of either twelve, or twenty-one, or thirty-six. In

---

845 *"Incidents of Travel in Central America, etc."*

these circles the centre place belongs to Assar, Azon, or the god in the circle, by whatever other name he might have been known. The thirteen Mexican serpent-gods bear a distant relationship to the thirteen stones of the Druidical ruins.

The T (Tau), and the astronomical cross of Egypt ⊕ are conspicuous in several apertures of the remains of Palenque. In one of the *basso-relievos* of the Palace of Palenque, on the west side, sculptured on a hieroglyphic, right under the seated figure, is a *Tau*. The standing figure, which leans over the first one, is in the act of covering its head with the left hand with the veil of initiation; while it extends its right with the index and middle finger pointing to heaven. The position is precisely that of a Christian bishop giving his blessing, or the one in which Jesus is often represented while at the Last Supper. Even the Hindu elephant-headed god of wisdom (or magic learning), Ganesha, may be found among the stucco figures of the Mexican ruins.

THE EGYPTIAN TAU AT PALENQUE

What explanation can the archæologists, philologists — in short, the chosen host of Academicians — give us? None whatever. At best they have but hypotheses, every one of which is likely to be pulled down by its successor — a pseudo-truth, perhaps, like the first. The keys to the biblical miracles of old, and to the phenomena of modern days; the problems of psychology, physiology, and the many "missing links" which have so perplexed scientists of late, are all in the hands of secret fraternities. This mystery *must be* unveiled some day. But till then dark skepticism will constantly interpose its threatening, ugly shadow between God's truths and the spiritual vision of mankind; and many are those who, infected by the mortal epidemic of our century — hopeless materialism — will remain in doubt and mortal agony as to whether, when man dies, he will live again, although the question has been solved by long bygone generations of sages. The answers are there. They may be found on the time-worn granite pages of cave-temples, on sphinxes, propylons, and obelisks. They have stood there for untold ages, and neither the rude assault of time, nor the still ruder assault of Christian hands, have succeeded in obliterating their records. All covered with the problems which were solved — who can tell? perhaps by the archaic forefathers of their builders — the solution follows each question; and this the Christian could not appropriate, for, except the initiates, no one has understood the mystic writing. The key was in the keeping of those who knew how to commune with the invisible Presence, and who had received, from the lips of mother Nature herself, her grand truths. And so stand these monuments like mute forgotten sentinels on the threshold of that *unseen* world, whose gates are thrown open but to a few elect.

Defying the hand of Time, the vain inquiry of profane science, the insults of the revealed religions, they will disclose their riddles to none but the legatees of those by whom they were entrusted with the MYSTERY. The cold, stony lips of the once vocal Memnon, and of these hardy sphinxes, keep their secrets well. Who will unseal them? Who of our modern, materialistic dwarfs and unbelieving Sadducees will dare to lift the VEIL OF ISIS?

CHAPTER XV

"STE. — Have we devils here? Do you put tricks upon us
with savages, and men of Inde?"

The Tempest, Act ii., Sc. 2

"We have now, so far forth as it is requisite for our design, considered the
Nature and Functions of the Soule; and have plainly demonstrated that she is a
substance distinct from the body."

DR. HENRY MORE, *Immortality of the Soule*, 1659

"KNOWLEDGE IS POWER; IGNORANCE IS IMBECILITY."

AUTHOR OF "ART-MAGIC", *Ghost-Land*

THE "secret doctrine" has for many centuries been like the symbolical "man of sorrows"
of the prophet Isaiah. "Who hath believed our report?" its martyrs have repeated from one
generation to another. The doctrine has grown up before its persecutors "as a tender plant
and as a root out of a dry ground; it hath no form, nor comeliness . . . it is despised and
rejected of men; and they hid their faces from it. . . . They esteemed him not."

There need be no controversy as to whether this doctrine agrees or not with the
iconoclastic tendency of the skeptics of our times. It agrees with *truth* and that is enough. It
would be idle to expect that it would be believed by its detractors and slanderers. But the
tenacious vitality it exhibits all over the globe, wherever there are a group of men to quarrel
over it, is the best proof that the seed planted by our fathers on "the other side of the flood"
was that of a mighty oak, not the spore of a mushroom theology. No lightning of human
ridicule can fell to the ground, and no thunderbolts ever forged by the Vulcans of science
are powerful enough to blast the trunk, or even scar the branches of this world-tree of
KNOWLEDGE.

We have but to leave unnoticed their letter that killeth, and catch the subtile spirit of
their hidden wisdom, to find concealed in the *Books of Hermes* — be they the model or the
copy of all others — the evidences of a truth and philosophy which we feel *must* be based
on the eternal laws. We instinctively comprehend that, however finite the powers of man,
while he is yet embodied, they must be in close kinship with the attributes of an infinite
Deity; and we become capable of better appreciating the hidden sense of the gift lavished by
the *Elohim* on *H'Adam:* "Behold, I have given you everything which is upon the face of all
the earth . . . *subdue it*," and "*have dominion*" over ALL.

Had the allegories contained in the first chapters of *Genesis* been better understood, even
in their geographical and historical sense, which involve nothing at all esoteric, the claims of
its true interpreters, the kabalists, could hardly have been rejected for so long a time. Every
student of the *Bible* must be aware that the first and second chapters of *Genesis* could not
have proceeded from the same pen. They are evidently allegories and parables;* for the two
narratives of the creation and peopling of our earth diametrically contradict each other in
nearly every particular of order, time, place, and methods employed in the so-called
creation. In accepting the narratives literally, and as a whole, we lower the dignity of the
unknown Deity. We drag him down to the level of humanity, and endow him with the

peculiar personality of man, who needs the "cool of the day" to refresh him; who rests from his labors; and is capable of anger, revenge, and even of using precautions against man, "lest he put forth his hand, and take also of the tree of life." (A tacit admission, by the way, on the part of the Deity, that man *could do it*, if not prevented by sheer force.) But, in recognizing the allegorical coloring of the description of what may be termed historical facts, we find our feet instantly on firm ground.

ACQUISITION OF THE "SECRET DOCTRINE"

To begin with — the garden of Eden as a locality is no myth at all; it belongs to those landmarks of history which occasionally disclose to the student that the *Bible* is not all mere allegory. "Eden, or the Hebrew גן־עדן GAN-EDEN, meaning the park or the garden of Eden, is an archaic name of the country watered by the Euphrates and its many branches, from Asia and Armenia to the Erythraian Sea."[846] In the Chaldean *Book of Numbers,* its location is designated in numerals, and in the cipher Rosicrucian manuscript, left by Count St. Germain, it is fully described. In the Assyrian *Tablets,* it is rendered *gan-dunyas.* "Behold," say the אלהם *Eloim* of Genesis, "the man is become as one of us." The *Eloim* may be accepted in one sense for *gods* or powers, and taken in another one for the *Aleim,* or priests; the hierophants initiated into the good and the evil of this world; for there was a college of priests called the *Aleim,* while the head of their caste, or the chief of the hierophants, was known as *Java Aleim.* Instead of becoming a neophyte, and gradually obtaining his esoteric knowledge through a regular initiation, an *Adam,* or man, uses his intuitional faculties, and, prompted by the Serpent — *Woman* and matter — tastes of the Tree of Knowledge — the esoteric or secret doctrine — unlawfully. The priests of Hercules, or Mel-Karth, the "Lord" of the Eden, all wore "coats of skin." The text says: "And *Java Aleim,* made for Adam and his wife בתגרת עזד "CHITONUTH OUR." The first Hebrew word, *chitun,* is the Greek χιτων, *chiton.* It became a Slavonic word by adoption from the *Bible,* and means a *coat,* an upper garment.

Though containing the same substratum of esoteric truth as every early cosmogony, the Hebrew Scripture wears on its face the marks of its double origin. Its *Genesis* is purely a reminiscence of the Babylonian captivity. The names of places, men, and even objects, can be traced from the original text to the Chaldeans and the Akkadians, the progenitors and Aryan instructors of the former. It is strongly contested that the Akkad tribes of Chaldea, Babylonia, and Assyria were in any way cognate with the Brahmans, of Hindustan; but there are more proofs in favor of this opinion than otherwise. The Shemite, or Assyrian, ought, perchance, to have been called the Turanian, and the Mongolians have been denominated Scyths. But if the Akkadians ever existed otherwise than in the imagination of some philologists and ethnologists, they certainly would never have been a Turanian tribe, as some Assyriologists have striven to make us believe. They were simply emigrants on their way to Asia Minor from India, the cradle of humanity, and their sacerdotal adepts tarried to civilize and initiate a barbarian people. Halevy proved the fallacy of the Turanian mania in regard to the Akkadian people, whose very name has been changed a dozen times already; and other scientists have proved that the Babylonian civilization was neither born

---

846 See *Paul to the Galatians,* iv., 24, and *Gospel According to Matthew,* xiii. 10-15.

nor developed in that country. It was imported from India, and the importers were Brahmanical Hindus.

It is the opinion of Professor A. Wilder, that if the Assyrians had been called Turanians and the Mongolians Scyths, then, in such a case the wars of Iran and Turan, Zohak and Jemshid, or Yima, would have been fairly comprehended as the struggle of the old Persians against the endeavors of the Assyrian satraps to conquer them, which ended in the overthrow of Nineveh; "the spider weaving her web in the palace of Afrasiab."[847]

"The Turanian of Prof. Müller and his school," adds our correspondent, "was evidently the savage and nomadic Caucasian, out of whom the Hamite or Æthiopian builders come; then the Shemites — perhaps a hybrid of Hamite and Aryan; and lastly the Aryan — Median, Persian, Hindu; and later, the Gothic and Slavic peoples of Europe. He supposes the Celt to have been a hybrid, analogous to the Assyrians — between the Aryan invaders of Europe and the Iberic (probably Æthiopic) population of Europe." In such a case he must admit the possibility of our assertion that the Akkadians were a tribe of the earliest Hindus. Now, whether they were Brahmans, from the Brahmanic planisphere proper (40° north latitude), or from India (Hindustan), or, again, from the India of Central Asia, we will leave to philologists of future ages to decide.

TWO RELICS OWNED BY A PALI SCHOLAR

An opinion which with us amounts to certitude, demonstrated by an inductive method of our own, which we are afraid will be but little appreciated by the orthodox methods of modern science, is based on what will appear to the latter merely circumstantial evidence. For years we have repeatedly noticed that the same esoteric truths were expressed in identical symbols and allegories in countries between which there had never been traced any historical affiliation. We have found the Jewish *Kabala* and the *Bible* repeating the Babylonian "myths,"[848] and the Oriental and Chaldean allegories, given in form and substance in the oldest manuscripts of the Siamese Talapoin (monks), and in the popular but oldest traditions of Ceylon.

In the latter place we have an old and valued acquaintance whom we have also met in other parts of the globe, a Pali scholar, and a native Cingalese, who has in his possession a curious palm leaf, to which, by chemical processes, a timeproof durability has been given, and an enormous conch, or rather one-half of a conch — for it has been split in two. On the leaf we saw the representation of a giant of Ceylonian antiquity and fame, blind, and pulling down — with his outstretched arms, which are embracing the four central pillars of a pagoda — the whole temple on a crowd of armed enemies. His hair is long and reaches nearly to the ground. We were informed by the possessor of this curious relic, that the blind giant was "Somona, the Little"; so called in contradistinction with Somona-Kadom, the Siamese saviour. Moreover, the Pali legend, in as important particulars, corresponds with that of the biblical Samson.

---

847 The appropriate definition of the name "Turanian" is, any ethnic family that ethnologists know nothing about.
848 See Berosus and Sanchoniathon; Cory's "*Ancient Fragments*"; Movers, and others.

The shell bore upon its pearly surface a pictorial engraving, divided in two compartments, and the workmanship was far more artistic, as to conception and execution, than the crucifixes and other religious trinkets carved out of the same material in our days, at Jaffa and Jerusalem. In the first panel is represented Siva, with all his Hindu attributes, sacrificing his son — whether the "only-begotten," or one of many, we never stopped to inquire. The victim is laid on a funeral pile, and the father is hovering in the air over him, with an uplifted weapon ready to strike; but the god's face is turned toward a jungle in which a rhinoceros has deeply buried its horn in a huge tree and is unable to extricate it. The adjoining panel, or division, represents the same rhinoceros on the pile with the weapon plunged in its side, and the intended victim — Siva's son — free, and helping the god to kindle the fire upon the sacrificial altar.

Now, we have but to remember that Siva and the Palentinian Baal, or Moloch, and Saturn are identical; that Abraham is held until the present day by the Mahometan Arabs as Saturn in the Kaaba;[849] that Abraham and Israel were names of Saturn;[850] and that Sanchoniathon tells us that Saturn offered his only-begotten son as a sacrifice to his father Ouranos, and even circumcised himself and forced all his household and allies to do the same,[851] to trace unerringly the biblical myth to its source. But this source is neither Phœnician, nor Chaldean; it is purely Indian, and the original of it may be found in the *Maha-Bharata*. But, whether Brahmanical or Buddhistical, it must certainly be much older than the Jewish *Pentateuch*, as compiled by Ezra after the Babylonian captivity, and revised by the Rabbis of the Great Synagogue.

JEALOUS EXCLUSIVENESS OF THE HINDUS

Therefore, we are bold enough to maintain our assertion against the opinion of many men of learning, whom, nevertheless, we consider far more learned than ourselves. Scientific induction is one thing, and *knowledge of facts*, however unscientific they may seem at first, is another. But science has discovered enough to inform us that Sanscrit originals, of Nepaul, were translated by Buddhistic missionaries into nearly every Asiatic language. Likewise Pali manuscripts were translated into Siamese, and carried to Burmah and Siam; it is easy, therefore, to account for the same religious legends and myths circulating in all these countries.

But Manetho tells us also of Pali shepherds who emigrated westward; and when we find some of the oldest Ceylonic traditions in the Chaldean *Kabala* and Jewish *Bible*, we must think that either Chaldeans or Babylonians had been in Ceylon or India, or the ancient Pali had the same traditions as the Akkadians, whose origin is so uncertain. Suppose even Rawlinson to be right, and that the Akkadians did come from Armenia, he did not trace them farther back. As the field is now opened for any kind of hypothesis, we submit that this tribe might as well have come to Armenia from beyond the Indus, following their way in the direction of the Caspian Sea — a part which was also India, once upon a time — and from thence to the Euxine. Or they might have come originally from Ceylon by the same

849 Movers, 86.
850 Ibid.
851 Sanchon., in Cory's *"Fragments,"* p. 14.

way. It has been found impossible to follow, with any degree of certitude, the wanderings of these nomadic Aryan tribes; hence we are left to judge from inference, and by comparing their esoteric myths. Abraham himself, for all our scientists can know, might have been one of these Pali shepherds who emigrated *West*. He is shown to have gone with his father, Terah, from "*Ur* of the Chaldees"; and Sir H. Rawlinson found the Phœnician city of Martu or Marathos mentioned in an inscription at *Ur,* and shows it to signify THE WEST.

If their language seems in one sense to oppose their identity with the Brahmans of Hindustan, yet there are other reasons which make good our claims that the biblical allegories of *Genesis* are entirely due to these nomadic tribes. Their name Ak-ad, is of the same class as Ad-Am, Ha-va,[852] or Ed-En — "perhaps," says Dr. Wilder, "meaning son of *Ad,* like the sons of Ad in ancient Arabia. In Assyrian, *Ak* is creator and Ad-ad is AD, the father." In Aramean Ad also means *one,* and Ad-ad the *only-one;* and in the *Kabala Ad-ant* is the only-begotten, the first emanation of the unseen Creator. *Adon* was the "Lord" god of Syria and the consort of Adar-gat, or Aster-'t,' the Syrian goddess, who was Venus, Isis, Istar, or Mylitta, etc.; and each of these was "mother *of all living*" — the *Magna Mater.*

Thus, while the first, second, and third chapters of *Genesis* are but disfigured imitations of other cosmogonies, the fourth chapter, beginning at the sixteenth verse, and the fifth chapter to the end — give purely historical facts; though the latter were never correctly interpreted. They are taken, word for word, from the secret *Book of Numbers,* of the Great Oriental *Kabala.* From the birth of Enoch, the appropriated first parent of modern Freemasonry, begins the genealogy of the so-called Turanian, Aryan, and Semitic families, if such they be correctly. Every woman is an euhemerized land or city; every man and patriarch a race, a branch, or a subdivision of a race. The wives of Lamech give the key to the riddle which some good scholar might easily master, even without studying the esoteric sciences. "And Ad-ah bare Jabal: he was the father of such as dwell in tents, and *of such as have cattle,*" nomadic Aryan race; " . . . and his brother was Jubal; he was the father of all such as *handle the harp and organ; . . .* and Zillah bare Tubal-Cain, an instructor *of every artificer in brass and iron,*" etc. Every word has a significance; but it is no *revelation.* It is simply a compilation of the most *historical* facts, although history is too perplexed upon this point to know how to claim them. It is from the Euxine to Kashmere, and beyond that we must search for the cradle of mankind and the sons of Ad-ah; and leave the particular garden of Ed-en on the Euphrates to the college of the weird astrologers and magi, the Aleim.[853] No wonder that the Northern seer, Swedenborg, advises people to search for the LOST WORD among the hierophants of Tartary, China, and Thibet; for it is there, and only there now, although we find it inscribed on the monuments of the oldest Egyptian dynasties. The grandiose poetry of the four *Vedas*; the *Books of Hermes*; the Chaldean *Book of*

---

852 In an old Brahmanical book called the "Prophecies," by Ramatsariar, as well as in the Southern MSS. in the legend of Christna, the latter gives nearly word for word the first two chapters of Genesis. He recounts the creation of man — whom he calls *Adima,* in Sanscrit, the 'first man' — and the first woman is called Heva, that which completes life. According to Louis Jacolliot ("*La Bible dans l'Inde*"), Christna existed, and his legend was written, over 3,000 years B.C.

853 *Adah* in Hebrew is עדה, and Eden, עדן. The first is a woman's name; the second the designation of a country. They are closely related to each other; but hardly to Adam and Akkad — ארם, אקד which are spelled with aleph.

Numbers; the *Nazarene Codex*; the *Kabala* of the Tanaim; the *Sepher Jezira*; the *Book of Wisdom*, of Schlomah (Solomon); the secret treatise on *Muhta and Badha*[854] attributed by the Buddhist kabalists to Kapila, the founder of the Sankhya system; the *Brahmanas*;[855] he *Stan-gyour*,[856] of the Thibetans; all these volumes have the same ground-work. Varying but in allegories they teach the same secret doctrine which, when once thoroughly eliminated, will prove to be the Ultima Thule of true philosophy, and disclose what is this LOST WORD. It is useless to expect scientists to find in these works anything of interest except that which is in direct relation to either philology or comparative mythology. Even Max Müller, as soon as he refers to the mysticism and metaphysical philosophy scattered through the old Sanscrit literature, sees in it naught but "theological absurdities" and "fantastic nonsense." Speaking of the *Brahmanas*, all full of *mysterious*, therefore, as a matter of course, absurd, meanings, we find him saying: "The greater portion of them is simply twaddle, and what is worse, *theological twaddle*. No person who is not acquainted beforehand with the place which the *Brahmanas fill* in the history of the Indian mind, could read more than ten pages *without being disgusted*."[857] We do not wonder at the severe criticism of this erudite scientist.

Without a clew to the real meaning of this "twaddle" of religious conceptions, how can they judge of the esoteric by the exoteric? We find an answer in another of the highly-interesting lectures of the German savant: "No Jew, no Roman, no Brahman ever thought of converting people to his own national form of worship. Religion was looked upon as private or national property. It was to be guarded against strangers. The most sacred names of the gods, the prayers by which their favor could be gained, were kept secret. No religion was more exclusive than that of the Brahmans."[858]

Therefore, when we find scholars who imagine, because they have learned the meaning of a few exoteric rites from a srotriya, a Brahman priest initiated in the sacrificial mysteries, that they are capable of interpreting all the symbols, and have sifted the Hindu religions, we cannot help admiring the completeness of their scientific delusions. The more so, since we find Max Müller himself asserting that since "a Brahman was born — *nay, twice-born*, and could not be made, not even the lowest caste, that of the Sudras, would open its ranks to a stranger." How much less likely that he would allow that stranger to unveil to the world his most sacred religious Mysteries, the secret of which has been guarded so jealously from profanation throughout untold ages.

---

854 The two words answer to the terms, *Macroprosopos,* or macrocosm — the absolute and boundless, and the *Microprosopos* of the "Kabala," the "short face," or the microcosm — the finite and conditioned. It is not translated; nor is it likely to be. The Thibetean monks say that it is the real "Sutrâs." Some Buddhists believe that Buddha was, in a previous existence, Kapila himself. We do not see how several Sanscrit scholars can entertain the idea that Kapila was an atheist, while every legend shows him the most ascetic mystic, the founder of the sect of the Yogis.
855 The *"Brahmanas"* were translated by Dr. Haug; see his *"Aitareya Brahmanam."*
856 The "Stan-gyour" is full of rules of magic, the study of occult powers, and their acquisition, charms, incantations, etc.; and is as little understood by its lay-interpreters as the Jewish "Bible" is by our clergy, or the "Kabala" by the European Rabbis.
857 *"Aitareya Brahmana,"* Lecture by Max Müller.
858 Ibid., *"Buddhist Pilgrims."*

No; our scientists do not — nay, cannot understand correctly the old Hindu literature, any more than an atheist or materialist is able to appreciate at their just value the feelings of a seer, a mystic, whose whole life is given to contemplation. They have a perfect right to soothe themselves with the sweet lullaby of their self-admiration, and the just consciousness of their great learning, but none at all to lead the world into their own error, by making it believe that they have solved the last problem of ancient thought in literature, whether Sanscrit or any other; that there lies not behind the external "twaddle" far more than was ever dreamed of by our modern exact philosophy; or that above and beyond the correct rendering of Sanscrit words and sentences there is no deeper thought, intelligible to some of the descendants of those who veiled it in the morning hours of earth's day, if they are not to the profane reader.

We do not feel in the least astonished that a materialist, and even an orthodox Christian, is unable to read either the old Brahmanical works or their progeny, the *Kabala*, the *Codex* of Bardesanes, or the Jewish *Scripture* without disgust at their immodesty and apparent lack of what the uninitiated reader is pleased to call "common sense." But if we can hardly blame them for such a feeling, especially in the case of the Hebrew, and even the Greek and Latin literature, and are quite ready to agree with Professor Fiske that "it is a mark of wisdom to be dissatisfied with imperfect evidence"; on the other hand we have a right to expect that they should recognize that it is no less a mark of honesty to confess one's ignorance in cases where there are two sides to the question, and in the solution of which the scientist may as easily blunder as any ignoramus. When we find Professor Draper, in his definition of periods in the *Intellectual Development of Europe,* classifying the time from the days of Socrates, the precursor and teacher *of Plato,* to Karneades, as "the age of faith"; and that from Philo to the destruction of the Neo-platonic schools by Justinian — the "age of decrepitude," we may be allowed to infer that the learned professor knows as little about the real tendency of Greek philosophy and the Attic schools as he understood the true character of Giordano Bruno. So when we see one of the best of Sanscrit scholars stating on his own unsupported authority that the "greater portion of the *Brahmanas* is simply theological twaddle," we deeply regret to think that Professor Müller must be far better acquainted with the old Sanscrit verbs and nouns than with Sanscrit thought; and that a scholar so uniformly disposed to do justice to the religions and the men of old should so effectually play into the hands of Christian theologians. "What is the use of Sanscrit?" exclaims Jacquemont, who alone has made more false statements about the East than all the Orientalists put together. At such a rate there would be none indeed. If we are to exchange one corpse for another, then we may as well dissect the dead letter of the Jewish *Bible* as that of the *Vedas.* He who is not intuitionally vivified by the religious spirit of old, will never see beyond the exoteric "twaddle."

When first we read that "in the cavity of the cranium of Macroprosopos — the Long-Face — lies hidden the aërial WISDOM which nowhere is opened; and it is not discovered, and not opened"; or again, that "the *nose* of the 'ancient of days' is *Life* in every part"; we are inclined to regard it as the incoherent ravings of a lunatic. And when, moreover, we are apprized by the *Codex Nazaræus* that "she, the *Spiritus,*" invites her son Karabtanos, "who is frantic and without judgment," to an unnatural crime with his own mother, we are pretty well disposed to throw the book aside in disgust. But is this only meaningless trash, expressed in rude and even obscene language? No more can it be judged by external appearance than the sexual symbols of the Egyptian and Hindu religions, or the coarse frankness of expression of the "holy" *Bible* itself. No more than the allegory of Eve and the tempting serpent of Eden. The ever-insinuating, restless spirit, when once it "falls into matter," tempts Eve, or Hava, which bodily represent chaotic matter "frantic and without judgment." For *matter*, Karabtanos, is the son of *Spirit,* or the *Spiritus* of the Nazarenes, the *Sophia-Achamoth,* and the latter is the daughter of the pure, intellectual spirit, the divine breath. When science shall have effectually demonstrated to us the origin of matter, and proved the fallacy of the occultists and old philosophers who held (as their descendants now hold) that matter is but one of the correlations of spirit, then will the world of skeptics have a right to reject the old Wisdom, or throw the charge of obscenity in the teeth of the old religions.

LYDIA MARIA CHILD ON PHALLIC SYMBOLISM

"From time immemorial,"[859] says Mrs. Lydia Maria Child, "an emblem has been worshipped in Hindustan as the type of creation, or the origin of life. It is the most common symbol of Siva [Bala, or Maha-Deva], and is universally connected with his worship. . . . Siva was not merely the reproducer of human forms; he represented the fructifying principle, the generative power that pervades the universe. . . . Small images of this emblem carved in ivory, gold, or crystal, are worn as ornaments about the neck. . . . The maternal emblem is likewise a religious type; and worshippers of Vishnu represent it on their forehead by a horizontal mark. . . . Is it strange that they regarded with reverence the great mystery of human birth? Were *they* impure thus to regard it? Or are we impure that we do *not* so regard it? We have travelled far, and unclean have been the paths, since those old Anchorites first spoke of God and the soul in the solemn depths of their first sanctuaries. Let us not smile at their mode of tracing the infinite and incomprehensible Cause throughout all the mysteries of nature, lest by so doing we cast the shadow of our own grossness on their patriarchal simplicity."

Many are the scholars who have tried, to the best of their ability, to do justice to old India. Colebrooke, Sir William Jones, Barthelemy St. Hilaire, Lassen, Weber, Strange, Burnouf, Hardy, and finally Jacolliot, have all brought forward their testimony to her achievements in legislation, ethics, philosophy, and religion. No people in the world have ever attained to such a grandeur of thought in ideal conceptions of the Deity and its offspring, MAN, as the Sanscrit metaphysicians and theologians. "My complaint against many translators and Orientalists," says Jacolliot, "while admiring their profound knowledge is, that *not having lived in India,* they fail in exactness of expression and in comprehension of the *symbolical* sense of poetic chants, prayers, and ceremonies, and thus too often fall into material errors, whether of translation or appreciation."[860] Further, this author who, from a long residence in India, and the study of its literature, is better qualified to testify than those who have never been there, tells us that "the life of several generations would scarce suffice merely to read the works that ancient India has left us on history, ethics *(morale),* poetry, philosophy, religion, different sciences, and medicine." And yet Louis

---

859 "*Progress of Religious Ideas through Successive Ages,*" vol. i., p. 17.
860 "*La Bible dans l'Inde.*"

Jacolliot is able to judge but by the few fragments, access to which had ever depended on the complaisance and friendship of a few Brahmans with whom he succeeded in becoming intimate. Did they show him *all* their treasures? Did they explain to him *all* he desired to learn? We doubt it, otherwise he would not himself have judged their religious ceremonies so hastily as he has upon several occasions merely upon circumstantial evidence.

Still, no traveller has shown himself fairer in the main or more impartial to India than Jacolliot. If he is severe as to her present degradation, he is still severer to those who were the cause of it — the sacerdotal caste of the last few centuries — and his rebuke is proportionate to the intensity of his appreciation of her past grandeur. He shows the sources whence proceeded the revelations of all the ancient creeds, including the inspired *Books of Moses,* and points at India directly as the cradle of humanity, the parent of all other nations, and the hot-bed of all the lost arts and sciences of antiquity, for which old India, herself, was lost already in the Cimmerian darkness of the archaic ages. "To study India," he says, "is to trace humanity to its sources."

"In the same way as modern society jostles antiquity at each step," he adds, "as our poets have copied Homer and Virgil, Sophocles and Euripides, Plautus and Terence; as our philosophers have drawn inspiration from Socrates, Pythagoras, Plato, and Aristotle; as our historians take Titus Livius, Sallust, or Tacitus, as models; our orators, Demosthenes or Cicero; our physicians study Hippocrates, and our codes transcribe Justinian — so had antiquity's self also an antiquity to study, to imitate, and to copy. What more simple and more logical? Do not peoples precede and succeed each other? Does the knowledge, painfully acquired by one nation, confine itself to its own territory, and die with the generation that produced it? Can there be any absurdity in the suggestion that the India of 6,000 years ago, brilliant, civilized, overflowing with population, impressed upon Egypt, Persia, Judea, Greece, and Rome, a stamp as ineffaceable, impressions as profound, as these last have impressed upon us?

"It is time to disabuse ourselves of those prejudices which represent the ancients as having almost spontaneously-elaborated ideas, philosophic, religious, and moral, the most lofty — those prejudices that in their naive admiration explain all in the domain of science, arts, and letters, by the intuition of some few great men, and in the realm of religion by revelation."[861]

We believe that the day is not far off when the opponents of this fine and erudite writer will be silenced by the force of irrefutable evidence. And when *facts* shall once have corroborated his theories and assertions, what will the world find? That it is to India, the country less explored, and less known than any other, that all the other great nations of the world are indebted for their languages, arts, legislature, and civilization. Its progress, impeded for a few centuries before our era — for, as this writer shows, at the epoch of the great Macedonian conqueror, "India had already passed the period of her splendor" — was completely stifled in the subsequent ages. But the evidence of her past glories lies in her literature. What people in all the world can boast of such a literature, which, were the Sanscrit less difficult, would be more studied than now? Hitherto the general public has had to rely for information on a few scholars who, notwithstanding their great learning and

---

861 *"La Bible dans l'Inde."*

trustworthiness, are unequal to the task of translating and commenting upon more than a few books out of the almost countless number that, notwithstanding the vandalism of the missionaries, are still left to swell the mighty volume of Sanscrit literature. And to do even so much is the labor of a European's lifetime. Hence, people judge hastily, and often make the most ridiculous blunders.

Quite recently a certain Reverend Dunlop Moore, of New Brighton, Pa., determined to show his cleverness and piety at a single stroke, attacked the statement made by a Theosophist in a discourse delivered at the cremation of Baron de Palm, that the *Code of Manu* existed a thousand years before Moses. "All Orientalists of any note," he says, "are now agreed that the *Institutes of Manu* were written at different times. *The oldest part of the collection probably dates from the sixth century before the Christian era.*"[862] Whatever other Orientalists, encountered by this Pennsylvania pundit, may think, Sir William Jones is of a different opinion. "It is clear," he says, "that the *Laws of Manu,* such as we possess them, and which comprise but 680 slokas, cannot be the work attributed to Soumati, which is probably that described under the name of *Vriddha Manava,* or *Ancient Code of Manu,* which has not yet been entirely reconstructed, although many passages of the book have been preserved by tradition, and are often cited by commentators."

"We read in the preface to a treatise on legislation by Narada," says Jacolliot, "written by one of his adepts, a client of Brahmanical power: 'Manu having written the laws of Brahma, in 100,000 slokas, or distichs, which formed twenty-four books and a thousand chapters, gave the work to Narada, the sage of sages, who abridged it for the use of mankind to 12,000 verses, which he gave to a son of Brighou, named Soumati, who, for the greater convenience of man, reduced them to 4,000.' "

Here we have the opinion of Sir William Jones, who, in 1794, affirmed that the fragments in possession of the Europeans could not be *The Ancient Code of Manu,* and that of Louis Jacolliot, who, in 1868, after consulting all the authorities, and adding to them the result of his own long and patient research, writes the following: "The Hindu laws were codified by Manu *more than* 3,000 *years before the Christian era,* copied by the whole of antiquity, and notably by Rome, which alone has left us a written law — the *Code of Justinian;* which has been adopted as the basis of all modern legislations."[863] In another volume, entitled *Christna et le Christ,* in a scientific arraignment of a pious, albeit very learned Catholic antagonist, M. Textor de Ravisi, who seeks to prove that the orthography of the name Christna is not warranted by its Sanscrit spelling — and has the worst of it — Jacolliot remarks: "We know that the legislator Manu is lost in the night of the ante-historical period of India; and that no Indianist has dared to refuse him the title of the most ancient law-giver in the world" (p. 350).

But Jacolliot had not heard of the Rev. Dunlop Moore. This is why, perhaps, he and several other Indiologists are preparing to prove that many of the Vedic texts, as well as those of Manu, sent to Europe by the Asiatic Society of Calcutta, *are not genuine texts at all,* but mostly due to the cunning tentative efforts of certain Jesuit missionaries to mislead science, by the help of apocryphal works calculated at once to throw upon the history of

---

862 *"Presbyterian Banner,"* December 20, 1876.
863 *"La Bible dans l'Inde."*

ancient India a cloud of uncertainty and darkness, and on the modern Brahmans and pundits a suspicion of systematical interpolation. "These facts," he adds, "which are so well established in India that they are not even brought in question, *must be revealed to Europe*" (*Christna et le Christ*, p. 347).

Moreover, the *Code of Manu*, known to European Orientalists as that one which is commented upon by Brighou, does not even form a part of the ancient Manu called the *Vriddha-Manava*. Although but small fragments of it have been discovered by our scientists, it does exist as a whole in certain temples; and Jacolliot proves that the texts sent to Europe disagree entirely with the same texts as found in the pagodas of Southern India. We can also cite for our purpose Sir William Jones, who, complaining of Callouca, remarks that the latter seems in his commentaries to have never considered that "the laws of Manu are *restricted to the first three ages*" (*Translation of Manu and Commentaries*).

THE AGE OF THE VEDAS AND MANU

According to computation we are now in the age of Kali-Yug, the *third*, reckoning from that of Satya or Kritayug, first age in which Hindu tradition establishes the laws of Manu, and the authenticity of which Sir William Jones implicitly accepted. Admitting all that may be said as to the enormous exaggerations of Hindu chronology — which, by the bye, dovetails far better with modern geology and anthropology than the 6,000 years' caricature chronology of the Jewish *Scripture* — still as about 4,500 years have elapsed since the fourth age of the world, or Kali-Yug, began, we have here a proof that one of the greatest Orientalists that ever lived — and a Christian in the bargain, not a Theosophist — believed that Manu is many thousand years older than Moses. Clearly one of two things should happen: Either Indian history should be remodelled for the *Presbyterian Banner*, or the writers for that sheet should study Hindu literature before trying their hand again at criticism of Theosophists.

But apart from the private opinions of these reverend gentlemen whose views very little concern us, we find even in the *New American Cyclopædia* a decided tendency to dispute the antiquity and importance of the Hindu literature. The *Laws of Manu*, says one of the writers, "do not date earlier than the third century B.C." This term is a very elastic one. If by the *Laws of Manu* the writer means the *abridgment* of these laws, compiled and arranged by later Brahmans to serve as an authority for their ambitious projects, and with an idea of creating for themselves a rule of domination, then, in such a sense, they may be right, though we are prepared to dispute even that. At all events it is as little proper to pass off this abridgment for the genuine old laws codified by Manu, as to assert that the Hebrew Bible does not date earlier than the tenth century of our era, because we have no Hebrew manuscript older than that, or that the poems of Homer's *Iliad* were neither known nor written before its first authenticated manuscript was found. There is no Sanscrit manuscript in the possession of European scholars much older than four or five centuries,[864] a fact which did not in the least restrain them from assigning to the *Vedas* an antiquity of between four or five thousand years. There are the strongest possible arguments in favor of the great antiquity of the *Books of Manu*, and without going to the trouble of quoting the opinions of various scholars, no

---

864 See Max Müller's "*Lecture on the Vedas*."

two of whom agree, we will bring forward our own, at least as regards this most unwarranted assertion of the *Cyclopædia.*

If, as Jacolliot proves, text in hand, the *Code of Justinian* was copied from the *Laws of Manu*, we have first of all to ascertain the age of the former; not as a written and perfect code, but its origin. To answer, is not difficult we believe.

According to Varro, Rome was built in 3961 of the Julian period (754 B.C.). The Roman Law, as embodied by order of Justinian, and known as the *Corpus Juris Civilis,* was not a code, we are told, but a digest of the customs of legislation of many centuries. Though nothing is actually known of the original authorities, the chief source from which the *jus scriptum,* or written law, was derived, was the *jus non scriptum,* or the law of custom. Now it is just on this law *of custom* that we are prepared to base our arguments. The law of the twelve tables, moreover, was compiled about A.U.C. 300, and even this as respects private law was compiled *from still earlier sources.* Therefore, if these earlier sources are found to agree so well with the *Laws of Manu,* which the Brahmans claim to have been codified in the *Kritayug,* an age anterior to the actual *Kali-yug,* then we must suppose that this source of the "Twelve Tables," as laws of *custom* and tradition, are at least, by several hundred years, older than their copyists. This, alone, carries us right back to more than 1,000 years B.C.

The *Manava Dharma Sastra,* embodying the Hindu system of cosmogony, is recognized as next to the *Vedas* in antiquity; and even Colebrooke assigns the latter to the fifteenth century B.C. And, now, what is the etymology of the name of *Manava Dharma Sastra?* It is a word compounded of *Manu; d'harma,* institute; and *sastra,* command or law. How then can Manu's laws date only since the third century before our Christian era?

The Hindu *Code* had never laid any claims to be divinely revealed. The distinction made by the Brahmans themselves between the *Vedas* and every other sacred book of however respectable an antiquity, is a proof of it. While every sect holds the *Vedas* as the direct word of God — *sruti* (revelation) — the *Code of Manu* is designated by them simply as the *smriti,* a collection of oral traditions. Still these traditions, or "recollections," are among the oldest as well as the most revered in the land. But, perhaps, the strongest argument in favor of its antiquity, and the general esteem in which it is held, lies in the following fact. The Brahmans have undeniably remodelled these traditions at some distant period, and made many of the actual laws, as they now stand in the *Code of Manu,* to answer their ambitious views. Therefore, they *must have done it at a time when the burning of widows (suttee) was neither practiced nor intended to be,* which it has been for nearly 2,500 years. No more than in the *Vedas* is there any such atrocious law mentioned in the *Code of Manu!* Who, unless he is completely unacquainted with the history of India, but knows that this country was once on the verge of a religious rebellion occasioned by the prohibition of *suttee* by the English government? The Brahmans appealed to a verse from the *Rig-Veda* which commanded it. But this verse has been recently proved to have been falsified.[865] Had the Brahmans been the sole authors of the *Code of Manu,* or had they codified it entirely instead of simply filling it with interpolations to answer their object not earlier than the time of Alexander, how is it possible that they would have neglected this most important point, and so imperilled its

---

865 See Roth's "*The Burial in India*"; Max Müller's "*Comparative Mythology*" (Lecture); Wilson's article, "*The Supposed Vaidic Authority for the Burning of Hindu Widows,*" etc.

authority? This fact alone proves that the *Code* must be counted one of their most ancient books.

TRADITIONS OF PRE-DILUVIAN RACES

It is on the strength of such circumstantial evidence — that of reason and logic — that we affirm that, if Egypt furnished Greece with her civilization, and the latter bequeathed hers to Rome, Egypt herself had, in those unknown ages when Menes reigned ,[866] received her laws, her social institutions, her arts and her sciences, from pre-Vedic India;[867] and that therefore, it is in that old initiation of the priests — adepts of all the other countries — we must seek for the key to the great mysteries of humanity.

And when we say, indiscriminately, "India," we do not mean the India of our modern days, but that of the archaic period. In those ancient times countries which are now known to us by other names were all called India. There was an Upper, a Lower, and a Western India, the latter of which is now Persia-Iran. The countries now named Thibet, Mongolia, and Great Tartary, were also considered by the ancient writers as India. We will now give a legend in relation to those places which science now fully concedes to have been the cradle of humanity.

Tradition says, and the records of the *Great Book* explain, that long before the days of Adam, and his inquisitive wife, He-va, where now are found but salt lakes and desolate barren deserts, there was a vast inland sea, which extended over Middle Asia, north of the proud Himalayan range, and its western prolongation. An island, which for its unparalleled beauty had no rival in the world, was inhabited by the last remnant of the race which preceded ours. This race could live with equal ease in water, air, or fire, for it had an unlimited control over the elements. These were the "Sons of God"; not those who saw the daughters of men, but the real *Elohim*, though in the Oriental *Kabala* they have another name. It was they who imparted Nature's most weird secrets to men, and revealed to them the ineffable, and now *lost* "word."

This word, which is no word, has travelled once around the globe, and still lingers as a far-off dying echo in the hearts of some privileged men. The hierophants of all the Sacerdotal Colleges were aware of the existence of this island, but the "word" was known only to the *Java Aleim*, or chief lord of every college, and was passed to his successor only at the moment of death. There were many such colleges, and the old classic authors speak of them.

We have already seen that it is one of the universal traditions accepted by all the ancient peoples that there were many races of men anterior to our present races. Each of these was distinct from the one which preceded it; and each disappeared as the following appeared. In *Manu*, six such races are plainly mentioned as having succeeded each other.

"From this Manu Swayambhouva (the minor, and answering to Adam Kadmon) issued from Swayambhouva, or the Being existing through himself, descended six other Manus

---

866 Bunsen gives as the first year of Menes, 3645; Manetho as 3892 B.C. "Egypt's Place," etc., vol. v., 34; Key.
867 Louis Jacolliot, in *"The Bible in India,"* affirms the same.

(men typifying progenitors), each of whom gave birth *to a race* of men. . . . These Manus, all powerful, of whom Swayambhouva is the first, have each, *in his period* — antara — produced and directed this world composed of movable and unmovable beings" (*Manu,* book i.).

In the *Siva-Purana,*[868] it runs thus:

"O Siva, thou god of fire, mayest thou destroy my sins, as the bleaching-grass of the jungle is destroyed by fire. It is through thy mighty Breath that Adhima (the first man) and Heva (completion of life, in Sanscrit), *the ancestors of this race of men* have received life and covered the world with their descendants."

There was no communication with the fair island by sea, but subterranean passages known only to the chiefs, communicated with it in all directions. Tradition points to many of the majestic ruins of India, Ellora, Elephanta, and the caverns of Ajunta (Chandor range), which belonged once to those colleges, and with which were connected such subterranean ways.[869] Who can tell but the lost Atlantis — which is also mentioned in the *Secret Book,* but, again, under another name, pronounced in the sacred language — did not exist yet in those days? The great lost continent might have, perhaps, been situated south of Asia, extending from India to Tasmania?[870] If the hypothesis now so much doubted, and positively denied by some learned authors who regard it as a joke of Plato's, is ever verified, then, perhaps, will the scientists believe that the description of the god-inhabited continent was not altogether fable. And they may then perceive that Plato's guarded hints and the fact of his attributing the narrative to Solon and the Egyptian priests, were but a prudent way of imparting the fact to the world and by cleverly combining truth and fiction, to disconnect himself from a story which the obligations imposed at initiation forbade him to divulge.

And how could the name of Atlanta itself originate with Plato at all? Atlante is *not* a Greek name, and its construction has nothing of the Grecian element in it. Brasseur de Bourbourg tried to demonstrate it years ago, and Baldwin, in his *Prehistoric Nations and Ancient America,* cites the former, who declares that "the words *Atlas* and *Atlantic* have no satisfactory etymology in any language known in Europe. They are not Greek, and cannot be referred to any known language of the Old World. But in the Nahuatl (or Toltec) language we find immediately the radical *a, atl,* which signifies water, war, and the top of the head. From this comes a series of words, such as *atlan,* or the border of or amid the water; from which we have the adjective *Atlantic.* We have also *atlaca,* to combat. . . . A city

---

868 *Purana* means ancient and sacred history or tradition. See Loiseleur Des-longchamp's translations of "Manu"; also L. Jacolliot's "*La Genese dans l'Humanite.*"

869 There are archæologists, who, like Mr. James Fergusson, deny the great antiquity of even one single monument in India. In his work, "*Illustrations of the Rock-Cut Temples of India,*" the author ventures to express the very extraordinary opinion that "Egypt had ceased to be a nation before the earliest of the cave-temples of India was excavated." In short, he does not admit the existence of any cave anterior to the reign of Asoka, and seems willing to prove that most of these rock-cut temples were executed from the time of that pious Buddhist king, till the destruction of the Andhra dynasty of Maghada, in the beginning of the fifth century. We believe such a claim perfectly arbitrary. Further discoveries are sure to show how erroneous and unwarranted it was.

870 It is a strange coincidence that when first discovered, America was found to bear among some native tribes the name of *Atlanta.*

named *Atlan* existed when the continent was discovered by Columbus, at the entrance of the Gulf of Uraha, in Darien, with a good harbor. It is now reduced to an unimportant *pueblo* (village) named Aclo."[871]

Is it not, to say the least, very extraordinary to find in America a city called by a name which contains a purely local element, foreign moreover to every other country, in the alleged *fiction* of a philosopher of 400 years B.C.? The same may be said of the name of *America,* which may one day be found more closely related to Meru, the sacred mount in the centre of the *seven* continents, according to the Hindu tradition, than to Americus Vespucius, whose name by the bye, was never Americus at all, but *Albericus,* a trifling difference not deemed worth mentioning till very lately by *exact* history.[872] We adduce the following reasons in favor of our argument:

1st. Americ, Amerrique, or Amerique is the name in Nicaragua for the high land or mountain range that lies between Juigalpa and Libertad, in the province of Chontales, and which reaches on the one side into the country of the Carcas Indians, and on the other side into the country of the Ramas Indians. *Ic* or *ique,* as a terminal, means great, as *cazique,* etc. Columbus mentions, in his fourth voyage, the village *Cariai,* probably *Caicai.* The people abounded with sorcerers, or medicine men; and this was the region of the Americ range, 3,000 feet high.

Yet he omits to mention this word. The name *America Provincia,* first appeared on a map published at Basle, in 1522. Till that time, the region was believed to be part of India. That year Nicaragua was conquered by Gil Gonzales de Avida.[873]

2d. "The Northmen who visited the continent in the tenth century,[874] a low level coast thickly covered with wood," called it *Markland,* from *mark,* a wood. The *r* had a rolling sound as in *marrick.* A similar word is found in the country of the Himalayas, and the name of the World-Mountain, Meru, is pronounced in some dialects as MERUAH, the letter *h* being strongly aspirated. The main idea is, however, to show how two peoples could possibly accept a word of similar sound, each having used it in their own sense, and finding it applied to the same territory. "It is most plausible," says Professor Wilder, "that the State of Central America, where we find the name *Americ* signifying (like the Hindu Meru we may add) great mountain, gave the continent its name. Vespucius would have used his surname if he had designed to give a title to a continent. If the Abbé de Bourbourg's theory of *Atlan* as the source of Atlas and Atlantic is verified, the two hypotheses could agree most charmingly. As Plato was not the only writer that treated of a world beyond the pillars of Hercules, and as the ocean is still shallow and grows sea-weed all through the tropical part of the Atlantic, it is not wild to imagine that this continent projected, or that there was an island-world on that coast. The Pacific also shows signs of having been a populous island-empire of Malays or Javanese — if not a continent amid the North and South. We know that

---

871 Baldwin, *"Prehistoric Nations,"* p. 179.
872 Alberico Vespuzio, the son of Anastasio Vespuzio or Vespuchy, is now gravely doubted in regard to the naming of the New world. Indeed the name is said to have occurred in a work written several centuries before. A. Wilder (Notes).
873 See Thomas Belt, *"The Naturalists in Nicaragua."* London, 1873.
874 Torfieus, *"Historia Vinlandiæ Antiquæ."*

Lemuria in the Indian Ocean is a dream of scientists; and that the Sahara and the middle belt of Asia were perhaps once sea-beds."

ATLANTIS AND ITS PEOPLES

To continue the tradition, we have to add that the class of hierophants was divided into two distinct categories: those who were instructed by the "Sons of God," of the island, and who were initiated in the divine doctrine of pure revelation, and others who inhabited the lost Atlantis — if such must be its name — and who, being of another race, were born with a sight which embraced all hidden things, and was independent of both distance and material obstacle. In short, they were the *fourth* race of men mentioned in the *Popol-Vuh*, whose sight was unlimited and who knew all things at once. They were, perhaps, what we would now term "natural-born mediums," who neither struggled nor suffered to obtain their knowledge, nor did they acquire it at the price of any sacrifice. Therefore, while the former walked in the path of their divine instructors, and acquiring their knowledge by degrees, learned at the same time to discern the evil from the good, the born *adepts* of the Atlantis blindly followed the insinuations of the great and invisible "Dragon," the King *Thevetat* (the Serpent of *Genesis*?). Thevetat had neither learned nor acquired knowledge, but, to borrow an expression of Dr. Wilder in relation to the tempting Serpent, he was "a sort of Socrates who *knew* without being initiated." Thus, under the evil insinuations of their demon, Thevetat, the Atlantis-race became a nation of wicked *magicians*. In consequence of this, war was declared, the story of which would be too long to narrate; its substance may be found in the disfigured allegories of the race of Cain, the giants, and that of Noah and his righteous family. The conflict came to an end by the submersion of the Atlantis; which finds its imitation in the stories of the Babylonian and Mosaic flood: The giants and magicians " . . . and all flesh died . . . and every man." All except Xisuthrus and Noah, who are substantially identical with the great Father of the Thlinkithians in the *Popol-Vuh,* or the sacred book of the Guatemaleans, which also tells of his escaping in a large boat, like the Hindu Noah — Vaiswasvata.

If we believe the tradition at all, we have to credit the further story that from the intermarrying of the progeny of the hierophants of the island and the descendants of the Atlantian Noah, sprang up a mixed race of righteous and wicked. On the one side the world had its Enochs, Moseses, Gautama-Buddhas, its numerous "Saviours," and great hierophants; on the other hand, its "*natural* magicians" who, through lack of the restraining power of proper spiritual enlightenment, and because of weakness of physical and mental organizations, unintentionally perverted their gifts to evil purposes. Moses had no word of rebuke for those adepts in prophecy and other powers who had been instructed in the colleges of esoteric wisdom[875] mentioned in the *Bible*. His denunciations were reserved for such as either wittingly or otherwise debased the powers inherited from their Atlantian ancestors to the service of evil spirits, to the injury of humanity. His wrath was kindled against the spirit of *Ob*, not that of OD. [876]

---

875 *2 Kings*, xxii. 14; *2 Chronicles*, xxxiv. 22.
876 As we are going to press with this chapter, we have received from Paris, through the kindness of the Honorable John L. O'Sullivan, the complete works of Louis Jacolliot in twenty-one volumes. They

are chiefly upon India and its old traditions, philosophy, and religion. This indefatigable writer has collected a world of information from various sources, mostly authentic. While we do not accept his personal views on many points, still we freely acknowledge the extreme value of his copious translations from the Indian sacred books. The more so, since we find them corroborating in every respect the assertions we have made. Among other instances is this matter of the submergence of continents in prehistoric days.

In his "Histoire des Vierges: Les Peuples et les Continents Disparus," he says: "One of the most ancient legends of India, preserved in the temples by oral and written tradition, relates that several hundred thousand years ago there existed in the Pacific Ocean, an immense continent which was destroyed by geological upheaval, and the fragments of which must be sought in Madagascar, Ceylon, Sumatra, Java, Borneo, and the principal isles of Polynesia.

"The high plateaux of Hindustan and Asia, according to this hypothesis, would only have been represented in those distant epochs by great islands contiguous to the central continent. . . . According to the Brahmans this country had attained a high civilization, and the peninsula of Hindustan, enlarged by the displacement of the waters, at the time of the grand cataclysm, has but continued the chain of the primitive traditions born in this place. These traditions give the name of *Rutas* to the peoples which inhabited this immense equinoctial continent, and from their speech *was derived the Sanscrit*." (We will have something to say of this language in our second volume.)

"The Indo-Hellenic tradition, preserved by the most intelligent population which emigrated from the plains of India, equally relates the existence of a continent and a people to which it gives the name of Atlantis and Atlantides, and which it locates in the Atlantic in the northern portion of the Tropics.

"Apart from the fact that the supposition of an ancient continent in those latitudes, the vestiges of which may be found in the volcanic islands and mountainous surface of the Azores, the Canaries and Cape Verd, is not devoid of geographical probability, the Greeks, who, moreover, never dared to pass beyond the pillars of Hercules, on account of their dread of the mysterious ocean, appeared too late in antiquity for the stories preserved by Plato to be anything else than an echo of the Indian legend. Moreover, when we cast a look on a planisphere, at the sight of the islands and islets strewn from the Malayan Archipelago to Polynesia, from the straits of Sund to Easter Island, it is impossible, upon the hypothesis of continents preceding those which we inhabit, not to place there the most important of all.

"A religious belief, common to Malacca and Polynesia, that is to say to the two opposite extremes of the Oceanic world, affirms 'that all these islands once formed two immense countries, inhabited by yellow men and black men, always at war; and that the gods, wearied with their quarrels, having charged Ocean to pacify them, the latter swallowed up the two continents, and since, it had been impossible to make him give up his captives. Alone, the mountain-peaks and high plateaux escaped the flood, by the power of the gods, who perceived too late the mistake they had committed.'

"Whatever there may be in these traditions, and whatever may have been the place where a civilization more ancient than that of Rome, of Greece, of Egypt, and of India was developed, it is certain that this civilization did exist, and that it is highly important for science to recover its traces, however feeble and fugitive they may be" (pp. 13-15).

This last tradition, translated by Louis Jacolliot from the Sanscrit manuscripts, corroborates the one we have given from the "Records of the Secret Doctrine." The war mentioned between the yellow and the black men, relates to a struggle between the "sons of God" and the "sons of giants," or the inhabitants and magicians of the Atlantis.

The final conclusion of M. Jacolliot, who visited personally all the islands of Polynesia, and devoted years to the study of the religion, language, and traditions of nearly all the peoples, is as follows:

"As to the Polynesian continent which disappeared at the time of the final geological cataclysms, its existence rests on such proofs that to be logical we can doubt no longer.

The ruins which cover both Americas, and are found on many West Indian islands, are all attributed to the submerged Atlantians. As well as the hierophants of the old world, which in the days of Atlantis was almost connected with the new one by land, the magicians of the now submerged country had a net-work of subterranean passages running in all directions. In connection with those mysterious catacombs we will now give a curious story told to us by a Peruvian, long since dead, as we were travelling together in the interior of his country. There must be truth in it; as it was afterward confirmed to us by an Italian gentleman who had seen the place and who, but for lack of means and time, would have verified the tale himself, at least partially. The informant of the Italian was an old priest, who had had the secret divulged to him, at confession, by a Peruvian Indian. We may add, moreover, that the priest was compelled to make the revelation, being at the time completely under the mesmeric influence of the traveller.

The story concerns the famous treasures of the last of the Incas. The Peruvian asserted that since the well-known and miserable murder of the latter by Pizarro, the secret had been known to all the Indians, except the *Mestizos* who could not be trusted. It runs thus: The Inca was made prisoner, and his wife offered for his liberation a room full of gold, "from the floor up to the ceiling, as high up as his conqueror could reach" before the sun would set on the third day. She kept her promise, but Pizarro broke his word, according to Spanish practice. Marvelling at the exhibition of such treasures, the conqueror declared that he would not release the prisoner, but would murder him, unless the queen revealed the place whence the treasure came. He had heard that the Incas had somewhere an inexhaustible mine; a subterranean road or tunnel running many miles under ground, where were kept the accumulated riches of the country. The unfortunate queen begged for delay, and went to consult the oracles. During the sacrifice, the chief-priest showed her in the consecrated "black mirror"[877] the unavoidable murder of her husband, whether she delivered the

---

"The three summits of this continent, Sandwich Islands, New Zealand, Easter Island, are distant from each other from fifteen to eighteen hundred leagues, and the groups of intermediate islands, Viti, Samoa, Tonga, Foutouna, Ouvea, Marquesas, Tahiti, Pournouton, Gambiers, are themselves distant from these extreme points from seven or eight hundred to one thousand leagues.

"All navigators agree in saying that the extreme and the central groups could never have communicated in view of their actual geographical position, and with the insufficient means they had at hand. It is physically impossible to cross such distances in a pirogue . . . without a compass, and travel months without provisions.

"On the other hand, the aborigines of the Sandwich Islands, of Viti, of New Zealand, of the central groups, of Samoa, Tahiti, etc., *had never known each other, had never heard of each other* before the arrival of the Europeans. *And yet, each of these people maintained that their island had at one time formed a part of an immense stretch of land which extended toward the West, on the side of Asia.* And all, brought together, were found to speak the same language, to have the same usages, the same customs, the same religious belief. And all to the question, 'Where is the cradle of your race?' for sole response, *extended their hand toward the setting sun*" (Ibid., p. 308).

877 These "magic mirrors," generally black, are another proof of the universality of an identical belief. In India these mirrors are prepared in the province of Agra and are also fabricated in Thibet and China. And we find them in Ancient Egypt, from whence, according to the native historian quoted by Brasseur de Bourbourg, the ancestors of the Quiches brought them to Mexico; the Peruvian sun-worshippers also used it. When the Spaniards had landed, says the historian, the King of the Quiches,

treasures of the crown to Pizarro or not. Then the queen gave the order to close the entrance, which was a door cut in the rocky wall of a chasm. Under the direction of the priest and magicians, the chasm was accordingly filled to the top with huge masses of rock, and the surface covered over so as to conceal the work. The Inca was murdered by the Spaniards and his unhappy queen committed suicide. Spanish greed overreached itself and the secret of the buried treasures was locked in the breasts of a few faithful Peruvians.

Our Peruvian informant added that in consequence of certain indiscretions at various times, persons had been sent by different governments to search for the treasure under the pretext of scientific exploration. They had rummaged the country through, but without realizing their object. So far this tradition is corroborated by the reports of Dr. Tschuddi and other historians of Peru. But there are certain additional details which we are not aware have been made public before now.

PERUVIAN RELICS

Several years after hearing the story, and its corroboration by the Italian gentleman, we again visited Peru. Going southward from Lima, by water, we reached a point near Arica at sunset, and were struck by the appearance of an enormous rock, nearly perpendicular, which stood in mournful solitude on the shore, apart from the range of the Andes. It was the tomb of the Incas. As the last rays of the setting sun strike the face of the rock, one can make out, with an ordinary opera-glass, some curious hieroglyphics inscribed on the volcanic surface.

When Cusco was the capital of Peru, it contained a temple of the sun, famed far and near for its magnificence. It was roofed with thick plates of gold, and the walls were covered with the same precious metal; the eave-troughs were also of solid gold. In the west wall the architects had contrived an aperture in such a way that when the sunbeams reached it, it focused them inside the building. Stretching like a golden chain from one sparkling point to another, they encircled the walls, illuminating the grim idols, and disclosing certain mystic signs at other times invisible. It was only by understanding these hieroglyphics — identical with those which may be seen to this day on the tomb of the Incas — that one could learn the secret of the tunnel and its approaches. Among the latter was one in the neighborhood of Cusco, now masked beyond discovery. This leads directly into an immense tunnel which runs from Cusco to Lima, and then, turning southward, extends into Bolivia. At a certain point it is intersected by a royal tomb. Inside this sepulchral chamber are cunningly arranged two doors; or, rather, two enormous slabs which turn upon pivots, and close so tightly as to be only distinguishable from the other portions of the sculptured walls by the secret signs, whose key is in the possession of the faithful custodians. One of these turning slabs covers the southern mouth of the Liman tunnel — the other, the northern one of the Bolivian corridor. The latter, running southward, passes through Trapaca and Cobijo, for

---

ordered his priests to consult the mirror, in order to learn the fate of his kingdom. "The *demon* reflected the present and the future as in a mirror," he adds (De Bourbourg, "*Mexique*," p. 184).

Arica is not far away from the little river called Pay'quina,[878] which is the boundary between Peru and Bolivia.

Not far from this spot stand three separate peaks which form a curious triangle; they are included in the chain of the Andes. According to tradition the only practicable entrance to the corridor leading northward is in one of these peaks; but without the secret of its landmarks, a regiment of Titans might rend the rocks in vain in the attempt to find it. But even were some one to gain an entrance and find his way as far as the turning slab in the wall of the sepulchre, and attempt to blast it out, the superincumbent rocks are so disposed as to bury the tomb, its treasures, and — as the mysterious Peruvian expressed it to us — "a thousand warriors" in one common ruin. There is no other access to the Arica chamber but through the door in the mountain near Pay'quina. Along the entire length of the corridor, from Bolivia to Lima and Cusco, are smaller hiding places filled with treasures of gold and precious stone, the accumulations of many generations of Incas, the aggregate value of which is incalculable.

We have in our possession an accurate plan of the tunnel, the sepulchre, and the doors, given to us at the time by the old Peruvian. If we had ever thought of profiting by the secret, it would have required the cooperation of the Peruvian and Bolivian governments on an extensive scale. To say nothing of physical obstacles, no one individual or small party could undertake such an exploration without encountering the army of smugglers and brigands with which the coast is infested; and which, in fact, includes nearly the whole population. The mere task of purifying the mephitic air of the tunnel, which had not been entered for centuries, would also be a serious one. There, however, the treasure lies, and there the tradition says it will lie till the last vestige of Spanish rule disappears from the whole of North and South America.

The treasures exhumed by Dr. Schliemann at Mycenæ, have awakened popular cupidity, and the eyes of adventurous speculators are being turned toward the localities where the wealth of ancient peoples is supposed to be buried, in crypt or cave, or beneath sand or alluvial deposit. Around no other locality, not even Peru, hang so many traditions as around the Gobi Desert. In Independent Tartary this howling waste of shifting sand was once, if report speaks correctly, the seat of one of the richest empires the world ever saw. Beneath the surface are said to lie such wealth in gold, jewels, statuary, arms, utensils, and all that indicates civilization, luxury, and fine arts, as no existing capital of Christendom can show to-day. The Gobi sand moves regularly from east to west before terrific gales that blow continually. Occasionally some of the hidden treasures are uncovered, but not a native dare touch them, for the whole district is under the ban of a mighty spell. Death would be the penalty. Bahti — hideous, but faithful gnomes — guard the hidden treasures of this prehistoric people, awaiting the day when the revolution of cyclic periods shall again cause their story to be known for the instruction of mankind.

According to local tradition, the tomb of Ghengiz Khan still exists near Lake Tabasun Nor. Within lies the Mongolian Alexander, as though asleep. After three more centuries he will awake and lead his people to new victories and another harvest of glory. Though this

---

878 Pay'quina, or *Payaquina,* so called because its waves used to drift particles of gold from the Brazil. We found a few specks of genuine metal in a handful of sand that we brought back to Europe.

prophetic tradition be received with ever so many grains of salt, we can affirm as a fact that the tomb itself is no fiction, nor has its amazing richness been exaggerated.

THE GOBI DESERT AND ITS SECRETS

The district of the Gobi wilderness and, in fact, the whole area of Independent Tartary and Thibet is jealously guarded against foreign intrusion. Those who are permitted to traverse it are under the particular care and pilotage of certain agents of the chief authority, and are in duty bound to convey no intelligence respecting places and persons to the outside world. But for this restriction, even we might contribute to these pages accounts of exploration, adventure, and discovery that would be read with interest. The time will come, sooner or later, when the dreadful sand of the desert will yield up its long-buried secrets, and then there will indeed be unlooked-for mortifications for our modern vanity.

"The people of Pashai,"[879] says Marco Polo, the daring traveller of the thirteenth century, "are great adepts in sorceries and the *diabolic* arts." And his learned editor adds: "This Pashai, or Udyana, was the native country of Padma Sambhava, one of the chief apostles of lamaism, *i.e.*, of Thibetan Buddhism, and a great master of enchantments. The doctrines of Sakya, as they prevailed in Udyana *in old times*, were probably strongly tinged with Sivaitic magic, and the Thibetans still regard the locality as the classic ground of sorcery and witchcraft."

The "old times" are just like the "modern times"; nothing is changed as to magical practices except that they have become still more esoteric and arcane, and that the caution of the adepts increases in proportion to the traveller's curiosity. Hiouen-Thsang says of the inhabitants: "The men . . . are fond of study, but pursue it with no ardor. *The science of magical formulæ has become a regular professional business with them.*"[880] We will not contradict the venerable Chinese pilgrim on this point, and are willing to admit that in the seventh century *some* people made "a professional business" of magic; so, also, do *some* people now, but certainly not the true adepts. It is not Hiouen-Thsang, the pious, courageous man, who risked his life a hundred times to have the bliss of perceiving Buddha's shadow in the cave of Peshawer, who would have accused the holy lamas and monkish thaumaturgists of "making a professional business" of showing it to travellers. The injunction of Gautama, contained in his answer to King Prasenagit, his protector, who called on him to perform miracles, must have been ever present to the mind of Hiouen-Thsang. "Great king," said Gautama, "I do not teach the law to my pupils, telling them 'go, ye saints, and before the eyes of the Brahmans and householders perform, by means of your supernatural powers, miracles greater than any man can perform.' I tell them, when I teach them the law, 'Live, ye saints, *hiding your good works, and showing your sins*.' "

---

879 The regions somewhere about *Udyana* and *Kashmere,* as the translator and editor of Marco Polo (Colonel Yule), believes. Vol. i., p. 173.
880 "*Voyage des Pelerins, Bouddhistes,*" vol. i.; "*Histoire de la Vie de Hiouen-Thsang,*" etc., traduit du Chinois en francais, par Stanislas Julien.

THIBETAN AND CHINESE LEGENDS

Struck with the accounts Of magical exhibitions witnessed and recorded by travellers of every age who had visited Tartary and Thibet, Colonel Yule comes to the conclusion that the natives must have had "at their command the whole encyclopædia of modern 'Spiritualists.' Duhalde mentions among their sorceries the art of producing by their invocations the figures of Laotsen[881] and their divinities *in the air,* and *of making a pencil write answers to questions without anybody touching it.*"[882]

The former invocations pertain to religious mysteries of their sanctuaries; if done otherwise, or for the sake *of gain,* they are considered *sorcery,* necromancy, and strictly forbidden. The latter art, that of making a pencil write *without contact,* was known and practiced in China and other countries centuries before the Christian era. It is the A B C of magic in those countries.

When Hiouen-Thsang desired to adore the shadow of Buddha, it was not to "professional magicians" that he resorted, but to the power of his own soul-invocation; the power of prayer, faith, and contemplation. All was dark and dreary near the cavern in which the miracle was alleged to take place sometimes. Hiouen-Thsang entered and began his devotions. He made 100 salutations, but neither saw nor heard anything. Then, thinking himself too sinful, he cried bitterly, and despaired. But as he was going to give up all hope, he perceived on the eastern wall a feeble light, but it disappeared. He renewed his prayers, full of hope this time, and again he saw the light, which flashed and disappeared again. After this he made a solemn vow: he would not leave the cave till he had the rapture to see at last the shadow of the "Venerable of the Age." He had to wait longer after this, for only after 200 prayers was the dark cave suddenly "bathed in light, and the shadow of Buddha, of a brilliant white color, rose majestically on the wall, as when the clouds suddenly open, and, all at once, display the marvellous image of the 'Mountain of Light.' A dazzling splendor lighted up the features of the divine countenance. Hiouen-Thsang was lost in contemplation and wonder, and would not turn his eyes away from the sublime and incomparable object." Hiouen-Thsang adds in his own diary, *See-yu-kee,* that it is only when man prays with sincere faith, and if he has received from above a hidden impression, that he sees the shadow clearly, but he cannot enjoy the sight for any length of time.[883]

Those who are so ready to accuse the Chinese of irreligion will do well to read Schott's *Essays on Buddhism in China and Upper Asia.*[884] "In the years *Yuan-yeu* of the Sung (A.D. 1086-1093) a pious matron with her two servants lived entirely to the Land of Enlightenment. One of the maids said one day to her companion: 'To-night I shall pass over to the Realm of Amita' (Buddha). The same night a balsamic odor filled the house, and the maid died without any preceding illness. On the following day the surviving maid said to her lady: 'Yesterday my deceased companion appeared to me in a dream, and said: "Thanks to the persevering supplications of our dear mistress, I am become an inhabitant of Paradise, and

---

881 Lao-tsi, the Chinese philosopher.
882 "*The Book of Ser Marco Polo,*" vol. i., p. 318. See also, in this connection, the experiments of Mr. Crookes, described in chapter vi. of this work.
883 Max Müller, "*Buddhist Pilgrims.*"
884 Berlin Academy of Sciences, 1846.

my blessedness is past all expression in words." ' The matron replied: 'If she will appear to me also, then will I believe all you say.' The next night the deceased really appeared to her. The lady asked: 'May I, for once, visit the Land of Enlightenment?' 'Yea,' answered the blessed soul; 'thou hast but to follow thine hand-maiden.' The lady followed her (in her dream), and soon perceived a lake of immeasurable expanse, overspread with innumerable red and white lotus flowers, of various sizes, some blooming, some fading. She asked what those flowers might signify? The maiden replied: 'These are all human beings on the Earth whose thoughts are turned to the Land of Enlightenment. The very first longing after the Paradise of Amita produces a flower in the Celestial Lake, and this becomes daily larger and more glorious as the self-improvement of the person whom it represents advances; in the contrary case, it loses in glory and fades away.'[885] The matron desired to know the name of an enlightened one who reposed on one of the flowers, clad in a waving and wondrously glistening raiment. Her whilom maiden answered: 'That is Yang-kie.' Then asked she the name of another, and was answered:

'That is Mahu.' The lady then said: 'At what place shall I hereafter come into existence?' Then the Blessed Soul led her a space further, and showed her a hill that gleamed with gold and azure. 'Here,' said she, 'is your future abode. You will belong to the first order of the blessed.' When the matron awoke, she sent to inquire for Yang-kie and Mahu. The first was already departed; the other still alive and well. And thus the lady learned that the soul of one who advances in holiness and never turns back, may be already a dweller in the Land of Enlightenment, even though the body still sojourn in this transitory world."

In the same essay, another Chinese story is translated, and to the same effect: "I knew a man," says the author, "who during his life had killed many living beings, and was at last struck with an apoplexy. The sorrows in store for his sin-laden soul pained me to the heart; I visited him, and exhorted him to call on the Amita; but he obstinately refused. His illness clouded his understanding; in consequence of his misdeeds he had become hardened. What was before such a man when once his eyes were closed? In this life the night followeth the day, and the winter followeth the summer; that, all men are aware of. But that life is followed by death, no man will consider. Oh, what blindness and obduracy is this!" (p. 93.)

These two instances of Chinese literature hardly strengthen the usual charge of irreligion and total materialism brought against the nation. The first little mystical story is full of spiritual charm, and would grace any Christian religious book. The second is as worthy of praise, and we have but to replace "Amita" with "Jesus" to have a highly Orthodox tale, as regards religious sentiments and code of philosophical morality. The following instance is still more striking, and we quote it for the benefit of Christian revivalists: "Hoang-ta-tie, of T'anchen, who lived under the Sung, followed the craft of a blacksmith. Whenever he was at

---

885 Colonel Yule makes a remark in relation to the above Chinese mysticism which for its noble fairness we quote most willingly. "In 1871," he says, "I saw in Bond street an exhibition of the (so-called) 'spirit' drawings, *i.e.*, drawings executed by a 'medium' under extraneous and invisible guidance. A number of these extraordinary productions (for extraordinary they were undoubtedly) professed to represent the 'Spiritual Flowers' of such and such persons; and the explanation of these as presented in the catalogue was in substance exactly that given in the text. It is highly improbable that the artist had any cognizance of Schott's Essays, and the coincidence was certainly very striking" (*"The Book of Ser Marco Polo,"* vol. i., p. 444).

his work he used to call, without intermission, on the name of Amita Buddha. One day he handed to his neighbors the following verses of his own composition to be spread about:—

> 'Ding dong! The hammer-strokes fall long and fast,
> Until the iron turns to steel at last!
> Now shall the long, long day of rest begin,
> The *Land of Bliss Eternal* calls me in!'

"Thereupon he died. But his verses spread all over Honan, and many learned to call upon Buddha."[886] To deny to the Chinese or any people of Asia, whether Central, Upper, or Lower, the possession of any knowledge, or even perception of spiritual things, is perfectly ridiculous. From one end to the other the country is full of mystics, religious philosophers, Buddhist saints, and *magicians.* Belief in a spiritual world, full of invisible beings who, on certain occasions, appear to mortals objectively, is universal. "According to the belief of the nations of Central Asia," remarks I. J. Schmidt, "the earth and its interior, as well as the encompassing atmosphere, are filled with spiritual beings, which exercise an influence, partly beneficent, partly malignant, on the whole of organic and inorganic nature. . . . Especially are deserts and other wild or uninhabited tracts, or regions in which the influences of nature are displayed on a gigantic and terrible scale, regarded as the chief abode or rendezvous of evil spirits. And hence the steppes of Turan, and in particular the great sandy Desert of Gobi have been looked on as the dwelling-place of malignant beings, from days of hoary antiquity."

Marco Polo — as a matter of course — mentions more than once in his curious book of *Travels*, these tricky nature-spirits of the deserts. For centuries, and especially in the last one, had his strange stories been completely rejected. No one would believe him when he said he had witnessed, time and again, with his own eyes, the most wonderful feats of magic performed by the subjects of Kublai-Khan and adepts of other countries. On his death-bed Marco was strongly urged to retract his alleged "falsehoods"; but he solemnly swore to the truth of what he said, adding that "he had not told *one-half* of what he had really seen!" There is now no doubt that he spoke the truth, since Marsden's edition, and that of Colonel Yule have appeared. The public is especially beholden to the latter for bringing forward so many authorities corroborative of Marco's testimony, and explaining some of the phenomena in the usual way, for he makes it plain beyond question that the great traveller was not only a veracious but an exceedingly observant writer. Warmly defending his author, the conscientious editor, after enumerating more than one hitherto controverted and even rejected point in the Venetian's Travels, concludes by saying: "Nay, the last two years have thrown a promise of light even on what seemed *the wildest* of Marco's stories, and the bones of a veritable RUC from New Zealand lie on the table of Professor Owen's cabinet!"[887]

The monstrous bird of the *Arabian Nights,* or "Arabian Mythology," as Webster calls the *Ruc* (or Roc), having been identified, the next thing in order is to *discover* and recognize that *Aladdin's* magical lamp has also certain claims to reality.

Describing his passage through the great desert of Lop, Marco Polo speaks of a marvellous thing, "which is that, when travellers are on the move by night . . . they will hear

---

886 Schott, "*Essay on Buddhism,*" p. 103.
887 "*The Book of Ser Marco Polo,*" vol. i., Preface to the second edition, p. viii.

spirits talking. Sometimes the spirits will call him by name . . . even in the daytime one hears these spirits talking. And sometimes you shall hear the sound of a variety of musical instruments, and still more commonly the sound of drums."[888]

In his notes, the translator quotes the Chinese historian, Matwanlin, who corroborates the same. "During the passage of this wilderness you hear sounds," says Matwanlin, "sometimes of singing, sometimes of wailing; and it has often happened that travellers going aside to see what those sounds might be, have strayed from their course and been entirely lost; for they were voices of spirits and goblins."[889] "These goblins are not peculiar to the Gobi," adds the editor, "though that appears to have been their most favored haunt. *The awe of the vast and solitary desert raises them in all similar localities.*"

Colonel Yule would have done well to consider the possibility of serious consequences arising from the acceptance of his theory. If we admit that the weird cries of the Gobi are due to the *awe* inspired "by the vast and solitary desert," why should the goblins of the Gadarenes (*Luke* viii. 29) be entitled to any better consideration? and why may not Jesus have been self-deceived as to his objective tempter during the forty days' trial in the "wilderness"? We are quite ready to receive or reject the theory enunciated by Colonel Yule, but shall insist upon its impartial application to all cases. Pliny speaks of the phantoms that appear and vanish in the deserts of Africa;[890] Æthicus, the early Christian cosmographer, mentions, though incredulous, the stories that were told of the voices of singers and revellers in the desert; and "Mas'udi tells of the *ghûls,* which in the deserts appear to travellers by night and in lonely hours"; and also of "Apollonius of Tyana and his companions, who, in a desert near the Indus by moonlight, saw an *empusa* or ghul taking many forms. . . . They revile it, and it goes off uttering shrill cries."[891] And Ibn Batuta relates a like legend of the Western Sahara: "If the messenger be solitary, the demons sport with him and fascinate him, so that he strays from his course and perishes."[892] Now if all these matters are capable of a "rational explanation," and we do not doubt it as regards most of these cases, then, the Bible-devils of the wilderness deserve no more consideration, but should have the same rule applied to them. They, too, are creatures of terror, imagination, and *superstition;* hence, the narratives of the *Bible* must be false; and if one single verse is false, then a cloud is thrown upon the title of all the rest to be considered *divine* revelation. Once admit this, and this collection of canonical documents is at least as amenable to criticism as any other book of stories.[893]

---

888 Ibid., vol. i., p. 203.
889 "*Visdelon,*" p. 130.
890 "*Pliny,*" vii., 2.
891 "*Philostratus,*" book ii., chap. iv.
892 Ibid., book iv., p. 382; "*Book of Ser Marco Polo,*" vol. i., p. 206.
893 There are pious critics who deny the world the same right to judge the "Bible" on the testimony of deductive logic as "any other book." Even exact science must bow to this decree. In the concluding paragraph of an article devoted to a terrible onslaught on Baron Bunsen's "Chronology," which *does not quite agree* with the "Bible," a writer exclaims, "the subject we have proposed to ourselves is completed. . . . We have endeavored to meet Chevalier Bunsen's charges against the inspiration of the "Bible" on its own ground. . . . An inspired book . . . never can, as an expression of its own teaching, or as a part of its own record, bear witness to any untrue or ignorant statement of fact, whether in history

There are many spots in the world where the strangest phenomena have resulted from what was later ascertained to be natural physical causes. In Southern California there are certain places on the sea-shore where the sand when disturbed produces a loud musical ring. It is known as the "musical sand," and the phenomenon is supposed to be of an electrical nature. "The sound of musical instruments, chiefly of drums, is a phenomenon of another class, and is really produced in certain situations among sandhills when the sand is disturbed," says the editor of *Marco Polo*. "A very striking account of a phenomenon of this kind, *regarded as supernatural,* is given by Friar Odoric, whose experience I have traced to the Reg Ruwan or flowing sand north of Kabul. Besides this celebrated example . . . I have noted that equally well-known one of the *Jibal Nakics,* or 'Hill of the Bell' in the Sinai desert; . . . Gibalul-Thabul, or hill of the drums. . . . A Chinese narrative of the tenth century mentions the phenomenon as known near Kwachau, on the eastern border of the Lop desert, under the name of "the singing sands."[894]

That all these are natural phenomena, no one can doubt. But what of the questions and answers, plainly and audibly given and received? What of conversations held between certain travellers and the *invisible* spirits, or unknown beings, that sometimes appear to whole caravans in tangible form? If so many millions believe in the possibility that spirits may clothe themselves with material bodies, behind the curtain of a "medium," and appear to the *circle,* why should they reject the same possibility for the elemental spirits of the deserts? This is the "to be, or not to be" of Hamlet. If "spirits" can do all that Spiritualists claim for them, why can they not appear equally to the traveller in the wildernesses and solitudes? A recent scientific article in a Russian journal attributes such "spirit-voices," in the great Gobi desert, *to the echo.* A very reasonable explanation, if it can only be demonstrated that these voices simply repeat what has been previously uttered by a living person. But when the "superstitious" traveller gets intelligent *answers* to his questions, this Gobi *echo* at once shows a very near relationship with the famous echo of the Théâtre Porte St. Martin at Paris. "How do you do, sir?" shouts one of the actors in the play. "Very poorly, my son; thank you. I am getting old, very . . . very old!" politely answers the echo!

What incredulous merriment must the *superstitious* and *absurd* narratives of Marco Polo, concerning the "supernatural" gifts of certain shark and wild-beast charmers of India, whom he terms *Abraiaman,* have excited for long centuries. Describing the pearl-fishery of Ceylon, as it was in his time, he says that the merchants are "obliged also to pay those men who *charm* the great fishes — to prevent them from injuring the divers whilst engaged in seeking pearls under water — one-twentieth part of all that they take. These fish-charmers are termed Abraiaman (Brahman?), and their charm holds good for that day only, for at night they dissolve the charm, so that the fishes can work mischief at their will. These Abraiaman know also how to charm beasts and birds, and every living thing."

And this is what we find in the explanatory notes of Colonel Yule, in relation to this *degrading* Asiatic "superstition": "Marco's account of the pearl-fishery is still substantially correct. . . . At the diamond mines of the northern Circars, Brahmans are employed in the analogous office of propitiating the tutelary genii. The shark-charmers are called in *Tamil,*

---

or doctrine. *If it be untrue in its witness of one, who shall trust its truth in the witness of the other?"* ("*The Journal of Sacred Literature and Biblical Record,*" edited by the Rev. H. Burgess, Oct., 1859, p. 70.)
894 Remusat, "*Histoire du Khotan,*" p. 74; "*Marco Polo,*" vol. i., p. 206.

Kadal-Katti, 'sea-binders,' and in Hindustani, *Hai-banda,* or 'shark-binders.' At Aripo they belong to one family, supposed to have the monopoly of the charm.[895] The chief operator is (or was, not many years ago) *paid by the government,* and he also received ten oysters from each boat daily during the fishery. Tennent, on his visit, found the incumbent of the office to be a *Roman Catholic Christian* (?), but that did not seem to affect the exercise of the validity of his functions. *It is remarkable that not more than one authenticated accident from sharks had taken place during the whole period of the British occupation."*[896]

Two items of fact in the above paragraph are worthy of being placed in juxtaposition. 1. The British authorities pay professional shark-charmers a stipend to exercise their art; and, 2, only *one life* has been lost since the execution of the contract. (We have yet to learn whether the loss of this *one* life did not occur under the Roman Catholic *sorcerer.*) Is it pretended that the salary is paid as a concession to a *degrading* native superstition? Very well; but how about the sharks? Are they receiving salaries, also, from the British authorities out of the Secret Service Fund? Every person who has visited Ceylon must know that the waters of the pearl coast swarm with sharks of the most voracious kind, and that it is even dangerous to bathe, let alone to dive for oysters. We might go further, if we chose, and give the names of British officials of the highest rank in the Indian service, who, after resorting to native "magicians" and "sorcerers," to assist them in recovering things lost, or in unravelling vexatious mysteries of one kind or another, and being successful, and at the time *secretly* expressing their gratitude, have gone away, and shown their innate cowardice before the world's Areopagus, by publicly denying the truth of magic, and leading the jest against Hindu "superstition."

Not many years ago, one of the worst of *superstitions* scientists held to be that of believing that the murderer's portrait remained impressed on the eye of the murdered person, and that the former could be easily recognized by examining carefully the retina. The "superstition" asserted that the likeness could be made still more striking by subjecting the murdered man to certain old women's fumigations, and the like gossip. And now an American newspaper, of March 26, 1877, says: "A number of years ago attention was attracted to a theory which insisted that the last effort of vision materialized itself and remained as an object imprinted on the retina of the eye after death. This has been proved a fact by an experiment tried in the presence of Dr. Gamgee, F. R. S., of Birmingham, England, and Prof. Bunsen, the subject being a living rabbit. The means taken to prove the merits of the question were most simple, the eyes being placed near an opening in a shutter, and retaining the shape of the same after the animal had been deprived of life."

If, from the regions of idolatry, ignorance, and superstition, as India is termed by some missionaries, we turn to the so-called centre of civilization — Paris, we find the same principles of magic exemplified there under the name of *occult* Spiritualism. The Honorable John L. O'Sullivan, Ex-Minister Plenipotentiary of the United States to Portugal, has kindly furnished us with the strange particulars of a semi-magical seance which he recently attended with several other eminent men, at Paris. Having his permission to that effect, we print his letter in full.

---

895 Like the *Psylli,* or serpent-charmers of Libya, whose gift is hereditary.
896 *"Ser Marco Polo,"* vol. ii., p. 321.

"I cheerfully obey your request for a written statement of what I related to you orally, as having been witnessed by me in Paris, last summer, at the house of a highly respectable physician, whose name I have no authority to use, but whom, after the usual French fashion of anonymizing, I will call Dr. X. "I was introduced there by an English friend, well-known in the Spiritualist circles in London — Mr. Gledstanes. Some eight or ten other visitors were present, of both sexes. We were seated in *fauteuils,* occupying half of a long drawing-room, flush with a spacious garden. In the other half of the room was a grand piano, a considerable open space between it and us, and a couple of *fauteuils* in that space, evidently placed there to be occupied by other sitters. A door near them opened into the private apartments. "Dr. X. came in, and discoursed to us for about twenty minutes with rapid and vehement French eloquence, which I could not undertake to report. He had, for over twenty-five years, investigated occult mysteries, of which he was about to exhibit some phenomena. His object was to attract his brethren of the scientific world, but few or none of them came to see for themselves. He intended before long to publish a book. He presently led in two ladies, the younger one his wife, the other (whom I will call Madame Y.) a medium or sensitive, with whom he had worked through all that period in the prosecution of these studies, and who had devoted and sacrificed her whole life to this work with him. Both these ladies had their eyes closed, apparently in trance. "He stood them at the opposite ends of the long grand piano (which was shut), and directed them to put their hands upon it. Sounds soon began to issue from its chords, marching, galloping, drums, trumpets, rolling musketry, cannon, cries, and groans — in one word, a *battle.* This lasted, I should say, some five to ten minutes. "I should have mentioned that before the two mediums were brought in I had written in pencil, on a small bit of paper (by direction of Mr. Gledstanes, who had been there before), the names of three objects, to be known to myself alone, viz., some *musical composer,* deceased, a *flower,* and *a cake.* I chose *Beethoven,* a *Marguerite* (daisy), and a kind of French cake called *plombieres,* and rolled the paper into a pellet, which I kept in my hand, without letting even my friend know its contents. "When the battle was over, he placed Mme. Y. in one of the two *fauteuils,* Mme. X. being seated apart at one side of the room, and I was asked to hand my folded, or rolled, paper to Mme. Y. She held it (unopened) between her fingers, on her lap. She was dressed in white merino, flowing from her neck and gathered in at the waist, under a blaze of light from chandeliers on the right and left. After a while she dropped the little roll of paper to the floor, and I picked it up. Dr. X. then raised her to her feet and told her to make "the evocation of the dead." He withdrew the *fauteuils* and placed in her hand a steel rod of about four and half or five feet in length, the top of which was surmounted with a short cross-piece — the Egyptian *Tau.* With this she traced a circle round herself, as she stood, of about six feet in diameter. She did not hold the cross-piece as a handle, but, on the contrary, she held the rod at the opposite end. She presently handed it back to Dr. X. There she stood for some time, her hands hanging down and folded together in front of her, motionless, and with her eyes directed slightly upward toward one of the opposite corners of the long *salon*. Her lips presently began to move, with muttered sounds, which after a while became distinct in articulation, in short broken sentences or phrases, very much like the recitation of a litany. Certain words, seeming to be names, would recur from time to time. It sounded to me somewhat as I have heard Oriental languages sound. Her face was very earnest and mobile with expression, with sometimes a slight frown on the brow. I suppose it lasted about fifteen or twenty minutes, amidst the motionless silence of all the company, as we gazed on the weird scene. Her utterance finally seemed to increase in vehemence and rapidity. At last she stretched forth one arm toward the space on which her eyes had been fixed, and, with a loud cry, almost a scream, she exclaimed: 'BEETHOVEN!' — and fell backward, prostrate on the floor.

"Dr. X. hastened to her, made eager magnetic passes about her face and neck, and propped up her head and shoulders on cushions. And there she lay like a person sick and suffering, occasionally moaning, turning restlessly, etc. I suppose a full half-hour then elapsed, during which she seemed to pass through all the phases of gradual *death* (this I was told was a re-enacting of the death of Beethoven). It would be long to describe in detail, even if I could recall all. We watched as though assisting at a scene of real death. I will only say that her pulse ceased; no beating of the heart could be perceived; her hands first, then her arms became cold, while warmth was still to be felt under her arm-pits; even they at last became entirely cold; her feet and legs became cold in the same manner, and they swelled astonishingly. The doctor invited us all to come and recognize these phenomena. The gasping breaths came at longer and longer intervals, and feebler and feebler. At last came the end; her head fell sidewise, her hands, which had been picking with the fingers about her dress, collapsed also. The doctor said, 'she is now dead'; and so it indeed seemed. In vehement haste he produced (I did not see from where) two small *snakes*, which he seemed to huddle about her neck and down into her bosom, making also eager transverse passes about her head and neck. After a while she appeared to revive slowly, and finally the doctor and a couple of men servants lifted her up and carried her off into the private apartments, from which he soon returned. He told us that this was all very critical, but perfectly safe, but that no time was to be lost, for otherwise the death, which he said was real, would be permanent.

"I need not say how ghastly the effect of this whole scene had been on all the spectators. Nor need I remind you that this was no trickery of a performer paid to astonish. The scene passed in the elegant drawing-room of a respectable physician, to which access without introduction is impossible, while (outside of the phenomenal facts) a thousand indescribable details of language, manner, expression, and action presented those minute guarantees of sincerity and earnestness which carry conviction to those who witness, though it may be transmitted to those who only hear or read of them.

"After a time Mme. Y. returned and was seated in one of the two *fauteuils* before mentioned, and I was invited to the other by her side. I had still in my hand the unopened pellet of paper containing the three words privately written by me, of which (Beethoven) had been the first. She sat for a few minutes with her open hands resting on her lap. They presently began to move restlessly about. "Ah, it burns, it burns," she said, and her features contracted with an expression of pain. In a few moments she raised one of them, and it contained a *marguerite*, the flower I had written as my second word. I received it from her, and after it had been examined by the rest of the company, I preserved it. Dr. X. said it was of a species not known in that part of the country; an opinion in which he was certainly mistaken, as a few days afterwards I saw the same in the flower-market of the Madeleine. Whether this flower was *produced* under her hands, or was simply an *apport*, as in the phenomenon we are familiar with in the experiences of Spiritualism, I do not know. It was the one or the other, for she certainly did not have it as she sat there by my side, under a strong light, before it made its appearance. The flower was perfectly fresh in every one of its delicate petals.

"The third word I had written on my bit of paper was the name of a cake — *plombières*. She presently began to go through the motions of eating, though no cake was visible, and asked me if I would not go with her to *Plombières* — the name of the cake I had written. This might have been simply a case of mind-reading. "After this followed a scene in which Madame X., the doctor's wife, was said, and seemed to be, possessed by the spirit of Beethoven. The doctor addressed her as "Monsieur Beethoven." She took no notice until he called the name aloud in her ear. She then responded with polite bows, etc. (You may remember that Beethoven was extremely deaf.) After some conversation he begged her to play, and she seated herself at the piano and performed magnificently both some of his known music and some improvisations which were generally recognized by the company as in his style. I was told afterwards, by a lady friend of Madame X., that in her normal state she was a very ordinary amateur performer. After about half an hour spent in music and in dialogue in the character of Beethoven, to whom her face in expression, and her tumbled hair, seemed to acquire a strange resemblance, the doctor placed in her hands a sheet of paper and a crayon, and asked her to sketch the face of the person she saw before her. She produced very rapidly a profile sketch of a head and face resembling Beethoven's busts, though as a younger man; and she dashed off a rapid name under it, as though a signature, 'Beethoven.' I have preserved the sketch, though how the handwriting may correspond with Beethoven's signature I cannot say. "The hour was now late, and the company broke up; nor had I any time to interrogate Dr. X. upon what we had thus witnessed. But I called on him with Mr. Gledstanes a few evenings afterwards. I found that he admitted the action of spirits, and was a Spiritualist, but also a great deal more, having studied long and deeply into the occult mysteries of the Orient. So I understood him to convey, while he seemed to prefer to refer me to his book, which he would probably publish in the course of the present year. I observed a number of loose sheets on a table all covered with Oriental characters unknown to me — the work of Madame Y. in trance, as he said, in answer to an inquiry. He told us that in the scene I had witnessed, she became (*i.e.,* as I presumed, was possessed by) *a priestess of one of the ancient Egyptian temples,* and that the origin of it was this: A scientific friend of his had acquired in Egypt possession of the mummy of a priestess, and had given him some of the linen swathings with which the body was enveloped, and from the contact with this cloth of 2,000 or 3,000 years old, the devotion of her whole existence to this occult relation, and twenty years seclusion from the world, his medium, as sensitive Madame Y., had become what I had seen. The language I had heard her speak was the sacred language of the temples in which she had been instructed, not so much by inspiration but very much as we now study languages, by dictation, written exercises, etc., being even chided and punished when she was dull or slow. He said that Jacolliot had heard her in a similar scene, and recognized sounds and words of the very oldest sacred language as preserved in the temples of India, anterior, if I remember right, to the epoch of the Sanscrit.

"Respecting the *snakes* he had employed in the hasty operation of restoring her to life, or rather perhaps arresting the last consummation of the process of death, he said there was a strange mystery in their relation to the phenomena of life and death. I understood that they were indispensable. Silence and inaction on our part were also insisted upon throughout, and any attempt at questioning him at the time was peremptorily, almost angrily, suppressed. We might come and talk afterward, or wait for the appearance of his book, but he alone seemed entitled to exercise the faculty of speech throughout all these performances — which he certainly did with great volubility, the while, with all the eloquence and precision of diction of a Frenchman, combining scientific culture with vividness of imagination. "I intended to return on some subsequent evening, but learned from Mr. Gledstanes that he had given them up for the present, disgusted with his ill-success in getting his professional colleagues and men of science to come and witness what it was his object to show them.

"This is about as much as I can recall of this strange, weird evening, excepting some uninteresting details. I have given you the name and address of Dr. X. confidentially, because he would seem to have gone more or less far on the same path as you pursue in the studies of your Theosophical Society. Beyond that I feel bound to keep it private, not having his authority to use it in any way which might lead to publicity.

"Very respectfully, Your friend and obedient servant, J. L. O'SULLIVAN"

In this interesting case simple Spiritualism has transcended its routine and encroached upon the limits of magic. The features of mediumship are there, in the double life led by the sensitive Madame Y., in which she passes an existence totally distinct from the normal one, and by reason of the subordination of her individuality to a foreign will, becomes the permutation of a priestess of Egypt; and in the personation of the spirit of Beethoven, and in the unconscious and cataleptic state into which she falls. On the other hand, the will-power exercised by Dr. X. upon his sensitive, the tracing of the mystic circle, the evocations, the materialization of the desired flower, the seclusion and education of Madame Y., the employment of the wand and its form, the creation and use of the serpents, the evident control of the astral forces — all these pertain to magic. Such experiments are of interest and value to science, but liable to abuse in the hands of a less conscientious practitioner than the eminent gentleman designated as Dr. X. A true Oriental kabalist would not recommend their duplication. Spheres unknown below our feet; spheres still more unknown and still more unexplored above us; between the two a handful of moles, blind to God's great light, and deaf to the whispers of the invisible world, boasting that they lead mankind. Where? Onward, they claim; but we have a right to doubt it. The greatest of our physiologists, when placed side by side with a Hindu fakir, who knows neither how to read nor write, will very soon find himself feeling as foolish as a school-boy who has neglected to learn his lesson. It is not by vivisecting living animals that a physiologist will assure himself of the existence of man's soul, nor on the blade of the knife can he extract it from a human body. "What sane man," inquires Sergeant Cox, the President of the London Psychological Society, "what sane man who knows nothing of magnetism or physiology, who had never witnessed an experiment nor learned its principles, would proclaim himself *a fool* by denying its facts and denouncing its theory?" The truthful answer to this would be, "two-thirds of our modern-day scientists." The impertinence, if truth can ever be impertinent, must be laid at the door of him who uttered it — a scientist of the number of those few who are brave and honest enough to utter wholesome truths, however disagreeable. And there is no mistaking the real meaning of the imputation, for immediately after the irreverent inquiry, the learned lecturer remarks as pointedly: "The chemist takes his electricity from the electrician, the physiologist looks to the geologist for his geology — each would deem it an impertinence in the other if he were to pronounce judgment in the branch of knowledge not his own. Strange it is, but true as strange, that this rational rule is wholly set at naught in the treatment of psychology. *Physical scientists deem themselves competent to pronounce a dogmatic judgment upon psychology and all that appertains to it, without having witnessed any of its phenomena, and in entire ignorance of its principles and practice.*"[897]

We sincerely hope that the two eminent biologists, Mr. Mendeleyeff, of St. Petersburg, and Mr. Ray Lankester, of London fame, will bear themselves under the above as unflinchingly as their living victims do when palpitating under their dissecting knives.

For a belief to have become universal, it must have been founded on an immense accumulation of facts, tending to strengthen it, from one generation to another. At the head of all such beliefs stands magic, or, if one would prefer — occult psychology. Who, of those who appreciate its tremendous powers even from its feeble, half-paralyzed effects in our civilized countries, would dare disbelieve in our days the assertions of Porphyry and Proclus, that even inanimate objects, such as statues of gods, could be made to move and exhibit a factitious life for a few moments? Who can deny the allegation? Is it those who testify daily over their own signatures that they have seen tables and chairs move and walk, and pencils write, without contact? Diogenes Laertius tells us of a certain philosopher, Stilpo, who was exiled from Athens by the Areopagus, for having dared to deny publicly

897 *"The Spiritualist,"* London, Nov. 10, 1876.

that the Minerva of Pheidias was anything else than a block of marble. But our own age, after having mimicked the ancients in everything possible, even to their very names, such as "senates," "prefects," and "consuls," etc.; and after admitting that Napoleon the Great conquered three-fourths of Europe by applying the principles of war taught by the Cæsars and the Alexanders, knows so much better than its preceptors about psychology, that it would vote every believer in "animated tables" into Bedlam.

Be this as it may, *the religion of the ancients is the religion of the future.* A few centuries more, and there will linger no sectarian beliefs in either of the great religions of humanity. Brahmanism and Buddhism, Christianity and Mahometanism will all disappear before the mighty rush of *facts.* "I will pour out my spirit upon all flesh," writes the prophet Joel. "Verily I say unto you . . . greater works than these shall you do," promises Jesus. But this can only come to pass when the world returns to the grand religion of the past; the *knowledge* of those majestic systems which preceded, by far, Brahmanism, and even the primitive monotheism of the ancient Chaldeans. Meanwhile, we must remember the direct effects of the revealed mystery. The only means by which the wise priests of old could impress upon the grosser senses of the multitudes the idea of the Omnipotency of the Creative *will* or FIRST CAUSE; namely, the divine animation of inert matter, the soul infused into it by the potential will of man, the microcosmic image of the great Architect, and the transportation of ponderous objects through space and material obstacles.

Why should the pious Roman Catholic turn away in disgust at the "heathen" practices of the Hindu Tamil, for instance? We have witnessed the miracle of San Gennaro, in good old Naples, and we have seen the same in Nargercoil, in India. Where is the difference? The coagulated blood of the Catholic saint is made to boil and fume in its crystal bottle, to the gratification of the lazzaroni; and from its jewelled shrine the martyr's idol beams radiant smiles and blessings at the Christian congregation. On the other hand, a ball of clay filled with water, is stuffed into the open breast of the god Suran; and while the padre shakes *his* bottle and produces his "miracle" of blood, the Hindu priest plunges an arrow into the god's breast, and produces *his* "miracle," for the blood gushes forth in streams, and the water is changed into blood. Both Christians and Hindus fall in raptures at the sight of such a miracle. So far, we do not see the slightest difference. But can it be that the Pagan learned the trick from San Gennaro?

"Know, O, Asclepius," says Hermes, "that as the HIGHEST ONE is the father of the celestial gods, so is man *the artisan of the gods who reside in the temples,* and who delight in the society of mortals. Faithful to its origin and nature, humanity perseveres in this imitation of the divine powers; and, if the Father Creator has made in His image the *eternal gods,* mankind in its turn makes its gods in its own image." "And, dost thou speak of statues of gods; O, Trismegistus?" "Verily, I do, Asclepius, and however great thy defiance, perceivest thou not that these statues are endowed *with reason,* that they are animated with a soul, and that they can operate the greatest prodigies. How can we reject the evidence, when we find these gods possessing the gift of predicting the future, which they are compelled to tell, when forced to it by magic spells, as through the lips of the divines and their visions? . . . It is the marvel of marvels that man could have invented and created gods. . . True, the faith of our ancestors has erred, and in their pride they fell into error as to the precise essence of these gods . . . but they have still found out that art themselves. Powerless to create soul and spirit, they evoke the souls of angels and demons in order to introduce them into the consecrated statues; and so make them preside at their Mysteries, by communicating to idols their own faculty to *do good as well as evil*."

It is not antiquity alone which is full of evidence that the statues and idols of the gods at times exhibited intelligence and locomotive powers. Full in the nineteenth century, we see the papers recording the capers played by the statue of the Madonna of Lourdes. This gracious lady, the French Notre Dame, runs away several times to the woods adjoining her usual residence, the parish church. The sexton is obliged to hunt after the runaway, and bring her home more than once.[898] After this begins a series of "miracles," healing, prophesying, letter-dropping from on high, and what not. These "miracles" are implicitly accepted by millions and millions of Roman Catholics; numbers of these belonging to the most intelligent and educated classes. Why, then, should we disbelieve in testimony of precisely the same character, given as to contemporary phenomena of the same kind, by the most accredited and esteemed historians — by Titus Livy, for instance? "Juno, would you please abandon the walls of Veii, and change this abode for that of Rome?" inquires of the goddess a Roman soldier, after the conquest of that city. Juno consents, and nodding her head in token of acquiescence, her statue answers: "Yes, I will." Furthermore, upon their carrying off the figure, it seems to instantly *"lose its immense weight,"* adds the historian, and the statue seems rather to follow them than otherwise.[899]

With *naivete,* and a faith bordering on the sublime, des Mousseaux, bravely rushes into the dangerous parallels, and gives a number of instances of Christian as well as "heathen" *miracles* of that kind. He prints a list of such walking statues of saints and Madonnas, who lose their weight, and move about as so many living men and women; and presents unimpeachable evidence of the same, from classical authors, who described their *miracles.*[900] He has but one thought, one anxious and all-overpowering desire — to prove to his readers that magic does exist, and that Christianity beats it flat. Not that the miracles of the latter are either more numerous, or more extraordinary, or suggestive than those of the Pagans. Not at all; and he is a fair historian as to facts and evidence. But, it is his arguments and reflections that are priceless: one kind of miracle is produced by God, the other by the Devil; he drags down the Deity and placing Him face to face with Satan, allows the arch-enemy to beat the Creator by long odds. Not a word of solid, evident proof to show the substantial difference between the two kinds of wonders.

Would we inquire the reason why he traces in one the hand of God and in the other the horn and hoof of the Devil? Listen to the answer: "The Holy Roman Catholic and Apostolical Church declares the miracles wrought by her faithful sons produced by the will of God; and all others the work of the spirits of Hell." Very well, but on what ground? We are shown an endless list of holy writers; of saints who fought during their whole lives with the fiends; and of fathers whose word and authority are accepted as "word of God" by the same Church. "Your idols, your consecrated statues are the abode of *demons,*" exclaims St. Cyprian. "Yes, it is these *spirits* who inspire your divines, who animate the bowels of your victims, who govern the flight of birds, and who, mixing incessantly falsehood with truth,

---

898 Read any of the papers, of the summer and autumn of 1876.
899 Tite-Livy, v. déc. i., — Val. Max., 1, cap. vii.
900 See *"Les Hauts Phenomenes de la Magie"*; *"La Magie au XIXme Siècle"*; *"Dieu et les Dieux,"* etc.

render oracles, and . . . operate prodigies, their object being to bring you invincibly to their worship."[901]

Fanaticism in religion, fanaticism in science, or fanaticism in any other question becomes a hobby, and cannot but blind our senses. It will ever be useless to argue with a fanatic. And here we cannot help admiring once more the profound knowledge of human nature which dictated to Mr. Sergeant Cox the following words, delivered in the same address as before alluded to: "There is no more fatal fallacy than that the truth will prevail by its own force, that it has only to be seen to be embraced. In fact the desire for the actual truth exists in very few minds, and the capacity to discern it in fewer still. When men say that they are seeking the truth, they mean that they are looking for evidence to support some prejudice or prepossession. Their beliefs are moulded to their wishes. They see all, and more than all, that seems to tell for that which they desire; they are blind as bats to whatever tells against them. The scientists are no more exempt from this common failing than are others."

We know that from the remotest ages there has existed a mysterious, awful science, under the name of *theopœa*. This science taught the art of endowing the various symbols of gods with temporary life and intelligence. Statues and blocks of inert matter became animated under the potential will of the hierophant. The fire stolen by Prometheus had fallen down in the struggle to earth; it embraced the lower regions of the sky, and settled in the waves of the universal ether as the potential *Akâsa* of the Hindu rites. We breathe and imbibe it into our organic system with every mouthful of fresh air. Our organism is full of it from the instant of our birth. But it becomes potential only under the influx of WILL and SPIRIT.

Left to itself, this life-principle will blindly follow the laws of nature; and, according to conditions, will produce health and an exuberance of *life*, or cause *death* and dissolution. But, guided by the will of the adept, it becomes obedient; its currents restore the equilibrium in organic bodies, they fill the waste, and produce physical and psychological miracles, well-known to mesmerizers. Infused in inorganic and inert matter, they create an appearance of life, hence motion. If to that life an individual intelligence, a personality, is wanting, then the operator must either send his *scin-lecca*, his own astral spirit, to animate it; or use his power over the region of nature-spirits to force one of them to *infuse* his entity into the marble, wood, or metal; or, again, be helped by human spirits. But the latter — except the vicious, earth-bound class[902] — will *not* infuse their essence into these inanimate objects. They leave the lower kinds to produce the similitude of life and animation, and only send their influence through the intervening spheres like a ray of divine light, when the so-called "miracle" is required for a good purpose. The condition — and this is a law in spiritual nature — is purity of motive, purity of the surrounding magnetic atmosphere,

---

901 "*De Idol. Vanit.*," lib. I., p. 452.

902 These, after their bodily death, unable to soar higher, attached to terrestrial regions, delight in the society of the kind of elementals which by their affinity with vice attract them the most. They identify themselves with these to such a degree that they very soon lose sight of their own identity, and become a part of the elementals, the help of which they need to communicate with mortals. But as the nature-spirits are not *immortal*, so the human elementaries who have lost their divine guide — spirit — can last no longer than the essence of the elements which compose their astral bodies holds together.

personal purity of the operator. Thus is it, that a Pagan "miracle" may be by far holier than a Christian one.

Who that has seen the performance of the fakirs of Southern India, can doubt the existence of *theopœa* in ancient times? An inveterate skeptic, though more than anxious to attribute every phenomenon to jugglery, still finds himself compelled to testify to facts; and facts that are to be witnessed daily if one chooses. "I dare not," he says, speaking of Chibh-Chondor, a fakir of Jaffna-patnam, "describe all the exercises which he performed. There are things one *dares* not say even after having witnessed them, for fear of being charged with having been under an inexplicable hallucination! And yet, ten, nay, twenty times, I saw and saw again the fakir obtain similar results over inert matter. . . It was but child's play for our 'charmer' to make the flame of candles which had, by his directions, been placed in the remotest corners of the apartment, pale and become extinguished at will; to cause the furniture to move, even the sofas on which we sat, the doors to open and shut repeatedly: and all this without quitting the mat upon which he sat on the floor.

THE MAGICIAN AIDS, NOT IMPEDES, NATURE

"Perhaps I will be told that I saw imperfectly. Possibly; but I will say that hundreds and thousands of persons have seen and do see what I have, and things more wonderful; has one of all these discovered the secret, or been able to duplicate these phenomena? And I can never repeat too often that all this does not occur on a stage, supplied with mechanical contrivances for the use of the operator. No, it is a beggar crouched, naked, on the floor, who thus sports with your intelligence, your senses, and all that which we have agreed among ourselves to style the immutable laws of nature, but which he appears to alter at will!

"Does he change its course? 'No, but he makes it act by using forces which are yet unknown to us,' say the believers. However that may be, I have found myself twenty times at similar performances in company with the most distinguished men of British India — professors, physicians, officers. Not one of them but thus summarized his impressions upon quitting the drawing-room. 'This is something terrifying to human intelligence!' Every time that I saw repeated by a fakir the experiment of reducing serpents to a cataleptic state, a condition in which these animals have all the rigidity of the dry branch of a tree, my thoughts have reverted to the biblical fable (?) which endows Moses and the priests of Pharaoh with the like power."[903]

Assuredly, the flesh of man, beast, and bird should be as easily endowed with magnetic life-principle as the inert table of a modern medium. Either both wonders are possible and true, or both must fall to the ground, together with the miracles of Apostolic days, and those of the more modern Popish Church. As for vital proofs furnished to us in favor of such possibilities, we might name books enough to fill a whole library. If Sixtus V. cited a formidable array of spirits attached to various talismans, was not his threat of excommunication for all those who practiced the art, uttered merely because he would have the knowledge of this secret confined within the precincts of the Church? How would it do for his "divine" miracles to be studied and successfully reproduced by every man endowed

---

903 L. Jacolliot, "*Voyage au Pays des Perles*."

with perseverance, a strong positive magnetic power, and an unflinching will? Recent events at Lourdes (of course, supposing them to have been truthfully reported) prove that the secret is not wholly lost; and if there is no strong magician-mesmerizer concealed under frock and surplice, then the statue of Notre-Dame is moved by the same forces which move every magnetized table at a spiritual seance; and the nature of these "intelligences," whether they belong to the classes of human, human elementary, or elemental spirits depends on a variety of conditions. With one who knows anything of mesmerism, and at the same time of the charitable spirit of the Roman Catholic Church, it ought not to be difficult to comprehend that the incessant curses of the priests and monks; and the bitter anathemas so freely pronounced by Pius IX. — himself a strong mesmerizer, and believed to be a *jettatore* (evil eye) — have drawn together legions of elementaries and elementals under the leadership of the disembodied Torquemadas. These are the "angels" who play pranks with the statue of the Queen of Heaven. Any one who accepts the "miracle" and thinks otherwise blasphemes.

PHILOSOPHY, RELIGION, ARTS AND SCIENCES BEQUEATHED BY MOTHER INDIA TO POSTERITY

Although it would seem as if we had already furnished sufficient proofs that modern science has little or no reason to boast of originality, yet before closing this volume we will adduce a few more to place the matter beyond doubt. We have but to recapitulate, as briefly as possible, the several claims to new philosophies and discoveries, the announcement of which has made the world open its eyes so wide within these last two centuries. We have pointed to the achievements in arts, sciences, and philosophy of the ancient Egyptians, Greeks, Chaldeans, and Assyrians; we will now quote from an author who has passed long years in India studying their philosophy. In the famous and recent work of *Christna et le Christ*, we find the following tabulation:

"*Philosophy* — The ancient Hindus have created from the foundation the two systems of spiritualism and materialism, of metaphysical philosophy and of positive philosophy. The first taught in the Vedantic school, whose founder was Vyasa; the second taught in the Sankya school, whose founder was Kapila.

"*Astronomical Science* — They fixed the calendar, invented the zodiac, calculated the precession of the equinoxes, discovered the general laws of the movements, observed and predicted the eclipses.

"*Mathematics* — They invented the decimal system, algebra, the differential, integral, and infinitesimal calculi. They also discovered geometry and trigonometry, and in these two sciences they constructed and proved theorems *which were only discovered in Europe as late as the seventeenth and eighteenth centuries*. It was the Brahmans in fact who first deduced the superficial measure of a triangle from the calculation of its three sides, and calculated the relations of the circumference to the diameter. Furthermore, we must restore to them the square of the hypotenuse and the table so improperly called Pythagorean, which we find engraved on the *gôparama* of the majority of great pagodas.

"*Physics* — They established the principle which is still our own to-day, that the universe is a harmonious whole, subject to laws which may be determined by observation and experiment. They discovered hydrostatics; and the famous proposition that every body plunged in water loses of its own weight a weight equal to the volume which it displaces, is only a loan made by the Brahmans to the famous Greek architect, Archimedes. The physicists of the pagodas calculated the velocity of light, fixed in a positive manner the laws which it follows in its reflection. And finally, it is beyond doubt, from the calculations of Surya-Sidhenta, that they knew and calculated the force of steam. "*Chemistry.* — They knew the composition of water, and formulated for gases the famous law, *which we know only from yesterday, that the volumes of gas are in inverse ratio to the pressures that they support*. They knew how to prepare sulphuric, nitric, and muriatic acids; the oxides of copper, iron, lead, tin, and zinc; the sulphurets of iron, copper, mercury, antimony, and arsenic; the sulphates of zinc and iron; the carbonates of iron, lead, and soda; nitrate of silver; and powder. "*Medicine.* — Their knowledge was truly astonishing. In Tcharaka and Sousruta, the two princes of Hindu medicine, is laid down the system which Hippocrates appropriated later. Sousruta notably enunciates the principles of preventive medicine or hygiene, which he places much above curative medicine — too often, according to him, empyrical. Are we more advanced to-day? It is not without interest to remark that the Arab physicians, who enjoyed a merited celebrity in the middle ages — Averroes among others — constantly spoke of the Hindu physicians, and regarded them as the initiators of the Greeks and themselves. "*Pharmacology.* — They knew all the simples, their properties, their use, and upon this point have not yet ceased to give lessons to Europe. Quite recently we have received from them the treatment of asthma, with the datura.

"*Surgery* — In this they are not less remarkable. They made the operation for the stone, succeeded admirably in the operation for cataract, and the extraction of the fœtus, of which all the unusual or dangerous cases are described by Tcharaka with an extraordinary scientific accuracy.

"*Grammar* — They formed the most marvellous language in the world — the Sanscrit — which gave birth to the greater part of the idioms of the Orient, and of Indo-European countries.

"*Poetry* — They have treated all the styles, and shown themselves supreme masters in all. Sakuntala, Avrita, the Hindu Phædra, Saranga, and a thousand other dramas have their superiors neither in Sophocles nor Euripides, in Corneille nor Shakespeare. Their descriptive poetry has never been equalled. One must read, in the *Megadata,* "The Plaint of an Exile," who implores a passing cloud to carry his remembrances to his cottage, his relatives and friends, whom he will never see more, to form an idea of the splendor to which this style has been carried in India. Their fables have been copied by all modern and ancient peoples, who have not even given themselves the trouble to color differently the subject of these little dramas. "*Music.* — They invented the gamut with its differences of tones and half-tones much before Gui d'Arezzo. Here is the Hindu scale:

Sa—Ri—Ga—Ma—Pa—Da—Ni—Sa.

"*Architecture* — They seem to have exhausted all that the genius of man is capable of conceiving. Domes, inexpressibly bold; tapering cupolas; minarets, with marble lace; Gothic towers; Greek hemicycles; polychrome style — all kinds and all epochs are there, betokening the origin and date of the different colonies, which, in emigrating, carried with them their souvenirs of their native art." Such were the results attained by this ancient and imposing Brahmanical civilization. What have we to offer for comparison? Beside such majestic achievements of the past, what can we place that will seem so grandiose and sublime as to warrant our boast of superiority over an ignorant ancestry? Beside the discoverers of geometry and algebra, the constructors of human speech, the parents of philosophy, the primal expounders of religion, the adepts in psychological and physical science, how even the greatest of our biologists and theologians seem dwarfed! Name to us any modern discovery, and we venture to say, that Indian history need not long be searched before the prototype will be found of record. Here we are with the transit of science half accomplished, and all our ideas in process of readjustment to the theories of force-correlation, natural selection, atomic polarity, and evolution. And here, to mock our conceit, our apprehensions, and our despair, we may read what Manu said, perhaps 10,000 years before the birth of Christ: "The first germ of life was developed by water and heat" (*Manu*, book i., sloka 8).

"Water ascends toward the sky in vapors; from the sun it descends in rain, from the rain are born the plants, and from the plants, animals" (book iii., sloka 76).

"Each being acquires the qualities of the one which immediately precedes it, in such a manner that the farther a being gets away from the primal atom of its series, the more he is possessed of qualities and perfections" (book i., sloka 20).

"Man will traverse the universe, gradually ascending, and passing through the rocks, the plants, the worms, insects, fish, serpents, tortoises, wild animals, cattle, and higher animals. . . Such is the *inferior degree*" (Ibid.).

"These are the transformations declared, from the plant up to Brahma, which have to take place in his world" (Ibid.).

"The Greek," says Jacolliot, "is but the Sanscrit. Pheidias and Praxiteles have studied in Asia the chefs-d'œuvre of Daonthia, Ramana, and Aryavosta. Plato disappears before Dgeminy and Veda-Vyasa, whom he literally copies. Aristotle is thrown into the shade by the *Pourva-Mimansa* and the *Outtara-Mimansa*, in which one finds all the systems of philosophy which we are now occupied in re-editing, from the Spiritualism of Socrates and his school, the skepticism of Pyrrho, Montaigne, and Kant, *down to the positivism of Littre.*"

Let those who doubt the exactness of the latter assertion read this phrase, extracted textually from the *Outtara-Mimansa*, or *Vedanta*, of Vyasa, who lived at an epoch which the Brahmanical chronology fixes at 10,400 years before our era:

"We can only study phenomena, verify them, and hold them to be relatively true, but nothing in the universe, neither by perception nor by induction, nor by the senses, nor by reasoning, being able to demonstrate the existence of a Supreme Cause, which could, at a fixed point of time, have given birth to the universe, Science has to discuss neither the possibility nor impossibility of this Supreme Cause."

Thus, gradually but surely, will the whole of antiquity be vindicated. Truth will be carefully sifted from exaggeration; much that is now considered fiction may yet be proved fact, and the "facts and laws" of modern science found to belong to the limbo of exploded myths. When, centuries before our era, the Hindu Bramaheupto affirmed that the starry sphere was immovable, and that the daily rising and setting of stars confirms the motion of the earth upon its axis; and when Aristarchus of Samos, born 267 years B.C., and the

Pythagorean philosopher Nicete, the Syracusan, maintained the same, what was the credit given to their theories until the days of Copernicus and Galileo? And the system of these two princes of science — a system which has revolutionized the whole world — how long will it be allowed to remain as a complete and undisturbed whole? Have we not, at the present moment, in Germany, a learned savant, a Professor Schoëpfer, who, in his public lectures at Berlin, tries to demonstrate, 1, that the earth is immovable; 2, the sun is but a little bigger than it seems; and 3, that Tycho-Brahe was perfectly right and Galileo perfectly wrong?[904] And what was Tycho-Brahe's theory? Why, that the earth stands immovable in the centre of the universe, and that around it, as around its centre, the whole of the celestial vault gravitates every twenty-four hours; and finally, that the sun and moon, apart from this motion, proceed on curved lines peculiar to themselves, while Mercury, with the rest of the planets, describes an epicycloid.

We certainly have no intention to lose time nor devote space to either combating or supporting this *new* theory, which suspiciously resembles the *old* ones of Aristotle and even the Venerable Bede. We will leave the learned army of modern Academicians to "wash their family linen among themselves," to use an expression of the great Napoleon. But we will, nevertheless, avail ourselves of such a good opportunity as this defection affords to demand once more of science her diploma or patents of infallibility. Alas! are these, then, the results of her boasted progress?

It was hardly more than yesterday when, upon the strength of facts within our own observation, and corroborated by the testimony of a multitude of witnesses, we timidly ventured the assertion that tables, mediums, and Hindu fakirs were occasionally levitated. And when we added that, if such a phenomenon should happen but once in a century, "without a visible mechanical cause, then that rising is a manifestation of a natural law of which our scientists are yet ignorant," we were called "iconoclastic," and charged, in our turn, by the newspapers, with ignorance of the law of gravitation. Iconoclastic or not, we never thought of charging science with denying the rotation of the earth on its axis, or its revolution around the sun. Those two lamps, at least, in the beacon of the Academy, we thought would be kept trimmed and burning to the end of time. But, lo! here comes a Berlin professor and crushes our last hopes that Science should prove herself exact in some one particular. The cycle is truly at its lowest point, and a new era is begun. The earth stands still, and Joshua is vindicated!

In days of old — in 1876 — the world believed in centrifugal force, and the Newtonian theory, which explained the flattening of the poles by the rotatory motion of the earth around its axis, was orthodox. Upon this hypothesis, the greater portion of the globular mass was believed to gravitate toward the equator; and in its turn the centrifugal force, acting on the mass with its mightiest power, forced this mass to concentrate itself on the equator. Thus is it that the credulous scientists believed the earth to rotate around its axis; for, were it otherwise, there would exist no centrifugal force, and without this force there could be no gravitation toward the equatorial latitudes. It has been one of the accepted

---

904 "*Ultimate Deductions of Science; The Earth Motionless.*" A lecture demonstrating that our globe does neither turn about its own axis nor around the sun; delivered in Berlin by Doctor Schoëpfer. Seventh Edition.

proofs of the rotation of the earth, and it is this deduction, with several others, that the Berlin professor declares that, "in common with many other scientists," he "rejects."

"Is this not ridiculous, gentlemen," he concludes, "that we, confiding in what we were taught at school, have accepted the rotation of the earth around its axis as a fact fully demonstrated, while there is nothing at all to prove it, and it *cannot* be demonstrated? Is it not cause of astonishment that the scientists of the whole educated world, commencing with Copernicus and Kepler, should have begun by accepting such a movement of our planet, and then three and a half centuries later be searching for such proofs? But, alas! though we search, we find none, as was to be expected. All, all is vain!"

And thus it is that at one stroke the world loses its rotation, and the universe is bereaved of its guardians and protectors, the centrifugal and centripetal forces! Nay, ether itself, blown out of space, is but a "fallacy," a myth born of a bad habit of using empty words; the sun is a pretender to dimensions to which it was never entitled; the stars are twinkling dots, and "were so expressly disposed at considerable distances from one another by the Creator of the universe, probably with the intention that they should simultaneously illumine the vast spaces on the face of our globe" — says Dr. Schoëpfer.

And is it so that even three centuries and a half have not sufficed the men of exact science to construct one theory that not a single university professor would dare challenge? If astronomy, the one science built on the adamantine foundation of mathematics, the one of all others deemed as infallible and unassailable as truth itself, can be thus irreverently indicted for false pretences, what have we gained by cheapening Plato to the profit of the Babinets? How, then, do they venture to flout at the humblest observer who, being both honest and intelligent, may say he has seen a mediumistic, or magical phenomenon? And how dare they prescribe the "limits of philosophical inquiry," to pass beyond which is not lawful? And these quarrelling hypothesists still arraign as ignorant and superstitious those giant intellects of the past, who handled natural forces like world-building Titans, and raised mortality to an eminence where it allied itself with the gods! Strange fate of a century boasting to have elevated exact science to its *apex of fame,* and now invited to go back and begin it's A B C of learning again!

Recapitulating the evidence contained in this work, if we begin with the archaic and unknown ages of the Hermetic Pimander, and come down to 1876, we find that one universal belief in magic has run through all these centuries. We have presented the ideas of Trismegistus in his dialogue with Asclepius; and without mentioning the thousand and one proofs of the prevalence of this belief in the first centuries of Christianity, to achieve our purpose we have but to quote from an ancient and a modern author. The first will be the great philosopher Porphyry, who several thousand years after the days of Hermes, remarks in relation to the prevailing skepticism of his century, the following: "We need not be amazed in seeing the vulgar masses (όι πολοι) perceive in statues merely stone and wood. Thus it is generally with those who, ignorant in letters, find naught in *stylæ* covered with inscriptions but stone, and in written books naught but the tissue of the papyrus." And 1,500 years later, we see Mr. Sergeant Cox, in stating the case of the shameful prosecution of a medium by just such a blind materialist, thus expressing his ideas: "Whether the medium is guilty or guiltless . . . certain it is that the trial has had the unlooked-for effect of directing the attention of the whole public to the fact that the phenomena *are asserted to* exist, and by a great number of competent investigators are *declared to be true*, and of the reality of which every person may, if he pleases, satisfy himself by actual inspection, thus sweeping away, thus and for ever, *the dark and debasing doctrines of the materialists.*"

Still, in harmony with Porphyry and other theurgists, who affirmed the different natures of the manifesting "spirits" and the personal spirit or will of man, Mr. Sergeant Cox adds, without committing himself any further to a personal decision: "True, there are differences of opinions . . . and perhaps ever will be, as to the sources of the power that is exhibited in these phenomena; but whether they are the product of the psychic force of the circle . . . or, if spirits of the dead be the agents, as others say, or elemental spirits (whatever it may be) as asserted by a third party, this fact at least is established — that man is not wholly material, that the mechanism of man is moved and directed by some non-material — that is, some non-molecular structure, which possesses not merely intelligence, but *can exercise also a force upon matter*, that something to which, for lack of a better title, we have given the name of soul. These glad tidings have by this trial been borne to thousands and tens of thousands, whose happiness here, and hopes of a hereafter, have been blighted by the materialists, who have preached so persistently that soul was but a superstition, man but an automaton, mind but a secretion, present existence purely animal, and the future — a blank."

"Truth alone," says Pimander, "is eternal and immutable; *truth* is the first of blessings; but truth is not and cannot be on earth: it is possible that God sometimes gifts a few men together with the faculty of comprehending divine things with that of rightly understanding truth; but nothing is true on earth, for everything has matter on it, clothed with a corporeal form subject to change, to alteration, to corruption, and to new combinations. Man is not *the* truth, for only that which has drawn its essence from itself, and remains itself, and unchangeable, is true. How can that which changes so as not to finally be recognized, be ever true? Truth, then, is that only which is immaterial and not enclosed within a corporeal envelope, that which is colorless and formless, exempt from change and alteration; that which is ETERNAL. All of that which perishes is a lie; earth is but dissolution and generation; every generation proceeds from a dissolution; the things of earth are but *appearances* and imitations of truth; they are what the picture is to reality. The things of earth are not the TRUTH! . . . Death, for some persons, is an evil which strikes them with profound terror. This is ignorance. . . Death is the destruction of the body; the being in it *dies not.*. . . The material body loses its form, which is disintegrated in course of time; the senses which animated it return to their source and resume their functions; but they gradually lose their passions and their desires, and *the spirit* ascends to heaven to become a HARMONY. In the first zone, it leaves behind itself the faculty of increasing and decreasing; in the second, the power of doing evil and the frauds of idleness; in the third, deceptions and concupiscence; in the fourth, insatiable ambition; in the fifth, arrogance, audacity, and temerity; in the sixth, all yearning after dishonest acquisitions; and in the seventh, *untruthfulness.* The spirit thus purified by the effect on him of the celestial harmonies, returns once more to its primitive state, strong of a merit and power self-acquired, and which belongs to it properly; and only then he begins to dwell with those that sing eternally their praises of the FATHER. Hitherto, he is placed among the powers, and as such has attained to the supreme blessing of knowledge. He is become a GOD! . . . No, the things of earth are not the truth."

After having devoted their whole lives to the study of the records of the old Egyptian wisdom, both Champollion-Figeac and Champollion, Junior, publicly declared, notwithstanding many biassed judgments hazarded by certain hasty and unwise critics, that the *Books of Hermes* "truly contain a mass of Egyptian traditions which are constantly corroborated by the most authentic records and monuments of Egypt of the hoariest antiquity."[905]

Closing up his voluminous summary of the psychological doctrines of the Egyptians, the sublime teachings of the sacred Hermetic books, and the attainments of the initiated priests in metaphysical and practical philosophy, Champollion-Figeac inquires — as he well may, in view of the then attainable evidence — "whether there ever was in the world another association or caste of men which could equal them in credit, power, learning, and capability, in the same degree of good or evil? No, *never!* And this caste was subsequently *cursed* and stigmatized only by those who, under I know not what kind of modern influences, have considered it as the enemy of men and — science."[906]

At the time when Champollion wrote these words, Sanscrit was, we may say, almost an unknown tongue for science. But little in the way of a parallel could have been drawn between the respective merits of the Brahmans and the Egyptian philosophers. Since then, however, it has been discovered that the very same ideas, expressed in almost identical language, may be read in the Buddhistic and Brahmanical literature. This very philosophy of the unreality of mundane things and the illusion of the senses — whose whole substance has been plagiarized in our own times by the German metaphysicians — forms the groundwork of Kapila's and Vyasa's philosophies, and may be found in Gautama Buddha's enunciation of the "four truths," the cardinal dogmas of his doctrine. Pimander's expression "he is become a god" is epitomized in the one word, *Nirvana*, which our learned Orientalists most incorrectly consider as the synonym of *annihilation!*

This opinion of the two eminent Egyptologists is of the greatest value to us if it were only as an answer to our opponents. The Champollions were the first in Europe to take the student of archæology by the hand, and, leading him on into the silent crypts of the past, prove that civilization did not begin with our generations; for "though the origins of ancient Egypt are unknown, she is found to have been at the most distant periods within the reach of historical research, with her great laws, her established customs, her cities, her kings, and gods"; and behind, far behind, these same epochs we find ruins belonging to other still more distant and higher periods of civilization. "At Thebes, portions of ruined buildings allow us to recognize remnants of still anterior structures, the materials of which had served for the erection of the very edifices which have now existed for thirty-six centuries!"[907] "Everything told us by Herodotus and the Egyptian priests is found to be exact, and has been corroborated by modern scientists," adds Champollion.[908]

Whence the civilization of the Egyptians came, will be shown in volume II., and in this respect it will be made to appear that our deductions, though based upon the traditions of

---

905 Champ.-Figeac, "*Egypte,*" p. 143.
906 Ibid., p. 119.
907 Ibid., p. 2.
908 Ibid., p. 11.

the Secret Doctrine, run parallel with those of a number of most respected authorities. There is a passage in a well-known Hindu work which may well be recalled in this connection.

"Under the reign of Viswamitra, first king of the Dynasty of Soma-Vanga, in consequence of a battle which lasted five days, Manu-Vina, heir of the ancient kings, being abandoned by the Brahmans, emigrated with all his companions, passing through Arya, and the countries of Barria, till he came to the shores of Masra" (*History of India*, by Collouca-Batta). Unquestionably this Manu-Vina and Menes, the first Egyptian King, are identical.

Arya, is Eran (Persia); Barria, is Arabia, and Masra, was the name of Cairo, which to this day is called, *Masr*, Musr, and Misro. Phœnician history names Maser as one of the ancestors of Hermes.

And now we will bid farewell to thaumatophobia and its advocates, and consider thaumatomania under its multifarious aspects. In vol. II., we intend to review the "miracles" of Paganism and weigh the evidence in their favor in the same scales with Christian theology. There is a conflict not merely impending but already begun between science and theology, on the one hand, and spirit and its hoary science, magic, on the other. Something of the possibilities of the latter have already been displayed, but more is to come. The petty, mean world, for whose approving nod scientists and magistrates, priests and Christians compete, have begun their latter-day crusade by sentencing in the same year two innocent men, one in France, the other in London, in defiance of law and justice. Like the apostle of circumcision, they are ever ready to thrice deny an unpopular connection for fear of ostracism by their own fellows. The Psychomantics and the Psychophobists must soon meet in fierce conflict. The anxiety to have their phenomena investigated and supported by scientific authorities has given place with the former to a frigid indifference. As a natural result of so much prejudice and unfairness as have been exhibited, their respect for scientists is waning fast, and the reciprocal epithets bandied between the two parties are becoming far from complimentary to either. Which of them is right and which wrong, time will soon show and future generations understand. It is at least safe to prophesy that the Ultima Thule of God's mysteries, and the key to them are to be sought elsewhere than in the whirl of Avogadro's molecules.

People who either judge superficially, or, by reason of their natural impatience would gaze at the blazing sun before their eyes are well fitted to bear lamp-light, are apt to complain of the exasperating obscurity of language which characterizes the works of the ancient Hermetists and their successors. They declare their philosophical treatises on magic incomprehensible. Over the first class we can afford to waste no time; the second, we would beg to moderate their anxiety, remembering those sayings of Espagnet — "Truth lies hid in obscurity," and "Philosophers never write more deceitfully than when plainly, nor ever more truly than when obscurely." Furthermore, there is a third class, whom it would compliment too much to say that they judge the subject at all. They simply denounce *ex-cathedra*. The ancients they treat as dreamy fools, and though but physicists and thaumatophobic positivists, they commonly claim a monopoly of spiritual wisdom!

We will select Irenæus Philaletha to answer this latter class. "In the world our writings shall prove a curious-edged knife; to some they shall carve out dainties, but to others they shall only serve to cut their fingers; yet we are not to be blamed, for we do seriously admonish all who shall attempt this work that they undertaketh the highest piece of philosophy in nature; and though we write in English, yet our matter will be as hard as Greek to some, who will think, nevertheless, that they understand as well, when they misconstrue our meaning most perversely; for is it imaginable that they who are fools in nature should be wise in books, which are testimonies unto nature?"

The few elevated minds who interrogate nature instead of prescribing laws for her guidance; who do not limit her possibilities by the imperfections of their own powers; and who only disbelieve because they do not know, we would remind of that apothegm of Narada, the ancient Hindu philosopher:

"Never utter these words: 'I do not know this — therefore it is false.' " "One must study to know, know to understand, understand to judge."

END OF VOLUME I

39738775R00326